THE MODERN WORLD
A HISTORY

Third Edition

Andrea Finkelstein | George J. Lankevich

Bronx Community College

PEARSON

Custom
Publishing

ISBN 0-536-83663-9

2004300026

AP/RO

Please visit our web site at *www.pearsoncustom.com*

PEARSON CUSTOM PUBLISHING
75 Arlington Street, Suite 300, Boston, MA 02116
A Pearson Education Company

For Our Students

and

in Memory of
Mark D. Hirsch
and
Samuel D. Ehrenpreis

Professor Hirsch founded the History Department at Bronx Community College and led it until his retirement in 1973. Professor Ehrenpreis guided and sustained it for the next sixteen years. We owe a profound debt to these two great men.

Contents

List of Maps and Tables

1

The World in 1750

Today, planet Earth is home to over six billion people speaking over a thousand different languages, following almost as many different faiths, and living in more than two hundred independent nation-states. The interactions between them are so complex and the rush of events so swift, that the wars and peace negotiations, droughts and floods, stock market peaks and economic reverses, scientific advances and epidemics, and elections and military takeovers filling our news media seem to follow no recognizable pattern. The present seems impossible to understand and knowledge of the past too vast to master.

History surveys remain part of the core curriculum because they offer students a framework for putting today's world in perspective. The word *history* comes from the Greek *'istoria*—learning through narrative (story-telling). At its most basic, history is the story we tell about how we came to be the way we are. The names and dates that many students dread having to memorize are not history; they are only the signposts that tell us where in the story we are at any given time. Of course, we cannot tell the whole story in a single book; we could not tell it in a million books, because every book written would be adding to the story itself. In the discipline of history, we tell only a small portion of the story at a time. What we choose from the historical record is determined by what aspect of present or past experience we wish to explain.

This textbook was designed to provide an outline of the three-hundred year long process of creating the world we know as *modern*. While *modern* can just mean *present day,* when we talk about *modern societies* we are applying a concept developed by twentieth-century historians and sociologists living in industrial democracies to describe their own cultures. According to this view, *modern* societies tend to protect individual freedom by keeping their governments under tight control. An important aspect of that freedom is the right of free inquiry: knowledge is open to all and open to the questioning of all. Modern societies tend to make a sharp distinction between knowledge and faith. Matters of faith are considered personal and private rather than matters of institutional and public concern. Modern societies believe that what they are today is a product of their history, and what they will become tomorrow is in their own hands. They believe in both the possibility and the desirability of progress through science and technology. Indeed, technology has become nearly as basic to their lives as breathing. What *modern* society needs, it makes by machine: machines harvest crops, weave cloth, cut timber for houses, produce medicine, preserve songs and stories, and carry people across land, sea, air, and even into outer space. Machines also organize and transport vast amounts of information at incredible speeds.

But if we were to take a world tour in 1750 we would find that nearly all of its less than half a billion inhabitants lived in *traditional* societies. Traditional societies see human beings as inherently unequal. In traditional cultures, human society is seen as the creation of a divine authority who gave each individual a different place in the social scale in order to guarantee the smooth working of society: a peasant, a serf, a peon, or a slave is destined by that divine authority to work while a noble, a warrior, or a king is destined to rule. A ruler's primary duty is to keep everyone in his/her place so the society does not collapse. Religion is closely tied to the government that, in turn, supports it. There is little or no room for religious dissent. To call one element of this society into question is to question every element in it. Access to knowledge is just as controlled as is access to power. Faith and knowledge are one and the same: truth is what tradition says it is, was, and always will be. Traditional societies try to prevent change because they view it as destructive. Traditional societies make what they need by hand or with the help of animal power.

The world we call *modern* is a world dominated by ideas, technologies, and institutions created by Europeans. To understand that world, we must begin by understanding the changes that transformed *traditional* European society itself and then move out into the greater world as the Europeans transformed it. As the world becomes more interconnected, its history becomes more global. In its simplest outline, that is the story this history book tells.

Of course, anyone traveling around the world today will soon realize that it is far from completely *modern*, but if we could go back in time only as far as 1750 and look around, very little that we call *modern* would even exist. In this introductory chapter, we will take a look at the world in 1750: a world without electricity or antibiotics, a world in which everything has to be handmade. The mountains, rivers, oceans, and continents are the same, but many of the countries that fill today's news cannot be found on any map printed in 1750 because they did not yet exist.

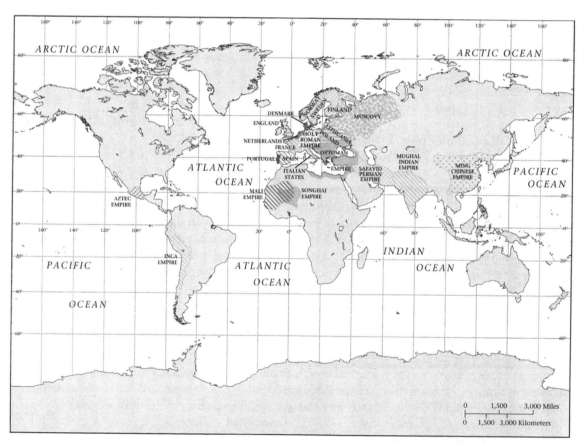

The World of Separate Civilizations, ca. 1500
From *Human Venture*, Fifth Edition, (2004), reproduced by permission of Prentice-Hall, Inc.

China

As globetrotting tourists in 1750, the oldest existing civilization we encounter is that of China, where state formation began under the Xia dynasty (c. 2205–1818 B.C.E.) about a thousand years after the rise of Pharonic Egypt. Chinese civilization began in the fertile river lands of the Huang Ho (Yellow) and Yangtze River valleys of East Asia. The Han people native to those territories were and are the overwhelming ethnic majority within China's borders. Despite the deserts and mountain ranges that tended to isolate China from its central Asian neighbors, outsiders occasionally overwhelmed Chinese rulers and imposed themselves on the land. The attraction of Chinese culture was so powerful, however, that successive waves of invaders were absorbed into Chinese civilization. And for ordinary people, family and clan were always more important daily realities than the names of those who ruled the empire.

Migrating southward from their home in Manchuria, the Manchu (Ch'ing Dynasty) had seized the Middle Kingdom (as China called itself) in 1644. They mobilized China's wealth to build huge armies and assert control over much of Asia. The Emperor Ch'ien Lung (1735–1796) reigned over China, Manchuria, Mongolia, Tibet, Korea, and Burma. In 1750, his territory included some 210 million people from many different ethnic groups. To govern his empire, Ch'ien utilized the services of a professional bureaucracy known as mandarins. The mandarins found guidance for their policies in ancient texts such as the writings of Confucius (551–479 B.C.E.), the Chinese philosopher who defined virtue as courtesy towards friends and respect for parents, tradition, authority, and maintenance of the social order. Entry into and promotion within the bureaucratic hierarchy was by examination in the classic Confucian texts. This insured the continued dominance both of traditional values and the traditional hierarchy, because, while the tests were open to all, schooling was private rather than public, and costly.

Like every other agricultural society, China's main means of production was its land, and control of that land was the main source of political power. But China, the world's largest civilization in 1750, also had a history of technological innovation: paper, printing, and gunpowder were numbered among its most famous exports. The populations of less technologically advanced societies, such as those in Europe, had long sought China's tea, silks, and the glazed porcelain pottery we still call "china." But China was not interested in the world outside Asia. The mandarins were certain all foreigners were barbarians and worked to keep China free from foreign influence. But the western world had already left its mark on the daily lives of the Chinese. Sweet potatoes, peanuts, maize, and the Irish potato were in common use by 1750 and contributed to a marked increase in China's population over the course of the eighteenth century.

Japan

The islands of Japan were independent of China in 1750, but remained within its cultural orbit. Japan drew the foundations of its written language, its Buddhism, and its arts from China. But to a greater degree than its mighty neighbor, Japan was, at first, more willing to deal with Europeans. Portuguese merchants and Catholic missionaries visited Japan during the sixteenth century. By 1600 over 300,000 Japanese had become practicing members of the Roman Catholic Church.

Neither China nor Europe exerted much impact on internal Japanese politics, a constant turmoil of warlord rivalry and civil war. According to tradition, the Emperor of Japan was a direct descendant of the sun goddess, Amaterasu-Ōmikami, from whose tears had sprung the Japanese people. But the Emperor had not really ruled Japan since the eleventh century. From that time forward, day-to-day control of the country had been in the hands of a *shogun*, a military dictator.

The Emperor remained a quasi-religious figurehead locked away in his imperial palace. Japan's most powerful clans had been fighting each other for the office of shogun for centuries. By 1615, that office was in the hands of the Tokugawa family, won for them by Tokugawa Ieyasu (1543–1616). The measures he took—murders, marriages, hostage takings, and relocations of powerful nobles—secured that office for his descendants for almost two hundred and fifty years. Military personnel occupied the top of the social order: they held the land, staffed the bureaucracy, and helped the shogun close off Japan from the rest of the world. Tokugawa rulers prohibited Japanese from leaving the islands, expelled foreign traders, and massacred Japan's large Christian community. A series of edicts governed every aspect of the peasants' lives, from how much rice they might eat to the kind of clothing they could wear. Japan entered into a long era of isolation that was virtually unbroken until 1853.

Mughal India

Two thousand miles west of Peking, at the edge of Chinese dominion, a second great center of civilization and culture flourished. The Indian sub-continent, called Bharat by its original settlers, comprises a large peninsula separated from the rest of Asia by three of the world's most rugged mountain chains. The Himalayas, the Pamir, and the Hindu Kush create a massive 2000-mile long curved barrier that protected and isolated the sub-continent from foreign invaders more effectively than did the man-made Great Wall of China. South of the mountains a wide array of peoples made their homes, a jumble of cultures speaking over 350 languages and dialects. Sometime between 4,000 and 3,500 years ago, the Hindi-speaking people conquered a large portion of the sub-continent and absorbed the original culture within their own. The Hindu faith divided the population into legally, economically, and socially distinct castes: *Brahmins* (priests), *Kshatriya* (warriors), *Vaisya* (tradesmen and farmers), and the *Sudra* (servants and laborers). At the bottom of the social hierarchy were the *Harijan* ("Untouchables"), individuals whose jobs (such as corpse washing or leather tanning) were considered so ritually impure that they were forced to live apart from other Indians. Although a majority of the population was Hindu in religious practice, the Mughal Dynasty that controlled much of the Indian north after 1500 was a mixture of Mongol and Turkish followers of Islam. They followed a path of conquest cleared earlier by fellow Muslims from Afghanistan. The Mughal capital was Delhi, a city with a wondrous array of beautiful palaces and monuments. Among the Mughal rulers was Shah Jehan (r. 1627–1658) who completed the world famous Taj Mahal in 1653. An agricultural society, India sent cotton cloth, tea, and spices westward to Europe in return for silver. But political infighting between Muslim rulers and religious struggles between Hindus and Muslims were already beginning to tear apart Mughal India and reduce its ability to resist foreign intervention.

The Ottoman Empire

Beginning in the seventh century, Arabian followers of the Prophet Muhammad (c. 570–632) launched wave after wave of conquest throughout the Middle East and into North Africa. By the year 1000 this Muslim empire stretched West to East from Morocco to Iraq and was beginning to push northward into Spain and Central Asia. This first Arab empire was itself gradually conquered by one of its own subject peoples, the Ottoman Turks, who brought a final end to the Roman Empire when they conquered the Byzantine capital of Constantinople in 1453. Renamed Istanbul, the city became a great cosmopolitan metropolis of some 700,000 people by 1600. Within the empire, foreign traders and subject peoples lived side by side with the ruling Turks. While pagans were given the choice of "Islam or the sword," Christians and Jews were officially tolerated minorities even if subject to special taxation. Those who converted to Islam became full citizens of the Ottoman Empire. Not all its subject peoples were content under Ottoman rule. The discontent of one small group, the Serbs, defeated at the Battle of Kosovo in 1389, would have a disproportionately large impact on modern world history.

Most of the trade that passed through the Ottoman Empire was in the hands of foreigners and protected minorities, but in 1750 Turkish armies continued to rule Egypt, Mesopotamia, Asia Minor, the Balkans, and most of North Africa. Much of that power was sustained by the *janissaries,* enslaved members of conquered populations trained to serve in the armies and bureaucracy. The Ottoman Empire was the strongest single state in Africa and a major power in western Asia, but its European empire had been in retreat since its losses at Lepanto (1571) and Vienna (1683). Ottoman authority existed on three continents, but it was a fading power looking to the past rather than the future.

Sub-Saharan Africa

Although the Turks dominated African lands along the Mediterranean Sea, most of the continent of Africa is located south of the Sahara Desert. While the dry climate of the north preserved even the fragile textiles of Ancient Egyptian civilization, climatic conditions south of the Sahara have destroyed much of that region's archaeological record, making the reconstruction of the history of central and southern African kingdoms extremely difficult. Much of what we know comes from the contact of those kingdoms with the Islamic empires of the north and east. In the heartland of the continent, small but sophisticated cultures such as the Nok (c. 500 B.C.E.–500 C.E.) and the Igbo-Ukwu (c. 800–1150) of modern Nigeria existed alongside great kingdoms such as Ghana (c. 700–1100), Mali (c. 800–1550), and Songhai (c. 1300–1600), which dominated the routes of commerce across the Sahara and had access to gold mines in the western areas of the Sudan. Some African rulers are known to have followed Islam. Mansa Musa (r. 1312–1337) and Askia the Great (r. 1493–1528) were famous for the wealth they displayed during pilgrimages to Mecca, but they did not demand that their subjects also convert. The Muslim rulers of the Hausa and Fulani kingdoms (c. 1200–1900), on the other hand, often launched religious crusades across what is now Mali, Niger, Nigeria, and Chad. The political and social structures of these kingdoms were as varied as their populations. Some were little more than loose federations of villages headed by quasi-independent chiefs; others were tightly organized military empires. Our 1750s tourists would find everything from pastoral nomads to walled cities and highly organized agriculture. But they would recognize all of those societies as traditional.

By 1750, however, many of Africa's famed kingdoms were gone and others increasingly beset by Muslim and European incursions. The oldest existing empire was the Orthodox Christian kingdom of Ethiopia, known to the ancient Egyptians as the Kingdom of Punt, a source of spices such as Myrrh. The Egyptians called the inhabitants of Punt *Habashat,* from which comes the term Abyssinia (another name for Ethiopia). The dynasty that ruled Ethiopia claimed descent from Menelik, the son, according to Ethiopian tradition, of Solomon and Sheba. But after several battles with the Ottoman Empire the Ethiopian state had fallen apart. Our travelers would have found a divided land of mostly Christian subsistence farmers and mostly Muslim pastoral nomads under the control of feuding warlords who, being descended from noble families, were the only ones who could actually own land. Ethiopian reunification did not begin until the middle of the nineteenth century.

Even in its divided state, Ethiopia was able to resist foreign penetration, but much of the African coast was not as fortunate. Large coastal sections were caught in a struggle between more established Muslim conquerors and newly arrived European invaders, neither of which was yet technologically dominant. The kingdom of Kongo fell to the Portuguese invaders, but the Portuguese lost Mombasa to the Arab Omani. Descendants of Dutch settlers held a small colony at Africa's southern tip. Christian-Muslim politico-economic rivalry had prompted Europe's first interest in Africa—a desire to cut out the Muslim middlemen who brought Africa's gold as well as eastern spices to Europe. Portugal's Prince Henry (1394–1460) sent out mapping and trading expeditions along Africa's western coast. By 1498, Vasco da Gama (1460–1524) had rounded the horn of Africa to established a sea-link to India as the Spanish seized islands off West Africa. Within the continent's heart new kingdoms were being born to replace the old.

A traveler to Asante (southern Ghana) in 1750 would have seen a tightly-organized empire whose outlying dependent provinces were kept under control by a well-organized bureaucracy and a heavily-armed military. The empire was the creation of Osei Tutu (d. 1712) who had forged an alliance of independent Asante chiefs in the 1680s and 1690s to wage a successful war for Asante independence (1698–1701) from an older Gold Coast Kingdom (the Denkyera). Under his successors, the Asante tripled the size of their territory with guns purchased from the British and the Dutch for slaves and gold. The center of the Asante kingdom was Kumasi, home of its founder. At the heart of Kumasi was the *sika 'dwa* (Golden Throne), embodying the spirit of the Asante people and brought down from heaven by Osei Tutu's right hand man, the priest Okomfo Anokye. A network of roads running from the capital to each province made it easy to send out the troops and bring back the tribute. Provincial chiefs were required to report to the Asantehene's (king's) court on a regular basis while a network of couriers kept him well-informed of events on his borders.

The trade in slaves and guns and gold brought knowledge of Africa's coastal kingdoms to Europeans. But the same geographical barriers that prevented European penetration into the African interior kept knowledge of most African history from the outside world. Central Africa was as unknown in Europe as it was unknowing of Western Europe's transformation from a traditional to a modern society.

Europe

Europe, the second smallest of all the continents, is located at the extreme western end of the Eurasian landmass, directly to the north of Africa. The Roman Empire had once encircled the Mediterranean Sea, uniting southern Europe, Western Asia, and Northern Africa, but its fall left Europe divided into numerous dukedoms, principalities, kingdoms, and empires, speaking dozens of languages.

Although most of Eastern and Central Europe had never been under Roman rule, Christian conversion linked it to the west. But Christian Europe had not been religiously united since the split between Orthodox (Eastern) and Catholic (Western) Christianity in the eleventh century. A further split within Catholic Europe in 1517 gave birth to several Protestant sects that competed with each other as well as with Catholicism and Orthodoxy for control. Islam dominated only in those portions of the Balkans under Ottoman control, and Judaism existed under political restraint on the fringes of Christian communities. But there was no "free market" in religion. Because these were traditional societies, each political entity had its own official religion and only limited toleration for those of its subjects who dissented from the official faith.

Russia was the largest European state, a multi-national empire extending well into Asia built by the conquests of the Dukes of Muscovy (Moscow). Poland was a dying state on Russia's western border; it was divided three times in the eighteenth century until it disappeared altogether into the territories of Russia, Austria, and Prussia. Prussia and Austria were, like the over three dozen independent Germanic states in central Europe, still technically part of the Holy Roman Empire begun under Charlemagne (768–814) in the ninth century.

The formal head of this shadowy Germanic Empire was the Habsburg family, a dynasty whose capital was Vienna but which held territory encompassing portions of today's Germany, Austria, Hungary, Czech Republic, Slovakia, Slovenia, Romania, and northern Italy. Despite their nominal authority over much of central Europe, the Habsburgs could not always control the peoples and politics of their varied possessions. German rulers within the Holy Roman Empire, and particularly in Prussia, were in reality quite independent. There was no single entity on the map of Europe called Germany. Neither was there an Italy, for that peninsula was divided into a series of independent kingdoms and imperial possessions.

Beneath the different political and social structures of all Europe's kingdoms, however, our tourists could discern key similarities left by that shared history of Roman conquest and Christianization. Russia was ruled by an all-powerful Tsar whose mere word was law while the neighboring Polish monarch was only elected for life, but all European kings ruled in cooperation with an aristocracy and church leaders whose parallel authority they had been striving for centuries to reduce. In the east especially, Europe was still a continent of subsistence peasant farmers under the legal control of the landowning hereditary nobility. But, in the West, a new Europe was being born.

Iberia and the "Columbian Exchange"

At the extreme southwest of Europe, where its landmass meets the Atlantic Ocean, is the Iberian Peninsula shared by the countries of Portugal and Spain. It was from Iberia that aggressive maritime explorations had established colonies in Africa and the Americas in the sixteenth century, following the voyages of Vasco da Gama and Christopher Columbus (1451–1506). Trading ships filled with spices from the Far East and gold and silver from the Americas made Iberia rich. But underneath, misguided control of the Spanish economy was rotting the empire from within. Spain concentrated on the production of wool for export. The *Mesta*, the royally chartered sheep-herding monopoly, maintained such a stranglehold on the Spanish economy that Spain was forced to import wheat to feed its people. The Jews and Muslims who made up most of Spain's commercial classes had been forced to convert to Catholicism, persecuted by the Inquisition, and then driven into exile altogether. The treasure that flowed from the Americas into Spain's coffers quickly flowed out again as Spain exported raw materials to and imported manufactured goods from her European neighbors to pay for its army and navy.

Of great interest to anthropologists, botanists, and historians is the impact of the "Columbian Exchange," the consequences of the meeting of Europe and the Americas, two previously unrelated parts of the globe. Europeans brought sugar cane, grapes, wheat, bananas, olives, horses, sheep, pigs, hens, and goats to the Americas, and took home tobacco, corn, cocoa, potatoes, peppers, tomatoes, the Brazil nut, and the Lima bean. But the Columbian Exchange was not all benign. By 1494 a new strain of syphilis appeared in Europe, more virulent than known there before. Much more deadly, however, were the measles, chicken pox, and smallpox viruses accidentally brought from Europe to the Americas. By 1600, perhaps as much as 90 percent of the native population of the Americas had perished in a pandemic of European diseases to which the native Americans had no immunity.

Another unexpected result of the Columbian Exchange was the African diaspora. The "Great Dying" of native American populations occurred just as sugar cane cultivation was being introduced to the Caribbean. The Iberian rulers of the New World needed labor for the evolving plantation system and to work their gold and silver mines. Estimates of the number of slaves taken from Africa to the Americas before the trade ended in the nineteenth century range upward from 11 million. Slavery was hardly a new institution. Virtually all pre-modern states used it to some extent, but because of the needs of the plantation economy African slavery became a major force in the history of five continents. West African kingdoms, Arab merchants, Islamic rulers, European shippers, and American shippers and purchasers all cooperated in the traffic. Arab slave dealers in East Africa had transported over one million Africans to Arabia, India, and China by 1800. Far Eastern plantations raising cloves or coconut palms found slave labor as useful as did the owners of sugar, tobacco, or cottons fields in the New World. Although only 5 percent of all slaves brought to the New World landed in the future United States, their impact on American history was especially profound. The diaspora of black Africans produced by the slave trade was the largest involuntary migration in human history.

Britain, France, and the Netherlands

Clinging to traditional economic and dynastic policies led to the decline of Spanish and Portuguese power during the seventeenth-century despite the continued influx of riches from their American and eastern empires. By 1750 a French family sat on the throne of Spain. The Netherlands, France, and Great Britain, a trio of commercial empires in Western Europe, had wrested the lead from Iberia.

The Netherlands, low-lying marshes in Northwestern Europe, had won their independence from Spain in the seventeenth century. Without mineral resources, the Dutch turned to commercial ventures and innovative agricultural techniques to reclaim land from the sea, drain the marshes for farmland, and build their economy through world trade. Their East India Company quickly established its dominance in the Indonesian islands and competed with the French and British for trading posts in India and Southeast Asia. Their West Indies ventures established outposts in North and South America. They named one of their settlements New Amsterdam; today we know it as New York. The Dutch even had a colony at the southern tip of Africa. But with their small population and meager natural resources they could not, in the end, compete with the bigger powers growing to their west.

In 1750, France was the richest nation in all of Europe, and its 16 million peasants made it the most populous as well. During the long reign of King Louis XIV (r. 1638–1715), whose personal rule began in 1661 and lasted fifty-four years, the power of France's nobility was successfully reduced and government was centralized in the person of the monarch. Without a national legislature to challenge his authority, Louis XIV was able to say that *"L'état, c'est moi* (I am the state)." Louis XIV's growing appetite for glory led him to wage a series of trade and colonial wars with the Netherlands and Great Britain. His successors followed his example.

During this protracted conflict, France's most tenacious opponent was Great Britain. Great Britain was created by the Act of Union (1707) that joined England and Scotland, two separate kingdoms making up the larger of the two main British Isles. Ireland, the kingdom on the smaller island, was as much a colony of Britain as was New York or New Jersey. During the seventeenth century both England and Scotland had endured a long period of turmoil as the landholding aristocracy fought to limit the power of monarchs who sought, like Louis XIV, to have absolute power. In contrast to France, the new kingdom of Great Britain emerged from this strife as a constitutional monarchy in which ultimate political power was held by a Parliament dominated by the aristocracy. Despite the turmoil, Britain developed greater economic diversity, better institutions of public finance, and a more independent commercial class than France.

While France was the wealthiest European power, that wealth was concentrated in the hands of the nobility and the great lords of the Church who together made up only two percent of the population. The average French peasant family, tenants on land owed by the nobility or the Church, was much poorer than the average independent British farming family. The greatest lords of the British aristocracy were certainly as wealthy as their French counterparts, but eighteenth-century travelers often remarked on the prosperity of the British farmers, town dwellers, and working classes. British brewers, bakers, masons, and farmers were better dressed, better fed, and more likely to be literate than their continental counterparts. They were freer as well. One result of the brutal French religious wars of the sixteenth century had been the Edict of Nantes (1598) granting religious toleration to France's Protestants, but Louis XIV revoked it in 1685, expelling dissenters and imposing religious uniformity on the French by force. In contrast, the British civil wars and revolutions of the seventeenth century resulted in the creation of a Bill of Rights (1689) guaranteeing toleration for most Protestant sects, protecting civil liberties, and subjecting the monarch to the rule of law. This was not a world of civil rights as we understand it: Catholics were still subject to stiff civil penalties, and only about six percent of the population met property and gender (male) qualifications for the vote. But this was a markedly more modern society than was generally found on the European mainland.

Contest for Empire

Although France and Great Britain were latecomers to the European quest for empire, they had taken the lead by the dawn of the eighteenth century and were each other's greatest rivals. France held power in Canada, the British along the Atlantic Coast of North America, and both had possessions among the sugar producing islands of the West Indies. Both were also establishing growing colonies on the Indian sub-continent. Wars between Britain and France could involve troops on three continents.

The long and bitter struggle for control of India is a case in point. Because eastern spices both flavored and preserved food, merchants flocked from Iberia to India in the sixteenth century. The Netherlands, Britain, and France followed in the seventeenth. By artful use of bribery, they established "factories," places for buying and selling, at strategic locations along the Indian coast. Each factory was both a collection of warehouses and a small fortress in which merchants of the competing East India Companies of Britain, the Netherlands, and France maintained mercenary troops to guard the goods awaiting shipment to Europe. Native Indians were soon recruited into the ranks of these private armies.

By 1700 the British East India Company had outstripped its competitors. It achieved virtual control of the ocean trade routes around India and constructed large trading stations at the Indian ports of Madras, Bombay, and Calcutta. But France, acutely aware of India's wealth, continued to maintain its trading center at Pondicherry to prevent a British monopoly. The situation in India became even more critical as the declining power of the Great Mughal increased the possibility of establishing European colonial control in parts of India. Skirmishes between the British and French companies reached their climax in 1757. At the Battle of Plassey (1757), Robert Clive (1725–1774) of the British East India Company led an army of 3,000 men, two-thirds of whom were *sepoys* (native troops), to victory against a Bengali-French army of 50,000. Eliminating French and Dutch traders from his area of dominion, Clive transformed the British East India Company into the most powerful commercial, military, and political force in India. It remained virtually an independent power within the greater British Empire for another century.

But the Battle of Plassey was only one episode in a wider conflict between the major European powers known as the Seven Years' War (1756–1763), a war which, as the reader will see in the next chapter, had a major impact on the future of France's and Britain's North American colonies.

It is commonplace in our world to claim that all human societies –industrial or agrarian, democratic or authoritarian, capitalist or socialist—are irretrievably part of a single, interdependent global reality. Like ripples caused when a stone enters a quiet pool, events in one part of the world have an inevitable impact on another. But "global interrelatedness"—both as an idea and a reality—is a modern construct, born out of European expansion. In 1750, Japan had closed itself off from the west, China tried to insulate itself from peoples it saw as barbarian, the Mughal Empire was in retreat, and the Ottoman Turks were already losing control of their farthest flung possessions in North Africa. While much of day to day life in Western Europe seemed the same as life in any other traditional society in the world, the process of modernization had already begun to change its culture, outlook, and power. In time, those changes would affect every society on the globe. The task of this book is to chart the course of those changes. We begin, then, with a series of revolutions within Europe and its American empires that helped launch the world we now call *Modern*.

2

An Age of Revolution

By the end of the nineteenth century, every inhabited continent had either been conquered, colonized, or had its trade controlled by Europeans (or their descendants), and their explorers were already challenging the vast ice deserts of Antarctica. The ideology and technology that enabled the inhabitants of this small continent to plant their flags all over the world emerged out of a series of revolutions that began in Europe in the sixteenth century: the Scientific Revolution, the Enlightenment, the American Revolution, the French Revolution, and the Revolutions of the European colonies in Latin America. The Scientific Revolution asserted the freedom of the human intellect and gave it an effective analytical method. The Enlightenment politicized the demand for intellectual freedom and turned scientific method to the analysis of society. The Americans created a Constitution out of Enlightenment "political science" and forged a nation dedicated to "life, liberty, and the pursuit of happiness." The French brought those lessons home to the European Continent and welded Nationalism to them. The descendants of European settlers in Central and South America used those same lessons and demands to free themselves from the rule of their forebears. The confidence and power unleashed by these revolutions continues to shape civilization around the world.

Europe's Scientific Revolution

During the sixteenth and seventeenth centuries European thinkers and scientists changed the way in which educated people thought about the nature of the universe and their place in it. The more they studied the workings of the earth and the heavens, the more they came to believe the universe was a natural machine whose operation they could ultimately explain. What the human eye could not see for itself, tools could be invented to discover: the thermometer appeared in 1598, the telescope by 1608, and the barometer in 1643. Viewing knowledge as power, they saw a guarantee of progress in their growing understanding of the laws of nature: science was the key to a better life. The energy and confidence generated by this new way of thinking played a vital role in the rising power of Europe.

Ancient learning as summarized in the *Almagest* of Ptolemy (d. 151) taught that the sun, moon, planets, and stars circled around an immovable Earth. Today, we call this theory the *geocentric* (*Earth* at the center) view of the universe. Using homemade instruments and data collected over centuries of sky watching, Nicholas Copernicus (1473–1543) came to realize the geocentric view was wrong. But Copernicus was a priest, and loyal to a Catholic Church that endorsed the *Almagest*, so he refrained from letting his radical conclusions be published until he was on his

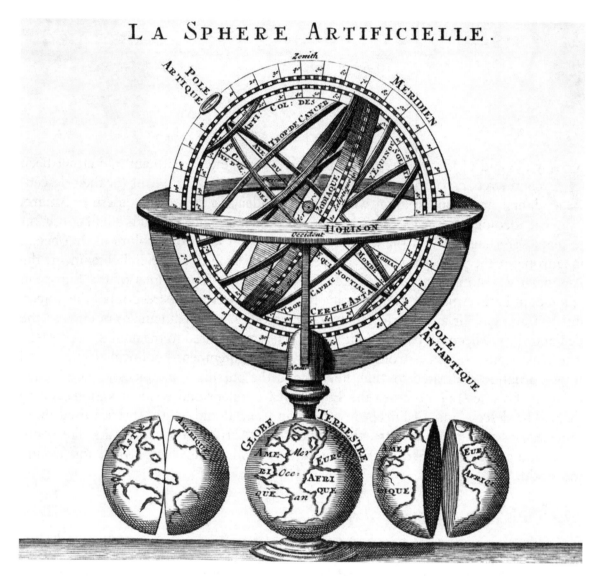

Armillary spheres helped seventeenth-century scientists calculate Solstices and Equinoxes according to the Copernican view of the solar system.
Copyright © CORBIS/Bettman

deathbed. When his *On the Revolution of the Heavenly Bodies* finally appeared in 1543, it argued that the Earth, moon, and planets moved in two different ways at the same time: each one rotated around a central axis daily while revolving around the sun. This view became known as the *helio*-centric (*sun*-centered) view of the solar system.

In the decades after Copernicus's death, a succession of mathematicians expanded on his revolutionary insights. The mathematical models of Germany's Johannes Kepler (1571–1630) demonstrated that planetary orbits were elliptical rather than circular; Kepler's laws of planetary motion were revealed to the world in his *New Astronomy* (1609). Italy's Galileo Galilei (1562–1642) used his own improved version of the telescope to show that other planets were circled by moons of their own, further supporting the heliocentric view in his *Dialogue on the Two Chief World Systems* (1632). But the Catholic Church refused to accept the "new learning." Its Inquisition forced Galileo to recant his views in 1633 and put him under house arrest. The "crime of Galileo" became a symbol of the struggle between free investigation and religious orthodoxy.

Outside the confines of the Church, the search for knowledge exploded in all directions. Among the landmark achievements of the age were the systematization of trigonometric tables (1550), the decimal system (1585), and logarithms (1616). Experiments in the comparative anatomy of humans and animals led England's William Harvey (1578–1657) to claim that the heart was a great mechanical pump circulating blood around the body from arteries to veins and back again (1628). England's Robert Boyle (1627–1691) explained the physics of gases (1660) while France's Blaise Pascal (1623–1662) proved the existence of a vacuum and invented the first mechanical calculator.

The ever-accumulating mass of knowledge led seventeenth-century philosophers to look for more systematic methods of investigation. Francis Bacon (1561–1626), an Englishman, published two books, the *Advancement of Learning* (1605) and *The New Atlantis* (1626), preaching the virtues of *experimental* philosophy. Bacon believed the only way to achieve useful knowledge was to base our conclusions only on the results of *experiments* (carefully controlled observations of the natural world). Very different but equally influential were the writings of René Descartes (1596–1650), a French philosopher who believed that only logical analysis could bring certain knowledge. In his *Discourse on Method* (1637) he turned skeptical doubt into a method of establishing undoubtable truth by claiming that his awareness of his own existence resisted all skeptical attack: *Cogito ergo sum* (I think, therefore, I am). Put together, the ideas of Bacon and Descartes created modern scientific method.

Across Europe scholars and inventors organized to discuss their findings. The Royal Society (1660) in London and the French Academy of Sciences (1666) were formed to "examine, question, experiment . . . and find truth." Members corresponded with each other and published their findings in journals put out by the societies. These scientific societies helped knowledge move ever more quickly across national boundaries.

That knowledge reached its peak in 1687, when England's Isaac Newton (1642–1727) published his *Mathematical Principles of Natural Philosophy*. In it, he demonstrated that the same natural laws of gravity and motion affected everything from the smallest particle of matter to the largest stars in the universe. No one really knows if he actually thought up the law of gravity after being hit on the head by a falling apple, but it is true that the same mathematical formula applies to the apple and the earth. Mathematics was the new language of physics, the science explaining the workings of the physical world. And two men, Isaac Newton and the German Gottfried Leibniz (1646–1716), were both working independently of each other on giving the world a new mathematics of motion, the calculus. Awarded a knighthood for his contributions to human knowledge, Sir Isaac became the first scientist to be buried in Westminster Abbey, the traditional burial place of English royalty. Even more revealing of how people thought of Newton were these lines written by Alexander Pope (1688–1744):

Nature and Nature's laws lay hid in night:
God said, Let Newton be! and all was light.

Sir Isaac Newton's work in physics remained unchallenged for over 200 years.
Copyright © Library of Congress

The Enlightenment in Europe

Eighteenth-century thinkers saw the universe as essentially orderly, mechanical, and rational. This was the view they inherited from over one hundred years of Scientific Revolution in Europe, years of experiment and observation culminating in the codification of the laws of motion and gravity, the development of the calculus, and the understanding that the sun (and not the earth as believed since ancient times) was the center of the solar system. Eighteenth-century intellectuals used the new methods of science to examine everything from the workings of the human mind to those of society itself. They believed that they lived in an "Enlightened Age." Their theories were many and not always compatible, but everywhere they posed common questions: Were human ideas fixed? Did inherited customs and belief systems meet the dictates of reason? Under their ceaseless questioning, Europe's settled existence would be shaken to its foundations, its religious establishments uprooted, and its governments overturned.

◆ John Locke

The English philosopher John Locke (1632–1704) was in the forefront of the new wave of thinkers who held that reason was the key to human progress. He believed that human knowledge derived from sense experience and that the ills of society were the result of inadequate education and the unquestioning acceptance of tradition. In his *Essay Concerning Human Understanding* (1690), Locke built an entire system of human psychology from the premise that the human mind was, at birth, a *tabula rasa* (blank slate). Sensory experience, and our mind's reflection upon it, created all our ideas, from those about size and color to those about right and wrong. Locke challenged the accepted idea that human ideas were *innate* (implanted in our minds by God before we were born) and not subject to human questioning. In *Two Treatises on Government* (1690), Locke extended his analysis to consider the origins of government itself. In 1688–1689, England had ousted a Catholic king, James II (r. 1685–1688), and installed his Protestant daughter Mary (r. 1689–1694) and her husband William (r. 1689–1702) on the throne. Locke was committed to justifying that revolution. He argued society was created by a "social contract" that gave political power to rulers only for the purpose of safeguarding people's natural rights to life, liberty and the free enjoyment of their property. The people always kept the right to amend or discard (through revolution) any government that failed to fulfill its end of the contract. It did not matter whether governments were run by Kings or Parliaments: government was the employee of society and not its master. Although Locke's political ideas had little immediate effect on Europe's kings and emperors, popular support for his ideas spread quickly.

◆ Deists and *Philosophes*

The "Laws of Nature" discovered during the Scientific Revolution led many to think of the universe as a kind of clock that God had wound up to run on its own (via those "laws" of gravity and motion discovered by Galileo and Newton). This approach to the Almighty was called Deism. Deists thought of God as a master craftsman who, having set the universe up to work according to Natural Law, let it run by itself. Deists believed reason was an ability given them by God to uncover the rules of His universe. They thought that, like the physical world, the social world must also run on natural laws. If human beings discovered those laws and let them guide their behavior, the future of humanity could only be brighter than its past.

As the Enlightenment spread across Europe, this secular faith in the future was preached with conviction by a group of writers in France who called themselves *philosophes*. They were not professional philosophers, however, but political propagandists who used satires, plays, essays, and novels as weapons to lift people out of ignorance, oppression, and poverty. Across Europe successful merchants, entrepreneurs, physicians, attorneys, and even members of the literate aristocracy were converted to rationalism by reading the volumes turned out by the *philosophes*.

Europe's most prominent *philosophe* was the French writer François-Marie Arouet, far better known as Voltaire (1694–1778). Playwright, poet, pamphleteer, and historian, Voltaire believed that his trade was "to say what I think." He did so fearlessly. The son of a lawyer, Voltaire's pride led him to mock the nobles who controlled French society and claimed superiority merely because of accidents of birth. He was twice imprisoned in the Paris Bastille for insults offered to these elites. During a three-year exile in Great Britain to escape another stay in prison, Voltaire was introduced to Newtonian science and thereafter placed his faith in the power of reason to improve human society. Voltaire's novel *Candide* (1759) made fun of those who saw change as sacrilegious because a

Voltaire championed the Enlightenment and Newtonian science in France.

Copyright © The Granger Collection

Divinely-created Earth was *necessarily* the "best of all possible worlds." Voltaire distrusted all established churches, but he particularly scorned the Catholic Church for its support of absolute monarchy and willingness to exploit the superstitious fears of ordinary believers. His writings advised humankind to *"écrasez l'infâme"* (crush the infamous thing) of religion and rely instead on the God-given ability to reason. Never one to back off from a fight, Voltaire narrowly escaped prison once more in his battle to clear the name of Jean Calas (1698–1762). Falsely accused by the Church of murdering his own son to prevent him from converting to Catholicism (the boy was a suicide), the Protestant Calas was tortured, strangled, and burnt at the stake for the crime of impiety. Voltaire's *Treatise on Tolerance* (1763), written to vindicate Calas, is still persuasive.

Knowledge remained a political battleground throughout the eighteenth century. The *Encyclopedia* (1751–1772), a twenty-eight volume compendium produced by an international group of Enlightenment writers under the editorial direction of Denis Diderot (1713–1784) was repeatedly censored and banned by the French government. Diderot also spent a short time in the Bastille for some of his other writings. In France, it was criminal to present ideas that attacked the claims of church or state. Yet Diderot persevered. The *Encyclopedia* summarized the latest and most radical scholarship about anything and everything from farming to comets, education, and political science. Thousands of copies of the *Encyclopedia* were quickly circulated throughout the states of western Europe and their colonies in the Americas.

◆ New Theories of Government

The *philosophes* believed that all human relationships would in time be shown to follow laws as unchangeable as that of gravity itself. They were the pioneers of the social sciences, but their newly created political science seemed to threaten the entire established social order. After all, Locke's *Two Treatises of Civil Government* justified revolution. Most European countries were governed by absolute monarchs who could barely be held accountable by the greatest nobles within their realms. Moreover, even among the business and professional classes few believed that ordinary people were capable of governing. Even Great Britain, with its constitutional monarchy and Parliament, limited the vote to holders of landed property. The *philosophes* themselves were divided over how much political change was desirable. Some looked to Britain's constitutional monarchy as a guide, others favored direct democracy, while still others believed social change was best brought about by Europe's absolute monarchs who could keep reform from becoming revolution.

Charles Louis de Secondat, Baron de Montesquieu (1688–1755) was the chief justice of one of France's regional courts. He spent a lifetime studying history to find out how a country could best be governed. He published his conclusions in *The Spirit of Laws* (1746). Montesquieu felt that no single type of government fit all societies. He thought that republics, because they were based on the virtue of participating citizens, were only effective in small states. On the other hand, despotism, because it utilized fear and coercion to maintain authority, was the most suitable form of government for vast empires. Monarchy was the best government for the middle-sized nations that predominated on the European continent, but not absolute monarchy. Only an "Enlightened" king whose power was counterbalanced by a strong nobility, town councils, and courts could bring permanent prosperity and power to any nation. Montesquieu took as his model a somewhat naive vision of the combination of "King, Lords and Commons" that governed England through Parliament. Even though Montesquieu's analysis of the English government was flawed, the *Spirit of Laws* may well have been the most influential volume of the century. With its dissection of the executive, legislative, and judicial functions of government, it was hailed as a blueprint for rational government and within eighteen months of its first publication had gone to twenty-one editions.

Montesquieu accepted the social inequalities of the European world as a given. But more radical *philosophes* such as Jean-Jacques Rousseau (1712–1778) did not. He thought successful societies were defined by their ability to create good citizens, not by their wealth or power. Achieving this goal was difficult because humanity had lost contact with nature; modern civilization had destroyed an original condition in which people had been happy, free, honest and healthy. In the *Social Contract* (1762), Rousseau advocated small republics ruled by the decisions of direct democracy: citizens could only live freely under rules created by the "general will" of the community. Only this way could they regain their lost natural virtue. But this meant that whoever refused "to obey the general will" must be "compelled to do so by the whole body" of society. Rousseau called this being "forced to be free."[1] Rousseau's vision of democracy offered no protection for minorities who disagreed with society's decisions.

◆ Enlightened Despotism

If Montesquieu looked to Britain and Rousseau to republics, most *philosophes* believed that social change had to be engineered by Europe's existing monarchs to be successful. Some of Europe's monarchs were willing to listen, at least to those ideas of the *philosophes* that might help them strengthen their own regimes. These rulers were known as "Enlightened Despots": *Enlightened* because they subscribed to some of the ideas of the *philosophes,* and *despots* because they would not tolerate any reduction of their personal political authority.

Frederick II of Prussia (r. 1740–1786) was called "The Great" both by contemporaries who feared his military skills and the *philosophes* who appreciated his bounty. Tenacious and gifted in battle, he expanded Prussia to the east by adding Silesia and parts of Poland to his domain. During the course of his long reign, Frederick built an honest civil service, ordered universal education for both sexes (though the curriculum for girls focused more on housekeeping skills than intellectual pursuits), and brought religious freedom to Prussia. Public money was spent to expand arable acreage and introduce the farming reforms that had fostered England's agricultural revolution.

Europe in 1714 The War of the Spanish Succession ended a year before the death of Louis XIV. The Bourbons had secured the Spanish throne, but Spain had forfeited its possessions in Flanders and Italy.
From *Heritage of World Civilization*, Sixth Edition, (2003), reproduced by permission of Prentice-Hall, Inc.

Prosperity increased, but Frederick's true goal was always to increase Prussia's military strength. His toleration stopped short of any challenge to his sole rule. As he explained in an *Essay on Forms of Government*, a monarch was "the first servant of the state," created by the people for "the preservation of the laws" and the "defense of the citizens." But he also likened the ruler of a nation to "the head" of "a man," so it was the ruler's "duty to see, think, and act for the whole community" on his own."[2] The result of his enlightened rule was substantial improvement in the wealth and prestige of Prussia, but no change in the militaristic attitude of Europe's most highly organized state.

Catherine II (Catherine the Great) of Russia (r. 1762–1796) was a German-born princess who came to power in Russia after a palace coup. During the early years of her marriage to Tsar Peter III (r. 1762), she survived the intrigues of a court hostile to a foreigner and educated herself by reading the works of the *philosophes*. Catherine came to believe only radical change could preserve Russia as a great power. After one of her many lovers killed the Tsar, she assumed the throne. Despite being a foreigner, a usurper, and a woman, she set about transforming Russia. She named a Legislative Commission that initiated the reform of Russian law in 1767 and granted local governments more authority. But after putting down a revolution by one of Russia's ethnic minorities, Catherine realized that her strongest support came from the nobility. She guaranteed their rights in the *Charter of the Nobility* (1785) at the expense of Russia's serfs whose condition was never worse than during her reign. The *Charter* gave the nobles hereditary rights over their lands and the serfs who lived on them. But Catherine also removed Russia's internal trade barriers, restricted the use of torture, and attempted to educate more Russians so that an efficient state bureaucracy might be created. She even founded a school for women. She collected the artwork that became the foundation of the Hermitage Museum and created the Library of St. Petersburg. She corresponded with Voltaire and invited Diderot to visit. Diderot was so impressed with her reforms that he called her the "North

Emperor Joseph II of Austria demonstrates his interest in agricultural improvement.
Copyright © Bildarchiv/ÖNB Wien

Star." But, like Frederick, Catherine approved of military expansionism. Her wars against the Ottoman Empire and Poland created the boundaries of contemporary Russia.

The ruler who most embodied the spirit of the Enlightenment was Joseph II, Emperor of Austria (r. 1780–1790), whose formal reign had been preceded by years of co-regency with his mother. He was a humane leader who believed that the monarch had an obligation to improve the situation of his people. Among the 11,000 laws Joseph issued were decrees that abolished serfdom, granted toleration and citizenship to Jews, imposed equality of taxation, and mandated equal punishment for crimes regardless of social class. Royal stipends allowed a quarter of Austria's children to attend primary school while other expenditures transformed Vienna into the medical center of Europe. Joseph's popular reforms went further than those of either Frederick or Catherine. But there were limits. In 1786 he reversed his earlier tolerance of a free press when he found it criticized his policies. The nobility opposed his efforts to restrict their privileges; the peasants rebelled because they thought his efforts did not go far enough. He angered Hungarians within the Empire by imposing German as the official language of their courts and schools. After his death, the land and tax reforms he had ordained were reversed, and Austria reverted to its traditional conservatism.

The American Revolution (1775–1781)

While they favored the extension of education and trade, the Enlightened Despots of Europe always kept political power in their own hands. They never even imagined trusting to the will of the people. So it was in the New World rather than the Old that the ideals of the Enlightenment first redirected world history.

Beginning with a settlement in Virginia in 1607, Britain had established a chain of thirteen colonies along the North American coastline. With a white population approaching 3,000,000 in 1760, the thirteen colonies together occupied a far greater landmass, had more landholders, and boasted a higher literacy rate than the British "motherland." Because the vast expanse of the Atlantic Ocean made communications between them difficult, the colonies had long been virtually self-governing despite the presence of royal governors. Founded at different times and under different charters, each had its own constitution, elected its own local legislators, and participated in international commerce under the protection of the Royal Navy. They considered themselves loyal subjects of the Crown, linked to Great Britain by a shared constitutional vision, the dominance of the Protestant religion (although America had many Catholics and a few Jews), and strong ties of blood and commerce, but resisted any hands-on interference by Britain in their day-to-day affairs. The colonists considered themselves heirs of the 1688–1689 revolution that gave the English a *Bill of Rights* (1689). They believed it was the king's job to safeguard their rights as Englishmen to "life, liberty and property." They did not, however, extend those same rights to the Africans living among them, slave or free.

The American colonists had loyally supported Britain during its long rivalry with France. Colonial militias fought alongside British troops in what they called "the French and Indian War," but which was really only the North American campaign of the Seven Years' War (1756–1763) that France and Britain fought in Europe, Asia, and the Americas. With the *Treaty of Paris* (1763) that ended the war, France lost almost all her North American lands to Britain, keeping possession only of the sugar producing islands of Haiti, Martinique, Guadeloupe, and St. Lucia. The cost of fighting the Seven Years' War tripled the national debt of Great Britain. A temporarily impoverished King and Parliament agreed that their colonies must pay a fair share of the costs of victory. But colonial merchants who had become rich by trading within the British imperial system detested the very thought of having to pay higher taxes to exercise privileges that had long been virtually free.

In the 1760s the theory of political economy that governed the relationship between European states and their colonies was Mercantilism. Mercantilists thought of wealth as power, but only thought of wealth as gold and silver. They sought to regulate trade in such a way as to bring precious metals into the mother country and discourage their export. Subsidies to domestic industries, combined with tariffs on imported goods, aimed at producing a favorable balance of trade (more exports than imports). Colonies were considered vital because they provided an exploitable source of raw materials and a secure market for the mother country's goods, without depleting an empire's gold reserves. Statesmen across Europe had endorsed the mercantilist model for two centuries, and applied it equally to commerce in Asian spices, Aztec gold, or Caribbean sugar.

After the soaring deficits created by the Seven Years' War with France, the British government passed new laws to regulate America's growing trade to Britain's greater advantage. The new regulations seemed eminently fair to taxpayers in Britain. The national debt had to be financed and salaries paid to royal officials and garrisons stationed in North America; North American colonists were expected to pay their fair share. Though Americans enjoyed the benefits of belonging to the British Empire, they resented

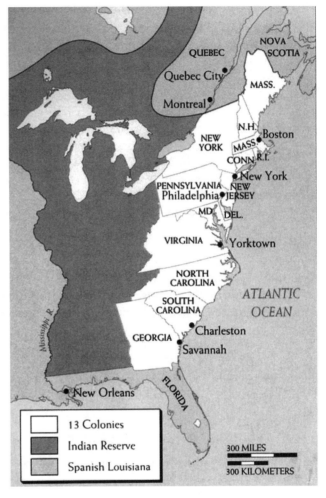

North America in 1763.
From *The Western Heritage, 6/e, Combined Edition,* by Donald Kagan, Steven Ozment, and Frank M. Turner. Copyright © 1998 by Prentice-Hall, Inc.

policy changes they had no voice in drafting, since Americans elected no representatives to Parliament. Resentment grew when Britain declared that all the lands beyond the Appalachian Mountains newly won from France would be closed to American colonists while the government decided how best to incorporate their French and Indian inhabitants into British rule.

Controversy erupted after March 1764, when Parliament passed a Revenue Act to regularize American commerce. Often called the Sugar Act, the measure actually reduced American customs duties but set up a better program for their collection, with British troops aiding in their enforcement. Americans protested against a plan designed to "tax (them) into obedience," but Parliament passed an even broader tax measure the following year. The Stamp Act (1765) imposed a "stamp tax" on certain uses of paper, a levy customary in Britain and other European lands but new to Americans. Nine colonies met in congress and worked out a Non-Importation Agreement. When the king's stamps arrived in the colonies they went unsold. It was the first time the colonies had cooperated with each other.

Benjamin Franklin (1706–1790), Pennsylvania publisher, member of the Royal Society, and the most famous living American, traveled to Britain to explain why, according to the theories of Britain's own John Locke, Parliament lacked the right to legislate internal taxes on its colonial citizens. Still asserting its right to tax the American colonists, Parliament repealed the Stamp Act in 1766. In its place, Parliament enacted a series of external trade taxes, an area in which it had long held unquestioned authority. But emboldened colonists immediately challenged this assumption as well. Radical groups like the "Sons of Liberty" were soon rallying American support behind banners proclaiming "no taxation without representation." Despite sporadic protests, the British managed to collect most of their taxes (after accommodating the colonists by repealing the most protested trade duties in 1767).

Relations between Britain and the thirteen colonies seemed to be improving, until Parliament granted the British East India Company the exclusive right to sell tea in the American colonies in 1773. Many in the Massachusetts colony, which supported itself primarily by trade, saw the measure as a threat to self-government and their profits. In December 1773, a group of merchants, poorly disguised as Mohawk Indians, destroyed 304 cases of imported tea before they could be unloaded from an East India Company vessel in Boston Harbor. The "Boston Tea Party" set off a furor in Parliament. Prime Minister North (1732–1792) rammed through a series of Coercive Acts (1774) to force the Massachusetts colony into obedience. Faced with the threat of military occupation, representatives from all thirteen colonies convened in a First Continental Congress on September 5, 1774. After considerable debate about the historic privileges of Englishmen, the Congress issued a notably mild *Declaration of Rights and Grievances* that recognized Parliament's right to tax its colonies. But continued boycotts led North to send more troops to Boston. In April 1775, those troops clashed with colonists in the town of Lexington and on a small bridge near Concord. The American Revolution had begun.

◆ *When in the course of human events . . .*

Britain's thirteen colonies had no history of close cooperation before the 1760s. What little unity they had arose from the shared belief that they were defending their traditional English liberties against violation by King and Parliament. By and large, the American establishment was slow to rebel. Fully a third of the colonial population opposed any break with Britain. A Second Continental Congress continued to send both declarations of rights and offers of negotiation to Britain while reluctantly putting together the infrastructure of an independent state. They set up a postal system, funded an army and a navy, issued currency, and opened their ports to the commerce of the world. But the last step—a declaration of their independence—still proved difficult to take.

Men such as Thomas Paine (1737–1809), who had emigrated from Britain to Pennsylvania in 1774, clearly perceived the logic of independence. In January 1776, Paine published *Common Sense*, a stirring pamphlet that condemned Britain's King George III (r. 1760–1820) as a "royal brute" ready to crush republican liberty. It was folly to believe that an island could rule a continent, wrote Paine, and free Englishmen would never forsake their rights and submit to control by a corrupt tyranny. *Common Sense* sold over 150,000 copies within six months and fired America's desire for independence. Finally, the Second Continental Congress unanimously approved a *Declaration of Independence* on July 4, 1776, a manifesto largely written by Thomas Jefferson (1743–1826) with substantial help from Benjamin Franklin and John Adams (1735–1826). America's *Declaration* restated the Enlightenment theory of natural rights and the social contract, asserting a "Right of the People to alter or to abolish" any government that did not protect their "self-evident" liberties. The nature of this newly declared nation had yet to be determined, but the neces-

During Boston's 1773 "Tea Party," the Sons of Liberty, disguised as Mohawk Indians, destroyed a cargo of British tea.
Copyright © Library of Congress

sity of reconciling the conflicting economic and social systems of the thirteen colonies dictated painful compromises from the beginning. The great manifesto of the rights of "life, liberty and the pursuit of happiness" ignored the issue of slavery in the colonies. It also ignored the question of women's rights.

From 1775 to 1781 Britain vainly attempted to prevent American independence. Advantages in manpower, financial resources, and naval strength enabled Britain to win most of the battles, and occupy several cities. But British armies failed to destroy the colonial forces under the American commander, George Washington (1732–1799), or break the morale of the populace. After an American victory at Saratoga in 1777, France agreed to enter into a formal alliance with the rebels. The French monarchy had no sympathy for freedom, but it wanted revenge for the humiliation imposed by Britain in 1763. Money, arms, and naval support from France helped America survive until the strain of fighting across an ocean convinced Britain that negotiations were necessary. Another *Treaty of Paris* (1783) confirmed the independence of the United States, but the new nation faced an uncertain future.

◆ Creating a Republic

Victory over Great Britain hardly guaranteed long-term survival for the United States. Under the *Articles of Confederation* that governed the United States from 1781 to 1787, the central government had far less power than the individual states. It could neither pay its war debt nor enforce its laws. The new union was threatening to break apart. In 1787 the desperate leaders of the American

Revolution once again convened in Philadelphia to create a new framework for government. Over the course of a brutally hot summer, fifty-five delegates from the thirteen sovereign states labored to create a federal system that would strengthen central authority while retaining significant powers for local leadership. Utilizing Montesquieu's theory of separation of powers, the Constitutional Convention created a system of three co-equal branches incorporating "checks and balances" designed to prevent the concentration of power at any level of government. Unlike the *Articles of Confederation,* the new *Constitution* established Executive and Judicial branches with powers independent of those enjoyed by the Legislature. The new *Constitution* was ratified by the states in 1788. Not until a *Bill of Rights* was added in 1791 did popular fears of a too-powerful government end.

Slavery once again proved a stumbling block to national unity. The new *Constitution* required a census every ten years in order to re-apportion legislative seats, but the same slaves who were treated as *property* under the fugitive slave laws made up more than a quarter of the population of some southern States. 39.1 percent of all the people in Virginia, the most populous state, were slaves of African descent. Not to count the slaves would create a Congress dominated by the North. To count them would create a legal precedent for their being free as soon as they fled to an anti-slavery state and a Congress dominated by the South. The *Constitution* of the United States has come to be the world's leading model of free government, but it began life under the cloud of the "Three-Fifths' Compromise":

> *Representatives and Direct Taxes shall be apportioned among the several states which may be included in this Union, according to their respective numbers, which shall be determined by adding to the whole numbers of free Persons, including those bound to Service for a Term of Years, and excluding Indians not taxed, three fifths of all other Persons.*

According to this compromise, the census-takers would count each slave as three-fifths of a person, balancing out the number of representatives from free and slave states in Congress. Otherwise slaves were not even three-fifths of a person; they were just property.

George Washington, the military hero who had presided over the Philadelphia Convention, was unanimously selected to serve as first President of the United States (1789–1797). Washington chose Alexander Hamilton (1755–1804), a young New York City lawyer as his Secretary of the Treasury, and Hamilton proved to be a financial genius. He successfully established the nation's credit, federal fiscal authority, and a national bank to administer revenues gained from excise duties and land sales. He used the national debt to bind investors to the government and transformed a potential liability into an engine for growth. Peace was needed if the new republic was to thrive, and Washington committed his administration to a foreign policy based on neutrality and non-involvement in European conflicts. Major treaties were signed with Great Britain and Spain as the United States sought peace, secure boundaries, and trade. Hamilton organized a pro-business Federalist Party that favored a strong central government. When Washington left office after eight years, free elections confirmed Federalism in power under President John Adams (1797–1801). Washington's *Farewell Address* cautioned his countrymen to avoid taking sides in the wars engulfing Europe; the neutrality he advised became an article of faith for many Americans. When the Federalist Party lost national elections in 1800 to a rival party led by Thomas Jefferson, there was general agreement that the changed "will of the people" had to be accepted. The new nation had survived the first test of democratic government, the orderly transition of power as President Jefferson (1801–1809) took office. Protected by its geographic isolation, the United States entered a new century free of European obligations and with a virtually limitless capacity for economic growth.

ALEXANDER HAMILTON (1755–1804)

Patriot, political philosopher and statesman.
Copyright © Art Resource, NY

Alexander Hamilton was born in Nevis, British West Indies, on January 11, 1755. His career was haunted by the fact that his mother, Rachel, was not divorced from her former husband until three years after Alexander's birth. After his father deserted his mother in 1765, Alexander left school at age eleven in order to work as a clerk in an import-export firm. Rachel's death in 1768 left him on his own. Hamilton quickly rose to become manager of the St. Croix branch of a New York mercantile firm, and his superiors sent him on to King's College (later Columbia University) in New York. As a student, he became an ardent supporter of the colonial cause, and, in March 1776, he raised his own artillery company. His service at the Battle of Trenton (1776) prompted an invitation to Hamilton to serve as aide-de-camp to General Washington. Lieutenant-Colonel Hamilton became Washington's trusted advisor and helped to reform the military system. Afterwards, Hamilton's eagerness to remain in the fight won him a battalion command in the Battle of Yorktown (1781).

Hamilton married Elizabeth Schuyler, a member of one of New York's most influential families in 1780. Once the Revolutionary Wars was over, he settled down to practice law in New York City. There, Hamilton continued to campaign for a stronger national government than was possible under the Articles of Confederation and was instrumental in the call for a Constitutional Convention. With James Madison (1751–1836) and John Jay (1745–1829), he co-authored the *Federalist Papers* that helped obtain ratification of the new *Constitution.* Hamilton became the first Secretary of the Treasury in Washington's administration. He instituted a comprehensive program to restore fiscal stability through the establishment of a national bank and federal taxation to pay the accumulated debt. He also recommended the use of protective tariffs, funding of internal improvements, and the development of domestic manufacturing in order to secure America's economic independence from Britain. Opposition to Hamilton's policies and to his failure to support the French Revolution led to a split among the "Founding Fathers" and the creation of America's first political parties: the Federalists supported Hamilton while the Democratic Republicans were led by Thomas Jefferson and Hamilton's old ally, James Madison.

In 1793, Hamilton helped convince Washington to keep the United States neutral in the European conflict set off by the French Revolution. The next year, he helped command the forces that crushed the Whiskey Rebellion. But financial pressures forced him to resign his government post in 1795. Resuming the practice of law in New York, his politics brought him into conflict with Aaron Burr (1756–1836) and the Democratic Republicans. His opposition to Burr's winning the governorship of New York in 1804 led to tragedy. Burr challenged Hamilton to a duel. Hamilton demurred, his eldest son having been killed in a duel only three years earlier, but Burr insisted. The men met on the heights of Weehawken, New Jersey, on July 11, 1804, and Hamilton fell. He died the following day, ironically leaving his widow and seven remaining children heavily in debt. Of all the Founding Fathers of the United States, none contributed more to the creation of an effective government.

The French Revolution (1789–1799)

Back in Europe, the news of the American Revolution and the birth of the new Republic seemed further proof of the possibility of social progress promised by the more radical propagandists of the Enlightenment. In 1786, Marie Jean Antoine Nicolas de Caritat, Marquis de Condorcet (1743–1794), anonymously published *The Influence of the American Revolution in Europe*, a pamphlet proclaiming the inevitability of that progress. In "poor and ignorant" America, a free people had shown how "rights so sacred and long forgotten" could transform society. Condorcet predicted Europe would now feel their power. France, governed by an absolute monarch, was about to find out what he meant.

In France's *Ancien* (old) *Régime,* the king occupied the top of the social pyramid, and all his 25 million subjects were ranked into three *estates* under his control. The clergy were called the *First Estate.* They made up only half of one percent of the population, but owned ten percent of the land and were exempt from taxes. The *Second Estate,* the nobility, included some 400,000 people who were also exempt from most taxes and held 25 percent of the nation's best land. All other Frenchmen, rich or poor, belonged to the *Third Estate.* They paid the taxes that kept the government in operation. By far the largest portion of the Third Estate was the peasantry. Fully 80 percent of the population, the peasants owned only one-third of the land. Peasants were subject to a variety of taxes including duties on land (*taille*), income (*vingtième*), salt (*gabelle*), labor (*corvée*), and religion (tithe), as well as local levies collected by the lord of their area. Also included in the Third Estate were urban day laborers and members of the *bourgeoisie* (middle classes): bankers, merchants, professors, lawyers, and physicians.

King Louis XVI (r. 1774–1793) had not supported the American rebels out of any desire for reform but in order to weaken Britain, France's ancient enemy. Louis was especially anxious to avenge France's defeat by Britain in the Seven Years' War, but helping the Americans proved so expensive that it tripled the French monarchy's debts. By 1787 France was essentially bankrupt, with half of all state revenues committed to paying the annual interest on its debt. A desperate Louis XVI proposed taxing all landed property regardless of the Estate of its owner. The First Estate, suddenly threatened with regular taxation, drastically reduced the generous "free gift" that it annually made to the state. High courts dominated by the nobility and merchants refused to register royal taxation decrees. A hastily called Assembly of Notables (1787), that spoke for the Second Estate and the richest members of the Third, refused to be taxed, standing on the Enlightenment principle that taxation without representation usurped their natural rights. In desperation, the crown decided to revive an institution called the Estates-General that, in centuries past, had been willing to authorize royal taxation. Although this body had not been convened since 1614, it was the closest approximation to a national legislature the French had. Under its traditional rules each Estate cast only a single vote, a procedure that prevented the Third Estate from challenging its social superiors. However, once the king called for a meeting of the Estates General, leading members of the bourgeoisie resolved to transform this medieval institution into a real national legislature.

◆ The Rights of Man and Citizen . . .

In the fall of 1788, leaders of the Third Estate asked to be granted 648 representatives to the Estates-General, twice the usual number for each of the other two Estates. Since each Estate was to cast only one vote, the government, after some hesitation, granted the request that December. It

In this French cartoon of 1789 the structure of society is caricatured by showing the monarchy, clergy, and parlements *all astride a blindfolded and shackled third estate. With a whip in his hand, Louis XVI is the "driver" in charge of this faltering structure, and the riders hold papers identifying their special interests and feudal rights. For a number of years the third estate supported the nobility and clergy in their struggle against royal despotism. But by 1788 the third suddenly changed its position, turned on its former allies, and took up the cause of the nation as its own war cry.*
Courtesy of Corbis Images/The Bettmann Archive.

assumed that after separate meetings of each Estate, the conservative forces representing the clergy and the nobles would still control the proceedings. But in May 1789, once the three groups began to meet at the palace at Versailles outside of Paris, it was clear that the leaders of the Third Estate wanted more than token reform. Lawyers, wealthy landowners, and merchants united behind the demand of one representative one vote. If this were allowed, the Third Estate would immediately control half of the Estates General. Support from only a few sympathetic nobles and priests would give them a majority. Louis XVI had no intention of sharing power with his subjects, however; he decided that each Estate must meet separately.

Before his ruling was even announced, an overly zealous bureaucrat locked the Third Estate out of its meeting hall. The delegates knew Louis was gathering troops at his palace of Versailles, just outside Paris; they thought the lock-out was a prelude to an attack. In self-defense, they barricaded themselves in a nearby indoor tennis court, taking a solemn oath (on June 20) not to disband until France had a constitution giving the French people a say in their own government. Joined by a few of the most liberal members of the First and Second Estates, the Third Estate converted itself into a National Assembly.

Louis XVI continued to mass his troops. Popular uprisings in Paris and the countryside saved the reform movement. Workers in the capital (called *sans-culottes,* because they wore long pants, rather than the knee-pants, or *culottes,* worn by the wealthy) seized control of city streets. On July 14, 1789, they showed their support for the National Assembly by assaulting the Bastille, an old royal fortress that dominated the east end of the city. One of the leaders of the assault was Anne-Josephe Théroigne de Méricourt (1762–1817), a professional singer who helped organize the women of Paris. After killing several royal officials, the mob paraded through the streets carrying their victims' heads aloft on pikes. At the same time peasants burned down noble estates throughout the country. As a "Great Fear" spread across the nation, demands for reform escalated. On the night of August 4–5 the National Assembly saw a wave of representatives from the First and Second Estates renounce all their special privileges. Henceforth, all Frenchmen would be free and equal citizens under the law. Before the month was over, the Assembly passed a *Declaration of the Rights of Man and Citizen* inspired by the American *Declaration of Independence* and the British *Bill of Rights.*

Like its models, the French *Declaration of the Rights of Man and Citizen* excluded women from most of its benefits. This prompted Olympe de Gouges (1748–1793), a feminist playwright, to write the *Declaration of the Rights of Woman and Citizen* (1791). The question of slavery in France's colonies was also not addressed. And, like the new nation across the Atlantic, the emerging French state faced tremendous financial problems and a crushing national debt. As a temporary measure, the Assembly decided to issue paper currency (known as *assignats*) secured by the value of lands confiscated from the Catholic Church. This effectively turned the Church into a branch of the government; priests were paid by the National Assembly, a move turned into law the following year by the *Civil Constitution of the Clergy* (1790). When the Pope condemned the *Civil Constitution,* an overwhelmingly Catholic France was forced to choose between its faith and its revolution.

By the summer of 1791, the National Assembly had turned France into a constitutional monarchy that was much more democratic than Great Britain's. The new French legislature had only one branch (no House of Lords), and it could ultimately override any royal veto. But there were limits to reform. Property qualifications restricted the new electorate to the wealthiest 60 percent of the adult male population. This group of so-called "active citizens" was also allowed to serve in the army while the remaining "passive citizens," although otherwise equal in rights, could not.

ANNE JOSEPHE THÉROIGNE DE MÉRICOURT (1762–1817)

THE WOMEN OF PARIS MARCHING TO VERSAILLES.

The march of Parisian women on Versailles (October 5, 1889) brought the king back under the control of the revolutionary government.
Copyright © Art Today

Anne Josephe Théroigne de Méricourt was born into a peasant family of French stock in Marcourt, Belgium, in 1762. When her widowed father remarried, Théroigne, still a child, did not get along with her step-mother. She was soon sent off into service, and eventually found employment with an Englishwoman who took the beautiful seventeen-year old back to London with her. In England, Théroigne began a lucrative career as a singer and courtesan. She toured the continent as a professional signer to great acclaim. Her fame and fortune made it possible for this daughter of a peasant to play a major role in the French Revolution.

When a now wealthy Théroigne arrived in Paris in 1789, she found it seething with discontent. King Louis XVI and the newly summoned Estates-General were locked in a political stalemate. Théroigne quickly organized French women during the crisis, and, dressed as an Amazon, she was one of the leaders of the crowd that marched on the Bastille on July 14, 1789. In October, she led the Women's March to Versailles to confront Queen Marie Antoinette, wife King Louis XVI. Under Théroigne's command, the royal family was returned to Paris where the revolutionaries would be better able to control it.

Théroigne spent her fortune fighting against the Royalist cause. She supported herself as a journalist and orator, but was forced to flee the country in 1790 during the virtual civil war raging between pro- and anti-revolutionary forces. As a known revolutionary, she was held for several months in an Austrian prison before winning her freedom after an audience with the Emperor Leopold II (r. 1790–1792). Returning to France in 1792 she fought simultaneously for the Revolution and the rights of women. She participated in the storming of the Tuilleries (the current royal residence) by radical republicans on the night of August 9–10, but she spent most of her time organizing women's clubs to fight for the republic and for female equality in any new constitution. Throughout France women had joined men in the propaganda war and on the barricades, but independent action by women was antagonizing the male revolutionary leadership.

After the execution of King Louis XVI on January 21, 1793, the most powerful revolutionary party split into two groups. Théroigne supported the *Girondins* who favored both political and economic liberalism. But the Girondins lost the power struggle to the more radical faction (the Jacobins) led by Georges Jacques Danton and Maximilien Robespierre in July 1793. The triumph of the Jacobins marked the beginning of the Reign of Terror. At the height of the Terror, Théroigne was beaten unconscious on the streets of Paris at the instigation of her enemies. Arrested again in 1794, she escaped the guillotine only because her jailers realized that injuries received in the earlier assault had affected her mind. Théroigne de Méricourt spent the last twenty years of her life interned in the asylum of Saltpétrière. She outlived her enemies by those twenty years, for Danton and Robespierre both died under *La Guillotine* in 1794, victims of their own Reign of Terror.

◆ The War and the First French Republic

While Louis the XVI appeared to accept the new constitution, he was secretly negotiating with his fellow monarchs in Austria and Prussia to send their armies to his aid. In June 1791 he attempted to flee the country with his family but was caught and brought back under guard. When the new Legislative Assembly convened that October, distrust and discontent were rampant. Some nobles and churchmen continued to support the king. Under the leadership of a radical group known as the Girondins, the new government declared a pre-emptive war against Prussia and Austria. The Girondins believed the threat of foreign attack would help unify France. The plan backfired when the joint Austro-Prussian force pushed the French army all the way back to the outskirts of Paris in 1792. Panic set in. Under the leadership of Georges Jacques Danton (1759–1794), the *sans-culottes* stormed the Legislative Assembly demanding the creation of massive new armies and the removal of the king. The new armies, created by a nationalist patriotic appeal, turned the tide, and the invaders were forced to retreat. The king was arrested, and a republic proclaimed based on universal manhood suffrage. The Legislative Assembly, reconstituting itself as a Constitutional Convention, began to create a second constitution for France, this time as a Republic (1792).

In January 1793, the new government executed Louis XVI. This act united all of Europe against France. Great Britain, Spain, and the United Netherlands joined in coalition with Austria and Prussia to put an end to the French Revolution. With foreign armies on its borders and monarchist sympathizers within, the new French Republic began a campaign to sustain itself through terror. The Jacobins, the dominant faction in the Convention, were controlled by Maximilien Robespierre (1758–1794), leader of the twelve-man Committee of Public Safety that acted as the new government's chief executive. A lawyer from Arras in northern France, Robespierre had first gained power through his campaign for universal manhood suffrage and equal rights for actors, Jews, and slaves. He hoped to create an honest government free from the corrupt selling of offices and justice that had marked the *Ancien Régime,* but Robespierre would not tolerate any opposition to his policies. He sentenced opponents to the guillotine after summary trials as he organized new armies to defend France. His victims included Queen Marie Antoinette (1755–1793) and his former ally, Danton. In a speech made February 5, 1794, Robespierre explained the rationale behind the Committee's "Reign of Terror":

> *If the driving force of popular government in peacetime is virtue, that of popular government during a revolution is both* virtue and terror: *virtue, without which terror is destructive; terror, without which virtue is impotent. Terror is only justice that is prompt, severe, and inflexible; it is thus an emanation of virtue; it is less a distinct principle than a consequence of the general principles of democracy applied to the most pressing needs of the* patrie *(fatherland).*[3]

As universal military service and total mobilization of national resources continued to turn the military tide, the Jacobins attempted to create a "Republic of Virtue" heavily influenced by the thought of Rousseau. Robespierre was a Deist who initially opposed the removal of religious institutions. Faced, however, with unyielding Church opposition to the French Republic, Robespierre decided the Catholic Church would have to go. He outlawed Catholicism and set up a new civic religion based on the worship of an undefined "Supreme Being" in its place. Robespierre's reforms were so thorough that the very calendar itself was discarded and a new, one, purged of all religious influence, was created instead. Under the new calendar, the year was divided into twelve months of thirty days. Since this added up to only 360 days, a series of annual festivals was added (between September 17 and September 22) to make up the difference. The five days of the annual festival were devoted in turn to Virtue, Genius, Labor, Opinion, and Rewards; the sixth festival day added in leap years was a Festival of the Revolution. Each month was then divided into three weeks (*décades*) of ten days each, with each tenth day being a "holiday." Having only three days of rest per month was supposed to increase the sobriety of the revolutionary worker and dislodge the Christian ideas associated with Sunday. The days of the new week had numbers rather than names (*Primidi, Duodi, Tridi, Quartidi, Quintidi, Sextidi, Septidi, Octidi, Nonidi, Décadi*) to further distance them from any religious associations. September 22, 1792 (the day the new republic had been instituted), was set as Day One of the Year One of the French Republic and the Revolutionary Calendar.

The Republic of Virtue was intended to last forever. But in July 1794 (the month of *Thermidor* in the new calendar), the Jacobins fell victim to their own "Reign of Terror" as Robespierre went to the guillotine followed by cries that "the blood of Danton" would drown him. By October 1795 yet another government had issued yet another new constitution. This one was called the Directory.

◆ The Directory and the Rise of Napoleon Bonaparte

The Directory was named for its executive branch, a committee of five Directors. Although it accomplished little within France, the Directory was able to use the huge armies created by Robespierre to conquer France's smallest neighbors. The wealth of these satellite republics fed France. The Directory's dependence on military power led to its downfall at the hands of one of its own generals, Napoleon Bonaparte (1769–1821). Bonaparte was born in Corsica, a small island off the coast of Italy that had been under French rule since 1768, although its people were an ethnic mix of Greek and Italian. Because Napoleon was born one year after the French took over the island, he was a French citizen, but he first used his training as an artillery officer in France to fight for Corsican independence. When that movement collapsed in 1789, Napoleon returned to France to take service in the Revolutionary armies. His extraordinary tactical skills led to victories on the Italian peninsula (1796–1797). Those victories, in turn, led to a temporary peace with France's enemies. This brought Napoleon to the attention of the Directors. He convinced them to let him take French forces into Egypt in 1798, in a move to damage Britain's economy by cutting off its trade with India. When he learned that his conquests in Italy had been lost to a newly reformed British-Austrian-Russian-Prussian Coalition, Napoleon abandoned his Egyptian campaign and returned to Paris. Arriving in November 1799, he plotted to end the Directory and "save" the Revolution.

Napoleon's *coup d'état* created a government called the Consulate (modeled on the ancient Roman Republic) with Napoleon as the First, and dominant, consul. Napoleon quickly regained control in Italy. When Russia suddenly withdrew its troops from the Coalition after arguing with Austria, Napoleon's position grew stronger. The young Consul even convinced Pope Pius VII (r. 1800–1823) to recognize the loss of Church lands in France. By 1802 he was able to negotiate a general peace (the *Treaty of Amiens*) with the Coalition and have himself made consul for life. Two years later, on December 2, 1804, he crowned himself Emperor of the French. Like all of Napoleon's acts, even the creation of another monarchy for France was confirmed by a vote of the French people.

This work by Jean-Jacques Louis David shows the young Napoleon as the champion of the ideals of the French Revolution.
Copyright © Giraudon/Art Resource, NY

◆ Napoleonic Europe

The revolutionary reforms introduced by Napoleon into the territories his army conquered were the most important legacy of the Napoleonic Empire that lasted until 1815. The ideas of equality under the law, freedom of religion, free markets in place of old guild restrictions, and trial by jury were enshrined in the Code Napoleon (1804), enforced in France as well as in all the conquered territories. To convince Europe that the Revolution was over, he returned France to the standard calendar in 1806. But as he centralized his authority over much of Europe, Napoleon often misunderstood the peoples he conquered. Spaniards of all classes resented the Code's imposition of religious freedom because it threatened their traditional values. Yet Napoleon's extension of Enlightenment principles forced even his enemies to grant some reforms. Prussia freed its serfs and established equality under the law in 1808.

Napoleon's rule was supported by a series of brilliant military victories. He could not overcome the superior power of the British navy, losing to it at Trafalgar in 1805, but he seemed unbeatable on land. He crushed the Austrian army in 1805, the Prussian in 1806, and the Russian in 1807. By 1808 Napoleon was the master of most of Europe, but he overreached himself by invading Spain. British forces intervened there and turned the Iberian Peninsula into a constant battleground. Napoleon responded with economic warfare, forbidding the import of British goods throughout his empire. In 1812, when Russia refused to abide by Napoleon's rules, he decided to invade. His troops advanced as far as Moscow before halting for the Russian winter, but Tsar Alexander I (r. 1801–1825), safe in retreat in the east, refused to negotiate surrender, and Napoleon's army began to degenerate into a rabble during their enforced inactivity. With the surrounding countryside scorched by the retreating Russian troops and his own supply lines dangerously over-extended, Napoleon was forced to retreat. His men died by the thousands in the snows during their forced return to Paris. Once again, the British, Austrians, Prussians, and Russians united against Napoleon, finally defeating him in 1813. Napoleon was removed from office and exiled to the island of Elba, off the Italian coast, in 1814. Briefly regaining power the following year, he was again defeated by Coalition forces in 1815 (at Waterloo). This time he was transported to St. Helena, an island in the south Atlantic Ocean 1200 miles west of Africa, where he remained in captivity until his death in 1821.

◆ The Congress of Vienna (1814–1815)

After a generation of warfare, the leaders of the Coalition against Napoleon felt a great obligation to establish order in Europe. Even before Coalition armies first occupied Paris in March 1814, British Foreign Minister Viscount Castlereagh (1769–1822) convinced other members of the alliance that France should be stripped of its Napoleonic conquests and its old dynasty, the Bourbons, restored. A Quadruple Alliance of Great Britain, Austria, Prussia, and Russia was created to guarantee the future peace of Europe. The leaders of the Quadruple Alliance convened in Vienna in September 1814 to finalize those terms. But the deliberations of this Congress of Vienna were interrupted by Napoleon's return. After Waterloo, the victors were even less charitably minded towards France. The Quadruple Alliance imposed a war indemnity on France and sent troops to occupy it until the indemnity was paid in full. France was not excluded from Congress deliberations, however; its status as a Great Power was never in doubt. Still, the Quadruple Alliance worried that King Louis XVIII (r. 1814–1824), brother of the executed Louis XVI, whom they installed as ruler of France, would not be able to control French expansionism. Further measures were needed.

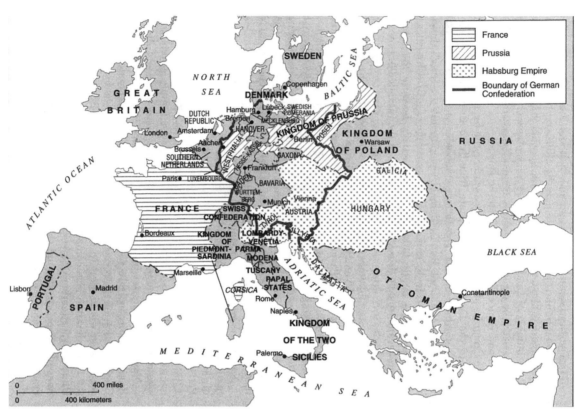

Europe After the Congress of Vienna, 1815   Changes in boundaries of states after the Congress of Vienna.
From *History of Modern Europe*, First Edition, (1996), W. W. Norton & Company.

In addition to Castlereagh, the negotiators at Vienna included Prince Clemens von Metternich (1773–1859) of Austria, who hosted the meetings, and Tsar Alexander of Russia. Along with King Frederick Wilhelm III of Prussia (r. 1797–1840) these leaders agreed to create a series of *buffer* states against the threat of a revival of the French revolutionary spirit. A buffer state allows its neighbors to prepare for an invasion by being large enough to slow down an enemy army's advance, but not large enough to threaten its neighbor's security. Belgium was folded into a larger United Netherlands, and centrally located Switzerland was enlarged. A strengthened Kingdom of Piedmont guarded France's southern border. Prussia received new territories along the Rhine River and in Saxony. Austria's control of the northern Italian provinces of Lombardy and Venetia was confirmed, and it was given the presidency of a newly created Germanic Confederation consisting of 38 smaller states that were expected to accept its leadership. Russia gained control of Poland, while Sweden's independence was reaffirmed to block any French advance to the north.

In addition, Tsar Alexander convinced the monarchs of Austria and Prussia to join with him in a Holy Alliance (1815) to defend Christianity within their realms against liberal revolution. Great Britain, fearing the goals of the Holy Alliance were uncertain and the purpose reactionary, chose not to enlist. Castlereagh was content just to sign a renewal of the Quadruple Alliance on

November 20, 1815. With the old dynasties restored to their thrones throughout Europe by the Alliance members and the French revolutionary virus apparently defeated, the statesmen of Vienna were proud of what they had accomplished. The settlement they arranged at the Congress of Vienna lasted almost intact for thirty-three years and prevented a general European war for a century.

Revolution in Latin America

Although, in Europe, the winds of revolution were temporarily calmed by the settlement of the Congress of Vienna, they were still blowing throughout the Americas. The European colonies of the Caribbean and Central and South America were eager to experience the freedoms won by their neighbor to the north, and the Napoleonic Wars provided them with just the opportunity they needed to achieve that freedom: as long as the nations of Europe fought each other they could not spare the troops needed to hold on to their territories overseas.

While the colonies of France, Spain, and Portugal may have looked to the newly formed United States as a model for independence, their colonial experience had actually been very different from that of Britain's North American colonies. Within a century of Columbus's voyages, Spain established a system of paternalistic landholding and despotic viceroys in virtually all its New World possessions. In these lands the Catholic Church combined with an imperial administration to convert the Indian populations and to plunder the natural wealth of the colonies for the benefit of Spain. When the native populations succumbed to such European diseases as chicken pox, mumps, small pox, Spain imported African slaves to work the plantations. The few Indians that remained found themselves tenant farmers on the land they had once owned, unable to leave the plantations because of the debts they owed the Spaniards. Mercantilist principles determined the pattern of trade between Spanish dominions and Madrid, but not even the vast influx of gold and silver from the New World could transform Spain into an economic power. After 1650, declining Spanish prestige allowed first France and later Great Britain to control the *asiento,* the contract to supply African slaves to plantation owners. Humiliated by its weaknesses, Spain tightened the mercantilist policies that guaranteed the economic subjection of its colonies and imposed a rigid censorship to prevent the ideas of the *philosophes* from infecting its colonies. Conditions were very similar in Portuguese Brazil and French Saint-Domingue (Haiti).

◆ The Creation of Haiti

Columbus had claimed Hispaniola, a small island in the Caribbean, for Spain back in 1492. Soon the eastern, more fertile, half of the island was a thriving sugar producing Spanish colony, Santo Domingo. As the native population succumbed to disease, African slave labor was brought in to work the plantations. Over time, French adventurers from the nearby island of Tortuga invaded the western half of Hispaniola and established tobacco plantations there. A century of intermittent warfare ended in 1697 with the partition of Hispaniola; the Spanish colony of Santo Domingo in the east and the French colony of Saint-Domingue in the west.

The colonies experienced periodic slave rebellions. An educated ex-slave named François Dominique Toussaint (c. 1743–1803) took over the leadership of one of those rebellions in Saint-Domingue in 1791; before he was finished, his forces controlled the entire island, French and Spanish colonies alike. He was soon dubbed "*L'Ouverture* (the opening)" for the striking success of his raids. When Toussaint marched into the capital of the Spanish colony in 1801 he abolished

TOUSSAINT L'OUVERTURE (C.1743–1803)

François Dominique Toussaint was born into slavery in Haiti sometime around the year 1743. His father was an educated slave who converted to Catholicism, and Toussaint received his elementary education in French from the Jesuits. Although his father had been freed before Toussaint was born, French law did not consider the children of freed slaves automatically free. However, Toussaint's talents so impressed his master that Toussaint was promoted to steward on the plantation and legally freed in 1777. Finally able to marry, Toussaint and his wife Suzan had two sons.

Haiti was a French colony, but the violent course of the Revolution in France (1789–1799) prevented the French government from attending to problems in its American possessions. When a slave rebellion broke out in Haiti in 1791, Toussaint first rescued his former master, but thereafter joined the freedom fighters. Some rebel leaders proposed an alliance with whites seeking independence from France, but Toussaint broke away to form a rebel army of black Haitians that waged a guerilla war against French plantation owners and their mulatto allies.

When France and Spain went to war in 1793, Toussaint's forces allied themselves with rebellious colonists in Santo Domingo (today's Dominican Republic), the Spanish colony occupying the rest of the island of Hispaniola. Known as L'Ouverture for his striking tactics, Toussaint broke with the Santo Domingo rebels (and their British suppliers) in 1794 when the French Republic abolished slavery but the rebels did not. For his belated loyalty to France, Toussaint was rewarded with the lieutenant governorship of Saint-Domingue (Haiti). Toussaint proved to be a successful administrator, promoting economic growth and racial reconciliation, although at the cost of imposing a military discipline on the island's black and mulatto workforce. The French government was impressed enough to accept Toussaint's self-promotion to Governor General in 1796.

Against Napoleon's orders, Toussaint's forces overran Spanish Santo Domingo in 1801. Toussaint now ruled the entire island, and he ordered the abolition of slavery in the former Spanish colony. But he also issued a constitution that made him Governor General for life. Napoleon had no intentions of accepting Haitian autonomy: 11,000 French troops landed on Haiti's shores in January 1802 to restore French rule. Many whites and mulattos defected to the French, unhappy at the prospect of coexisting with a free black majority under Toussaint's rule. When many black leaders defected as well, Toussaint opened peace negotiations. In return for a French promise not to restore slavery, Toussaint agreed to lay down his arms in May 1802. He was originally allowed to retire to a plantation on the island, but was soon arrested on suspicion of plotting a new rebellion. Assured of a pardon if he would only go to Paris to defend himself, Toussaint surrendered. He was sent to Fort-de-Joux in France where he died on April 7, 1803.

Toussaint may have thought he died a failure, but, in 1803, an outbreak of Yellow Fever decimated French forces in Haiti. Another rebellion led by Toussaint's followers completed the defeat of the French and secured Haiti's independence, making it the second oldest free state in the Western Hemisphere.

slavery throughout Hispaniola. Brought up on Enlightenment ideas, Toussaint did not seek independence. He believed the island would fare best as part of the great French Revolutionary state, now headed by Napoleon Bonaparte. The French Revolution, after all, had been fought to bring "liberty, equality, and fraternity" to all. Issuing a Constitution, Toussaint proclaimed himself Governor General for life of a French colony with the right to make its own laws. But Napoleon

Founding father of Haiti.
Copyright © Historical Pictures/Stock Montage

decided it was necessary to maintain a much closer hold on the island's government because of the wealth Haitian sugar brought France. He sent a French force of 11,000 men to retake the island; they landed in January 1802. Tricked by the promise of vindicating himself in Paris, Toussaint surrendered to the French. Although he died in a French prison without ever seeing his native Haiti again, Toussaint's revolution continued as his men fought for the ideals of the French Revolution against France itself. On January 1, 1804, the island declared its independence as the republic of Haiti, although it took another five years of fighting to totally dislodge French troops from the eastern half of the island. The new nation, the second republic to be born in the Americas and the first to abolish slavery was led by Jean-Jacques Dessalines (1758–1806), one of Toussaint's lieutenants. He was succeeded by the self-proclaimed King Henri Christophe (r. 1807–1820), who attempted to foment slave rebellions in Surinam, Barbados, Guadeloupe, and Jamaica. Fighting off French attempts to reconquer it in 1814 and 1816, the new Haitian republic quickly degenerated into a dictatorship. The eastern half of the island, claimed by both Haiti and Spain, remained a virtual battleground until its final break from both powers in 1844, when it became the Dominican Republic.

◆ Spanish America

Stretching from what is now the northern border of California to the southern tip of South America, Spain's American territory was divided into five colonies: the Viceroyalty of New Spain (now the southwestern United States, Mexico, and all of Central America north of Panama), the Viceroyalty of New Granada (modern day Colombia, Venezuela, and Ecuador), the Viceroyalty of Peru (modern day Peru and north-western Bolivia), the Viceroyalty of la Plata (modern day Argentina, Uruguay, Paraguay, and the rest of Bolivia), and the Audiencia of Chile. Society within these colonies was highly stratified. Economic power was held by the *Creoles*, colonists of Spanish descent whose families had lived in the Americas for generations. The Creoles owned the plantations and served as the officer class in the colonial military. But the highest political offices in each colony were reserved for *Peninsulares*, officials sent over from Spain and reporting directly back to the Spanish crown. The majority of the inhabitants were neither of purely Spanish descent nor newly arrived from Spain. The colonies were peopled primarily by Indians, African slaves, and

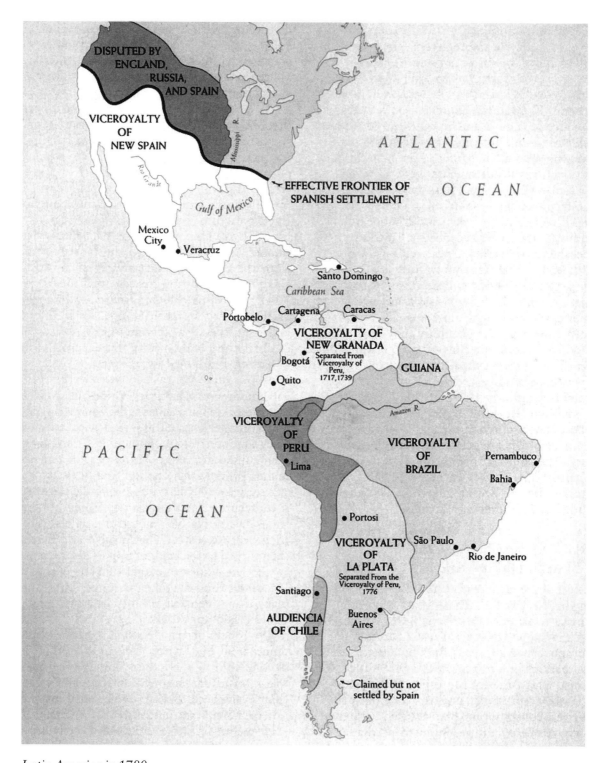

Latin America in 1780.
From *The Western Heritage, 6/e, Combined Edition,* by Donald Kagan, Steven Ozment, and Frank M. Turner. Copyright © 1998 by Prentice-Hall, Inc.

Latin America in 1830.
From *The Western Heritage, 6/e, Combined Edition,* by Donald Kagan, Steven Ozment, and Frank M. Turner.
Copyright © 1998 by Prentice-Hall, Inc.

people of various racial mixtures that resulted from centuries of living together. These were the *Mestizos* (a mixture of Spanish and Indian descent), *Mulattos* (a mixture of Spanish and African descent), and *Zambos* (a mixture of Indian and African descent) who worked on the plantations and in the mines, in varying degrees of servitude.

In 1780 an Indian rebellion briefly succeeded in controlling sections of Peru and Bolivia. It was led by the Peruvian rebel José Gabriel Condorcanqui (1742–1781) who renamed himself after Túpac Amaru (r. 1571–1572), the last Emperor of the Incas. The Creoles joined forces with Spain to crush the revolt. The Creoles wanted self-rule, but they had no wish to alter a system that guaranteed their economic and social pre-eminence.

◆ Mexico

In 1808, Napoleon Bonaparte invaded Spain. Several years of guerilla warfare followed as Spanish loyalists resisted French occupation. Spain's internal problems kept it from controlling affairs in its American colonies, although its colonial armies tried to hold those territories for Spain. In the town of Dolores, on the morning of September 16, 1810, a *Creole* priest named Miguel Hidalgo y Costilla (1753–1811), inspired by his reading of the *philosophes,* called on the largely Indian and Mestizo population of his parish to rebel against Spanish control. His revolutionary manifesto, the *Grito de Dolores,* inspired his untrained followers to a series of early victories, but Hidalgo was eventually captured, shot, and beheaded by Spanish troops stationed in Chihuahua. Neither his spirit nor his demand for changes in the colonial landholding system were so easily silenced. After a decade of battle between Spanish royalists and independence-minded patriots, Agustín de Iturbide (1783–1824) declared Mexico an independent state in 1821. Iturbide, a former royalist general, claimed that he favored racial equality and individual liberty, but his arrogance led him to follow the example of Napoleon and proclaim himself emperor. He was overthrown within two years. In 1824 Mexico became a republic. While its constitution was strikingly similar to that of the United States, the freedoms it promised were rarely made available to the masses of the nation's people.

◆ Bolívar's Pan-American Vision

Creole plantation owners in New Granada were also growing increasingly tired of being ruled by Spanish Peninsulares. In 1806, one of those Creole aristocrats, Francisco de Miranda (1750–1816), aided secretly by Britain and the United States, attempted to create a republic in Venezuela. His efforts failed and he fled to exile in Britain. When Napoleon Bonaparte invaded Spain in 1808, Miranda's followers thought the time was ripe to try again. After all, if Spain were busy defending itself against Napoleon, it could not simultaneously use all its power to hold on to its colonies. The man who led the revolution was Simón Bolívar (1783–1830). A Creole sent to France at age 16 to finish his education, Bolívar was exposed to the ideas of Locke, Montesquieu, Voltaire, and Rousseau. That, and what he saw in the United States on his way back home to Venezuela, convinced him that Spanish America must fight for its independence.

Venezuela declared its independence from Spain in 1811. Miranda was taken prisoner by Spanish troops when he tried to return to Venezuela. That left Bolívar in charge of the rebel troops. He defeated the Spanish armies in six battles and took control of Caracas (the capital city of Venezuela) in 1813. A grateful Venezuelan congress named him *El Libertador* (the Liberator). When Venezuelan troops loyal to Spain took back Caracas a year later, Bolívar was forced into exile. He soon returned with aid from Haiti's King Henri Christophe. After several years of fighting, Bolívar took Bogotá, the capital of Colombia, in 1819. He proclaimed it the capital of the new Republic of Gran Colombia, a federation of Colombia, Venezuela, and Ecuador. After three more years of war, Bolívar became the first president of Gran Colombia in 1822. This was only the first step in Bolívar's plan to unite all of Spanish America in a league strong enough to resist all outside interference. His armies marched into Peru in 1823. When they took it from Spain a year later, Bolívar became the president of Peru. In 1825, the region in La Plata known as Upper Peru was captured by Bolívar's lieutenants. It renamed itself Bolivia to honor Bolívar and named him its first president.

One year later, in 1826, Bolívar convened the world's first Pan-American Conference to lay the plans for his grand league of Spanish-American Republics. But Bolívar's own Gran Colombia was already awash in civil war as Venezuela and Ecuador each sought to break away from Bolívar's autocratic rule. Bolívar decided that Montesquieu's theories of checks and balances did not fit the realities of life in Spain's former colonies; he preferred constitutions with weak legislatures and strong executives elected for life. By 1830, Gran Colombia was no more: the independent states of Venezuela, Ecuador, and Colombia had taken its place. A deposed Bolívar retreated to his estate along the Colombian coast, where he died of tuberculosis in 1830 at the age of forty-seven.

◆ O'Higgins and San Martin

While Bolívar was fighting Spain in the north, Bernardo O'Higgins (1776/78–1842) and José de San Martin (1778–1850) were fighting Spain in the south. Bernardo O'Higgins was the illegitimate son of the Spanish-Irish governor of the Audiencia of Chile and a Creole Chilean mother. Sent at 16 to finish his education in Spain, he moved on to Britain where he was greatly influenced by the patriotism of the exiled Francisco de Miranda. He returned to Chile after his father's death in 1801 and spent the next several years working a large estate left him by his father. But in 1810 a group of Creole leaders took advantage of the chaos caused by Napoleon's invasion of Spain to take over the government of Chile. They established a congress (1811), and wrote a constitution (1813), only to find themselves invaded by forces loyal to Spain from the neighboring Viceroyalty of Peru (1814). O'Higgins left his estate to take up arms and quickly rose to the leadership of the revolutionary army. Badly outnumbered, O'Higgins and his troops fled into the Andes mountains on Chile's eastern border. By the end of 1814, it seemed as though Chile might never become independent. But there was hope further south.

José de San Martin was born into a Creole family in the portion of the Viceroyalty de la Plata that is now Argentina. His family moved to Spain when he was six, and, after completing his education there, San Martin became a officer in the Spanish army. He served that army loyally for twenty years. In 1811, however, after three years of fighting against the Napoleonic army that had invaded Spain, San Martin returned to the Americas. Arriving in Buenos Aires, the center of revolutionary activity in the Viceroyalty de la Plata, José de San Martin decided that his native land came first, and joined the revolution against Spain in 1812. After four years of fighting, San Martin's forces saw the Viceroyalty gain its independence as the United Provinces of the Rio de la Plata in 1816. Fearing that no Spanish-American republic would be secure as long as Spain held a single colony on the mainland, San Martin aimed at driving the Spanish out of their last stronghold, the Viceroyalty of Peru. Unable to reach it through the jungles to the north, San Martin led his armies over the Andes mountains and linked up with Bernardo O'Higgins. Together they reconquered Chile. With O'Higgins now its leader, Chile became an independent state in 1818. San Martin could now move up the coast to Peru. In 1821, he forced the Spanish out of Lima, Peru's capital city. But Bolívar had his eye on Peru. Bolívar and San Martin met on July 26, 1822, to decide how to finish the liberation of Spanish America. What happened at that meeting is not known, but San Martin left the liberation of the rest of Peru to Bolívar's troops. A disenchanted San Martin quit the Americas to spend the rest of his life in Europe.

Bernardo O'Higgins fared little better than his colleagues. Because he angered the Church and the Creole plantation owners by trying to make them pay taxes, and angered the business classes by failing to protect their interests, he was forced out of office in Chile in 1823. He ended his life in exile in Peru.

◆ Portuguese America

Brazil, the largest colony in South America, belonged to Portugal. Its fate took an unexpected turn when the Portuguese royal family fled there in 1807 to escape Napoleon's armies. The exiled royal family declared Brazil an independent state. Brazil was far richer in natural resources and a hundred times larger than Portugal. When the Congress of Vienna restored the royal family to their Portuguese throne in 1814, they were reluctant to leave Brazil. When King João VI (r. 1816–1826) finally returned to Portugal in 1820, he appointed his son Pedro as regent of Brazil, and secretly encouraged him to resist any reversion to colonial status. By the end of 1822 Dom Pedro asserted the full independence of Brazil and became its reigning Emperor as Pedro I (r. 1822–1831). Pedro attempted to rule Brazil as an enlightened despot, but when he lost a border war against Argentina he forfeited the confidence of his aristocrats. He was forced to abdicate in 1831 in favor of his five-year old son and successor, Pedro II (r. 1831–1889). When Pedro II came to rule, he instituted systemic reforms in education and trade, and permitted Brazil to become a constitutional monarchy. But in Brazil, as in the Spanish republics, true independence was reserved exclusively to the Creole aristocracy.

◆ Independence and Disintegration

The new Latin American states were unstable republics under the control of Creole soldiers and plantation owners. The majority of the population, the Mestizos, Mulattos, Zambos, Indians, and enslaved Africans were no better off under their new Creole rulers than they had been under Spanish or Portuguese control. In many instances the new republics faced decades of intermittent civil war as the disenfranchised majority tried to wrest power from the new dictators. The republics were also in the process of breaking up. As mentioned earlier, Gran Colombia broke up into Venezuela, Colombia, and Ecuador. Even as José de San Martin sailed backed to the Viceroyalty of La Plata, its northeastern province declaring its independence from both Spain and the La Plata as the new country of Paraguay (1811). La Plata continued to splinter: Bolivia (1825) and Uruguay (1828) broke away, and all that was left of La Plata was Argentina.

Mexico also lost much of its territory. All of modern day Central America north of Panama had been one administrative unit inside Spain's Viceroyalty of Mexico. As Mexico fought for independence from Spain, the Creole leaders in Central America fought amongst themselves (some wanted to join with Mexico, others wanted to go it alone) and against Mexico. At a conference in 1823, a new country was born: the United Provinces of Central America. By 1840, it had broken up into the countries of Guatemala, El Salvador, Honduras, Nicaragua, and Costa Rica.

The age of revolution achieved decidedly mixed results. The constitutional structure of the United States offered opportunities for "the pursuit of happiness" that were denied to the masses by Europe's rigid social hierarchy. Still, it was not revolutionary enough to eliminate slavery. Revolutions in Latin America brought independence without social or political equality. France's revolution began with a king (Louis XVI) and ended with an Emperor (Napoleon I). The Congress of Vienna that followed put the old ruling families back on their thrones, but the liberal ideas loosed by the Enlightenment and the French Revolution continued to undermine the political stability of Europe throughout the nineteenth century.

At the same time, Science and the Enlightenment were producing yet another revolution in Europe, the Industrial Revolution. Every time we turn on the faucet, switch on a light, start our cars, or get into our favorite pair of jeans we reap the benefits of that revolution. The Industrial Revolution is the subject of the next chapter in our history of the *modern* world.

◆ Notes

1. Jean-Jacques Rousseau, *Du contract social,* edited by J.-L. Lecercle (Paris: Éditions Sociales, 1968), 72 [I.7].

2. *Posthumous Works of Frederic II*, Vol. 5: *Political, Philosophical and Satyrical Miscellanies,* translated by Thomas Holcroft (London: G. and J. Robinson, 1789), 8–15, 17–18.

3. Marvin Perry et al, *Sources of the Western Tradition,* 4th ed. (Boston: Houghton Mifflin Company, 1999), 109–111.

3

Industrialization and Its Consequences

The *philosophes* looked forward to a golden age of humanity based on the scientific investigation of human society. Published one year after his execution during the Reign of Terror, Condorcet's *Outlines of an Historical View of the Progress of the Human Mind* (1795) still proclaimed to the world that "the prosperity, resulting from the progress that will be made by the useful arts, in consequence of their being founded upon a sound [scientific] theory" and the "improved legislation, built upon the truths of the political sciences" would "naturally dispose men" to "benevolence" and "justice," leading to the "infinite improvement" of human life.[1]

While the wars resulting from the French Revolution cast doubt on the soundness of Enlightenment political ideals, a very different kind of revolution—an Industrial Revolution—challenged its faith in a technologically created paradise. Two essential elements define the Industrial Revolution: the invention of machines that produced goods rapidly and efficiently, and the replacement of human or animal power by non-animal sources of energy. Industrialization created a new kind of production: labor, machinery, raw materials, and management were all focused in a single location, the "mill" or "factory." Using a principle known as the "division of labor," the production of any item was broken down into separate stages, with specialized machines performing each task in the process. Machine manufactured goods could be mass produced at a vastly cheaper price than handmade items because of this centralization and specialization. Machines altered the fabric of daily life, changing where people worked and how long they worked, where they lived, and the products available to them.

Industrialization led to a surge in wealth and population. Between 1750 and 1900 Europe's population grew from 140 to 400 million. The wealth that flowed from a machine-based economy enabled the industrialized nations of Europe and North America to impose their will upon the rest of the world while revolutionizing their own internal social structures. Urbanization, changes in the status of women and children, and new ideologies of liberty and social equality were as much consequences of the Industrial Revolution (1750–1850) as were factories, cheaper consumer goods, and weapons capable of enslaving whole continents. No portion of the world is unaffected today by the process of industrialization that began over two centuries ago in Great Britain.

Great Britain and the Industrial Revolution

◆ Why Great Britain?

Britain was a leading commercial nation in the middle of the eighteenth century and intensely proud that its worldwide trade had increased by almost 500 percent since 1700. Its military successes against France were gaining it an ever growing overseas empire. But there were several differences between the political, economic, and social structures of Great Britain and its continental rivals that made Britain the birthplace of the industrial world.

Britain's government was more stable than any other of the monarchies of Europe. While Britain was a monarchy, its real rulers were the landed aristocrats of Parliament. In France, a nobleman who engaged in business risked *dérogation*, loss of his legal privileges. In Britain nobles and commoners alike flocked to invest in state-chartered trading monopolies and the Bank of England (whose initial shareholders included pharmacists, sailors, and cloth workers as well as 30 Members of Parliament and nine Peers of the Realm). The active pursuit of international trade brought tremendous capital resources into Great Britain, and the Bank of England (established 1694) guaranteed merchant investors a solid currency. The enterprising owners of London's coffee houses chalked up the latest stock prices on slate boards, creating the world's first stock exchange.

Equally important was the Agricultural Revolution, a series of agricultural innovations initiated by men like Jethro Tull (1674–1714). Traveling through France in 1711, Tull saw peasants hoeing the furrows around grapevines in vineyards. Aerating the soil allowed plants to make more effective use of water and raised crop production even without fertilization. Tull returned home to argue for the use of iron plows. He even developed a drill planter that eliminated the need to "broadcast" seed; it put each seed at just the right depth for every crop. Lord Charles Townshend (1674–1738) taught British farmers how to use fertilizer in sandy soils, and, by rotating their crops as the Dutch did, to restore productivity of their lands. Growing wheat, turnips, barley, and clover in sequence brought new life to once depleted land. With more fodder available to feed animals, farmers were soon making use of Robert Blakewell's (1725–1795) scientific breeding to raise animals that were healthier and produced more milk and meat. Together, the changes introduced by these men altered forever the eating patterns and improved the nutrition of Britain. Arthur Young (1741–1820) edited the leading agriculture journal in Britain and made certain that each advance was well publicized. By the 1790s Young could report that Great Britain had the richest and healthiest peasantry in Europe. England's agricultural output just about doubled between 1700 and 1800 even though there had been a 28 percent drop in the farming population.

The new agricultural methods were most efficient when they were used on large tracts of lands, but England's landed estates had been subdivided into small tenancies for centuries. Many tenants held formal rights to graze their farm animals on large open tracts called "commons" because the tenants shared the use of the pasture. Other workers, called "cottagers" because they lived in small houses (cottages) supplied by the landowner, were also allowed to use the "commons" without a having a formal lease. Between 1760 and 1840 Parliament passed hundreds of measures permitting over seven million acres of these "commons" to be enclosed for private use. These laws required tenants to pay for fencing the land they enclosed. Those who could not afford to do so lost the right to use the commons. Cottagers were not even given the opportunity to pay for fencing because they had no leases. Much of the enclosed land was used for sheep grazing instead of for farming because woolen cloth was Britain's largest and most profitable export. These Enclosure Acts benefitted the larger economy, but forced thousands of once self-sufficient farmers off the land. Some became day laborers on those farms, but many more moved to the cities and became the world's first industrial work force. Better diet and commercial farming supported a population revolution. Great Britain's population soared from 8.3 million in 1770 to 14.2 million by 1821.

Despite these changes, the Industrial Revolution would never have happened in Britain had it lacked iron and coal reserves. These natural resources were vital requirements for industrial growth and both were abundant in Great Britain. British capital, the wealth accumulated by merchants and businessmen, financed the rapid development of national coal and iron deposits during the eighteenth century. The government of Great Britain was particularly determined to develop coal as a fuel reserve because the island was being progressively deforested. In 1705, Thomas Newcomen (1663–1729) invented a steam-powered pump to clear water out of deep mine shafts. This early steam engine made the collieries (coal mines) far more productive and profitable. The increasing supply of coal made possible the creation of large amounts of coke, a carbonized residue of coal vital to iron smelting. Spurred on by the profits to be won from the military contracts supporting Britain imperial expansion, Abraham Darby (1678–1717) pioneered the use of coke in his iron mills at Coalbrookdale. His innovations resulted in a more moldable iron produced on a much larger scale than ever before. A "puddling" process developed by Henry Cort (1740–1800) in 1784 to burn away additional carbon from large batches of molten iron ore made iron that was even easier to shape, increasing its usefulness. Britain's annual iron production jumped from 17,000 tons in 1740 to 2 million tons by 1840, making it the world's top producer. The cannon and shot formed from some of that iron helped Britain triumph in its wars against Napoleon.

Half-naked men, women, and children spent their days crawling underground to coal-power Britain's Industrial Revolution.
Copyright © Bildarchiv Preussischer Kulturbesitz

◆ Revolution in the Textile Trade

No industry so well demonstrates the transforming effects of industrialization as does the production of textiles (cloth), one of the oldest human crafts. Ever since the British East India company introduced Indian cottons to the British market during the seventeenth century, Britain's consumers had flocked to buy them. Local producers wanted to increase their profits by bringing in raw cotton from India and manufacturing the cloth themselves. In 1733, John Kay (1704–1764) invented a "flying shuttle" that automatically moved thread across a loom. Because weavers no longer needed an assistant to move the shuttle across a wide bolt of cloth, one person could now do the work of two. Weavers were thrown out of work because the production of thread, still spun by hand on a wheel, could not keep pace with the demands of the larger, faster looms. In 1761 the Royal Society offered a prize for a faster spinning machine, which may have inspired James Hargreaves (1732–1778) to invent his "spinning jenny" (1764), a machine that spun eight threads at the same time. One spinner now did the work of eight.

The textile mills of the early Industrial Revolution were located near streams since waterpower could drive machinery more efficiently than could human muscle. The "water frame," developed by Richard Arkwright (1732–1792) in 1769, a further adaptation of spinning machinery, could put thread on over a hundred spindles at once. Manufacturers soon discovered that nature was an unreliable business partner, however: streams could run dry. A more secure power source was necessary, and, fortunately, James Watt (1736–1819) of Glasgow had developed a more efficient version of the steam engine. Watt's engine could be used not only to pump out a flooded mine (as had Newcomen's engine), but also to transfer power to the cranks, cogs, pulleys, and belts of a textile factory efficiently. Freed from dependence on waterpower, factories could now be located anywhere, and owners immediately took notice of the many laborers available in the cities. Productivity soared. By 1830 British factories were churning out 347 million yards of cotton cloth a year. "Body linen" (so called because it was made of linen cloth, a luxury product) had once been the privilege of wealth. Now every factory worker could afford cheap cotton underwear.

These technological innovations were transforming British society just as political revolution was beginning in France. The violence and turmoil that flowed from the French Revolution (1789–1799) and the Napoleonic Wars prevented the rest of Europe from even trying to catch up to Britain. As the armies of France, Britain, Austria, and Prussia fought each other on the mainland, the island of Great Britain continued to transform itself. New cities devoted to the textile trade, such as Manchester in the Midlands, became industrial giants. A modest town of 17,000 in 1750, Manchester exploded to a population of 367,000 a century later. The mechanical production of cloth was the stimulus that transformed British society and made Great Britain the "workshop of the world."

◆ The Impact of Industrialization

The ripples caused by the mechanization of Great Britain's textile industry soon became evident around the world. Despite the fact that France was at war with Great Britain, Napoleon ignored his own boycott of British goods and accepted the smuggling of British cloth so that his armies could be clothed more cheaply. Napoleon's decision increased British wealth and ultimately helped his enemy overthrow him. Great Britain's enormous demand for raw cotton even changed the history of the United States. Most of the cotton grown in the United States was unsuitable for

JAMES WATT (1736–1819)

James Watt was born on January 19, 1736, in Greenock, Scotland, the son of a successful builder. A sickly child (he suffered from migraines his whole life), Watt spent much of his time in his father's workshop making models of simple machines. After training at Glasgow University and in London, he became a scientific-instrument maker for Glasgow University in 1757. In 1764, James married his cousin Margaret Miller. They had four children (two of whom died in infancy) before Margaret's death in child-birth in 1773.

In 1764, Watt's primary responsibility was repairing Glasgow University's Newcomen engine. Watt was struck by the amount of energy it wasted, and, within a year, invented a separate condenser to correct the problem. To support his rapidly growing family, Watt had accepted work as a land surveyor in Scotland, but, in 1768, he started a company with John Roebuck (1718–1794) of the Carron Iron Works to turn out his new engines. To insure the profitability of his company, Watt took out a patent for his unique condenser in 1769. His inventive genius soon created more improvements, and he obtained patents for rotary motion, double-acting pistons, parallel rods, and a pressure gauge. In 1784 he even registered a patent for a steam-powered carriage. When Roebuck went bankrupt in 1772, Watt started a new company with Matthew Boulton (1728–1809), owner of the Soho Iron Works in Birmingham, England. The recently widowed Watt moved his family to Birmingham in 1774, and there, in 1775, he married Anne MacGregor (d. 1832) with whom he would have two more children.

Each improvement to Watt's steam engine increased the demand for it. By 1790, Watt's engines were in use in mines, ironworks, cotton mills, paper mills, distilleries, and canals. The success of his engines made James Watt a wealthy man, and brought him several honors from the scientific community. He was elected to the Royal Society in 1785, received a law degree from the University of Glasgow in 1806, and was created one of eight foreign associates of the French Academy of Sciences in 1814. Nor were his interests limited to engineering. Watt was one of two Englishmen (the other was Henry Cavendish, 1731–1810) to independently discover that water was composed of oxygen and hydrogen. Watt vainly hoped this discovery would lead to a cure for his son Gregory, who died of tuberculosis in 1804.

Watt's eldest son James (1769–1848) caused him considerable concern when he became involved with the radical element of the French Revolution. But James Jr. quarreled with Robespierre and the Jacobeans in 1793, and returned home to work in his father's company. When Watt retired in 1800, James Jr. took over management of the firm along with Boulton's son Matthew. In retirement, James Sr. invented a machine that could reproduce original sculptures. In 1817 the never satisfied inventor had the ship *Caledonia* fitted out with his engine, and she became the first steamship to sail from England. Watt died at home on August 25, 1819.

textile manufacturing because each boll had so many seeds that hand cleaning was not cost effective. But, in 1793, Eli Whitney (1765–1825), the Yale-educated son of a Massachusetts farmer, developed the cotton gin (short for cotton engine) to remove the seeds mechanically. The export trade of the United States boomed, and cotton quickly became its number one product. Southern states prospered as a result, and thriving plantation owners defended black slavery as a "positive good" for the nation.

The Industrial Revolution in Europe, 1815–1860   Areas of industrial concentration and growth in Britain and on the continent.
From *History of Modern Europe*, First Edition, (1996), W. W. Norton & Company.

Machines altered forever the scale of production. With ships still powered by the wind in their sails, all British warships needed dozens of pulley blocks to haul the sails up and down to catch the wind. Those pulley blocks needed frequent replacement. For most of the eighteenth century, a great arsenal at Portsmouth had employed a skilled work force of 110 men who hand-shaped the pulleys needed by the world's most powerful navy. In 1808, a panel of admirals approved an engineering plan to use forty-three newly designed machines driven by a single steam engine to manufacture the blocks. From then on the 100,000 pulley blocks used each year by the navy were produced by just ten unskilled laborers. The British navy saved a fortune in labor costs, but over a hundred skilled workmen had to find new employment.

In another example of the ripple effects of industrialization, John Wilkinson (1728–1808) used hardened steel to create the tougher cutting edge necessary to precisely bore engine cylinders. Boring machines with Wilkinson's blades were so sharp they could cut iron efficiently, transforming a process that had been slow and labor-intensive. The jobs lost in the transformation were more than equaled by those created by the increased demand for iron and steel. Wilkinson's innovation helped make possible both Watt's high-efficiency steam engines and larger cannons that were more accurate because their barrels were cut straighter and more precisely. The same technology that made Watt's steam engine possible also increased the destructive capacity of British artillery and helped it sweep Napoleon's navy from the seas.

As factories began to proliferate across the British landscape, it was soon apparent that a better transportation network was needed to get the raw materials to the factories and the manufac-

Eli Whitney's cotton gin made the American plantation system (and slavery) profitable.
Copyright © CORBIS/Bettmann

tured goods from the factories to market. Britain already possessed a vast fleet of ships to handle trade with its colonies and the world, and Parliament had approved government spending to improve Britain's harbors. Then, in 1807, the American Robert Fulton (1765–1815) successfully mounted a steam engine on a ship and inaugurated a new type of water travel. By the end of the nineteenth century the time it took to cross the Atlantic Ocean had been reduced from two months to about a week. Speedy delivery of raw materials for the industrial system was assured. On land, however, Britain's roads proved inadequate to handle the enormous horse and wagon traffic necessary to supply raw materials to factories and haul their products to port. New roads had to be constructed, and new methods of paving them were introduced. Because the earliest factories were constructed alongside streams and land transportation was so expensive, Britain needed more canals, man-made waterways linking up its mines, factories, rivers, and ports. The Sankey Navigation Canal (1757), connecting coal fields to the Mersey River, was the first step in tying the country together. By 1850, Britain's canal system had grown from 1,000 to 4,250 miles.

Canals were only one of the transportation innovations fostered by the Industrial Revolution. The steam-powered railroad engine changed Great Britain even more than had the canals. Several British inventors, including James Watt, had patented locomotive designs, but the first one to prove practical was that designed in 1814 by mine mechanic George Stephenson (1781–1848) to move coal from the mine to waiting canal barges. It could only run at four miles per hour up hill loaded with 30 tons of coal, but it was still doing the work of fifty horses. On September 18, 1830, his new engine, the *Rocket* (clocked at 29 miles per hour in test runs) inaugurated the brand new sixty-mile-long Liverpool and Manchester Railroad line, demonstrating

GEORGE STEPHENSON (1781–1848)

Inventor and self-made locomotive magnate. Copyright © National Museum of Photography, Film & Television/SSPL

Geoorge Stephenson was born on June 8, 1781, in Wylam, England, to working class parents. His father operated a New-comen engine at the local coal mine; his mother was the daughter of a cloth dyer. There was no school in Wylam, and neither George nor his four brothers and sisters learned to read until they were adults. At the age of eight, George was sent out to tend cows for a local farmer at two pence a day. At ten he became a "picker" at the mine, sort-ing coal from rock for all of six pence a day. By the age of 14, he was working as his father's assistant and earning a grown man's salary—one shilling (twelve pence) a day—because of his talent for keeping the Newcomen engine working. At eigh-teen he was finally making enough money to afford the one-guinea (252 pence) annual fee for night classes at a trade school where he learned to read, write, add, subtract, multiply, and divide.

Stephenson courted Elizabeth Hindmarsh, the daughter of a wealthy local farmer, but was rejected by her father because of his poverty. Disappointed, he turned for comfort to Frances Henderson, a servant at a local farm, and they wed in 1802. To earn extra income for his new family, Stephenson taught himself to repair clocks and watches. When Frances died of con-sumption in 1806, George took over the care of their young son Robert (1803–1859), making sure the boy went to a proper day school.

Stephenson's ability to handle both New-comen and Watt engines earned him the position of chief mechanic at the Killingworth mine. There,

in 1813, he saw a steam boiler on wheels built by John Blenkinsop (1783–1831) haul coal from the mine shaft to the waiting barges. The machine had frequent breakdowns, and Stephenson con-vinced Killingworth's owner that he could design a better one. The *Blucher,* his first locomotive, was built in 1814. But Stephenson was not satis-fied with it, and his 1815 patent for a "steam blast"—a method of increasing an engine's draft by exhausting steam through a chimney—made steam locomotives truly practical. With his increas-ing success, Stephenson was able to afford the eighty pounds needed to send his son Robert to Edinburgh University for one term. And he felt himself able to remarry. Finally winning the approval of Mr. Hindmarsh, George wed his Elizabeth in 1820. They remained happily wed, although childless, until her death in 1845.

With investment capital from his friends, Stephenson set up the Newcastle Rail Works (1823) to manufacture rails and locomotives. Hearing of plans to build a tram road from Stock-ton to Darlington using horse-drawn carts, Stephenson convinced the builders to try one of his locomotives instead. On September 27, 1825, a Stephenson locomotive pulled the thirty-six cars of the first public passenger train from Darlington to Stockton at the unheard of speed of 12 miles per hour. Stephenson's new engine, the *Rocket,* was chosen to inaugurate the Liver-pool and Manchester railway line in 1830. By now quite wealthy, Stephenson spent the rest of his life designing and building locomotives, rail-ways, and bridges.

He was wed for a third time, to his house-keeper, one Miss Gregory, in January 1848, just five months before his sixty-seventh birthday, but died of a recurring pleurisy on August 12. Robert, who had been managing the Newcastle Rail Works since his father's 1845 retirement, went on to become a famous designer of bridges; he constructed the Victoria Bridge at Montreal, the longest bridge in the world when it opened in 1859.

that human bodies, defying dire medical predictions, were able to stand the physical stress of such speed. One of the invited guests decided to make too close an inspection of the track and became railroading's first fatality, but the accident was hushed up for fear of scaring off potential customers.

For the first time in the history of the world it was cheaper to ship goods by land than by sea. By 1850 locomotive speeds of 50 m.p.h. were commonplace. Originally intended to serve factory needs, railroads soon became the preferred mode of passenger travel. Britain's 800 miles of track in 1840 grew to 6,600 miles by 1850. Entrepreneurs in the United States, inspired by reports of British advances, opened the first American railroad in 1830, with France following in 1837.

◆ The Spread of Industrialization

The first century of the world's industrial transformation was dominated by Great Britain. "Steam is an Englishman" was the lament of Britain's competitors, but the techniques and methods pioneered by British firms could not long be kept secret. Within the course of another fifty years rapid developments in the oil, steel, and electric industries ended British supremacy. The second phase of the Industrial Revolution saw the nations of Western Europe challenge British domination while the United States gradually displaced it as the manufacturing center of the globe. Most of the countries of Europe possessed the necessary iron and coal reserves and contained masses of laborers to staff the new factories. Starting their industrialization later than Britain, they began by installing the latest technology instead of having to update older versions as Britain was soon forced to do. European inventors were soon keeping up with, and sometimes outpacing their British counterparts. One such example was the rapid adoption of open-hearth steel making in Prussia after 1866. Karl Wilhelm Siemens (1823–1883) had emigrated from Prussia to Britain. He was a naturalized British citizen—awarded a knighthood for his innovations in producing high quality steel—but when Prussia needed the process Siemens invented, he gave it to his brother. The improved furnace, in which high quality steel was made by combining pig and scrap iron, enabled his native country to match British steel production by 1900.

Yet the country that eventually seized world industrial primacy was the United States of America. Conceived as an agricultural republic by Thomas Jefferson, the United States was already beginning to change as the Napoleonic Wars came to an end. By the 1820s the factory system became permanently established in places such as Lowell, Massachusetts, and industrialization proceeded rapidly in the northern United States as turnpikes, canals, and railroads eased internal commerce and fostered an emerging national marketplace. By 1836 Lowell alone had twenty major mills employing 7,000 workers, most of them young women. In Lowell, as in Britain, wages were low; average pay for a six day, 72 hour week was $3.50. The response to industrialization, indeed its very course, was different in America than in Britain, however. Workers such as the "Lowell girls" rarely considered themselves victims of the new economy. Without the centuries of craft tradition that had existed in Europe and with labor needs generally outstripping demand, factory efficiency seemed more natural in the United States. The sheer vastness of the country mean that American railroads had to be more extensive than Britain's. In addition American inventiveness soon challenged Britain's accomplishments. Eli Whitney also developed the technology of assembling manufactured goods from interchangeable parts, a technique that came to be called "the American system." New inventions, such as the telegraph and code (1844) developed by Samuel Morse (1791–1872), began to flow out of the United States. As leadership in technology gradually shifted across the ocean after 1840, British investors poured capital into the United States and helped to solidify its industrial base.

THE LOWELL GIRLS

In 1813 Francis Cabot Lowell (1775–1817) organized the Boston Manufacturing Company in Waltham, Massachusetts, putting all cotton textile operations under one roof. He had traveled to Britain to study mill operations there and was heavily influenced by the value placed on the worker in Robert Owen's New Lanark Mills. When Lowell's company needed a larger facility in 1826, he was able to incorporate many of those values in the new "textile city" he built along the Merrimac River.

Hundreds of young, unmarried girls from rural New England were recruited from poor families willing to let daughters make their own way but concerned that they not face city life unprotected. The average work career at the mills was only three years. Most of the women hoped to earn enough to contribute towards a future marriage. Some saved for their own continued education, and many for their brothers'. Company tradition had it that a quarter of the men who attended Harvard went through on the earnings of their sisters. The firm built chaperoned boarding houses, provided educational programs and libraries, and churches for their moral instruction. Most boarding houses even had a piano. The work was hard: six days a week, twelve hours a day from March to September, breakfast at six and only 45 minutes for lunch. Curfew at the boarding houses was ten o'clock. Still, the young women even found time to publish their own magazine (*The Offering*).

Children under 15 who worked as bobbin-doffers were taken out of the mills for the three months' schooling required by state law. Lucy Larcom (1824-1893), a popular poet, was probably the best known graduate of the Lowell mills. The daughter of a boardinghouse-keeper, she began as a bobbin-doffer for a dollar a week plus room and board until she was old enough for the spinning machines. Weaving was the highest paid job available to the women: only men were supervisors. But Larcom turned down a promotion to the looms to work in a lower paid but quieter part of the mill, the cloth room, where workers were actually allowed to read between measuring and folding bolts of cloth.

As competition grew, owners cut piece-work rates; in October 1834, over 800 girls turned out in protest. New hires undercut their organizing effort but they did recover half the original wage cut. In 1836, when boardinghouse rates were raised, a strike involving half the workforce was more successful. As the cooperative spirit waned, recruiting efforts focused on Irish immigrants rather than native New Englanders. The twenty Lowell mills had only 4% foreign-born workers in 1836, but the percentage grew to 60% by the 1860s when there were forty mills employing 10,000 workers. An Irish-led strike in 1859 was totally crushed. Although agitation for the ten-hour day began at Lowell in the 1840s, the reform was not adopted until 1875. By then the workforce had been transformed into an industrial proletariat drawn from the immigrant class.

◆ Steel and Vertical Integration

A major area in which the United States outpaced Britain was in the manufacture of steel. As late as 1850 Britain led the world in producing iron, pouring 2.5 million tons a year, but only 60,000 of those tons were steel. Steel was expensive to make because of the difficulty of removing all the contaminants contained in iron ore. An American, William "Pig Iron" Kelly (1811–1888), solved this industrial dilemma in 1851 by using a blast of air to "decarburize" molten iron, converting it to steel quickly and cheaply. The Englishman Sir Henry Bessemer (1813–1896), who also experimented with an air blast furnace, bought out Kelly's patent and further developed the process that still bears his name. Once the Bessemer converter and the Siemens open-hearth furnace had been developed, steel became the basic commodity for the construction of railroads, ships, bridges, skyscrapers, and weapons. America, with plentiful iron ore and coal deposits, made huge quantities of Bessemer steel for the railways that spanned the continent by 1869, and seized leadership of the steel industry.

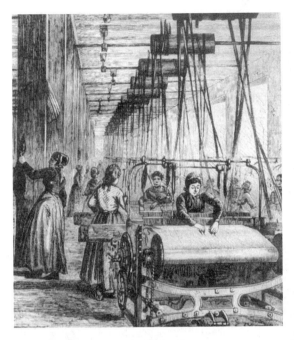

Young women formed the bulk of the workforce in nineteenth-century textile mills.
Copyright © Bildarchiv Preussischer Kulturbesitz

Andrew Carnegie (1835–1919), a Scot who emigrated to the United States at the age of thirteen, was the man most responsible for the American victory in the race to produce and market steel products. One of the 35 million Europeans who came to the United States in the century after 1820, Carnegie first worked as a mill bobbin boy for $1.20 a week, then as a telegraph operator whose talent made him secretary to the general superintendent of the Pennsylvania Railroad. While learning managerial techniques, he also learned that rails made of steel lasted twenty times longer than those made of iron. Then he struck out on his own. After 1873, Carnegie focused entirely on developing steel products as he ruthlessly constructed the most efficient company in the world. Carnegie made use of the most advanced science, hired only the most talented managers, rationalized production to save the smallest part of a penny, bought out his major competitors, beat back unionization, and plowed back profits to build an ever-larger manufacturing base. He bought up iron ore reserves, constructed his own railroads, marketed his varied products, and "integrated" the multifaceted operations of Carnegie Steel until they meshed perfectly. He created a vertical corporation, one that held complete control of a product as it advanced from raw material to marketable goods. By 1890 United States' steel makers surpassed Great Britain in steel ingots production; Carnegie Steel alone poured 322,000 tons. Ten years later it produced 3 million tons, and out-produced all of Great Britain by itself.

John David Rockefeller (1839–1937) hated competition as much as Carnegie did. Entering the new oil industry in 1863, Rockefeller consolidated 95 percent of the refining capacity of the United States into a "horizontal corporation" called Standard Oil. Standard Oil's virtual monopoly of refining facilities made it necessary for all independent oil producers to make use of Rockefeller's services. Rockefeller eliminated competitors by price slashing, obtaining illegal rebates, and planting industrial spies. Pipelines, oil fields, railroads, and marketing outlets were soon added to Standard Oil's empire, as it followed Carnegie's lead to become a vertically integrated company. By 1880 Rockefeller had achieved his goal of creating a monopoly, a "trust" to control the market for petroleum products, making himself America's first billionaire in the process. Split up by the United States government in 1911, Standard Oil's heirs are Exxon, Texaco, and Amoco.

Modern skyscrapers depend on the cheap production of steel made possible by the Bessemer converter.
Copyright © CORBIS/Bettemann

Carnegie, who sold off his steel company in 1901, spent the rest of his life giving away his $480 million proceeds. He believed that to die rich was to die in disgrace. Two universities, a Foundation for the Advancement of Teaching, the Endowment for International Peace, a Peace Palace in the Hague, Netherlands, and a plethora of public buildings are evidence of his attempts to distribute his wealth. Despite giving away over 7,500 church organs and building 2,500 libraries, the steel maker failed to accomplish his goal, and he died rich. The effort he initiated continues, however, and the foundations he established have given away over $5.5 billion. Rockefeller's largesse surpassed even Carnegie's, once he was convinced that philanthropy made for a good business image. Rockefeller family foundations have dispersed sums of money far surpassing the ten-billion-dollar mark. Both these American "robber barons" came to believe that wealth was "a sacred trust" to be used for the good of all.

Reactions to Industrial Capitalism

◆　　Explaining Capitalism

The dynamic nature of the Industrial Revolution is far easier to understand looking backward than it was for people who actually experienced its often drastic changes. Those who lived through it knew that the economic world was changing, but rare saw the changes forming any

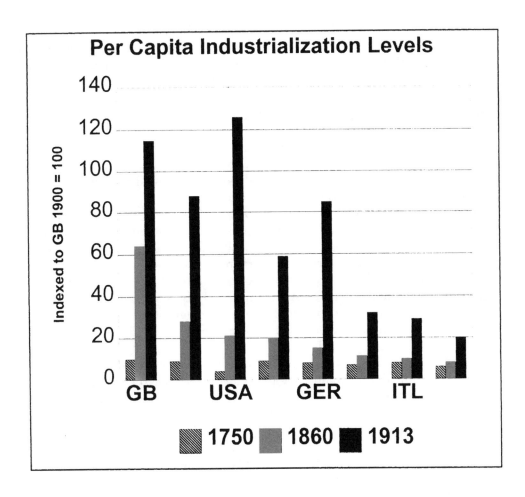

Per Capita Industrialization Levels

Indexed to GB 1900 = 100

GB   USA   GER   ITL

1750   1860   1913

Source: P. Bairoch, "International Industrialization Levels from 1750 to 1980," *Journal of European Economic History* 11 (Spring 1982): 294.

coherent pattern. The task of explaining the evolving system was undertaken by Adam Smith (1723–1790). Born in the Scottish village of Kirkcaldy, the son of a customs official, Smith went on to become a Professor of Moral Philosophy at Glasgow University. A nobleman impressed by Smith's writings on moral truth hired him as a tutor to his son, and they together they traveled to Paris. In the French capital, Smith participated in discussions with the *philosophes*, especially with the economic theorists known as *Physiocrats*. Led by François Quesnay (1694–1774), the *Physiocrats* stressed two economic principles: first, there should be free trade between nations and second, that land was the source of all wealth. Smith joined the debates, carefully defined his disagreements and, slowly over a decade, wrote *An Inquiry into the Nature and Causes of the Wealth of Nations* (1776).

Published in the same year as the American *Declaration of Independence* and *Common Sense*, Smith's *Wealth of Nations* analyzed the emerging economic order of industrial capitalism. Smith had learned from Quesnay that "when left alone, the world moves of its own accord," and he transformed this insight into the great principle of *laissez-faire*. According to Smith, it was the enterprising spirit of individual investors that created the conditions that fostered industrial growth. The government ought to stay out of economic affairs, permit the marketplace to operate, and allow entrepreneurs to make their own economic decisions. The market that Smith described operated best when left alone. The laws of supply and demand kept an economy in balance without government interference. The same division of labor that ensured efficient factory production ensured efficient social production: motivated by self-interest, human beings naturally gravitated to those specialized tasks they did best. So, they naturally divided up the labor of producing everything a society needed between themselves, increasing that society's productivity. And, for Smith, product, which he defined as labor applied to natural resources, was wealth. With the "invisible hand" of supply and demand balancing human efforts, those self-interested individuals worked for the good of all in society without even knowing they were doing so.

Smith's ideas undermined the rationale supporting *mercantilism,* the then dominant economic theory. Because mercantilists thought only gold and silver were wealth, they encouraged governments to regulate the economy to prevent gold and silver from leaving the country to pay for imported goods. Smith argued that government efforts to create a positive balance of trade (more exports than imports) by means of tariffs, monopolies, and regulations were counterproductive. Instead governments should recognize that the native skills, natural resources, and climate unique to each country determined its productive capacity. Logically, therefore, a program of free trade in locally produced products would be most beneficial for each individual nation and for all combined.

Economic liberalism, the ideology that blended Enlightenment political principles with Smith's work, argued that individuals should have the right to set their own courses towards wealth, and to acquire it without governmental interference. Nineteenth-century liberals believed that if government stayed out of economic affairs—except for its necessary roles in defending the nation, political justice, citizen safety, and constructing public works—the market would gradually improve the lives of everyone in society. Smith's ideas have made him the "patron saint" of capitalism; the economic liberalism he advocated was fundamental to the evolution of Classical Economics.

◆　　Abuses Within the Factory System

In the first few decades after Smith's *Wealth of Nations* appeared, however, the life of a factory worker became harder, not easier. Prices went up faster than wages. Technological changes created waves of unemployment in trade after trade, and the old safety-net of Poor Relief (taxes to support the indigent ill and elderly collected within each parish) was straining at the seams. Total annual expenditure on Poor Relief had jumped from £400,000 in 1696 to over £1.5 million in 1776 and would more than double again to nearly £4.3 million by 1802.

Tenant farmers ousted by the enclosure movement, home weavers displaced by steam-powered looms, and thousands of craftsmen made irrelevant by machinery constituted a new class of workers, called the *proletariat*. This *proletariat* was made up of urban factory workers whose income was totally dependent upon their ability to sell their labor. In a capitalist economy the means of production (machinery) is owned by the entrepreneurs who organize the manufacturing process to produce goods for the market and wealth for themselves. Labor is merely one of the necessary components that *bourgeois* managers have to obtain for the manufacturing process to be successful. Applying to labor the same principles that pertained to raw materials, machinery, or rent, owners believed the cost of labor must always be minimized so that profit might be maximized. Workers, required to labor at machines for a set period of time each day, lost control over their lives. The expenses involved in running a factory demanded that machines operate at full capacity whenever possible. Weavers, farmers, smiths, and craftsmen of all kinds, once able to determine their own pace on the job, were now ruled by the tyranny of the time-clock. Displaced and unemployed workers saw machine production as a threat, and sometimes reacted with violence, as in the case of the Luddite riots of 1811–1816 in Great Britain. Factory owners suppressed these outbursts with government support and sometimes even with government troops.

Factory life was hard and brutal, demanding long hours on the job for meager pay. A typical day began at six in the morning and ended after dusk, with only one meal break and no overtime pay. Workers who could not keep pace with the machines were fired. The earliest machines were so bulky they could only be operated by men. As machines became easier to use, women and children, paid only half as much as men, became the preferred mill hands. Conditions within the factories were appalling: lighting was poor, there was little ventilation, sanitation was primitive, and the machinery dangerous. Accidents occurred frequently since safety standards were non-existent. Injured workers received neither compensation nor insurance; if they could no longer perform they were replaced. At the start of the Napoleonic wars, Great Britain made unions illegal (1799), seeing them as revolutionary organizations. Economic liberals felt that anti-labor legislation was justified because they believed only free competition and *laissez-faire* could create wealth. Industrialists everywhere considered worker organizations to be illegal efforts to restrict national trade and prosperity.

The exploitation of the proletariat hardly ended when they finished work. In manufacturing towns and industrial cities the rentable row housing available to workers was uniformly miserable and expensive. Solid rural family values were now tested by oppressive, constricted slum conditions, and many were shattered by the experience. Factory laborers may actually have worked a shorter workday than did farmers, but city life meant crowding, foul air, dirty streets, and polluted water. Although hardly created by the Industrial Revolution, family violence, drunkenness, illegitimate births, and prostitution were all intensified in the city. Beggars were everywhere, and disease was prevalent in tenements that lacked even the rudiments of sanitation. Tenants in the slums were wracked by water-borne diseases such as cholera and typhoid, while textile workers were prone as well to "Factory fever," lung afflictions caused by the humid conditions, dust, and air-borne fibers common in the mills. Unemployed children of six or seven played in filthy streets. Since there was no public schooling, the best life could offer an uneducated child was a job in the factory.

Misery, however, does not represent the entire story of early industrialization. Workers had jobs that paid them weekly money, as opposed to farmers who often had no coins in their pocket until the harvest. Most families survived the traumas of city life and stayed intact. The marvels of mass production made useful commodities, like cotton goods, available to all members of society at a cheap price. Cotton could be laundered repeatedly and changed frequently, so the level of personal sanitation improved. Cheap cotton goods meant a great advance in the battle against fleas and lice. Pipes made of mass-produced iron eventually introduced running water to the foulest slum. The Industrial Revolution provided workers with more consumer goods than ordinary people had ever before possessed.

◆ Classical Economic Theory

The science of economics, as presented in the *Wealth of Nations*, concerned itself with explaining the production and distribution of commodities, and was little concerned with the lives of those who suffered in the process. Indeed, the successors of Adam Smith generally held that the condition of the proletariat could not be improved. Thomas Robert Malthus (1766–1834) was the first person to be appointed a professor of the new discipline of economics. In 1798 he published an *Essay on the Principle of Population* that marshaled statistics to present an extremely bleak case for the future of the human race. The rapid population gains that accompanied the Industrial Revolution were now a matter of record, and Malthus used these figures to demonstrate that while population tended to grow geometrically, food production increased only arithmetically. Using United States census figures because America was considered to be closer to a natural state of existence, Malthus concluded that population would double and redouble until it outran the food supply. War, famine, and disease were nature's way of correcting the balance between population size and food supply. Malthus argued that men and women ought to cooperate with nature by using moral restraint with regard to begetting children. He believed government should stop trying to defy nature as well, and eliminate measures that only encouraged the poor to over breed. His ideas had an immediate impact on Britain's welfare laws. Prime Minister William Pitt (1759– 1806) had promised to increase payments to larger families, and so create more workers for Britain's new industries. After reading Malthus in 1800, Pitt decided not to proceed with this legislation. Malthus views were also an important tool in the hands of those seeking to transform Britain's Poor Relief system into a early form of "workfare." In 1834, Poor Relief was converted to a "Workhouse" system. The Workhouse was a combination of factory and dormitory in which, segregated by sexes, all but the infants and the most ill and elderly had to work in order to eat. Workhouses were intended to be self-supporting, and food was deliberately kept to meager to encourage the able-bodied to seek jobs in the private sector.

Malthus, Prophet of the "Population Bomb."
Copyright © Library of Congress

David Ricardo (1772–1823), a successful stockbroker who retired early to study economics, was greatly influenced by Malthusian theory. Ricardo was deeply pessimistic regarding the future well-being of the working class prospects. His *Principles of Political Economy and Taxation* (1817) claimed there was an "Iron Law of Wages" that kept worker income at a subsistence level. Ricardo described labor as a commodity whose value fluctuated with the available supply. If workers were scarce, employers raised wages to attract and keep them on the job. In the larger economy, any increase in wages became a higher cost for capitalists and soon translated into higher prices for goods. However, when workers made more money they became optimistic about the future and betrayed their own economic interest by producing more children. Soon there would be more laborers than the economy needed and wages would sink back to a subsistence wage level. Ricardo was not unfeeling; he appreciated the ambitions of the working classes and argued that the real value of goods derived from the labor put into them. But he maintained that the *Iron Law of Wages* was as *natural* and as unbreakable a law as gravity. The pessimistic conclusions of what became known as the Classical School of Economics gave the subject its reputation as the "dismal science." Misery seemed to be the inevitable lot of the vast majority of humanity.

◆ Origins of Factory Reform

Despite the pessimistic conclusions Classical Economics, the evils of the factory system prompted increasing numbers of concerned citizens to demand changes. Workers lacked the political power to alter their situation since the right to vote was limited to those who owned property. The impetus to create more humane conditions was actually initiated by members of Parliament who were members of the landed classes. Generally, they belonged to the conservative group known as Tories and their primary concern was not to aid workers, but to blunt the competition they felt from the growing economic power of the factory owners. The first Factory Act (1802) was a toothless piece of legislation that failed to authorize any government inspection of factory conditions but did caution employers that it was their duty to see to the welfare of child laborers. Workers were permitted to unionize themselves after 1825, but they were still denied the right to strike. As the result of an investigation (1831–1832) carried out by a Parliamentary Committee chaired by Michael Thomas Sadler (1780–1835), Parliament enacted more vigorous measures in the Factory Act of 1833, excluding children under nine from work, capping the workday at eight hours for 9–13 year-olds and twelve hours for 14–18 year-olds, and creating four factory inspectors to see the law was carried out. The law also called for two hours of elementary schooling a day for the youngest children at the factory owner's expense. The main effect of that provision was the employers' firing of women with children. Women and young children continued to labor in mine shafts under horrific conditions until Parliament finally banned the practice in the Mines Act (1842). The Ten Hours Act (1847) limited the work day of most women and children under the age of 18, even though it permitted exceptions that allowed some to work up to eleven hours.

The struggles between factory workers and factory owners for the control of industrialization's future in Great Britain spread to every other European country that tried to catch up to Britain's industrial lead. As they did, a new ideology emerged, one that took a very different view of capitalism from the position put forward by the Classical Economists.

The Socialist Alternative

Adam Smith argued that capitalism was dependent on risk-takers, people with ambition who were willing to invest their money in pursuit of the goal of achieving wealth. Capitalists put up investment money, bought machines, hired laborers, obtained raw materials, recruited managers, and often lost fortunes as they sought success. The rewards that flowed from their efforts by right belonged to them. Both Smith and his disciple Ricardo freely admitted that the actual value of the goods created was the result of the laborers' toil, but they considered the contribution of the capitalist far more vital to the industrial process.

Socialism, a word that began to be commonly used only in the 1830s, offered a very different view of free enterprise. John Locke had argued that every individual has a natural right to life, liberty, and property. Socialists argued that every human being had a right to *social equality*, and there could be no true equality where property was private. Crime, disease, ignorance, and immorality were not the products of human nature but of social inequality. If labor created value, then that value belonged to the laborer. If laborers had collective ownership of the factories, all would receive their fair share of the wealth the factories produced. Crime, disease, ignorance, and immorality would be minimized or, perhaps, disappear altogether. Most socialists did not long to return to a pre-industrial world, but wanted a more equal allocation of the wealth industrial society created; they just could not agree on how best to achieve this goal. Unlike capitalism, which was based upon the competitiveness of human nature, early socialism was infused with idealistic visions of human cooperation. Its earliest advocates are sometimes called Utopians, a disdainful label given them by more radical groups.

◆   Utopian Socialism

Utopian Socialists believed that a better social order must be based upon cooperation rather than competition. Claude Henri de Saint-Simon (1760–1825) was a French nobleman, a veteran of the American Revolution, and an advocate of modern technology. He believed that a modern society could more easily sacrifice 30,000 aristocratic landholders than 3,000 top businessmen and scientists. The old agricultural world was ending, but if humans adopted Christian virtues, if the government owned manufacturing equipment and had it managed by experts, the future age would be one of peace and shared success. A decent civilization would utilize the skills of all and provide rewards to each member of society according to the work accomplished. The charismatic Saint-Simon inspired a group of young followers who kept his vision alive for the rest of the century, and fought unending battles to abolish inheritance rights, achieve full equality for women before the law, and finance useful public works. Saint-Simonian socialists believed that economics was a determining cause of history and that wealth could be peacefully and more equitably distributed throughout society.

Some Utopian Socialists advocated withdrawing from the existing society altogether. Charles Fourier (1772–1837), a French cloth merchant impoverished by the Revolution, dreamt of a system in which violence would be replaced by voluntary cooperation. His *Grand Treatise* (1822) denounced the degrading conditions of factory life that alienated workers from their labor and suggested that political revolutions brought only the illusion of liberty. Instead, Fourier argued that equal numbers of men and women living in communities of 1,620 persons (phalanxes), performing up to eight different jobs each day and mutually sharing profits, could create a society more congenial to human needs. There would be no property rights, and the acquisitive passion of each member would be channeled into their labor. Among his other suggestions were large common kitchens and an end to forced monogamy. No rich sponsor appeared to finance the community envisioned by Fourier, but he spent years eagerly awaiting such a visit. In the meantime, dozens of small experiments in both France and the United States demonstrated his influence and the growing disillusionment with unrestricted capitalism.

The most well-known of the Utopians was the Welshman Robert Owen (1771–1858), who financed his socialist convictions with his own money. Owen was self-educated, but talented enough to move from the factory floor to the rank of manager. He married a factory owner's daughter, and, when he inherited the estate, created a model industrial town at New Lanark, Scotland. He used company profits to build worker housing, establish schools, and set-up cooperative stores. Owen successfully demonstrated that an owner could reduce factory hours while paying top wages and still make a profit. His workers loved him, and his mills prospered, but few British owners followed Owen's example. After 1825 the frustrated reformer established a "village of cooperation" in New Harmony, Indiana, a community based upon his ideals and supposedly free of the corruption of existing capitalism. Within three years the experiment failed, both financially and spiritually. Bitter worker dissension over the division of communal profits highlighted the difficulties of socialist cooperation in a capitalist environment. Ironically, the New Harmony site is today maintained as a museum by the government of the world's most successful capitalist nation. Owen also worked for factory reform, the creation of a single union for all British workers, and the organization of consumer cooperatives. He became infatuated with spiritualism in his later years and ultimately died in poverty. More conventional English businessmen scoffed at a man who sacrificed his personal wealth to pursue a futile dream.

◆ Karl Marx and Scientific Socialism

The leading advocate of using violent revolution to achieve socialism was the German, Karl Marx (1818–1883). Marx was the grandson of a rabbi and the son of a wealthy lawyer who converted to Christianity. Whatever personal faith Marx possessed was lost during the course of his university education as he earned a doctorate in philosophy (1842). While studying in Berlin, Marx first read Georg Wilhelm Hegel (1770–1831), a philosopher whose writings developed the concept of the *dialectic* to describe the manner in which knowledge was acquired. Hegel said people learn by resolving the conflicts inherent in opposiing positions. In this dialectical process, a dominant known position (thesis) was challenged by its opposite (antithesis) until something new, a synthesis, was achieved. This synthesis was not a compromise, but a higher level of understanding that transcended the two original positions. Both Marx and Hegel believed that synthesis, once attained, was superior to what previously existed, but the process did not stop there; each synthesis in turn became a new thesis to be challenged. Hegel believed that dialectical growth took place in the mind after which the results were applied to society. Marx, having embraced atheism and materialism, rejected the primacy of ideas and held that the dialectical process operated in the physical world. Accordingly, after obtaining his doctorate he chose a career in journalism rather than education. He dedicated himself to the interests of the working classes and aspired to lead their efforts to change capitalism.

Marx devoted his life to discovering and explaining the laws he believed determined the process of history: whatever shaped the past forged the future. He was convinced that economic conditions alone controlled human actions. Ricardo's "Iron Law of Wages" proved to radicals like Marx that capitalists lived in luxury by stealing the labor of workers. Marx also condemned monarchy, and he was successively forced to flee both Germany and Belgium. He arrived in Paris in 1847 and soon became a member of the Communist League of the Just. It was there that he met Friedrich Engels (1820–1895), the son of a rich German capitalist who had become passionately devoted to the cause of workingmen's rights while living in Britain.

Late in 1847, Marx and Engels agreed to write a statement summarizing the beliefs of their fledgling Communist organization. The little pamphlet they produced became the most successful revolutionary document in world history. Their *Communist Manifesto* appeared in January 1848, offering a reinterpretation of all history based upon a materialistic reading of human activity that saw all ideas, from patriotism to honor to religious faith, as mere reflections of economic reality. Property and class were the truly compelling forces in the chronicle of humanity's past, and its future could be predicted by analyzing present conditions. Marx's contended that human destiny was knowable and predictable because it was based on scientific economic laws. So he called his version of socialism "scientific" in contrast to the dreams of the Utopians. Insisting that history was determined by these economic laws, Marx promised Communists that economic forces already at work would inevitably result in the triumph of the working class, and urged them to dedicate their

Karl Marx's "Scientific Socialism" transformed political and economic thought.
Copyright © The Granger Collection

efforts to that end. In a very real way, Marx offered a vision of the future as vital as any heaven promised by religious faith. For his followers, serving the cause of proletarian revolution became a means to personal salvation.

In a series of works culminating in *Das Kapital* (1867), Marx declared that a society's social and political theories and organization were determined by its prevailing method of production–agricultural or industrial—and exchange. In the Middle Ages, kings and nobles ruled because they owned the productive land. Their rule could not be successfully challenged until changing economic conditions created a class that was neither king nor noble nor peasant, the urban bourgeoisie. As commerce and manufacturing became ever more important to society, the political power of the bourgeoisie grew apace. Nineteenth century capitalism was so powerful an economic force that the bourgeoisie was able to seize control of modern society and all its institutions. Industrial capitalism's tendency to concentrate wealth in fewer and fewer hands was fast creating a world in which there were only two classes: the factory owners and the factory workers. The bourgeoisie (factory owners) and the proletariat (factory workers) were the real-world equivalent of Hegel's *thesis* and *antithesis*. But in the *real* world, the creation of a transcendent *synthesis* would not be bloodless. Marx argued that the increasing productive capacity of industrial capitalism would soon create more goods than the market could absorb. Factory owners would have to lay-off workers. Wageless workers would no longer be able to purchase goods, prompting factor owners to larger layoffs until a vast depression engulfed the industrialized world. Desperate capitalists would attempt to crush unions, undermine worker unity, and crush discontent, but they were destined to fail. The working class could never be destroyed because it was essential to the continuation of industrial production. In Marx's striking phrase, capitalism "created its own gravediggers." After violent struggles the proletariat—that "immense majority" of humankind—would eliminate their oppressors and take control of the means of production. After a transitional stage, which he called the "dictatorship of the proletariat," the state that had originally been created to control the masses would "wither away." No one needed a state if there was no one to control. In the resulting socialist society, everyone would be an owner-worker and everyone would be equal. If everyone belonged to the same class, society would be classless. The economic dialectic of history would come to an end. Marx believed that his work would help socialists understand the interaction of economic forces that made the future predictable, and that such knowledge would hasten the inevitable triumph of communism.

In 1849 Marx fled the turmoil of continental Europe and moved to London where he spent the rest of his life studying in the British Museum. His lifetime of research and writing was financed by Engels, who had inherited a fortune. Marx was not content just to theorize. He became an organizer and spokesman for the International Workingmen's Association (1864). This First International hoped to unite the working people of all nations into a mighty force to prepare for the revolution Marx predicted, but in practical terms it accomplished very little. Part of the reason was Marx's political ineptitude, but far more important was the growing evidence that his predictions were not being realized. The *Manifesto*'s dire vision of degraded workers living precariously on the edge of subsistence became increasingly less true. In every industrialized nation the condition of the proletariat markedly improved as the century progressed: real wages rose, unions were legalized, safety conditions improved, and the benefits of mass production were more widely distributed. The workday was shortened to ten hours or less, the work week to five and half days with Saturday afternoons and Sundays off. Even more impressive was the fact that workers were granted the vote by several countries. Marx's insistence that there could never be change from within a corrupt economic system was being widely questioned by socialists even before Marx died in 1883. Even Engels, who oversaw the publication of two additional volumes of *Capital* after the death of his friend, appeared less certain that revolution was imminent.

◆ Democratic Socialism

By the time a Second International was established in 1889, the socialist dream of a united working person's movement had fragmented into separate parties within each of the various European countries. Even more troubling for communists was the emergence of a less radical form of socialism associated with Eduard Bernstein (1850–1932). Bernstein claimed that Marx's conclusions needed to be reexamined and "revised" in the light of changing industrial conditions. In his *Evolutionary Socialism* (1899), Bernstein suggested that a violent revolution was neither inevitable nor desirable. Capitalism had demonstrated both staying power and an ability to reform itself. It was an evolving system, one that had already rewarded labor with material benefits, and which might be further improved as workers participated in politics. Bernstein concluded that if unions had helped improve the workers' position in the factory and using the ballot box had brought workers political power, the best thing workers could do was work *within* the democratic system to *gradually* gain greater and greater control. The political parties in Western Europe who adopted Bernstein's position took to calling themselves "democratic" socialists because they aimed at creating social equality through democratic means rather than revolution. Those socialists who stayed loyal to a strict Marxist view denounced Bernstein and the democratic socialists as "revisionists" for daring to revise Marx. Democratic socialism remained most influential in the wealthier industrialized states while Marxist Communism was more influential in less developed nations with a profound effect on the political history of the twentieth century.

◆ *Rerum Novarum*

Late in the century, the Catholic Church too voiced its disillusionment with unrestricted capitalism and its concerns for the violence and anti-religious bias of Marxist Communism. Taking a middle view, Pope Leo XIII (r. 1878–1903) defended the legitimacy of both private property and unionization in the encyclical *Rerum Novarum* (1891). The pope was skeptical about socialist theory and rejected the conception of inevitable class warfare; he believed that a richer future for all persons could be attained under a reformed capitalism with the guidance of the Catholic Church. The debate over a fair society consumed the energies of a host of nineteenth century thinkers, as they attempted to understand the dislocations brought about by the Industrial Revolution.

Industrialization, a process by which human beings create machines to automatically perform productive work, was and is the most far-reaching change in human history since the development of farming. With the advent of the Industrial Revolution the focus of human activity shifted dramatically, away from the agricultural village and the seasonal way of life to the clock-driven urban existence of modern society. New classes—the capitalist factory owner and the urban factory worker—came to dominate the economic life of Europe and contend with each other and with Europe's traditional land-owning aristocracy for political power. New ideologies—economic liberalism and socialism—contended for the hearts and minds of those new classes. New products and technologies—locomotives, telegraphs, steel-supported skyscrapers twelve stories high, cotton underwear—found their way into everyday life and changed it forever. And a self-consciously proud society held industrial expositions (fairs) to brag of their glorious technology to all the world. For the Paris Exposition of 1889 (the hundred year anniversary of the French Revolution), Alexander Eiffel (1832–1923) constructed a tower of 12,000 steel parts, held together by several million rivets, and rising a then mind-boggling 986 feet above the ground. Although many of the fair's visitors thought it a monstrosity, the Eiffel Tower still stands, a symbol of Paris, and a symbol of the power of industrialization.

As industrialization transformed the social and economic organization of Europe another ideology—nationalism—challenged its political organization with consequences that also continue to shape world affairs, for the modern world is nothing if not a world of independent nation-states.

◆ Note

1. Marie Jean Antoine Nicolas de Caritat, Marquis de Condorcet, *Outlines of an Historical View of the Progress of Humankind* (London: J. Johnson, 1795), 355.

4

Nationalism and the Modern State

John Locke's *Essay Concerning Human Understanding* (1690) portrayed human beings as essentially identical "blank slates" at birth, differing as adults only because of their different experiences. So he proposed a one-size-fits-all explanation of government's origin and purpose in his *Two Treatises on Civil Government* (1690). This emphasis on universality was a key feature of most Enlightenment political thought. It grew out of the Enlightenment's infatuation with the physical sciences: if gravity was the same everywhere, were not the laws of political science just as universal? But the French Revolution (1789–1799) and the Napoleonic era (1799–1815) that followed it led many to reject the Enlightenment beliefs they saw as the Revolution's cause. Many agreed with the French monarchist Joseph de Maistre (1753–1821) when he said:

> there is no such thing as man *in the world. During my life, I have seen Frenchmen, Italians, Russians . . . but I must say, as for* man, *I have never come across him anywhere. . . . A constitution that is made for all nations is made for none: it is a pure abstraction, an academic exercise of the mind, according to some hypothetical ideal.*[1]

Even those who did not reject the Enlightenment outright remembered that Montesquieu had said each "nation" had its own unique "general spirit," a unique culture developed over generations, and thus needed laws that fit that spirit.

The roots of the word *nation* lie in *natio*, Latin for "birth." As far back as the fourteenth century, *nation* had been used to mean people tied together by a common culture (language, religion, values, and customs) and history. But in societies divided into groups with differing rights and duties, most people's primary loyalty was to their family, clan, or estate. Nobles did not think of peasants as belonging to the same nation. In the wake of the French Revolution, however, a new word entered the English language: *nationalism*. Nationalism can be defined as the ideology that 1) sees humanity as divided into nations (groups sharing a common culture and history), and 2) believes these national identities are the most important factors in creating our individual nature. Thus it holds that 3) our nations are owed our greatest loyalty, and 4) because of the uniqueness of each nationality, no one nation should be ruled by another: each nation should have its own independent territory (called a *nation-state*).

But at the beginning of the nineteenth century, most Europeans and Asians did not live in independent nation-states. Some, like those who called themselves Germans, were split up among a few large kingdoms (Prussia and Austria) and many small ones: some way would have to be found to join these independent states together before all Europe's Germans could have one nation-state. Others, long conquered by neighboring armies, were now part of multi-national empires that would have to be ripped apart to create individual nation-states. Hungarians, Romanians, Czechs, Slovaks, Slovenes, and Croats lived under Austrian rule. Cossacks, Tartars, Lithuanians, Finns,

Latvians, and Uzbeks lived under Russian rule. Bosnians, Serbs, Bulgarians, Albanians, Macedonians, and Arabs were among those ruled by the Ottoman Turks. The Poles had been split up between Russia, Prussia, and the Austrian Empire. The Hindus, Sikhs, Pathans, Gurkas, and Bengalis of the Mughal Empire on the Indian subcontinent did not have their own states. Chinese emperors ruled over Mongols, Manchurians, and Tibetans.

This chapter looks at the spread of nationalism in the nineteenth century. It looks at the strategies used to create nation-states and the problems their citizens faced even after achieving unification or independence. For nationalism created as many problems as it solved. What happened, for example, when independence was won before any clear sense of nationalism was developed? The northern and southern states of the United States of America began to develop two different cultures while still British colonies. How were America's two national identities (slave v. free, industrial v. agricultural) to be meshed into one? The former Spanish and Portuguese colonies of Latin America were populated by several racially and culturally distinct groups (Creoles, Indians, Africans, Mestizos, and Mulattos) but run by Creoles who did not see the other groups as their compatriots. Could the people of those countries find a common national identity? What happened when a country with a traditional social structure (rulers, nobles, warriors, peasants) was challenged by an industrial power? Could a traditional kingdom such as Japan find a way to use industrialization to maintain its independence without losing its unique Japanese identity? Even in long established nation-states, the struggle for full membership in the nation—the right to vote, to hold office—was far from over in the nineteenth century. These are the questions examined in this chapter.

The Evolution of the Nation-State in Europe

◆ France

The combined might of Great Britain, Austria, Prussia, and Russia defeated Napoleon, but their leaders did not seek to dismember France, only to prevent any further outbreak of the French Revolution's "liberty, equality, and fraternity." The decision was made at the Congress of Vienna to give France back its king. As Louis XVI had been guillotined in 1793, and his son Louis XVII had died in a French Republican prison two years later at the age of ten, the oldest surviving brother of Louis XVI was crowned by the Congress of Vienna as Louis XVIII, King of France, in 1814. Understanding that the reforms fought for by the revolutionaries could not be entirely undone despite the wishes of some returning nobles, Louis XVIII (r. 1814–1824) wisely issued a Charter protecting, and in some areas extending, the political rights won during the revolutionary era. His regime marked the beginning of a long struggle between French liberals and conservatives. Liberals believed that government should be based on human reason and natural rights, not simply on past practice. Conservatives believed that tradition guaranteed social stability and resisted abrupt change. Louis XVIII tried to find a middle ground. He was a conservative monarch who tried to work with the nationally elected legislature while winning back for France the respect of its neighbors. Through his efforts the Quadruple Alliance (Britain, Austria, Russia, and Prussia) evolved into a five-sided "Concert of Europe" in which France played a major role.

But reactionary politics returned to France when Louis's death brought his younger brother to the throne as Charles X (r. 1824–1830). An advocate of absolute rule, Charles curtailed voting rights, religious toleration, and freedom of the press. His backward-looking policies ignored thirty-five years of change. In July 1830 a popular revolution ousted Charles X and installed his relative, Louis Philippe (r. 1830–1848), as "King of the French." Louis Philippe's new title was meant to show that the monarchy was a creation of the people rather than separate and above them. Support for the new regime came primarily from the *bourgeoisie*—the professionals, shop owners, and factory owners—whose importance to the state grew as France industrialized. Recognizing this, Louis Philippe pledged to uphold liberal tenets in both political and economic affairs. He even adopted the business-like dress of the *bourgeoisie*. But a series of riots in Paris during a severe recession in 1848 ended up replacing his monarchy with a Second Republic. As conservatives, liberals, and socialists struggled for control, French voters looked back nostalgically to the country's past glory and elected Louis Napoleon (1808–1873), Bonaparte's nephew, as their new president in November, 1848.

Louis Napoleon won voter support in 1848 by invoking his uncle's name. Three years later he did it again, this time to win popular support for his decision to make himself Emperor. He controlled France's destiny until 1870 as Emperor Napoleon III. He argued that France thrived only under strong leadership and that his destiny was to restore its primacy in Europe. But, unlike his uncle, he vowed to pursue "social, industrial, commercial (and) humanitarian" gains peacefully rather than fight wars of aggression across Europe. After his *coup* was endorsed by a popular vote, Napoleon III embarked on programs to rebuild Paris, construct worker housing, finance industrial growth in steel and textiles, and create a nationwide railway system. Prosperity increased his popularity.

Despite his domestic achievements, Napoleon III never dared resist the pursuit of glory on an international scale. As the inheritor of the Napoleonic mantle, he supported construction of the Suez Canal in Egypt (1859–1869) while his armies expanded French holdings in Algeria and seized New Caledonia (1853). He willingly acceded to pressure from the Catholic Church to intervene against the secularist government of Mexico, and sent in French troops to support the imposition of an Austrian archduke as Emperor of Mexico. French arms and money were of little use against the aroused fury of the Mexican people. The execution of Archduke/Emperor Maximilian in 1867 was a personal disaster for Napoleon III. Four years later Napoleon III's regime collapsed entirely when he led France into the disastrous Franco-Prussian War (1870–1871).

Defeated by Prussia, a chastened France resumed its endless debate over the style of government best able to restore national glory. In Paris, a socialist Commune seized power and promised to build an egalitarian France. But the radicals won little support from a French electorate that remained bourgeois and conservative. It took a "Bloody Week" of civil war (May 21–28, 1871), and almost 20,000 dead, to reestablish the power of the central government. A Third Republic, approved in September 1871, lasted until 1940, but it failed to settle the national debate between conservatives who yearned for strong leadership, liberal advocates of individual rights, and supporters of socialist alternatives. The Third Republic was wracked by scandals, such as the notorious Dreyfus Affair (1896–1906), that threatened its very survival. Captain Alfred Dreyfus (1859–1935), the first Jewish officer on the army General Staff, was convicted of spying for Germany in 1894 on fabricated evidence. When sentence was first pronounced against Dreyfus on January 5, 1895, a crowd of nearly 20,000 people surrounded the court, yelling "Death to the Traitor! Death to the Jew!" He languished in prison for years, despite evidence of his innocence. Public apathy, fed in good measure by anti-Semitism, allowed the army high command to save face by shielding the reputation of the real spy. Dreyfus was sacrificed in the name of the nation, and his eventual rehabilitation in 1906 strained the politic fabric of the Republic. The Roman Catholic Church campaigned against any effort to exonerate him even after it was revealed that the key piece of evidence against him was a forgery. The army command demoted his defenders and promoted his accusers. The question of whether a member of a religious minority would be allowed to be a full member of the nation continued to trouble France well into the next century.

◆ Great Britain

As the first state to undergo the Industrial Revolution, Great Britain quickly became the greatest power in Europe. But neither its inventive bourgeoisie nor the laboring proletariat had much influence over the state's direction in 1815. Parliament was an institution dominated by aristocrats and the landed gentry. Control of land was the traditional source of power in Britain, and parliamentary measures like the Corn Law of 1815, which imposed a heavy tariff on imported grain, were designed to protect landowners' profits regardless of their effect on the price of bread. Such measures set off sporadic rioting among the urban proletariat, still trying to adjust to the periodic waves of unemployment set off by industrialization. Radical agitation for Parliamentary reform precipitated a series of clashes between protestors and soldiers. When several protestors in a crowd at Saint Peter's Fields in Manchester were killed in 1819 in the worst of these incidents, Parliament responded by enacting Six Acts that curtailed individual freedom and increased the government's repressive powers.

During the 1820s the conservative landowners who dominated Parliament did make some concessions to reform. The restrictions on trade unions in the Combination Act of 1799 were relaxed in 1824 and 1825. The Test Act (which limited office holding to members of the Church of England) was repealed in 1828, and other restrictions on Catholics were removed by the Emancipation Act of 1829. But conservatives stoutly resisted any attempt to make Parliament more representative.

Internal migration during the Industrial Revolution had depopulated older towns while creating new cities in different parts of the country. Because there had been no major Parliamentary redistricting since 1689, industrial centers such as Manchester were under-represented in Parliament, while depopulated rural areas were still guaranteed their traditional seats. Perhaps the most famous example of these "rotten boroughs" was Dunwich-Under-the-Sea, once a thriving seaside town long since covered over by the North Sea but still sending a member to Parliament.

A new reform effort was launched, with support from the new Prime Minister, Lord Grey (1764–1845), after King William IV (r. 1830–1837) came to the throne. The bill passed the House of Commons but was blocked by the House of Lords. Grey convinced William to threaten the House of Lords with the creation of 50 new peers from the mercantile classes if they did not change their minds. Only then did conservative opposition cease and the measure become law. The Reform Act of 1832 redistributed seats from the rotten boroughs and enfranchised business owners, but it did not create democracy. It still maintained high property requirements for suffrage. As a result, although it increased the number of enfranchised Englishmen by 50%, only one in every eight men was eligible to vote.

Neither of the two parties that dominated political life in England spoke for the majority of the people. The Conservative Party (called the "Tories") drew their support from the largely aristocratic landowners. The Liberal Party (called the "Whigs") drew theirs from the wealthiest factory owners. Neither party had much sympathy for the working class. Working men and women, aware they could expect little help from the established parties, rallied during the 1830s to the reform movement known as *Chartism*. Demanding an end to industrial exploitation and the creation of a more popularly based government, Chartist leaders attempted to mobilize working class support by circulating a *People's Charter* with six specific proposals for government reform: universal male suffrage, the secret ballot, abolition of property requirements for election to Parliament, salaries for members of Parliament, equal electoral districts, and annual Parliaments. When finally presented to the House of Commons in July 1839, the *People's Charter* held over 1.2 million signatures. Nevertheless, a scornful bipartisan vote rejected any discussion of its demands. After a series of marches and strikes, a second petition containing almost 3 million signatures was resubmitted in 1842; by a vote of 287–49 the House of Commons again refused to accept it.

Even though unsuccessful, the Chartist movement convinced some leaders in the Liberal and Conservative parties of the potential strength of the working class. The question was, which established party would win their support? In 1867, Conservative Prime Minister Benjamin Disraeli (1804–1881) pushed a Second Reform Bill through Parliament. It doubled the electorate by adding urban workers to the enfranchised: one out of every three adult males could now vote. But if Disraeli thought the workers hated their bosses enough to make common cause with the Conservatives against the Liberals, he was quickly proven wrong. Most of the new voters sided with the Liberals in the next election, making Liberal leader William Gladstone (1809–1898) the next Prime Minister.

During Gladstone's "Great Ministry"(1868–1874), Parliament enacted measures that further reduced the power of the Anglican Church, reformed army and civil service rules to reward talent rather than birth, and revised existing legal codes to fully protect union privileges. The secret ballot was approved (1872), and the passage of the Education Act (1870) created the first national school system. Elected again in 1880, Gladstone's ministry pushed through a Franchise Act (1884) extending the vote to agricultural workers, achieving virtually complete suffrage for males. This broadened participation in government fostered national pride. While other nations struggled violently to create unity, the English bragged about the flexibility of their parliamentary system.

◆   Nationalism and the Concert of Europe

Although conservative opinion dominated Europe after 1815, no part of the continent proved immune to the doctrines of nationalism and liberalism spread by the Napoleonic Wars. In 1820 there were revolts in Spain, Portugal, and Naples, and in 1821 in northern Italy. The great powers of the Congress of Vienna had agreed to consult each other on European matters on a regular basis. After a hasty conference chaired by Austria's Prince Metternich, most agreed that armed intervention was necessary to crush the spreading dissent, and Austrian troops put down the Italian rebels in 1821. As Great Britain's refusal to condone military action threatened to splinter the Quadruple Alliance, Metternich persuaded the French support to send troops to crush the Spanish revolt in 1823. That action won France back a place in the "Concert of Europe," as the consultation system set up by the Congress of Vienna was called.

How the Concert Powers reacted to revolution depended on whether they saw it as helping or hurting their own interests. When the Greek provinces of the Ottoman Empire declared their independence in 1822, Britain, France and Russian supported the rebels in order to gain greater influence over the Balkan Peninsula, the Ottoman Empire's foothold in Europe. After Greece won its independence in 1829, the Concert Powers installed a German prince, Otto of Bavaria (r. 1832–1862), as Greece's king. Back in 1815, the Congress of Vienna had folded Catholic Belgium into the Protestant Netherlands in order to create a buffer against the future spread of French revolutionary ideas. But, inspired by the French Revolutionaries of 1830, Belgium threw out its Dutch rulers. Liberal outbreaks in their own empires prevented Austria and Russia from sending troops against the Belgian rebels. By 1839, Belgium's new constitutional monarchy was recognized even by a reluctant United Netherlands, and the Concert Powers had signed a treaty to support Belgium's declared perpetual neutrality.

France's overthrow of King Louis Philippe in 1848 led to a sudden outbreak of the virus of liberal revolt across Europe. Before the end of the year, the Concert Powers were faced with nearly 50 rebellions, as rebels from Sicily to Cracow to Budapest attempted to emulate the French example and create governments more acceptable to the people. Yet although the French monarchy fell immediately, the results everywhere else were devastating to those who expected liberal victories. The forces of change were everywhere defeated; early liberal successes were followed by conservative counterattacks that regained control.

FLORENCE NIGHTINGALE (1820–1910)

During the Crimean War (1854–1856), wounded British soldiers blessed the care given them by the "Lady of the Lamp." Her name was Florence Nightingale, and she was born on May 12, 1820, into a family of wealthy landowners. Like her elder sister, Florence was educated at home and helped her mother with charity work. Florence became interested in the care of the sick, but a career in that field did not seem possible in England where women could not be trained as physicians. Nursing was neither a profession nor respectable in Britain, since it was most often left to untrained prostitutes. In some countries on the continent, however, nursing was also an activity pursued by nuns. Nightingale toured the continent to learn the methods used by these nursing sisters. In the town of Kaiserworth in Germany, she discovered a school for Protestant Deaconesses that included instruction in nursing, and remained there to take the course herself. Her reports on the nursing profession won her the post of superintendent at the new Hospital for Invalid Gentlewomen in London in 1853.

When the Crimean War broke out in 1854, Nightingale used her family's political connections to obtain a commission to inspect the field hospitals. Taking thirty-eight nurses (nursing sisters and trainees from her own hospital) with her, Nightingale immediately began to bring order to slapdash military facilities that lacked clean water, soap, towels, clothing, bedding, and unspoiled food. So primitive were health conditions that soldiers, doctors, and nurses alike succumbed to cholera and typhus in greater numbers than to enemy fire. Rarely on her feet for less than twenty hours a day, her time not tending the wounded was spent sending dispatches home to raise a relief fund and badger the government into adopting sanitary reform. Nightingale's efforts reduced the death rate in frontline hospitals from 42 to 2.2 per cent. In a time when soldiers' families still provided support services for the army, Florence Nightingale found herself organizing laundries and kitchens for the wives and children of the men on the battle lines. Near death herself at one point, she did not return to England until five months after the peace was concluded in March 1856. She refused to leave Russia until the last hospital was closed though her exertions left her a semi-invalid for the rest of her life.

On her return to London, Nightingale devoted all her efforts to reforming hospital care and creating schools for nurses. With funds raised in a public subscription, the Nightingale School and Home for Nurses was established at St. Thomas's Hospital, London, in 1860. Her *Notes on Nursing* (1859) became the standard textbook in the field, and she inspired the British government to found an army medical college and a military hospital. Nightingale's expert advice was sought by the United States government during the Civil War and by the German and French governments during the Franco-Prussian War.

She died in her home in London on August 13, 1910. Her inspiration lives on in the profession she created.

The "Lady with the Lamp."
Copyright © Globe Photos, Inc.

Then, a war fought in the Crimean Peninsula in Southern Russia from 1854 to 1856 transformed the European *status quo*. Russia was eager to expand southwards towards Mediterranean waters, but the Ottoman Empire lay in its path. The Ottoman Empire controlled both sides of the Bosporus and the Dardanelles, the Straits that linked Russia's warm water ports on the Black Sea to the Mediterranean. Tsar Nicholas I (r. 1825–1855) launched a war against the Ottoman Turks in 1854 to get that access, but Great Britain and France intervened to protect their trading interests in the Ottoman-ruled Middle East. In the battles that followed, the Ottoman Turks were forgotten as the armies of Britain and France confronted the Russians. Although the Crimean War brought about the professionalization of nursing under the direction of Florence Nightingale (1820–1910), it was a disaster for all involved. Administrative and military ineptitude led to a standstill that ended only when Austria threatened to join the Anglo-French coalition, forcing Russia to the negotiating table. Peace was established after a conference in Paris (March 1856), but the Crimean War had brought the Concert of Europe to an end.

◆ Creating Italy and Germany

For centuries the Italian and German peoples had been divided into separate, small states. The 38 Germanic states were politically independent of each other, although they did cooperate in some areas. 30 of them participated in the *Zollverein*, a customs union established under Prussian leadership in 1819, and all 38 held membership in a Germanic parliament (the *Diet*) whose presidency was held by Austria, the largest German-speaking state. But political rivalries and competing great power interests stood in the way of German unification. The situation was even more complicated on the Italian peninsula where several of the territories were under foreign rule.

The revolutions that followed on the heels of the Congress of Vienna were revolutions of liberal nationalism, a form of nationalism that placed as much emphasis on the equality of the people within the nation as on its political independence. But liberal nationalism had failed to create a unified Italy or a unified Germany. Its most well known advocate on the Italian peninsula, Giuseppe Mazzini (1805–1872), briefly led the Roman republic set up in the failed revolution of 1848, but had to flee to exile in Britain before invading Austrian troops. German professors who prepared a liberal constitution for a united Germany at a conference in Frankfurt in 1849 (the so-called "Frankfurt Parliament") discovered that the monarchs of the largest German states were not interested in constitutions that limited their powers.

In the 1850s, two statesmen, Count Camillo Benso di Cavour (1810-1861) of the northern Italian kingdom of Piedmont and Otto von Bismarck (1815-1898) of Prussia, turned to a new form of nationalism—*Realpolitik*—to unify their nations. *Realpolitik* was a term popularized by a Prussian journalist, August Ludwig von Rochau (1810–1873), in his *Principles of Realpolitik, Applied to Political Conditions of Germany* (1853). According to Rochau, "To rule means to exercise power, and only he who possesses power can exercise it. This direct connection of power and rule forms the fundamental truth of all politics and the key to all history."[2] If politics was all about power, then *realism* in *politics* (the literal meaning of *Realpolitik*) meant doing whatever was necessary to preserve the power of the state or nation. The end justified the means in the name of national development, and the best defense was often a good offense.

The Unification of Italy, 1859–1870   *The unification of Italy by Piedmont-Sardinia included territory acquired in 1859, 1860, 1862, and 1866.*

From *History of Modern Europe*, First Edition, (1996), W. W. Norton & Company.

Cavour was the Prime Minister of the Kingdom of Piedmont, which also included the island of Sardinia. While Piedmont was independent, two other northern regions of the Italian peninsula—Lombardy and Venetia—were in Austrian hands. Cavour believed that by aligning himself with France (Austria's old rival), he could gain those territories as a first step towards a united Italy. So, in 1855, even though Piedmont had no grievances against Russia, Cavour sent 10,000 troops to the Anglo-French side in the Crimean War. This gave Cavour the right to attend the peace conference, where he was careful to strike up a friendship with France's leader, Napoleon III. He used that friendship to get Napoleon III to agree to let Piedmont keep Lombardy and Venetia if Piedmont could win them from Austria (with French aid). Cavour maneuvered Austria into declaring war against Piedmont in April 1859. At first, Napoleon III kept his promise to aid the Piedmontese army, but, beginning to doubt the wisdom of creating too strong a state on his southeastern border, Napoleon III struck a compromise with the Austrians in July, letting them keep Venetia while Piedmont got Lombardy. Trying a different tactic, Cavour negotiated a series of plebiscite votes in the Italian states of Parma, Modena, Tuscany, and Romagna in 1860 that joined them to Piedmont.

Then, in the spring of 1860, a professional revolutionary named Giuseppe Garibaldi (1807–1882) launched a rebellion in the southern Italian Kingdom of the Two Sicilies. In May, Garibaldi and a thousand red-shirted followers landed in Sicily and quickly captured Palermo. Although Cavour had originally opposed the expedition, he quickly provided secret aid to Garibaldi and sent Piedmontese armies south to occupy the Papal States. In November, another round of plebiscites merged the newly conquered territories with Piedmont. On March 17, 1861, King Victor Emmanuel II of Piedmont became King Victor Emmanuel I (r. 1861–1878) of the Kingdom of Italy. Rome was still under the control of the papacy and Austria still controlled some territory in Italy's north but Cavour lived long enough to see his nation united and independent.

German unification followed shortly thereafter. After the failure of the Frankfurt Parliament, advocates of German unity gradually turned for leadership to Prussia, the largest Germanic state outside Austria, and the least liberal. Its constitution barely controlled the vast power of the Junkers, landholding aristocrats who provided leadership for the Prussian military. Prominent among leading Junker conservatives was Otto von Bismarck, who served Prussia at the *Diet* of the Germanic Confederation set up by the Congress of Vienna and as ambassador to France and Russia. Bismarck watched with great interest as Cavour's *Realpolitik* advanced Italian nationalism. Then in 1862, shortly after Italy unified, King Wilhelm I (r. 1861–1888) of Prussia appointed Bismarck his chief minister. Wilhelm had been unsuccessful in getting funding from a liberal-dominated legislature for his plans to modernize and enlarge Prussia's army. He had twice tried dissolving the legislature and calling new elections only to be faced with increased liberal majorities. Bismarck showed him a way to break the constitutional deadlock by deliberately misinterpreting a temporary spending bill passed only to keep the government going until the budget crisis could be resolved. Wilhelm got his army and Bismarck became chief minister.

With the failures of liberal conferences in 1848 and 1849 to unify Germany still rankling, Bismarck believed that the unification of the German states could only be achieved through "iron and blood." He faced two main problems. First, he had to prove to the smaller German states that they were better off surrendering their independence to join a larger one. Secondly, he had to convince them that Austria should not be a part of any newly created Germany. Austria was the only Germanic state powerful to challenge Prussia for the leadership of a unified Germany, and Bismarck was determined to maintain Prussian control.

Bismarck's first opportunity came as a legacy of the territorial adjustments made at the Congress of Vienna in 1815. The Congress had given the king of Denmark the right to administer

Holstein, a small region of German-speakers on Denmark's southern border, as a buffer against French power. When Denmark's king attempted to tie Holstein more closely to Denmark in 1864, Bismarck rapidly arranged a military alliance with Austria to protect German "honor." Ignoring British attempts to prevent fighting, a joint Prusso-Austrian military expedition made quick work of the Danes (Prusso-Danish War, 1864). Denmark was forced to cede Holstein to Austrian control and Schleswig (another primarily German-speaking province) to Prussian control.

But Bismarck had a bigger prize in mind. He isolated Austria internationally by supporting Russian repression of a Polish insurrection, promising Napoleon III territory along the Rhine, and promising Italy to help it get Venetia from Austria. In the meantime, he tried to convince the *Diet* that Austria had plans to grab more German states. It did not take Bismarck long to provoke Austria into attacking Prussia. The Austro-Prussian War (1866) is more commonly known as the Seven Weeks' War, for it took only that long for Prussia's modernized military to secure victory. The *Treaty of Prague* (1867) joined Hanover, Schleswig, Holstein, Nassau, and Hesse-Cassel to Prussia. Twenty-two other German states were organized into a North German Confederation

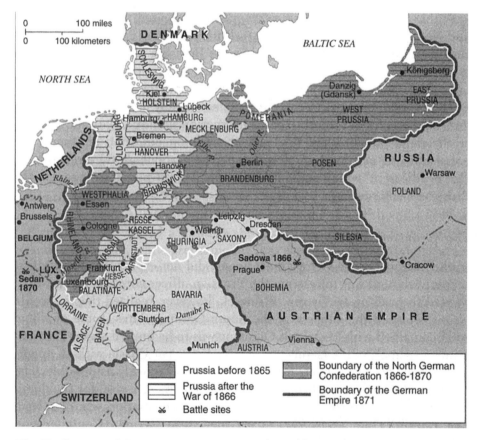

The Unification of Germany, 1866–1871   The unification of Germany by Prussia included territory acquired after the Austro-Prussian War (1866) and the Franco-Prussian War (1870–1871).
From *History of Modern Europe*, First Edition, (1996), W. W. Norton & Company.

whose hereditary ruler would be the King of Prussia. Austria was left entirely isolated from its fellow German states and Venetia was given to Italy.

Despite Prussia's triumph, there was still no united Germany. There could be none so long as major German states like Bavaria, Baden, and Württemberg retained their independence. Bismarck's plans would have to wait until an opportunity presented itself to convince those states to join Prussia. An unexpected crisis in Spain gave him the opportunity he sought. In September, 1868, Spain expelled Queen Isabella II (r. 1833–1868) and invited Prince Leopold, a member of the Prussian royal family (the Hohenzollerns), to become its new king. France reacted strongly against having Hohenzollern rulers on both its borders. Bismarck used French hostility to foster feelings of patriotic unity among all Germans. He quickly negotiated defensive treaties with Bavaria, Baden, and Württemberg. When King Wilhelm renounced the candidacy of his nephew Leopold in 1870 the danger of war over Spain eased, but the ever-inventive Bismarck still intrigued against France. During a July vacation in Ems, Belgium, King Wilhelm held a friendly conversation with the French Ambassador, sending a dispatch (an official telegram) back to Berlin to keep his chief minister informed of the negotiations. After receiving the Ems Dispatch, Bismarck released an edited version that made it appear that France had insulted Wilhelm. Napoleon III, eager to win military glory, snapped at Bismarck's bait. On July 19, 1870, just as Bismarck had intended, France declared war on Prussia. Once again an "innocent" Prussia was under attack.

The Franco-Prussian War (1870–1871) was a turning point in the story of nationalism in Europe. The independent states of southern Germany allied themselves with Prussia, while France fought alone against a well-prepared enemy. When retreating French armies had to be reinforced with troops that had long protected the Papal States, Italian forces filled in the vacuum and were finally able to occupy Rome. Thus the Franco-Prussian War completed the unification of two nations. French forces proved no match for the Prussian war machine commanded by General Helmuth von Moltke (1800–1891). The French armies surrendered, Napoleon III was captured, and unified German armies soon surrounded Paris. France was humiliated and the reign of Napoleon III ended. On January 18, 1871, Bismarck watched proudly as King Wilhelm of Prussia became the Kaiser (Emperor) of a single united Germany. The *Treaty of Frankfurt* (1871) gave Germany Alsace and Lorraine, two French border provinces with predominantly German-speaking populations. The Treaty also imposed a one billion dollar indemnity on France and occupation by German troops until it was paid. After three wars in six years, Bismarck's version of *Realpolitik* had created a second German *Reich* (state) that dominated continental Europe.

As Chancellor of Germany from 1871 to1890, Bismarck never again fought a war. He encouraged rapid industrialization, and by 1890 Germany surpassed England in the production of coal, steel, chemicals, and machinery. By 1900 German steel mills produced more than Britain and France combined. German scientists, musicians, engineers, and physicists became world famous in this period of prosperity. Adopting policies calculated to develop national pride in the new German nation, Bismarck oversaw the creation of a common legal code, judicial system, coinage, postal system, and railways. The Chancellor's only misstep came when he attempted to utilize religion to foster national feeling. In alliance with the Liberal Party, Bismarck enacted legislation to restrict Catholic education and prevent the Vatican from filling vacant bishoprics. The program, labeled the *Kulterkampf* (culture struggle) by its supporters, foolishly divided Germany's northern Lutheran population from the Catholic south. Once Bismarck realized its threat to unity, he order an end to the *Kulterkampf*. After 1878, the specter of religious strife in Germany was buried for another half-century.

Bismarck proclaims the Second Reich, January 18, 1871.
Copyright © Hulton Getty Picture Collection

Despite universal male suffrage, the government remained virtually unaccountable to the people and the social upheavals of rapid industrialization strengthened the membership of the Marxist oriented Social Democratic Party. To undercut its revolutionary potential, Bismarck combined the passage of an Anti-Socialist Law with a package of benefits designed to make Germany's working class loyal to the state: National Health Insurance (1883), Accident Insurance (1884), and Old Age and Invalidity Insurance (1889). In his domestic agenda, Bismarck demonstrated that *Realpolitik* was as useful a tool within a nation as without.

◆ Russia

Nineteenth-century Russia was a multi-ethnic empire, not a nation-state: less than 50 percent of its population was actually Russian. The majority of the population was composed of other Slavic, Baltic, Germanic, and Central Asiatic populations whose lands had been conquered by the

Russians over almost four centuries of Russian expansion. Tsar Alexander I of Russia (r. 1801–1825) dedicated himself to isolating Russia from the liberal ideas he saw as threatening that conquest and the autocratic order that supported it. But total isolation was impossible to achieve. After his death in 1825, a small group of westernized army officers in St. Petersburg attempted to install his younger brother, Constantine, as Tsar, in December. Their liberal demands for "Constantine and Constitution" were easily crushed by regiments loyal to Tsar Nicholas I (r. 1825–1855).

Despite its failure, the threat seen in this Decembrist Revolution guaranteed that Russia would support Austria's attempts to crush liberalism in Eastern Europe. At home, Russia's Tsars made little attempt to modernize their empire politically, economically, or socially until after their embarrassing defeat in the Crimean War (1854–1856). Then, Tsar Alexander II (r. 1855–1881) launched a series of modernizing reforms: rebuilding the army, updating the legal code, granting villages some self-government, fostering university education, and building railroads. His most dramatic reform was the March 1861 Edict emancipating Russia's 20 million serfs, permitting them to choose their occupation, move off their lord's estate, and own land. But the terms of the land reform were so stringent that most peasant allotments were too small for subsistence farming, while larger landowners did not receive enough funds to invest in capitalist farming. Further edicts in 1864 created regional assemblies (*zemstov*) for local control of public works, health and sanitation, education, and poor relief, but they were kept on too tight a financial rein by the central bureaucracy to achieve real independence. And even this first flush of reform soon gave way to efforts to extend Russian imperial control into the Far East, Central Asia, and the Balkans.

As reform withered, disappointed advocates of change began to organize. Mikhail Bakunin (1814–1876) was an officer in the Imperial Guard who resigned his commission in 1848 after witnessing the slaughter of Polish nationalists by Russian forces. Convinced that all forms of government were oppressive by nature, Bakunin became an advocate of active resistance, accepting terrorism as a legitimate response to autocratic power. He claimed that "the passion for destruction" was "also a constructive passion." His ideas earned him a six-year term in a Siberian prison, but such measures only increased his popularity among dissidents. *The People's Will,* one of the many secret groups inspired by Bakunin, "sentenced" the Tsar to death in 1879 for his failure to enact democratic reforms. Several assassination attempts were made before a bomb ended the Tsar's life on March 13, 1881, the very morning he was to approve the creation of a limited Constituent Assembly for Russia.

The assassination of his father convinced Alexander III (r. 1881–1894) that only harsh repression could preserve his power. He attempted to crush both political dissent among native Russians and nationalist feeling among the various ethnic groups conquered in the four hundred years of Russian expansion across Europe and Asia. Alexander's policy of *Russification* aimed at the forced substitution of the Russian religion, language, and values for the patchwork of Slavic, Baltic, Finnish, Germanic, and Turkic customs strung across his multi-national empire. Even curriculum reform in secondary schools and universities was designed to eliminate sources of nationalist sentiment. Groups excluded from *Russification* fared even worse. After 1882, Russian Jews were subjected to "Temporary Rules" that kept them in territorial isolation in a region known as "the Pale of Settlement" (hence the expression, "beyond the pale") and inflicted officially encouraged massacres (*pogroms*) of Jews.

Alexander III had no objection to increasing Russia's economic potential. His ministers negotiated loans from Western bankers and used the funds to foster industrial growth. The Tsar also approved the construction of the Trans-Siberian Railway in 1891. By the time of Alexander's death,

Russia's annual industrial growth rate of eight percent made it the fastest growing economy in the world even though it was sill the least developed Great Power.

The United States

Unlike Italy and Germany, the United States was already an independent—and expanding—state when the nineteenth century began. President Thomas Jefferson (1801–1809), convinced that American's future lay in agriculture, purchased the Louisiana Territory from a cash-strapped Napoleon Bonaparte in 1803. The new territory doubled the size of the United States. A treaty with Spain added Florida to the United States in 1819. Emigrants from the United States succeeded in wresting the province of Texas from Mexico in 1836 and joining it to the United States in 1845. A war with Mexico (1846–1848) brought the southwest (Arizona, California, Nevada, Utah, and parts of New Mexico, Colorado, and Wyoming) into the Union, and a treaty with Britain (1846) the northwest. Americans began to brag of their expansion across the continent

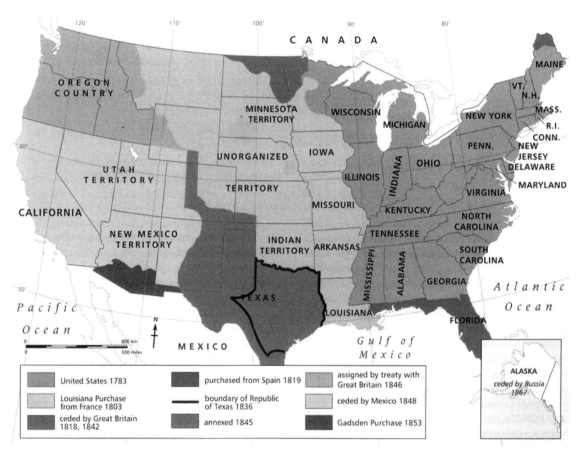

Territorial Expansion of the United States to 1860.
From *World History: An Atlas and Study Guide*, edited by Gerald A. Danzer. Copyright © 1998 by Prentice-Hall, Inc.

from the Atlantic Ocean to the Pacific as their "Manifest Destiny." Great engineering triumphs like the Erie Canal (1825) and a widening web of railways tied far-flung American states ever more closely together and contributed to the sense of national unity, as did the creation of a universal white male suffrage during the presidency (1829–1837) of Andrew Jackson.

Although the American nation appeared united in spirit, its unresolved sectional and moral differences hurled it into civil war before its first centennial. By the 1830s, America's industrializing northern states had all outlawed slavery. However, slavery remained fundamental to the plantation economy of the American south, even though the majority of southern farmers never owned slaves. Britain's Industrial Revolution fostered an insatiable demand for raw cotton, and Eli Whitney's cotton gin made the South the world's greatest cotton producer. Cotton was "king" of the southern economy, and cotton was grown, tended, and harvested by slaves. America's four million slaves made up twenty percent of its entire population.

While cotton remained America's biggest export, the southern states were able to keep Congress from even discussing abolition. Northern opponents of slavery organized an "underground railroad" to conduct blacks into freedom and opposed the effort of slave-catchers to return them to bondage. Frederick Douglass (1818–1895), himself an escaped slave, became a leading abolitionist speaker; his life and accomplishments provided daily proof that blacks were fully capable of participating as equals in American society. But it was the nation's continued territorial expansion that starkly demonstrated how the issue of slavery could threaten the existence of the Union. As each new territory petitioned for statehood, Congress had to decide whether the new states would be slave or free. Compromise after compromise maintained an increasingly fragile balance between slave and free states in the nation. Guerrilla warfare between abolitionist and pro-slavery settlers in the Kansas territory after 1854 was a clear sign that balance was falling apart. By 1860, many southerners advocated establishing a separate nation where their freedoms and rights—especially the right to own slaves—would be secure.

In the presidential election year of 1860, Republican Party candidate

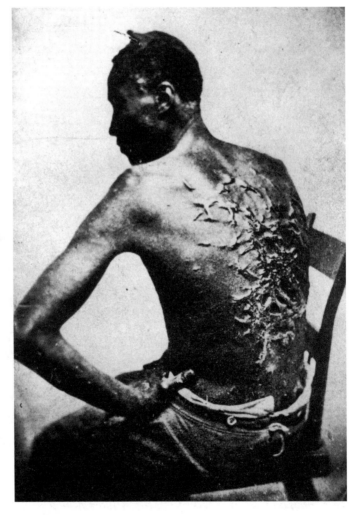

The treatment of "property" in the pre-Civil War Southern United States.
Copyright © National Archives

Abraham Lincoln (1809–1865) ran on a platform that would prevent any extension of slavery into the territories. The South refused to accept Lincoln's assurances that he was not going to disturb the institution of slavery where it existed under Constitutional protection. Even before Lincoln's inauguration in March 1861, seven states had seceded from the Union, and four others followed after southern forces attacked Fort Sumter, South Carolina, in April 1861. The bloodiest war ever fought by the United States followed, as half the nation fought to prevent the other half from becoming the Confederate States of America. The more populous north, aided by the productivity of modern industry and making full use of its extensive railroad system, ultimately would triumph. The war marked the debut of a machine gun (1861) invented by American Richard Jordan Gatling (1818–1903). Using the same type of shells as a handgun, the earliest Gatling Guns could fire off 350 rounds per minute; later versions could fire as many as 1200 rounds per minute.

When Northern ships blockaded Southern ports, cutting off the flow of supplies to the South, they also cut off the flow of cotton to Britain's mills. British capitalists favored intervention in the Civil War on the Southern side. To win the support of Britain's workers and liberal abolitionists,

This painting, The Storming of Fort Wagner, *shows the attack on the fort near Charleston, South Carolina, by the 54th Massachusetts African American Regiment on July 18, 1863. The attack failed, and more than half the members of this first Union all-black regiment and their white commanding officer, Robert Gould Shaw, were killed.*
Lithograph by Kurz and Allison, 1890. Courtesy of the Library of Congress.

and to shore up morale in the North, Lincoln issued the Emancipation Proclamation on January 1, 1863. It proclaimed an end to slavery in rebel states, but not in those loyal to the union or held by martial force. The four million slaves in rebel territory could not enjoy this proclaimed freedom until those areas were retaken by Union troops. Even then, the freedom granted would not be permanent until guaranteed by a Constitutional amendment. Victory for the North came at Appomattox Court House on April 11, 1865. 620,000 Americans, black and white alike, died in the war. Three days later, President Lincoln was assassinated by the actor John Wilkes Booth (1838–1865), born in Maryland and a southern sympathizer.

The American Civil War (1861–1865) transformed a collection of sovereign states into an indivisible nation ready to compete on the world scene. In the next generation, northern industrialists led America to economic greatness even though the south remained largely agricultural and underdeveloped. Lincoln's plan for reconstruction of the Union had emphasized "malice towards none and charity for all," but the passionate feelings stirred by during the Civil War overwhelmed most benevolent intentions. Before defeated Confederate states were readmitted to the Union they were required to approve a Thirteenth Amendment (1865) to the Constitution abolishing slavery, experience military occupation, and accept black citizenship (under the Fourteenth Amendment, 1868), and the vote for black men (under the Fifteenth Amendment, 1870).

Neither the southern economy nor its attitude towards black people altered as the larger nation prospered. As the last federal troops withdrew from Southern soil in 1877, southern whites regained political control of their states. The largely rural black population of the South became an exploited underclass unable to exercise its rights, while the North concentrated on its own industrial development. Despite bitter protests by some Abolitionists, including black leaders such as Frederick Douglass and Sojourner Truth (1797–1883), African-Americans were abandoned by the federal government. Even in the states of the victorious North full equality remained elusive. In a series of decisions culminating in the case of *Plessy v. Ferguson* (1896), the United States Supreme Court ensured the survival of segregation by deciding that "separate but equal" public facilities did not violate the Fourteenth Amendment.

Nationalism in Latin America

Most Latin American states their independence from Spain or Portugal in revolutions led by their Creole elite. The status of the majority of the inhabitants—the Indians, Africans, mestizos, and mulattos—was not altered by the change from colonial to independent rule. Lacking both experience with and sympathy for popular government, the Creole elite tended to favor autocratic rule by *caudillos* (leaders) who, in alliance with the Catholic Church, invoked nationalism only as a means of bolstering their own authority.

◆ Argentina

Even as newly independent Argentina was losing the provinces that became the independent states of Paraguay, Bolivia, and Uruguay, disputes between the Buenos Aires, the Argentine capital, and the rest of the country threatened to tear it apart. Buenos Aires supported a strong, centralized ("Unitarian") constitution while ranchers in the outlying provinces wanted a decentralized ("Federalist") government with more power for the provinces than for the capital. A state of intermittent civil war helped make possible the dictatorial regime of Juan Manuel de Rosas (1793–1877), a cattle rancher from Buenos Aires province. From 1829 to 1852 he was the most important man

FREDERICK DOUGLASS (1818–1895)

Abolitionist and Human Rights advocate.
Copyright © CORBIS/Bettmann

According to the Tuckahoe, Maryland, plantation records of Aaron Anthony, Frederick Augustus was born in February 1818 to the slave Harriet. But slaves were deliberately kept in the dark about such matters, and the boy who grew up to be Frederick Douglass was certain neither of his birth date or year; he believed all his life he had been born in 1817. His fellow slaves told him his father was a white man, possibly even his own master. Young Frederick played no part in the decision that shaped his life, for, when he was only eight, he was sent to Baltimore as a house servant. His new master's wife taught him his ABCs until her husband explained they could be sent to jail for teaching a slave to read. Frederick Douglass picked up the rest of his letters on the sly: he traded food to white boys on the street for a glimpse at their lessons.

Sent to work in the Baltimore shipyards, Douglass learned the trade of ship's caulker and saved what little he was allowed to keep out of his own wages to buy his first book, a textbook in oratory. He also met and courted a free black woman, Anna Murray (d. 1883). Disguised as a sailor, Douglass escaped to New York with Murray in 1838, where they wed before moving further north to Massachusetts.

In 1841, William Lloyd Garrison (1805–1879), the abolitionist editor of *The Liberator,* helped organize an anti-slavery conference in Nantucket, Massachusetts. Hearing that there was an escaped slave in the audience, Garrison asked him to speak. Douglass's first anti-slavery speech was a resounding success, and he became a regular speaker for the Massachusetts Anti-Slavery Society. In 1845, he published his autobiography, the *Narrative of the Life of Frederick Douglass,* but spent the next two years hiding in England, afraid that publicity from the book would lead his master right to him. Friends raised funds to purchase Douglass from his owner and emancipate him, so it was as a free man that Douglass returned to the United States in 1847 to begin publishing his own newspaper, the *North Star.*

When the Civil War began, Douglass campaigned without success for black enlistment. After issuance of the *Emancipation Proclamation* paved the way for military service for blacks, Douglass became a recruiter for black units. His sons Charles and Louis joined the 54th Massachusetts, and Sgt.-Major Louis Douglass fought in and survived the regiment's famous assault on Fort Wagner (seen in the film *Glory*).

After the end of the Civil War, Douglass held a number of public offices culminating in his appointment as U.S. Minister to Haiti (1889–1891). He was always newsworthy, because he refused to limit his civil rights campaigns to abolition and male suffrage. In 1848 he was one of the few men to endorse the *Declaration of Sentiments* of the women's rights convention in Seneca Falls, New York. When the Fifteenth Amendment (1870) gave black men the right to vote without addressing women's rights, many feminists accused Douglass of betraying their cause. He remained a controversial figure until his death (February 20, 1895), because his second wife (Helen Pitts) was white.

in Argentina, gradually extending the authority of Buenos Aires over the entire country. Rosas ruled by force, tolerated no dissent, and restricted personal liberties, but he greatly expanded Argentine trade with Great Britain. Argentina prospered as an exporter of beef and an importer of manufactured goods.

Justo José de Urquiza (1801–1870), a *caudillo* from the state of Entre Rios, overthrew Rosas in 1852 with help from Brazil and Uruguay. As Rosas fled to Britain, Urquiza pledged to end government by terror. He issued a Constitution in 1853 that was similar to that of the United States. When Buenos Aires threatened to boycott the federal republic in 1859, Urquiza went to war and conquered the capital province. Not for another twenty years would the relationship between Argentina and its greatest city be settled, but the brief civil war of 1859 ensured that Argentina would remain a single state. Urquiza, however, was assassinated in 1870 by one of his rivals for power in Entre Rios. With the support of the military, Urquiza's National Autonomous Party remained in control of Argentina until 1916.

In an effort to settle the conflict between the capital and the rest of the country once and for all, the city of Buenos Aires was detached from its surrounding territory in 1880 and granted separate provincial status. That same year, the army defeated rebellious Indian tribes south and west of Buenos Aires, clearing the land for wheat farming. With the advent of refrigerated shipping, sales of Argentine beef to Europe soared. Anxious to industrialize and lacking an educated workforce, Argentina offered inducements that lured hundreds of thousands of European immigrants. Large numbers of Italian and Spanish newcomers, and the skills they brought with them, made Argentina the most European of all Latin American nations. Under a series of able presidents, notably Julio Roca (1880–1886, 1898–1904), Argentina began a long period of sustained economic growth. As its population soared from 1.5 million in 1860 to almost 8 million in 1914, Argentina became one of the most stable and prosperous of all Latin American nations, although most of the wealth remained in Buenos Aires or in the hands of the ranch owners.

◆ Brazil

Brazil, a country that occupies half of the South American landmass, is the only Portuguese speaking nation in Latin America. It became independent in 1822 under the leadership of the Portuguese royal family, which had fled there during the Napoleonic Wars. When Pedro I was forced to abdicate the throne of Brazil on April 7, 1831, authority fell to his five-year-old son. After a ten-year regency, Pedro II (r. 1831–1889) assumed power in 1840, presiding as a constitutional monarch over a huge territory with a disproportionately small population (just under three million in 1870). The long and remarkable cooperation between Dom Pedro II and the political leadership of both conservative and liberal parties permitted Brazil to develop peacefully, creating a strong sense of national unity. Until the 1860s Dom Pedro deftly allowed politicians from all parties to participate in government, often as joint members of a "conciliation cabinet." He also was responsible for the fall of the Argentine dictator Juan Rosas in 1852, and led Brazil in the 1865–1870 war against Paraguay that cemented its good relations with Argentina.

Dom Pedro's regime provided his nation both respectability and pride. However, his government took few initiatives to develop the economy, relying instead on foreign firms for any technological aid. Agriculture remained the dominant source of wealth, with sugar and rubber being second only in importance to coffee among Brazil's exports. By 1900, Brazil was growing three quarters of the world's coffee supply. But coffee production made use of slave labor, and by 1871 Brazil was the only nation in the Americas that had not yet abolished slavery.

While all Latin American cultures were a mixture of the European, the Indian, and the African, Brazil's culture was the most African of any Latin American nation. This was because just about half of Brazil's three million people were African slaves. To avoid disrupting brazil's economy, Dom Pedro favored gradual emancipation. In 1871 the Law of the Free Womb declared the children of slave women to be free, but granted masters the right to their labor for twenty-one years. Abolitionist sentiment grew, and in 1885 the Parliament granted freedom to all slaves over sixty. When army officers refused to enforce the laws keeping slavery alive, Dom Pedro avoided the issue by departing for medical treatment in Europe. A reform Parliament then passed the May 1888 Golden Law abolishing slavery. It was signed by the emperor's daughter while he was away.

Dom Pedro returned to a dissatisfied nation. Taking their cue from Argentina, Brazilian coffee planters began offering bounties to Europeans who were willing to work in the coffee fields. Almost three million immigrants, primarily from Italy, Spain, and Portugal flooded the country between 1887 and 1914, changing its cultural make-up. The campaign for abolition had given birth to a strong republican movement that wanted Brazil to adopt a constitution like that of the United States. In mid-1889 Dom Pedro announced plans for decentralizing authority and winning foreign investment, but the initiative came too late. A military coup led by Manuel Deodoro da Fonseca (1827–1892) overthrew the monarchy, exiled Dom Pedro to Portugal, and proclaimed a republic (November 16, 1889). General Fonseca ruled while an American-style constitution was written. By 1891 Brazil became a federal republic with twenty states, although real power still remained in the hands of the agricultural and military elite. Slavery had been abolished, but the franchise was limited to literate males. No more than eight percent of Brazil's male population was eligible to vote in any election until 1930.

◆ Mexico

At war with Spain since Father Hidalgo had issued his call for independence and land redistribution in 1811, the final peace of 1821 left Mexico far more ravaged than either Argentina or Brazil. Its transportation and communication systems were shattered; its mines had caved in; its fields had been trampled by contending armies. All its politicians could agree on was the expulsion of all Spaniards, a decree that eliminated the most educated part of the nation. The Catholic Church held about half of all Mexican land and was in firm alliance with the land-holding Creole elite. Most of the people were landless tenants in perpetual debt to the Church and other powerful landowners. Iturbide, who had declared himself Emperor after negotiating the final treaty with Spain, was overthrown two years later by one of his own generals, Antonio López de Santa Anna (1797–1876). Santa Anna remained in control of Mexico, sometimes as president, sometimes as the power behind the office, until he was finally forced out in 1854. But even his relatively long regime was punctuated by mutinies whenever the government did not have enough money to pay its army. Borrowing from foreign banks to fund the government only increased Mexico's debt, siphoning off monies that could otherwise have been used for desperately needed services. Further aggravating Mexico's plight was the successful revolution of the American settlers in the province of Texas in 1836 and the loss of half of Mexico's territory in the Mexican-American War (1846–1848) provoked by the United States.

Mexico was a humiliated and weak land in the 1850s as *La Reforma* began. *La Reforma* was a liberal movement designed to ensure civilian rule, win foreign investments, separate church and state, and improve the situation of Mexico's poor. Having deposed Santa Anna for the last time in 1855, the reform leaders attempted to break up large agricultural estates and reduce the power of the Church and the military. Benito Juárez (1806–1872), a Zapotec Indian and one of the leaders

BENITO (PABLO) JUÁREZ (1806–1872)

Statesman and champion of liberal reform.
Copyright © Art Today

Benito Juárez was born on March 21, 1806, in the Indian community of San Pablo Guelatao in Mexico. Orphaned at the age of three, he lived, from the age of twelve, at his sister's home in Oaxaca where formal schooling was available. Intended by his family for a career in the church, Juárez instead attended the Oaxaca Institute of Arts and Sciences where he could study law. He graduated in 1831 and immediately won a seat on the municipal council. His personal life seemed promising as well after his marriage to Margarita Maza in 1843.

But his political career came to a sudden halt when conservatives came to power in 1853; Juárez spent a two-year exile in New Orleans working for a liberal victory. Juárez was a liberal in both the economic and political senses; he favored free market capitalism and opposed the tremendous influence exercised by the Roman Catholic Church through its large land holdings. He wanted Mexico to adopt a United States style federal constitution that would prevent excessive centralization of power and maintain a firm separation of church and state. When the liberals regained power in 1855, Juárez returned home as Minister of Justice and Public Administration. He won passage of the *Ley Juarez* (1855), eliminating special courts for members of the military and clergy, and he supported the *Ley Lerdo* (1856) that forced the Church to sell some of its property. In 1857, Mexico got the liberal constitution of which Juárez had dreamed, capping the period known as *La Reforma.*

Juárez was appointed Chief Justice of the Supreme Court in 1857, a post which also made him vice president, but when President Ignacio Comonfort (1855–1858) was ousted by a conservative counter-rebellion in 1858, Juárez was unable to take office as president and was forced, instead, to retreat to Veracruz. Controlling only a portion of the country, Juárez's government began a concerted attack on the Catholic Church in an attempt to weaken its alliance with the conservatives: Church property was confiscated, marriage was made a civil affair, and freedom of religion was granted to all. By 1861 Juárez was back in Mexico City, a President with true constitutional authority. As he struggled to get the bankrupt nation back onto its feet, Juárez announced a two-year suspension of foreign debt payments that alarmed Britain, Spain, and France, Mexico's major creditors. Troops sent by the three countries landed at Veracruz in 1862, but Britain and Spain withdrew their forces when they realized that Napoleon III intended to make Mexico a puppet state under Archduke Maximilian of Austria. French victories forced Juárez to flee the capital in 1863, and his government retreated to the United States-Mexican border. But renewed efforts by the Mexican army, American pressure, and public opinion back in France turned the tide in 1867: French troops left Mexico, Maximilian was captured and executed, and Juárez returned to power.

A triumphant Juárez called new elections in August 1867 and proposed sweeping constitutional changes to strengthen the power of the executive branch. Although he was reelected, the proposed amendments were resoundingly defeated by members of the legislature who feared that the presidency might become a dictatorship. Debilitated by the loss of his wife and a stroke suffered in 1870, Juárez was reelected for the last time in 1871. He spent the last months of his life, until he died of a heart attack on July 18, 1872, working to restore peace to Mexico.

of *La Reforma,* was instrumental in the construction of a new Constitution in 1857. It guaranteed freedom of the speech and press, abolished slavery, separated church and state, subordinated the military to civilian control, and increased the power of the central government over its feuding states. While remaining Mexico's official constitution until 1917, it was rarely in full force. The Church did not accept it and excommunicated any government official who swore to support it. The military led a rebellion against it. Juárez and his supporters were forced to retreat to Veracruz as the conservative military-church alliance set up a rival government in Mexico City. With supplies from the Americans, Juárez recaptured Mexico City in 1861, only to find himself facing French armies invited in by Mexican conservatives.

Napoleon III took advantage of America's absorption in its own Civil War (1861–1865) to try and recreate the power and glory France had known under his uncle Napoleon Bonaparte. Dreaming of a "Latin League" that would stretch from Italy to the Americas, Napoleon III was convinced by exiled Mexican conservatives that Mexico would welcome any leader who promised to restore the power of their beloved church. Backed by a French army, Archduke Maximilian of Austria (1832–1867) arrived in May 1862 to serve as Napoleon's puppet emperor of Mexico. The *Juáristas* hated Maximilian, and he alienated conservatives when he refused to undo the nationalization of Church property by Juárez. Mexico already had one national holiday, the commemoration of Miguel Hidalgo's declaration of independence from Spain on September 16, 1810. The success of the outnumbered Mexicans against Maximilian's French forces at the Battle of Puebla on May 5, 1862, gave Mexico its second independence day, *Cinco de Mayo.* But that victory was not enough to end the war. The end of the American Civil War brought increasing American pressure on France to withdraw its aid to Maximilian, as did mounting protests within France at the war's cost. In response, French troops began their withdrawal from Mexico in February 1867. By June, Juárez's troops had captured and executed Maximilian. For the next several years, Juárez labored to consolidate national power over Mexico's northern provinces where independent *caudillos* still ruled. He laid the foundations for a secular public education system, extended concessions allowing British firms to complete the Veracruz-Mexico City railroad, and began work on tariff reform.

La Reforma did not long outlive its chief architect. Four years after the death of Juárez died, General Porfirio Díaz (1830–1915) seized power. Díaz, a mestizo born of a Mixtec mother and a Spanish father, came from Juárez's home state of Oaxaca. Díaz had been one of the heroes of the fight against Maximilian, but criticized Juárez for moving too quickly toward a democracy for which Mexico was not ready. As Mexico's new leader, Díaz claimed to be schooling his country for eventual freedom, but remained in power until he was ousted by another revolution 1911. Maintaining the outward forms of the 1857 Constitution, he packed both Congress and the Judiciary with his supporters to keep the government in line. He won the support of the Church by letting it buy back some of the land stripped from it under *La Reforma.* He created a paramilitary militia called the *rurales* to maintain order in the countryside. Diaz was often ruthless; he used both the army and his *rurales* to wage a genocidal war to exterminate the last Indian resistance to his rule. The Yaqui Indians of Northwestern Mexico had been at war with each succeeding Mexican government since independence in an attempt to preserve their culture and communal land ownership. Unable to convince them to settle down to western-style farming on individual plots, Díaz ordered in the troops in 1902, slaughtering thousands of Yaquis and deporting the remainder to forced labor on the plantations of southern Mexico.

Recognizing that Mexico lacked the entrepreneurial class it needed to develop, Díaz invited British and United States investors to develop Mexican mineral wealth. During the years of the *Porfiriato* industry grew and the elite prospered as never before. But the situation of the peasants

Generalissimo Porifirio Díaz was dictator of Mexico from 1876 to 1911.
Copyright © Brown Brothers

remained dismal, and in 1900 no more than three percent of rural families owned any land. On the great *haciendas* (plantations) of Mexico's heartland, laborers were not paid in cash but in scrip that could only be used at the company store. Underpaid for their labor and their crops, peasants were reduced to peonage—unable to leave the hacienda because they were unable to pay off their debts. Diaz gave Mexico economic growth and political stability, but the benefits were limited to the upper classes. When Diaz was finally displaced in 1911, there was still no united Mexican "nation" even though the country had been independent for nearly a century.

Japan Embraces Modernity

Contact with the west brought the problems of nationalism to Asian shores. Japan is a chain of islands, an archipelago strung out over a thousand miles off the eastern coast of the Asian mainland, with a total land mass about the size of California. Less than a fifth of that land is suitable for farming, but with a centuries old tradition of intensive farming, the four main islands of Japan supported a population of about 30 million by the middle of the nineteenth century. By comparison, the total population of the United States as the time was only about 20 million.

At the pinnacle of Japanese society was the Emperor, but the Emperor had not exercised direct control over Japan for centuries. Instead, Japan was governed by a *shogun*, a military commander who exercised power in the Emperor's name, while the Emperor was reduced to a religious figurehead. Since 1615, the office of Shogun had been in the hands of the Tokugawa family. They controlled the country through a military bureaucracy made up of the great nobles (*daimyo*) who acted as governors of the provinces and their armed swordsmen (*samurai*). Long prosperity made both the merchant class and the landed aristocracy supporters of the Tokugawa, but the life of the exploited peasantry was harsh and under constant government scrutiny.

Ever since Tokugawa expelled the Jesuit Order of missionary priests in 1614, Japan had existed in almost total isolation from western influence, although the Dutch were allowed to maintain a small trading outpost on an island off the port of Nagasaki. The defeat of China by Britain in the First Opium War (1839–1842) made the Japanese government wonder how long it could keep out the West.

In July 1853 Commodore Matthew Perry (1794–1858) of the United States anchored his four-ship squadron in Edo (Tokyo) Bay. Perry brought a letter of greeting (and a request for a trade treaty) from the American government, but it was the military power represented by his ominous "black ships" (steam-powered and heavily armed) that impressed the Japanese. Abe Masahiro (1819–1857), senior councilor to the Shogun, argued strongly that Japan must accommodate the American proposals or suffer the fate of China. Abe's counsel prevailed, and when Perry returned nine months later, Japan signed its first agreement with a modern state. The *Treaty of Kanagawa* (1854) established better treatment for shipwrecked foreign sailors, approved an American coaling station, and opened two Japanese ports to American trade. Similar concessions were gained by Britain, the Netherlands, and France within eighteen months.

Foreign pressure kept Japanese tariffs on imported goods quite low, while interest charges on development loans extended to Japan were high. Moreover, foreigners residing in Japan enjoyed the right of extraterritoriality (the privilege of being judged only by their own officials and laws). Samurai campaigns to "expel the foreigners" only led to armed interventions by western forces (1863–1864) further demonstrating Japanese weakness. By 1867 some samurai leaders decided that salvation lay in adopting the administrative and technical skills of the west. They forced the resignation of the Tokugawa Shogun. Authority was restored to the Emperor Mutsuhito, a boy of fifteen, whose long reign (1868–1912) is called "The *Meiji* (Enlightened Government) Era. To

ITŌ HIROBUMI (1841–1909)

Statesman and advocate for Japanese Modernization.
Copyright © CORBIS/Bettmann

Itō Hirobumi was born into a modest samurai family on October 14, 1841, in Suō Province, Japan. His career was shaped by the desire of many Japanese to westernize the country after the shameful capitulation of the Tokugawa Shogunate in the *Treaty of Kanagawa* (1854). With the support of the Choshu clan, he was sent to England in 1863 to study naval technology. He would eventually be part of the delegations sent to the United States (1870) and Europe (1871–1873) to study western budgetary methods and negotiate treaty revision.

Itō first rose to real power in 1878, when he was made minister of home affairs. His great achievement was to convince the government of the importance of adopting a western style con-stitution. Itō returned to Europe (1882–1883) to study such governments, before deciding on a German style constitution, which favored exec-utive over legislative power. Many Japanese opposed any kind of constitutional government, so the adoption of the German model was a con-siderable victory for supporters of liberal reform. The Meiji Emperor proclaimed the constitution in 1889, and a *Diet* (parliament) was created the following year.

Itō Hirobumi served several terms as Prem-ier (1885–1888, 1892–1896, 1898, and 1900–1901), during which he created a national upper house (the House of Peers) to act as a balance against regional forces in the Diet. He also formed a new political group, the *Rikken Seiyūkai* (Friends of Constitutional Government), to further smooth the passage of reform.

He played a moderating role in the growth of the Japanese Empire as well. It was under him that Japan defeated China in 1895, thus acquir-ing its first colony, the island of Taiwan. As resi-dent general in Korea, however, he attempted to prevent the outright Japanese annexation of the country, although he was still unable to win the confidence of the Korean people. But his break with the other senior statesmen (*genro*) allowed Yamagata Aritomo (1838–1922), the founder of the modern Japanese army, to become the domi-nant force among senior government officials during Itō's last years. His government continued to honor Itō, however, making him a Prince (*Koshaku*) in 1907.

Itō was assassinated on October 26, 1909, in Harbin (Manchuria), by a member of the Korean independence movement. With his moderating influence removed, Korea was annexed to the Japanese Empire the following year. His political legacy is ambiguous. He played a primary role in creating a Japanese constitution, yet he also sup-ported Japan's early aggression against China and Korea, and gave the country a constitution that could be used by militarists in the 1930s to destroy parliamentary government.

symbolize this new beginning, Japan's capital was transferred to from Kyoto to Tokyo. But the emperor was not to rule; power was exercised by a bureaucracy determined to save Japan by modernizing it. Feudalism was abolished, and samurai were ordered to give up the swords that marked their status. A hasty rebellion by incensed traditionalists was crushed by a conscript army in 1877. Modernizers within the samurai class were then able to implement major changes in society.

Within two decades the Meiji reformers transformed Japan. Technical missions returning from abroad introduced the use of chemical fertilizers and hardy new strains of seed into the agricultural economy. Between 1870 and 1920 population grew from 35 to 56 million. Other Japanese travelers brought back the secrets of the Industrial Revolution; steel mills and textile factories soon dotted the country. By 1910 Japan was exporting as much silk as China. The reformers set up a national bank, created a national currency based on the decimal system, established a postal service, put the country on a Western calendar, and created Japan's first compulsory education system (four years of primary schooling for both sexes in 1872). Although Japan's first railroad was not opened until 1872, there were over two thousand miles of railroad track in operation by 1894. The Japanese army was rebuilt on the Prussian model while a navy was constructed following the British example. Before the 1870s ended, Japan had ironclad ships, a conscript army led by expert officers, and a General Staff to coordinate military affairs. Finally, enlightened Japanese leaders became aware that modern states boasted of their constitutions. Itō Hirobumi (1841–1909), a leader of the Meiji movement, developed a constitution for Emperor Mutsuhito to confer on his people as a "voluntary gift" in 1889. Heavily dependent on the German model, the Japanese Constitution kept political control in the hands of Japan's aristocrats just as surely as Bismarck had assured it to the Junkers. Under the terms of the Peerage Ordinance of 1884, Japan's former daimyo were transformed into barons, counts, and princes. His person "sacred and inviolable," the emperor was the supreme commander of the armed forces, held an irreversible veto power over the legislature (the *Diet*), was the only one who could initiate constitutional amendments, and administered the nation through a cabinet not subject to recall by the legislature. The upper branch of the legislature (the House of Peers) was filled by Japan's new nobility. Although membership in the lower branch (the House of Representatives) was by election, only about one percent of the population could vote: all women, all men under the age of twenty-five, and all men who did not meet a minium income tax level were denied the franchise. The position of the emperor was further enhanced by the state's sponsorship of Shinto. Shinto (the "Way of the Gods") was Japan's native religion, and despite the infusion of Buddhism, Shinto's core value—ancestor worship—remained fundamental to Japanese culture. According to Shinto tradition, Japan (the "land of the Gods") was the creation of the Sun Goddess, Amaterasu-Ōmikami, and the Emperor was her direct descendant, the earthly incarnation of the divine will. These beliefs became a key part of the curriculum written by the government for the new public schools.

As the last decade of the century began, Japan had constructed an industrial base despite the fact that it lacked great natural resources. Its people were better fed, clothed, and educated than ever before in its history. Among its samurai elite, the code of *Bushido* (the way of the warrior) remained paramount: honor, loyalty, and courage were valued above money. But many among the ruling class believed that Japan's future prosperity could be assured only by the establishment of its own empire. Thanks to its newly modernized military, Japan was able to win its own sphere of influence in China after defeating it in the Sino-Japanese War (1894–1895), increase that sphere by defeating Russia in the Russo-Japanese War (1904–1905), and annex Korea in 1910. Within a generation, Japan had become a modern nation state without losing a sense of its destiny and culture. The reconstruction of Japan during the Meiji Era introduced a major new player into the game of international politics, a major power whose military expenditures were averaging over 33 percent of its total budget.

Of all the "isms" generated by Europeans during their period of global ascendancy, nationalism has proven to be the most powerful and the least predictable. It can impel a population to common action or tear it apart. It can result in greater individual freedom or less. Conservative and militaristic forces dominated unification movements in Germany, Japan, and much of Latin America. The United States was nearly ripped apart by Civil War. France went through two monarchies, three republics, and a second empire in its quest for lasting order.

Throughout the nineteenth century, nationalism's most potent enemy was the imperialism exercised within Europe by its multinational empires (the Russian, the Austrian, and the Ottoman) and exercised within Asia and Africa by Europe's industrializing nation-states. The next chapter tells the story of empire building in the nineteenth century.

◆ Notes

1. Joseph de Maistre, *Considerations on France* (1796), in *The Works of Joseph de Maistre*, translated by Jack Lively (New York: Macmillan Company, 1965), 77.

2. Hajo Holborn, *History of Modern Germany*, 3 vols. (Princeton, NJ: Princeton University Press, 1982), 2:117.

5

The Age of Imperialism

The term *Imperialism* comes from two Latin words: *imperator,* the title awarded Roman generals who conquered foreign armies, and *imperium,* the right to impose capital punishment. However, imperialism, the practice of exploiting the resources of foreign lands, predates the Roman Empire by millennia. It has been practiced by Egyptians, Babylonians, Persians, Chinese, Greeks, Romans, Aztecs, Incas, Mongols, Mughals, Arabs, and Ottoman Turks, as well as by modern European nation-states. The forms of imperialist exploitation range from the imposition of unequal trade treaties to outright annexation with the enslavement or displacement of the native population. Imperialist domination can be political, economic, social, military, or cultural, or all of the above. Imperialism is always ethnocentric. It thrives on the belief that a more powerful society has the "right," if not the absolute duty, to impose its authority, attitudes, and values on cultures and peoples it sees as inferior.

In dealing with the empires created by modern European nation-states, historians traditionally distinguish two distinct periods of expansion. The first occurred during the sixteenth and seventeenth centuries. It is usually referred to as the era of *Colonialism.* In this period thousands of individuals from Spain, Portugal, England, France, and the United Netherlands colonized the Americas and displaced the native populations. European languages, religions, values, forms of government, and economic organization came with them and dominate the Americas to this day.

During this same period, however, European nations also established small settlements along the coasts of Asia and Africa to make it possible for their ships to ply the East Indies trade in spices, silks, porcelains, jades, tea, and other luxury goods. These settlements gradually grew larger over the centuries until they became jumping off points for a second wave of European expansion in the last third of the nineteenth century. This period is usually called the Age of Imperialism (or the "New" Imperialism to distinguish it from the "Old" Colonialism). In less than half a century almost all of Africa, the Indian subcontinent, and Southeast Asia came under direct European control. In addition, China's coast was carved up into European and Japanese spheres of influence, while the United States acquired colonies in the Caribbean and the Pacific. These new territories were used primarily as sources of cheap raw materials and native labor, rather than as places for European settlement. Comparatively few Europeans moved into these new colonies and even fewer remain in those areas today. While European-style political and social systems were imposed on the native populations, no effort was made to include them as equals.

The motives behind this expansion varied. Economic and political interests were powerful factors. As the nations of continental Europe industrialized, they enacted protective tariffs to shelter their developing industries from British competition. Britain, losing her economic advantage in Europe, concentrated on expanding her Indian and African beachheads in search of new markets

An American cartoonist in 1888 depicted John Bull (England) as the octopus of imperialism, grabbing land on every continent. Notice the hand at the left poised over Egypt.
"The Devilfish in Egyptian Waters," courtesy of the Granger Collection, New York

and cheap raw materials. As the unification of Italy and Germany altered the balance of power in Europe, older powers like France hurried to catch up with Britain's colonial lead and forestall any imperial ambitions on Germany's part. Economic interests turned into problems of political and military strategy. To safeguard a canal, an entire country might have to be subdued. Philanthropic motives also played a part: the spread of liberalism led Europeans to reconsider their role in the slave trade. Banning slavery from their own territories, they sought to eradicate it in Africa as well. Missionaries sought not only to convert native populations to Christianity (which they believed was a superior religion), but they also tried to put an end to such practices as female infanticide, polygamy, or *suttee* that oppressed women.

Whatever the motive, the "New" Imperialism was a phenomenal success from a territorial standpoint. By 1914 more than half the surface of the Earth was in European hands.

Imperialism and the Indian Subcontinent

◆   India and the British East India Company

The story of nineteenth-century imperialism has its roots in the same quest that set-off the Age of European Colonialism in the Americas: the desire to gain direct access to the spices of southern Asia. This was the part of the world that Europeans called the East Indies (from a mispronunciation of one the area's major languages, Hindi). In the sixteenth century the Portuguese and Spanish empires staked out a trading monopoly in the East Indies. In the seventeenth, the Dutch, English, and French launched their own "East India" Companies to compete. These East India companies were state-sanctioned monopolies with private armies that fought each other as often as they fought the "natives."

On the Indian subcontinent the main rivalry was between the British and French East India Companies. The prizes sought were not only spices, but also calico, chintz, and gingham, types of cotton cloth from India that were immensely popular in Europe. The "India" into which the British and French Companies were moving, however, was not a single nation but a conglomeration of hundreds of small kingdoms. In the north, many of these kingdoms had been under some form of Mughal control since a series of invasions by these Muslims from Turkey, Afghanistan, and Persia in the sixteenth century. In the south, independent Hindu states still prevailed. With concessions granted by the native rulers, the competing European companies set up their first trading posts on the subcontinent. The British-French rivalry reached its peak in 1757 at the Battle of Plassey, an early battle in the Seven Years War' (1756–1763) that also saw France lose its Canadian colony to Britain. The victory of British forces over the French secured the British East India Company's dominance in Indian affairs.

Christian missionaries arrived in India in 1813. While attempting to convert the Hindu population, missionaries also supported British East India Company efforts to ban the existing practices of widow burning (*suttee*), female infanticide, child marriage, and ritual murder (*thuggee*). These were no minor crusades since *thuggee* alone was responsible for some 20,000 deaths each year, all done in the name of the goddess Kali. During the 1830s an educational system modeled on that of Great Britain was introduced, but it was available to relatively few persons, and illiteracy remained widespread. Telegraph service began in 1839, and massive railway construction began to unite the far-flung areas of the two million square miles under British East India Company control.

Many Indians supported the East India Company's efforts to reduce princely privileges and introduce the technical advances of the Industrial Revolution, but others worried that the Hindu majority was simply exchanging one master for another. And all the while British control was expanding into neighboring Burma to the east and Afghanistan to the west. A series of battles fought by British and East India Company troops against Afghan natives (1838–1843) ended in virtual deadlock in Afghanistan, but similar campaigns in Burma (1823–1826 and 1852–1853) resulted in the cession to British India of several Burmese provinces. In India itself, the Sikh state in the Punjab launched a preemptive strike against the encroaching British on December 3, 1845. Two wars and four years later, the Punjab became part of British India.

By the 1850s, the mix of regular soldiers and privately financed armed forces controlling India for Britain and the East India Company numbered more than 400,000 men. Native Hindu and Muslim fighters known as *Sepoys* comprised almost 80 percent of East India Company troops. In the northern province of Bengal, a combination of poor pay, material deprivation, and the arrival of a particularly racist group of British troops caused an explosive situation. Taking full advantage of the religious faith of the soldiers, agitators in the service of unhappy princes told Sepoy regiments that the cartridges for their new Enfield rifles were being coated with beef or pork fat before distribution, respectively offending Hindu and Muslim religious sensibilities. The tale was not true: the grease was vegetable based, but the harm was done. Pledging loyalty to the Mughal Emperor and his court, perhaps a quarter of the Sepoys, largely Hindu, rose up in mutiny and began an ill-organized but extremely bloody march up the Ganges River Valley to capture Delhi. En route, rebellious Sepoys slaughtered a garrison force that had already surrendered and filled the central well at Cawnpore with the bodies of women and children. The British began a series of equally savage reprisals, burning entire villages with all their inhabitants and summarily executing suspected mutineers. A combination of loyal Sepoy troops and British Imperial forces took over a year to restore order.

The name given to any war in history books is rarely a neutral one. In British textbooks, the conflict that raged in the Bengal region of India from 1857 to 1858 is called "The Sepoy Mutiny" or "The Great Mutiny." The Indians, on the other hand, see it as part of their history of resistance to British rule, and call it "The Great Rebellion."

The immediate result of the war was the transfer of control of India from the British East India Company to the British government. Parliament made British India a Crown Colony in 1858, although many princely states within the sub-continent retained some self-rule under the general administrative umbrella. The period of the British Raj (1858–1947) had officially begun.

◆ The British Raj

The trade and tax policies that followed the India Act of 1858 were designed to transform India into a vast marketplace for British manufactured goods. The colony was encouraged to produce more raw materials for export. Indian weavers had once enjoyed a higher standard of living than their British counterparts because of the cheaper cost of food in India and the greater worker protection. But under British rule, India's thriving domestic textile industry was destroyed, while it became a leading exporter of jute, oilseeds, wheat, and raw cotton. The result was a favorable trade balance for Great Britain, but India remained an agricultural society as Britain continued to industrialize. British rule did bring India railroads, telegraph and postal services, and western medical techniques that lowered the high death rate, enabling the population to increase by 50 percent to nearly 300 million.

An ancient functional and ritual division within the Hindu religion, the caste system, divided the Hindu population into four main groups: *Brahmins* (priests), *Kshatriya* (warriors), *Vaisya* (farmers and traders), and *Sudra* (servants and laborers). Beneath this hierarchy were the *Harijan* ("Untouchables"), individuals whose jobs (such as corpse washing or leather tanning) were considered so ritually impure that they were forced to live apart from other Indians in dire poverty.

Successive British Viceroys made some efforts to improve the social status of lower-caste and untouchable Indians, but jobs were restricted to agricultural pursuits and lower level positions in the colonial Civil Service. Traditional caste distinctions and the reluctance of the British to open their administration combined to restrict access to a Western-style education to members of the Hindu and Muslim elite. By 1900 university attendance more than doubled to 23,000, while 633,000 students attended secondary schools, although national literacy was still only 15 percent. That small elite would soon be agitating for independence.

The spiritual father of Indian national consciousness was Ram Moan Roy (1772–1833), a Bengali Hindu who once worked for the East India Company. Roy's goal was to combine the best elements of European Christian practice with the piety and naturalism of Hindu thought. He was a committed modernizer whose writings condemned both British paternalism and "backward" Indian practices such as *suttee*. As a teacher at the Hindu School of Calcutta, Roy influenced a generation of students; with his encouragement, they demanded more rights from the governing authorities. In 1884 the viceregal government approved the creation of an Indian National Congress to debate matters of general concern, but gave it no power to force British governors to take its advice. Established in December, 1885, the All-India National Congress included both Hindu and Muslim delegates from the professional classes. Pro-British Hindu moderates normally controlled the elected Congress, but after 1890 this elite domination was challenged by Bal Gangadhor Tilak (1856–1920). "Educate, Agitate and Organize" was his program, and he demanded the creation of labor unions, a minimum wage, universal suffrage, and compulsory education for all classes. After famine struck the land in the 1890s, and Bombay suffered an outbreak of plague in 1897, Tilak's appeal to the lower classes grew.

Tilak's emphasis on the use of the Hindu religion as a means of unifying the country alienated India's sizable Muslim minority, a group with its own traditions of national consciousness. If Ram Moan Roy was the spiritual father of Hindu Indian national consciousness, Sir Syed Ahmed Khan (d. 1898) was the spiritual father of Muslim Indian national consciousness. An advocate of education for India's Muslims, he started a school in 1875 that developed into India's first Muslim University (1920). His shift from fighting for a united India to one split into separate Hindu and Muslim countries was sparked by an 1867 Hindu attempt to replace the local Urdu language in the courts with Hindi. The movement he started took a more organized form in 1906 with the founding of the All-India Muslim League.

These divisions between India's Hindus and Muslims hampered their ability to win concessions from the British. Nevertheless, Tilak ultimately did win some administrative reform. In 1909 the Indian Councils Act (Morley-Minto Reforms) provided that Indians elect a majority of the members of provincial legislatures and, for the first time, permitted an Indian to serve on the Viceroy's Executive Council. The measure marked an initial step towards national self-government.

China and Southeast Asia

◆   The "Opening" of China

China's Manchu Emperors ruled over an empire containing twice the population and four times the landmass of Europe. Over the centuries Europeans had borrowed China's advanced technologies of paper-making, printing, and gunpowder, and imported its porcelains, silks, and tea, only to find that China was not especially interested in anything "barbarian" Europe had to sell. While China bought shark fins, Indian cotton, and African sandalwood from European traders, the

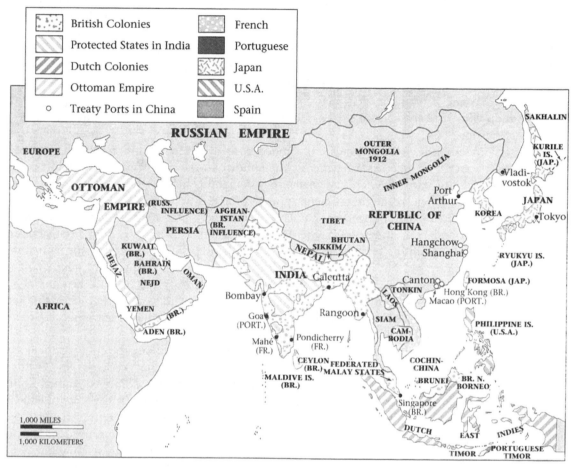

Imperialism in Asia to 1926.
From *Human Venture*, Fifth Edition, (2004), by permission of Prentice-Hall, Inc.

Chinese government preferred payment in silver for its exports and allowed Europeans limited use of only one port (Canton) in which to transact their business.

By the 1830s, the unfavorable balance of trade between China and Britain was straining the entire British economy. British textile mills needed the Indian cotton that once might have gone to China. Desperately seeking an alternative commodity for China to buy, the British decided to offer opium produced in India. The narcotic was shipped eastwards to China, carefully packaged into three-pound balls wrapped in poppy leaves, and sold to a vast and willing market. Opium was still a legal substance in Britain, and the Chinese themselves believed moderate use of the drug was harmless. By 1832, the increasing volume of the opium trade caused an outflow of silver for the first time in China's commercial history. Four years later, Chinese authorities took the unprecedented step of banning opium. They moved aggressively to close smoking parlors and execute known dealers. In 1839 Imperial Commissioner Lin Tse-hsü (1785–1850) petitioned Queen Victoria to halt the trade, arguing that China was being "paid in smoke" for its riches. That June, his agents seized and destroyed 2,613,879 pounds of British opium. Great Britain prepared for war to recoup its losses.

The First Opium War between Britain and China began in November 1839 when a British merchant ship fought off an attack by Chinese vessels. Substantial British forces arrived off Canton the next summer, and for the next two years, with some aid from France, English squadrons devastated Chinese shipping. In one exploit, HMS *Nemesis* destroyed five Chinese forts, one battery, two military stations, and nine war ships. The one-sided destruction did not end until the *Treaty of Nanking* was negotiated in August 1842. China paid a fine equivalent to 21 million dollars to indemnify Great Britain for the destruction of the opium. China also agreed to open five port cities to British traders. A resident British consul protecting British interests was to be stationed in each city. The island of Hong Kong was ceded to Britain, and for the next 175 years it remained a symbol of Western power in the Far East. The *Treaty of Nanking* fostered a vast extension of trade in tea, porcelain, wallpapers, lacquerware, and silk. Within two years China was forced to grant similar to France and the United States, which had been active in the opium trade since about 1804. The *Treaty of Wanghia* (July 1844), between China and the United States, further insulted Chinese dignity by insisting on the right of *extraterritoriality* for Americans in China. Article 21 of that treaty stated that

> *"citizens of the United States who may commit any crime in China shall be subject to be tried and punished only by the consul or other public functionary of the United States thereto authorized."*[1]

Despite the great concessions won in 1842, British merchants complained that Chinese markets were difficult to penetrate. In 1856 a Second Opium War began when England joined with France to punish supposed Chinese restrictions on their trade. The subsequent *Treaty of Tientsin* (1858) extorted another indemnity, opened additional treaty ports, explicitly guaranteed the safety of Christian missionary activities, permitted foreign travel throughout China, gave the British in China the right of extraterritoriality, and legalized the opium trade. Despite the settlement, the Chinese court proved reluctant to implement the treaty and hostilities sputtered on until the British captured the Chinese capital in 1860. China's losses in these wars came as a shock to a court that had long held the West in disdain, but demonstrated the ability of industrialized states to impose their will over the furthest corners of the globe.

The Chinese peasantry found itself supporting an imperial regime that could not defend its borders, its trade or its culture. Matters were particular difficult in Kwangsi and Kwantung, the southern provinces most affected by the Opium Wars. Banditry and piracy were everyday occurrences in a countryside overburdened by taxes and rife with ethnic strife between the dominant Han Chinese and the Hakka ("Guest People") minority that had migrated from the north. Rebellion against the Chinese government was not long in coming. The Taiping Rebellion (1850–1864) was led by Hung Hsiu-ch'üan (1814–1864), a onetime schoolteacher turned mystic. He proclaimed himself the younger brother of Jesus, and pledged to cleanse China of sin and achieve equality for women. Western diplomacy and arms bolstered whatever side happened to be losing the fight, with the goal of weakening all opposition to their position. The result was an unmitigated disaster for Manchu China. Before the Taiping rebels, and collateral rebellions by Nien and Muslim groups were repressed, over 20 million lives were lost. After the slaughter, Manchu rule continued, but its control over China was seriously weakened.

HUNG HSIU-CH'ÜAN (1814–1864)

Mystic and leader of a religious, agrarian, and nationalist revolution.
Copyright © J.M. Callery and M. Yvan

Hung Hsiu-ch'üan was born on January 1, 1814, to a Hakka family in Guangdong province in southern China. The Hakka people, who had migrated from the north centuries before, were known for their love of education, and Hung became a schoolteacher. He hoped to enter the imperial bureaucracy, the surest route in traditional China to power, prestige, and wealth, but suffered a nervous breakdown after his third failure to pass the entrance examination in 1837. The hallucinations he then suffered changed his life. After he failed the examination a fourth time, he became interested in Christian doctrine, and decided that during his earlier delirium he had visited heaven and talked with God and Jesus Christ. He decided he was the second Son of God, baptized himself, and set about saving China for God.

Hung's promises of salvation and eternal life in heaven won him many followers in the poverty-stricken south. Not surprisingly, he condemned most of Chinese culture (including the examination system) as the work of demons. He also opposed opium smoking, foot binding, gambling, and prostitution. Such was the power of his message that his insistence upon sexual abstinence, which extended even to married people, did nothing to reduce the appeal of his message. This rule, however, did not include Hung or his captains, all of whom kept large harems.

Demanding that all property be shared in common, and calling for an end to foreign Manchu rule, Hung began a rebellion in 1850. He soon recruited an army of over one million disciplined soldiers, organized in separate men's and women's regiments. He proclaimed a new dynasty, the *Tai Ping Tien-guo* (the Great Peace Heavenly Kingdom) and himself *Tien-wang* (Heavenly King). The Taiping rebels captured Nanking (China's southern capital) in 1853, and soon much of the Yangtze was in their hands. But after a failed attempt to capture the northern Manchu capital of Peking, the Taiping leaders began to fall out among themselves. Hung had his chief minister murdered for disagreeing with him and then executed the general who killed the minister.

The Taiping attempt to capture Shanghai in 1860 was defeated, in part through the efforts of General Charles ("Chinese") Gordon. Hung's movement began to lose ground. He had never bothered to recruit the local gentry who rejected his attacks on Confucianism. They joined with the Manchu and organized the armies that retook Nanking in 1864. After a lingering illness, Hung Hsiu-ch'üan committed suicide on June 1, 1864, but over 100,000 of his followers refused to abjure their faith, and were massacred by Manchu troops. Before all Taiping resistance ended in 1866, over 20 million Chinese were killed.

◆ French Indochina

The Manchu regime was also losing its influence over the rest of East Asia. Many Asian areas with non-Chinese populations had once been ruled by or paid tribute to China. Vietnam to the south had been independent since 935, but its laws, writing system, and civil service derived from Chinese models. Its government always resisted domination from its great northern neighbor, but the Europeans proved harder to keep out. The Portuguese planted an enclave in 1535. The Dutch and the French followed shortly thereafter. By the first decades of the nineteenth century, the Vietnamese ruler, Minh Mang (r. 1819–1841), was battling internal rebellions aided by the Christian missionaries he was trying to eject from his kingdom. His successors resorted to summary executions of French missionaries, a policy that caused a public outcry in France. China's losses in the Opium Wars (1839–1842 and 1856–1858) proved that it could not defend itself, let alone the Vietnamese, from foreign intervention. A French armada sailed into Tourane (modern Da Nang) in August 1858, advancing to Saigon early the following year. Vietnamese resistance proved so powerful, however, that the French needed reinforcements from the Spanish Philippines to secure the surrounding countryside. By 1864, the French occupied Cambodia, by 1867 southern Vietnam, and by 1882 the north. France consolidated its new possessions into French Indochina (modern Vietnam, Cambodia, and Laos). Controlling the new colony was far more difficult than naming it. War raged on in Indochina between the French and Vietnamese guerilla forces for years before the colony was finally pacified in 1897.

On paper, the native government remained in place, but Vietnamese emperors who refused to serve the French were routinely deposed. The highest positions in the bureaucracy were reserved for the French, and the economy was directed to provide raw materials (rubber) and agricultural products (rice) for export to France or its chosen markets. The railroads, harbors, bridge, and canals built under French rule were designed to make this cash-crop economy function as efficiently as possible, not to bring the industrial revolution to Vietnam. The consolidation of small plots into great farms did not benefit the Vietnamese peasant: the plantations were sold off to a few aristocratic Vietnamese collaborators and hundreds of French speculators. The Vietnamese peasant became a landless laborer or tenant farmer who owed his landlord up to 60 percent of his crop. Before the arrival of the French three-quarters of Vietnam's land was in the hands of peasant families. By 1930, half the Vietnamese owned no land at all while 45 percent of the land was in the hands of less than 3 percent of the population.

◆ Russia and Japan Join the Battle for Asia

To China's north, Russian expansion reached the Pacific Ocean in 1860 with the founding of Vladivostok. Russia's diplomatic efforts to negotiate an Anglo-French withdrawal from Peking later that year garnered it control of both banks of the Amur River and concessions along the Korean border. In central Asia, the advancing Russian armies occupied Tashkent (1865), Bukhara (1868), Khiva (1873), and Merv (1884). Cotton cultivation was introduced into Uzbekistan, while the Trans-Siberian Railway linked Russia's Asian and European territories. Long-standing Chinese claims to lands in Central Asia were ignored as Russia moved to consolidate its territorial gains. Although China negotiated a treaty with Russia that restored China's power over much of western Mongolia (1881), its once dominant position in Asia was obviously on the wane.

Korea, a nation whose culture was strongly influenced by China, was strategically located between Chinese, Japanese, and Russian ambitions. The Japanese, in fact, had tried to annex it as early as 1598. It was a Japanese mission that finally opened Korea to world trade in 1876. China and Japan openly contended for influence over Korean affairs. A war between them was narrowly avoided in 1884 with the signing of the *Li-Itō Convention* assuring mutual disengagement. But a second Sino-Japanese conflict became open war in 1894. At the request of the Korean king, the Chinese government sent troops to quell a religious rebellion. The Japanese saw this as a violation of the *Li-Itō Convention* and sent in 8,000 Japanese troops. A Japanese attack on Chinese war-ships that July became a prelude to a Japanese declaration of war on August 1. China counter-attacked, but the Japanese soon won control of the sea and strongholds on the Chinese mainland. With Japanese troops marching up to Peking, and the Chinese unable to get aid from Russia or Britain, the Chinese government had no choice but to agree to Japan's demand for an uncondi-tional surrender. Not even the most acute Westerners were prepared for the overwhelming Japan-ese victory. Europeans had little comprehension of the extent to which Meiji reforms had transformed Japan into a modern society. China, lacking an industrial base and debilitated by the incursions of the other imperialists, was a helpless victim of Japanese aggression. By the *Treaty of Shimonoseki* (1895) that ended this Sino-Japanese War (1894–1895), China was forced to pay a large indemnity to Japan, cede both Formosa and the Liao-tung Peninsula in southern Manchuria (including Port Arthur) to Japan, and recognize an independent Korea.

The scramble to "carve up the Chinese melon" intensified after Japan's easy victory in 1895. In 1898 Germany obtained a 99-year lease on Kaio-chau harbor and the right to develop coal mining facilities in Shantung Province, France "leased" Kwang-chou-wan, Britain occupied the port of Weihaiwei, and Russia advanced into Port Arthur. The United States attempted to cut itself in without seeming to do so, by proclaiming an "Open Door Policy" in March 1899, a program that endorsed the territorial integrity of China even as it demanded equal economic opportunity for all nations in Asia.

Meanwhile, differences between traditional Chinese values and those of the missionaries were proving increasingly disruptive to Chinese society. In the Confucian system, the father had com-plete control over all members of the family, whether the children were grown or not. He owned all the family property and arranged his children's marriages without needing their consent. He could take a second wife (a concubine) at will, but his widow was not supposed to re-marry. While Christian missionaries saw themselves as aiding Chinese women by attacking the crippling custom of foot-binding and trying to eliminate concubinage, traditional authorities saw them as attacking the values that upheld Chinese society. When Christian missionaries took the sides of their con-verts in village disputes, violence was often the result. Underlying the friction was the worsening condition of the average Chinese peasant. In the years since the *Treaty of Nanking* (1842), China's population had grown from over 150 million people to nearly 300 million, but the increase in land under cultivation was nowhere near as great, so that the amount of cultivated land per per-son by 1900 was less than two-thirds of what it had been fifty years before. Hunger was the Chi-nese peasant's constant companion, and an increasing tax burden imposed by the Chinese government only made matters worse.

The Chinese government was as indecisive in dealing with its internal problems as it was in dealing with foreign governments. The government was in the hands of the Empress Dowager Tz'u-hsi (1835–1908), a former concubine and the widow of the late Emperor Hsien-feng (r. 1851–1861). She ruled as regent on behalf first of her underage son (T'ung-chih, r. 1862-1874) and then of her nephew (Kuang-hsü, r. 1875–1908). Like most traditional Chinese, she resented China's weakness with respect to the industrialized powers but resisted all efforts to modernize. Aware of the widespread anger against "foreign devils," the Empress and her court secretly

Tz'u Hsi, Empress Dowager of China, was unable to rid her domain of foreign control.
Courtesy of the Freer Gallery of Art, © Smithsonian Institution, Washington, D.C.

encouraged a religious society known as the Righteous and Harmonious Fists (known to foreigners as the "Boxers") to expel all foreigners. The Boxers had their origin in a self-defense organization created during the earlier Taiping Rebellion and had originally been both an anti-government and anti-Christian group, but after a secret 1898 pact with the government, the Boxers organized into militia openly attacking missionary outposts and settlements of Chinese Christians. Popular hatred of foreigners was exacerbated by the starvation caused by a series of floods and a severe drought in northern China. In a frenzy of orchestrated violence during 1898–1899, over 240 missionaries were killed and many other foreign civilians murdered. In June 1900, the Boxers laid siege to Peking's foreign legation quarter. Boxer troops murdered the German minister and a member of the Japanese legation. The Boxers believed that their amulets made them impervious to bullets but soon discovered their error. It took an international force, drawn from American, British, French, Italian, Japanese, and Russian troops less than two months to relieve the legations, even though the Boxers were aided by the Chinese army. The Boxers were destroyed and the Chinese court humiliated by imposed indemnities. A beaten China was totally at the mercy of its exploiters. Western forces were placed on permanent station in Peking while Russia utilized the opportunity to seize full control of Manchuria.

The overlapping concessions by which Japan and the European powers dominated China's trade eventually led to war. Japan deeply resented that it had been denied the Shantung peninsula after its victory over China in 1895. That resentment turned to rage when its Russian rival occupied the Shantung Peninsula and Port Arthur in 1898. After securing the neutrality of Great Britain by signing a naval treaty (*Anglo-Japanese Naval Treaty,* 1902), the Japanese launched a surprise attack against Russian forces in Port Arthur on a Sunday morning in 1904. During the ensuing Russo-Japanese War (1904–1905), the small island nation proved that modernization under the Meiji regime had transformed it into a global power. Russia's army was defeated at Mukden and its navy at Tsushima in 1905. When exhaustion in Japan and revolution in Russia made both sides willing to consider a truce, President Theodore Roosevelt of the United States brokered a settlement in Portsmouth, New Hampshire (1905). Japan replaced Russia as the controlling power in the Shantung Peninsula, and acquired the Russian lease over the Manchurian railway and the southern half of Sakhalin Island. Japan's victory over Russia demonstrated how quickly a nation determined on technological development could become a significant power in world politics. To consolidate its foothold on the east Asian mainland, Japan formally annexed Korea in 1910.

The Conquest of Africa
◆The Creation of South Africa

European penetration of southernmost Africa began as no more than a byproduct of the limitations of seventeenth-century travel: the sail-powered ships of the Dutch East India Company could not reach their Asian ports of call without stopping for food and fresh water several times along the way. The harbor of the Cape of Good Hope was one such convenient way-station. Cape Town, the settlement founded around that harbor in April, 1652, also served as a base for Dutch farmers who claimed title over what they called "empty lands." They ploughed under the foraging range of the native San and Khoi hunter-gatherers. Cape Colony residents soon began to call themselves Afrikaners, and their sense of uniqueness was enhanced as they developed a local variant of their native Dutch, called Afrikaans. The poorest of these first Dutch settlers, always in search of fresh pastures, were called *trekboers* (wandering farmers). Gradually, the term *Boer* came to describe all white settlers in the colony. To the Boers, the San and Khoi were ignorant savages (*kaffirs*), good for nothing but forced labor.

The Boers soon faced a more formidable foe. The British were also looking for way-stations on the route to India, the main source of raw cotton for Britain's textile mills. Cape Town harbor was not only a convenient place to refit and resupply Britain's merchant fleet; it could be used as a "choke point" in case of naval warfare with her imperial rivals. Only the Boers stood in Britain's way. Britain used her power to demand that the Cape Colony be ceded to her at the Congress of Vienna (1814–1815), but Britain's victory did not make the Boers willing British subjects. The outnumbered Boers deeply resented Britain's abolition of the slave trade (1807), the proclamation that English was Cape Town's official language (1822), and laws that permitted blacks to testify in courts and purchase their freedom (1826). When Britain abolished slavery altogether in 1833, many Boers decided to leave Cape Town and British authority behind. Led by Andrius Pretorius (1799–1853) and Piet Retief (d.1838), nearly 10 thousand Boers moved inland from the Cape Colony in the "Great Trek."

The Boer migration into the heart of southernmost Africa was not a journey into "empty land," but a movement into the home range of the Xhosa, a cattle-herding people whose kingdom

SHAKA (c. 1787–1828)

Founder of the Zulu kingdom.
Copyright © Cambridge University Library

Shaka was son of Senzangakhona (1760s–1816), chieftain of the Zulu, and Nandi (1760s–1827), an orphaned princess of the neighboring Langeni. The Langeni and the Zulu were two of many small groups of Nguni-speaking peoples in the Natal region of South Africa. The most important element in Nguni social structure was the clan (ritual bloodline), which cut across several Nguni villages. Tradition forbade marriage within the same clan even if the couple were from different villages. Because his parents belonged to the same clan, Shaka was considered illegitimate. In disgrace, Nandi took Shaka back to her own village where she was also repudiated. In 1802, Nandi and Shaka sought refuge with another group of Nguni speakers, the Mthethwa.

Like all young men in the Mthethwa villages, Shaka was eventually called up for service in the army of Dingiswayo, the Mthethwa leader. During six years of service, Shaka advanced through the ranks until he became Dingiswayo's favored lieutenant. Dingiswayo had begun to dream of uniting all the Nguni peoples into one great king-dom, and he looked on Shaka as a possible successor. With Dingiswayo's support, Shaka took the Zulu throne from his half-brothers upon the death of Senzangakhona in 1816. When Dingiswayo himself died a year later, Shaka became leader of the Mthethwa as well. Although the Zulu were the smallest of the Nguni groups, under Shaka's leadership they became the nucleus of a vast Nguni empire that would henceforth bear their name: KwaZulu. By 1824, Shaka's KwaZulu encompassed all of the Nguni-speaking peoples of the Natal. Shaka's military innovations were both technical and organizational. His development of the stabbing spear (*assegais*) and regimental system (*impi*) forged an army in which allegiance was to the Zulu nation rather than to the village or clan. But his creation of KwaZulu rested on a military ruthlessness so bloody it threatened to depopulate the Natal. Clans fleeing his armies moved southward in the civil war known as the *Mfecane* (crushing).

Shaka never took an official wife, and his mother remained one of his chief advisors until her death in 1827. Her death sent Shaka off into a grief so violent it threatened to destroy the kingdom he had built. He ordered the deaths of all pregnant women, along with their husbands. He refused to allow the Zulu to plant any crops and slaughtered the cows whose milk was a staple of the Zulu diet. In 1828 he ordered raids into Boer territory to the south and then sent his armies north without a rest between campaigns. His lieutenants finally rebelled, and Shaka was assassinated on September 22, 1828, by his half-brother Dingane (c. 1795–1840) who then took the Zulu throne.

Although his methods were bloody and his rule authoritarian, Shaka's legacy was an empire that survived his death by almost 50 years. Only the modern weaponry and technological superiority of British imperial forces enabled them to take the Zulu capital in 1879. In modern South Africa, the Zulu remain a unified people whose influence remains vital in determining the future of the nation.

was already splitting in two under internal pressures. Border wars with the Xhosa (Hintsa's War, 1834–1835) gave way to even larger struggles with related groups to the North. Nguni-speaking pastoralists had moved into what is now South Africa as early as the eleventh century. This ancestral group split off into two main stocks: the Xhosa to the south and the people we now call the Zulu to the north. By the middle of the fifteenth century, the clans of the northern branch were the dominant group in the fertile lands around the Tugela River, but their semi-independent villages proved little threat to white settlement until their unification in the 1820s by Shaka (c. 1787–1828), the chief of the small Northern-Nguni group called the Zulu. Shaka, an exile who seized power in his father's village in 1816, was a gifted military leader who revolutionized battle tactics in the Natal area by perfecting the *impi*, a highly disciplined regiment formed over years of training. His armies were composed of mature soldiers forbidden to marry until their mid-30s. He increased their effectiveness even further by making their primary weapon a short, stabbing spear (the *assegais*). Under his leadership, Zulu armies ravaged the land and created an empire (KwaZulu) for their king. KwaZulu, centered in present day Natal, comprised some quarter of a million inhabitants. Shaka's centralizing policies were speedily replacing the feudal sub-chief structure and clan divisions with a sense of national identity, but Shaka's increasingly violent behavior and erratic actions led to his eventual assassination.

Shaka's successor, and half-brother, Dingane (r. 1828–1840) was left to deal with the Boer incursions. As the Boers advanced into his lands, Dingane ordered the massacre of a scout party led by Retief. Both sides recognized that battle was inevitable, and on December 16, 1838, the opposing forces met at Blood River. The Boers won an overwhelming victory, killing 3,000 Zulu warriors and forcing the rest to retreat northward. The British intervened to force a truce, and the Zulu ceded a portion of their lands to the Boers. The victorious Boers then proclaimed this land the Republic of Natal (1839). But the British continued to encroach. By 1845 they had annexed Natal and assumed the responsibility for keeping the peace between the Boer settlers and the Zulu. Rather than submit to British rule, many Boer families emigrated northward, creating two Boer Republics, the Transvaal (1852) and the Orange Free State (1854), in lands they hoped to maintain independent of British authority and Zulu threats. While the Boers regrouped, the British became entangled in a series of Frontier Wars against the resurgent Xhosa (in 1846 and 1850–1853). Battles between the British and the Boers (in 1848) further prevented any permanent settlement of the competing territorial claims.

The discovery of diamonds in the Cape Colony in 1868 opened up the land to a new type of competition. Among the adventurers drawn to the mines was Cecil Rhodes (1853–1902), a young Briton who succeeded in putting together the great DeBeers diamond syndicate within ten years of his arrival in Cape Town in 1870. Mining claims and counter claims exacerbated the growing tensions between the British, the Boers, the Xhosa, and the Zulu. The last of the Frontier Wars between the British and the Xhosa was fought in 1877–1878 although final incorporation of the last Xhosa kingdom into the British colony did not come until 1885. While the British fought the Xhosa, the Boers continued to push into Zulu lands. Cetshwayo (c. 1832–1884), ruler of KwaZulu since 1872, complained repeatedly to the British authorities without avail. Gathering up the *impi* in preparation for a campaign against the Boers, he was ordered to disband his troops by the British. When he refused, British troops moved into KwaZulu. The Zulu attacked, gaining a first victory at Isandhlwana (January 21, 1879) against the overconfident British. The regrouped British, aided by the Gatling gun, were able to capture the Zulu capital by the beginning of July. The kings of KwaZulu reigned from then on only as puppets of their British overlords. All the while, skirmishes continued between the British and the Boers.

CECIL RHODES (1853–1902)

The colossus of British Imperialism.
Copyright © Library of Congress

Cecil John Rhodes was born on July 5, 1853, in Hertfordshire, England, the son of a wealthy vicar. Poor health kept him out of university, and he went to Natal, South Africa, in 1870 to manage a cotton farm already established by his brother. Having acquired a large stake in Transvaal mines soon after the discovery of gold there in 1885, he founded the Gold Fields of South Africa Company two year later. During the great diamond rush in Kimberley, he worked ceaselessly to create a diamond monopoly under his control. By 1891 his De Beers Consolidated Mines Ltd., controlled ninety percent of the world's production of diamonds, but Rhodes regarded his great wealth primarily as a means to extend the British Empire. An almost mystical imperialist, his admonition "Remember, you are an Englishman, and therefore have won first prize in the lottery of life," summed up his belief in the superiority of the Anglo-Saxon "race." He even dreamed of returning the United States to the British Empire.

The charters of both the De Beers and South Africa companies allowed for northward expansion, and Rhodes was determined to acquire all of southern Africa for Britain. The mining concessions Rhodes created north of the Cape Colony eventually led to the colonization of Bechuanaland (Botswana) and Nyasaland (Malawi), as well as the territories originally named for him, Southern Rhodesia (Zimbabwe) and Northern Rhodesia (Zambia). But his plans for an even greater empire were foiled by the German acquisition of South-West Africa (Namibia), and the decision of the British government to maintain Portuguese Angola and Mozambique. His hopes for a Cape Town to Cairo railway on contiguous British territory were ended by German settlement of Tanganyika (Tanzania).

As Prime Minister of the Cape Colony between 1890 and 1896, Rhodes hoped to convince both British and Boers to support his northern policy. Despite his appeals, President Kruger of the Boer Transvaal Republic continued to refuse political rights to British and other foreign prospectors (called *Uitlanders* by the Boer leadership). A frustrated Rhodes decided to encourage an *Uitlander* revolt to overthrow Kruger. Leander Starr Jameson (1853–1917), the British physician appointed administrator of Matabeleland by Rhodes, invaded the Transvaal in December 1895. The raid was a total failure; Jameson went to prison, and Rhodes was forced to resign.

Even in defeat, Rhodes continued to play an important political role in South Africa, supporting the suspension of the constitution during the last Anglo-Boer War (1899–1902). He died of incurable heart disease on March 26, 1902, but his will established the Rhodes scholarships that still allow young men from Britain and their "kindred" in Germany and Britain's former colonies to study at Oxford University. He hoped his legacy would encourage "a more disinterested kind of imperialism," but he would not be pleased to learn his scholarships have been extended to women and people of color.

In 1885 gold was discovered in the Transvaal. Backed by the power of the DeBeers syndicate, Cecil Rhodes quickly eliminated rival Boer claimants and established the Gold Fields of South Africa Company (1887). Rhodes now added the income of gold mines to his fortune; his personal income in 1890 was estimated at $5 million. Inevitably, Rhodes became Prime Minister of Cape Colony (1890–1896) and continued to expand Britain's imperial position. He founded the city of Salisbury, later the capital of a country (Rhodesia) named in his honor. After annexing Nyasaland in 1892, Rhodes began to plot the ouster of the Boers, the final obstacle to British expansion to the north. Rhodes believed that he would see the day when railroads would bring travelers from Cape Town to Cairo completely through British possessions. He dreamed of a world dominated by Anglo-Saxon entrepreneurs. However, his unscrupulous support of an 1895 attempt to overthrow the Boer government of the Transvaal State led by Paul Kruger (1825–1904) forced Rhodes's resignation.

All was not well in the Boer states. Even though the Xhosa and the Zulu seemed pacified, a continuing influx of Europeans threatened to make the Boers a minority in their own republics. Kruger began a campaign of discriminatory measures against the *Uitlanders* (Foreigners) to prevent their taking control of the Transvaal and the Orange Free State. British-Boer diplomacy failed to resolve the crisis and war erupted between the two in the fall of 1899. This last Anglo-Boer War raged on until 1902 as the British found it more difficult than they expected to defeat the guerilla tactics of the outnumbered Boers. The British claimed victory when the Boers finally surrendered, but the settlement offered something to both sides: the extension of the right of self-government resulted in the unification of British and Boer territories in the self-governing dominion of South Africa in 1909. The Xhosa and the Zulu had no say in the decision.

◆   France in North Africa

While the Dutch and the British moved into Africa from the south, France took aim at the north. Napoleon Bonaparte led the first French troops into Africa in 1798 when he invaded Egypt in an attempt to outflank the British in Malta. The attempt failed, and Napoleon's European conquests soon occupied all of France's energies. For the French, the years immediately after Napoleon's final defeat in 1815 were dedicated to rebuilding their country and regaining their place in the European community. By 1830, a resurgent France began to look for new places in which to build an empire. A long-running dispute with the Ottoman ruler of Algeria over trade and piracy set the stage for French imperial expansion in Africa. A personal insult to the French Consul provided the excuse: Husayn (r. 1818–1830), the Ottoman *Dey* (governor) in Algeria, struck the French consul in the face with a fly whisk. When a three-year blockade of the port of Algiers brought no apologies for the insult, French forces occupied the city in 1830. Husayn fled into exile, but native forces under 'Abd al-Qadir (1808–1883) held off the French for fifteen years before ultimately succumbing. The struggle between al-Qadir's guerillas and the French expeditionary forces of General Thomas Bugeaud (1784–1849) set the pattern for warfare in Africa for decades to come: hit-and-run native resistance to the invaders and a scorched earth response by the Europeans.

The results of Bugeaud's victories were mixed. The French held the coast, but even after their final victory in 1847, elements of the population remained rebellious and parts of the interior were never safe for Frenchmen. 'Abd al-Qadir's revolt was actually as much a part of a native Algerian movement against the Ottoman Empire as it was a result of French intervention. Al-Qadir's father, a director of one of the region's religious schools, had been trying to organize his own Muslim State. This form of Muslim nationalism would also prove important in shaping Northern Africa's future.

The French made every effort to incorporate Algeria into France itself: French became the language of the schools and the bureaucracy. By 1875, French settlers in Algeria sent representatives to the French national legislature back in Paris. But those French settlers only accounted for ten percent of Algeria's population. The native Algerians who made up ninety percent of the colony's population enjoyed no such privileges. This two-tier system became the model for French colonies everywhere. The large-scale confiscation of cultivable land benefitted only the French and the Spanish, Italians, and Maltese settlers who joined them.

◆ From Suez to Fashoda

Throughout the nineteenth century, the French and the British were rivals for territory in Asia, but the main route to Asia was the long and costly voyage around the continent of Africa. The more territory the rivals gained in Asia, the more they needed a shorter route to those territories. The most logical place for the construction of such a shortcut was the Isthmus of Suez, the narrow strip of land between the main body of Egypt and the Sinai peninsula separating the Mediterranean from the Red Sea. The ruling family of Egypt was technically under the control of the Ottoman Empire, but the Egyptian *Pasha* (governor), Muhammad 'Ali (r. 1805–1849), was determined to pursue an independent policy of modernization. He encouraged the development of commercial agriculture and European settlement, sent his grandson Isma'il to school in France, and began borrowing heavily from French and British bankers to finance his plans and enrich his family's holdings. The sons and grandsons who succeeded him—Ibrahim (r. 1848), 'Abbas I (r. 1848–1854), Sa'id (r. 1854–1863), and Isma'il (r. 1863–1879)—followed in his modernizing footsteps. Sa'id granted the French a contract to cut a canal through the Isthmus of Suez in 1859. In 1869, after ten years of work under the supervision of the French engineer, Ferdinand de Lesseps (1805–1894), the Suez Canal opened to great fanfare. It had been funded by the creation of the Suez Canal Company. The *Pasha* was given 51 per cent of the shares and the rest sold to French investors.

Isma'il used the canal money to step up the pace of modernization. He opened Egypt's first schools for girls, a national library, and more large-scale irrigation projects. But Isma'il's policies exceeded his budget; Egypt was on the verge of bankruptcy. To bail his country out, Isma'il sold his Suez Canal shares to the British in 1875. This infuriated the French who had raised most of the funds to build the canal, but the proceeds were still not enough cover Isma'il's debts. The governments of Britain and France combined to force his hand: control of Egypt's finances was turned over to their commissioners in 1876.

National resentment soon boiled over. The Egyptian Nationalist Party was formed in 1879 under the leadership of Colonel Ahmad 'Urabi (1839–1911), whose efforts forced the abdication of Isma'il in 1879 and marked the beginning of modern Egyptian nationalism. The country was in open revolt by 1881. British troops defeated 'Urabi's forces in 1882 and occupied Egypt. Henceforth Egyptian governors ruled only as puppets of the British. The British consul general Sir Evelyn Baring (1841–1917), had the final say in Egyptian affairs from 1883 on. Baring introduced modern irrigation methods, constructed railroads, built the first Aswan Dam, and restored Egypt's financial solvency, but blocked all efforts to open a university in Cairo because he feared it would prove a breeding ground for nationalism.

To the south of Egypt lay Sudan, a desert region under Egyptian control since 1822. Taking control of Egypt made Britain responsible for Sudan as well. But the Sudan was in the middle of a nationalist revival with a religious focus. Claiming to be *Al-Mahdi*, a promised Muslim Messiah, Muhammad Ahmed (1844–1885) organized Sudanese tribes in opposition to Egyptian rule. British troops were sent to Sudan in 1883, but after an indecisive and expensive campaign, fought

AL-MAHDI (1844–1885)

Courtesy of the Mansell Collection/Getty Images.

The man who claimed to be the *Mahdi* ("Right Guided One"), the political savior of Islam, was born Muhammad Ahmed Ibn as-Sayyid'abd Allah on August 12, 1844. He was the son of a shipbuilder in Dongola, a city in Sudan that was part of the ancient kingdom of Nubia. While he was still an infant, his family moved farther up the Nile River to a village just outside of the city of Khartoum, a region in which the mystic tradition of Sufi Islam held great sway. Muhammad Ahmed was schooled in a Sufi tradition that rejected worldly values and embraced a strict Islamic discipline. By 1870, the charismatic Muhammad Ahmed moved deeper into the Sudanese desert to instruct a growing band of disciples.

The political situation in East Africa was complicated. Sudan was nominally under the control of Egypt, which was part of the multinational Ottoman Empire. Both Egyptians and Nubians, like many of the peoples subject to the Ottoman Turks, were growing restless under their control. They also resented the growing threat to their native traditions posed by domineering and exploitative European merchants.

Convinced that the Sudan's Egyptian and Turkish overlords were traitors to Islam who colluded with the British and French, Muhammad began to preach rebellion. On June 29, 1881, he proclaimed himself *al-Mahdi*. Within two years Muhammad had forged an army that seemed invincible; he destroyed three Egyptian armies, wiping out the last force of 8,000 almost to the last man. His movement spread throughout Muslim Africa and as far as the very gates of Mecca. The British felt the power of his rhetoric (and his armies) when he laid siege to Khartoum and took it from the British garrison on January 26, 1885. At the end of the battle, General Charles Gordon, the British commander, was killed.

Muhammad established the capital of his purified Islamic State at Omdurman, a village across the Nile from Khartoum. His government was a theocracy based on a "pure" version of Islam as he believed it was practiced in the days of the Prophet. But the Mahdi did not long enjoy the fruits of his victory, dying less than six months later, on June 22, 1885, possibly of typhus. He was succeeded by his chief of staff, 'Abd Allah ibn Muhammad (1846–1899).

The Mahdi's Islamic State did not long outlast him. General Gordon had originally been sent to Khartoum only to evacuate it, not to hold it against the Mahdi's forces. But when word of the siege reached the British press, there was a public call to relieve the garrison. When word came of the defeat and Gordon's death, Parliament was vilified by the press for failing to rescue Gordon. Fearful of a general Arab uprising and further French incursion into Africa, the British government finally decided to avenge Gordon. In 1898, General Kitchener's troops wiped out 'Abd Allah's forces at the battle of Omdurman. Kitchener ordered the Mahdi's body dug up and decapitated. The body was thrown into the Nile while Kitchener kept the head until his superiors ordered it re-interred. The Mahdi's state disappeared, and Sudan became part of the British Empire. 'Abd Allah withdrew into the desert with what remained of his troops and died fighting the British a year later.

by British and Egyptian troops, Britain British decided to abandon the region. General Charles Gordon (1833–1885) was sent to Sudan in 1884 with orders to evacuate the remaining Egyptian troops from the Sudanese capital, Khartoum. Believing he could save Sudan, Gordon decided to hold Khartoum. By March 1884, the city was under siege by the Mahdi's forces. The British government of anti-imperialist liberals seemed willing to abandon the intransigent Gordon, but a public outcry forced their hand. Dubbed "Chinese Gordon" in the British press, General Gordon had been a popular hero in Britain since his victories over the Taiping Rebels in China. Prime Minister Gladstone reluctantly ordered a rescue attempt on September 19, 1884. Facing native resistance all the way, a British column arrived forty-eight hours after the Mahdi's forces had taken Khartoum and decapitated Gordon. The Mahdi himself died soon after, although his Islamic State lived on until its final defeat by the British in 1898.

The British withdrew from Sudan after the failure at Khartoum. But, in 1892, General Horatio Kitchener (1850–1916), newly appointed commander of the Egyptian forces, began training troops to re-take it. Also under his command were the black Sudanese, the people of southern Sudan who had long resented their domination by the Arab Sudanese of the north. Constructing a railway along the Nile to solve the problem of moving troops and heavy equipment through the desert, Kitchener's column was on the move early in 1896. On September 2, 1898, his combined British, Egyptian, and Sudanese troops met the forces of the Mahdi's successor at Omdurman, the Islamic capital the Mahdi had ordered built across the Nile from Khartoum. In a single morning, Kitchener's troops killed some 11,000 Arabs at the cost of 48 British dead. The key to the British victory was the fire-power of the Maxim machine gun. The first fully automatic machine gun, it was invented (c. 1884) by Sir Hiram Stevens Maxim (1840–1916) an American-born British engineer. The British public was soon boasting of its imperial victories with the ditty: "Whatever happens we have got, the Maxim Gun and they have not." Winston Churchill wrote of crossing the field after the battle of Omdurman and seeing rotting corpses lying "so thickly as to hide the ground."[2] As far as the British public was concerned, Gordon was avenged.

While the British were moving southward along the Nile, the French, having recovered from the set-back of the Franco-Prussian War (1870–1871), were moving eastward across northern Africa from their stronghold in Algeria. They occupied Tunisia in 1881. A French resident-general was installed to keep a close eye on the native governor and an even closer eye on the neighboring British. The French were still angry over Britain's purchase of a controlling interest in the Suez Canal and were determined to stop the spread of British rule in Africa. Jean Baptiste Marchand (1863–1934) was a French officer who had risen through the ranks during the campaigns in West Africa. In 1897 he was given command of a French expedition charged with extending France's African territory to the Nile. By July 10, 1898, he had reached Fashoda. The British administration, incensed by what seemed a French incursion into their backyard, ordered Kitchener on to meet them. At the sight of Kitchener's vastly superior numbers, Marchand backed off. A formal agreement between the British and the French in 1899 set the boundaries of their respective domains. The French continued to consolidate their colonies in the South West, having taken Timbuktu in 1892, Guinea and the Ivory Coast in 1893, and Madagascar and Dahomey in 1894. By 1900 almost 3.5 million square miles of the continent were under French authority and the fate of 40 million Africans was determined in Paris.

◆ The Scramble for Africa

The confrontation between the British and the French at Fashoda belongs to a period in world history often called "the Scramble for Africa," a great race between the major European powers for

The irresistible force of western imperialism—the Maxim machine gun.
Courtesy of the Director, National Army Museum, London

colonies that began in the 1870s and ended in 1900 with only Liberia and Ethiopia escaping European domination. A student looking at a map of Africa the day the Suez Canal opened would see how little of the mainland, except for a few coastal settlements, actually "belonged" to Europeans in 1869. What set off the land rush that followed?

The underlying causes had been building up over the nineteenth century. The spread of liberal sentiment throughout Western Europe led to a campaign first against the slave trade and then against slavery itself. This belated recognition of the humanity of Africans fostered missionary zeal within Christian Europe. Many denominations were soon making plans to "save" the pagan peoples of this "unknown" continent. This could not be done, however, until the continent's vast interior was mapped. In the age of science it seemed inconceivable that the globe still possessed so many "unknown" spaces. English, French, German, and American adventurers directed their efforts toward mapping the lakes, rivers, and natural riches of Africa. Perhaps the most famous of the explorers was Dr. David Livingstone (1813–1873), a Scottish missionary who crisscrossed sub-Saharan Africa. In support of his missionary goals, he mapped the Zambezi River and "discovered" Lake Nyasa. When he was not heard from for several months during an 1867 trip, the *New York Herald* dispatched a reporter to find him. Henry Morton Stanley (1841–1904) did locate Livingstone, and his report of the four months they spent in central Africa gave the Welsh-born American journalist world renown.

Missionary zeal and scientific curiosity were only part of the complicated web of motives that turned European attention toward Africa. The creation of Italy and Germany had altered the balance of power in Europe. Industrialization was occurring at an ever-increasing pace; even countries as small as Belgium were becoming major economic powers. These new industrial powers were on the prowl for cheap sources of labor and raw materials as well as markets in which to sell their goods. Britain was losing her lead and looking for ways to regain it as her continental rivals erected high tariff barriers to protect their fledgling industries from British competition.

But the immediate spark of the "Scramble for Africa" was lit by King Leopold II of Belgium (r. 1865–1909) when he hired Stanley in 1878 to explore the Congo region of Central Africa and secure control of its resources. The Congo River stations that Stanley established, and the lands he explored, became the geographic foundation of the Free State of the Congo that Leopold proclaimed in 1879. Stanley's initiative provided Belgium with a colony eighty times the size of the homeland. Other European states resented Belgium's access to such resources. France and Portugal immediately made counterclaims to lands around the mouth of the Congo River. Germany, for its part, building on the travels of Karl Peters (1856–1918) in Tanganyika, claimed three different strips of East Africa. Alarmed at the inroads made by her continental rivals, Britain, as we have seen, turned south from the Suez Canal.

By 1885 the major states of Europe had been at peace with each other for fifteen years, but their sudden rivalry over the acquisition of African lands made war between them a serious possibility. Having used wars to unify Germany, Otto von Bismarck now saw any war as dangerous to Germany's security. He invited contending European states to convene in Berlin to set some guidelines for the conquest of Africa. At the Berlin Conference (November 1884–February 1885), Bismarck and the other diplomats re-configured the map of Africa. Leopold's control of the Congo was accepted, as was the British position in Niger, and Germany's hold over Tanganyika. Resolutions to end slavery were also an important part of the settlement. But the major accomplishment of the Berlin Conference was to establish mutually accepted criteria whose fulfillment would secure title of African lands for a claimant. The key factors were "effective occupation" and control of the African coast. Powers "effectively" in control of coastal holdings had first claim on the adjacent interior. Powers claiming new coastline had to give other signatories notice so counter claims could be settled peacefully. At Berlin, the European signatories pledged to "protect the natives in their moral and material well-being," but these humanitarian goals were largely ignored. The main accomplishment of the Conference was to minimize the chance of colonial disputes between Britain, France, Germany, Portugal, and the International Association of the Congo. Bismarck convinced Europe that African colonies were not important enough to justify war amongst themselves. The "scramble" to colonize Africa could proceed.

The last years of the nineteenth century marked the height of European power in Africa. From 1885 to 1908 Leopold II held the Congo, a land mass equal in size to Western Europe, as his private possession. As many as 10 million people, half of the population, died from forced labor harvesting the Congo's rubber, copper, and gold. Germany, late to the "scramble" because of Bismarck's opposition to colonial expansion, formally assumed control of Southwest Africa in 1888, adding to its existing possessions on the Indian Ocean coastline. Treaties and consultations peacefully separated the Great Powers while giving them free hands within their designated spheres: Germany occupied Rwanda and Burundi while British authority was recognized in Kenya, Uganda, Nigeria, and Zanzibar. Lesser powerful European states claimed their share of Africa as well. Portugal took Angola and Mozambique. Spain claimed a strip south of Morocco. Italy moved into Libya and Somalia.

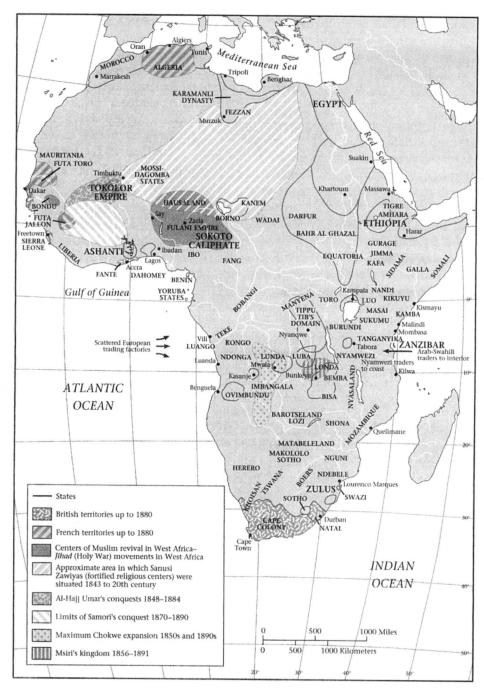

19th Century African Empires
From *Human Venture*, Fifth Edition, (2004), by permission of Prentice-Hall, Inc.

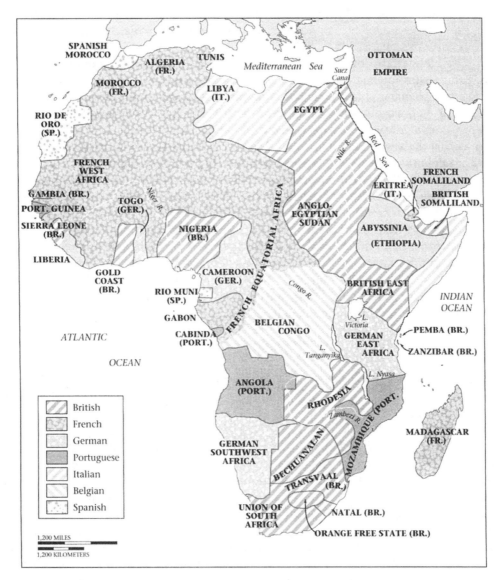

European Empires in Africa, 1910
From *Human Venture*, Fifth Edition, (2004), reproduced by permission of Prentice-Hall, Inc.

◆ Liberia and Ethiopia

The only African states able to resist the invasion were Liberia and Ethiopia. Liberia was a creation of the United States. In 1817, the American Colonization Society was formed to return blacks—free and enslaved—to Africa. President James Monroe's administration (1817–1825) gave the Society $100,000 and helped secure territory for the repatriated Africans. For his support, the capital, Monrovia, was named after him. Most of those who actually emigrated to Liberia were ex-slaves freed by the Civil War. American protection kept Liberia safe from

European conquest during the "scramble for Africa," but created a situation in which a majority African population was ruled by a minority descended from Westernized African-Americans.

Ethiopia (or Abyssinia as it was then known) had been an established kingdom for over a thousand years. It was also the only Christian kingdom in Africa. Its mountainous terrain and centralized administration had kept it safe from invasion by the Arabs and Ottoman Turks. Faced with the much more dangerous menace of industrialized imperialism, Menelik II (r. 1889–1912) assured Ethiopia's independence by exploiting the rivalries of the Europeans, modernizing his army, suppressing the slave trade, weakening the power of the nobility, and promoting literacy. He had obtained his throne with Italian assistance and rewarded Italy for that aid by signing the *Treaty of Ucciali* (1889). He believed the treaty only required him to consult with Italy on matters of foreign policy, but the Italian government saw the treaty as granting it the right of directly administering Ethiopia's foreign relations. Italy already exerted a considerable influence in the coastal state of Eritrea, and proclaimed it a colony in January 1890, although Ethiopia considered Eritrea a satellite state of its own. Menelik used the Italian proclamation as an excuse to repudiate the foreign policy clause of the *Treaty of Ucciali*. By early 1895 Italian troops had occupied most of Eritrea, but by the end of the year they were hard pressed by opposing Ethiopian forces. The final conflict came at Adowa on March 1, 1896, when Menelik's troops decimated the Italian army. The peace treaty finally agreed to by Italy in 1900 left Italy with a severely limited colony in Eritrea and secured Ethiopia's continued independence.

The United States Looks South and East

While the major European powers were carving out colonies in Asia and Africa, the United States had been moving to increase its territory within the Americas and gain a foothold in the Pacific. Having signed a trade treaty with China in 1844, the United States forced similar concessions from Japan with the *Treaty of Kanagawa* in 1854, while American missionaries moved into the Hawaiian Islands. But these overseas adventures were only minor themes in the main storyline of American development, the push to dominate the North American continent. Victory in the Mexican-American War (1846–1848) had doubled the size of the United States at Mexico's expense. More land was added when the United States purchased Alaska from Russia in 1867, but land added was not necessarily land controlled. The Hispanic populations of the lands taken from Mexico had to be put under American rule. The indigenous Indian nations who opposed the westward expansion of the United States were swept aside in a series of short yet brutal wars culminating in the slaughter of non-combatant Sioux at Wounded Knee Reservation in December 1890.

The American people and their government evinced no interest in the "Scramble for Africa." Liberia had been established as an independent country in a utopian scheme to avoid racial confrontation in the United States, not to plant the flag abroad. But the Pacific was another matter. To protect its trade with China and Japan the United States sought to establish a series of fueling stations and naval bases linking the Far East with California, on America's Pacific Coast. The United States annexed the Island of Midway in 1867, and took a lease on the mouth of the Pearl River (Pearl Harbor) on the island of Oahu in Hawaii in 1884. The seven main islands of the Hawaiian chain were formally annexed in 1898. Yet even in this theater of imperialism the United States seemed uncertain how far to go. Its Open Door Policy (1900) demanded commercial opportunity in China for the United States, but refused to agree to the actual dismemberment of that country. Although many nations received indemnification after the Boxer Rebellion, only the United States used the money to fund scholarships for Chinese students. In its own backyard, the United States proved to be a more aggressive neighbor. It had already exerted its power to settle disputes with

Chile (1891) and Venezuela (1895) when a growing crisis in Spanish Cuba opened up new opportunities in the Caribbean.

Spain had constructed Europe's first overseas empire, but lost most of it to Latin-American independence movements in the decades immediately following the Napoleonic Wars. Maintaining Spanish rule in the few islands still under its control became increasing difficult. Like the Spanish colonies that had already gained their independence, Spain's Cuban colony was home to a mixture of races in which the controlling Europeans made up less than half the population. An 1846 census listed 660,000 African slaves, 200,000 free Africans and Mulattos, and 565,000 mostly Creole Europeans; those groups competed with each other as well as against Spain for political control. Spain placed Cuba under martial law from 1825 to 1844 in order to crush a series of slave rebellions only to face a Ten Years' War (1868–1878) against Creole plantation owners, and still another rebellion in 1895, this one taking the life of Cuban poet and patriot José Marti (1853-1895). Cuba was placed under martial law once again as Spain tried to wipe out any lingering resistance. American businessmen, with investments of over $50 million in Cuba, certainly did not favor any US intervention that might disrupt trade. But New York City's tabloid newspapers and an active Cuban exile community that sent arms to the rebels in 1895, combined to attack the barbarity of Spanish control over Cuba and to lionize the "freedom fighters" who died opposing Spanish tyranny. Jingoism and propaganda whipped the American public into a moral fury. A battleship, the USS *Maine*, was sent off to Havana to protect American citizens and property from the anti-Spanish rioting. When the *Maine* exploded due to unknown causes in Havana Harbor on February 18, 1898, war seemed to become inevitable.

In the summer of 1898 the United States fought what Secretary of State John Hay (1838–1905) called a "splendid little war," and won all the battles. While an army of regulars and volunteers defeated the Spanish in Cuba, Commodore George Dewey (1837–1917) led a squadron into Manila Bay in the Philippines, destroying the Spanish fleet in a single day (May 1, 1898) with the Americans suffering only seven casualties. Taking over that Spanish colony would provide a strong link in the chain of naval bases the United States was building in the Pacific, but first it would have to be pacified, because the Filipinos were in the middle of their own rebellion against Spain. The exiled leader of that rebellion, Emilio Aguinaldo (1869–1964), was brought back to the Philippines on an American battleship on May 19 on Dewey's orders. Aguinaldo's forces helped the Americans drive the Spanish out of the colony. But when Aguinaldo declared Philippine independence on June 12 he soon found himself facing American troops. Open warfare turned into guerilla warfare and the last of Aguinaldo's resistance forces did not surrender until June 1902. What finally pacified the new American colony, however, were the measures taken by the United States to let literate or property-owning Filipino men vote for their own local officials, and to redistribute 430,000 acres of church lands to Filipino tenant farmers.

Four territories—Cuba, Puerto Rico, the Philippine islands, and Guam—were ceded to the United States by Spain in the *Treaty of Paris* (1898) that ended the Spanish–American War (1898). Spain also agreed to pay the United States a $20 million indemnity for damages done to American property. But Americans were divided over what to do with the four territories. In order to get money from Congress to fight the Spanish, President McKinley's administration (1897–1901) had guaranteed Cuba's independence, so Cuba could not be kept. It became an independent nation, but the Platt Amendment (1901) added to the constitution written for Cuba by the United States restricted Cuba's right to make foreign alliances, ordered Cuba to cede land to the United States for an American military base "to maintain the independence of Cuba," and granted America the privilege of intervening in Cuban affairs for "the protection of life, property and individual liberty."[3] These provisions allowed the United States to occupy Cuba from 1906 to 1909 and again

JOSÉ MARTI (1853–1895)

Poet, patriot, and martyr for Cuban independence.
Copyright © CORBIS/Bettmann

José Julian Marti y Pérez was born in Havana, Cuba, on January 28, 1853. At the age of sixteen, he was first arrested for the revolutionary agitation that shaped his entire life. He was sentenced to six years at hard labor in a limestone quarry while fettered in leg-irons, the most extreme punishment Spanish rule could inflict. After six months, partially blind and in a weakened condition, Marti was released and exiled to Spain in 1871. There, he enrolled in the University of Saragossa, where he received a law degree. By 1874 he was in Mexico, where he met his future wife, Carmen Zayas Bazan, the daughter of Cuban exiles living in Mexico City. For Marti, the temptation to abandon his revolutionary goals must have been strong, but he refused to betray his homeland. He spent three years teaching literature and philosophy at the University of Guatemala, but returned to Cuba in 1879 one year after his marriage to join in its struggle for freedom from Spanish control. His activities brought him a second exile in Spain.

Marti was a revolutionary, but he was also Cuba's greatest poet. Between revolutionary campaigns, he found time to compose *Versos Sencillos* (*Simple Verses,* 1871), which began a new school of Spanish poetry. Marti's writing was not based on existing Spanish literary styles; instead his innovations made his work the forerunner of the *Modernismo* movement. His fight for Cuban independence was forcefully presented in a series of essays that focused on Cuba's quest for freedom. An outstanding speaker, Marti addressed his audiences in clear and brilliant prose.

Marti was closely identified with the United States. After his second Spanish exile ended, he arrived in New York City with his wife and infant daughter Maria in 1881 to serve as Consul for Uruguay, Paraguay, and Argentina. Marti earned a living by writing articles on American politics for South American newspapers and the New York *Sun.* Marti greatly admired the United States but feared its growing influence over Latin America.

It was during his years in New York that Marti organized the movement for Cuban independence. In January 1892, he formed the Cuban Revolutionary Party. He also belonged to a Cuban Junta, a council concerned with the coordination of the numerous rebel groups in the United States. Marti established a newspaper, *La Patria* (*The Fatherland*), to spread the revolutionary message. In December 1894 Marti organized an expedition in Florida for an attack on Cuba with an army disguised as agricultural workers. The plan was betrayed to Spanish authorities, who promptly protested to the United States government. Federal officials seized the vessels intended to transport the rebels to Cuba, and the planned expedition collapsed.

Leaving his family behind in New York, Marti finally reached Cuba in 1895 and joined the rebel troops. Marti was told to remain in the rear, but could not. He rode on horseback to the front lines and was killed in his first battle, at Boca de Dos Rios, on May 19, 1895. Only forty-two, Marti's martyrdom made him the symbolic leader of the Cuban independence movement.

in 1912. The Philippine islands were not given their independence until 1946. The United States justified holding on to the Philippines on the grounds that European or Japanese imperialist ambitions would swallow them up if America failed to keep the Philippines under its protective wing. Puerto Rico and Guam remain under American control to this day, military bases on those islands providing the United States with strategic oversight points in the Caribbean and Pacific.

One hero of the Spanish American War was Theodore Roosevelt (1858–1919), who used his victories to gain the vice-presidency of the United States. When President William McKinley (1843–1901) was assassinated in 1901, Roosevelt became president (1901–1909). Roosevelt was determined to win the United States a greater role on the world scene. His first foreign policy venture in the Americas concerned Panama, a province of the Republic of Colombia. Colombia had refused an offer of $10 million to let the United States cut a canal through Panama. Instead, Colombia wanted $25 million and guarantees of a smaller American presence. In order to gain that strip

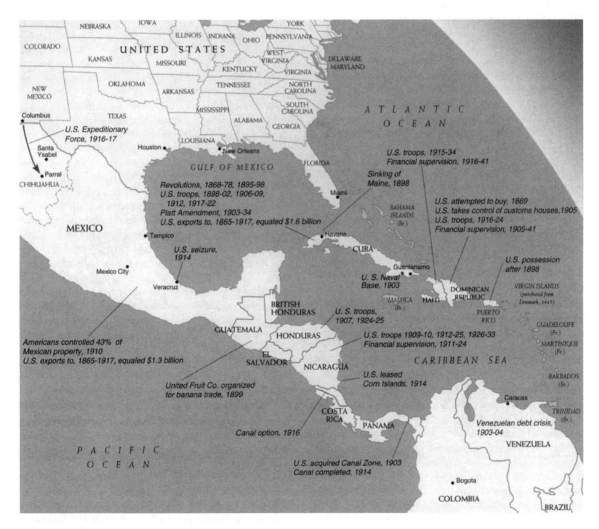

The United States in the Caribbean, 1865–1933.
From *Out of Many: A History of the American People, Second Edition,* by Faragher, Buhle, Czitrom, and Armitage. Copyright © 1997 by Prentice-Hall, Inc.

of land on the Isthmus of Panama, Roosevelt fomented a revolution among the local planter elite. Panama declared its independence from Colombia in 1903, and the United States obtained the right to build its canal. Construction began in 1904 and, in 1914, the canal finally opened. The Panama Canal and the Canal Zone remained in American hands until it proved too small for the largest ships in the US Navy. It was returned to Panamanian control at the end of 1999.

Speaking softly and carrying a big stick, Theodore Roosevelt upheld the primacy of the United States in the Western hemisphere.
Copyright © Archive Photos

As far back as 1823, President James Monroe (1758–1831) announced that the United States would protect the newly born Latin American republics from being taken back by their former European owners. This foreign policy initiative became known as the Monroe Doctrine. In 1904, President Theodore Roosevelt revised that Doctrine by adding a corollary asserting that the United States had a right to intervene in those Latin America states to deal with cases of "chronic wrongdoing." The immediate cause for the policy change initiated in the "Roosevelt Corollary" was the threat by several European nations to invade the Dominican Republic to collect debts owed to their bankers. Roosevelt's response was to send in the United States Marines to oversee customs collection in the Dominican Republic until the debts were repaid. The next year Roosevelt explained that his Corollary to the Monroe Doctrine was necessary because only the United States could be trusted to perform such duties honorably. The United States, said Roosevelt, must serve the larger cause of world peace as an "honest broker."

The greatest impact of the Age of Imperialism was felt by the colonized peoples: their societies were upended, their land taken, their economies redirected to profit European firms, their traditions disregarded, and their very languages replaced by foreign tongues. After the failure of successive native rebellions against the modern weaponry of the colonizing powers, resistance to foreign control took two main forms, the traditionalist and the modernizing. Traditionalists, usually members of the pre-colonial elite, sought to maintain the old way of life, the village, and the chieftainship. They tried to refrain from interaction with the colonial administration as much as possible. But measures such as hut taxes—cash only impositions on native villages—were specifically designed to break-up the native economy and procure a labor force for the new mines, plantations, and railroads. Modernizers, usually members of the younger generation whose eventual accession to power had been short-circuited by European intervention, sought out a Western-style education. They hoped to use the economic and political skills gained from the West to make their countries strong enough to gain independence from the West. In their efforts lay the great paradox of the imperial challenge to traditional cultures: in order to preserve their autonomy they had to sacrifice some of their individuality. They had to seek a way to reconcile modernization and their cultural uniqueness.

But Europe itself was also undergoing a political, economic, and cultural transformation. The emergence of new nations, such as Italy and Germany, within Europe itself brought new players onto the world scene creating dangerous rivalries in the "scramble" for colonies and trade. Conferences like that held in Berlin about Africa (1884–1885) seemed to channel these rivalries away from Europe itself, but under the surface, tensions between the European powers continued to mount. The spread of industrialization upset the continent's economic balance as wealth moved from the older, traditional empires to the smaller, modernizing states. By the end of the century, even tiny Belgium was eight times as wealthy per capita as was giant Russia. New ways of working, traveling, communicating, and living were transforming European society from within. Women and minorities were demanding their right to be full members of the nation. The next chapter looks at the changes within European society that accompanied the growth of their empires.

◆ Notes

1. Franz H. Michael and George E. Taylor, *The Far East in the Modern World*, (New York: Holt, Rinehart and Winston, Inc., 1964), 133.

2. Joel H. Wiener, editor, *Great Britain: Foreign Policy and the Span of Empire, 1689–1971, A Documentary History,* 8 volumes (New York: Chelsea House Publishers & McGraw Hill Book Co., 1972), 4:2898.

3. Charles I. Bevans, editor, *Treaties and Other International Agreements of the United States of America, 1776–1949,* 13 volumes (Washington, DC: Department of State, 1968–1976), 8:1971.

6

The Nineteenth-Century Mind

The nations of Europe spent much of the last half of the nineteenth century imposing their *Modern* western values on the peoples of Africa and Asia. But, back home, the Europeans were not as secure in those values as they might have seemed to the people in their colonies. Europeans were still trying to work out what liberty or equality or science meant. Their uncertainty should not surprise us. The people of the nineteenth century were the first to truly live in a world we would recognize as *Modern,* but it was not a world in which they were entirely at home. For all its technological comfort, much about it seemed inhumane, perplexing, and downright frightening. The nineteenth century was a battleground of ideologies and counter-ideologies: scientific rationalism v. theological tradition, the near-worship of industrial innovation v. the deification of the hand-made, imperialism v. the striving for national independence, claims of equal rights for all against racism, sexism, and religious bigotry. No one living through the century was certain which would emerge triumphant. This chapter looks at some of those conflicting ideologies.

The Struggle to Define and Achieve Equality

◆ Utilitarianism

The economic and political liberals of the Enlightenment believed that society could reach its greatest potential only when it did away with traditional restrictions on individual opportunity imposed by church and state. But as practiced during the early stages of the Industrial Revolution, *laissez-faire* capitalism merely replaced the traditional inequality of legal status with a new inequality based on socio-economic class. This created an ideological and political struggle between economic liberals who argued for *laissez-faire,* and social democrats who sought to revise those policies and open the political process in order to create greater social equality. One result of the conflict was the emergence of utopian, scientific (Marxist), and democratic socialism. Another outcome was the development of the "New Liberalism," theories that sought to balance liberalism's original emphasis on individual freedom with a greater emphasis on political and social equality.

Foremost among these early revisionist liberals was Jeremy Bentham (1748–1832). Admitted to Oxford when he was only twelve and trained as a lawyer, Bentham spent his adult life trying to dismantle the traditions that had nurtured him. In the process, Bentham gradually developed a system he called Utilitarianism. According to Bentham, existing British institutions reflected the established power and values of the upper classes and were of little use to the majority of the population. He took it as given that men and women always acted in their self-interest, which he defined as trying to maximize their pleasure and avoid pain. According to Bentham, the "Principle of Utility" argued that a properly functioning society ought to aim at achieving the greatest amount of happiness for the greatest number of its people. Since the British system ignored the suffering of the many in order to preserve the happiness of the few, it failed the test of *utility* (usefulness) and so should be changed. Bentham's plans for remodeling British society went far beyond altering its government. He designed model schools and prisons, drew up plans for rationalizing the judicial system, and even created a job-training scheme.

By the end of the Napoleonic Wars, the increasing speed of industrialization was putting great pressure on traditional British society. Even conservative landowners began to see socio-political reform in a more positive light, if only as a way of heading off revolution. The 1825 repeal of Combinations Act (prohibiting collective bargaining), the 1828 repeal of the Test Act (keeping Catholics and Protestant dissenters from public office), and the passage of the Reform Act of 1832 (expanding suffrage to include factory owners) were in keeping with Bentham's view that laws must work for the happiness of the many rather than for that of the few.

Following in Bentham's steps, the writer John Stuart Mill (1806–1873) continued to expand the meaning of liberalism. Mill was a child prodigy who mastered Classical Greek at the age of three and wrote his first book when only twelve years of age. His *Principles of Political Economy* (1848) upheld the value of a marketplace free from government interference. But Mill also deplored the factory abuses that flourished under strict *laissez-faire*, and his work favored government action to ease human suffering. Increasingly influenced by his wife and writing partner Harriet Taylor (1807–1858), Mill suggested that government programs include public education, trade union protection, and additional factory safety laws. He pushed, as well, for votes for women, and a freer press to present minority opinions.

Mill's most famous volume, *On Liberty* (1859), is primarily remembered as the greatest liberal statement of individualism and a person's right to be free of government control. Its origin lay in Mill's conviction that "the only purpose for which power" could "be rightfully exercised over any member of a civilized community, against his will" was "to prevent harm to others." Mill believed that "the worth of the state" was no more than "the worth of the individuals" who comprised it, but those individuals could not reach their full potential without the liberty to choose. Those who let society choose for them, Mill believed, needed no other faculty than "the ape-like one of imitation."[1] The best argument for individual freedom, therefore, according to Mill, was its social *utility*. The question was whether nineteenth-century society would see and act on that utility.

◆ The Campaign Against Slavery

Enlightenment doctrine believed in the value of every individual, and some nineteenth-century reformers followed this view to its natural conclusion. Believing slavery to be the greatest evil of the era, they devoted themselves to its abolition. Opposition to slavery also arose among Utilitarians, but many abolitionists, such as William Wilberforce (1759–1833), drew their inspiration from personal religious conviction. Wilberforce, who had undergone a personal conversion to evangelical Christianity, was an energetic politician who might have risen to prime minister had he not devoted his energies to ending the slave trade. He was a pioneer in the crusade against it, introducing abolition bills in 1789, 1791, and 1795. By 1804 his measure won the support of the House of Commons, only to be ignored by the House of Lords. Not until 1807 did Parliament agree to end the slave trade, and its decision went into effect a year later. The United States Congress, conforming to Constitutional limits, enacted an American ban on the slave trade to take effect after January 1, 1809. Revolutionaries in Venezuela and Mexico outlawed it in 1810.

British Foreign Secretary Castlereagh was able to convince the Congress of Vienna to condemn it in 1815. Action by France (1815), Spain (1820), and Portugal (1820) followed, but British efforts to create an international maritime force to capture slaving ships failed during the 1820s.

Many states were outlawing the slave trade, but only the Republic of Haiti had abolished slavery itself. Wilberforce concentrated on removing it from the British Empire. He died knowing he had succeeded, although the Slavery Abolition Act was not signed into law until one month after his death in 1833. Progress in the United States was slower. Only in 1865, after the Civil War, was slavery abolished there, and it was not entirely banished from the New World until Brazil finally outlawed slavery in 1888.

◆ ## The Expansion of the Electorate

In Great Britain, the right to vote was limited to male property owners. This meant that not even a factory owner could vote, because "property" was defined as "land." These limitations dated from a time when the economy was overwhelmingly agricultural. But the industrial revolution was quickly making the factory worker the largest class in Britain. Workers wanted laws protecting their rights, but they could not have them unless they had the vote. Factory owners wanted laws protecting them from unions, but they could not have them unless they had the vote. Landowners did not want to lose their power, but wanted to avoid the kind of revolutionary violence they had seen in France. Shifting alliances between various factions resulted in a gradual widening of the right to vote. The 1832 Reform Act gave the vote to manufacturers; additional laws in 1867 and 1884 extended the vote to factory and farm workers, though none of these laws included women. Equally important was the Ballot Act of 1872, which, by introducing the secret ballot, set the stage for meaningful participatory democracy. Workers and tenants would not have to declare their votes with their employers and landlords looking on. Laws passed in 1828 and 1829 allowed Protestant Dissenters and Catholics to become Members of Parliament; a law adopted in 1847 allowed Jews to do so as well.

In the United States, the last property requirements were abolished in the 1830s, making all white male citizens eligible voters. But the abolition of slavery in 1865 opened up a new quandary: were the ex-slaves citizens, and did recognition as citizens mean that males among them could vote? Frederick Douglass had no doubts that black men should be given the vote. Not to give black men the vote, he said, would label them as inferior, but with the franchise they would be able to stand on their own as free citizens. The Fifteenth Amendment (1870) to the Constitution achieved a universal male franchise, though it required the presence of federal troops to enforce the franchise in some states.

The First French Republic had proclaimed universal manhood suffrage in 1793 but that law did not outlast France's revolutionary convulsions. Eventually it was restored by the Second French Republic in 1848. The constitution that created Germany in 1871 included universal manhood suffrage. One *man* one vote would be achieved in Russia in 1905, Austria in 1907, and Italy in 1911. Broad male citizen participation in government was becoming a key feature of *modern* society.

With electoral participation came governmental reform. Except for Russia, the Ottoman Empire, and Montenegro, written constitutions were in place everywhere by 1871. But not every written constitution was a liberal one. Many of the new constitutions gave sweeping powers to monarchs and nobles: political parties, expanded suffrage, religious toleration, and *laissez-faire* economics were tolerated, but an independent judiciary was more the exception than the rule. In

Eastern Europe, especially, individual freedoms were less firmly established and less likely to survive in times of crisis.

◆ Expansion of Education

Ever since the work of John Locke, human beings were seen as primarily the product of their experiences. So it was not surprising that access to education became a key concern of eighteenth and nineteenth-century society. The demand that education become more widely available had other sources as well. Industrialists needed literate workers to operate ever more complicated machinery. With Factory Laws excluding more and more children from the workplace, those children could now go to school. The question of *public* education, however, opened up new debates over how secular or religious a *public* education should be, how open to religious and ethnic minorities, whether the sexes should be educated together or separately, what education was or was not appropriate for each sex or class, and who should pay for it.

In the United States, education was a matter reserved to individual state control under the constitutional division of powers. Massachusetts was one of the pioneers in the field of public education. Its 1827 High School Law required towns with at least 50 families to provide at least one teacher "to instruct children in orthography, reading, writing, English grammar geography, arithmetic, and good behavior" for six months out of every year. Towns in Massachusetts with at least five hundred families also had to provide instruction in "the history of the United States, bookkeeping by single entry, geometry, surveying, and algebra" for ten months each year, with at least one teacher in the school who could instruct the students in Latin and Greek.[2]

In Germany education was also a matter for the individual states that had combined to form Germany in 1871, but they generally followed a pattern similar to Prussia's. There, according to the 1894 regulations, girls attended secondary school for fewer hours per week than boys and were required to take "Household Arts" and "Needlework" instead of college preparatory classes. Britain passed an Education Act in 1870 that mandated the formation of parish-run elementary schools to supplement the private schools then in existence, but the parish schools were not free, except for a limited number of hardship cases. Parliamentary funds to support the schools were first mandated in the Education Act of 1891. The children attending these schools were often those who had been closed out of the workplace in the Factory Act of 1833 and the Mines Act of 1842. While France required the building of at least one elementary school per district in 1833, it did not make primary education compulsory for boys or girls until 1882. The primary schools set up in Russia by Alexander II's Education Statute of 1864 were government funded but not mandatory. Peasants could refuse to send their children to school if they were needed in the fields. Girls were kept home even more frequently, because most peasants believed female education was unnecessary.

Western Europe and the United States became literate societies, even though higher education was a privilege offered to very few. Perhaps as few as eight of every 10,000 students ever went to college. This was not always a matter of choice. In Britain, an 1827 law excluded Roman Catholics, Protestant Dissenters, and Jews from admission to Oxford and Cambridge, then the only universities in England. It was not repealed until 1856. The University of London was created in 1836 in part to offer degrees without without religious restrictions; in 1878 the University of London took a further step on the road to innovation and admitted women for degrees. Oxford and Cambridge admitted female students, but did not begin awarding them degrees until after World War One.

Even where there were no religious or gender restrictions, many just could not afford a university education. Most of the jobs available in the nineteenth century did not require one, but employers were finding they increasing needed technically trained workers. George Birkbeck

(1776–1841) founded a Mechanics Institute in Scotland in 1823 to bring technological training to working class men; similar institutions were soon created in England to train the mechanics and engineers needed for the new industries. George Stephenson (the inventory of the first practical locomotive) was one of those who paid their annual fee of one guinea to learn their skills at these trade schools.

◆ Nineteenth-Century Feminism

If workers' benefits had been the result of workers' political power, then women's rights had to be sought through their political power. But at the start of the nineteenth century, women had no political power. Under the Common Law of Great Britain, women lost their name, their property, and their legal existence once they married: husbands and wives were considered one legal person represented by the husband. English Common Law also formed the basis for the law codes of Canada, Australia, and the United States.

Since the revolutions of the late eighteenth century, however, a few bold women and men had been trying to change that view. In the United States, Abigail Adams (1744–1818), in a letter she wrote to her husband John in March 1776, urged him to "remember the ladies" when the time came to draft new laws, warning him of the consequences if the new government did not do so. "If particular care and attention is not paid to the ladies," she wrote, "we are determined to foment a rebellion, and will not hold ourselves bound by any laws in which we have no representation."[3]

In revolutionary France, the Marquis de Condorcet (1743–1794), in a *Plea for the Citizenship of Women* (1790), claimed that "Either no individual of the human race has genuine rights, or else all have the same; and he who votes against the rights of another, whatever the religion, the color or the sex of that other, has henceforth abjured his own."[4] The feminist playwright Olympe de Gouges (1748–1793) issued the *Declaration of the Rights of Woman and Citizen* (1791) demanding full political equality for women and exhorting women to liberate themselves from the tyranny of men. Later she campaigned for a national assembly of women to secure women's rights to inheritance and property as well as the right, regardless of marital status, to legitimate their children. Like many other visionaries of the early days of the French Revolution of 1789, both Condorcet and de Gouges later fell victim to the Reign of Terror.

Responding to events in France, Mary Wollstonecraft (1759–1797) wrote *A Vindication of the Rights of Women* (1792), the first major feminist tract in English and one that would have an enormous influence on American women. She encouraged women to look beyond the home and to pursue the education that men denied them, arguing that "truth must be common to all, or it will be inefficacious with respect to its influence on general practice." Believing that God had endowed both men and women with natural rights, she concluded that just as God had not intended that tyrants enslave men, so it was not God's intention for men to enslave women. "I do not wish [women] to have power over men," she said, "but over themselves."[5] But despite the appearance of a new literature aimed at securing women's social, economic, and political rights, the first decades of the nineteenth century brought no great alteration in their situation. Among middle class women, a "cult of domesticity" arose to justify the traditional role of women as wives and mothers. And even those women who exchanged work at home or on the farm for work in the factories found that their political status remained unchanged.

The formation of an organized women's rights movement in the United States was tied to the abolitionist movement. In 1840, at the World Anti-Slavery Convention in London, male delegates voted to exclude women from participation and segregated them in a gallery, separating them from the men by a low curtain. Among those so humiliated were the Americans, Elizabeth Cady

Stanton (1815–1902) and Lucretia Mott (1793–1880). They resolved to return home and form a society to advance their own rights. Eight years later the event that marks the birth of modern feminism in the United States took place in the Wesleyan Chapel in Seneca Falls, New York. On two hot July days in 1848, over three hundred delegates considered, and a majority approved, a *Declaration of Sentiments*, drafted by Stanton. Patterned after the American *Declaration of Independence*, this new declaration was written in the conviction that "all men *and women* are created equal." A split along sex lines marked the vote. Most of the men who attended the Seneca Falls Convention were not willing to sign its *Declaration*. Frederick Douglass was one of the few who did. As a declaration, it was not very different from the manifesto penned by de Gouges, but the organizers of the Seneca Falls Convention were already seasoned veterans of the age's reform movements and had a more activist agenda in mind.

Lucretia Mott was a Quaker minister and former teacher who founded the Philadelphia Female Anti-Slavery Society in 1833, harbored fugitive slaves, and ran the Philadelphia Association for the Relief and Employment of Poor Women. Elizabeth Cady Stanton studied law with her father. Although forbidden by law to practice, she became involved in the women's suffrage movement through her campaigns for women's property and custody rights in divorce cases.

In 1851 Stanton met Susan Brownell Anthony (1820–1906), a Quaker teacher whose father's abolitionist sentiments led her to work with fugitive slave Harriet Tubman (1821–1913) on the Underground Railroad. Quaker beliefs in the equality of all human beings before God led many of their faith into the age's reform movements, and their insistence on educating children of both sexes produced many prominent female reformers. The women's movement founded by Stanton, Mott, and Anthony did not limit itself to campaigning for female suffrage. Anthony worked strenuously for equal pay and representation for female teachers in the New York State Teachers' Association and campaigned successfully for the passage of the New York State Married Women's Property Act (1860). This law allowed married women to own property, including any salary they made while working, instead of its falling under their husband's control.

Working for women's rights did not mean abandoning the cause of abolition. Mott organized aid for slaves fleeing north or freed by the

Susan B. Anthony was one of the pioneers of the Women's Rights Movement in the United States.
Copyright © CORBIS/Bettmann

144

advance of Union armies. Stanton worked for the Women's Loyal League. Anthony continued to work for the American Anti-Slavery Society. Tubman became a nurse, scout, and spy for the Union Army.

But the abolition and women's rights movements parted company after the Civil War. Stanton and Anthony had pushed for a Fifteenth Amendment that guaranteed the right to vote to women as well as all men, but most abolitionists felt the cause of male black suffrage to be more important. That split led to the formation, by Anthony and Stanton, of the National Women Suffrage Association (NWSA) in 1869 and the International Council of Women in 1889. Harriet Tubman became one of the NWSA's most prominent speakers. But African-American civil rights leaders such as Harriet Tubman and Ida B. Wells-Barnett (1862–1931) who campaigned for both African-American and women's rights often found themselves caught between the aims of the separate movements. Wells-Barnett was asked by Anthony not to attend women's rights meetings in Southern States, for example, to avoid alienating white patronage. For the NWSA nothing was more important than gaining the vote.

Susan B. Anthony was arrested and put on trial for voting in the 1872 presidential elections. Although the Nineteenth Amendment, granting women the right to vote everywhere in the United States, was not ratified until 1920, Stanton and Mott did live to see victories for women suffrage in several western states and territories: Wyoming (1869), Utah (1870), Colorado (1893), and Idaho (1896). Washington joined them in 1910, California in 1911, Arizona and Oregon in 1912, and Montana and Nevada in 1914. Also, by the time of Stanton's death, women were admitted to over half the nation's colleges and universities.

In Europe, the effort to actively organize women was delayed because of greater governmental restrictions on public association and public speech. But there, too, the organizing impetus came from women who were already participants in other reform efforts, most often movements tied to nationalism or social-democratic aims. Jeanne Deroin (c. 1805–1894) was a self-educated schoolteacher and journalist who had been active in the French Revolution of 1848. In 1849, she petitioned the Democratic Socialist Party to become a candidate for the Legislative Assembly but was rejected because of her sex. When she tried to organize joint associations of female and male workers (such associations were illegal) she was imprisoned for six months in St. Lazare, the prostitute's prison. Fleeing to Great Britain in 1852, she remained active in women's issues, publishing a *Women's Almanac* and editing two journals. Not until 1866 was a women's rights organization formed in France.

Luise Otto-Peters (1819–1895), a writer of novels about working class problems under the male pseudonym Otto Stern, joined the liberal revolution of 1848 to campaign for the rights of German women only to see those rights ignored in the state created by Bismarck in 1871. She was the first President of the General German Women's Association that petitioned in 1876 and 1888 for the reform of Germany's discriminatory marriage laws that protected the rights of the husband over those of the wife in cases of divorce and child custody disputes.

Despite these pioneering efforts, the path to political rights for women proved slow and painful throughout the Western world. The women of Europe did not gain the franchise until the twentieth century. But across the Pacific Ocean, New South Wales in Australia granted women the vote in 1867, and New Zealand did so in 1886. Liberal Britain lagged far behind its Dominions. In 1867 during the debates on the Second Reform Bill extending suffrage to urban workers, John Stuart Mill proposed amending the bill's language by substituting the word *person* for *man*. Although the bill passed, Mill's amendment did not. In 1869 Mill published *The Subjection of Women*, in which he denounced the cruelties by which men distorted women's character. With characteristic irony, Mill wondered why women might sit on the throne of England but not vote.

IDA BELL WELLS-BARNETT (1862–1931)

Journalist and Civil Rights activist.
Copyright © Schomburg Center for Research in Black History

I da B. Wells was born into slavery in Holly Springs, Missouri, in 1862, and was educated at one of the freedmen's schools set up during Reconstruction. Her parents died during the Yellow Fever epidemic of 1878, leaving the sixteen year old Ida to support her younger brothers and sisters as a teacher in Memphis. But when Federal troops were withdrawn from the south after 1877, Reconstruction ended and the southern backlash against African-American education cost Wells her teaching job. In 1891, she turned to journalism to fight racism, founding her own newspaper, the *Memphis Free Speech.*

In 1892, the Memphis grocery store owned by Will Stuart, Calvin McDowell, and Thomas Moss was attacked at the prompting of a competing white grocer. Stuart, McDowell, and Moss were arrested and executed without trial. Ida Wells used her newspaper to publicize the case and urge her fellow African-Americans to leave Memphis for better lives in the Midwest. Thousands responded and soon Memphis, a town almost half-black, found itself hurting financially. Wells stepped up the pressure by coordinating a successful black boycott of the city's new trolley system. Warned out of town for being "uppity," she moved north to escape the limitations of the Jim Crow system and worked on newspapers in New York and Chicago. She led protests when blacks were excluded from exhibiting in the World Columbian Exposition in Chicago in 1893.

In the United States, there had been 197 lynchings in 1894 alone, and Well's first book, *A Red Record* (1895), made lynching an international issue. Recognizing England's importance as a purchaser of southern cotton, Wells traveled to Europe to raise awareness of the lynching problem. Thanks in large part to her campaigns, there were no lynchings in Memphis for two decades after her book appeared.

Ida Wells-Barnett was one of the founders of the National Association for the Advancement of Colored People (1909) and Chair of the Chicago Equal Rights League (1915). Married to the lawyer Ferdinand Barnett (on June 27, 1895), she continued to work for the rights of African-Americans and of women of all races, organizing the Alpha Suffrage Club of Chicago to mobilize African-American women for the fight for the vote. Her last major crusade took place in 1919, when a group of black farmers in Arkansas tried to start a union to get higher prices for their crops. When whites attacked an organizing meeting, men on both sides of the struggle were killed, but it was the black farmers who were arrested for "starting" the "Arkansas Race Riot." After twelve black farmers were sentenced to death, Wells ran a successful campaign against the injustice, and the farmers were released.

Ida Wells Barnett died in Chicago on March 25, 1931, eleven years after the Nineteenth Amendment gave women the right to vote but 34 years before the Voting Rights Act of 1965 put an end to the Jim Crow system she battled her entire life. Her posthumously published autobiography is entitled *Crusade for Justice.*

During the later years of the century, the National Union of Women's Suffrage Societies (NUWSS) was led by Millicent Fawcett (1847–1929), a self-taught economist who wrote *Political Economy for Beginners* (1870). The NUWSS tried to exert political pressure through marches and peaceful protests. But it was the more militant Emmeline Pankhurst (1858–1928) and her daughters Christabel, Adela, and Sylvia who seized the public consciousness. In 1903 the Pankhursts organized the Women's Social and Political Union (WSPU). When their lobbying efforts were ignored, the WSPU turned militant. Mobilizing women of all social classes, WSPU members broke windows, threw themselves under racehorses, chained themselves to the gates of Parliament, and pelted its members with tomatoes. Hundreds of suffragettes were imprisoned and force-fed when they fasted in protest. Challenged to justify her tactics by other feminist groups as well as by male opponents, Emmeline Pankhurst reminded one and all that the male franchise had only been extended after male workers turned to violent protest; reason alone had not worked. Despite all these efforts, the British franchise remained exclusively male until after World War I. As a reward for their contributions to the war effort, suffrage was extended to women, but only to those who were property owners and at least thirty years old. Not until 1928, shortly before Emmeline Pankhurst's death, was a full female franchise enacted.

While unable to win their ultimate goal of the franchise in Europe in the closing years of the nineteenth century, the women's movement was able to make strides in the welfare of women in the traditional societies of Asia as a by-product of imperialism. The Japanese, in their race to catch-up with the west and avoid the humiliations imposed on China, quickly opened up schools for women. Elementary education for both sexes was compulsory by 1872, and an 1899 law mandated the creation of at least one secondary school for women in each prefecture (county). Ninety percent of Japanese women had at least an elementary school education by 1904.

In China, by contrast, less than 10 percent of Chinese women were literate by 1904. Throughout the nineteenth century the only schools available to Chinese girls were those run by western missionaries, although some girls from the wealthiest families might be privately educated at home. In the wake of the failed Boxer rebellion, the desire to ensure a Chinese (rather than a western) education for Chinese women prompted reformers to push for an amendment of a 1901 education law that excluded women. Further reforms in 1906 approved elementary and teacher education for women, in principle, but the Dowager Empress did little to implement them. Not willing to wait for the government to move, many Chinese women traveled to Japan for an education just as their brothers had done before them in order to gain access to western skills frowned upon by the Chinese establishment. Since Japanese schooling for women concentrated on the formation of "good wives and mothers," Chinese families saw it as compatible with their society. They did not realize that an increasingly westernized Japan would expose young Chinese women to alien values. One of the leading exponents of using 'safe' Japanese schools to educate good Chinese wives and mothers was Shimoda Utako (1854–1936), author of several books on household management for women and creator of a publishing house designed to spread her ideas throughout China.

By 1907 there were 100 Chinese women studying in Japan, most at the Practical Women's School founded in Tokyo in 1899 by Shimoda specifically for Chinese students. While the school curriculum focused on basic literacy skills, teacher training, handiwork, and the Confucian view of the importance of "women's work," students were picking up western ideas about the role of women and citizens on the Japanese streets. One of the Chinese women to attend school in Tokyo with Shimoda's aid was Qiu Jin (1875–1907) whose women's rights articles and participation in a failed 1907 attempt to replace China's emperors with a republic cost her life. Other graduates of the Practical Women's School would join the 1911 revolutionary movement that finally did create a Chinese republic.

EMMELINE PANKHURST (1858–1928)

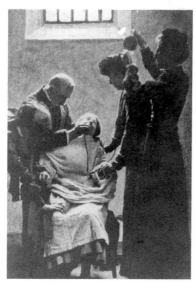

Emmeline Pankhurst was among those Women's Rights advocates who were forcefed if they used hunger strikes to protest their arrest.
Copyright © Bildarchiv Preussischer Kulturbesitz

Emmeline Goulden was born on July 4, 1858. Her father, Robert Goulden, owned a calico factory and her mother, Sophia, was active in the age's abolition, labor reform, and women's rights movements. Emmeline was only fourteen when she attended her first women's suffrage meeting, but she suffered because educational opportunities for young women were very limited. Although Emmeline's brothers went to university, she had to settle for a finishing school in Paris, where young ladies learned about art, music, literature, and the social graces.

In 1879 she wed Richard Pankhurst, a barrister several years her senior, who had himself been active in the women's suffrage movement in Manchester. Despite the death of their eldest son, the Pankhursts' marriage was a happy one, and they had four other children before the death of Richard Pankhurst in 1898. The Pankhursts ardently supported the Married Women's Property Bill (1882): he drafting it for Parliament and she campaigning for it. Frustrated by the lack of Liberal or Labour Party support for women suffrage, and tired of the lack of success of the polite tactics of advocates for female suffrage, Emmeline Pankhurst founded the Women's Social and Political Union in 1903 to wage an independent campaign for women's rights both in Great Britain and the United States.

Unable to get results by genteel persuasion, Mrs. Pankhurst's followers resorted to more strident methods: they were ejected from Liberal and Labor Party meetings, broke windows, and chained themselves to the railings outside Parliament. Every arrest of a "Suffragette" brought more publicity, more members, and more funds. Mrs. Pankhurst was arrested a number of times, most notably in 1912, after the Liberal government reneged on its promise to consider a Suffrage bill. Thrown into Holloway Prison, Mrs. Pankhurst began a hunger strike that brought her release when it jeopardized her health. But the government then passed a special act requiring all hunger strikers to be returned to prison whenever their health recovered. Force-feeding was also employed to break down Suffragette resistance, but to no avail. Mrs. Pankhurst was in and out of prison until the outbreak of World War One: released from her cell as hunger strikes injured her health and returned to prison whenever her health improved. Her daughters Christabel (1880–1958), Sylvia (1882–1960), and Adela (1885–1961) joined their mother on the barricades and in prison.

The need to mobilize all the nation's resources during the Great War brought a truce between the government and the Suffragettes. Mrs. Pankhurst devoted her energies to the war effort, and, in 1918, in gratitude for the efforts of women throughout Great Britain, a partial suffrage law was passed by Parliament. Emmeline Pankhurst then began to campaign for child welfare in Britain and Canada. She died in London on June 14, 1928, just after the Second Representation of the People Act finally awarded full and equal suffrage to British men and women.

Science, Progress and the Soul

◆ Romanticism and Nationalism

The heritage of the Enlightenment, its faith in science, logic, and progress, was at the heart of nineteenth-century liberalism. But many artists and writers found eighteenth-century rationalism emotionally unfulfilling, and their reaction against it sparked the counter trend called the Romantic Movement. Romantic writers might be found at any point on the political spectrum, but they were united in their revolt against a culture that placed its faith solely in reason, and offered instead a pre-Enlightenment belief in personal salvation through religious faith. In France, René de Chateaubriand (1768–1848) summed up these sentiments in *The Genius of Christianity* (1802), arguing that only through traditional faith could humanity make advances in art, morals, and true liberty. The youngest child of an impoverished noble family who had fled the political chaos of the French Revolution for the natural life of the Indians and fur traders along the American-Canadian border, Chateaubriand inspired a wider cultural movement that preferred nature to science, poetry to logic, and belief to mathematics. Like many Romantics, he looked back to the time when a single Christian religion had united all of Europe, before science and skepticism destroyed what he believed was the beauty of the Middle Ages.

Romanticism proved especially enduring in the Germanic states. The poet and author Wolfgang von Goethe (1749–1832) was a product of middle class society who saw its cautious calculation as fatal to the development of individual personality. Goethe's *Faust* (1806) recounted the story of a hero who was willing to accept damnation in his relentless search for knowledge, experience, and fulfillment. In the end, only chaste love (a metaphor for the love of Christ) could save him.

The natural world played a persistent but ambivalent role in the Romantic Movement; it could serve as a healing alternative to modern materialism, stand in for the struggle of the individual genius to achieve fulfillment, or warn humanity of the perils of scientific pride. William Wordsworth (1770–1850) penned lyric depictions of the English countryside celebrating "emotion recollected in tranquility." For Wordsworth, absorption in nature was a way of achieving psychological balance and, on a personal level, helped him cope with the loss of a beloved brother. Mary Wollstonecraft Shelley (1797–1851), the daughter of the English feminist, wrote *Frankenstein: or The Modern Prometheus* (1817). It depicted the tragic fall of Dr. William Frankenstein, who was so blinded by the power of science that he ripped the secret of life from the very fabric of the universe to animate an Adam stitched together from corpses. At the tale's climax, the creator and created were locked in eternal struggle in the frigid Arctic wastes.

As French armies, first under the banner of the Republic and then under the command of Napoleon, sought to spread the Enlightenment at the point of a sword, the Romantic Movement became closely associated with Nationalism. While most Enlightenment writers based their political systems on the universality of human nature, Romantics saw each nation as possessed of a unique spirit that had a right to develop in its own way. The German theologian Johann Gottfried von Herder (1744–1803), in his *Ideas Toward a Philosophy of the History of Mankind* (1784–1791), decided that the survival of different languages and customs even among peoples living side by side for centuries was proof of their value: each people had its own unique contribution to make to human civilization. The Scottish poet, historian and novelist, Sir Walter Scott (1771–1832), created a new genre, the *historical* novel, with his tales of banished knights (*Ivanhoe*) and outlaws (*Rob Roy*). Many of his novels depicted a Scotland struggling to maintain its own character after the 1707 Union with England. In Italy, Giuseppe Verdi (1813–1901), the son

Delacroix's painting of Liberty Leading the People in the French Revolution of 1830 shows the link between Romanticism and Nationalism.
Copyright © Giraudon/Art Resource

of an illiterate tavern and grocery keeper, first became a national idol for weaving the theme of national liberation into operas set during the Babylonian captivity of the Jews (*Nabucco*) and France's 100-year long struggle against English invasion (*Giovanna d'Arco*). He became so associated with the idea of Italian unification that his very name was said to spell out **Vittorio Emanuele Re D'Italia** (Victor Emanuel, King of Italy).

◆ Positivism and Materialism

If the Romantics attacked the rationalism of the Enlightenment and the mechanism of its science, other schools of thought arose to defend them. One in particular, positivism, built the Enlightenment's faith in progress into a new philosophy of science. Auguste Comte (1799–1857), a French engineer born in Montpellier who served as Saint-Simon's secretary and built on his ideas, developed and popularized this theory in two major works, *The Course of Positive Philosophy* (1830–1842) and *The System of Positive Philosophy or Treatise on Sociology* (1851–1854). Comte argued for an evolutionary view of civilization. His "law of three stages" held that society had advanced from a "theological" stage (belief in the supernatural), through a "metaphysical" stage (seeking abstract explanations of events), to the "scientific" stage (recognition that a physical explanation underlies all reality). Europe was finally ready, according to Comte, to enter that final stage, to create a new "science of society" (sociology) that could be used to place human institutions on a scientific foundation. But Comte himself mixed Positivism with Romanticism, trying to build a "Religion of Humanity" out of his theories.

The enshrining of science and the reduction of all phenomena to manifestations of physical reality also set the stage for the emergence of materialism and atheism. Materialism is the belief that there is no reality beyond the physical, tangible world. Atheism denies the existence of a divine creator. The two beliefs often went hand in hand. The German philosopher, Ludwig Feuerbach (1804–1872), an early proponent of materialistic atheism, dismissed religion as superstitious mythmaking. According to his *Essence of Christianity* (1841), "God" was the product of people's imaginations, a projection of the powers they themselves desired to wield, but which only succeeded in making them feel powerless. Only by placing themselves at the center of the universe could human beings escape this self-imposed tyranny of religion. The idea that shedding the illusion of religious faith would yield freedom and a greater sense of well-being was central to the materialist outlook.

Although most people in the western world continued to practice the religions of their ancestors, traditional religions were increasingly put on the defensive in the second half of the nineteenth century. Advances in linguistics, history, and archaeology suggested that the *Pentateuch* (the first five books of the Bible) was not the work of a single Moses, but of several different authors whose texts had been spliced together. German scholars proposed that the Gospels were in large part drawn from one common source, now lost. These suggestions did not sit well with Europe's religious establishment.

The World Science Built

◆ The Triumph of Technology

Nineteenth-century society became ever more susceptible to materialism as industrialization continued to alter everyday life. At the beginning of the century sailing ships took weeks to cross the Atlantic, but steam-engine-powered ships measured the trip in days before the century's end. Transportation overland also accelerated dramatically as networks of railroads spread across Europe, North America, India, and parts of South America. By 1905 the 5,542 miles of the Trans-Siberian Railroad, running from Moscow to Vladivostok, united Russia's Asian lands with Europe. With each decade the produce of far-flung areas was made ever more available to manufacturers and consumers. Communications across nations and empires were speeded up by the development of the commercial telegraph (1844) and the laying of the Atlantic Cable (1876) that allowed it to cross an ocean, by the telephone (1876), and the wireless (1895), the precursor of radio and television. By the end of the century a single inventor, Thomas Edison (1847–1931), a self-taught former telegraph operator, held over 1,000 patents, and was responsible for such diverse changes as the lighting of cities, the phonograph (1877), and the motion picture (1896). London's steam-powered railway opened in 1863. On October 27, 1904, New York's first subway line, the IRT, opened after four years of tunneling; eventually there would be more than 700 miles of track in the world's most extensive rapid transit system. The first internal combustion engines were powering cars, boats, and cycles by century's end, and on a cold and windy December 17, 1903, Orville (1871–1948) and Wilbur Wright (1867–1912), two bicycle mechanics from Dayton, Ohio, ushered in the age of the airplane with their flights over the North Carolina coast. It was hardly surprising that most of Western society was confident technology would secure its control over the world's riches and ensure its material well-being.

Karl Benz in his automobile, 1887
"Modern World," courtesy of Foto Deutsches Museum, München.

◆   Atoms, Elements, and Germs: Science Reveals the Universe

A new scientific revolution easily kept pace with the technological advances of the age. Ever since the ancient Greeks, Europeans had assumed that all matter was made up of four "elements": earth, air, fire, and water. Not until the 1780s, when Antoine Lavoisier (1743–1794), the father of modern chemistry, began to study the nature of fire was that notion finally abandoned. A lawyer, and also France's chief tax collector, Lavoisier was an ardent scientist as well. Testing the properties of oxygen, only just isolated, Lavoisier showed that fire was not an element but a compound of more basic ingredients. His research led to the conclusion that in nature no matter was ever lost (the Law of the Conservation of Matter). Lavoisier ended his distinguished career by drawing up a list of thirty-two known elements, preparing the way for advances by his successors. In 1808, John Dalton (1766–1844), an English physician who experimented with gases, decided that each of Lavoisier's elements was composed of identical atoms and that each element could be distinguished from another by its atomic weight. His calculation of the weights of various atoms led to a theory about how elements form compounds. When, in 1869, Russian chemist Dimitri Mendeleev (1834–1907) put all known elements in order of atomic weight, he found they grouped themselves into several families sharing common properties. Since some families were missing some elements, he assumed (correctly) that these would subsequently be discovered, or even created, by humans. Mendeleev's Periodic Table of the Elements, the foundation of physical chemistry, remains one of the greatest achievements of nineteenth century science.

Shortly after mid-century the German botanist Ferdinand J. Cohn (1828–1898) discovered microscopic plants he called "bacteria," which he suggested were the causes of many diseases. Scottish surgeon Joseph Lister (1827–1912) created new antiseptic practices that helped fight infection by killing these bacteria. Hungarian Ignaz Semmelweiss (1818–1865) rapidly applied these insights and gave the world the weapons it needed to end childbirth fever, though he died, ironically of a wound infected during an operation, long before the medical profession accepted his findings. This "Germ Theory of Disease" was finally proven by Louis Pasteur (1822–1895) in France and Robert Koch (1843–1910) in Germany. A paper on "Germ Theory and its Application to Medicine and Surgery" read by Pasteur before the French Academy of Sciences on April 29, 1878, dealing with his experiments on the anthrax virus and septicemia bacterium is usually taken to mark the public debut of "germ theory."

A crude but occasionally effective inoculation against smallpox, originally developed in China, had been known in Europe for centuries. But only during Pasteur's fight against anthrax (a disease affecting sheep) in the 1870s did he begin to understand why vaccinations worked. Applying his insights to humans, Pasteur developed an effective smallpox vaccine using a mild form of the disease. Persons who received the vaccination escaped the more severe effects of the disease which killed a majority of its victims. Pasteur always emphasized the practical applications of his theoretical experiments. We see this every time we pick up a container of *pasteurized* milk, although Pasteur first developed the process to help France's beer industry. So eager was Pasteur to further knowledge of science that he used his prestige to institute evening university classes for working men.

In Germany, Robert Koch, who had been a field surgeon during the Franco-Prussian War (1870–1871), pioneered research into other "germs," eventually discovering the organisms that caused eleven different diseases, including cholera (1884) and tuberculosis (1882). He was awarded the Nobel Prize in Physiology and Medicine in 1905 for his development of the "scratch test" for exposure to tuberculosis, still in use today. He also developed many of the techniques still used to grow bacteria in a laboratory.

These medical discoveries began to have an immediate impact on the lives of people in industrial societies as governments suddenly found themselves in the business of keeping things clean. Great Britain passed laws in 1875 requiring local authorities to maintain sewers, forbade the building of any new houses without a toilet, and outlawed the selling foods colored or stained to look fresher than they were.

Some historians of science believe the greatest advances of the century were made in physics. Many of these grew out of the process of industrialization. Working to improve techniques for boring metal cannon in 1798–1799, the American Benjamin Thompson (1753–1814) demonstrated that the activity generated a limitless amount of heat. Since no material body could be produced in unlimited quantities, his experiments proved that heat was a kind of energy, not a material thing. Using these findings, Hermann von Helmholtz (1821–1894) of Germany was able to formulate the Law of the Conservation of Energy (1847). A counterpart of Lavoisier's Law of the Conservation of Matter, Helmholtz's Law held that, although energy could be converted from one form into another, there could be no addition to, nor subtraction from, the total

Using a quill pen and primitive equipment, Pasteur brought medicine into the Modern Age.
Copyright © Library of Congress

amount of energy in the universe. Because this law applies not only to heat, but also to electricity, magnetism, and light, it was one of the most important scientific generalizations of the nineteenth century. But advances in physics were not limited to theory; many of them had an immediate impact on everyday life. In Great Britain, Michael Faraday (1791–1867) helped develop the dynamo, a machine that allowed the transmission of electric current over long distances. Faraday's ingenuity made possible Edison's lighting systems, Bell's telephone, and the development of the electric motor.

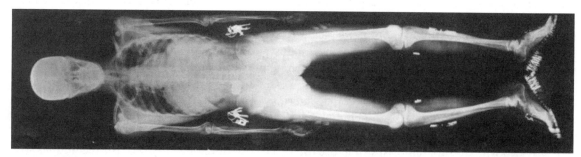

An early x-ray taken by Wilhelm Röntgen.
Copyright © Deutsches Museum

By the century's end, however, physicists were challenging the accepted nature of the universe itself. Not only were atoms not the smallest units of matter in the universe, many of them were also structurally unstable. Physicists themselves were startled in 1895 when Wilhelm Röntgen (1845–1923) of Germany reported a strange ray he detected while sending electric current through a glass tube from which most of the air had been removed. Röntgen named what he saw the "X-ray" because he was uncertain of the ray's exact nature, although he believed it was a form of electromagnetic radiation like light but of a shorter wavelength. Future experiments proved his belief correct. For his discovery, Röntgen was later awarded the very first Nobel Prize in Physics (1901). In France, Henri Becquerel (1852–1908) discovered that uranium compounds also gave off a form of radiation; the papers he published in 1896 gave modern physics a new direction. Marie Skłodowska Curie (1867–1934) coined the term "radioactivity" in 1898 for the phenomenon first observed by Becquerel. Building on Becquerel's work, she and her husband Pierre (1859–1906) demonstrated that radioactivity was an atomic property of uranium and isolated two more radioactive elements, radium and polonium. The Curies and Becquerel shared the Nobel Prize for Physics in 1903. After the discovery of the electron in 1897, Ernest Rutherford (1871–1937) suggested that each atom had a central, positively charged nucleus, which was separate from its negatively charged electrons. Radioactivity was caused by electrons escaping from unstable atoms.

X-rays, radioactivity, and the electron theory challenged one of the most dearly held beliefs of science, the idea that matter was indivisible and continuous. The work of Röntgen, Becquerel, the Curies, and Rutherford cleared the way for a new understanding of the universe. The universe was neither solid nor stable, but composed of energy only precariously bound into atoms. The single, simple "theory of everything" the Scientific Revolution thought it had found in the theories of Sir Isaac Newton receded further and further into the distance.

◆ Charles Darwin and the Revolution in Biology

The most controversial scientist of the nineteenth century, Charles Darwin (1809–1882), never intended to be a public figure. A doctor's son, Darwin was sent to Cambridge by his father to study theology after failing at medical school, but he was too fascinated by the study of plants and animals to enter the Church. Darwin became a naturalist instead. From 1831 to 1836 he served on the HMS *Beagle*, a naval survey ship engaged in a mapping expedition off the coasts of South America. When the ship stopped at the Galapagos Islands off Ecuador, Darwin discovered small birds, the descendants of flocks brought centuries before by storms. Living in isolation on various islands, they had adapted to local conditions and available food sources until they were clearly different from related species on the South American mainland. When the ship returned to Britain, Darwin published several well-received books based on his observations. Then, in 1859, he published *On the Origin of Species by Means of Natural Selection*. In it, Darwin offered a theory of evolution through time as the best means of understanding the variety displayed by all forms of life. No scientific book has ever had a greater impact on the mind of an era.

Darwin's theory of evolution was the most revolutionary, and also the most controversial, product of nineteenth century science. For religious people, the century's discoveries in chemistry and physics were seen as demonstrating the intricacy of God's design. They seemed to reaffirm religion's confidence in the beneficence of the Creator. Only the new science of Geology offered any challenge to traditional religious belief. Geology, the study of the forces governing changes in the earth, developed quickly in the late eighteenth century, encouraged by industry's need to identify underlying deposits of coal and minerals. Its pioneering genius was the Englishman Charles

MARIE CURIE (1867–1934)

Maria Skłodowska was born on November 7, 1867, in Warsaw, while Poland was part of the Russian Empire. Her father taught mathematics and physics, and her mother ran a school for girls. But the death of her mother from tuberculosis when little Manya (as she was called) was only eleven marked a severe change in the family's fortunes. Both Manya and her older sister Bronya (Bronislava) had to go to work after graduating from the Russian *lycée* (secondary school). There was no university education for girls in Poland, but both Skłodowska girls wanted to be scientists, so they worked out a plan to take turns paying for each other's way to Paris. Manya tutored Polish working women as part of a nationalist "free university" and worked as a governess to pay Bronya's way to medical school in Paris. Then, in 1891, with Bronya's help, Manya followed her sister to Paris and took university degrees at the Sorbonne in physics (1893) and mathematics (1894). In 1894 she also met Pierre Curie (1859–1906) who had risen from laboratory assistant at the Sorbonne (1878) to supervisor at the School of Physics and Industrial Chemistry in Paris (1882). In 1895, shortly after Pierre successfully defended his doctoral dissertation on magnetism (or Curie's law: the magnetic coefficients of attraction of paramagnetic bodies vary in inverse proportion to the absolute temperature), and Pierre and Marie (as she was called in France) were wed on July 25.

In 1896, while working with uranium ore, Henri Becquerel (1852–1908) discovered the phenomenon that Marie Curie would later name "radioactivity." Searching for a topic for her own doctoral dissertation, Marie looked to extend Bec-querel's discoveries to other substances. Marie and Pierre first worked with pitchblende (a major source of uranium) and together discovered two new elements in 1898: polonium (named by Marie for her homeland) and radium. Becquerel and the Curies shared the 1903 Nobel Prize for Physics for their work on radioactivity. The Prize won Marie her Doctorate, but Pierre got the job, a professorship at the Sorbonne in 1904.

The Curies had two daughters—Irène (in 1897) and Ève (in 1904)—before Pierre was killed on April 19, 1906, when he was run over by a horse-drawn cart. Marie had been working as a lecturer in physics at a Normal School for girls (a teacher's college) since 1900, but on May 13, 1906, she was appointed to fill Pierre's professorship, the first woman to be so honored. In 1911, she won a second Nobel Prize, this time in Chemistry, for her continuing work on radium. The Radium Institute at the University of Paris was opened under her direction in 1914. Throughout the First World War, assisted by her daughter Irène, Marie Curie worked on the medical uses of X-radiography. She set up x-ray units for military hospitals and herself braved the dangers of the trenches.

Working for the League of Nations after the War, Marie publicized the practical and theoretical uses of radioactive materials. Irène and her husband Frédéric Joliot continued to advance Marie's work, and their discovery of artificial radioactivity also won a Nobel Prize. On July 4, 1934, just a few months after her daughter's discovery, Marie died of leukemia probably caused by her years of exposure to radiation.

Lyell (1797–1875). Based on the book of Genesis, conservative religious teaching maintained that the Earth resulted from a special creation by God some 6,000 years ago. In his *Principles of Geology* (1830–1833), Lyell maintained the shape of the Earth as we knew it was created by natural processes operating uniformly over *millions* of years. Darwin, influenced by Lyell's work, supposed that life of Earth had also changed slowly over those millions of years, challenging the Biblical idea of one single creation.

Marie and Pierre Curie, pioneers of Radioactivity, at work in their laboratory.
Copyright © Ullstein Bilderdienst

Darwin was not the first to suggest or try to explain the variety of life. In France, the Chevalier de Lamarck (1744–1829), struggling to classify various plants and animals, noted the existence of subtle differences between closely related species. In *Philosophie Zoologique* (1809) he argued that plants and animals were occasionally forced to change, to better adapt to their environment. Giraffes, he conjectured, in order to reach leaves at the tops of trees, had, through generations of stretching, consciously lengthened their necks. Lamarck's theory, that characteristics animals acquired during their lifetimes could be passed on to their offspring, was widely criticized by scientists, and finally disproved in 1890s by the German biologist August Weismann (1834–1914) whose work in human heredity was the forerunner of modern DNA theory.

Origin of Species was taken with far greater seriousness than Lamarck's ideas because Darwin's careful observations made the theory of evolution plausible. Darwin was uncertain how the observed changes had come about, but he theorized that random variations within each species favored the survival of some individuals over others in a changing world. An ever-changing environment was not the only threat to the survival of any one species. Darwin also drew on the work of Malthus to conceive of an eternal over-population crisis in the plant and animal kingdoms causing a constant struggle for survival. Individuals possessing some characteristic, no matter how minor, that made them better able to secure food were more likely to survive to mate. Thus they were more liable to pass their characteristics on to the next generation. Over many generations, the accumulation of more and more of these small changes produced a plant or animal so different from its ancestors as to be an entirely new species. For example, if a color variation helped an animal hide from predators, it was more likely to survive and pass on the helpful color to its offspring. In this way the natural world was "selecting" those individuals or species most suited to their environments. Darwin called this principle of preservation, "Natural Selection," though it became more popularly known as "survival of the fittest."

Many in the scientific community accepted Darwin's conclusions, but much of the British public did not. When Darwin's subsequently applied his theory of evolution to human development in *The Descent of Man* (1872) there was even more vigorous dissent; he now seemed to be attacking the special place in creation that Judeo-Christian theology assigned to humanity. Darwin was aware of the weaknesses in his theory: he was unable to explain the mechanism by which variations were passed from parent to offspring and the fossil record did not reveal the intermediate forms one would expect as species evolved. The fossil of the most famous intermediate form, Archaeopteryx, an early bird retaining some dinosaur-like features, would not be discovered for another two decades. Neither Darwin's attackers or defenders were aware, as well, of the pioneer work in genetics being carried out at this same time by an Austrian monk, Gregor Johann Mendel

A contemporary caricature ridicules Darwin's theory of Natural Selection.
Copyright © Barnaby's Picture Library

(1822–1884). The laws of inheritance Mendel formulated in 1866 helped provide a scientific basis for Darwin's theory, but his work did not gain recognition until long after his death. Questions concerning Natural Selection remained unresolved well into the twentieth century, and Darwin's ideas are still rejected by some religious groups.

◆ Social Darwinism

Darwin's theories form the basis of modern biology, but his ideas had an even greater impact on political and social thought. "Social" Darwinists attempted to apply biological theories regarding the struggle for existence and survival of the fittest to contemporary human society. Social Darwinists claimed that science endorsed the victors in any struggle, whether in business, between nations, or in the competition for empire. Their belief that evolutionary theory justified the victorious was certainly a misapplication of biology, but many people were persuaded by it.

In Britain, the publication of *Social Statics* (1850) by Herbert Spencer (1820–1903) marked the beginning of sociology as a modern intellectual discipline. Spencer considered changes in society, like those being observed elsewhere in nature, to be part of a universal evolutionary process. He believed that progress was not an accident but a necessity. It was Spencer who first wrote that evolution was a mechanism placed into nature by an Unknowable Power that assured the "survival of the fittest." Like Malthus before him, Spencer also believed the Laws of Nature demonstrated the folly of welfare legislation that only encouraged the weakest elements in society to over breed. Taking Darwin's work as a confirmation of his own theories, Spencer saw the marketplace as a perfect example of the struggle for existence: economic failure was proof of biological or cultural inferiority.

Racism, which certainly long preceded Darwinism, was greatly strengthened by Social Darwinist thought. In France, Count Joseph Arthur de Gobineau (1816–1882), in *The Inequality of Human Races* (1853–1855), argued that there was a hierarchy of races, culminating in the blond, blue-eyed inhabitants of northern France, England, Belgium, and Germany. This special breed, if it avoided mixing with inferior Semitic and Negroid races, could eventually rule the world. "Gobinism" proved exceedingly popular in Germany, where it was taken up by the composer Richard Wagner (1813–1883). Wagner celebrated the Middle Ages, Christian faith, and the soul of the

German people in "musical dramas" like his four-opera Ring Cycle of Germanic mythology. The American writer Madison Grant (1865–1937), in *Passing of the Great Race* (1916), worried that Anglo-Saxons were already so infected with "Semitic skepticism" they might no longer be strong enough to save "Civilization." The notion of "Aryan" superiority was a prime factor in the mind of men such as Cecil Rhodes as they launched imperial ventures around the world. In an age when Britain, Germany, and America were the three greatest industrial powers of the world, their technological superiority was often explained as being the result of a presumed northern European racial superiority. As the nineteenth century turned into the twentieth, eugenicists in America, Germany, and Great Britain sought to "improve" the human race by framing laws to sterilize the dissolute, the "weak-minded," and those with heritable diseases.

The colossus of British Imperialism.
Copyright © Library of Congress

Living with the Modern World

◆ Realism and the Middle Classes

Realism and naturalism were the literary counterparts of the materialism that dominated the late nineteenth century. Realists scoffed at literature that showed a world peopled by demons, individuals laboring under curses, and medieval lords and maidens. Instead, realist writers found the drama in the lives of ordinary people in everyday surroundings. They were as critical of modern society as were the Romantics, but preferred to expose the harsh reality of modern life in the hope of improving it. Honoré de Balzac (1799–1850), whose 91-volume *Human Comedy* appeared between 1827 and 1847, was the founder of French Realism. A prodigious writer who put in 14–16 hours days fueled by endless pots of coffee, he spent his off hours in an equally extravagant social whirl that kept him in constant debt. The son of a peasant and a woman of middle class background, he knew France from the bottom up. His novels threw a merciless light on the greed and jealousy within middle class society.

The heyday of Realism was also the first great era of mass culture. As urban growth rates exceeded the growth rate of the population at large, the middle and working classes became prominent forces in the cultural life of their nations. Middle-class novels, often appearing in weekly installments in the popular press before being packaged as books, added a sentimental gloss to the harsh Realist vision. In Britain, Charles Dickens (1812–1870), who was forced into factory work when his father was imprisoned for debt, combined realism with Victorian sentimentality. His *Oliver Twist* (1838) told the story of a young boy born into a Workhouse who, after many misadventures among London's criminal classes, ends up in the arms of his long-lost upper-middle class family. Samuel Clemens (1835–1910), the American river boat pilot and journalist who wrote under the pen name

Mark Twain, was the most successful writer in the United States. He even set up his own publishing company to keep up with the demand for his works. Twain's novels included warts-and-all depictions of the pre-Civil War south (*Huckleberry Finn,* 1884, and *Tom Sawyer,* 1876) that remain controversial classics to this day.

The new middle classes were avid readers, but they preferred their literature discreet. Gustav Flaubert (1821–1880) turned to writing as a profession when a nervous condition (thought to be epilepsy) sidelined his legal career. His *Madame Bovary* (1857) was the story of a bored provincial middle class wife who betrayed her husband. When she, in turn, was betrayed by her lover, she committed suicide. The novel's sympathetic description of her adultery so offended public sensibilities that Flaubert was tried—although not convicted—for scandal.

At the same time, department stores began selling a seemingly endless variety of affordable machine-made goods. Advertising and mail-order marketing became facts of everyday life. And professional teams provided spectator sport for the masses. The first professional football teams were organized in Britain in 1893, and the first automobile race was held in France in 1894. Storefront theaters began to spring up to show off the brand new invention of moving pictures. Mass culture had arrived.

◆　Alternate Visions

But mass culture did not arrived unopposed. Impressionism, which developed, primarily in France, as early as the 1860s, rejected both Romantic melodrama and the high finish of classical realism. The founders of the movement were fascinated by the role of light in determining the appearance of the physical world. They hoped to capture the fleeting and ever changing impression that objects made on the eye. The development of the camera in the 1840s had seemed to threaten the future of painting as a recorder of reality. But by the changing effects of light on objects, Impressionists cast doubt on the whole notion of an "objective" visual reality. Originally shunned by the art establishment, the Impressionists were eventually adopted by an increasingly confident middle class delighted to see itself depicted in the colorful canvases of such painters as Pierre Auguste Renoir (1841–1919).

The painters known as Post-Impressionists or Expressionists rejected the sunlit depictions of middle class picnics and flower gardens that were common subjects of the Impressionists. Paul Gauguin (1848–1903) abandoned his family and a career in the stock exchange to explore the mysteries of primitive peoples by living and painting in the French colony of Tahiti. He asserted that "primitive" art still retained that sense of wonder at the world that Western Civilization had lost, and his paintings attempted to portray the mystical elements of Polynesian life. In France, Paul Cezanne (1839–1906) rebelled against the legal career his well-to-do parents had laid out for him and pursued the artistic life of bohemian Paris. Eventually rejecting the representational painting of the Impressionists, Cezanne developed a style based on geometric forms that led to Cubism in the twentieth century.

The most forceful rejection of the Modern world came from the pen of the German philosopher Friedrich Nietzsche (1844–1900) who denounced what he termed the "slave morality" of Christianity in such works as *The Birth of Tragedy* (1872), *Thus Spake Zarathustra* (1883–1884), and *Beyond Good and Evil* (1886). Nietzsche rejected the existing system of Christian ethics and called for a new, heroic world-view that would affirm life in all its irrational instincts, including violence, the desire for power, and the thirst for beauty. Emphasizing the changes that could be made through a single person's will, Nietzsche predicted the emergence of a higher type of human being whose "will to power" would transcend the flabby conventions of nineteenth century Europe and reassert

FRIEDRICH NIETZSCHE (1844–1900)

Philosopher of a New World Order.
Copyright © CORBIS/Bettmann

Friedrich Nietzsche was born in Saxony on October 15, 1844. His father, a Lutheran minister, died when he was only five, leaving young Nietzsche in a household of five women. Classically educated, he was such a brilliant student at Bonn and Leipzig (1864–1868) that he was given a doctorate without writing a dissertation or taking an examination. Nietzsche's professorship at Basel was interrupted by service as a medical orderly during the Franco-Prussian War (1870–1871), where his health was permanently damaged by the experience.

In Switzerland, Nietzsche became friendly with the composer Richard Wagner and his wife. But during the 1870s Wagner's extreme nationalism, his anti-Semitism, and his expectation of homage led to a rupture of the relationship. Nietzsche's *Birth of Tragedy from the Spirit of Music* (1872), was a celebration of Wagner that also lamented the influence of Socratic rationalism and recommended adding Dionysian enthusiasm to Western culture. After Nietzsche resigned his university position in 1879 for health reasons, he began a decade of feverish writing that produced almost a book a year even as he struggled against unending headaches and growing physical infirmity. He spent winters in Italy in a futile effort to recover his health, and ruefully remarked that "pleasure is the absence of pain."

In works such as *Thus Spake Zarathustra* (1883–1884), *Beyond Good and Evil* (1886), *Genealogy of Morals* (1887), and the *Twilight of the Idols* (1888), Nietzsche passionately criticized Western culture, Christianity, and human conformity. He believed Christianity was based on deep resentment of this world; it fostered a "slave morality" that must and would be overcome as the world came to accept that "God is dead." In the future, a finer type of man, the *Übermenschen* (supermen), would emerge free of foolish illusion and capable of moving humanity to a higher level of existence. Characterized by their courage, intellectual energy and beauty of character, these new men were destined to become the "lords of creation." Although he believed no moral viewpoint could be imposed on all individuals, Nietzsche believed in the future greatness of mankind and success for nations such as Great Britain, Russia, and the United States.

The year 1888 was Nietzsche's last lucid period. In January 1889 he collapsed in Turin, and was institutionalized for the rest of his life. His sister Elizabeth published his volumes *Antichrist* (1895), *The Will to Power* (1901), and *Ecce Homo* (1908), but she added a veneer of anti-Semitism and incoherence to her brother's writing. Nietzsche said, "some men are born posthumously." When he died on August 25, 1900, insane from the effects of tertiary syphilis, Nietzsche was a virtual unknown even within the confines of Academia. But his impact on twentieth century philosophy, literature, and psychology has been profound. Freud, who gained the idea of sublimation from reading Nietzsche, thought he had "more penetrating knowledge of himself" than had any other man.

the primacy of instinct over reason. He argued that the emergence of a race of *Übermenschen* (supermen) was inevitable and would lead humanity into a better future. In Nietzsche's view, all that sprung from power was healthy, while all that sprung from weakness was evil. Nietzsche's increasing blindness and final descent into insanity (as a result of untreated syphilis) made it easier for the age to ignore his prophetic voice. Most educated Europeans remained confident about the future, but their views would soon be challenged by the events of the twentieth century.

Perhaps the highest celebration of Europe's self-confidence was the Paris *Exposition Universale* of 1889. Millions of tourists descended on Paris to visit the 200-acre site of the largest World's Fair ever held. It celebrated the triumphs of modern technology, "the living connection between men and things." Tourists gazed in awe at the Eiffel Tower, the tallest structure in the world, and felt sure that progress would continue indefinitely and that Europeans would lead it. The Fair ushered in *La Belle Époque,* a time of peace and shared confidence in the future. It was easy for bourgeois society to believe that technology would harness nature to create ever greater wealth for modern nations. Social Darwinists reassured western Europeans that imperial possessions were rightfully theirs because they were the "fittest," the highest product of human evolution. Any problems that remained were only material, and these would be ended as the technological revolution continued.

Under the surface calm of *La Belle Époque,* however, the problems of the nineteenth century remained. European intellectual life was a battlefield of opposing opinions whose conflicts had not been resolved. Belief in science, progress, and positivism continued strong, but not everyone shared in middle class prosperity. The capitalist world economy was thriving, the bourgeoisie reveled in the sanctity of private property, and Britain was still the center of world finance. But Marxist socialists in every nation, convinced of the illegitimacy of capitalism, sought a future of collective ownership, the elimination of states, and an economy of shared wealth. Liberals preached the virtues of constitutional government, individual freedoms, and parliamentary representation, while in Eastern Europe ancient autocracy remained predominant. Half the human race was denied basic rights because it was female. Social Darwinists documented immutable differences between the human "races" and predicted a pitiless biological struggle that would end in the enslavement or extermination of some peoples. Democracy and imperialism, civil rights and racism, and capitalist economies and Marxist political parties co-existed uneasily. Despite its wealth and power, Europe was deeply uncertain of its future direction. The good life of *La Belle Époque* would soon end as the nations of Europe found themselves involved in the very kind of war they thought their civilization had rendered impossible.

◆ Notes

1. John Stuart Mill, *On Liberty and Other Essays,* edited by John Gray (Oxford: Oxford University Press, 1991), 14, 65, 125.

2. *Laws of Massachusetts,* January Session, 1827, CXLIII.

3. *The Book of Abigail and John: Selected Letters of the Adams Family, 1762–1784,* edited by L. H. Butterfield, Marc Friedlaender, and Mary-Jo Kline (Cambridge, MA: Harvard University Press, 1975), 121.

4. *Oeuvres de Condorcet,* 12 volumes, edited by A. Condorcet O'Connor and M. F. Arago (Paris: Didot Frères, 1847), 10:122.

5. Mary Wollstonecraft, *A Vindication of the Rights of Men and A Vindication of the Rights of Women,* edited by D. L. Macdonald and Kathleen Scherf (Peterboro, CAN: Broadview Press, 1997), 102 and 130.

7

The First World War, and After

5

Industrialized nations dominated global affairs at the close of the nineteenth century. Their empires stretched across Asia, Africa, and the Pacific Ocean; the wealth of the world was theirs for the taking. The last decade of the nineteenth century, a period termed *La Belle Époque* by Europeans, was a time of optimism and extravagance that mirrored their unrivaled power. Rare was the person who warned that this pride was misplaced. Yet *La Belle Époque* was followed by the most terrible century in humanity's history, a century marked by wars of unprecedented scope and ferocity.

The war we call World War I (1914–1918) was known as the Great War to those who fought and lived through it. It introduced the world to the ravages of a conflict fought with such modern weapons as machine guns, submarines, warplanes, and chemical warfare. The havoc these weapons inflicted destroyed Europe's economic and moral preeminence. The war years represent a distinct historical watershed: before 1914 we see a smug and dominant European culture; after 1918 we see a devastated Europe no longer capable of asserting leadership. Understanding the pivotal nature of the Great War is essential to understanding the twentieth century. This chapter begins by tracing the steps that led the greatest powers in the world into a war they could not survive unbattered. Then it explores their efforts to recapture their previous positions of strength and their dependencies and possessions attempt to chart independent futures.

The Legacy of German Unification

◆ The Bismarckian System

Otto von Bismarck, the "Iron Chancellor" whose wars of *Realpolitik* created a united Germany, was the leading statesman of Europe from 1870 to 1890. Once his goal of unifying Germany was achieved, Bismarck used his long tenure in power to maintain Continental peace because he believed that was the best way to assure Germany's future. So he concentrated on acting as an "honest broker" between the competing claims of Europe's most powerful empires. One area of potential conflict was the Balkan Peninsula, lying between the Mediterranean, Black, and Adriatic Seas. Nominally under Ottoman control except for the small Greek kingdom, the Balkans contained many rival ethnic groups aspiring to national independence, but unable to obtain it without external assistance. The growing inability of the Ottoman Empire to control such movements provided a tempting opportunity for Austria and Russia to increase their influence in the region. Germany had little interest in the area for its own sake, but Bismarck found Russia's Balkan policy troubling. The Russian government trumpeted their historic "mission" to aid the liberation of all their fellow Slavic peoples. Russian advocates of Pan-Slavism expected that the small Slavic states that would be created by breaking up the Ottoman Empire would look to Russia for protection, if not outright union. Moreover, the resulting cluster of dependent states would not be strong enough to block Russian access to the Mediterranean through the Black Sea (the location of

Russia's only warm water ports). Austria, on the other hand, feared that a victory for Slavic nationalism within the Ottoman Empire would set off revolutions among the ethnic minorities within the Austro-Hungarian Empire itself.

As the weakness of Ottoman rule became ever more apparent, the forces of Tsar Alexander II (r. 1855–1881) attacked, pushing towards Constantinople in April 1877. Both Austria-Hungary and Britain were angered by the aggressive nature of the Russo-Turkish War (1877–1878). Their anger increased when Russia imposed a punitive peace on the Ottoman regime in March 1878, increasing Russia's territory and carving an independent Bulgaria, Serbia, Montenegro, and Romania out of the Ottoman empire.

Bismarck offered his mediation. At the Congress of Berlin (June-July 1878), he negotiated a settlement that reduced Russia's territorial gains, but further weakened the Ottoman Empire in order to pacify the other European powers. Austria-Hungary obtained the right to "occupy and administer" the land south of its border called Bosnia, a territory inhabited by Croats and Serbs with a large minority of Muslims. Britain obtained full control of Cyprus. France, although uninvolved in the conflict, was permitted to expand its imperial position in Tunisia. No one really believed that the Balkan issue was finally settled, but Bismarck, by asking for nothing, had managed to temporarily reconcile all interests. The political balance in the Balkans remained stable for a few more decades.

After winning the Franco-Prussian War (1870–1871), Bismarck had imposed a harsh peace settlement on a defeated France. The *Treaty of Frankfurt* (1871) mandated a huge indemnity, and German occupation of parts of France continued until it was paid in full. Most bitter in French eyes was Germany's annexation of Alsace and Lorraine. In defeat, France nurtured a great desire for revenge and the reconquest of its territory. Bismarck sought to prevent this with a series of alliances aimed at keeping France isolated. In 1873, he created a Three Emperors' League (*Dreikaiserbund*) committing the conservative monarchs of Germany, Austria-Hungary, and Russia to a joint defense of their regimes against the democratic subversion that might emerge from republican France. But the Balkan confrontation proved to Bismarck that his *Dreikaiserbund* was flawed because his allies were too deeply divided over that area's future status. Bismarck needed one primary ally, and ties of language and history favored Austria for that role. On October 7, 1879, the two Germanic states signed a treaty binding them together. Renewed at five-year intervals, this Dual Alliance was a decisive element in explaining the origins of the First World War. In May 1882, Bismarck persuaded Italy to join the combination and the Triple Alliance was created. The Triple Alliance was a mutual defense pact. According to its terms, if any member of the Alliance was attacked by an outsider, the other members would come to its defense.

The Tsar had withdrawn from the Three Emperors' League in the wake of the Berlin Congress of 1878. To avoid any alliance between Russia and France, Bismarck negotiated a second *Dreikaiserbund* in 1881, pledging the three parties to friendly neutrality in the event any of the three went to war with a fourth power. Bismarck believed this pact would keep the Balkans calm by having his allies, Austria and Russia, consult him rather than permit their rivalry to escalate. In his mind, the entire peninsula was "not worth the bones" of a single German soldier. He intended to keep the Balkans peaceful, but the conflicting desires of his allies proved uncontrollable. In 1887 the Three Emperors' League failed again. Never at a loss for an alternative policy, Bismarck quickly signed a secret *Reinsurance Treaty* (1887) with Russia that bound them to neutrality in case of war. There were two exceptions. In the first, Russia was not bound to neutrality if Germany attacked France, which Bismarck had no intention of doing. According to the second exception, Germany would not be bound to neutrality if Russia attacked Austria. In that case the terms of the Triple Alliance would become binding, and Germany would come to Austria's defense. Together, the *Reinsurance Treaty* and the Triple Alliance made Germany the friend and ally of two major European powers while maintaining the isolation of France. Bismarck seemed to have succeeded.

◆   Creating the Entente

On March 9, 1888, Kaiser Wilhelm I died and was succeeded as German Emperor by his son Frederick III. But Frederick was already dying of cancer, and after only three months his son Wilhelm came to the throne. Wilhelm II (r. 1888–1918), who became Kaiser at the age of twenty-nine, was the product of a strict military education and advocated the extension of German influence throughout the world. Armed with the arrogance of youth, Wilhelm II often disregarded the advice of Bismarck, and in March 1890, the Kaiser dismissed the 75-year old "Iron Chancellor." Wilhelm II intended to set a "new course" for Germany, and his first policy decision was not to renew the *Reinsurance Treaty* with Russia. Germany's decision left the Tsar as diplomatically isolated as was republican France.

In 1892 France and Russia began a rapprochement prompted in part by Wilhelm II's policies. Sizable French development loans to infant Russian industries helped draw the two states closer together. By January 1894 the banking and trade arrangements between France and Russia had evolved into a mutual defense pact called the Dual Alliance. Europe suddenly was divided into two rival power blocs. If any member of one bloc attacked a member of the other, five countries might soon be fighting. Yet the mere existence of two camps did not mean Great Power cooperation was impossible. France and Germany did unite to force Japan to give up her gains against China in 1895, and joint Russo-German action was undertaken against Chinese ports in 1897. All three states participated in crushing the Boxer Rebellion and joined in the general criticism of Great Britain's war against South Africa's Boers. Still, as the twentieth century began, the rival alliances seemed ever more suspicious of each other's intentions.

Great Britain remained the only major European power uncommitted to an alliance when the new century began. Industrial power, a vast empire, and a magnificent fleet had once permitted it to stand aloof from its neighbors' affairs. But Britain's productive and financial primacy had passed. Non-involvement was a luxury it could no longer afford. Many British leaders believed that Germany was Great Britain's natural ally. Wilhelm II was half English (his mother was a daughter of Queen Victoria), and the two countries were major trading partners. But Germany was also Britain's leading trade rival, as well as a growing imperial competitor. In 1896 the Kaiser alienated Britain by congratulating the Boers on crushing the Jameson raiders, and in 1898 he declared himself ready to protect the culture and autonomy of the world's Muslims, most of whom lived under the British flag. But the most troubling German action was its construction of an ocean-going fleet to protect its growing colonial empire. Signing the Naval Bills of 1898 and 1900, Wilhelm II approved the building of a High Seas Fleet, later boasting that, by so doing, Germany had "conquered" for itself "a place in the sun."[1] So challenged, Britain announced it would maintain a fleet superior to those of the next two greatest naval powers combined. The naval arms race had begun. In October 1905, Britain laid the keel of a new class of ship, the Dreadnought—the first "all big-gun" battleship. Dreadnoughts had ten of these 12-inch guns, eleven inches of armor-plating, and turbine engines able to propel the ship at 21 knots, faster than any previous battleship. Dreadnoughts made all other warships obsolete, but any nation willing to pay the price of their construction could now rival the British. Wilhelm II made clear his intention to compete. By the summer of 1914, Germany had thirteen Dreadnoughts to Britain's twenty, and an even more powerful ship, the "Super-Dreadnought" was joining the lines. Super-Dreadnoughts had 15-inch guns, and reached speeds of 25 knots.

Great Britain's declining world position, combined with its apprehension of Germany's aggressive behavior, worked together to end Britain's traditional isolation. In January 1902, Britain signed a naval pact with Japan intended to halt Russian advances in the Far East. Even more significantly, Britain proved willing to listen to French suggestions for mutual accommodation. For hundreds of years the French-English rivalry had shaped global affairs, but in April 1904 the historic enemies signed an *Entente Cordiale* (Friendly Agreement) settling their imperial differences in West Africa, Madagascar, and Newfoundland. The agreement permitted France a "free hand" in Moroccan affairs while conceding Britain's primacy in Egypt. Egypt had been a sore point between the two states since Britain's purchase of the majority interest in the Suez Canal. The *Entente Cordiale* was not aimed against Germany and did not provide for joint military cooperation, but it brought the British into the stream of Continental diplomacy. French mediation soon enabled Great Britain to settle its outstanding differences with Russia over their respective spheres of influence in Afghanistan and Persia. British and French loans to Russia allowed it to recover from the disaster of losing the Russo-Japanese war (1904–1905). The next move in turning Britain, France, into a block to rival the Triple Alliance of Austria, Germany, and Italy would be Germany's.

◆   A Decade of Crisis

Between 1904 and 1914, a series of crises made the Great Powers increasingly willing to consider war as a way of settling their differences. Germany initiated the process by trying to test the solidity of the understanding between Britain and France. In March 1905 the Kaiser visited Tangier to personally endorse the cause of Moroccan independence and deny the primacy of French interests there. At a conference convened in Algeçiras, Spain (1906), to settle the problem, Britain supported France against Austria-Hungary and Germany. After a worried Russia concluded its own Entente with Britain in 1907, Wilhelm II was convinced that Germany was surrounded by enemies and vowed to attend no further conferences. Britain, France, and Russia were now linked together by the series of understandings usually called the Triple Entente, but there was as yet no mutual defense pact among the three powers. In fact, in 1907, Britain had no intention of signing one, but Germany's actions would bring the Entente powers closer and closer together over the next few years.

In 1908 the bitterest rivals within the two alliance systems, Russia and Austria-Hungary, made a serious attempt to reconcile their disagreements in the Balkan Peninsula. Russia agreed that Austria could formally annex the province of Bosnia, which Austria had administered since 1878. In return, Russia won Austrian approval for Russian warships to pass through the Bosporus and Dardanelles' Straits and enter the warm waters of the Mediterranean Sea. Ratifying this, however, required British and German attendance at another international conference and neither power was willing to go. Because Austria went ahead and annexed Bosnia anyway, Russia, the protector of the Slavs, appeared to have been outwitted by Austria.

In 1911 a second Moroccan crisis exploded when French troops occupied the town of Fez. Wilhelm argued that this unilateral action benefited only France. He demanded that all the other imperial powers get some compensation in return. To emphasize his anger, the Kaiser dispatched the gunboat *Panther* to the scene. France agreed to cede a sliver of the French Congo to Germany, but tempers were rising all around. Joint military cooperation by Entente members intensified as the diplomatic gulf between the blocs widened. Military spending in all nations continued to grow. Adding to the uneasiness was the fact that an African war had actually been fought in 1911 when Italy seized Tripoli from the weak hold of the Ottoman Turks. Other nations now planned raids on the Ottoman Empire, the "sick man" of Europe.

In 1912 Bulgaria, Greece, Serbia, and Montenegro united to fight their former Ottoman overlords, and quickly carved large chunks out of what remained of the Ottoman Empire's European possessions. After their easy victory in this First Balkan War, the allies fell to arguing over who was to get which piece of territory. In 1913, the Ottoman government was able to unite with Serbia, Greece, and Romania to defeat Bulgaria in a Second Balkan War. Austria then intervened to create an independent Albania and frustrate the expansionist dreams of Serbia. But Serbia was not about to give up.

Crisis and War

◆   From the Third Balkan War to the First World War

On June 28, 1914, the heir to the throne of Austria, Archduke Franz Ferdinand (1863–1914) accompanied by his wife Sophie, was in the middle of an inspection tour of military maneuvers in Bosnia, the province Austria had annexed in 1908. The Archduke was a reformer who planned to modernize the empire while integrating its many minorities into a single nation. His policy was condemned by Serbian nationalists who sought back all the land, including Bosnia, that had once been part of a medieval Serbian kingdom. As the Archduke and his wife were driven through the city of Sarajevo in Bosnia, their car came within steps of Gavrilo Princip (1894–1918), a member of the "Black Hand," a secret society of Bosnian-Serb nationalists. Taking the name *Ujedinjenje ili Smrt* (Union or Death), the society had been founded in 1911 "for the purpose of realizing the national ideal: the union of all Serbs" through "terrorist" and "revolutionary action in all territories" in the Austrian and Ottoman Empires "inhabited by Serbs."[2] True to his organization's mandate, Princip shot and killed the Archduke and his wife.

Austrian officials quickly amassed evidence pointing to Serbia's involvement in the assassination, although the final proof that the Black Hand had been armed by Serbia's Chief of Military Intelligence using Russian funds was not obtained until after 1918. Convinced of Serbia's guilt, Austria-Hungary argued that Germany was morally bound to stand by her oldest ally. On July 5, 1914, the Kaiser granted Austria a pledge of unconditional support for a punitive campaign against Serbia.

The Great Powers may not have wanted a European-wide war, but the alliance structure intended to keep the peace began to spin out of control. With German support, Austria sent an ultimatum to Serbia on July 23. Five days later, after two of its terms were rejected, Austria declared what it expected to be a small, punitive war on Serbia (the Third Balkan War). Meanwhile, Russia prepared to support Serbia and was assured of French support. Assuming that Austria had Germany's support, Russian generals ordered their forces to mobilize on the Russo-German border as well as close to the Balkans. But mobilization within the close confines of Europe was universally considered a prelude to actual war. Germany fired off an ultimatum to Russia demanding it demobilize. France supported Russia's refusal to back down and began mobilizing as well. As a result, Germany formally declared war on Russia at 7 P.M., August 1, 1914. The Great War had begun.

Squeezed between two potential enemies—France and Russia—Germany had long sought a way to avoid fighting a two-front war. In 1905, the German Chief of Staff, General Alfred von Schlieffen (1833–1913), devised a war plan that promised military success but depended on speed.

Using the Franco-Prussian War as a model, Schlieffen reasoned that Germany could defeat France in six weeks by hurling vast armies through Belgium and Luxembourg. This way, German troops would outflank French defenses on the French-German border, and capture Paris in a grand assault. After victory over the French was secured, German armies would head back east to defeat the advancing Russian forces who were expected to mobilize more slowly. A modified version of this "Schlieffen Plan" remained the basis of Germany's strategy on August 1, 1914, even though Germany's quarrel was with Russia and not with France. German armies entered Luxembourg and Belgium on their way towards Paris. Belgian forces resisted but were not large enough to halt the German advance. When Belgium had been given its independence by the great powers, they had all signed a treaty in 1839 guaranteeing to protect its neutrality. Germany had just violated that treaty. Germany's unprovoked assault on Belgium decided the position of Great Britain. On August 4, Great Britain declared war on Germany for violating international law. France declared war on Germany as well. Austria declared war on Russia. By now every major European power and all their colonies in Africa, Asia, and the Americas were at war. On one side were the Allies (led by Great Britain, France, and Russia of the Triple Entente) and on the other the Central Powers (led by Germany and Austria of the Triple Alliance). Italy decided to back out of the Triple Alliance and remain neutral because its allies had not been attacked but had done the attacking.

◆　　The War in Europe

Although it is a myth that, on his deathbed, General Schlieffen said "keep the right wing strong," the story ought to be true. In 1914, the German General staff changed Schlieffen's plan in several particulars, taking troops from the right (attacking) wing and altering the line of advance towards Paris. On September 6, French General Joseph Joffre (1852–1931) attacked the exposed German flank along the River Marne and, in a bitter week-long battle, halted the German advance. Despite enormous German victories over poorly led Russian armies attempting to advance in the East, the Schlieffen Plan had failed. Germany was faced with fighting a two-front war. By Christmas, French forces in cooperation with the British Expeditionary Force established a defensive line extending from the English Channel off Belgium to the mountains of Switzerland. Within that battle zone about 500 miles long but rarely more than two miles wide, both sides constructed elaborate trench systems separated only by the short distance of "no-man's land." Millions of men died over the next four years charging across those terrible acres defended by machine guns and rapid-fire rifles. Expectations of a brief conflict ended as both sides mobilized their complete populations, retooled their industries, and prepared to fight a "total war." As the casualty lists lengthened, prospects of a negotiated settlement faded. "They shall not have died in vain" became the common battle cry. No politician could make peace, and no general knew how to win this new kind of war.

As the war dragged on it intensified. In April 1915 Germany introduced the use of poison gas (chlorine gas) in battle. Allied forces shortly retaliated, but both sides found the effects of gas attacks so unpredictable that its use was soon limited. The year's major fighting occurred in the East where German forces joined with Austrians to inflict 2 million casualties on Russian armies and occupy vast tracts of Russian territory. Despite tremendous losses, Tsar Nicholas II (r. 1894–1917) managed to keep armies in the field even as his regime at home began to deteriorate. In May 1915, the Allies convinced Italy to join their side by promising it Austrian land and African concessions. But Italian attacks northwards only succeeded in widening the battle area. By October 1914 yet another battle front was opened on the Greek border as Bulgaria joined the Central Powers. Serbia, exhausted after staving off three Austrian attacks, soon fell victim to a Bulgarian advance, giving the Central Powers a strong base in the Balkans by the end of 1915.

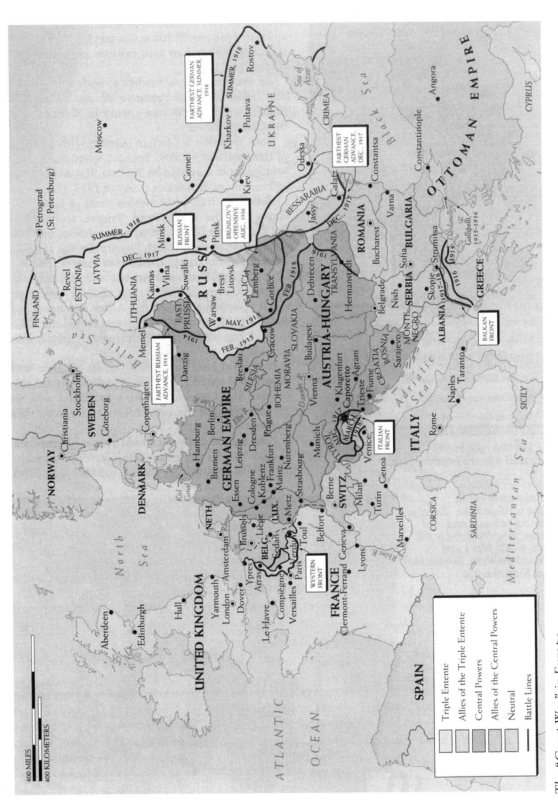

The "Great War" in Europe.
From *The Western Heritage, 6/e, Combined Edition,* by Donald Kagan, Steven Ozment, and Frank M. Turner. Copyright © 1998 by Prentice-Hall, Inc.

Trench Warfare.
"British Soldiers in Trench," courtesy of the Hulton-Deutsch Collection/CORBIS Images.

The war on the Western Front (the Franco-Belgian front) is best described as outright carnage. After a year and a half of war, European armies were in stalemate. Generals on both sides continued to hope that "one big push" would result in a decisive victory and end the war, but the generals were wrong. Despite the fact that machine guns and massed artillery gave the military advantage to the defenders in their trenches, the Allies prepared to launch major assaults in 1916. Instead of waiting, the Germans seized the military initiative early in February of that year. They attacked the area around Verdun in France, firing a million shells on the first day of their assault. German strategy during this six-month battle was simply to bleed the defending armies of French General Henri Pétain (1856–1951) until they collapsed. But by July the Germans had lost nearly as many men as had Verdun's defenders and the citadel still flew the French flag. The British high command decided to relieve the pressure on France by launching their own attack on the Germans defending the Somme River. On July 1, after a week of bombardment, 110,000 British and Australian troops began a "race against death" to see if they could occupy German trench lines before the defenders could reorganize. The British lost the race. German machine guns killed or wounded 60 percent of the officers and 57, 470 British troops became casualties within the first eight hours of battle. Yet the attacks continued for weeks, ultimately gaining 125 square miles of land without breaking through the German trenches at a cost to both sides of another million casualties. During this first battle of the Somme, the British deployed a new weapon, an armored vehicle called a "tank," but without a practical method of incorporating the new weapon into existing attack strategies, the tank made little difference to the battle's outcome.

Before the war both Britain and Germany expected to use their new Dreadnoughts in a major naval engagement resulting in a decisive victory. In fact, the two naval forces clashed only once, at the battle of Jutland (May 31–June 1, 1916), and the result was inconclusive: the two sides were too equally matched to overcome each other without fatal damage to themselves. Rather than risk its destruction in a war of attrition, the Kaiser decided to keep his expensive High Seas Fleet safe at home in German ports.

The only substantial gains of 1916 were attained by Russian forces in the more open conflict on the Eastern Front. In June 1916 the Russians moved against Austrian forces threatening Italy. By September, German reinforcements brought the Russian advance to a halt, but not before Russia regained much of the territory lost in 1915. The Russians also took about half a million German prisoners. But the Russians lost a million men in the advance, their supply system was collapsing, and their hungry soldiers were beginning to desert in record numbers.

Stalemate followed stalemate as a victory on one front was followed by a loss on another. Encouraged by Russia's seeming progress, Romania joined the Allies in August 1916 but was defeated by the Austrians that January, giving the Central Powers access to Romanian oil and wheat. By 1917 mutinies swept the contending armies as men on both sides began to refuse orders to attack.

◆ The War in the World, 1914–1917

Germany, fearful of losing its fleet to the British, did not use its navy to defend its African empire. When the Great War began British and French forces quickly occupied Togoland and the Cameroons in Central Africa while additional English units landed in Southeast Africa. The Boer commandos of the South African Republic defeated the Germans in Southwest Africa (present-day Namibia). Despite extraordinary resistance by German settlers, the allied powers kept a tight hold on Germany's African colonies throughout the war.

Japan, the only industrialized state in Asia, aimed at eliminating German influence in the Far East in order to establish its own hegemony there. Japan declared war upon Germany on August 23, 1914. By the close of the year, Japan had secured military control of the Marshall, Mariana, and Caroline Islands; only New Zealand's occupation of German Samoa on behalf of Great Britain stemmed Japan's progress. Moreover, in conjunction with a small British contingent, Japanese forces seized all of Germany's holdings in China: the defenders of Kiao-chow surrendered in November after enduring a two-month siege. Allied with Britain since their 1902 *Naval Treaty*, Japan claimed that its gains were undertaken only in support of a friend. But Japan's next step, an ultimatum of *Twenty-One Demands* delivered to China on January 18, 1915, could not be so justified. Japan demanded industrial, mining, and railroad concessions. An embattled Britain could not control its "ally," and the weak Chinese Republic, already suffering from internal divisions, had no choice but to accept the *Demands* and Japan's subsequent control over the Shantung Peninsula and Manchuria.

As fighting continued in Europe, only diplomatic pressure applied by the United States limited Japan's ambitions. At the end of 1917, Japan's Foreign Minister reluctantly pledged to respect the independence and territorial integrity of China and abide by the Open Door Policy. Although the

MATA HARI (1876–1917)

Spy or double agent?—a legend of WWI.
Copyright © CORBIS/Bettmann

Margaretha Geertruida Zelle, better known by her stage name Mata Hari, has become the universal symbol of the seductive female spy. Born in the Netherlands on August 7, 1876, her conventional early life gave no hint of her later notoriety. Her father was a prosperous businessman, and she was educated in convent schools and trained as a kindergarten teacher. At eighteen she married Captain Campbell MacLeod, a Scot serving in the Dutch colonial army, and bore him two children. From 1897 to 1902 the family lived in Java and Sumatra, but upon their return to the Netherlands, Margaretha MacLeod divorced her husband and moved to Paris. As Lady MacLeod, she became notorious as a dancer and courtesan, but soon took the name Mata Hari, perhaps from a Malay expression meaning "Eye of the Day."

Tall and extremely attractive, Mata Hari won fame throughout the capitals of Europe for her exotic East Indian dances, her skimpy (nearly nude) costumes, and her many lovers, government officials and military men prominent among them. When World War I broke out, Mata Hari was in Germany, but she returned to France in 1915. At this point accounts of her activities vary widely, as do theories about what secrets she sold to which side and why. Although an extensive mythology has grown up around the legend of the "greatest woman spy of World War I," no one is certain either of her crimes or her accomplishments.

By her own account, Mata Hari agreed to act as a French spy in German-occupied Belgium. She neglected to inform the French that she had already had some dealings with a German consul in the Hague who offered to pay her for military information obtained during her trips to France. Mata Hari freely admitted giving outdated information to a German intelligence officer, but claimed that indiscretion was part of an approved effort to win a prominent German nobleman to the Allied cause. Once French intelligence learned of her negotiations with the German official in the Hague (probably through British sources), they arrested Mata Hari in Paris on February 13, 1917.

By the time Mata Hari was tried in July, morale in the French Army had collapsed and half of its units had been mutinous. This crisis may have played a role in the secret proceeding of the French military court that found Mata Hari guilty of espionage. One of nine women executed by France during the Great War, Mata Hari died on October 15, 1917. After her execution, the records of the investigation leading to her arrest, as well as the proceedings of the trial, were ordered sealed for 100 years. Speculation raged for decades about Mata Hari's espionage activities, and the truth is still obscure.

United States clearly rejected any permanent reassignment of Chinese territory based upon Japan's *Twenty-One Demands,* it conceded that territorial proximity gave Japan a special interest in China's future development. But the long-term rivalry between the United States and Japan over the future development of Pacific Asia would put them on different sides in the next world war.

The only major addition to Central Power strength during the Great War occurred when the Ottoman Empire joined the German-Austrian bloc in November 1914. But the Ottoman troops soon found themselves locked in the same stalemate against Russia as the Germans, Austrians, British, and French were in the west. The Ottoman Turks had ruled several Armenian provinces for hundreds of years, but since the mid-nineteenth century those provinces had grown increasingly rebellious. Angered by their support of Russia, the Ottoman army began massive assaults against its Armenian subjects in 1915–1916. At least a million Armenians were slaughtered in the twentieth century's first outbreak of systematic genocide.

The Ottoman Empire's participation in the war led Britain and France to immediately make additional promises to Tsar Nicholas; a secret protocol in 1915 accepted Russia's ambition to annex Constantinople and its surrounding territory. Only the Russian Revolution in 1917 prevented this treaty from being implemented. Moreover, in the *Sykes-Picot Agreement* (1916), Britain and France secretly agreed to partition the Middle Eastern portion of the Ottoman Empire between themselves at war's end. Now that the battle zone included Turkey (the heartland of the Ottoman Empire), Britain raised an expeditionary force that attacked the Gallipoli Peninsula south of Constantinople in April 1916. The aim was to outflank the trenches and find a new way to bring the war to a close by attacking the weakest member of the Central Powers. Excellent preparations by German engineers and a gallant defense by the Turkish commander Mustafa Kemal (1881–1938) halted the invasion, and Allied armies withdrew early the next year following heavy losses.

The Ottoman Empire's presence as a Central Power transformed the Middle East into an area of critical Allied concern. Russians and Turks fought great battles seeking control of Mesopotamia (modern Iraq) and Persia (modern Iran) in 1916, and a sudden Ottoman move to take the Suez Canal had to be repulsed. Britain turned for aid to once ignored Arab leaders, among them Husayn ibn 'Ali (c. 1854–1931), the Grand Sharif of Mecca. Despite the secret terms of the *Sykes-Picot Agreement,* Britain agreed to Husayn's demand for Arab independence from the Ottoman Turks after an Allied victory. After British forces took Baghdad in March 1917, Colonel Thomas E. Lawrence (1888–1935) and Prince Faisal (1885–1933), Husayn's son, organized an Arab fighting force. By the summer of 1917 the Arab rebels were disrupting Ottoman communications and capturing their cities. Britain also moved to obtain the support of the Jewish Zionist movement. On November 2, 1917, the British Foreign Minister, Arthur, Lord Balfour (1848–1930), wrote a letter to Lionel, Baron Rothschild (1868–1937) endorsing "the establishment of a national home for the Jewish people" in Palestine. The conflict between Britain's pledges to Jews and Arabs, and British ambitions as indicated by the Sykes-Picot arrangement, seemed of little importance in 1917 when winning the war was all that mattered. Nevertheless, these conflicting promises were to have enormous repercussions on future world politics.

In the midst of the war, the United States emerged from its traditional isolation and began to play an important role. After war erupted in 1914, the administration (1913–1921) of President Woodrow Wilson at first proclaimed American neutrality. But maintaining economic neutrality proved impossible, as Britain controlled the high seas and routinely seized American merchant vessels heading for Germany or its neighbors. Although Britain compensated ship owners, some Americans believed that the violation of neutral trading rights was sufficient cause to go to war against Britain, but the unending stream of propaganda from the trenches convinced the nation that righteousness was on the Allied side. Democratic sentiment was strengthened by economic self-interest. By the time America entered the war in 1917, its citizens held $2.3 billion in Allied securities as opposed to a mere $20 million in German bonds. Equally important, trade with the Central Powers had fallen to less than $2 million as Allied trade rose to $3 billion.

Faced with exclusion from America's economic bounty, Germany declared a "war zone" around the British Isles in February 1915, an area in which Germany's submarine fleet would sink enemy ships without warning and neutral vessels entered at their own risk. On May 7, 1915, the British liner *Lusitania* was torpedoed and sunk off the coast of Ireland with the loss of over 1,200 lives, 128 of them American. A wave of anti-German hysteria swept the United States despite prior German notification of the danger and the revelation of contraband munitions aboard the *Lusitania*. A reluctant Germany promised not to sink any more liners and pay compensation for the lost lives. But Britain's refusal to lift her blockade on neutral shipping to the Continent left a loophole for renewed German action.

During the American presidential campaign of 1916, Wilson ran as the candidate who "kept us out of war," even though he had approved a national preparedness program that expanded the American army, created officer-training centers, and planned national industrial mobilization. Wilson was not maneuvering for war, but preparing for its increasing likelihood. On February 1, 1917, Germany announced it was resuming unrestricted submarine warfare and would allow only one American ship per week to enter the ports of Great Britain. Wilson immediately suspended diplomatic relations with Germany. Further trouble was already brewing. In January, German Foreign Minister Arthur Zimmermann (1864–1940) had proposed an alliance with Mexico. If Mexican troops would keep the Americans bottled up at home, Germany promised Mexico to help it recover the territory lost in the Mexican-American War (1846–1848). British intelligence intercepted the note Zimmerman sent to Mexico with the terms of the proposed alliance and released the text of the "Zimmerman Note" on March 1. Americans were outraged, but not unanimously in favor of war. On April 6, 1917, a still divided United States Congress declared war on Germany. It was not until December that the United States decided to fight Austria, and it never declared war against the Ottoman Empire.

◆   Mobilization

The scope, expense, and technological demands of the Great War put unprecedented strains on the economies and social structures of the nations that fought it. The United States soon discovered the complexities of total mobilization. The Food Administration imposed price controls on staples and launched patriotic appeals for "Wheatless Mondays, Meatless Tuesdays, and Porkless Thursdays." American shipments of foodstuffs to the Allies tripled. Capital expenditure in manufacturing increased by 300 percent; American plants were soon producing two ships for every one the Germans sank. But the long hours, cramped conditions, and strain of wartime production brought on a wave of strikes during 1917. In consequence, the government created the National War Labor Board (NWLB) to mediate industrial disputes and keep factories producing. The presence of national union leaders on the NWLB brought a new respectability to organized labor, and union memberships doubled.

Not all labor trouble was simply job related, however. Close to half a million African-Americans left the rural south for northern cities in search of jobs in the wartime economy. Many businesses recruited black workers as a way of getting around the wage demands of white labor unions. Union led or sanctioned attacks on black migrants were often the result. The worst such attack occurred on July 2, 1917, when at least 200 African-Americans were killed by whites in East St.

HORATIO HERBERT KITCHENER (1850–1916)

Famed as the avenger of General Gordon, Kitchener became a recruiting tool in WWI.
Copyright © Canadian War Museum

Horatio Herbert Kitchener was born on June 24, 1850, in County Kerry, Ireland. The son of a soldier and member of the Anglo-Irish gentry, Kitchener began his career in the British army as an engineer. He established his reputation by able survey work in Palestine and Cyprus between 1874 and 1880, and by excellent intelligence reports on Upper Egypt in 1884. Rising rapidly, Kitchener was appointed Adjutant-General to the Egyptian army in Cairo in 1889. In 1892, though still only a colonel, Kitchener was appointed *Sirdar,* or commander-in-chief of the Egyptian army. From 1896, he led the re-conquest of the Sudan from forces under the control of the Mahdi. After an exhausting two-year campaign up the Nile—the so-called River War—Kitchener finally destroyed the Arabs at the Battle of Omdurman on September 2, 1898. Using modern artillery, Maxim machine guns, and rifles, 25,800 British and Egyptian troops lost fewer than 200 men as they defeated an enemy force almost twice as large; eleven thousand Arabs were killed. Kitchener then proceeded to Fashoda where he prevented a small French force from claiming territorial rights. Kitchener won a peerage for his re-conquest of the Sudan.

During the last Anglo-Boer War (1899–1902) Kitchener accompanied Field Marshall Frederick S. Roberts (1832–1914) to South Africa as chief of staff. Roberts returned to England in 1900, leaving Kitchener to face continuing guerrilla warfare by Boer farmers. To frustrate roving guerrilla bands, Kitchener built a network of blockhouses and barbed wire crisscrossing the country and then methodically surrounded and defeated the Boers in each sector. To prevent the Boers from receiving supplies, Kitchener denuded the countryside of flocks and grain, burning hundreds of farms and placing civilians in internment camps. These measures were harshly criticized, but the Boers surrendered in May 1902. From 1902 to 1907 Kitchener served in India as commander-in-chief, where he reformed and greatly improved the administration of the colonial army. On leaving India, Kitchener was promoted to field-marshal and, as consul-general in Egypt, distinguished himself as an innovative social reformer.

Returning to England in June 1914, Kitchener was rewarded with an earldom for his service in Egypt. When World War I broke out in August, Kitchener was appointed secretary of state for war. Almost alone among statesmen and soldiers of Europe, Kitchener predicted the war would be long and widespread, and he advocated increasing the size of the army from 20 to 70 divisions. By 1916, Kitchener had accomplished this unprecedented expansion. With the help of a recruiting poster using his portrait, more than 3 million men were inspired to volunteer (33,000 of them on a single day in September 1914). They were equipped and sent to France with the help of a mobilized British industry in the world's first "total" war.

Kitchener's more than 40 years of service in the British army ended tragically. While on a military mission to Russia on June 5, 1916, his ship hit a mine and Kitchener drowned.

Louis. Racial prejudice was also strong in the military. Blacks who served in the military were assigned to segregated units used mostly for menial tasks. One exception was the Army's 369th Infantry Regiment, made up of soldiers from Harlem, awarded the *Croix de Guerre* by the French government for gallantry in battle in the western trenches where the 369th had fought side-by-side with French soldiers.

With men leaving the factories to join the armed forces, women moved into the industrial workforce in greater numbers than ever before. Some 2.25 million women were directly engaged in the war effort as munitions plant workers, train engineers, and streetcar conductors. These jobs were only "for the duration." The war's end meant the replacement of female factory workers by returning veterans. But wartime gains in jobs normally held by women, such as telephone operators, secretaries and clerks, proved to be more permanent. The contribution to the war effort of American women played a large role in gaining acceptance for female suffrage in 1920.

The national tax structure was revamped to pay for the war, increasing the number of Americans who paid income taxes from 437,000 in 1916 to 4,425,000 in 1918. The richest Americans faced 70 percent tax brackets. The sale of Liberty Bonds to Americans raised $23 billion for the war effort, but more had to be borrowed. Federal debt jumped from $1 billion in 1915 to $20 billion by 1920.

Men and women alike worked round the clock to meet the demands of global war.
Copyright © Imperial War Museum

Simply staffing the war required major social dislocations. In May 1917, Congress passed the Selective Service Act, the first compulsory draft legislation since the American Civil War. Twenty-four million men between the ages of 18 and 45 registered by the end of the Great War. Three million draftees and two million volunteers were inducted. Maintaining discipline among such a large number of men created new challenges for the American government. The War Department found itself distributing condoms to soldiers in a campaign against the spread of venereal disease. The army even established five-mile wide "pure zones" around training camps to keep prostitutes away from recruits.

Discipline was not simply a military matter. The Espionage Act of 1917 set penalties of up to 20 years' imprisonment for obstructing recruitment. The Sedition Act of 1918 outlawed "any disloyal, profane, scurrilous, or abusive language intended to cause contempt, scorn, contumely, or disrepute" to the Constitution, government or flag. The mailing rights of forty-five newspapers were revoked in the first year alone. The Espionage and Sedition Acts were upheld by the Supreme Court because of the perceived "clear and present danger" to American survival (*Schenck v. United States*, 1919).

Americans were experiencing the same constraints and upheavals faced by their European allies since the first wave of patriotic fervor in 1914 settled down into the hardships of total war. Government-planned production, rationing, and price and wage controls soon became the norm in all the combatant powers. In Germany, civilian mobilization went much further than in the United States. The German War Materials Board set up in 1914 rationed everything from oil to manure. The German Auxiliary Services Law of 1916 drafted all men between the ages of 17 and 60 not in the military into war work in the factories. But increasing shortages meant that by the last years of the war, milk was available only to children and pregnant women; the average German survived on less than a thousand calories a day. The combatant powers on both sides were edging closer to total collapse.

◆ The End of the War

The German High Command believed that the use of unrestricted submarine warfare could starve the Allies into defeat, but the U-boats failed to isolate Britain despite the losses they inflicted. The development of depth charges and a magnificent convoy system for supplies from the United States overcame their presence. In 1918 the navies of Britain and the United States were able to transport two million fresh troops to the battlefields of France without the loss of a single soldier. The Central Powers faced a growing threat on land as well, as the British began to discover the potential of their tanks to break the stalemate of trench warfare. At the battle of Cambrai in 1917, the British opened with a flying assault of nearly 400 tanks, driving a five-mile wedge into the German lines before lack of reserves and a German counter assault brought them to halt. Still, the ability of the tank to break the stalemate created by the machine gun was proven. The tactic would be used again, and with more success. The war in the air was also going badly for the Germans. Although German air raids on Paris (1914) and London (1916) caused considerable property damage and loss of human life, they did not affect the battlefront. As Britain gained air superiority, the German economy was further drained by the loss of many of its planes during aerial combat. The entry of the United States into the war only worsened the odds. By April 1918 the Americans had three air squadrons at the front, by November they had forty-five.

Only an unexpected revolutionary upheaval in Russia during 1917 provided hope for Germany, and gave it the will to fight on. The war-weary Russians overthrew Tsar Nicholas II in March 1917. By summer's end Russian military pressure on the Eastern Front virtually ceased. In

The new technology met the old in WWI.
Copyright © Imperial War Museum

November, after months of chaos, a Bolshevik minority took power in Russia and indicated its willingness to make peace; on March 3, 1918, Russia's surrender was negotiated at Brest-Litovsk. Stores of food from the granaries of the Ukraine and thousands of battle-hardened troops from the Eastern Front suddenly became available to an exhausted Germany. General Erich Ludendorff (1865–1937) prepared a last great offensive in the West, even as the first American regiments began to appear in trenches there. By the end of May 1918, some German units had advanced to within a day's march of Paris, but French General Ferdinand Foch (1851–1929), the Supreme Commander of Allied forces, gradually pushed the Germans farther and farther back. On August 8, British tank forces aided by airplanes shattered the remaining German defensive positions. Armored forces and air support were the technological innovations that finally permitted the combatants to escape from the trenches. The long nightmare of static warfare ended, and in its final weeks World War I was a blizzard of movement.

On September 30, Bulgaria surrendered, and the Ottoman Empire shortly followed suit. Even as British armies occupied the Hindenburg Line (Germany's last defense in France), the American army under General John "Black Jack" Pershing (1860–1948) won its first victory, in the Argonne region. The German military at last confronted the truth it had denied since 1914—the *Reich* could not win the war—and now sought to avoid responsibility for its loss. Ludendorff handed

ERICH LUDENDORFF (1865–1937)

Ludendorff's genius brought Germany its greatest victories against Russian forces.
Copyright © CORBIS/Hulton-Deutsch Collection

Erich Ludendorff was born in Kruszewnia in East Prussia on April 9, 1865. He was a brilliant student with a passion for technical studies who entered cadet school two years ahead of his class. When war erupted in 1914, Ludendorff was posted to the Western Front. There, he participated in the capture of the Citadel, one of the great Belgian forts defending Liège. Transferred to the Eastern Front, he and his superior, Paul von Hindenburg (1847–1934), annihilated the invading Russian armies at Tannenberg and the Masurian Lakes. Barely one month into the war Ludendorff was a national hero. Within two years Hindenburg was the Supreme Commander of the entire German army, and Ludendorff was his Quartermaster-General, responsible for commanding the war economy, systematizing recruitment, and crushing internal dissent as he organized German society for conquest and total war.

When impending defeat brought revolution to Germany in 1918, the war hero fled to safety in neutral Sweden disguised in a fake beard and blue sunglasses, but support from radical nationalists (who shared his vision of a Germany betrayed from within) soon brought him home. Ludendorff contributed to the instability of the Weimar Republic when he encouraged right-wing nationalists and officers to stage a coup in March 1920. The Kapp Putsch ended in failure and Ludendorff fled from Berlin to Munich, where he met Adolf Hitler. On November 9, 1923, Hitler and Ludendorff led a coup attempt in Munich, but were defeated by police resistance. Some Nazis were killed, but Ludendorff, showing bravery reminiscent of his glory days at Liege, calmly walked through police lines and surrendered. Hitler, previously a minor figure unknown outside of Bavaria, immediately earned a national reputation as a patriot because of his association with Ludendorff.

When German President Friedrich Ebert (1871–1925) died in February 1925, Ludendorff ran for office, but gained a mere one percent of the vote. After Hindenburg was elected with Nazi support, Ludendorff accused his recent allies of betrayal. Divorced by first wife in 1926, he married psychologist Mathilde Spiess von Kemnitz who advocated a spiritual philosophy of Aryan supremacy. Ludendorff built a nationalist organization, the Tannenbergbund, dedicated to teaching German racial awareness. So many of his followers belonged to the Nazi party that some of its leaders wondered if he planned to lead an opposition movement from within. But Hitler never forgot the help he had received from Ludendorff in the first years of the Nazi movement. After Ludendorff's death on December 20, 1937, Hitler approved a lavish funeral for his former comrade.

power over to civilian leaders and fled to Sweden. Early in October, the government requested an armistice from President Wilson and, as negotiations proceeded, Germany unilaterally ended unrestricted submarine warfare (October 28). After Austria surrendered on November 4, Kaiser Wilhelm II abdicated and fled to exile in Holland. Finally, at 11 A.M. on November 11, 1918, hostilities ceased on the battlefield. The worst war civilization had yet known was over.

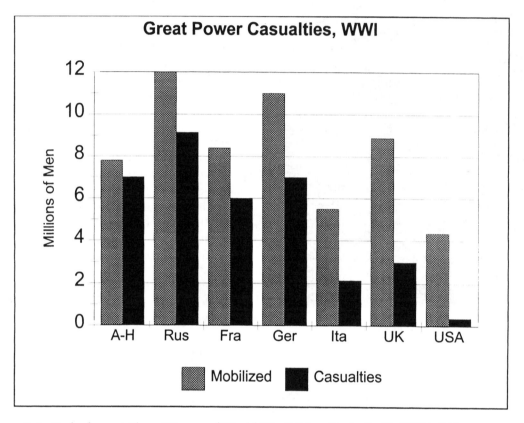

Source: J. L. Stokesbury, A Short History of World War I *(New York: Quill, 1981), 310.*

The Consequences of the Peace

◆   Peacemaking, 1919

No European statesman and only a few military leaders foresaw the duration and destructiveness of the Great War. No one was prepared for the total mobilization of men, resources, and industry required by modern warfare. Entire populations were reorganized to meet unprecedented demands for labor, food production, industrial production, and transportation. Time itself was adjusted as Daylight Saving Time was invented to meet the production demands of total war. The cost of the war topped $330 billion. The human loss was even more staggering. Ten million soldiers died and at least twenty million more were wounded. The casualties would affect the ability of Europe's population to maintain itself for generations: 50 percent of all French males between the ages of twenty and thirty had died. And as if more suffering was needed, the world experienced its worst plague since the Middle Ages. First reported in Kansas training camps of the American army, a virulent strain of influenza spread to Europe by the end of 1918. The influenza pandemic of 1918–1920 claimed an additional 20 to 40 million lives.

On January 18, 1919, peace negotiations formally opened in the palace of Versailles, near Paris. Although 70 delegates representing 27 victorious Allied nations attended, the terms of the resulting treaties were determined by the leaders of the allied Big Three: Woodrow Wilson of the United States, Georges Clemenceau (1841–1929) of France and David Lloyd George (1869–1945) of Great Britain. The Central Powers were excluded altogether from the discussions held to determine their future. President Wilson's idealistic *Fourteen Points* proposal of January 1918 had formed the basis for the armistice with the Central Powers. Based upon the principle of national self-determination, the *Fourteen Points* implied that honorable terms would be presented to Germany. That negotiators took only a week to approve his fourteenth point—the creation of a League of Nations—seemed a good sign. But Wilson did not play the dominant part in the negotiations that many had assumed; he was willing to accept the punitive agendas of his allies in order to ensure their support for the League.

Lloyd George had won reelection in 1918 on a pledge to "squeeze" Germany like a lemon "until the pips squeaked." Clemenceau, who personally remembered his nation's humiliating defeat in 1870–1871, planned a similar humiliation for Germany. Wilson proved incapable of moderating the demands of his allies, and the *Versailles Treaty* (1919) with Germany rapidly assumed a punitive form. Alsace and Lorraine were to be immediately returned to France, German lands along the Rhine River were to be permanently demilitarized, and the ore-rich lands of the Saar were placed under international supervision for fifteen years. German territory was also granted to Belgium as well as to the newly created Polish and Czech nations; the German cities of Memel and Danzig became free cities under League authority. Beyond these territorial losses in Europe, all German colonies were to be ceded to the League of Nations to be reassigned as "mandates" administered by Allied powers. Theoretically the mandates were to be prepared for independent existence, but in practice they became protectorates of the occupying power. While Germany was far from entirely dismembered, it lost 25,000 square miles of its European lands, home to six million people, and its entire overseas empire. Nor was Austria's vote to join together with its fellow German state recognized: *Anschluss* (union) between Germany and Austria was specifically forbidden. Germany was limited to an army of 100,000 men and had its General Staff disbanded. The new German Republic would have no tanks, no warplanes, no heavy artillery, no submarines, and no draft. Ordered to surrender its remaining fleet, the angry nation sunk it instead.

According to Article 231 of the *Treaty of Versailles*:

> *The Allied and Associated Governments affirm and Germany accepts the responsibility of Germany and her allies for causing all the loss and damage to which the Allied and Associated Governments and their nationals have been subjected as a consequence of the war imposed upon them by the aggression of Germany and her allies.*[3]

This meant that despite the fact that the German Republic was bankrupt, the "guilty" nation was ordered to repay all the losses inflicted on civilian property during the course of the war. In 1921, the Reparations Commission set the total bill at $33 billion, half of which would go to France.

John Maynard Keynes (1883–1946) had come to the peace negotiations as one of the economists from the British treasury department. Assigned to work up material on Germany's economic potential, he quit his job over what he saw as the basic injustice of the *Versailles Treaty*. Returning home to Britain, he quickly published a book, the *Economic Consequences of the Peace* (1919), that outlined the series of economic disasters he thought would follow any attempt to dismember the German economy. His predictions of German default, massive hyper-inflation, global depression, and global war would be proved substantially true within twenty years. But in 1919, no one was listening.

Germans, having expected a treaty along the lines of Wilson's *Fourteen Points,* condemned the *Treaty of Versailles* as a *diktat,* a dictated peace. Wilson recognized that its terms were one-sided, but expected the League of Nations to moderate their rigor. Because the League Covenant was used as a preamble to the Treaty, all nations that accepted the peace were automatically members of the League. German representatives were informed that the penalty for failure to sign was Allied occupation. Many resigned. On June 28, 1919, two little known German delegates signed the *diktat* that, for the next twenty years, would provide a convenient target for nationalist demagogues.

The work of the negotiators continued for another year. Subsequent treaties with Austria at St. Germain (1919), with Bulgaria at Neuilly (1919), with Hungary at Trianon (1920), and with Turkey at Sevres (1920) redrew the map of Eastern Europe: the new nations of Poland, Czechoslovakia, Hungary, Austria, Lithuania, Latvia, Estonia, and a combined Kingdom of the Croats, Slavs and Slovenes (the future Yugoslavia) were created by the victors. Though the Allies seemed to be abiding by Wilson's principle of national self-determination, their desire to punish the losers and create states large enough not to be easily reabsorbed by their former rulers cut across national territories. Most of the new states contained ethnic minorities alienated from their governments, leaving open the possibility of a new round of ethnic wars such as those that led to the Great War.

◆ The Achievements of the League of Nations

Even as Germany accepted the *Treaty of Versailles,* Britain, France, and the United States were signing a defensive alliance. Although that alliance never became operative, it seems clear that the Big Three intended to hedge their bets regarding the effectiveness of the new League of Nations. If European leaders thought the League assured the ongoing cooperation of the United States, they were soon disappointed. Wilson's view of America's role in world affairs was not shared by most of his countrymen. He also had to convince the Senate that American membership in the League posed no threat to national sovereignty. In September, Wilson began a grueling railroad tour to explain the League to the American public, but during the trip he suffered a stroke. The illness affected his political judgment, and when the Senate prepared to approve the *Versailles Treaty* subject to fourteen amendments that did not actually its basic terms, Wilson ordered his supporters to reject the compromise. As a result, the Senate refused to ratify the *Versailles Treaty,* thus rejecting the League membership that came with it. It also voted down the proposed defensive alliance with Britain and France. The United States was taking an isolationist position in world affairs. On July 2, 1921, the United States made a separate peace with Germany through a joint resolution of Congress.

Responsibility for administering the League of Nations now fell to European powers. The League set up headquarters in Geneva, Switzerland. Each year a General Assembly convened, the Executive Council (Britain, France, Italy, Japan, and several rotating members) set an agenda for discussion, and a Secretariat supervised the operations of the League. Mandates created from German and Ottoman territories were assigned to supervising nations and plebiscites were administered in disputed areas. But the League was weakened from the start by lack of American

The Versailles Peace Settlement.
From *The Western Heritage, 6/e, Combined Edition*, by Donald Kagan, Steven Ozment, and Frank M. Turner.
Copyright © 1998 by Prentice-Hall, Inc.

participation, and it never had an armed force with which to enforce its decisions. Nor was it ever truly universal: Germany was not permitted to join until 1926 and Turkey not until 1932. Soviet Russia, clearly one of the major forces in the post-war world, was denied membership until 1934 because of its Communist ideology. In 1926 Brazil, angered at its failure to win a permanent place on the Council, became the first of several nations to leave the European-dominated organization.

In reality, the League could deal effectively only with issues upon which the Great Powers agreed. Yet the League did enjoy several substantial successes. The Permanent Court of International Justice had settled forty-one cases by 1937. League mediation settled outstanding issues between Sweden and Finland, Poland and Germany, and Britain and Turkey. Perhaps the most effective League service was its assistance to war refugees during the troubled years of the 1920s. Fridtjof Nansen (1861–1930), delegate to the League from Norway, won a Nobel Peace Prize for his famine relief efforts in Russia. The League provided reconstruction loans to the nations of the Danube Basin, and its International Labor Organization worked to better working conditions around the world. International agreements against opium use, the arms trade, and poison gas were signed in 1925. League investigations documented the continuation of slavery in Africa. One mark of the League's lasting value was how few changes in its structure were necessary to transform it into the United Nations in 1945.

The Eclipse of Europe

At the start of the twentieth century Europeans believed their "superior" civilization gave them the right to rule the world. But Europe's assumed moral superiority died in the trenches of the Western Front. No colonized people could ever again take seriously Europe's claim to an inherent right to rule. Although Europe's empire was not immediately lost, its fading authority made it possible for nineteenth century dreams of nationalism to flourish elsewhere across the globe. National independence for subject peoples became the great cause of the twentieth century, and in some ways its abiding affliction.

◆ Inventing Turkey

Before the Great War the "Young Turk" reform movement of 1908 attempted to reclaim the prestige of the Ottoman past, but its inept military leadership blundered into the Balkan Wars and then into an unwise alliance with the Central Powers. Peace brought only additional shame. The *Treaty of Sevres* (1920) removed the Balkan Peninsula and the Arab Middle East from Ottoman rule, and put the strategic Dardanelles and Bosporus Straits under international control. Humiliation and anger merged to demand a Turkish leader who could restore national pride. In 1920, General Mustafa Kemal rebelled against the Ottoman administration and proclaimed a rival government in the newly founded city of Ankara. In 1922 he regained control of European Turkey by agreeing to keep the Bosporus and Dardanelles open to the ships of all nations. Later that year, he ordered the abolition of the Ottoman Sultanate and placed the army in control of Turkish society. On October 29, 1923, a Turkish Republic was proclaimed.

For the rest of his life, Kemal ruthlessly transformed Turkey into a modern state. Clerical courts were dismantled as church and state were separated and religious toleration enacted in law. Wearing the traditional Muslim hat (the *fez*) was banned, polygamy was abolished, civil ceremonies were required for marriages, and divorce allowed. Women were encouraged to shun the veil, give up their "harem mentality," and obtain an education as they gained the right to vote in

1934. Universal suffrage, a ministry responsible to the legislature, and secularization led to enormous changes in a once closed and religious society. In 1928 Kemal ordered Turks to adopt the Latin alphabet, and made bureaucrats attend school until they mastered the new system. Civil, criminal, and commercial law codes based on Western European models were strictly enforced. Agricultural, mining, and industrial complexes were constructed using state funds. The Ottoman debt was ordered repaid and non-aggression pacts secured Turkey's long frontiers. In July 1932 Turkey was permitted to join the League of Nations. Grateful for all Kemal had accomplished, the Turkish legislature suggested that Kemal accept the name *Ataturk* (Father of the Turks). The success of this dictatorial transformation was not lost upon later leaders of nationalist causes.

◆ Africa and Pan-Africanism

To the American sociologist William E. B. Du Bois (1868–1963), the end of the Great War presented an opportunity for black people everywhere to assert their rights and gain recognition for their hopes and sacrifices. After all, tens of thousands of Africans had born arms as soldiers in the armies of the Allied Powers and hundreds of thousands more had worked in support positions. Ten thousand soldiers and 195,000 porters had volunteered in Kenya alone. In 1919, as the Versailles delegations hammered out peace with Germany, Du Bois convened a second Pan-African Congress (the first had been held in London in 1900, organized by Booker T. Washington) to present the case for the legal, economic, and social rights of African peoples. Fifty-seven delegates representing fifteen nations attended the Paris Pan-African Congress, although most came from the United States and the Caribbean. But the Great Powers had no intention of applying Wilson's principles to Africa. The Versailles settlement merely turned German colonies into Allied mandates. In Africa, however, war was still being waged against colonization. The Maji-Maji rebellion (1898–1914) in German East Africa had only just been put down at the start of the Great War. Sayyid Muhammad ibn 'Abd Allah Hasan (1864–1920) continued his jihad (1899–1920) against the British and Italians in Somalia, while 'Abd-al-Krim (1880–1963) fought the French and the Spanish in Morocco (1921–1926). The Italians encountered fierce Bedouin resistance in Libya (1912–1931).

The failure of European leaders to acknowledge the legitimacy of African claims to independence left the Pan-African movement up in mid air. Losing faith in the good will of Europe's leaders, Du Bois turned his attentions to the plight of his fellow African-Americans. The Pan-African Congress held in New York City the following year focused on the racial situation in the United States. Although it took a Second World War to dislodge Europe's hold on Africa, the Pan-African movement did succeed in establishing Africa as a legitimate area of scholarly research. In 1926 an International Institute of African Language and Culture was created in New York, and courses in African history began to appear in the catalogues of universities in Europe and the United States. The academic rediscovery of Africa's past was crucial to an understanding of its present problems.

In the United States itself, the movement for Black Nationalism was not led by the scholarly Du Bois but rather by the more flamboyant Marcus Garvey (1887–1940). The Jamaican-born Garvey founded the Universal Negro Improvement Association, a self-help movement that included a "Back to Africa" component. He inspired millions of black people to be proud of their heritage, and his Black Star Steamship Line carried some American colonists back to their ancestral homes. Leaving America in 1927, Garvey propagated his cause first from Jamaica and later from London, but he convinced few of his listeners to return to Africa. His dream of a "mighty African Nation" did not take into account either the continent's diversity or the strength of its colonial rulers, but it remained a rallying point for later generations.

◆ The New Middle East

Arab leaders saw the Mandate System incorporated into the *League of Nations Charter* as a betrayal of Allied promises of Arab independence in return for Arab aid against Turkey. That sense of betrayal brought on the "Year of Catastrophe," a wave of unsuccessful national uprisings in Syria, Palestine, Iraq, Egypt, Afghanistan, and Persia in 1920. Instead of the promised independence, the Mandate System awarded control of Turkey's former possessions to Britain and France. Britain received Iraq, Palestine, and the Transjordan region. France received Syria.

In March 1920 Prince Faisal, who had loyally supported the war against the Turks, dared to proclaim himself King of Syria, only to have French forces dethrone him. But armed intervention still did not secure French control; after subdividing the Syrian mandate into two provinces, France faced a fierce insurrection by Druse nationalists. Intent on creating a loyal Christian client state in the Middle East, the French government expediently recognized the more peaceful southern half of their mandate as the Republic of Lebanon (May 23, 1926). When the charter of the new state divided governmental authority between Muslim, Druse, and Christian groups, it virtually guaranteed future difficulties. France also pledged to grant greater independence to Syria. Elections held in 1932 returned a moderate government with strong ties to Paris; indeed France retained veto power over Syrian finance, foreign relations, and military affairs for another generation. Only in 1944, during the Second World War and as a means of winning Arab support for the Free French, did Syria receive full sovereign powers.

Just south of French-controlled areas, the existence of competing Jewish and Arab national aspirations made the history of Britain's Palestine mandate a troubled one. Zionism, as defined by Theodor Herzl (1860–1904), hoped "to secure for the Jewish people a home in Palestine" and return a dispersed people to their Biblical homeland (Israel, or Zion). During the war in 1917, Britain had endorsed this goal in a letter sent by Foreign Secretary Arthur James Balfour to Lord Rothschild, a leader of the Zionist Federation. It pledged British support for a "national home" for the Jews in Palestine as long as nothing was done to "prejudice the civil and religious rights" of Palestinian Arabs in the process. This "Balfour Declaration" pleased neither the Palestinian Arabs nor the Palestinian Jews and set the stage for the rivalries plaguing the region to this very day.

Zionists interpreted the Balfour Declaration as a promise of statehood, but Britain had made similarly vague pledges to secure the support of Arab leaders during the Great War with no intention of delivering the newly mandated lands to the control of either group. When the French expelled Faisal from Syria, Britain made no objection. Similarly, it showed vast unconcern when Jewish immigrants in Jaffa were murdered during Arab street rioting in 1921. Arab-Jewish rivalries enabled Great Britain to consolidate its position in the Middle East.

In July 1922 the League of Nations confirmed Britain's Palestine mandate and British Colonial Secretary Winston Churchill (1874–1965) decided that efficient administration of the area required dividing the territory along the Jordan River. Transjordan, the eastern half of the mandate, was granted autonomy in 1923. Although Great Britain formally recognized its independence five years later, Britain retained control of both financial and military matters even after Emir Abdullah (1882–1951), the brother of Prince Faisal, became king of Jordan in 1946. Churchill's administrative scheme was interpreted by Palestinian Jews, comprising less than a fifth of the population of the area west of the Jordan, as a necessary first step toward the recognition of a Jewish state. Zionists pointed out that their untiring labor had reclaimed desert land, tapped the Jordan River as a power source, and created Tel Aviv as a modern city; they believed it was time for the promises of the Balfour Declaration to be fulfilled. But Britain demurred. In 1929 a dispute over the right of Jews to pray at Jerusalem's "wailing-wall" (the last remnants of the ancient Temple) led to extensive Jewish-Arab rioting. Britain's response was to restrict new Jewish immigration and land acquisition rights. By the spring of 1937 a state of virtual war existed between Jewish and Arab communities in Palestine, with Britain caught in the middle.

The only Mid-Eastern nation to enter the original League of Nations was Persia, a land long dominated by Great Britain. Inspired by the example of Kemal in Turkey, a patriotic young Persian officer named Reza Khan (1878–1941), seized control of the Persian government from the reigning Shah in 1921. Reza Khan modernized the Persian army, suppressed dissent, built a road system, and began construction of a railroad linking the Caspian Sea to the Persian Gulf. Soon the Shah was forced into exile, and on April 25, 1926, Khan took the throne as Reza Shah Pahlavi. The new Shah was well aware of the economic potential of Persia's oil reserves and, even as he introduced Western laws and a national banking system, he permitted foreign corporations to develop those resources. As Persia's "black gold" began to flow to the nations of the industrialized West, the wealth generated by oil allowed the Pahlavi dynasty to maintain control of the nation to which they restored its ancient name, Iran (1935). As long as Reza Shah favored Britain and the West his authority was recognized by them as absolute.

Geographically adjacent to Iran, Iraq in 1919 was little more than a British protectorate transformed into a mandate by the Versailles settlement. Immediately thereafter, Britain asserted its authority and crushed a nationalist uprising by Arabs who had expected independence. In 1921, Britain permitted a plebiscite in which 96 percent of the propertied classes endorsed the candidacy of Prince Faisal, recently ousted as King of Syria. Assuring Britain of his cooperation, Faisal became King of Iraq on August 23, 1921. He secured his throne by allowing the British Treasury to control Iraq's finances. A parliament was established in 1924, and Britain recognized Iraq's independence in 1927 in return for three permanent air bases. In October 1932, Iraq entered the League of Nations with British sponsorship. Although nation building apparently had succeeded in Iraq, democratic procedures existed mostly on paper and power remained in the hands of the ruling family. After Faisal's death in 1933, his son Ghazi became king (r. 1933–1939), but in name only. General Bakr Sidqi (1890–1937) seized power and quickly ended even the pretense of democratic government. As a nationalist, the General also limited British control. After Sidqi's assassination in 1937 by a military faction opposed to his policies, Britain established another protectorate on behalf of Ghazi's son, the three year old Faisal II (r. 1939–1958). Although nominally independent, Iraq and its valuable oil reserves were again under British control.

◆ Gandhi and Indian Independence

No colony so loyally supported Great Britain in the Great War as did India, long the "jewel" of her enormous empire. In modern New Delhi, the India Gate commemorates the 1,200,000 soldiers and laborers who served the Allied cause, more than 90,000 of whom died to defeat Germany. When war began, Mohandas Gandhi (1869–1948) was a resident of South Africa coordinating a resistance campaign he had initiated to end discrimination against Indians residing there. A British educated lawyer, Gandhi deeply believed that the moral force generated by passive resistance was the best means for a subject population to oppose oppression. After a long struggle, Gandhi successfully negotiated an agreement with South African Premier Jan Smuts (1870–1950) to protect the rights of South Africa's 200,000 Indian residents. Gandhi returned in triumph to India where he at first supported the war effort of the mother country. But Indian nationalism was rising, and a radical Hindu movement inspired by Bal Gangadhar Tilak (1856–1920) opposed Britain's continued domination of India.

Gandhi's loyalty to traditional technology shows his ambivalence toward the Modern World.
Copyright © Photo Researchers, Inc.

In the face of growing opposition to its rule, Britain did not deviate from its longtime policy of cooperation with the Congress Party. Additional Indians were given administrative positions in the civil service government service, but neither Tilak's radicals nor Gandhi's moderates found such minor concessions acceptable. After the Armistice, peaceful work stoppages and deadly rioting caused great tension across the sub-continent. Especially aggravating to the British government was the stance taken by the Muslim Khilafat movement; these radicals advocated solidarity with the Ottoman Turks, Britain's former opponent in the World War. When the British parliament passed the Rowlatt Acts in 1919 allowing trials of political cases in India without juries, lawyers or appeals, the Khilafat joined the Indian National Congress Party in calling for a nationwide strike (*hartal*). Violence escalated on both sides despite Gandhi's calls for peaceful demonstrations. The greatest atrocity, however, was committed by British troops at Amritsar in the Punjab. On April 13, 1919, fifty native soldiers under the command of Brigadier-General Reginald Dyer (1864–1927) fired 1650 rounds into an unarmed crowd of *hartal* demonstrators; at least 379 persons died and hundreds more were injured. The carnage provided martyrs for the cause of independence, and the intensity of public demonstrations against British rule escalated.

In response, Britain attempted to broaden Indian control over local government. The Government of India Act (1919) created *dyarchy*, a dual track government that split authority between British and Indian hands. Britain retained control over executive affairs, while locally elected Indian Legislative Council managed such social matters as sanitation and education. A two-house All India Parliament was added, but its decisions were not binding on Britain's Viceroy. Gandhi convinced the Congress Party to reject these reforms and intensify the national efforts of non-cooperation (*satyagraha*) and economic boycott. His attempts to incorporate rich and poor, Hindu and Muslim alike, in the national effort to oust Britain earned him the honorific *Mahatma* (Great Soul). He crisscrossed India encouraging the development of village industry; his spinning wheel became a symbol of India's determination to be independent. But the Mahatma was powerless to stop incidents of terrorism. In 1922, after nationalists killed over twenty policemen, he called off the national campaign of civil disobedience. Nevertheless, he was imprisoned by the British, the first of four jail sentences he endured in his battle for Indian freedom.

The Khilafat movement collapsed in 1924 when the Ottoman Empire disappeared, but Muslim nationalism continued to grow. In 1925 an attempt to set up an independent Muslim kingdom in Madras province was decisively crushed by the British: dozens of arrested Muslim leaders were so badly beaten that they died before reaching the jail.

Great Britain's refusal even to discuss the issue of independence provoked a series of national strikes in 1928. By 1930 Gandhi, now ably seconded by Jawaharlal Nehru (1889–1964), felt strong enough to proclaim another nationwide civil disobedience campaign. The centerpiece of this effort was a twenty-four day, 341-mile "march to the sea" to extract salt, a vital commodity taxed by the British. Gandhi's simple plan to undermine the tax system incensed British politicians. Jailed once more in May 1930, Gandhi had to be released from prison in January to negotiate a settlement with the Viceroy. He traveled to London in September 1931 to attend a Roundtable Conference on responsible government and minority rights.

The Statute of Westminster (1931) changed the British Empire into a British Commonwealth. The *Dominions* of the old Empire—Canada, Australia, South Africa, and New Zealand—were given true autonomy. No act passed by Parliament in London could become law in a Dominion until approved by its own parliament, and acts passed by Dominion parliaments did not have to be approved by London. But these measures did not affect India as long as it remained a *colony*. Gandhi's hope for dominion status for India went unfulfilled. On his return to India the Mahatma was jailed once more under the provisions of the Rowlatt Acts and this time he pledged to "fast unto death" on behalf of freedom and against the exploitation of India's "untouchables." The intensity of public response to his fast caused the Congress and the British government to reach a compromise ending the segregation of the untouchables in the electorate, and Gandhi broke off his fast.

Britain approved further reforms in 1935. India was divided into eleven provinces, the social powers of the regional Legislative Councils increased, and an All-Indian Federation was promised, but the Viceroyalty retained complete authority over finance, defense, and foreign affairs. Gandhi came to believe that Britain was never going to grant India true independence, and, despite his efforts, India remained a British colony until 1947.

◆ Sun Yat-sen and the Chinese Republic

On October 10, 1911, a military uprising near Wuhan, a major city on the Yangtze River, signaled the end of the Manchu Dynasty that had ruled China since the seventeenth century. The inspirational figure behind this event was a doctor named Sun Yat-sen (1866–1925) from the Chinese

Founder of the Chinese Republic.
Copyright © CORBIS/Bettmann

province of Canton still in exile after leading a failed revolt against the Manchu in 1896. This time, returning to China in triumph, Sun was elected president in December 1911. The last Chinese emperor, six-year-old Pu Yi (1906–1967), was forced to abdicate. Sun began to implement a program designed to modernize China. The *San Min Chu I,* his *Three People's Principles* of "Nationalism, Democracy and Livelihood (economic development)," aimed at giving China the will and ability to free itself from foreign exploitation. Before his program could win wide acceptance, Sun was again forced into exile by a military coup led by General Yüan Shih-k'ai (1859–1916). But Yüan quickly forfeited popular support when he tamely accepted the *Twenty One Demands* made by Japan in January 1915. His unexpected death paved the way for Sun Yat-sen to return to China in 1916. But while Sun's *Kuomintang* (Nationalist Party) dominated the lands around Canton, it never effectively controlled all of China. Independent warlords followed Yüan's example and seized most of China's northern territory. These local rulers cooperated with Japan, collected taxes, raised private armies, and ignored Sun's republic. Although Sun's government actually entered the Great War on the side of the Allies in 1917, its capabilities were limited, and its contributions were negligible.

Sun and other Chinese leaders expected the Versailles negotiators to restore the German terri-tories in China seized by Japan during the Great War. They also hoped for an end to the extra-territorial privileges enjoyed by foreigners during a century of imperial exploitation. When the peace negotiators ignored these issues, and Japan showed no sign of yielding its gains, a wildfire of nationalistic enthusiasm swept China as thousands of university students and tobacco, cotton, and flour workers joined in what became known as the May Fourth Movement (1919) to con-demn foreign exploitation, set up a boycott of Japanese goods, and make it impossible for China's delegation to sign the completed Treaty of Versailles. China felt itself a nation as never before.

Sun Yat-sen always believed that until China developed a national consciousness, it would remain prey to foreign exploitation. When the Chinese Communist Party was organized in Shang-hai (July 1921), it too appealed to patriotic feeling. President Sun admired the example of the Russian Revolution, and agreed that eliminating imperialism and increasing the wealth of the masses would benefit China. During the 1920s his Kuomintang worked with the Communists, accepted help from the Soviet Union, and welcomed Russian advisors as China struggled to end its subordination to modern states. When Sun died of cancer in 1925, he left a still incompletely uni-fied China.

The Great War was a catastrophe for Europe. Before 1914 the world was dominated by the eco-nomic, imperial, and intellectual vitality of the Earth's second smallest continent. After the horror of trench warfare, that age of privilege and power came to an end. The cost of the war must be measured not only in the deaths of millions of men, women, and children, and the loss of billions of dollars, but also in the loss of European prestige. The Versailles settlement further fragmented an imperial system already in disarray, even though the winning Great Powers not only held on to their empires but had them briefly enlarged by the mandates they assumed in Africa and the Mid-dle East. Still, it was a greatly weakened Europe that faced the arduous task of reconstruction after the Great War. The next chapter looks at the efforts of winners and loser alike to deal with the economic devastation and political upheaval of the Great War and its aftermath.

◆ Notes

1. *Speech to the North German Regatta Association, 1901* in C. Gauss, *The German Kaiser as Shown in His Public Utterances* (New York: Charles Scribner's Sons, 1915), 181–183.

2. Marvin Perry et al, *Sources of the Western Tradition,* 4th edition (Boston: Houghton Mif-flin Company, 1999), 295.

3. U. S. Department of State, *The Treaty of Versailles and After; Annotations of the Text of the Treaty* (Washington, DC, 1947), 413.

8

Dictatorship and Democracy:
The Inter-War Years

European civilization was severely damaged—psychologically as well as physically—by the Great War. Ten million soldiers were killed, but the peace treaties failed to achieve long-term stability. The new ideologies of Communism and Fascism offered themselves as fresh alternatives to exhausted peoples whose trust in government had been buried in the mud of the Western trenches and frozen in the snows of the East. Challenging the faith in capitalism, democracy, and progress that had previously defined *Modern* society, these new ideologies proposed to remake every element of human society from the family to the factory, from the nation to the state.

In characterizing these regimes, historians and political scientists use the terms *authoritarianism, dictatorship,* and *totalitarianism.* Authoritarianism can best be understood by contrasting it with liberalism. A liberal constitution protects its citizens' freedom by limiting the power of the government to interfere in people's lives through a combination of checks and balances between the branches of government and written guarantees of basic civil rights. An authoritarian constitution protects the authority of the state by limiting the political freedom of the citizens. While an authoritarian government restricts the citizens' freedom of expression, it does not generally interfere with their private life. A dictatorship is an extra-constitutional government; that is, it works outside the limits put upon any government by its constitution. Dictatorships do not have to be created by force: Hitler and Mussolini were voted dictatorial powers by their legislatures. Traditionally, dictatorships are authoritarian rather than liberal: dictators restrict the freedom of the citizenry in order to preserve their own power. The word totalitarian was invented to describe a new type of dictatorship that emerged in Europe after World War I. In a totalitarian regime, all aspects of life are subordinated to the goals of the leadership. While an authoritarian regime works through and with intermediate agencies (army, church, social elite), totalitarian regimes see these intermediate agencies as rivals and seek to eliminate them (or at least destroy their capacity for independent action). Instead of using these intermediaries, totalitarian regimes rely on mass indoctrination and institutional terror to directly control the population's economic, political, social, and intellectual life in the service of some overriding ideology.

Real life governments rarely fit precisely into categories drawn up by academic analysts. At the end of World War I, with European confidence shattered and older methods of governance discredited, both authoritarian and totalitarian dictatorships (as well as regimes with some features of each) arose in some European states with amazing speed and threatened the liberal constitutions of others. Nations such as China and Japan that had no liberal traditions fell victim to such regimes as well. This chapter looks at the growth of the dictatorial threat in the two decades following World War I.

Russia

◆ Origins of the Russian Revolution

Tsar Nicholas II (r. 1894–1917) began his reign by blundering into a disastrous war with Japan (Russo-Japanese War, 1904–1905). The humiliating defeat of Russia's army and navy did not convince Nicholas II of the need to further modernize his empire. Nor did "Bloody Sunday" (January 20, 1905). On that day a procession of workers in St. Petersburg, professing loyalty to the Tsar but petitioning for a Constituent Assembly and an eight hour work day, was fired upon by palace troops. Over 130 demonstrators were killed and hundreds more injured. After the crew of the battleship *Potemkin* mutinied, a general strike brought the nation to a halt. On October 30, Nicholas II reluctantly issued a constitution allowing the election of a representative assembly (called a *Duma*), but disagreements among the reformers allowed the Tsar to change the electoral procedures to ensure a governmental majority. The *Duma* met only to discover it had no power.

In 1914, Russia found itself even less well prepared for modern warfare than did the other Great Powers. The Tsar's best trained forces were decimated in the great battles of Tannenberg and the Masurian Lakes (August-September 1914). Changing the name of the capital from the German-sounding St. Petersburg to the Russian Petrograd in 1914 did little for morale and less for the war effort. In September 1915, the Tsar himself took command in the field in a vain effort to rally his armies, leaving Empress Alexandra (1872–1918) behind as regent. Alexandra, however, further tarnished the prestige of the monarchy by permitting Gregori Rasputin (1872–1916), a debauched Siberian monk, to influence her political decisions. She listened to Rasputin because she believed he could heal hemophiliac Prince Alexei (1904–1918), the heir to the throne. Russian nobles murdered Rasputin in December 1916, but the monarchy was already beyond saving.

◆ The Revolutions of 1917

Since August 1914 the Russians had fought valiantly and suffered more than five million casualties, but their leadership was so inept that by the winter of 1917 city dwellers were starving. As strikes and bread riots paralyzed Petrograd, troops were called out on March 8 to disperse the demonstrators. Instead, the troops refused to follow orders and joined in the protests. Four days later the *Duma* rejected the Tsar's order to disband and appointed a Provisional Government led by Prince Lvov (1861–1925). The new government immediately issued a general amnesty for political and religious prisoners and a declaration calling for equality under the law, universal suffrage, a secret ballot, the right to strike, and freedom of speech and the press.

On March 15, Nicholas II abdicated the throne; by March 20, he and his family were under arrest. So unstable was the political situation that Lvov's authority was soon under attack from a quickly organized Marxist Council (*Soviet*) of Workers', Peasants' and Soldiers' Deputies. This Petrograd Soviet was replicated in cities across Russia. Each Soviet organized militias, distributed confiscated food supplies, and spread the ideology of "scientific socialism" in its local newspapers. As peasants across the nation seized land and soldiers refused to fight, Russia seemed about to collapse. Army Order # 1, issued by the Petrograd Soviet on March 14, 1917, only made matters worse. It called for political elections within military units, ordered the soldiery to wrest control from their officers and obey only those Provisional Government measures that did not "conflict with the orders and resolutions of the Soviet."[1]

Into this chaos a Russian exile calling himself Lenin arrived at the Finland Station in Petrograd on April 16. Lenin, born Vladimir Ilyich Ulyanov (1870–1924), was a sixteen-year-old law stu-

GREGORI YEFIMOVICH RASPUTIN (1872–1916)

Advisor to the Tsarina: mystic or charlatan?
Copyright © CORBIS/Hulton-Deutsch Collection

Gregori Yefimovich Rasputin was born into a Siberian peasant family some time in 1872. Known for his debauched habits since early adolescence (*Rasputin* means "debauched one"), he had a religious conversion at 18, and for a time prepared to become a monk. He failed in that goal, but he remained deeply religious, albeit in an unorthodox fashion. Married at 19, he left his struggling wife and four children to make pilgrimages to Jerusalem and to Mount Athos in Greece. He gained the reputation of being a *starets* (holy man) in the Russian tradition of wandering preachers and faith healers.

Rasputin arrived in St. Petersburg in 1903. He soon made influential friends among the aristocracy who saw its own romantic view of the Russian peasantry confirmed in Rasputin's illiteracy and coarse manners. His mysticism convinced a confidant of the Empress Alexandra that he was a true man of God, and the *starets* was brought to royal attention in 1908. Alexei, the heir to the throne, was a hemophiliac. Rasputin was able to use his hypnotic powers to ease the boy's suffering. The grateful Empress became his devoted follower, and Rasputin exercised great influence over her and her indulgent husband, Nicholas.

Rasputin led a double life in the capital. The Empress, convinced of his sanctity, refused to hear any criticism of his very disorderly personal life. Rasputin became a ruthless power broker who used his influence to control government appointments. Yet Rasputin often gave good advice, decrying the foolishness of the government's longstanding policy of persecuting its Jewish subjects, and warning that a general European war could end the Romanov dynasty.

The outbreak of the First World War in 1914 increased Rasputin's power. When Nicholas II joined his troops at the front in 1915, he left the Empress and Rasputin in charge in the civilian government. Rasputin's nomination of a suspected German spy as both foreign minister and prime minister was a governmental catastrophe. With Russia losing the war, and confidence in the government in decline among all classes of society, a group of conservative politicians and noblemen decided to end the baleful influence of the *starets*. Rasputin was poisoned, shot, beaten, and ultimately drowned sometime during the night of December 30, 1916. His death devastated Alexandra, but his murder came too late to save the monarchy. The entire imperial family followed Rasputin to the grave in 1918.

dent at Simbrisk Academy when his older brother Alexander was hanged for plotting against the life of Tsar Alexander III. His brother's death radicalized the young student, and he embraced the revolutionary socialism of Karl Marx. In 1895 Lenin supported striking workers in St. Petersburg and was sentenced to a three-year term in a Siberian prison. In 1900 he left Russia for an exile in Western Europe spent organizing the militant wing of Russia's Social Democrats. In 1903, during the second Congress of the Social Democratic Party meeting in exile, Lenin's supporters won a vote on a minor organizational matter. From then on they called themselves the *Bolsheviks* (majority). The defeated more democratic wing became known as the *Mensheviks* (minority).

Except for one secret visit in 1905, Lenin had not revisited his homeland for seventeen years. But when the Tsar abdicated, German agents decided that if they returned this revolutionary thinker to Russia he might further weaken resistance to their armies, and so they sent his train on to Petrograd. For the next few months, events in Russia seemed to prove Germany's views correct. As casualties mounted and privation increased, Lenin's calls for "Bread, Peace and Land," factories controlled by workers, "abolition of the police, the army, [and] the bureaucracy," and "all power to the Soviets"[2] brought the Bolsheviks ever-increasing popularity. But a failed Bolshevik coup attempt in July forced Lenin into temporary refuge in Finland.

Immediately afterwards, on July 21, Alexander Kerensky (1881–1970) became Prime Minister of Russia. The new assaults he authorized against German lines fared no better than before. Most Russians detested the war, and the failure of the government's summer offensive only made matters worse. In August, factory workers in Moscow went on strike, calling for an immediate end to the war. The weakness of Kerensky's government gave the Bolsheviks a second opportunity to seize power. In October, Leon Trotsky (1879–1940), recently returned from exile in the Bronx, New York City, became Chairman of the Petrograd Soviet, and used it to further Lenin's goal.

On the night of November 6–7, the Bolsheviks took possession of bridges and communication facilities in Petrograd. In the morning, a Bolshevik assault on the Winter Palace of the Tsar routed Kerensky's supporters and sent him into exile. On November 9, Lenin was installed as Chairman of the Council of People's Commissars by action of the All-Russian Congress of Soviets. The Bolsheviks controlled Petrograd, but German troops were still on Russian soil, and opposition to the Bolsheviks was spreading. Lenin would spend the rest of his life consolidating his party's control over Russia.

◆ Peace with Germany and Civil War

By the end of November 1917 Lenin's "War Communism," a program inspired in large measure by Erich von Ludendorff's total mobilization of German resources, was instituted in Russia. Banks, landed estates, and most industries were nationalized. Food supplies were requisitioned from unwilling peasants to feed the starving urban populations. Opposition newspapers were closed. All military operations against Germany were ended even before an armistice was negotiated on December 5. But the Bolsheviks were still a minority party, and on November 25 elections previously scheduled by the ousted Kerensky were held. Lenin and his followers polled 9.8 million votes, a quarter of the ballots, giving them only 175 seats in the new Constituent Assembly. Nationalist parties in the non-Russian states did almost as well, polling 7.6 million votes, but the largest number of votes (17 million) and seats (370) went to the peasant dominated Social Revolutionary Party. At the opening of Assembly's first session on January 18, 1918, Lenin declared that Russia's "most advanced elements" had favored the Bolsheviks and used military force to prevent opposition delegates from taking their seats. Lenin's opponents began to raise their own armies. By May 1918 a civil war had begun.

Even before that civil war began, the Bolsheviks had delivered on their pledge to end Russia's war with Germany. The *Treaty of Brest-Litovsk* (March 3, 1918) transformed the western border-lands of the Russian Empire: Poland, the Baltic States (Latvia, Lithuania, and Estonia), Ukraine, Finland, and the Caucasus were now independent in name and under German control in reality. Although monetary compensation to Germany was limited to only $1.5 billion, the Russian Empire lost seventy percent of its coal and iron resources, a quarter of its cultivated land, and a third of its population. Lenin won approval from his assembly only by threatening to resign. Committed Marxists like Lenin easily accepted territorial losses that they believed were only temporary. They believed working class anger was about to engulf capitalist societies everywhere. International borders would have no significance in a proletarian world. Staking a claim to lead that new, proletarian world, Lenin's party dropped the strictly Russian *Bolshevik* label in favor of the more internationally recognized designation of the Communist Party.

Many different groups opposed Lenin's regime, but their own rivalries prevented them from cooperating with each other during the civil war. Among Lenin's opponents were the Mensheviks, troops led by officers still loyal to the Tsar, and independence-seeking ethnic groups such as the Cossacks, Estonians, and Asian tribesman. The Allied Powers, angered at the defection of Russia from the war with Germany, supported "White" counter-revolutionary forces against the Communist "Reds" whenever they could. British Prime Minister Lloyd George even dispatched an expeditionary force to keep 60,000 tons of military materials stored in the ports of Murmansk and Archangel from being used by Lenin. During the summer of 1918, another British force landed in Georgia in southern Russia. Its supposed role was to guard against Turkish assaults, but it really attempted to provide an opportunity for an anti-Leninist. French units in Odessa supported a rival Russian government established by White armies in the Ukraine, while a portion of Russia's Pacific coastline was attacked by a joint American-Japanese-British expedition. These Allied interventions were naturally resented by the Communists.

In order to remove any symbol that might unite his opponents against him, Lenin approved the execution of the imprisoned Tsar Nicholas and his family (July 1918). To fight the civil war from a central location, he transferred the Russian capital from Petrograd to Moscow. To create an army as disciplined ideologically as it was militarily, he named Trotsky Commissar of War. By the end of 1918, Trotsky commanded a mobile army of over half a million men and had commissioned 50,000 former Tsarist officers willing to fight. But Trotsky attached political officers to every unit to ensure that every soldier toed the Bolshevik party line. Nearly ten million people died in three years of civil war, but, in the end, the Red Army was victorious. Now the Bolsheviks faced the much greater task of building the world's first socialist state.

◆ Lenin's Russia

Indeed, the fate of the Russian Revolution in a war-ravaged land was far from clear. Nature itself seemed to turn against the Communist regime when a severe drought in 1920–1921 brought death from starvation to some three million Russians, while millions more survived only with aid from the Red Cross, the League of Nations, and the United States. The rigors of War Communism had reduced agricultural production to only a third of pre-war levels while industrial production was only 13 percent of former output. By March 1921, economic deprivation was so severe that the socialist sailors of the Kronstadt Naval Base in the Gulf of Finland rose against Lenin's government. The mutiny lasted for sixteen days before it was crushed by loyal forces.

Lenin responded to the economic crisis by instituting a New Economic Policy (NEP) in 1921. The NEP permitted partial capitalism on the grounds that Russia was not yet ready for full socialism. Peasants were permitted to own land, pay taxes in kind (produce), and sell the bulk of their crops on the open market. Banks, transportation, and major industry remained under state control, but individual enterprise and internal trade were encouraged. As the profit motive was reintroduced, domestic conditions improved, exports soared, and a circulating currency based on gold was introduced. By 1928, the nation regained pre-war 1914 economic levels.

Lenin proved to be just as pragmatic in the international arena. The Bolsheviks had created the Communist Third International (COMINTERN) in 1919 "to carry into effect the revolution of the proletariat" worldwide. Yet Lenin made no attempt to recapture the five states (Lithuania, Latvia, Estonia, Finland, and Poland) that had declared their independence from Russia and signed trade agreements with capitalist Great Britain and Germany. Lenin decided Russia needed investment capital more than it needed world revolution.

Despite his pragmatic approach to "socialist" government, Lenin was not about to tolerate ideological opposition at home. In December 1917 he had approved the creation of the *CHEKA* (named for the Russian initials of the first two words in its official name, the "Extraordinary Commission to Fight Counter-Revolution"), the first of a series of political police agencies designed to eliminate the sources of dissent. Lenin gave the CHEKA a mandate to detain all "saboteurs, strikers" and "counter-revolutionaries" without due process, and confiscate their property and their ration cards. By July 1918 all other political parties were outlawed. The Kronstadt mutiny demonstrated to Lenin that even revolutionaries could not always be trusted. As a result, he ruthlessly ordered rival socialist thinkers into prison, exile, or the grave. The party itself was led by the Politburo, an executive council dominated by Lenin, the hero of the Revolution. It was Lenin who first created the aura of infallibility, the "cult of personality" that surrounds totalitarian leaders. He was the first totalitarian dictator.

Beginning in 1922, Russia's nationalities were brought under the federal Union of Soviet Socialist Republics (USSR). In theory, over fifty ethnic groups and a hundred different linguistic families were linked in perfect equality. In practice, however, the Russian Republic became as dominant culturally as the Communist Party was politically.

◆ The Triumph of Stalin

Five days after Lenin's death on January 21, 1924, from a massive stroke, a stricken nation renamed the city of Petrograd "Leningrad" in honor of its fallen leader. Settling the question of who would succeed him took three years. Lenin had been ill for two years before his death, and during those years a power struggle had broken out between Commissioner of War Trotsky and Josef Stalin (1879–1953), Secretary-General of the Party. Trotsky's enormous contribution to the Communist victory in the civil war made him the immediate favorite (as he had been Lenin's), but Stalin proved to be the better politician. As Party Secretary, Stalin set the agenda for meetings, dispensed patronage, and led the commission that drafted the Soviet Constitution of 1924. He solidified his political base with patronage appointments, even naming many supporters of Trotsky to ambassadorial positions that took them outside the country.

In 1924 Trotsky called on the Russian Communist Party to spread "permanent revolution" across the globe. Stalin suggested that Russia was obligated to build "Socialism in one country" before exporting it abroad. He added that the NEP, despite its accommodation with capitalism, was a perfectly proper Leninist means to accomplish this end. Stalin maintained that Trotsky and the other "left deviationists" who opposed the NEP and called for revolution actually hindered the triumph of socialism by betraying Lenin's legacy. By the Fifteenth Party Congress in 1927, Stalin was able to have Trotsky expelled from the party and ordered into internal exile. Less than

Lenin and Stalin: creators of Soviet totalitarianism.
Copyright © Culver Pictures

two years later, in January 1929, Trotsky was exiled from the USSR, now completely under Stalin's control. Trotsky spent the rest of his life advocating the overthrow of capitalism, writing his version of Russia's Revolution, and wondering where he went wrong. He was assassinated by a Stalinist agent in Mexico City in August 1940.

◆   Stalin's Russia

The son of a shoemaker, Josef Djugashvili, known to the world by his revolutionary alias of *Stalin* ("steel"), was born in Georgia, a once independent state annexed by Russia in the eighteenth century. Groomed by his mother to be a priest, Stalin was expelled from a seminary in 1899 for advocating Marxist revolution, but he continued to serve the socialist cause as a bank robber, editor of the newspaper *Pravda* (1917), and Commissar of Nationalities. By 1922 he was Party Secretary.

Leader of the Soviet Union for a quarter century, he transformed Russia into a modern, industrial state. In the process, he eliminated all those who opposed his plans. After exiling Trotsky, Stalin immediately adopted his former rival's proposals to dump the NEP and centralize the Russian economy. Massive state planning through successive Five-Year Plans (1928, 1933, 1938) soon replaced the limited private enterprise of the NEP. A central state agency, called *Gosplan*, drew up industrial plans and imposed them on the nation without regard to the suffering they caused. Stalin's goal was a self-sufficient Russia, fully armed and possessing the latest technology, capable of out-producing the capitalist powers.

At first, central planning led to extraordinary gains in steel, coal, chemical, electricity, and oil production. By 1938 the USSR led the world in the production of tractors and locomotives, and its reconstructed railroad system carried five times the freight of 1913. Russia had the world's largest automobile plant and biggest electricity generating station. As befit the new "Soviet Man," individual workers performed prodigies of labor. After Alexei Stakharov (d. 1977) mined 102 tons of coal in a single shift in 1935, he was named a "Hero of Socialist Labor." Every subsequent August 30 was celebrated as National Coal Miner's Day in his honor. All was not revolutionary heroism, however: the White Sea Canal and the Kotlas-Vorkuta and Norylsk Railways were built almost entirely by forced labor from the growing number of political prisoners.

Yet industrial growth was only one of the goals of the Five-Year Plans. The *Gosplan* of 1928 cautiously suggested that a fifth of all farmland should become state-owned, a seemingly unlikely goal in a nation where 25 million families held land by permission of Lenin's NEP. But Stalin would not settle for anything less than 100 percent collectivization. In 1929 he ordered farmers to surrender all privately owned lands, livestock, and equipment to the local collective farm. The USSR's most efficient farmers, members of the *kulak* class, had prospered under the NEP and violently opposed Stalin's policies. Armed soldiers and Communist Party officials were dispatched to the countryside to evict them. State sponsored class war soon engulfed the nation as the kulaks burnt their crops, slaughtered their animals, and poisoned their lands. More than seven million people died in the resulting famine while Stalin did nothing to alleviate their suffering.

Implementing the Five-Year Plans totally altered Soviet society. By 1939, ninety-six percent of the farmland had been reorganized into a quarter of a million collective farms. Millions of people deserted the land during the 1930s, and by 1940 a third of Russian citizens lived in bleak and overcrowded cities. New industrial complexes east of the Ural Mountains brought mass production techniques and electricity into the heart of Asia. Central planning allowed more Russians to live better than ever before. They did not live nearly as well as their capitalist counterparts, however, due to Stalin's unyielding emphasis on heavy industry and military spending over consumer goods. Housing was in such short supply that most families crowded into one room, sharing kitchens and toilets with their neighbors. On the other hand, massive efforts to create an educated workforce led to a decline in illiteracy from 50 to 20 per cent by 1940, and higher education was opened up to women as well as men. By 1950, three-quarters of all the doctors in the Soviet Union were women.

Nothing and no one was allowed to deviate from the Party line. In 1929 religious organizations were forbidden to engage in any function except worship, eliminating all religious instruction outside the home. Many churches were closed outright or turned over to government use.

Even loyal party members were not allowed to speak their minds. On December 1, 1934, the popular party boss of Leningrad, Sergey Kirov (1886–1934), was assassinated. Without any evidence that Kirov disagreed with his policies, Stalin had over a hundred of Kirov's supporters executed. The years between 1934 and 1938 became known as the time of the "Great Purges." During these four years, Stalin ordered a series of massive arrests and show trials to eliminate any possible opposition. Millions of party members, from the highest officials to the lowest rank and file were arrested by the secret police, now called the NKVD (the "People's Commissariat of Internal Affairs," renamed the KGB, "Committee for State Security," in 1953). A climate of fear gripped the national bureaucracy, trust became impossible, and survival possible only if one followed Stalin's ever-shifting party line. Sometimes even slavish obedience was not enough to ensure survival. All the remaining "Old Bolsheviks" who had worked with Lenin in 1917 were killed, along with fifty of the seventy-one members of the Central Committee of 1934. A dozen ambassadors, two Commissars of Foreign Relations, ninety percent of trade union officials, the police who collected evidence, the judges at the trials, and countless others became victims of Stalin's paranoia. The purges were then extended to the Red Army, which Stalin knew had been built by Trotsky; eighty percent of all officers above the rank of captain were replaced. When the "Great Purges" ended in 1938, fully five percent of Russia's population (over eight million citizens) was in prison labor camps called *gulags* scattered across the vast Soviet federation. Stalin reigned as totalitarian dictator over a nation and party from which all potential rivals had been eliminated.

Fascism in Italy

In 1915, Italy transferred its allegiance to the Allied side in World War I in return for promises of territorial gain. At a cost of 650,000 dead and a million wounded, it won a place at the peace conference only to have its claims largely ignored. The demobilization of its soldiers destabilized its already weak economy. In 1919 Italy endured 1600 strikes, two million unemployed, and general disillusionment regarding its future. It would become the first European State to adopt a Fascist form of government.

Benito Mussolini (1883–1945), the son of a blacksmith, rose to become a leading Socialist editor in the years immediately before World War I. In 1915 he broke with the Socialist's antiwar stance and endorsed Italy's entrance into the war, eventually serving in the army himself. In March 1919 Mussolini forged a political party out of returned soldiers as disgruntled and as undirected as himself. He named his group the *Fasci di Combattimento*, or *Fascisti*, after the *Fasces*, a bundle of rods tied around an ax used in ancient Rome as a symbol of authority. The *Fascisti* opposed the monarchy, the Church, and socialism, and the treaties that shortchanged Italy's wartime efforts.

Numbering only 30,000 members in 1920, Fascist Party rolls surged to 100,000 within a year as Italy's traditional political parties blamed each other for the country's problems instead of trying to solve them. In the May 1921 elections, the Fascists won five seats in the legislature. Mussolini promised voters he would regain respect for Italy, but his party seemed more concerned with terrorizing its opponents, beating up opposition leaders, and destroying printing presses. By 1922, with the government in total disarray and the Cabinet resigning, Mussolini reached for power. In October, he ordered his followers to "March on Rome" and demand that he be named Prime Minister. Thousands of Fascists converged on the capital from all over Italy. Even though the Fascists held fewer than ten percent of the seats in Parliament, Mussolini's bluff succeeded. King Victor Emmanuel III (r. 1900–1946) named Mussolini Prime Minister of Italy.

At first Mussolini led a coalition government of Fascists and nationalists, but he quickly maneuvered to obtain dictatorial powers. He became *Il Duce* (the Leader), and his Fascist militia was quickly transformed into a National Guard. Dissenters were slowly expelled from his cabinet as his popularity grew. Still uncertain of public support, the Fascists enacted the Acerbo Law (1923) that virtually ended democracy in Italy. Under its provisions, the party that received 25 percent of the vote in the 1924 elections would receive two-thirds of the seats in Parliament. Mussolini professed shock when his Fascist candidates actually won 65 percent of the vote. The results

To symbolize his commitment to autarky, Mussolini poses on a threshing platform in 1938.
Copyright © Archive Photos

so emboldened him that he permitted Fascist thugs to murder Giacomo Matteotti (1885–1924), leader of the moderate wing of the Italian socialist movement. Matteotti's murder on June 10 ended real political opposition to Mussolini's dictatorship. It took several years before the complete mechanisms of Fascist authority could be implemented, but by 1928 the only choice voters had was to approve or disapprove a single slate of candidates named by the Fascist Grand Council, a body led by Mussolini.

In the meantime, press censorship, the creation of a secret police (the *OVRA*), the exiling of political opponents, and the banning of non-Fascist trade unions proceeded systematically. Granted the right to govern by decree in 1926, Mussolini's proudest creation was the Corporate State that placed the capitalist economy under governmental direction. First, a tariff to protect small Italian industries was enacted. Then the nation was divided into large economic segments with separate corporations called *Syndicates* that represented management and workers in each industry. Strikes were prohibited, and any disputes between labor and owners were settled by the Minister of Corporations, Benito Mussolini. In dealing with agriculture, *Il Duce* proclaimed the "Battle of Wheat." He ordered swamps drained to create productive farmland and increased farm production. Urban unemployment was reduced with a large program of public works, the centerpiece of which was the construction of Rome's huge memorial to King Victor Emmanuel I. Unlike prior Italian rulers, *Il Duce* attacked and virtually destroyed both the Sicilian and Neapolitan Mafias.

Perhaps the most important of Mussolini's initiatives was to end sixty years of national conflict with the Roman Catholic Church. Ever since Italian forces occupied Rome and seized Church lands in 1870, animosity between the two powers had made Italy the most anti-clerical government in Europe. In retaliation, successive popes had instructed good Catholics not to give their allegiance to the secular state. In order to unify his nation, Mussolini negotiated the *Lateran Treaty* with Pope Pius XI (r. 1922–1939) in 1929. The pact recognized an independent Vatican City under papal control and compensated the Papacy for its lost territory. Roman Catholicism became the official faith of Italy, religion was taught in the public schools, and Catholic organizations were exempt from Fascist controls. In return, Mussolini's government won formal recognition from the Papacy, and Catholics were permitted to join the Fascist Party. Italians believed their nation was finally becoming a European Great Power.

Germany

◆ Weimar Germany, 1919–1929

Despite opposition from extremists at both ends of the political spectrum, a German constitution establishing a federal republic was adopted in the city of Weimar on July 31, 1919. It provided for a head of state (a president) to be elected by universal suffrage. The chancellor, or head of government, would be the leader of the party (or coalition of parties) holding a majority of seats in the legislature. Under the leadership of its first president, Friedrich Ebert (1871–1925), Germany began the slow process of reconstruction. The democratic aspirations of the Weimar Republic pleased foreign leaders like Woodrow Wilson, but they were less than attractive to Germans. Angry soldiers, already convinced they had been "sold out" by the Republic that signed the Versailles Treaty, returned to a bankrupt nation. Unemployed, they often united in quasi-military organizations (*Freikorps*) and engaged in acts of vandalism.

But nothing posed as great a threat to the democratic experiment as Germany's war debt. Economists like John Maynard Keynes argued that the reparations imposed on Germany were unreasonable, but the Allies, led by France, resisted all efforts to reduce them. Ebert's government made valiant efforts to repay the levies, until, plagued by inflation, labor unrest, and domestic violence, Germany defaulted on the annual reparations installment due in 1922. Rather than negotiate an extension, France decided to occupy the Ruhr and confiscate the region's industrial output in lieu of cash. The Weimar government encouraged German workers in the Ruhr to strike rather than produce for the French and printed enormous amounts of money to pay the strikers. Inflation soared out of control, and the stability of the republic was further undermined when several government officials were assassinated. By December 1923, the *Reichsmark*, once valued at four to the dollar, had become valueless at four trillion to the dollar. Savings accounts were wiped out, and workers received several raises each day just to keep up with the accelerating inflation. It took a suitcase full of money to buy a loaf of bread, and it became cheaper to burn money than to use it to buy fuel.

The economic crisis gave Adolf Hitler (1889–1945) his first chance at political power. The son of an Austrian customs official, Hitler arrived in Germany just as World War I was getting underway. He enlisted in the German Army where he served with distinction, twice winning the Iron Cross. In 1919, convinced that Germany had been betrayed by its civilian leaders, Hitler joined the small German Workers' Party and rapidly transformed it into his personal power base. A mesmerizing orator and gifted propagandist, Hitler became the leader (*Der Führer*) of the National Socialist (NAZI) Party. He recruited disaffected soldiers, dressed them in brown shirts, and marched them under the symbol of the *swastika* (twisted cross). At first Hitler and his National Socialist Brown Shirt "Storm Troopers" seemed nothing more than a poor imitation of Mussolini's Fascists. In November 1923, as the economic crisis brought the nation to the verge of anarchy, Hitler announced in a Munich beer hall that a "national revolution" was underway. His planned march on Berlin in imitation of Mussolini's March on Rome was ended by the police, and Hitler was sentenced to five years in jail for treason. Serving less than a year of his sentence, Hitler used the time to draw up his own manifesto. The book he wrote, *Mein Kampf* (1925), laid out his claims that the *Treaty of Versailles* strangling Germany was the result of an international conspiracy of Jewish bankers and communists. In *Mein Kampf*, Hitler argued the Germans were a "master race" that would never achieve its destiny without room to breathe: Germany must expand eastward into Europe, absorbing the lands of the "slave" (Slavic) races. To ensure German purity, Europe had to be purged of such degenerate racial mixtures as Jews and Gypsies. Much of the book seemed to be copied straight out of Gobineau's *Inequality of the Races*.

In the hyper-inflation of the early 1920s, Germans found it cheaper to burn currency than to buy wood.
Copyright © CORBIS/Bettmann

In 1924, Ebert's new chancellor, Gustav Stresemann (1878–1929), began to reform the German economy. He introduced a new *Deutschmark,* raised taxes, reduced government costs, and ended the passive resistance in the Ruhr. Just as crucial was international recognition that an unstable Germany could undermine global economic recovery. In April 1924, the American banker Charles G. Dawes (1865–1951) issued a report on the German economy that helped Stresemann's efforts. American bankers had previously made substantial loans to the Weimar Republic, and now Germany was permitted to market its bonds to American purchasers and use the income to pay reparations to Great Britain, France, and Belgium. America's former Allies then used the money to repay the loans they had received from the United States Treasury during World War I. At the cost of increased unemployment, Germany obtained economic stability. In the elections of 1925 Stresemann's coalition increased its power, despite the death of President Ebert. The new president, seventy-seven year old Field Marshal Paul von Hindenburg (1847–1934), named Stresemann Foreign Minister and the reforms continued.

As German industrial production gradually increased in 1925, Stresemann convinced France that democracy could not survive in Germany if it could not defend its borders: France must leave the Ruhr. After France withdrew, Stresemann negotiated the *Locarno Pact* (1925) that established inviolable borders between France, Belgium, and Germany. In 1926 Germany was admitted to the League of Nations. In 1928 it was one of the signatories of the *Kellogg-Briand Pact* outlawing war. For his efforts on behalf of European peace Stresemann, like Dawes the year before, was awarded the Nobel Peace Prize. Because of the initiatives taken by these two men, the prospects of the Weimar Republic improved annually until 1929. In that year, German democracy had to endure the twin shocks of a stock market collapse and Stresemann's death. Not even a second reduction in reparation payments was sufficient to overcome these blows. The combination of economic disaster and a leadership vacuum gave Hitler his second chance to overthrow the republic.

◆ Nazi Germany

The unremitting violence of the *Schutzstaffel* (SS), the Nazi Party militia commanded by Heinrich Himmler (1900–1945), and the blatant anti-Semitism of Hitler's fiery rhetoric alienated most Germans. Consequently, the National Socialist Party remained a minor force in German politics until after the stock market crash. Then, when other German parties failed to ease the growing economic suffering, many voters turned to the Nazis. The Nazis, who held only twelve seats in the *Reichstag,* suddenly became its second largest party by winning 107 seats in the September 1930 elections. But no party wanted to align itself with Hitler, an extremist whose speeches extolled the violence of war, Aryan (Germanic) purity, and hatred of the Jews. For two years, as successive coalitions were created only to quickly fall apart, Hitler and the Nazis had no responsibility for determining national policy. During that time Germany plunged ever more deeply into the Great Depression, and by the end of 1932 over 7,000,000 German workers were unemployed. Although Hitler led the largest single party in the *Reichstag,* he was still a political pariah, but one who confidently asserted he could reverse the decline. Because every other party had failed to cope with the Depression, a reluctant President Hindenburg finally decided that Hitler must be offered the opportunity to form a governing coalition. On January 30, 1933, under the provisions of a democratic constitution he despised, Hitler legally became Chancellor of Germany.

It took the *Führer* only a few months to transform the democratic republic of Germany into a dictatorship. When a fire consumed the *Reichstag* building on February 27, Hitler blamed the Communists and persuaded President Hindenburg to issue an Emergency Decree suspending civil liberties. Assuming the opposition had been destroyed, Hitler scheduled new elections for March 5.

The Nazi Party received only 43.9 percent of the vote, but the arrest and removal of all Communist deputies allowed Hitler to control the legislature. An Enabling Act pushed through on March 23 suspended the Weimar Constitution and granted Hitler the power to rule by decree. Using its authority, Hitler created the *Gestapo* (secret police) in April. He ordered books with "alien" philosophies burnt in public (May 10) and banned all other political parties in July. His first decrees against Jews in government or university positions were issued in June. By November their rights to citizenship and the vote was revoked. Although Jews comprised less than one percent of Germany's population, the Nazis now accused them of causing all its misfortunes. After the November 1933 elections, there were only two non-Nazi deputies in a *Reichstag* of 661 members.

Opposition to Hitler became ever more difficult because he fulfilled his pledge to solve the economic crisis. Although the currency was devalued on the international market, strict government controls maintained its purchasing power at home. High taxes kept inflation low and provided the Nazis with money to fund a massive program of public works, Germany's world famous superhighways (the *autobahns*) among them. Unemployment fell by 3 million people in less than a year. All corporate profits above six percent were confiscated by the Nazis and use to fund a Four-Year Plan of economic development. Germany's rural population loved Hitler, who prohibited banks from foreclosing on family farms. Nazi bureaucrats quickly organized state sponsored monopolies for gas, rubber, and steel production. Hitler himself participated in designing a mass-produced automobile, the *Volkswagen*, or people's car. Independent labor unions were replaced with Nazi-run alternatives (the Nazi Labor Front), and though wages remained low every worker was granted a state sponsored vacation. By 1937, with unemployment ended, Germany basked in the sunshine of an economic miracle while its neighbors still lived in the shadow of the Great Depression (1929–1939). A grateful Germany proved equally willing to endorse the *Führer*'s attempts to reverse the sanctions imposed by the *Treaty of Versailles*.

Economic success made it easy for Germans to accept the cruelties of Nazi policies. In June 1934 the original leadership of the Storm Troopers was purged and eliminated during the "Night of the Long Knives" for advocating a truly socialist revolution. The death of President Hindenburg that August removed another check on the Nazis, for voters then permitted Hitler to merge the offices of president and chancellor. As Germany's sole authority, he could implement a program of state-sponsored racism directed at Jews, gypsies, and other non-Aryan elements of the population. The Nuremberg Laws (September 1935) codified the many restrictions against Jews, now defined as a separate race, and intensified persecution of them. During the 1930s over 300,000 Jews emigrated from Germany, fleeing slave labor camps such as Dachau where despised ethnic groups and homosexuals were incarcerated along with political and religious dissenters. Racial purity was the goal of the Nazis, and "Aryan" marriages were encouraged; indeed every new couple received a copy of *Mein Kampf* as a wedding present.

Pastor Martin Niemöller (1892–1984), a leading German theologian interned in Dachau for his opposition to Hitler, poignantly summarized the course of Nazi success:

> *When Hitler attacked the Jews I was not a Jew, therefore I was not concerned. And when Hitler attacked the Catholics, I was not a Catholic, and therefore, I was not concerned. And when Hitler attacked the unions and industrialists, I was not a member of the unions and I was not concerned. Then, Hitler attacked me and the Protestant church—and there was nobody left to be concerned.*[3]

On November 7, 1938, a Nazi official stationed in Paris was assassinated by a Polish Jew. The murder provided Hitler with an excuse to terrorize Germany's remaining Jewish population. On November 9, 1938, rioters acting with the approval of the Nazi government destroyed over 7,500

JOSEPH GOEBBELS (1897–1945)

Propagandist of the "Master Race."
Copyright © CORBIS/Bettmann

Paul Joseph Goebbels was the third of five children born into the family of a factory clerk in the Catholic Rhineland on October 29, 1897. He received a Ph.D. in philology from Heidelberg University in 1922. But he had suffered an attack of osteomyelitis at age seven, an operation for which had left his left leg permanently shorter than his right, rendering him unfit for military service. This was a severe social disadvantage in Germany's militaristic culture. Anti-bourgeois and anti-capitalist since his student days, Goebbels joined the socialist wing of the Nazi Party in 1924. His inability to publish his novels, which he attributed to the Jews, had made him a rabid anti-Semite even before he heard Hitler speak. Goebbels broke with the socialists in the Party and joined the followers of the so-called *Führer,* Adolf Hitler.

The small Nazi Party was still merely a Bavarian organization when Hitler gave Goebbels the task of organizing a Berlin wing in 1928. For his success, Goebbels was rewarded with the new Ministry of Propaganda after Hitler came to power in 1933. As Minister of Propaganda, Goebbels brought all newspapers, publishing, and radio under strict government control. He organized the public burning of the works of Jewish, socialist, and pacifist authors in front of the University of Berlin. He fired all Jewish musicians and banned all works by Jewish composers from concert halls and the radio. But he almost lost his place in the Nazi hierarchy over an illicit love affair. Wed in 1931, Goebbels and his wife Magda had six children, but in 1937 he began an affair with a Czech film star that lasted for over a year before Hitler put a stop to it.

The role of the Propaganda Ministry was primarily domestic while the war went Hitler's way: he preferred his victories to speak for themselves. But Goebbels did play an important part in popularizing the euthanasia program that gassed over 70,000 institutionalized mental patients by 1940 as part of Hitler's plans to "purify" the German "race." Goebbels produced the film *I Accuse* to explain the "virtues" of these "mercy" killings. He also oversaw creation of *The Wandering Jew* and *The Jew Suss,* movies that depicted Jews as subhuman, to gain support for Hitler's "Final Solution."

After the German defeat at Stalingrad, Goebbels joined those pushing for a regime of austerity and "total war." For helping to defeat an attempted coup against Hitler in July 1944, Goebbels was named Reich Plenipotentiary for Total War. Despairing of Hitler's refusal to appear at public rallies after Germany began to lose the war, Goebbels visited bombed out cities and worked hard to rally support for the Reich. To the very end, he insisted that Germany would win. His propaganda campaigns were so effective that many Germans still believed in their invincibility as Allied troops closed in on Hitler's underground bunker in April 1945. Goebbels remained loyal to the last. Following Hitler's own suicide, Goebbels poisoned his children (aged 3 to 12) before having himself and his wife shot by soldiers in the bunker on May 1, 1945.

The master of demagoguery, Hitler at a Nazi rally in 1934.
Copyright © Canadian War Museum

businesses, burned 267 synagogues, and murdered 91 Jews. 25,000 of Germany's remaining Jews were forced into slave labor camps in the wake of *Kristallnacht* ("the night of broken glass"). Hitler had transformed the Jews into a national scapegoat.

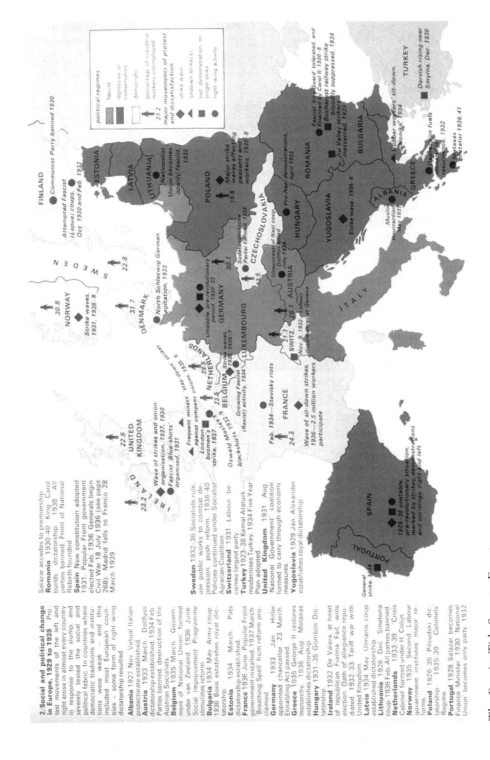

The Fascist Tide Sweeps Europe.
From *The Times Atlas of World History,* edited by Geoffrey Barraclough. Copyright © 1979 by Times Books Ltd., London

◆   Fascism in Europe

Maintaining republican institutions proved difficult for Europeans in the twenty years separating the two World Wars. The nations created in the Versailles settlement had little experience with democracy; many turned for leadership to right-wing dictators. These men promised stable governments, pledged economic reform, and denounced communists as the greatest danger to society. Militaristic governments in the Baltic States, Poland, Hungary, Romania, Bulgaria, Norway, Greece, Spain, and Portugal all reflected the spread of Fascist ideology. Just as Mussolini beguiled Italians with a vision of a revived Roman Empire, the new leaders of Eastern Europe guaranteed a restoration of past glory to the populations of their depressed lands. Nations with large peasant populations and little modernization proved quite susceptible to these appeals.

But not even an ancient democracy such as Great Britain was immune from the appeal of such thinking. In London, Sir Oswald Mosley (1896–1980) led a strong "Black Shirt" movement that caused Parliament to pass a Public Order Act (1936) banning the wearing of political uniforms. In France, Charles Maurras (1868–1952) adapted the Social Darwinist ideas of de Gobineau to his Fascist *Action Française* movement. Britain's longstanding democratic tradition allowed it to defeat any internal Fascist threat although France briefly succumbed in 1934 to a Fascist coup.

The United States and the Great Depression

◆   The Roaring Twenties

The Great War solidified the position of the United States as the world's strongest economy. Benefitting from its late entry into the conflict, America lost fewer soldiers than any of the other great powers and, as no battles were fought on American soil, suffered none of the agricultural or industrial damage inflicted on the other combatants. Yet the United States chose not to participate in the League of Nations, a choice that disillusioned internationalists but gave joy to isolationists. During the 1920s the United States largely ignored the chaos in a shattered Europe as it sought to recapture its pre-war "good life."

Recapturing that world proved to be impossible. The rapid demobilization of over two million soldiers led to unemployment and labor unrest. In 1919 a wave of 3,630 strikes involving over four million workers swept across the nation as labor attempted to regain wages and privileges lost during the wartime emergency. America's steel industry virtually closed down in September, a five-month stoppage that caused horror among business leaders and scared the Democratic Administration. Some Americans feared the strike was part of a Communist plot to export revolution to the shores of the United States. In 1919–1920 American leaders discovered that condemnation of the "Red Menace" was good politics. State militias were mobilized to repress a general work stoppage in Seattle and to crush a police strike in Boston.

In November 1919, Attorney General A. Mitchell Palmer (1872–1936) authorized a series of police raids that arrested thousands of "radicals" across the nation. In time, over 700 aliens were deported as a result of the "Red Scare." The New York Assembly even expelled five legitimately elected Socialist representatives. In Massachusetts, the judge presiding over a trial of two immigrants accused of armed robbery called the defendants, Nicola Sacco (1891–1927) and Bartolomeo Vanzetti (1888–1927), "anarchist bastards." He sentenced them to death even though the evidence against them was highly questionable. They languished in prison for seven years before their executions were finally carried out. Strident patriotism, even xenophobia, characterized the post-war period as the American Legion was created (1919), immigration restrictions

CHARLES MAURRAS (1868–1952)

Charles-Marie-Photius Maurras was born in France on April 20, 1868, into a Royalist Roman Catholic family. But, after an illness at school left him deaf, he rejected his parents' religion for the ancient Roman philosophy of Stoicism, or at least for its idea of submerging individual desires to the greater needs of the state. He moved to Paris in 1891. There he founded a group of young writers opposed to the anti-establishment modernism of contemporary French writing. Instead, they promoted a return to the Stoic classicism of French literature as it existed under the absolute monarchy of Louis XIV. Maurras' literary movement became a political cause during the trial of Captain Alfred Dreyfus, the French Jew unjustly accused of treason in 1894. In 1899, Maurras started a magazine, *L'Action Française,* devoted to what he called "integral nationalism," a theory based on the supremacy of the state over the rights of the individual. Maurras believed in the sanctity of an ethnically authentic French character: Jews, Socialists, Republicans, abstract artists, and ultramontane Catholics (those who put the Papacy before their country) were not part of it. His magazine railed against the supposed contamination of the French "race" by alien blood and praised the works of the Social Darwinist, Joseph Arthur de Gobineau. In 1908 the magazine became a daily newspaper as the official organ of the Royalist party. One of its first editorials condemned the government for daring to rehabilitate Dreyfus.

In his private life, Maurras wrote many successful poems, stories, and essays. His political ideas were mainly laid out in his *Enquiry Concerning Monarchy* (1900) and *The Future of Intelligence* (1905). Many of his supporters were Catholic, but his insistence that religious life be subordinate to the state earned him the official enmity of the Catholic Church. His books and newspaper were put on the Papal Index of banned books in 1926. During the 1930s, *Action Française,* a political movement that took its name from his newspaper, campaigned for the overthrow of the Third Republic and aligned itself with other Fascist groups. Its quasi-military youth group, the *Camelots du Roi,* smashed the storefronts of so-called "enemies" of the state, just as the Nazis had in Germany and the Fascists had in Italy. *Action Française* joined in the *coup d'état* of 1934 that briefly brought France under a right-wing dictatorship.

As Europe lurched toward World War II, Maurras continued to be a respected author and was inducted into the *Académie Française* in 1938. When Germany invaded France in 1940, he sided with the Nazis and supported Germany's puppet state in Vichy, France. Arrested by the Allies after the liberation of France in 1944, Maurras was sentenced to life imprisonment and stripped of his literary honors. Because of ill health, Maurras was released from prison in 1952. He died a few months later on November 16 in a clinic in Tours. Discredited by its alliance with the Vichy government, *Action Française* lapsed into silence.

imposed against Eastern Europeans (1924), black citizens lynched or attacked in record numbers, and the Ku Klux Klan enlisted over five million members.

Nothing so dramatically illustrates the national obsession with an imagined virtuous past as America's experiment with Prohibition. The Eighteenth Amendment to the Constitution (1919) prohibited the sale of any beverage containing more than one half of one percent alcohol. Prohibition had long been the dream of rural America, but most Americans now lived in cities, and they had no intention of giving up their right to drink. Millions of American citizens openly ignored the Constitution, and enterprising businessmen provided them with whatever drinks they wished. Al

"Scarface" Capone (1899–1947) arrived in Chicago in 1920 a penniless young man, but led a $60 million organized crime enterprise by 1927, leaving scores of dead bodies in his wake. A failed experiment, the Eighteenth Amendment was repealed in 1933.

The social scene was made more complex by the emancipation of women. Women had moved into traditionally male jobs in record numbers during World War I and had been rewarded with the ratification of the Nineteenth Amendment (1920) granting all citizens the right to vote regardless of sex. After the war, many women simply refused to return to their traditional place in society. Young women drank, smoked, danced, stayed out all night if they chose; some even spoke of divorce on demand and "free love." The uninhibited "flapper" became one of the defining figures of the decade.

Political life in the United States after 1920 was dominated by the conservative policies of the Republican Party. As Calvin Coolidge (1872–1933) put it during his presidency (1923–1929), "The business of America is business."[4] He cut the surcharge on the incomes of the wealthy, reduced the estate tax, and balanced the budget. In the election of 1928, a self-satisfied nation continued to endorse Republican rule.

◆ The Crisis of Capitalism

Herbert Hoover (1874–1964), a gifted mining engineer with a distinguished record of public service, began his presidency in 1929 in a complacent America. While the top five percent of the nation controlled a third of all income, 87 percent of Americans lived comfortably while earning less than $2,500 a year. By September 1929 the New York Stock Exchange reached all-time highs. It was the last good news of the "Roaring Twenties." In late October the market collapsed in the Great Crash. America, the economic success story of the 1920s, now led the world into a period of extended economic depression.

The Crash was not the true cause of the Great Depression (1929–1939), just the spark that set it off. Less than 1.5 percent of the American population even owned stock. The Great Depression was really the result of the accumulated economic misjudgments of a decade. American industry had been on a credit-financed expansion binge that outpaced the ability of the American consumer to consume. There was a vast inventory surplus and, after the market crashed, corporations attempted to salvage their investments by cutting labor costs, effectively eliminating workers as potential consumers. The result was a deflationary spiral: not enough purchasing power and too many goods. A similar pattern devastated American agriculture. The gradual return to production of European farms after 1919 combined with increased American investment in land and farm machinery to produce a worldwide glut of grain. Prices dropped to levels not seen in centuries. Similar disasters afflicted the producers of cotton, corn, sugar, and cocoa. High tariffs closed the American marketplace to foreign production, but made it impossible to dump surplus American goods abroad.

During the Hoover Administration (1929–1933), American investment shrank by 90 percent, industrial production fell by 50 percent, and wages by 60 percent. Banks saw their stock dividends vanish, so they curtailed personal and business loans. As consumer demand for goods vanished, unemployment soared to 25 percent nationwide and 50 percent among minority workers. Five thousand bankrupt banks cost nine million depositors their life savings. Hoover pleaded with corporations not to cut wages or lay-off workers but frightened capitalists ignored his advice. Congress approved his Reconstruction Finance Corporation to aid failing businesses, but failed to appropriate sufficient funding.

A symbol of the Great Depression: selling apples in the nation's capitol.
Copyright © CORBIS/Bettmann

In May 1931 the American Depression became an international disaster when the central bank of Austria collapsed, setting off a tidal wave of similar bankruptcies across Europe. Attempts to stem the tide by currency devaluation broke on the shoals of panic-prompted tariffs. World trade fell from $2.9 trillion in 1929 to only $1 trillion in 1933. A final German default in 1932 left over $25 billion in war debt unpaid. Across the globe over 50 million industrial workers were unemployed. Several Eastern European nations became so impoverished they reverted to barter. Only the Soviet Union, insulated from the capitalist world by its government-controlled socialist economy, seemed immune from the spreading economic plague.

◆ The New Deal

The American presidential election of 1932 occurred in an atmosphere of despair and anger. Hoover, once the most admired man in America, was now its whipping boy. Democratic candidate Franklin Delano Roosevelt (1882–1945), Governor of New York, promised a "New Deal" for the "forgotten" American if he were elected. He was. His Inaugural Address assured a traumatized nation that the "only thing we have to fear is fear itself." His pledge to "wage war" on the Depression rekindled hope.

Roosevelt's New Deal began in piecemeal experimentation. He arrived in Washington without a clear plan of action, but with a conviction that he must "try something" to relieve the pain of the Depression. He declared a "bank holiday" while national reforms were enacted to safeguard bank deposits though the Federal Deposit Insurance Program (FDIC), and began a series of radio "fireside chats" to explain his program to the American public. When the banks reopened, more funds came in than went out. Stocks began their slow climb out of the gutter. During the first three months of his presidency, Roosevelt proposed sixteen major measures, and a willing Congress enacted them all. This legislation attempted to raise price levels, restore purchasing power, and provide relief to the unemployed. Expert advisors flocked to Washington to staff the "alphabet agencies" established by the new laws: the AAA (Agricultural Adjustment Administration), CCC (Civilian Conservation Corps), CWA (Civil Works Administration), and TVA (Tennessee Valley

Crippled by polio, President Roosevelt nevertheless symbolized America's optimistic spirit.
Copyright © AP/Wide World Photos

Authority). Dozens of programs were created to curb capitalist excess and achieve fairer competition. As the New Deal matured, reforms included stock market regulation (SEC), collective bargaining for unions (NLRB), social security (SSA), minimum wage and maximum hour standards (FEPC), and massive public works spending (WPA). Government action was no longer resented but considered a necessary ingredient of modern society. "Liberalism" originally stood for the idea that individuals fared best when the government kept its hand off their freedoms and out of their pockets. Under Roosevelt's New Deal a "New Liberalism" came to mean using the government's power to better individual lives.

Not surprisingly, Roosevelt was overwhelmingly reelected in 1936. But he never approached dictatorial power. When Roosevelt suggested expanding the number of Supreme Court Justices in order to alter the majority that had declared some of his measures unconstitutional, his own party turned against him. The proposal to "pack the court" went down to stinging defeat in the Congress. In other nations, war and economic distress led to authoritarianism, but in the United States constitutional democracy remained the rule. The New Deal preserved the capitalist system by curbing its excesses, and by 1939 the GDP was back to pre-Depression levels although unemployment remained widespread.

Source for both charts: *Historical Statistics of the United States: Colonial Times to 1957* (Washington, DC: United States Government Printing Office, 1961).

Authoritarianism in Asia

◆ Japanese Militarism

During the last decades of the nineteenth century, Meiji reformers had overseen the rapid industrialization of Japan. As in every other industrial nation, this transformation had not been without problems. The low wages, long hours, and influx of women into the workforce that marked Japan's "industrial revolution" set off a round of strikes. The government's response was to enact stiff penalties for anyone caught encouraging workers to strike (the Peace Preservation Law, 1900). By 1911, Japan had passed its first child labor law, forbidding the factory employment of children under the age of twelve, and limiting the workday of children from twelve to fifteen to a maximum of twelve hours a day. Twelve hours was also set as the maximum workday for women. When food shortages and rising prices set off a round of "Rice Riots" in 1918, the government tried fixing prices. It used troops to break up demonstrations in Japan and confiscated rice from its Korean colony for the home market. By 1920, changes in the world market brought Japan its first economic recession.

Post-war Japan was an industrialized state eager to participate in global affairs whose "special interest" in China was recognized by the United States, and whose naval power was conceded by Great Britain. But an industrial Japan was not necessarily a democratic Japan. The Constitution of 1889, given to Japan as a "gift" from the Emperor kept effective power in the hands of the emperor, the samurai military class, and an aristocratic political elite. After 1890, the House of Representatives succeeded in taking effective control of budgetary expenditures and gradually reduced the influence of the military in politics, but not entirely: the nation's ministers of war and of the navy were generally chosen from officers on active service and approved by the military hierarchy. Military spending still absorbed more than one-third of the state's total budget, peaking at 49 percent in 1921. The military's role in Japanese society was bolstered by its victories over China (1894–1895), Russia (1904–1905), and its successful participation in World War I. The Suffrage Reform Law of 1925 created a universal male franchise, but the Peace Conservation Law passed the same year gave police the right to arrest and detain anyone they believed was attempting to undermine "the Japanese way." Still, when Emperor Hirohito (1901–1989) was installed in 1926, Japan looked forward to an age of *Shōwa* (enlightened peace).

The fatal weakness of the Meiji Constitution was its failure to place the military under the direct control of civilian authority. Although successive civilian governments were elected during the 1920s, the Japanese military remained proudly independent; leaders of the armed services were not directly responsible to the Prime Minister but only to the Emperor. The military establishment resented budget cuts imposed by civilian leaders and saw only humiliation in a tariff treaty that recognized a free China. Many angry young officers joined violence-prone groups such as the "Black Dragons," while more moderate soldiers were purged from the officer corps. Hamaguchi Osachi (1870–1931), leader of the *Minseito* (Progressive Party), became Prime Minister in 1929, but was shot by a military assassin on a Tokyo street less than a year later. Moreover, the onset of the Great Depression caused major economic dislocations as Japanese goods were priced out of world markets, and the income of both farmers and urban workers collapsed. Japan's banking system was already in disarray; a financial panic in 1927 had caused a general run on the banks. Widespread bank failures quickly wiped out the life savings of the average Japanese family. By 1931, with 3 million unemployed and famine in the northeastern parts of the country, the nation was in turmoil. When neither democratic party seemed capable of effective action, military units in the provinces seized the initiative.

Instilling patriotism Japanese style, Empire Day celebrations, 1934.
Copyright © CORBIS/Bettmann

Japanese military leaders stationed in Manchuria, the northernmost province of China, had long influenced policy through the decrees of client warlords. The Japanese high command watched with anxiety as Chiang Kai-shek (1887–1975), successor to Sun Yat-sen as leader of China, slowly expanded the Chinese Republic's area of effective control northwards to threaten Japan's territorial buffer against Russia. The military leadership came to believe that Japan's hard-won position on the mainland of Asia was threatened by the increasing strength of China's Kuomintang regime. When Japan's clients began to favor Chiang Kai-shek's policies over Japan's, the Japanese military decided to act. Japanese occupation forces in Manchuria exploded a bomb on the railway outside Mukden on September 18, 1931, and used the staged violence as a pretext to seize full control of China's richest province. In February 1932, Japan proclaimed Manchuria to be the independent state of Manchukuo and appointed the former Chinese Emperor PuYi to act as its puppet ruler. China appealed to the League of Nations for assistance. Although most League

Modern warfare: Shanghai following a Japanese air attack, 1937.
Copyright © CORBIS/Bettmann

members refused to recognize the new Manchukuo government, British opposition killed a League attempt to impose economic sanctions on Japan. Japan, for its part, withdrew from the League. When China tried to impose a unilateral boycott on Japan, Japan responded by bombarding Shanghai.

Within Japan itself, the military was also making its final moves in a long campaign to control the government. In May 1932, junior officers of the army and navy launched coordinated attacks against Japan's financial institutions, police, and civilian party headquarters. Inukai Tsuyoshi (1855–1932), leader of the *Rikken Seiyūkai* (Friends of Constitutional Government Party) was elected Prime Minister in 1931. When he was murdered in 1932 by military reactionaries, democratic government in Japan effectively came to an end. Faced with anarchy and rebellion, the leaders of the *Rikken Seiyūkai* agreed to accept Saitō Makoto (1858–1936), supposedly a moderate naval commander, as Japan's next prime minister. The military remained in control of Japan until September 1945.

◆ Kuomintang China

When Dr. Sun Yat-sen died in 1925, he believed that China, his divided and backward nation, had succeeded in reversing decades of misrule by the Manchu dynasty. Sun was confident that his guiding three principles—Democracy, Nationalism, and the People's Livelihood—had transformed China's prospects for the future. Western countries might criticize his acceptance of Communist advisors and note that his Canton based administration controlled less than a third of the country, but Sun died believing China was on the verge of national unity, prosperity, and international recognition. But Chiang Kai-shek, Sun's brother in law and successor, placed more faith in force than in an idealistic platform. Chiang decided to end Kuomintang cooperation with Chinese Communists and to eliminate independent provincial warlords; he relied on the army to achieve the national unity that had eluded Sun. In July 1926 Chiang launched the Northern Expedition, a military offensive aimed at adding the economically vital lands of the lower Yangtze River valley to the republic. Communists were officially expelled from the Kuomintang early the next year, while Chiang's advancing troops exterminated Communist-led labor unions in Shanghai and purged the party from China's other major cities. Kuomintang forces gained control of the old imperial capital of Peking in June 1928. Proclaiming a new capital for a new China in Nanking, Chiang negotiated a series of twelve treaties with Western nations that recognized his republic as China's sole legitimate government. Chiang had achieved superficial unity, but whether the Nanking government was capable of building a cohesive nation out of 500 million illiterate peasants remained to be seen.

A new Provisional Constitution was adopted in 1931, but the sole determining element in government policy remained Chiang and his Kuomintang elite. The generation of young leaders who served Chiang and the Kuomintang established banks, schools, newspapers, and a bureaucracy to administer the nation, but these real accomplishments only benefitted the middle and upper classes. In China 85 percent of the people remained poverty-stricken landless tenants in a rural economy, unaffected by policies that ignored their economic plight. Chiang's regime protected the authority and the privileged position of the land-owning classes and never gained the support of the peasantry whose quality of life it failed to improve. The republic failed at the task of nation building because it never addressed the hopes and needs of the larger population.

It also faced dangerous opposition from within. In 1931, within the wilderness of Kiangsi and Fukien Provinces in southern China, Mao Tse-tung (1893–1976) and his allies were reorganizing the survivors of Chiang's attack on the Communists. Mao's goal was to transform China's peasantry into a socialist revolutionary force, in defiance of the traditional Marxist view that the proletariat (urban factory workers) must play that role. Mao's Kiangsi Republic constantly challenged Chiang's authority; its growth led Chiang to undertake four "extermination" campaigns against it. Sun Yat-sen's goal of a united China seemed impossibly utopian in the early 1930s as Japan consolidated its hold over Manchuria and civil war between Kuomintang and Communist forces engulfed southern China.

Chiang's unrelenting animosity toward the small communist state led him to import mercenary German generals to advise his troops. Their presence brought some military success; by October 1934 Kuomintang armies forced almost 100,000 Communists to flee Kiangsi. Their epic retreat is now revered in China as "The Long March." During a 6,600 mile running battle that lasted for an entire year, Communist units crossed eighteen mountain ranges, twenty-four rivers, and eleven provinces. Only 20,000 survived to reach safe haven in Shensi Province deep in China's isolated north. There, Mao once again began the task of creating a Communist alternative to the Kuomintang, but no one expected him to succeed. In 1935, Chiang could plausibly believe that his battle against Mao was won. Ignoring the remnants of the Communist republic, Chiang's government turned instead to improving China's industrial production, increasing railway mileage, and collecting ever greater taxes from an impoverished population. The imposition of these levies caused additional peasant discontent, and China's agricultural productivity fell sharply late in the decade. Sun Yat-sen's nationalist pledge that government would serve "the people's livelihood" was not central to the policies of the Nanking regime.

The authoritarian and totalitarian regimes that emerged after World War I mobilized their peoples against a world that seemed to be spinning out of control. Japanese militarists and Chinese Nationalists shored up the authority and military strength of their governments at the expense of the welfare of their populations despite promises of a better future for all. Bolsheviks in Russia and Fascist leaders across Europe assured unhappy populations that a better society would emerge in time. Lenin and Stalin promised a Socialist Utopia while Fascists emphasized the restoration of national glory. These leaders were widely supported despite their worst political abuses.

Yet it is wrong to interpret the years from 1919 to 1939 as an inexorable move towards dictatorship. Democracy continued to flourish in much of western Europe and the United States. Under Franklin Roosevelt, the New Deal demonstrated the resilience of capitalism. Liberal principles

Generalissimo Chiang Kai-shek, leader of Nationalist China.
Copyright © CORBIS/Bettmann

continued to influence global political and economic life even as the new breed of dictators mobilized their societies against these beliefs. If the liberal governments of the West failed in anything, it was in their underestimation of the aggressive nature of the new dictatorships. Engaged in unending revolutions that had to spread or die, these regimes turned to conquest to justify their existence. The failure of the world's democratic powers to confront the expansionist aims of these dictators led the world into yet another World War, one far deadlier than the first.

◆ Notes

1. F. A. Golder, *Documents of Russian History 1914–1917,* (New York: Appleton-Century Crofts, Inc., 1927), 386–387.

2. *Great Issues in Western Civilization II: From Louis XIV through the Cold War,* 4th edition, edited by Brian Tierney, Donald Kagan, and L. Pearce Williams (New York: McGraw-Hill, Inc., 1992), 533–535.

3. *Congressional Record,* October 14, 1968, page 31636.

4. Calvin Coolidge, Speech before the Society of Newspaper Editors, January 17, 1925, cited in *The Oxford Dictionary of Quotations,* 3rd ed., (Oxford: Oxford University Press, 1967), 162 [#11].

9

World War II and Its Aftermath

In 1939, less than twenty-one years after the guns were stilled on the Western Front of the "Great War," the world was once again embroiled in a global conflict. Suddenly, it became necessary to refer to the confrontation of 1914–1918 as World War *One* to distinguish it from the conflagration that raged from 1939 to 1945. How did this happen? When Adolf Hitler was appointed Chancellor of Germany in 1933, Stalin was still preaching the wisdom of "Socialism in One Country," Mussolini was admired for bringing order to the chaos of postwar Italy, and Japan seemed content with its Manchurian Empire. France and Britain seemed to be climbing out of the Depression, and Franklin Delano Roosevelt was inaugurating his New Deal for the Forgotten American.

But the democratic powers misunderstood the nature of the new dictatorships that arose in Europe and Asia. They had not read or had refused to believe the emphasis on glory, war, and conquest in the writings of these dictators. They had forgotten the lure of the militaristic fix for a devastated economy: put several hundred thousand men into uniform and you put millions more to work supplying them. They had overlooked the bitterness left behind by the Versailles settlement and the unstable nature of the multinational states created in its wake. The actions of Adolf Hitler in Germany and Emperor Hirohito and Prime Minister Tōjō in Japan would ultimately disabuse them.

Aggression and Appeasement

◆   Germany Rearms

In retrospect, the events of 1933 played a pivotal role in setting Europe on the road to a second world war. At the end of January, President Hindenburg appointed Adolf Hitler Chancellor of Germany. In February, Japan learned that the League of Nations would take no military action against Japanese aggression in China. Within a month the military-controlled Japanese government had withdrawn from the League. From February to October, a League sponsored Disarmament Conference attempted to negotiate substantial arms reductions by all the European powers. Even though the plan would have allowed Germany to rearm to the level of France, Hitler rejected the proposal, the conference, and membership in the League.

Throughout 1934, Hitler laid the foundations for the *Luftwaffe* (air force), the *Kriegsmarine* (navy), and the *Wehrmacht* (army), in defiance of *Versailles Treaty* sanctions. He also signed a non-aggression pact with Poland, driving a wedge through France's attempts to encircle Germany with a ring of French defensive alliances. On July 25, the anti-Nazi Austrian Chancellor, Engelbert Dollfuss (1892–1934), was murdered by National Socialists. On October 9, King Alexander of Yugoslavia (r. 1921–1934), a Serb who had established a royal dictatorship, was assassinated by

Croatian Fascists. The Fascist tide had begun to swell. Then, on March 16, 1935, Hitler formally denounced the *Treaty of Versailles* while announcing plans for a draft to fill an army over five times the size allowed by that treaty. In April the League condemned Hitler's actions, but could nothing about them. Meeting separately in Stresa, the leaders of France, Italy, and Great Britain were unable to arrive at any concrete security agreements. In May, unable to act alone, France settled for a five-year alliance with Stalin against possible German aggression. In June, Britain essentially consigned the military provisions of the *Versailles Treaty* to the scrap heap by signing an *Anglo-German Naval Pact.* The pact allowed Germany to build up a fleet of battleships and cruisers to 35 percent and submarines to 45 percent the size of Britain's. Faced with the challenge of rebuilding economies ravaged by the Great Depression, the leaders of Europe's democracies were reluctant to confront the real nature of the enemy they faced in Fascism. Britain, in particular, could not afford to divert production from exports to military uses without derailing its economic recovery. And within Germany, the campaign against the "enemies" of the *Reich* continued as the Nuremberg Laws (1935) deprived German Jews of citizenship and civil rights.

◆   Mussolini Invades Ethiopia

The failure of the Stresa conference convinced Mussolini he, too, would meet no opposition. In October 1935, Mussolini's armies attacked Ethiopia, ostensibly in retaliation for Ethiopian raids on Italian Eritrea. The League of Nations invoked sanctions, but its sanctions were ineffective in stopping Mussolini's imperial campaign because the list of forbidden products failed to include oil, pig iron, and steel. Britain, worried about its African empire, and France, worried about losing a possible ally against Hitler, did not see any reason to harm their own trade with Italy when Italy was free to buy goods from such non-League members as the United States or Germany. The forces of Ethiopian Emperor Haile Selassie (1892–1975) were no match for the air power and poison gas of the Italian army. By May 1936, King Victor Emmanuel III of Italy (r. 1900–1946) was the new Emperor of Ethiopia. The League had lost its last chance to influence world events.

While Italian aggression riveted the world's attention, Hitler took his greatest gamble. In March 1936 he announced the "reoccupation" of the Rhineland—the territory between the Rhine River and Germany's borders with Belgium and France—that had been "forever" demilitarized by the *Treaty of Versailles.* Though prepared to retreat at the first sign of Allied action, Hitler discovered Britain would take no such action and France would not act alone. France was entangled in the second year of a political crisis that did not end until a coalition of socialist parties (the Popular Front) took office later in 1936. Britain was in the middle of a constitutional crisis set off by the death of George V (r. 1910–1936) and the expressed desire of his heir, Edward VIII (r. 1936), to marry Wallace Simpson, an American divorcée. As the Church of England did not recognize divorce and the King was constitutionally the head of the Church of England, he could not marry Wallace Simpson (1896–1986) and keep his throne. Edward was forced to abdicate in favor of his younger brother, George VI (r. 1936–1952).

◆   The Spanish Civil War

On July 18, 1936, General Francisco Franco (1892–1975) raised the flag of revolt against the Spanish government. The Spanish Civil War (1936–1939) that resulted was the culmination of several years of crisis. The monarchy had fallen in 1931 after the collapse of a coup led by General Miguel Primo de Rivera (1870–1930) and King Alfonso XIII (r. 1886–1931). The Republic that resulted tried to follow a path of moderate reform but this satisfied neither the conservatives nor the radicals while also alienating Catalan and Basque separatists. When a Popular Front coalition of reformers, socialists, and anarchists won the 1936 elections, Spanish Fascists (the *Falange*) began a campaign of terror against the Republic. Franco's revolt was the culmination of the *Falange* campaign.

In retrospect, the Spanish Civil War seems a rehearsal for the greater conflict to follow. Hitler and Mussolini armed the Fascists and sent troops to their support. The Soviet Union helped equip the Anarchists, but Stalin was too involved with his Great Purges to send more than nominal aid to the socialist Republic. And while liberals and socialists from the United States and Europe volunteered in the Republican cause, no official help was offered by any of the democracies. With substantial aid from Germany and Italy, Franco established a Fascist dictatorship in Spain. It lasted until his death in 1975.

◆ From Axis to *Nazi-Soviet Pact*

Throughout October 1936 Germany and Italy negotiated a series of Protocols linking their countries in "the Axis," a term coined by Mussolini when the alliance was formalized in November. An *Anti-Comintern Pact* signed by Germany and Japan in November, and by Italy the following year, further cemented an alliance that reached its final stage with the signing of the *Tripartite Pact* between Germany, Italy, and Japan, in September 1940. At the same time, Hitler informed his General Staff that he intended to advance German claims to all of Austria, as well as to portions of Czechoslovakia, Poland, and the Ukraine.

Austria was his first and not entirely unwilling target. It had actually voted to join Germany in 1918, but the Allied Powers had put an end to that *Anschluss* (union) in the post-war treaties. Allied opposition to such a union was one of the few points of agreement at the Stresa conference in 1935. But in February 1938, Hitler summoned Austrian Chancellor Kurt Schuschnigg (1897–1977) to Germany and gave him a choice between *Anschluss* or invasion. Schuschnigg scheduled a vote on unification for March 13. Although Hitler expected the vote to carry, he ordered his army to move on March 12 rather than wait for the results of the vote. With German tanks in their streets, 99.75 percent of Austria's citizens voted for the *Anschluss*.

Since Britain and France did nothing to oppose his interpretation of Wilson's principle of national self-determination, Hitler turned his sights to the Sudetenland, a crescent of land along Czechoslovakia's border with Germany/Austria predominantly occupied by people of German descent and possessing most of Czechoslovakia's coal and mineral resources. The Sudetenland's 3.5 million ethnic Germans demanded virtual autonomy from the Czech government, an autonomy the multi-ethnic nation felt it could not give and survive, since the Slovaks and Ruthenians within its borders would then be sure to demand autonomy as well. Throughout the spring and summer Hitler's agents fostered pro-Sudeten riots. But Czech President Edvard Beneš (1884–1948) remained defiant, relying on his ties with France and Russia to aid him in his stand against the dismemberment of Czechoslovakia, a nation created, after all, by the Allied peace settlement.

In an effort to appease Hitler and bring peace, British Prime Minister Neville Chamberlain (1869–1940) worked in combination with France to force Beneš to concede autonomy to the Sudeten Germans. But this was not enough for Hitler, and he ordered the *Wehrmacht* to prepare an invasion. Only a last minute intervention by Mussolini convinced Hitler to hold a conference (in Munich on September 29–30, 1938) to settle the issue. There Chamberlain and France's Édouard Daladier (1884–1970), reluctantly agreed to award the Sudetenland to Hitler. Beneš resigned. Stalin, who had been deliberately excluded from the Conference, learned from the Munich Agreement that his former Allies in the Great War could not be trusted. Chamberlain assured the British people he had won "peace in our time." A more realistic Winston Churchill described the appeasement of Hitler as a "disaster of the first magnitude."

Hitler had pledged to seek no more land in Europe, but six months later he occupied the rest of Czechoslovakia. Later that March, he retook the city of Memel, which Germany had ceded to Lithuania in the *Versailles Treaty*. He also demanded the return of Danzig, given to Poland in the same treaty. On March 31, 1939, Britain and France issued a public guarantee of Poland's independence. Hitler's response was to renounce the limitations of the *Anglo-German Naval Pact* of 1935 and the *Nazi-Polish Security Pact* of 1934. Although Hitler believed the British and French were unwilling to "die for Danzig," he also knew he could not launch a unilateral attack against Poland without risking Soviet reprisals. At the same time, Stalin knew that the Soviet Union could not launch an attack to recover the territory it lost in the *Treaty of Brest-Litovsk* (1918) without Hitler's agreement. Since both sides had more to gain by reaching some agreement before their armies moved than by fighting each other, they opened negotiations. The result was the *Nazi-Soviet Pact* of August 23, 1939. Ostensibly a non-aggression pact between Germany and the Soviet Union, it had secret provisions that called for a division of much of Eastern Europe between Germany and the USSR. The Baltic states of Estonia and Latvia, the Romanian province of Bessarabia, Finland, and eastern Poland would go to the Soviet Union, while Lithuania and the rest of Poland were reserved for German expansion.

World War II

◆ Blitzkrieg

Once Hitler was assured that Stalin would not interfere with his plans, he waited barely a week to strike. At 8 P.M. on August 31, 1939, Nazi agents staged a raid on a German border town, leaving behind fake evidence pointing to Polish aggression. On the morning of September 1, well-prepared German armies struck across the border. Rapidly moving armored columns, closely supported by aircraft, slashed through Poland's outmoded defenses. Britain and France declared war against Germany on September 3, but neither could do anything but watch as the Germans advanced. World War II had begun. Stalin's troops marched into Poland from the east on September 17. Warsaw fell to the Germans on September 27.

The German campaign in Poland introduced the world to a type of warfare: *Blitzkrieg* (Lightning war). *Blitzkrieg* was made possible by a combination of new technology and older tactics. As Field Marshal Erwin Rommel (1891–1944) defined the tactics, *Blitzkrieg* was "the art of concentrating [one's] strength at one point" in the enemy's defenses, "forcing a breakthrough, rolling up and securing the flanks on either side, and then penetrating like lightning, before the enemy" had "time to react."[1] Although air support was also vital, *Blitzkrieg*'s technology centered on the tank. The tractor-treaded, all-terrain armored vehicle was first introduced by the British in the last months of World War I, but now all the elements of a division—the infantry, artillery, signals and engineers—were motorized so they could move alongside the tanks without slowing them down. The Germany army had been massing these *Panzer* (armored) divisions throughout the 1930s. Six were ready for the thrust into Poland. The effect was devastating. The days of trench warfare were over; the new war would be fully mobile. The greatest irony was that *Blitzkrieg* was a tactic stolen from the British. At the Battle of Cambrai in 1917, during World War I, Britain launched a massed assault of over 400 tanks that changed the nature of warfare forever. The assault was led by John Frederick Charles Fuller (1878–1966), chief of staff of the British tank corps and advocate of military mechanization. After World War I ended, Fuller published several books pushing the effec-

FIELD MARSHALL ERWIN ROMMEL (1891–1944)

The "Desert Fox," defender of "Fortress Europe."
Copyright © Hulton Getty

Erwin Rommel was born in Warttemberg, Germany on November 15, 1891, to a middle class family with no military tradition; his father and grandfather were schoolmasters and mathematicians. One of five children, Rommel had a pleasant and uneventful childhood and his decision at the age of nineteen to join the Imperial German army was unexpected. In 1910 Rommel became an officer cadet in the 124th infantry regiment, and was commissioned a 2nd lieutenant two years later. During World War One he served with distinction in France where he was twice wounded and won the Iron Cross, Germany's highest decoration for bravery. Posted to the Romanian front Rommel learned about mountain warfare and later perfected infiltration techniques on the Italian front.

After the war, Rommel held various regimental commands, and was a valued instructor at the Dresden Infantry School (1929–1933) and the Potsdam War Academy (1935–1938). During his time at Dresden, Rommel wrote an infantry manual, *Infanterie Greift An* (*Infantry Attacks*), based on his wartime experiences. The 1937 edition of the book caught Hitler's eye, and in 1938

Colonel Rommel commanded the battalion charged with Hitler's safety during the march into Czechoslovakia. Rommel's reward was a field command, and in 1940 he led the 7th Panzer Division during the conquest of France. In 1941, after promotion to lieutenant general, he was given command of the German troops in Libya, a force soon to become famous as Rommel's *Afrika Korps*.

By November 1941, Rommel acquired control of all the Axis forces in North Africa when 20 Italian corps were transferred to his *Panzergruppe*. Most famous as a tank commander, Rommel led his armored forces brilliantly against the British in the desert, driving them back from Cyrenaica into Egypt as far as El Alamein. In June 1942, Rommel was promoted to field marshal for this accomplishment, the youngest in the history of the German army. However, as Hitler concentrated on his campaign in Russia and failed to support the *Afrika Korps* with adequate supplies and reinforcements, Rommel was unable to advance further to capture Alexandria. Eventually he was driven back to Benghazi and then into Tunisia where he was faced with fresh Allied forces. After a battle at Medenine on March 5, 1943, Rommel was forced by ill health to return to Germany, and the war in North Africa soon ended in German withdrawal.

After November 1943 Rommel was charged with the coastal defense of "Fortress Europe" from Denmark to Spain. Denied sufficient troops to repel the Allies on the beaches, he was unable to prevent the Allied landings in Normandy on D-Day, June 6, 1944. On July 17, Rommel was severely wounded by fire from an Allied plane and returned home to recover. Never a member of the Nazi party, Rommel was charged with complicity in the unsuccessful July 20 plot to assassinate Hitler. On October 14, 1944, he was forced to end his own life by taking poison. Rommel, known as the "Desert Fox" for his exploits in North Africa, was even admired by his adversaries for both his bravery and his brilliant military achievements.

tiveness of massed tank groups, but it was the German military and not the British that adopted Fuller's advice.

For the moment, however, there seemed to be no war. Hitler used the winter of 1939–1940 to consolidate his Polish gains and prepare for battle against his western enemies. No fighting took place in Western Europe during these months of *sitzkrieg,* or "phony war," and Hitler carefully fostered the hopes of many in Britain and France that some accommodation could be reached. In the meantime, Stalin funneled vast amounts of supplies and resources to Hitler under the terms of the *Nazi-Soviet Pact.* On November 30, Stalin launched a "Winter War" against Finland. The League of Nations expelled the Soviet Union for its unprovoked aggression against Finland, but without effect. On March 13, 1940, after a heroic resistance, Finland surrendered to the Soviet Union.

The "phony war" came to a sudden halt in April 1940. Denmark fell to a German airborne assault in one day. Despite the efforts of the British Royal Navy and an Anglo-French landing force, Norway fell within a week. In May the *panzers* swept across the Low Countries (Belgium and the United Netherlands) in two weeks. France thought itself secure behind the defensive emplacements of the Maginot Line, a series of fortifications along its border with Germany. However, in a modification of the old Schlieffen Plan, the German assault bypassed the fixed defenses of the Maginot Line to cut through the Ardennes Forest. The *panzer* advance cut a wedge between France's troops and the British Expeditionary Forces rushed over to reinforce them. The Royal Navy, aided by hundreds of civilian ships, managed to evacuate over 338,226 men from the Channel port of Dunkirk back to England, but almost all of their heavy equipment was lost. Prime Minister Winston Churchill (1874–1965), who had replaced Chamberlain in May, reminded his nation that, however praiseworthy the rescue operation, "wars are not won by evacuations." Mussolini, scrambling to win some of his Axis ally's glory, belatedly declared war on France, and attacked in the south on June 10. A demoralized France signed an armistice on June 22, in the same railroad car in which Germany had signed the armistice in World War I. German troops quickly occupied half the nation. In unoccupied France, Marshal Henri Philippe Pétain (1856–1951), the hero of Verdun in the Great War, established a collaborationist regime headquartered in the southern city of Vichy. Before the end of 1942 Vichy, too, was under direct German control.

A few Frenchmen escaped to Britain, and, led by General Charles de Gaulle (1890–1970), organized themselves as the Free French to fight with allied forces for the overthrow of the Axis powers and the liberation of their homeland. Great Britain was now the only European state still at war with Germany. Sweden, Switzerland, and Spain remained nominally neutral, but the rest of the continent was either in the hands of Hitler's forces or maintained some sort of alliance with him, all within nine months from the day the tanks had crossed into Poland. Europe was now *Festung Europa,* Hitler's "Fortress Europe."

Ever since the days of *Mein Kampf,* Hitler had dreamed of expanding the German empire eastward, of creating *Lebensraum* (living space) in which the German people could achieve their true greatness, but Stalin stood on his eastern front, and Britain to his west. To avoid a war on two fronts, Britain had to be subdued before any Russian campaign began, but Great Britain could not be taken by *panzers.* With the English Channel in the way, *Blitzkrieg* gave way to "the *Blitz*" as Germany prepared an aerial campaign to soften up Britain for an invasion. What came to be known as the "Battle of Britain" raged throughout the late summer of 1940 as German planes attacked fighter bases, communications networks, and, eventually, urban population centers. At great loss to itself, the Royal Air Force (RAF), aided by still experimental radar technology, inflicted debilitating losses on the attacking Germans, kept control of the skies, and forced Hitler

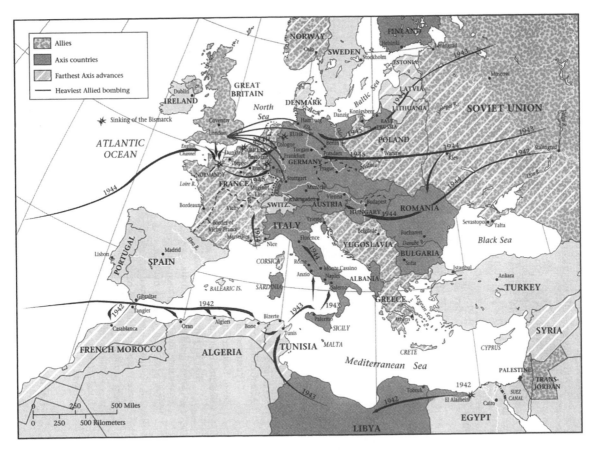

World War II European and Mediterranean Theaters, 1939–1945.
From *Human Venture*, Fifth Edition, (2004), reproduced by permission of Prentice-Hall, Inc.

to call off the planned invasion. In a speech to the House of Commons, Churchill acknowledged Britain's debt to the RAF with the words "Never in the field of human combat was so much owed by so many to so few,"[2] but he knew Britain could not win the war without help. He began a long relationship with President Roosevelt that bore almost immediate fruit when the United States exchanged fifty outdated World War I destroyers for British naval bases in the Caribbean. The Destroyer Deal of September 1940 provided Great Britain with additional sea power to protect its merchant fleet and keep open the sea lanes vital to supplying the British Isles. In March 1941, passage of the Lend Lease Act by the American Congress assured Great Britain of the resources it needed to continue its lonely fight. During the year and a half that it fought Germany alone, British morale never faltered despite the nightly bombardment. The *Blitz* was Hitler's first failure.

◆ Operation Barbarossa

Despite his failure to subdue Britain, Hitler felt he had the island nation bottled up so that it could not interfere with his eastern plans. Though angered by American support for Britain, he ordered his U-Boats not to attack American shipping to avoid having another hostile nation to his west as he turned his attention eastward. The existence of the *Nazi-Soviet Pact* did not stop Hitler from making plans for an invasion of the Soviet Union. The formal directive for "Operation Barbarossa" was issued on December 18, 1940, with Finland, Romania, and Bulgaria acting as staging points. Romania had joined the Axis in November, and Bulgaria would join in March. After intercepting German intelligence messages, Britain warned Stalin of an imminent Nazi assault, but Stalin continued to trust Hitler. His folly was brought home to him on June 22, 1941, when over three million German soldiers massed in 186 divisions invaded the Soviet Union. The Germans faced 2.9 million Soviet troops equipped with twice as many tanks and nearly three times as many aircraft, but the Soviet army had not learned that tanks must be massed in their own groups with adequate support to be effective. Many of the Soviet planes were destroyed on the ground in the first day of fighting. An alarmed Stalin joined Churchill and de Gaulle in the alliance against Nazi Germany as German armies captured an area twice the size of France within a month. The Germans took 150,000 prisoners, 1200 tanks and 600 big guns in the first ten days alone. Confident that the Soviet Union would soon fall, an elated Hitler ordered cutbacks in German military production, but an early winter slowed the German advance. Although more than two million Russians were dead and an equal number captured before the close of the year, Stalin had gained the breathing space he needed to rally his forces, beef up military production, and inspire his people to fight the "Great Patriotic War" against the fascist invader. A heroic Soviet defense halted the German advance outside Moscow in 1942.

◆ Japan's War

As Hitler took the first steps to create his Nazi empire, Japan was building an empire of its own in Asia. It already had a base in Manchukuo, the puppet-state in Manchuria that Japan established after they occupied it in 1931. On July 7, 1937, the generals in charge of Manchukuo provoked a violent incident at the Marco Polo Bridge near Peking and used the resulting bloodshed to justify an invasion of central China. Without a declaration of war, the Japanese advanced into Canton, occupying it by October. The Japanese advance down the coast and into the Chinese heartland forced Chiang Kai-shek's Nationalists and Mao Tse-tung's Communists into a defensive alliance against the invaders, but to no avail. Shanghai fell to the Japanese in November after a street by street defense, and Nanking followed in December. Within a month the population of Nanking was decimated as the victorious Japanese carried out an unprecedented slaughter. Over one quarter of a million people died in the "Rape of Nanking," the first of many atrocities that marked the Japanese advance. On March 30, 1940, Japan set up a puppet government at Nanking that obediently recognized Japan's right to control all of occupied China. Mao's forces continued to fight in the northwest while Chiang fled further inland to Chunking, but half of China remained in Japanese hands.

In the United States, an isolationist Congress, trusting in the protection provided by the Atlantic and Pacific Oceans, was reluctant to move against either Germany or Japan. Remembering how financial ties to the Entente powers had helped draw the United States into the Great War, Congress passed a series of Neutrality Acts between 1935 and 1937 to limit the exportation of war materials except on a "cash and carry" basis. Neither the Japanese invasion of China nor the Japanese attack on the American gunboat *Panay* in December 1937 changed Congress's mind. When the Japanese apologized for the *Panay* attack and offered reparations, the United States continued to supply Japan with materials used to attack China. Individual Americans might volunteer—the Flying Tiger Volunteer Air Corps fought the Japanese in China as the Abraham Lincoln

Brigade had fought Franco in Spain—but official American policy remained neutral. In fact, the United States seemed to be playing both sides against the middle, supplying Japan while extending $25 million in credits to the Chinese government in 1938, mostly to maintain the Burma road through which Britain was funneling supplies into China to aid it against Japan.

In September 1940, Japan persuaded the Vichy government in France to cede the northern portion of its Indochina colony to Japanese control. Japan's path was taking it ever closer to American bases in the Philippines. The United States prohibited the exportation of oil, scrap metal, and aviation fuel to Japan. More loans were negotiated to aid the struggling government of Chiang Kai-shek and re-equip the Nationalist Army. Under the provisions of the Lend Lease Act of March 1941, over fifty billion dollars in aid was made available to Hitler's enemies as the United States became the "arsenal of democracy." The navy was authorized to escort supply convoys halfway across the Atlantic until they could be taken under the protection of British warships. After April 1941, the American fleet was, in effect, participating in an undeclared naval war against Germany. In August, Roosevelt and Churchill signed the *Atlantic Charter,* outlining allied war aims four months before the United States formally entered the war.

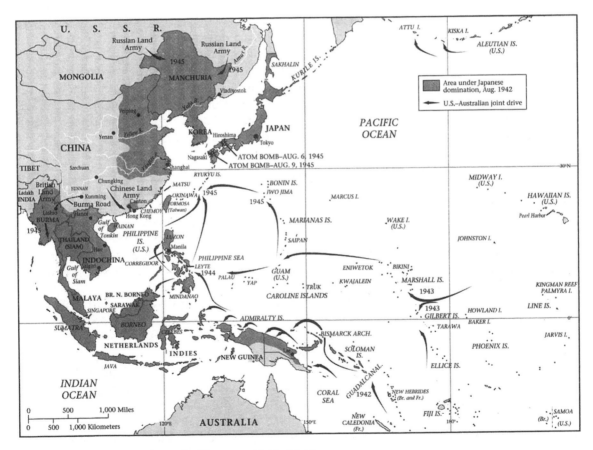

World War II Asian and Pacific Theaters, 1941–1945.
From *Human Venture*, Fifth Edition, (2004), reproduced by permission of Prentice-Hall, Inc.

Meanwhile, emboldened by Germany's victories in the Netherlands and France and by its aerial attacks on Britain, Japan began to move out of China and into British Burma, and islands of the Dutch East Indies. On July 23, 1941, Japan occupied southern French Indochina. Three days later Roosevelt ordered a freeze on all Japanese assets in the United States as the British government simultaneously froze Japanese assets in all British dominions. If left in place, the sanctions would have eventually starved Japan of the oil it needed to power its fleet. Negotiations to lift the sanctions sputtered on and off for months without result, because the Japanese rejected the American requirement that Japan must first withdraw from China. Incensed, the Japanese military began to plan a crushing attack against the American Pacific Fleet. Such a blow would give Japan time to replace resources lost to it by the American embargo by securing the material resources of Southeast Asia before the United States could rebuild its navy and retaliate. The Japanese assumed that by the time the United States could rebuild its fleet, the Japanese empire in Asia would be so secure that the Americans would decide to negotiate rather than fight. Even before General Tōjō Hideki (1884–1948) became Prime Minister of Japan on October 16, it was clear that war would be the most likely result of the Japanese-American impasse; what Japan needed to do was to win that war before running out of the raw materials usually purchased from the United States. As negotiations over the sanctions dragged on into November, a Japanese task force advanced secretly across the Pacific Ocean towards the American naval base at Pearl Harbor in Hawaii. At dawn on December 7, 1941, Japan's surprise attack, made without a declaration of war, decimated the United States Pacific Fleet. Although nineteen ships were sunk or disabled and over 2,300 sailors died, the assault failed to destroy the drydocks, fuel reserves, and aircraft carriers. Responding to President Roosevelt's request—in which he termed the assault "a date which will live in infamy"[3]—Congress declared war on Japan on December 8. Three days later, Hitler declared war on the United States. Four great powers—the United States, Great Britain, France, and the Soviet Union—now stood together in one "Grand Alliance" against the forces of Germany, Italy, and Japan, known collectively as the "Axis Powers."

◆   The Final Solution and the General Plan East

While most analysts agree that Hitler's attack on Russia, combined with his unnecessary declaration of war against the United States, made his defeat inevitable, it did not seem so in the spring of 1942, when the Axis, led by Hitler, Mussolini, and Tōjō, appeared triumphant everywhere. And everywhere Axis forces advanced, a new order was imposed. While Japan brutalized civilians and prisoners of war alike, forcing Chinese and Korean women into service in Japanese brothels, Hitler set about cleansing Europe of undesirable "races."

Considering Slavic peoples to be subhuman, Hitler's occupying forces murdered and imprisoned uncounted Russians. Behind his advancing troops special units called the *Einsatzgruppen* carried out the execution of thousands of Jews, expanding a program already begun in Poland. In late September 1941, German units operating in conjunction with Ukrainian militia slaughtered 33,711 Jews over a two-day period at Babi Yar. But these uncoordinated shootings, suffocations, and burnings wasted time and materiel. It was decided that a more efficient method was required to solve what Hitler called Europe's "Jewish problem" once and for all.

Nazi officials met in January 1942 at the Wannsee Conference to implement "the Final Solution" of the Jewish problem. With almost two-thirds of the world's Jews under Fascist control, the conference agreed on the creation of a string of slave labor and death camps throughout occupied Europe. All the productive innovations of the Industrial Revolution—division of labor, specializa-

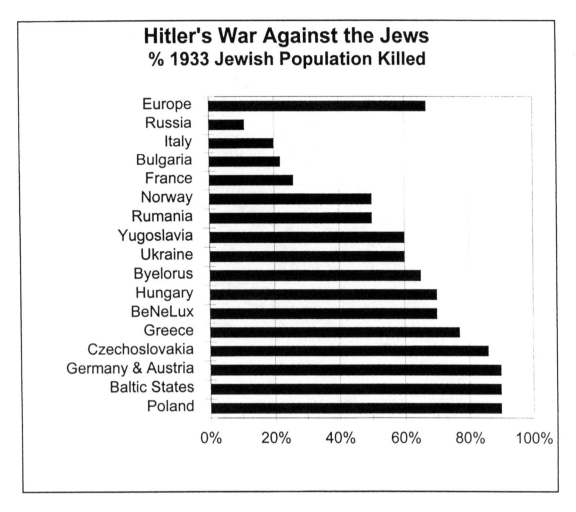

Hitler's War Against the Jews
% 1933 Jewish Population Killed

Source: Lucy S. Dawidowicz, *The War Against the Jews, 1933–1945*, 10th ed. (New York: Bantam Books, 1986), 403.

tion, the assembly line, time-management—were turned to the end of mass murder. German police, members of the army, special units, and willing volunteers from occupied lands all participated in the genocide. The most notorious of the death factories was Auschwitz, a complex of camps in southern Poland where over 1.2 million Jews died in gas chambers. And new camps were being built every day. As Germany's productive capacity strained to meet the needs of Hitler's army, the first orgy of murder gave way to a more systematic process as the able-bodied were worked almost to death in slave labor camps such as Dachau before they were gassed and buried. The killing never let up. At the same time plans were laid for the repopulating of Eastern Europe with a new German aristocracy after the war. Under the "General Plan East" adopted in June 1942, 80–85 percent of the Poles, 65 percent of the Ukrainians, 75 percent of the White Russians, and 50 percent of the Czechs were to be expelled to make room for their new German masters.

At the Nordhausen concentration camp, slave laborers were worked to death building V-bombs—one small part of the Nazi Holocaust.
Copyright © National Archives

Almost six million Jews died in this Holocaust, two-thirds of Europe's entire Jewish population. And some five million others—clergymen, Communists, gypsies, homosexuals, political dissidents, the physically handicapped and mentally ill, Slavs, and socialists—were murdered along with them as Hitler's forces consolidated their hold over continental Europe.

It is clear that British intelligence understood what might happen as early as 1941, and reports about what was happening in Poland were received in 1942, but these reports received little credence. Even to a world that lived through the horrors of World War I, such atrocities seemed impossible in the twentieth century. The world still argues over what could or could not have been done. Would Allied bombing of the rail lines over which the trains brought Hitler's victims to the camps have slowed the murder or just derailed the Allied campaign against Hitler's armies?

◆ The Turn of the Tide, 1942–1943

The Grand Alliance of Great Britain, the Free French, the Soviet Union, and the United States only began to halt the Axis advance in 1942. After destroying a large part of the American Pacific fleet in December 1941, Japanese forces went on to capture Guam, Wake, and the Philippine islands; they moved almost unimpeded through Indo-China and the southwest Pacific. Using land-based bomber aircraft Japan sank the two major British warships in the Far East, enabling its army to take the vital British base of Singapore in February 1942. By the end of May the Japanese were in total control of Burma and seemed poised to attack British India itself. Some ten thousand Indian soldiers in the British Imperial joined their Axis captors to fight against their colonial masters as Indian National Congress politicians called on Britain to "Quit India." But Japanese forces were advancing over an ever-widening perimeter; any defeat along that line would slow their momentum everywhere. In May 1942 their advance southwards towards Australia was checked by Allied naval forces at the Coral Sea, the first naval battle in which all the fighting was done by carrier-based aircraft. The forces afloat never even saw each other. Even more decisive was the American victory at Midway (June 3–6, 1942), where Japan lost four irreplaceable aircraft carriers and several hundred pilots to naval forces commanded by Admiral Raymond A. Spruance (1886–1969). Prophetically named, Midway marked the limit of Japanese success in the Pacific. The success of the long campaign (August 1942 to January 1943) to free Guadalcanal in the Solomon Islands set

NAVAJO CODE TALKERS IN WORLD WAR II

When Carl Gorman, a Navajo artist and former teacher at the University of California (Davis), died on January 29, 1998, he was the oldest of the 400 Navajo Code Talkers so instrumental to America's World War II victory in the Pacific. But few people had ever heard of their exploits because the secret was so vital to American security that the code talkers were not even allowed to tell their own story until 1969, when they were given belated recognition for saving thousands of American lives.

The Navajo are the largest Native American nation in the United States. Today they number roughly 150,000, three times their number in 1941, but they still live mostly on four reservations in northeastern Arizona, northwestern New Mexico, and southeastern Utah. At the outbreak of World War II, many Navajo left the reservation for the first time to work in munitions plants or to serve in the military. The Marine Corps sent 400 of these Navajo enlistees to the Pacific as "Code Talkers." Their use of the Navajo language over the radio for vital military communications foiled all Japanese attempts at code-breaking. Beyond the native Navajo, only about thirty people possessed any knowledge of their language, and none of them was Japanese. The Japanese, who broke most American military codes, were never able to break the Marines' Navajo code. In 1942, the first twenty-eight Navajo code talkers joined the Marine Corps' island-hopping campaign in the Pacific. Code Talkers took part in every major battle from Guadalcanal to Tarawa, Saipan, Peleliu, Iwo Jima, and Okinawa. They usually worked in pairs, two men in action near enemy lines and two more at headquarters. Using the radio, they transmitted orders from commanders to men in the field, reported on their own and enemy troop movements, and relayed requests for ammunition, supplies, or reinforcements. During the battle of Tinian (1944), the Code Talkers directed bombing runs of the B29 bombers stationed there. The Japanese (who spoke excellent English) could not send false messages to disrupt these operations, because they could not speak Navajo. Had they learned Navajo, the Japanese would still not have understood the code. As Navajo did not contain direct translations of modern military terminology, the Code Talkers were using poetic substitutions: torpedo planes became "swallows" and bombers became "buzzards." American Commanders issued orders and received information secure in the knowledge that even if enemies were picking up the transmissions they could never decipher the meaning of the messages.

Being a Navajo in the United States was far from easy. And given the long government campaign to suppress Native American languages, it was a wonder that enough Navajo speakers remained to make such a code work. Carl Gorman could remember being chained to an iron pipe for a week for using Navajo at a Mission School. Being a Navajo in the United States military was even more difficult. Because the Navajo looked like the Japanese to many of the other Marines, the Code Talkers were in some danger from their own side in the early days of the war. They had to be accompanied by a white man who could vouch for their identity. But the Code Talkers soon earned the recognition, respect, and gratitude of their fellows as well as of the high command, proudly calling themselves *Washingdon be Akalh B-kosilai* (United States Marines).

---

the Japanese permanently on the defensive. Just as importantly, attacks by American submarines on Japanese shipping were making tremendous inroads on Japanese war production, slowly starving it of rubber, tin, nickle, copper, and oil.

The summer of 1942 saw the resurgence of the German advance into southern Russia. Hitler wanted the oil-rich lands of Georgia and the Caucasus, but before these areas could be taken his armies began an epic struggle with Russian forces at the city of Stalingrad on the Volga River. The battle for the Soviet Union's third largest industrial city became a test of wills as Stalin decreed the city be held at all costs and Hitler refused to end the siege. For six months, from August 1942 to February 1943, the Russian defense held as German reserves dwindled and winter storms isolated them from support. Only 100,000 German soldiers, less than one-third the original attacking force, lived to surrender. Stalingrad marked the limit of the German march to the east.

Rommel's *Afrika Korps* seemed also to have met its match. Sent into Northern Africa in 1941 to help the Italians fend off a British assault on Libya, Rommel's two-division tank corps seemed unstoppable, only to be nearly turned back by the British in December 1941. After ten months of stalemate in which the British kept Rommel from taking the Suez Canal, British forces went on the offensive in Egypt and tasted victory at El Alamein in October 1942 under the command of Field Marshal Bernard L. Montgomery (1887–1976). Then, in November, Operation Torch saw American and British troops under the command of General Dwight D. Eisenhower (1890–1969) land in Morocco. Moving westward from Egypt and eastward from Morocco, Allied troops met in Tunisia in May 1943, having swept the Germans from Africa.

The tide turned as well in the Battle of the Atlantic, strengthening the supply line from the United States to the European theater. In 1942, over eight million tons of Allied shipping had been sunk in Atlantic waters. But by 1943, the Allies began protecting convoys with "baby carriers" and land-based B-17 Flying Fortresses and B-24 Liberators, which, together with high frequency direction finders and radar, the breaking of German naval codes, and innovative tactics, blunted the German threat. Just as importantly the vast American productive capacity virtually flooded the Atlantic with new ships and supplies.

◆   The Home Front

The Second World War, like the First, was a war of total mobilization. The assembly lines that had once cranked out automobiles and hosiery now turned out jeeps, tanks, and parachutes. The Gross National Product of the United States rose from $88.6 billion in 1939 to $198.7 billion in 1944. Military production rose from two percent of that total in 1939 to 40 percent by 1943. For every young man drafted off the assembly lines and into the armed forces, an American, British, or Russian "Rosie the Riveter" took his place; only Nazi Germany discouraged female workers, preferring German women to stay home and bear children for the future of the empire. In Allied countries, women moved into the blue-collar workplace in unprecedented numbers. In the United States alone, 19.5 million women were employed by 1945, an increase of over 50 percent from pre-war levels. Married women, barred from many jobs during the Great Depression, became the majority of the female workforce as recruitment posters encouraged them to take a job *"for the duration."* Many were eager to trade in waitress jobs that paid only 20 cents an hour for factory wages of $1.15 an hour. Women were also leaving the home front for the theaters of war in larger numbers than ever before and in a wider capacity. Before World War II, women were generally relegated to clerical jobs or served as nurses in military hospitals. World War II saw the creation of the WAC (Women's Army Corps), WAVES (the Navy Women division), the Women's Airforce Service Pilots, and the Marine Corps Women's Reserve. Over 350,000 women served in World War II as nurses, clerks, and pilots, and, although never officially on combat duty, many of them served under fire.

Other groups traditionally under represented in the American economy made their first strides toward equality because of the unceasing demands of wartime production. Begun in 1942, the *Bracero* program brought over 200,000 Mexicans into the country to help with the harvests. Over

"Women's Army Corps, Ready for War"
Courtesy of the National Archives and Records Administration.

46,000 American Indians found jobs in agriculture and industry. More than a million African-Americans were added to the workforce. Many of those African-Americans owed their jobs to the efforts of Asa Philip Randolph (1889–1979), the African-American labor leader who forced President Roosevelt to desegregate defense plants (Executive Order 8802, issued June 25, 1941) by threatening a massive protest march on Washington. Over one million African-Americans served in the still segregated armed forces.

The strains of military production began to tell even in prosperous America. Maintaining a family was a complicated job with meat, sugar, coffee, and dairy products rationed. Family cars were garaged for the duration as the government rationed gasoline. Even shoes had to be rationed because of the military's need for leather. With fathers overseas, mothers working in defense plants, and not nearly enough federally funded daycare centers, juvenile delinquency became a significant problem. Many teenagers dropped out of high school to find work; the US Office of Education issued a public appeal to employers in 1944 to raise their hiring ages.

Americans often refer to World War II as the last "Good War," but not all was well in wartime America. Intermittent racial violence plagued the war effort. The Sojourner Truth Homes were a block of federally funded apartments opened in Detroit in 1942 to house some of the 1.2 million African-Americans who had migrated north to work for the war effort. When 20 families attempted to move into the new apartment blocks, over 700 white protestors blocked the moving vans and

REAR ADMIRAL GRACE MURRAY HOPPER, USNR (1906–1992)

Grace Brewster Murray was born on December 9, 1906, in New York City, the oldest of three children of an insurance salesman. After education in private schools, she graduated from Vassar College in 1928 and received a Ph.D. in mathematics from Yale University in 1934, a rare achievement for a woman at that time. In 1930, she married Vincent Foster Hopper and kept her married name after her divorce in 1945.

Between 1931 and 1943, Hopper rose from instructor to associate professor of mathematics at Vassar. In 1943, following in the footsteps of her great-grandfather, a Civil War rear admiral, Hopper joined the WAVES (navy women). Commissioned a lieutenant (junior grade) in June 1944, she was assigned to the Bureau of Ships Computation Project at Harvard University. The Navy used Harvard's Mark I computer, one of the first in the United States, to run calculations for ballistics tables, underwater sound propagation, and implosion data for the atomic bomb. One of the country's first programmers, Hopper soon mastered the Mark I and spent the rest of her career in computer work.

After World War II, Hopper joined the Eckert-Mauchly Computer Corporation as a Senior Mathematician. In 1952 she became a systems engineer and Director of Automatic Programming Development at UNIVAC, rising to Senior Scientist for systems programming in 1964. Hopper's pioneering efforts in compiling systems and natural language instructions became a fundamental part of the widely used computer programming language COBOL.

Hopper remained a navy reservist after the war, and took a military leave from UNIVAC when she was recalled to active duty in 1967. She was 61 years old, but the navy could not do without her unique skills. Her first navy project was to develop a Tactical Data System for atomic submarines, and later she was charged with imposing order on the navy's proliferating programming languages. In August 1973 she was promoted to captain, and, a decade later, became a rear admiral by special presidential appointment. By her final retirement on August 14, 1986, Hopper was the oldest serving officer in the US Navy. She had become the Navy's foremost expert in programming languages, the chief propagandist for its computer program, and an important role model for women.

During her long career, Hopper published over fifty papers and articles on software and computing languages, while continuing to teach university classes. She consistently preached innovation and refused to be tied to the "old" way of doing things. The recipient of numerous medals, awards, and honorary degrees, Grace Hopper became the first Data Management Association's Computer Services "Man-of-the-Year" (1969) and the first woman awarded the National Medal of Technology (1991). She died on January 1, 1992, and is buried in Arlington National Cemetery.

burned a cross on the project's grounds. In the end, a thousand state-troopers were needed to get the families into their homes.

On February 19, 1942, President Roosevelt signed Executive Order 9066, suspending the civil rights of Japanese-Americans and authorizing the removal of some 110,000 from states along the west coast to internment camps in the western desert. Despite public protests, the Supreme Court upheld the relocation in 1944 (*Korematsu v. US*) on the grounds of national security. The last of the camps did not close until March 1946. Japanese-Americans lost homes and businesses worth half a billion dollars. Not until 1988 did Congress make a public apology and offer reparations of $20,000 to each of the remaining former internees.

Grace Murray Hopper and the Mark I computer, 1944.
Copyright © Smithsonian/National Museum of American History (negative no. 97–3400)

◆   Wartime Diplomacy: Tensions in the Grand Alliance

Throughout the war, leaders of the Allied nations held a series of conferences to forge a combined battle strategy. Roosevelt and Churchill met in Washington, D.C., just weeks after the United States declared war on Japan; they agreed to put the reconquest of Europe ("Germany first") before any allied aid to the US campaign against Japan. Out of that meeting also came the Combined Chiefs of Staff (CCS), the joint British-American committee that would hammer out future military strategy. In January 1943, with the Axis on the defensive, Churchill and Roosevelt met again in Casablanca to plan future campaigns against Hitler. Stalin, still in the middle of directing the defense of his namesake city, refused to leave Russian soil. Churchill and Roosevelt reaffirmed their commitment to defeating Germany before diverting allied resources to help the United States against Japan. They also set a policy of accepting only "unconditional surrender" from the Axis powers. This policy was intended, in part, to alleviate Stalin's fears that the USSR might be left alone to battle Germany. But how was Germany to be defeated? The Americans wanted to move directly on Germany. Churchill, worried about the consequences of a Soviet march on Germany through Russia's old territories in Eastern Europe, successfully argued for opening up a second front in Sicily. If British and American forces moved up through Southern Europe to the German border, they might be able to prevent Eastern Europe from falling into Communist hands.

ASA PHILIP RANDOLPH (1889–1979)

Union leader and Civil Rights activist.
Copyright © New York Public Library

Asa Philip Randolph was born on April 15, 1889, in Crescent City, Florida, the son of a minister in the African Methodist Episcopal Church (AME). He was educated at Edward Waters College, an industrial school run by the AME, but moved to Harlem in 1911. While studying acting at City College, he became a supporter of the Socialist labor leader Eugene Debs (1855–1926). In 1912, Randolph set up an employment agency for blacks with a new friend, Chandler Owen. In 1917, they created a magazine, *The Messenger* (later renamed the *Black Worker*), to oppose black enlistment until the government ended segregation in the military and defense industries. In 1914, Randolph met and married a widow, Lucille Green (1883–1963), who had left a teaching job at Howard College to open a salon specializing in the cosmetics for black women developed by Mrs. C. J. Walker (1867–1919). Lucille's income supported Randolph's struggles to unionize black workers.

The sleeping cars manufactured by George Pullman (1831–1897) were the most elegant means of long-distance travel in the days before jet airplanes. By 1920, railroads were the largest employers of blacks in the United States, but their sleeping-car porters were represented only by a company-controlled union. On August 25, 1925, Randolph met secretly with 500 porters and convinced 200 of them to join an independent union. By 1926 Randolph's Brotherhood of Sleeping Car Porters had locals in over 20 cities. The battle for recognition was long and hard, but the Brotherhood finally won its first major contract with the Pullman Company in 1937. Although most unions barred blacks from membership, Randolph had the Brotherhood join the great union alliances—the American Federation of Labor (AFL) and the Congress of Industrial Organizations (CIO)—to benefit from their strength and encourage the opening up of unions to African-Americans. He eventually became vice president of the AFL-CIO (1955) and created the Negro American Labor Council (1960) to fight for African-American equality within AFL-CIO ranks.

Even before the United States entered World War II, the government began to accelerate defense production, but such jobs were closed to black workers. With the support of his union, Randolph called for a protest march in Washington by 100,000 workers. A week before the July 1 march date, Roosevelt issued Executive Order 8802 (June 25, 1941), barring discrimination in defense industries. Randolph called off the march. After the war, he founded the League for Nonviolent Civil Disobedience Against Military Segregation to protest President Truman's peacetime draft. On July 26, 1948, Randolph won another victory when Truman issued Executive Order 9981, barring segregation in the armed forces. Randolph's organizational expertise was again evident in the 1963 March on Washington for Jobs and Freedom, where he gave the opening speech. President Johnson invited Randolph to the signing of the Civil Rights Act of 1964.

Even though he suffered from chronic illness, Randolph remained president of the Brotherhood of Sleeping Car Porters until 1968, when he retired from public life. He died on May 16, 1979.

In July 1943 Allied forces landed in Sicily; their advance to the Italian mainland in September caused the fall of Mussolini. Germany was forced to invade northern Italy to hold it for the Axis. But further meetings between Roosevelt and Churchill in Washington (May) and Quebec (August) postponed the planned main invasion of Europe until 1944. Stalin suspected his allies of delaying the invasion so that the Russian and German armies might destroy each other and leave Eastern Europe free. Despite Anglo-American rhetoric about the rights of national self-determination, Stalin intended to keep all the territories he had gained from the *Nazi-Soviet Pact* of 1939 and to exact harsh reparations from Germany.

At a conference of foreign ministers held in Moscow in October 1943, tensions within the Grand Alliance began to surface. The Russians rejected the claims of the London-based Polish government in exile for control of the still-to-be-liberated Poland, in favor of Polish communist exiles in Moscow. Nevertheless the sessions went well due to Allied military advances. Stalin was assured that the main invasion of Europe would go forward in 1944. In return, he agreed to declare war on Japan once Germany was defeated. All agreed that a new international organization should be formed to replace the discredited League of Nations. Nor was China's fate ignored by the Allies. At the Cairo Conference of November 22–23, 1943, Roosevelt and Churchill met with Chiang to assure him that their unconditional surrender terms applied to Japan as well. The territories seized from China would be restored to the Nationalists, and Korea would become free "in due course."

From November 8 to December 1, 1943, Roosevelt, Churchill, and Stalin conferred in Tehran, the capital of Iran. There, they endorsed a proposal to create a United Nations as a successor to the failed League and laid out some tentative zones of postwar control. Stalin was assured that any postwar Polish government would be friendly towards the USSR, and that Polish territory would be expanded at Germany's expense to insure the viability of Poland as a buffer state between the USSR and Germany. The date for the main invasion of Europe was set for May 1, 1944, but the choice of the invasion route opened another rift between the Allies. Churchill, convinced the Soviet Union would not retreat from any land it liberated from the Nazis, wanted a southern route. Stalin refused to consider it. Roosevelt agreed with Stalin on a western course. Churchill found himself overruled.

Churchill refused to accept a secondary role for Britain, traveling to Moscow in October 1944 to negotiate with Stalin on his own. The result was a "sphere of influence" power sharing scheme: in Greece, 90% British/10% Russian; in Romania, the reverse; in Yugoslavia and Hungary 50:50; and in Bulgaria 75% Russian/25% British. The scheme was never carried out, largely due to American objections.

◆ The End of the War in Europe

As 1944 began the Third Reich was under assault from every direction. Soviet armies pushed steadily west, Allied forces in Italy inched towards Rome, and fleets of aircraft daily dropped tons of bombs on German cities. The attempt to destroy Hitler's wartime production failed, but the skies belonged to the Allies, an advantage of vital importance in the planned invasion. Allied naval forces controlled the Atlantic shipping lanes, conveying vast quantities of men and materiel to staging areas in England. Rome was taken on June 4. Two days later, June 6 (D-Day), the Allied armies began to come ashore in Normandy, on the northern coast of France; the main invasion of *Festung Europa* had begun. Operation Overlord, as it was called, was the largest amphibious operation ever mounted. 150,000 men, 1500 tanks, and thousands of guns and supplies were moved onto the Normandy beaches. To get them there, the Allies used over 5,000 ships, landing

D-Day plus two: Allied forces dig in on Normandy Beach.
Copyright © Archive Photos

craft, and prefabricated harbors ("Mulberries"). Over 12,000 planes provided air support. A sixty-mile-long beachhead was established within days, but fierce German opposition, led by Rommel, kept the Allies from breaking out for almost seven weeks. The losses on both sides were enormous. In impeccably kept cemeteries along the Normandy coast, row upon row of white crosses still bear tribute to the dead.

While the British and Americans moved in from the west, the Soviet Union closed in on Hitler from the east. On June 26, the Russians launched a fresh assault against the Germans, although they halted temporarily outside Warsaw to allow German troops to put down a Polish uprising that might later have threatened Stalin's plans. By August, Soviet troops were pushing through Romania and Bulgaria.

Meanwhile millions of Allied troops were pouring into France through the Normandy beachhead and from a second landing in southern France. Finally pushing inland, Allied troops captured Paris on August 25. Belgium was rapidly cleared, but the defeat of a British force at Arnhem made it clear the war was not going to end in 1944. Mustering three *panzer* armies, Hitler ordered a winter attack on the weakly defended Ardennes front in northern France and Belgium. On

December 16, 1944, the Battle of the Bulge began as Germans, aided by the bad weather that grounded Allied planes, pushed fifty miles into Allied lines. But they failed to make a decisive breakthrough, and by the end of January 1945 the "Bulge" was gone and so was Germany's last opportunity. Anglo-American forces crossed the Rhine River by the end of March as Russians mounted a final assault on Berlin.

With the outcome of the war no longer in doubt, the Allied leaders met at Yalta in the Crimea, in February 1945, to discuss the final drive against Hitler and the future of Europe. All agreed on the carving up of Germany and its capital, Berlin, into zones of occupation. But Roosevelt, already suffering from advanced heart disease, struggled to gain Soviet support for the Pacific campaign against Japan and for the planned United Nations. Stalin's price was territorial concessions in the Far East, and, while he pledged to allow free elections in all the liberated territories, he did so knowing his forces were already in control in Eastern Europe.

Allied forces continued to advance on all fronts, but Roosevelt did not live to see the victory; he died of a cerebral hemorrhage on April 12 and was succeeded by his vice-president, Harry S. Truman (1884–1972). Neither did Mussolini survive the war. Italy's ousted Fascist leader was murdered by partisans on April 28, his corpse hung upside down at a gas station in a Milan square. The Soviet and American armies linked up at the city of Torgau in Germany on April 25, by which date Soviet troops were already advancing through the devastated streets of Berlin. There, on April 30, 1945, Adolf Hitler committed suicide in his underground bunker. His successor, Admiral Karl Dönitz (1891–1980), dispatched envoys to Reims, France, where General Alfred Jodl (1890–1946) formally signed Germany's surrender on May 7. Since the surrender took effect at one minute after midnight, May 8 became V-E (Victory in Europe) Day. Hitler's planned thousand-year *Reich* had lasted only twelve. The war in Europe was over.

◆   The End of the War in the Pacific

After securing Guadalcanal early in 1943, American forces commanded by General Douglas MacArthur (1880–1964) and Admiral Chester W. Nimitz (1885–1966) began a two-year "island hopping" campaign, targeting major bases and leaving lesser islands for later mopping up as they moved ever closer to Japan. The capture of Saipan, Tinian, and Guam in August 1944 brought Kyushu, one of the four main islands that make up Japan, within Allied bombing range (using the B-29 Superfortresses) for the first time in the war. The defeat of the Japanese navy at Leyte Gulf in the Philippines in October ended its ability to pose an offensive threat to the American advance. By November, US planes were bombing Japan on a regular basis, and MacArthur returned in triumph to the Philippine Islands that he had been forced to leave in 1942. But the Japanese refused to accept the inevitable. *Kamikaze* ("divine wind"), the Japanese term for typhoons, was also the name for a strategy of suicide aerial attacks. In the battle for Luzon in the Philippines (January 4–13, 1945) kamikaze pilots used obsolete airplanes as suicide bombs, deliberately crashing them into American ships. They managed to sink 17 American ships and damage another 50. In February-March 1945, Iwo Jima was taken after the most vicious fighting of the Pacific War: one third of all the US Marines who died in World War II died capturing that small island. Located only 750 miles from Tokyo, Iwo Jima provided an excellent base for the saturation bombing of Japanese cities. On April 1, four US Army and four US Marine divisions landed on Okinawa, an island just over 300 miles south of Japan's home islands. The Americans wanted Okinawa as a base for the planned invasion of Japan. The American blockade had so weakened Japanese production that the Japanese navy had to sideline some of its remaining battleships for lack of fuel, but the Japanese on Okinawa resisted so fiercely, it was June 21 before the island was secured by US forces. Kamikaze pilots managed to sink another 15 American ships and damage 200 more.

Before the planned invasion of Japan was undertaken, the Allied leaders met once again, this time at Potsdam, south of Berlin from July 12 to August 2. The meeting marked the changing of the guard. Truman now represented the United States, and Clement Attlee (1883–1967), the Labour Party leader, replaced Churchill as Prime Minister of Britain in the middle of the conference. Only Stalin remained of the original leaders of the Grand Alliance. The meeting also underscored the widening divide between eastern and western plans for a post-war world. Knowing the western allies were not willing to fight on for several more years to liberate eastern Europe from Soviet control, Stalin refused Truman's demands for free elections in the eastern states. Questions of requiring reparations from the Axis powers and Poland's borders and government remained unresolved. On July 24, Truman informed Stalin that the United States had successfully tested a new weapon that might shorten the Pacific war considerably. Stalin merely nodded acknowledgment. Told by his spies of the successful bomb test of July 16 (at Alamogordo, New Mexico), Stalin had already ordered the development of a similar weapon for the USSR. The conference ended with the Big Three issuing a warning to Japan of total destruction if it did not surrender. The weapon in question was the atomic bomb, the result of a government-sponsored, military-run research effort (the "Manhattan Project") begun in 1942 to counter a suspected Nazi atomic research project.

On board ship while returning from the Potsdam Conference, Truman approved the use of the atomic bomb against Japan. Fewer than ten thousand of Okinawa's 120,000 defenders had been captured alive. The Japanese had not only fought to the death but massacred the civilian population as they went. The Americans expected a similarly fanatical defense of Japan's Home Islands. The hope was that the bomb, by convincing the Japanese of the futility of such a defense, would make an invasion unnecessary and save the tens of thousands of expected American casualties. A quick defeat of Japan would also be a campaign won without Soviet assistance and without Soviet claims for territory thereafter. On August 6, a B-29 bomber (the Enola Gay) dropped a single uranium bomb on Hiroshima that leveled much of the city and killed over 80,000 people. On the eighth, Stalin fulfilled his Yalta pledge and declared war on Japan. The Soviet Union launched an invasion of Manchuria and laid claim to all the territorial concessions it had been promised, including Korea north of the 38th parallel. The Japanese stood fast. On August 9, a second bomb, this one using plutonium instead of uranium, destroyed the city of Nagasaki. Despite the unprecedented destruction, only the personal intervention of Emperor Hirohito could bring the Imperial War Council to finally consider surrender. Peace overtures were made on August 14. The formal surrender was signed before the representatives of 41 Allied nations on the deck of the battleship *Missouri* on September 2, 1945. The most destructive war in human history was finally over. 61 countries, comprising 75 percent of the world's population fought on one side or the other. Mobilizations topped 110 million with more than half those mobilized to fight coming from the Soviet Union, Germany, and the United States alone. At an estimated direct cost of one trillion dollars and trillions more in damaged property, it was more expensive than all the other wars in human history combined. The loss of human life was so vast no accurate count can be established down to the last individual, but with over 25 million soldiers and more than 53 million civilians killed, it was by far the bloodiest war in human history as well.

Atlee, Truman, and Stalin at Potsdam—the last meeting of the "Big Three" Allies of WWII.
Copyright © CORBIS/Bettmann

Aftermath

◆ Creating the United Nations

The unprecedented loss of life and property during the Second World War convinced the members of the Allied coalition that an international agency dedicated to preventing such catastrophes was essential. President Roosevelt had campaigned for a new global organization almost as hard as he had worked to defeat the Axis powers. As far back as January 1942, the Allies had pledged to support political and economic freedom and maintain harmonious international relations after the defeat of Fascism. Still, the problems of creating a viable international organization, given the collapse of the League of Nations, were immense. In many respects the 1942 Declaration of the United Nations reflected America's naive expectation that freely elected governments, guaranteed citizen rights and liberal capitalist economies would surely follow victory. By the time the *United Nations Charter* was signed on April 25, 1945, in San Francisco, those expectations had faded, but the work went forward.

The United Nations went into operation in London in January 1946 when Trygve Lie (1896–1968) of Norway was elected its first Secretary General. The organization quickly took its current form. Modeled on western ideas of government, the United Nations possesses legislative, executive, and judicial branches, although these branches do not have the same powers as the branches of a national government. The General Assembly forms the "lower" house of the "legislature." All member nations have one vote in the General Assembly, which elects the Secretary General and deals with issues of human rights, economic development (through its Economic and Social Council), decolonization (through its Trusteeship Council) and international order. The General Assembly has the right to meditate, condemn, and impose economic sanctions, but it cannot enforce its decisions.

The power to use military force rests with the "upper" house, the Security Council. The five largest Allied powers—The United States, the Soviet Union, Great Britain, France, and (Nationalist) China—were awarded permanent seats on the Security Council. The other members of the General Assembly organized themselves into regional groups, with each group electing one of its members to fill a rotating seat on the Council. The number of rotating seats has been increased over the years but the only change in the Permanent Seats has been the substitution of Communist for Nationalist China. Two rules apply to votes taken in the Security Council: all measures must be passed by a majority vote, and each Permanent Member has an absolute veto over all Council measures. The veto assured the Allied powers that measures against their interests would not move forward—and satisfied Congress that American sovereignty would not be violated—but it also prevented the United Nations from taking action in cases where the superpowers were divided. The Security and Peacekeeping forces are made up of soldiers from the member nations and cannot be sent into any country without that country's express request.

The Secretariat, headed by the Secretary General, acts as the "executive" branch of the United Nations, supervising its bureaus worldwide. The Secretary General often acts as the organization's chief diplomat and mediator. The International Court of Justice established at The Hague in the Netherlands functions as the "judicial" branch of the United Nations. It resolves disputes between any two members that wish to bring a case before it. However, without an international state to enforce it, international law lacks the sanction power of national law. Therefore, the Court cannot force members to appear before it or enforce its decisions on its own.

Shifting from temporary locations in London and Geneva, the United Nations was given a permanent home in the United States. In 1952 a complex of buildings was erected on land donated by the Rockefeller family in New York City, and for more than half a century the leaders of the world have convened in Manhattan in search of world cooperation.

◆ A Framework for Peace

No one single Treaty or general Peace Conference marked the end of World War II (1939–1945). The new world order was put together piece by piece in an era of shifting political alignments. The borders of Germany were redrawn at the Potsdam Conference (1945): the southern section of East Prussia (including Danzig) was given to Poland, the northern section to Russia. Several territorial adjustments were not resolved until 1947: Italy's recently acquired African empire was disbanded and a small portion of the Italian province of Venezia was given to Yugoslavia; one province of Finland went to Russia; Hungary lost territory to Czechoslovakia and Romania, while Romania lost territory to Russia and Bulgaria. But none of these reallocations directly addressed the problem of maintaining peace and creating equality within multi-national states. Relatively modest reparations were imposed on the Axis Powers and their satellite states, ranging from $70 million for Bulgaria to $360 million for Italy. When the United Nations received its Charter in 1945, the

Axis Powers and their satellites were originally excluded from membership, as were the formally "neutral" states such as Sweden, Switzerland, and Spain.

A growing internationalism marked the postwar settlement and world. One important attempt to foster shared values was made when the Grand Alliance put dozens of their former enemies on trial in Nuremberg, Germany. No such proceedings had followed World War I, when only a few German officers had been convicted in national trials; the Kaiser had been permitted to live out his life in exile. But the unprecedented crimes of the Nazi regime seemed to require a definitive world response. Since it was impossible for the millions who supported the Nazis to be put on trial, the major powers—the United States, the Soviet Union, Great Britain and France—convened an International Tribunal to hold representative Nazi figures accountable. Twenty-two German leaders from the government, the army, the police, and industry were the first to be tried in Nuremberg. At the end of their year-long trial, nineteen were found guilty of conspiracy to wage aggressive war and crimes against humanity. The defense of just "following orders" was not accepted as an excuse for committing atrocities. Although Hermann Göring (1893–1946), *Luftwaffe* chief and director of Hitler's economic planning, escaped judgment by committing suicide, a dozen Nazi leaders were hanged in 1946 and the rest imprisoned. At additional trials over a three-year period, judges, doctors, and corporate officials were brought before the bar of international justice. Similar trials in the Far East brought 28 Japanese defendants before a panel of eleven international judges. The most prominent defendant was former Prime Minister Tōjō, who was hanged along with six other Japanese leaders in December 1948. Historians, politicians, and legal experts still debate the legality, the efficacy, and the morality of the sentences and the tribunals that imposed them.

◆ Occupied Japan

On August 15, 1945, Emperor Hirohito told his nation that the "unendurable must be endured" and announced that Japan would surrender to the Grand Alliance. Having used biological weapons against China and terribly mistreated prisoners of war, the Japanese expected a harsh occupation. As six million Japanese soldiers slowly made their way home from areas they had once conquered, American General Douglas MacArthur was given the task of remodeling Japan and overseeing its return to the world community. That task was made easier in December 1945 when the Truman Administration, in an unofficial arrangement, agreed to Soviet control of Bulgaria and Romania in return for a free hand in Japan.

For the next six years MacArthur ruled the island nation as Supreme Commander for the Allied Powers (SCAP), with dictatorial power. His first job was demilitarization. While only seven Japanese officials had been executed for their role in World War II, over 200,000 soldiers and administrators were removed from the positions from which they had directed the imperial war effort. The stranglehold of the samurai class on the government of Japan was broken.

The next issue was the reform of the government itself. At first many Japanese believed that the United States intended to end their monarchy, but because American policy permitted Emperor Hirohito to retain his title, the population became more supportive of the proposed changes. State Shinto, the combination of native Japanese animism and emperor worship that had been a distinctive feature of traditional Japan, was abolished: the Emperor was now no more than the ceremonial head of state. A new constitution, written in 1947, created a parliamentary democracy in which the population elected all the members of both houses of the legislature (the *Diet*), guaranteed all citizens freedom of speech, religion, and the press, and made all citizens equal under the law by eliminating noble rank and giving the vote to women as well as to men. The first elections had already been held in 1946, when the newly formed Liberal Party led by Yoshida Shigeru (1878–1967) began its still almost unbroken string of electoral triumphs.

MacArthur initiated a series of social reforms to be completed by the new government. The educational system was purged of teachers who had actively supported military aggression: 25 percent of all teachers were replaced. To bring the benefits of higher education to a greater number of Japanese, MacArthur increased compulsory education for both sexes from six years to nine, made co-education the norm rather than the exception, decentralized control of the secondary schools which were set up on American models, and introduced global social studies into the Japanese curriculum. Textbooks were rewritten to give Japanese students a more realistic view of their country's past behavior. MacArthur's land reforms created a thriving class of small farmers while American-encouraged labor unions began to play a role in industrial life. The largest of the vertically integrated industrial syndicates were broken up as well, although they would soon reform along modified lines. Because American aid rebuilt Japan's economy along with its cities, the American occupation helped provide the foundation for the "economic miracle" that began in the 1950s and transformed Japan into one of the largest economies in the world.

This economic powerhouse would prove to be a peaceful powerhouse. The new Japanese constitution included a clause renouncing "war as a sovereign right of the nation." The new Japan had only self-defense forces and relied on the United States military for wider protection. A peace treaty ending World War II was signed on September 8, 1951, and under its terms the United States secured the right to have military bases on Japanese territory. To help ease international concerns about a rebuilt Japan, the United States also signed mutual security pacts in 1951 with Australia and New Zealand (the ANZUS Pact) and with the Philippines.

◆ Occupied Germany

According to the agreements reached at the Yalta and Potsdam Conferences in 1945, Germany was to be divided into three zones of occupation with each of the three occupying powers—the Soviet Union, the United States and Great Britain—in charge of "denazification," demilitarization, and re-education within its respective zone. With the consent of the United States and Great Britain a fourth zone was carved out of their territories for French occupation. Berlin, the German capital since 1871, was inside the Soviet zone, but it was similarly divided among the four powers. Each occupying power was also given the authority to exact reparations in the form of capital equipment and external assets, but not out of current production. The partition was not intended to be permanent. Progress towards rehabilitation was to be rewarded by re-unification. In the western zones, regional parties were allowed to form within each *Länder* (state) within a year.

Austria was also divided into occupation zones. It was freed from Allied control and reunited in 1955. Germany, however, would not be re-united until 1990. The reasons for this delay will be discussed in the following chapter.

◆ Summing Up

As a military venture, the Second World War (1939–1945) was very different from the First (1914–1918). The First World War had been a war of trenches and fixed positions. The great powers turned their industrialized weapons upon each other only to find they had no effective defenses except to burrow into the ground. The Second World War was highly mobile, making the machine gun-proof tank the centerpiece of its armored forces and relying on wireless technology to keep track of its speeding armies. The First World War saw the introduction of submarine and

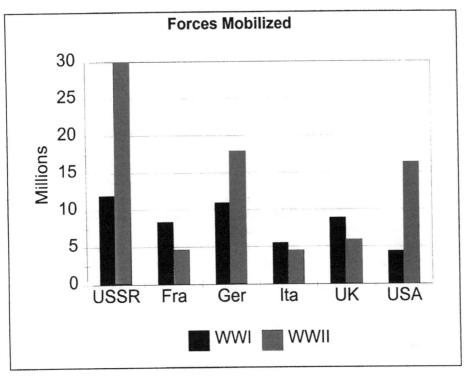

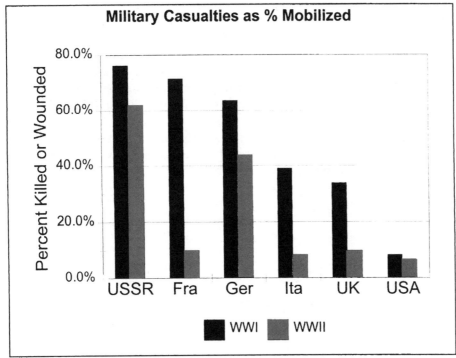

Sources for both charts: J. L. Stokesbury, *A Short History of World War I* (New York: Quill, 1981), 310; John Ellis, *World War II, A Statistical Survey* (Facts on File), 253–254; Robert Gorlaski, *World War II Almanac* (New York: Putnam, 1981), 425–428.

aerial warfare. The Second brought destroyers to combat the submarines, radar to detect enemy aircraft, and aircraft carriers to bring the air war to the seven seas. The great bombers of the Second war dwarfed the biplanes of the First. The First war brought poison gas; the Second, the atomic bomb. As high as the casualties were in the First War, the improved weaponry of the Second sent the numbers soaring. Military deaths were more than twice as high and civilian deaths three times as high as in the First World War. Every nation involved saw its losses mount, but the nations hardest hit were the Soviet Union, with 29 million dead including 17 million civilians, and China, with 21.4 million dead including 20 million civilians. Property damage was in the trillions.

To feed the vast and deadly armies, fully industrialized economies turned, for the duration, into the largest producers of war machines the world had ever seen. And, in the end, it was those economies that made the difference. It was Germany's economic strength that allowed Hitler to make his first conquests and, enlarged by the use of slave labor in the conquered territories, to hold an empire greater than Napoleon's. But it could not last against the combined military might of the United States and the Soviet Union, or even the economic power of the United States alone. The largest economy the world had ever seen was capable not only, it seemed, of endlessly resupplying its own forces, but endlessly resupplying those of its allies as well. No war is, of course, ever won because of a single reason; the strategy and tactics chosen, the size of the armies and the morale and motivation of the opposing forces all play their part. But more than in any previous wars, the balance of economic power tipped the scales in World War II.

One final distinction between the two World Wars must be mentioned. The horrors of the First World War dealt a blow to the self-confidence of European civilization from which it never entirely recovered, but the Second institutionalized unprecedented mass murder and extermination camps. Attacks on noncombatants had been a minor note in the First World War, but a daily occurrence in the Second, and each attack was rendered more terrible by the deadlier firepower of the Second World War. Japan's "Rape of Nanking" and Hitler's Blitz were met by the Allied fire bombings of Dresden (February 13–15, 1945) and Tokyo (March 9–10). While true concentration camps were found only in German and Japanese territory, the internment of civilians was common to both sides. Japanese Americans found themselves imprisoned within their own country as war fever reached its highest pitch. No outrage, no atrocity, no saturation bombing, however, approached the horror that awaited the liberating armies as they crossed the eastern half of *Festung Europa*. The piles of half-burned bodies, the walking skeleton survivors, the bales of human hair awaiting recycling as mattress stuffing and human ash as soap—neither words nor pictures will ever capture the horror of Hitler's assembly line of death.

◆ Notes

1. *The Rommel Papers*, edited by B. H. Liddell Hart, translated by Paul Findlay (New York: Da Capo Press, 1982), 124.

2. *Bartlett's Familiar Quotations*, 15th edition, edited by Emily Morrison Beck (Boston: Little, Brown, and Co., 1980), 744 [#6].

3. *Bartlett's Familiar Quotations*, 780 [#15].

10

The Cold War

The "Cold War" was a term coined in 1947 to describe the mounting antagonism between the victorious members of the Grand Alliance that defined superpower relations for some forty-five years after the fall of Nazi Germany, as the United States and the Soviet Union competed to win allies and influence national policy around the world. It was fought in the theaters of science, technology, military potential, economic productivity, political ideology, and even in the arenas of athletic competition and artistic achievement. It was a war without a clearly defined beginning and it seemed to have no conceivable end. Then, in 1989, almost without warning, the Soviet bloc began to collapse. Germany was reunited in 1990. The Soviet Union fell apart in 1991. This chapter charts the construction, course, and conclusion of the "Cold War."

Constructing the Cold War

◆ From Conflicting Aims to Conflict

During successive Allied conferences held during the Second World War, it became increasingly clear that the "Big Three" (the United States, Great Britain, and the Soviet Union) had incompatible visions of the post-war order. Stalin's main concerns in Europe were strategic security and economic compatibility. This meant achieving political control over the countries on the Soviet Union's western border, many of which had been Nazi satellites or hostile to Communism. It also meant maintaining a controlling influence in post-war Germany. Stalin was determined to prevent a third German invasion of the Russian heartland. Establishing a line of "people's republics" along the Soviet Union's European border would serve was a buffer zone against any future German expansion, while providing the Soviet economy with compatible trading partners in the long term and desperately needed capital resources and food in the short. Stalin also expected to be treated as a victorious partner by his capitalist Allies; he expected to have an equal voice in international affairs. He intended to expand Soviet influence if and when suitable opportunities to do so presented themselves, just as he expected his Allies to attempt to expand their spheres of influence. He believed that every state imposed its political system as far as its armies could reach.

Great Britain was an imperial power entering a period of economic and political decline. Traditionally, Britain had preserved its own security by maintaining a "balance of power" within Europe: if one state became so strong as to prove a threat to Britain's interests, Britain would respond by making alliances with other European states to counter-balance it. Now the Soviet Union was about to assume military dominance within Europe. Moreover, whether under the Tsar or under the Communists, Russia had long been Britain's rival in the Middle East and Central Asia. In 1943 Churchill had lobbied hard for an Anglo-American invasion of Nazi-occupied Europe from the south rather than from the west. If Allied forces came up via the Mediterranean, they would liberate large portions of South East and Central Europe before Soviet forces could reach them. This would limit the post-war sphere of influence available to Stalin. Churchill's plans, however, had been vetoed by Roosevelt.

Roosevelt saw aggressive power politics, competing "spheres of influence," and imperialist rivalries as the root cause of both world wars. He expected that the combination of America's role in an Allied victory and America's economic power would bring about a different world order, one based on the principles in the *Declaration of the United Unions* signed by the Allies in 1942. This *Declaration* pledged the Allies to support political and economic freedom for all nations, and to maintain peaceful international cooperation and collective security. The Americans expected their own values to spread swiftly in such a world order.

In 1946, the "Big Three" clashed over the future of Iran. Western forces had occupied Iran during the war, but Soviet military forces stationed in northern Iran supported breakaway nationalist movements in Iran's northern provinces of Kurdistan and Azerbaijan in the hope of turning them into autonomous Soviet client states. The United States and Great Britain backed an Iranian complaint about the USSR made at the first session of the United Nations (January 14, 1946). The Soviet Union agreed to withdraw its forces in return for an oil concession and partial self-government in northern Iran, but American military aid to the Shah of Iran soon helped him repudiate the agreement and crush the separatists.

The battled lines hardened throughout 1946. In February, Stalin spoke of western "enemies," predicted war between the capitalist and Communist systems, and refused to participate in a United Nations plan to control atomic energy. In a "long telegram" from Moscow on February 22, American diplomat George Kennan (b. 1904) warned of historic Russian ambitions to control Central Europe and expand southward towards the Middle East; the solution he proposed was "firm and vigilant containment" of Soviet expansion. On March 5, in a speech given at Westminster College in Missouri, Winston Churchill warned the world that "an iron curtain has descended across the Continent" and behind its cover Soviet-sponsored "police governments" were moving to destroy democracy.[1] The Soviet Union was already putting pressure on Turkey to cede its northern province of Kars (a former possession of Tsarist Russia) to the USSR and allow Soviet warships through the Bosporus and Dardanelles, the straits connecting Soviet ports in the Black Sea to the Mediterranean. To coerce Turkey into making those concessions, Soviet troops massed on the border of neighboring Bulgaria. Truman began aiding the modernization of Turkey's armed forces to counter Stalin's attempts to control the Bosporus and Dardanelles.

◆ Rebuilding Europe

The conflict deepened in 1947. Early in the year it became clear that an independent Communist regime in Yugoslavia was using Albania and Bulgaria as conduits for arms shipments, in support of a Communist led insurrection (ELAS) in Greece. British troops had prevented an earlier Communist takeover in Athens in 1944, but this time an impoverished British government informed the United States that it could no longer provide military or financial aid to Greece. Unless the United States acted quickly, a Communist victory seemed assured. On March 12, the President asked Congress for $400 million in military and economic aid for Greece and Turkey. Congress, angered by Stalin's refusal to settle the future of Germany, agreed. The aid program and the policy that grew out of it have become known as the Truman Doctrine. Truman declared that "it must be the policy of the United States to support free peoples who are resisting attempted subversion by armed minorities or by outside pressures,"[2] committing the United States to halt the spread of world Communism. In the decades to come a ring of military alliances and dozens of aid packages would follow, but, the immediate effect of the Doctrine was to convince Stalin that cooperation with the west was impossible. The coalitions between Communists and other anti-Fascist parties he had allowed in Eastern Europe would have to go. Communists seized power in Bulgaria, Romania, and Hungary, coordinating their rule through the Communist Information Bureau (COMINFORM) set up later that year.

World War II had taken an enormous toll on Europe's productive capacity. Former Allies and Axis members alike were on the verge of bankruptcy, and the winter of 1946–1947 saw the worst European weather in a century. By late spring hunger, power shortages, and inflation were rampant. Such conditions had facilitated the rise of Communist and Fascist dictatorships only a few decades before. The question was how to prevent the cycle from repeating itself. The announcement of the Truman Doctrine and Stalin's reaction to it made a joint response impossible. The United States decided to act unilaterally. In a speech delivered at Harvard University on June 5, 1947, American Secretary of State George C. Marshall (1880–1959) proposed that the United States fund European economic recovery. The shock of a Communist takeover in Czechoslovakia in February 1948 prompted quick acceptance of the "Marshall Plan" by the American Congress. Enacted into law as the European Recovery Act, the Marshall Plan offered extensive aid grants and guarantees to all the states of Europe. However, while Marshall Plan aid would be channeled through a European administrative body, the United States expected to assume a guiding role in that administration. It also expected to gather economic intelligence about aid recipients. Alarmed by the thought of American economic oversight, Stalin refused to allow any of his European satellite states to participate in the program. Sixteen nations ultimately agreed to accept Marshall Plan aid, and over $13 billion was dispensed between 1948 and 1952, with seven-eighths of it in the form of grants. The Marshall Plan provided the economic foundation for western European recovery. By 1953 the output of the major Marshall Plan recipients was 35 percent above pre-war levels. The Plan undercut the appeal of Communism and secured allies and trading partners for the United States. The United States also profited directly from those grants to its European Allies; seventy percent of the aid was spent on goods from the United States.

The Soviet Union began its own aid program to its European satellites in 1947. Designed by Vyacheslav Mikhailovitch Molotov (1890-1986), the Russian negotiator of the Nazi-Soviet Pact, the "Molotov Plan" also aimed to prevent the formation of ties among the satellites by making their economies individually dependent on the USSR. By January 1949, the Molotov Plan had evolved into the Council of Mutual Economic Assistance (COMECON), charged with coordinating the central economic planning of Eastern Europe. Yugoslavia was the only Eastern European country to escape Soviet control. Since 1945, Yugoslavia had been under the control of Communist guerilla forces led by Josip Broz (1892–1980), a Croatian who called himself Marshal Tito. He established a one-party dictatorship and governed a federal state that provided cheap raw materials to the USSR. Not only did Tito refuse to become part of any Soviet "sphere of influence," he had visions of creating his own "sphere" in Communist southeast Europe. It was Tito's actions that had created the crisis in Greece in 1947. Outraged by Tito's refusal to follow his lead, Stalin withdrew economic and military aid, expelled Yugoslavia from COMINFORM, and used COMINFORM to enforce a commercial boycott of Yugoslavia that lasted until 1955.

◆ Arming Europe

Postwar life was proving to be very different in the four zones of occupied Germany. The Russians, claiming the reparations promised them at Yalta, were busy stripping their eastern zone of industrial resources, while the three western powers (Britain, France, and the United States) cooperated to reconstruct the economy of their zones under the Marshall Plan. Building on the regional political organizations they fostered in 1946, the three western allies also convened a congress of *Länder* (state) legislatures in 1948 to help draft a new constitution for the western zones. Approved by the Allies in the following year, the *Basic Law of 1949* created a federal system of modified parliamentary government with checks and balances, judicial review, universal suffrage, limitations on military use, and a mix of proportional and direct representation designed to prevent the sort of breakdown that had led to Hitler's appointment as Chancellor in 1933.

At the same time, the three western powers created a new currency for Germany. The *Deutschmark* replaced the Allied military currency in use since the occupation. While this currency reform stabilized the western German economy it threatened to destabilize the eastern. The western Allies offered to merge Berlin into the Soviet currency zone if they were given executive powers in the economic administration of the Soviet zone. Stalin demanded an equal say in the administration of western Germany's steel-rich Ruhr Valley in return, and the negotiations broke down. Stalin decided to act. On June 22, 1948, the Soviet Union closed off all overland rail and highway access to Berlin in an attempt to force the western powers to accept his terms. Truman's new policy of containment mandated that no further territory be ceded to the Soviet Union. In an unprecedented effort to meet the needs of a city of over 2 million people while avoiding a military confrontation, the Western allies instituted a massive airlift. Using three twenty-mile wide air corridors, Allied planes landed in Berlin sometimes as often as once every two minutes for the next ten months. Their 277,567 flights helped convince Stalin of the Allied will to maintain a free Berlin. To further intimidate him, the United States also moved two groups of B-29 atomic bombers to Britain to be closer to Berlin. The Soviet Union had yet to construct its first nuclear bomb. Stalin ended the blockade in May 1949. By September the three western zones had been transformed into the Federal Republic of Germany (West Germany) under the leadership of its first Chancellor, Konrad Adenauer (1876–1967). Less than a month later, Stalin approved the transformation of the Soviet zone into the German Democratic Republic (East Germany).

In March 1948, shortly before the blockade began, Ernest Bevin (1881–1951), Britain's Secretary of State for Foreign Affairs, orchestrated the *Treaty of Brussels,* in which Britain, France, Belgium, Luxembourg, and the Netherlands joined together in a mutual defense pact. In April, the American Congress passed the Vandenberg Resolution, authorizing President Truman to conclude defense treaties with nations threatened by the USSR. One year later, in April 1949, the North Atlantic Treaty Organization (NATO) was created by the United States, Great Britain, France, Italy, Belgium, Canada, Denmark, Iceland, Luxembourg, the Netherlands, Norway, and Portugal. The members of this mutual defense pact and collective security agreement were committed not just to treating an attack on one member as an attack against all, but also to establishing a joint military command for the defense of Western Europe. With American troops serving in NATO forces on NATO bases in Western Europe, a first response to Soviet aggression would not be slowed down by the long process of mobilization: American troops were already on the front lines. Stalin's response was the first successful test of a Soviet atomic bomb on August 29, 1949. By December, Truman authorized the development of the hydrogen bomb, a thermonuclear device far more powerful than the atomic weapons already in use. In April 1950, the National Security Council (NSC) recommended increasing American military spending from $13 to $50 billion per year, or about one-fifth of the country's total GNP. The recommendation came in a report (NSC-68) underlining the importance of globally deploying air, ground, and naval forces "superior" in number and capacity to those of the Soviet Union, without which "containment" would be nothing but a "dangerous policy of bluff."[3] Events would soon convince Congress to act on NSC-68.

DAG HAMMARSKJÖLD (1905–1961)

Advocate of a stronger United Nations.
Copyright © Hulton Getty

Dag Hjalmar Agne Carl Hammarskjöld was born on July 29, 1905, in Jönköping, Sweden into a family of distinguished civil servants. His father served as Prime Minister of Sweden (1914–1917) and chairman of the Nobel Prize Foundation (1929–1947). Hammarskjöld, having trained in law and economics at the universities of Uppsala and Stockholm, preferred politics to academia and decided to follow in his father's footsteps. After service in the Ministries of Finance and Foreign Affairs and as president of the board of the Bank of Sweden, he became vice chairman of Sweden's delegation to the United Nations General Assembly in 1951 and its chairman in 1952.

In the early 1950s, the United Nations was being torn apart by American-Soviet Cold War antagonisms. The USSR was convinced that Trygve Lie, the Norwegian serving as Secretary General, was little more than an American stooge who followed the American line on excluding Communist China, battling North Korea, and permitting FBI screening of UN personnel. Lie's forced resignation in November 1952 coincided with a virtual boycott of the organization by the Soviet Bloc. Only when Britain and France convinced the Soviet Union to accept Hammarskjöld as Secretary General (April 10, 1953) was the organization saved.

A respected administrator from a neutral country, Hammarskjöld's even-handed methods restored the promise of the United Nations. In January 1955 he flew to Communist China to secure the release of Americans held captive after the end of the Korean War. In 1956 he mediated the ending of the Suez Crisis and pioneered the UN's use of military peacekeepers, installing a United Nations Expeditionary Force (UNEF) along the Egypt-Israel border. Unanimously re-elected to a second five-year term in 1957, he helped resolve international crises in Lebanon (1958) and Laos (1959). In the process, he won grudging acceptance from both super powers.

Hammarskjöld's peacemaking skills were tested to the full when civil war erupted in the newly independent Republic of the Congo (1960). Over the complaints of the Soviet Union, Hammarskjöld again employed United Nations troops as peacekeepers. He visited the Congo repeatedly, seeking peace between the government of President Joseph Kasavubu and the secessionist movement of Moise Tshombe in the rich mining province of Katanga. During one such mission, on September 18, 1961, Hammarskjöld's aircraft crashed while attempting to land at Ndola airfield on the border between Katanga province and Northern Rhodesia. All aboard were killed in the crash, and Hammarskjöld was succeeded as Secretary General by U Thant of Thailand.

Though Hammarskjöld was unable to resolve the Congo crisis before his death, he left behind a United Nations whose worth as an international security organization was accepted by both the super powers. During the 1960s new nations rapidly swelled its membership as imperialism continued to recede around the globe.

Cold War Europe.
From *Out of Many: A History of the American People, Second Edition,* by Faragher, Buhle, Czitrom, and Armitage. Copyright © 1997 by Prentice-Hall, Inc.

In the meantime, NATO continued to expand. Greece and Turkey were admitted to NATO in 1952 as part of the commitment made in 1947 to keep them free of Communism. Spain did not join NATO but was drawn into its orbit through a separate treaty with the United States in 1953. And in 1954, the decision was made to admit West Germany to full membership in NATO. The leadership of the Soviet Union decided that a counter alliance was needed. COMINFORM was converted into a defensive military alliance when the Warsaw Pact was signed in May 1955 by the Soviet Union and its satellite states—Albania, Bulgaria, Hungary, Poland, Czechoslovakia, Romania, and the German Democratic Republic (East Germany). On either side of what Churchill had called the "iron curtain" dividing Europe, there now stood a military alliance headed by a superpower possessing nuclear weapons.

Fighting the Cold War: The Global Front
◆   A Third Power: the Emergence of Communist China

When the use of atomic weapons ended World War II in the Pacific, China had been at war with Japan for over eight years. From 1937 to 1945, the long and bitter internal conflict between Chiang Kai-shek and the Communist Party was put aside in favor of a "United Front" against the Japanese invaders. While Communist armies did most of the fighting, Chiang represented China in the Allied Coalition, and his Nationalist government was awarded a permanent seat on the United Nations Security Council.

The Chinese United Front quickly fell apart after the surrender of Japan. Soviet troops occupied Manchuria under the terms of the surrender. They used their position to transfer captured military resources to the Chinese Communists who already controlled vast areas of northeast China. President Truman dispatched George Marshall to negotiate an extension of the eight-year truce between the Chinese factions, but open war erupted between the Communists and the Nationalists in 1946. American transport facilities and financial assistance were made available to Nationalist Party leader Chiang Kai-shek. Despite being outnumbered by the Nationalists by more than three to one, a coalition of Communists, peasants, workers, and middle-class supporters led by Mao Tse-tung (1893–1976) seized an early advantage in the fighting. Most of the cities remained in Nationalist hands. But the identification of the Communist movement with land reform, active resistance to the Japanese, and general incorruptibility gained it great popularity in the Chinese countryside. By the beginning of 1949, Nationalist forces were everywhere in retreat, while expanding Communist armies outfitted themselves with equipment captured from fleeing Nationalists.

In a last ditch effort to negotiate a peace, Chiang gave up the presidency, but to no avail. The Nationalist capital of Nanking was taken on April 24. As the Communists secured southern China, Chiang confiscated all of China's gold reserves and led his defeated government into exile on Taiwan, a small island 100 miles off the China coast. The Nationalists had been making preparations for the move to Taiwan since 1947, but some ten thousand Taiwanese were executed before Chiang's authority was accepted. Meanwhile, the triumphant Communist Party leader Mao Tse-tung proclaimed the establishment of the People's Republic of China (PRC) on the mainland on October 1, 1949.

With over 540 million people, China immediately surpassed the Soviet Union to become the most populous Communist state. Unlike its Communist neighbor, however, the PRC was still a peasant society. Modernization had to be its first priority, but technical aid was only available through the Soviet Union. In December 1949, Mao traveled to Moscow to solicit Stalin's help in transforming China into a socialist society. Mao, recognizing that his hold on China was still fragile, was willing to accept the primacy of the Soviet Union within the Communist world for the time being. He was rewarded with a 30-year treaty of alliance and pledges of immediate assistance. Mao carried those promises back to a nation whose economy was so weak it had reverted to barter. Broad programs to raise literacy, improve health, and create jobs through public works were quickly instituted. Mao expected that the United States would eventually recognize the new state because America had already accepted the Soviet satellite system in Eastern Europe, but problems in Korea made that recognition impossible.

MADAME CHIANG KAI-SHEK (SOONG MEI-LING) 1897–2003

Born on March 5, 1897, in Kwantung province, China, Mei-ling was the third and youngest daughter of the wealthy Soong family. Her father, Charles Soong, an American-educated businessman, was a Christian who made his fortune selling Bibles to newly converted Chinese. The Soong "dynasty" is perhaps the most important in modern Chinese history. One of Mei-ling's two sisters (Ch'ing-ling) married the revolutionary leader (and first president of the Chinese Republic) Sun Yat-sen, while the other (Ai-ling) wed a premier of China. Her brother (Soong Tse-wen, or T. V. Soong as he was known in the west) was a wealthy banker who eventually became premier of China himself.

In 1908 Mei-ling was sent to the United States and graduated from Wellesley College, Massachusetts, in 1917. Returning to Asia, Mei-ling met Chiang Kai-shek, a young officer in Sun Yat-sen's military service who had risen to the leadership of Southern and Central China after Sun's death in 1925. They wed in December 1927, and not long afterward, Chiang became a Christian. Madame Chiang introduced her husband to Western culture, and became one of his chief advisers. In 1936, when her husband was kidnaped by rival troops, Madame Chiang helped to negotiate his release. Though she held no official position, her influence was recognized when Madame Chiang became one of the first women to receive a decoration from the Chinese government.

In the early years of World War II, Madame Chiang was a tireless and highly effective member of the "China lobby" attempting to influence American policy. She wrote two books—*This is Our China* (1940) and *China Shall Rise Again* (1941)—aimed at gaining the American public's support for China's struggle against the invading Japanese. Her articles on China were featured in American magazines, and she made frequent visits to the United States to publicize her country's cause and secure aid. In 1943 Madame Chiang became the first Chinese, and only the second woman, to address a joint session of Congress. For many years Madame Chiang's name appeared on American lists of the ten most admired women in the world.

During the civil war in China between the Communist forces of Mao Zedong and the Kuomintang, Madame Chiang continued her fund-raising activities in the United States on behalf of Chiang Kai-shek and the Nationalists. When the Nationalists lost, she joined her husband on Taiwan in 1950 and remained there until his death in 1975. Moving back and forth between the United States and Taiwan, Madame Chiang died in her home in New York City in October, 2003, at the age of 105.

◆   War in Korea (1950–1953)

Korea had been a divided nation since its Japanese occupiers agreed to surrender it in pieces to the USSR and the USA with the 38th parallel as the dividing line. Koreans in both halves of the nation hoped for the establishment of a self-governing state free of Japanese control for the first time since 1905. Conflicts between Soviet and American aims ended that hope. The Soviet Union created a Provisional People's Committee (PPC) for North Korea in February 1946. This de facto Communist government was led by Kim Il-Sung (1912–1994), who had gained considerable popularity in Korea by aligning himself with Mao's struggle against the Japanese. The United States set up a provisional government in the south, half of whose legislative members were appointed by the American occupation. While the United States and the Soviet Union continued to discuss holding unified elections, their disagreements over the proportion of legislative seats between North and South Korea and over which groups could field candidates for office made joint elec-

Mei-ling Chiang, Nationalist China's "ambassador" to the west.
Copyright © National Archives (208-PU-34-D-1)

tions impossible. The Russians solidified their hold on the north by transforming the PPC into the Democratic People's Republic of Korea. The Americans backed a government in the South headed by Syngman Rhee (1875‑1965). Rhee had spent the years of Japanese control in exile. He had been brought back by the Americans to shore up their shaky client state, whose officials were reliably anti-Communist but had spent the last decades collaborating with Japanese rule. Faced with two competing administrations, the United Nations recognized Rhee's government in December 1948. With American military aid, Rhee crushed a guerilla war waged by Communist peasants in rural South Korea.

Although Soviet forces left North Korea in December 1948, Russian advisors continued to equip and train its military. American troops pulled out of the South by June 1949. Early the following year, concerned that Mao was replacing him as a revolutionary model for Asia and uncertain of the extent of American commitment to Korea, Stalin approved Kim's plan for invading the weaker South. Kim's armies launched their assault against the Republic of Korea on June 25, 1950. Rhee's capital at Seoul was taken within three days. Truman, incensed by the attack on an American supported state, asked for a United Nations response. Like any other permanent member

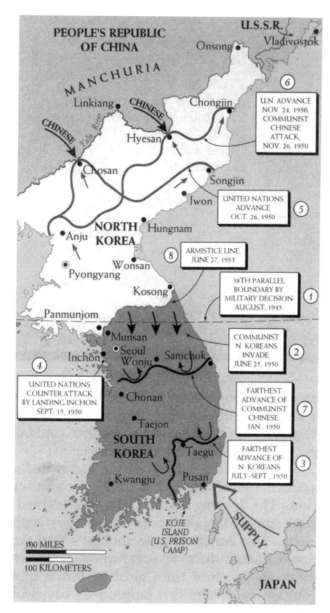

PEOPLE'S REPUBLIC OF CHINA

MANCHURIA

U.S.S.R.

Onsong

Vladivostok

Linkiang

CHINESE

Chongjin

⑥ U.N. ADVANCE NOV. 24, 1950, COMMUNIST CHINESE ATTACK, NOV. 26, 1950

CHINESE

Yalu River

Hyesan

Chosan

Songjin

Iwon

⑤ UNITED NATIONS ADVANCE OCT. 26, 1950

NORTH KOREA

Anju

Hungnam

⑧ ARMISTICE LINE, JUNE 27, 1953

Pyongyang

Wonsan

Kosong

① 38TH PARALLEL BOUNDARY BY MILITARY DECISION AUGUST, 1945

Panmunjom

Munsan

Seoul

Wonju

Samchok

② COMMUNIST N. KOREANS INVADE, JUNE 25, 1950

Inchon

④ UNITED NATIONS COUNTER ATTACK BY LANDING INCHON SEPT. 15, 1950

Chonan

⑦ FARTHEST ADVANCE OF COMMUNIST CHINESE, JAN. 1950

Taejon

SOUTH KOREA

Taegu

③ FARTHEST ADVANCE OF N. KOREANS JULY–SEPT., 1950

Kwangju

Pusan

SUPPLY

100 MILES

100 KILOMETERS

KOJE ISLAND (U.S. PRISON CAMP)

JAPAN

The Korean "Police Action," 1950–1953.
From *The Western Heritage, 6/e, Combined Edition,* by Donald Kagan, Steven Ozment, and Frank M. Turner. Copyright © 1998 by Prentice-Hall, Inc.

of the UN Security Council, the Soviet Union had the power to veto any resolution put before the Council. But the Soviet Union was boycotting the Council in protest over its refusal to recognize Mao's People's Republic of China in place of Nationalist China. So, on June 26, with no Soviet Union present to veto the resolution, the UN Security Council condemned Kim's invasion of South Korea and authorized a joint military defense of the South. Armed with UN approval, Truman committed American forces to battle the next day.

By the end of August, United Nations troops had been forced back into a single area in the extreme southeast of the country. On September 15, UN Commander General Douglas MacArthur counterattacked with a daring amphibious landing far behind Communist lines at Inchon. By October he was rapidly approaching the Yalu River, Korea's border with China. Before MacArthur could destroy all North Korean resistance, the intervention of "volunteer" Chinese units in late November turned the United Nations "Police Action" into a bloody stalemate.

After his Inchon victory, MacArthur publicly campaigned for the extension of UN operations into China with the support of Chiang's Taiwanese forces, raising the threat of nuclear war. Such posturing led Truman to dismiss MacArthur for insubordination in March 1951. The Korean front returned once again to the 38th parallel. Fighting continued for another two years before a cease-fire was reached in July 1953. Nearly 34,000 Americans and 3 million Koreans and Chinese lost their lives in a war that still has not yet formally ended. American and North Korean troops continue to patrol the demilitarized zone between the two Koreas.

Worried by the geographic expansion of the Cold War, Truman increased American military aid to France's fight against the Communist Viet Minh national liberation movement in French Indochina (modern Vietnam, Laos, and Cambodia). The ring of Western Alliances was expanded eastward. The 1951 security treaty with Japan was followed by the creation of a joint security pact with Australia and New Zealand (the ANZUS Pact) both of which had contributed forces to the Korean Police Action. In 1954, Great Britain (with American encouragement) formed the Baghdad Pact with Iraq, Turkey, Iran, and Pakistan. That same year the United States formed the South East Asia Treaty Organization (SEATO) with Britain, France, Australia, New Zealand, Thailand, the Philippines, and Pakistan. Older alliances were redirected to aid the security effort. In 1947 the *Treaty of Rio* had joined the 35 independent countries of the Americas in the Organization of American States (OAS), in a pact designed to facilitate cooperation in regional security and economic development. The United States now began to use the OAS as a vehicle for stopping the spread of Communism in its own backyard.

The containment barrier against Communist invasion seemed complete, but the problem of internal Communist threats to pro-western states remained. In 1953 the American Central Intelligence Agency (CIA) directed a successful coup against Prime Minister Muhammad Mossadeq (1880–1967) of Iran, a radical nationalist passionately opposed to the rule and policies of Shah Muhammad Reza Pahlavi (1919–1980). A similar CIA coup overthrew President Jácobo Arbenz Guzmán (1913–1971) of Guatemala in 1954 because of his supposedly Communist land reform proposals. Not so coincidentally, these reforms impinged on the holdings of the American United Fruit Corporation.

◆ The Home Front

Despite the measures taken by President Truman, his Republican opponents attacked his anti-Communist measures as inadequate. Some even argued that the Democratic Party and its supporters in the American media, unions, civil service, civil rights movement, and universities were secret Communists, Communist sympathizers, or outright Soviet spies. Congressman Richard M. Nixon (1913–1994) of California played a major role in the anti-Communist hearings held by the House Committee on Un-American Activities (HUAC), while Senator Joseph McCarthy (1908–1957) of Wisconsin chaired those held by the Senate Investigations Sub-Committee on Un-American Activities (SISUAC). Two sensational convictions added credence to their "witch hunts." The HUAC believed it had discovered Communist sympathies in former President Roosevelt's diplomatic aide, Alger Hiss (1904–1996). Prosecuted for passing documents to Soviet agents in 1948, Hiss was eventually convicted of perjury and imprisoned. He protested his innocence throughout his life. Russian documents released in the 1990s seemed to demonstrate his guilt, but failed to end the political controversy over his conviction. McCarthy claimed to have uncovered Russian spies in the American nuclear weapons development programs. The Soviet Union rolled out its first hydrogen bomb on August 12, 1953, just under ten months after the Americans tested their first H-Bomb on November 1, 1952. How the Soviet Union caught up so quickly was certainly suspicious. McCarthy claimed that Soviet atom bomb development had benefitted from espionage by disloyal nuclear scientists. McCarthy's influence caused the FBI to begin rigorous investigations of the Manhattan Project's security that led to the persecution of J. Robert Oppenheimer (1904–1967), the director of the Project. In 1951 two members of the New York Communist Party—Ethel (1915–1953) and Julius Rosenberg (1918–1953)—were convicted of passing atomic secrets to the Soviet Union. The Rosenbergs were sent to the electric chair in 1953. The extent of their involvement in the transfer of nuclear information to the Soviet Union remains a subject of debate although Russian records show at least some connection.

Aside from these two notorious cases, few charges were ever successfully brought by either Congressional committee. In the anti-Communist hysteria of the time, however, virtually any attempt at self-defense was treated as contempt of Congress. The defendants were considered

J. ROBERT OPPENHEIMER (1904–1967)

Scientific chief of the Manhattan Project.
Copyright © Hulton Getty

Julius Robert Oppenheimer was born on April 22, 1904, in New York City, the son of a German textile importer. As an undergraduate at Harvard University, Oppenheimer was as well known for his poetry as for his physics, but when he graduated in 1925, he put aside his literary interests to undertake atomic research at the Cavendish Laboratory in Cambridge. After graduate work at Göttingen University in Germany, he returned to the United States to teach physics at the University of California at Berkeley and the California Institute of Technology.

Oppenheimer's interest in the workings of subatomic particles and the implications of the new relativity and quantum theories might have remained merely academic had it not been for the outbreak of World War II. Physicists like Albert Einstein (1879–1955) warned of international disaster if Nazi Germany were the first to construct an atomic bomb, and military intelligence reported that Hitler's scientists were engaged in just such an effort. President Roosevelt authorized atomic research, and in August 1942, put the American military in charge of organizing

Allied nuclear development under the code name "Manhattan Project." The logical choice for its scientific leader was J. Robert Oppenheimer who was already working in California to separate uranium-235 from natural uranium, the key to the first atomic bomb.

To construct and test an atomic bomb, Oppenheimer helped choose a team of British and American physicists and picked Los Alamos, New Mexico (the locale of his childhood boarding school) as the place where the team would work. On July 16, 1945, Oppenheimer oversaw the testing of the world's first nuclear device. Atomic bombs dropped on Hiroshima (August 6) and Nagasaki (August 9) brought World War II to a close and ushered in the Atomic Age.

Oppenheimer resigned from Los Alamos in October 1945, and became head of the United States Atomic Energy Commission (1947–1952). Even after he helped produce the world's first hydrogen bomb in 1949, Oppenheimer fell victim to the fear of Communism that marked the United States during the first years of the Cold War. On December 21, 1953, Oppenheimer was accused of having associated with communists when he was young. During the Spanish Civil War in 1936, Oppenheimer had publicly supported the republicans, many of whom were socialists, and he had given money to anti-fascist organizations fighting Hitler. Although he never joined the Communist Party and publicly repudiated even his socialist connections over Stalin's treatment of Soviet scientists in the 1930s, his idealism made him suspect during the McCarthy Era. Though eventually cleared of the treason charges brought against him, he lost his security clearance and all connections with government research. Only in 1963 did President Johnson award him the Enrico Fermi Award of the Atomic Energy Commission. But Oppenheimer would not long enjoy his political rehabilitation; he died of throat cancer on February 18, 1967.

tainted, and barred from working at their professions by "blacklists." Often the only way to avoid prosecution was to "name names" and accuse friends and colleagues. Public institutions and private organizations voluntarily fired personnel considered ideologically questionable, ignoring Constitutional guarantees of freedom of opinion.

At first, the inauguration of a Republican President, former Supreme Allied Commander General Dwight D. Eisenhower, in January 1953, seemed to make no difference to the witch hunters. But in 1954, McCarthy attempted to launch an investigation of alleged pro-Communism within the senior ranks of the United States Army. Eisenhower, who had remained silent even when McCarthy attacked Truman and his Secretary of State, George Marshall, was galvanized into action. The counter attack by the Army's attorneys led to an eventual Senate censure and the end of McCarthy's career.

◆   "Peaceful Co-Existence"

Josef Stalin died on March 15, 1953. For the first time in over a quarter of a century, the Soviet Union was without a supreme leader. Laurenti Beria (1899–1953), Stalin's feared state security chief, courted popular acclaim by proposing to decentralize political authority, relax censorship, and re-orient the economy toward consumer production. But Beria's position was undermined in June when East German workers went on strike against higher production quotas. Beria's innovations now looked too much like concessions. After the German protests were crushed by Soviet

Attorney Joseph Welsh reacts to Senator Joseph McCarthy's testimony during the Army hearings of 1954.
Copyright © CORBIS/Bettmann

troops, Beria's rivals united to arrest him for treason. Executed in December 1953, his bid for power had lasted only nine months.

Premier Georgi Malenkov (1902-1998) and Communist Party First Secretary Nikita Khrushchev (1894-1971) now shared power. Recognizing the futility of winning a war waged with hydrogen bombs, Malenkov pushed for "peaceful co-existence," replacing military competition between the two super powers with economic, diplomatic, and ideological competition. But Malenkov had been too close to Stalin to win the trust of the party membership. Khrushchev, who had fought his way up from rural poverty, adopted an energetic populist style. Enthusiastically co-opting his rival's vision of "peaceful coexistence," Khrushchev closed Soviet bases in Finland and China, offered economic aid on attractive terms to newly independent Asian states whether Communist or not, reopened long-stalled negotiations on Germany, and gave his support to a 1954 peace settlement in Indochina. He even attempted to repair relations with Yugoslavia. This whirlwind of activity left his rival Malenkov in the dust. By February 1955 Malenkov had been replaced as Prime Minister by Nikolai Bulganin (1895–1975), one of Khrushchev's supporters, and Khrushchev was the undisputed leader of the Soviet Union. Malenkov ended his days as manager of a power plant in Siberia.

Meanwhile, western governments remained uncertain whether Khrushchev's actions represented a real change in Soviet policy or were just designed to cover some new expansion. Everyone was pleased when extended negotiations resulted in the signing of an *Austrian State Treaty* in May 1955, giving Austria full sovereignty as a neutral power. Allied forces occupying Austria were speedily withdrawn. In the same month Khrushchev met with West German Chancellor Konrad Adenauer in Moscow, and the two states established diplomatic relations despite Adenauer's refusal to recognize the German Democratic Republic. Still, a Big Four Grand Alliance Summit of Great Britain, France, the United States, and the Soviet Union in Geneva in July 1955 produced few hard agreements; West Germany's membership in NATO remained a major stumbling block.

While Khrushchev consolidated his hold over the Soviet Union, Eisenhower began to modify Truman's containment policy by increasing American reliance on the deterrent power of thermonuclear weapons. Compared to the expense of ringing the world with conventional bases, the successful development of the hydrogen bomb provided massive destructive power at relatively little cost. If Soviet forces dared to cross the containment perimeter, Eisenhower's "New Look" Defense Policy (1953) threatened to launch an immediate nuclear attack on the Soviet Union itself. "Massive Retaliation," as preached by Secretary of State John Foster Dulles (1888–1959), was intended to so frighten Soviet policy makers that they would not dare start a war. Following the American example, Khrushchev also began to favor nuclear over conventional weapons. The Soviet Union's display of its new Bison bomber airplane prompted the United States to speed up development of the B-52 bomber. The B-52 was a long-range heavy bomber capable of carrying atomic weapons or massive loads of conventional bombs to the Soviet Union at a top speed of 595 miles per hour. Improved versions in the late 1960s had a maximum range of 10,000 miles (the B52-G) and could deliver 40,000 pounds of conventional bombs. The arms race was in full swing.

Meanwhile, Dulles based America's Far East policy on what he called the "Domino Theory," his belief that Asian states were so weak they would fall over like a row of dominoes if just one of them succumbed to Communism. French Indochina proved to be the key domino. Japanese occupying forces had left the shell of French colonial administration intact, while directing it from behind the scenes, but it was in total disarray when the Japanese surrendered in 1945. When the Japanese left, Ho Chi Minh ("Bringer of Light") declared Vietnam independent and began a war against the French. Born Nguyen Sinh Cung (1890–1969) in a village in central Vietnam, Ho had shipped out on a French freighter in 1911 not to return to his homeland until 1941. Wandering about the world, he spent time as an itinerant laborer in Brooklyn and an assistant pastry chef at the Carlton Hotel in London. His attempt to give Woodrow Wilson a nationalist petition for Vietnamese independence at the Paris Peace Conference in 1919 brought him to the attention of the French Communist Party. Ten years later, a Moscow trained agitator, he organized the Indochinese Communist Party. After a stay in China, Ho slipped back into French Indochina in 1941, disguised as a Chinese journalist, and organized the Viet Minh. His declaration of independence in 1945 set off the first round of a thirty-year long war.

Ho Chi Minh's initial victory over the French in 1954 in the battle of Dien Bien Phu convinced Dulles that to prevent the loss of all of Asia, every state in the region had to be propped up by American aid. The 1954 Geneva Peace Accords recognized Ho as the head of a provisional Democratic Republic of Vietnam (DRV) north of the 17th parallel. When France ceded the northern portion of Vietnam to Ho's forces in 1954, they also agreed to hold general elections in the south in 1956 to determine the fate of the whole country. However, Ho's popularity as a national liberator seemed to assure a Communist victory in the elections. The United States did not consider itself bound by Peace Accords it had not signed, so it sponsored a separate Republic of Vietnam (RVN) in the south under Ngo Din Diem (1901–1963). With American support, Diem prevented the balloting. Keeping Vietnam half pro-west became ever more important to American policy as the years passed.

◆ "Destalinization"

Khrushchev realized that Communism had to prove itself an appealing alternative to capitalism if it were to attract the interest of the newly independent states emerging from the collapse of Europe's colonial empires. He ordered massive economic reforms in the USSR to prove the success of the Communist system. Grain farming schemes to open virgin Siberian land in 1954 were supposed to achieve agricultural parity with the United States by 1970. Housing construction was dramatically increased as part of a new emphasis on consumer oriented production. But his decisive commitment to reform came at the Twentieth Congress of the Soviet Communist Party in February 1956. Addressing a closed session of Soviet and foreign delegates, Khrushchev charged Stalin with pathological brutality against the Soviet people and denounced him as the creator of a malevolent "cult of personality." Numerous victims of Stalin's purges were rehabilitated, many posthumously. State censorship was relaxed so that the "Destalinization" of the Soviet Union could proceed. But Mao considered Khrushchev's speech a betrayal of Communist solidarity. This led to an ever widening divide within the Communist movement.

More immediately, the spread of Khrushchev's reformist sentiments to Poland and Hungary proved to have disastrous results for those satellites. Poland was permitted to organize a new government in June 1956, but similar demands in Hungary began to undermine the dominant position of Communist ideology. Under intense public pressure, the new Hungarian Prime Minister, Imre Nagy (1896–1958) dismantled the security services and formed a coalition cabinet with non-Communists in October 1956. Even more threatening to Soviet security than the talk of multi-party elections was Nagy's announcement on November 2 that Hungary would withdraw from the Warsaw Pact and adopt a policy of neutrality. Khrushchev, after first agreeing to withdraw Soviet troops from Hungary, reversed his position and ordered Red Army units to attack. They seized control of Hungary on November 4. Ignoring condemnation by the United Nations, Soviet forces installed a reliable Communist administration under Premier Janos Kadar (1912–1989).

Khrushchev capitalizes on the capture of a U-2 spy plane (1960).
Copyright © AP/Wide World Photos

Nagy was arrested, held incommunicado, and finally executed. Kadar continued with Destalinization, but within strictly controlled limits. The United States did nothing to intervene although it did grant asylum to those freedom fighters who escaped across the border.

Khrushchev scored another coup when Russian scientists successfully launched the world's first artificial satellite, Sputnik, in October 1957; American policy makers worried about a growing "missile gap," while Khrushchev boasted of the USSR's superior technology. But all was not well within the USSR. Khrushchev's goals for a consumer revolution could not be met by the rigidly organized and poorly managed Soviet economy. His decentralization policies threatened the security of party bureaucrats without making measurable changes in Soviet productivity. The result was a failed attempt by the Politburo to replace Khrushchev in June 1957. A shaken Khrushchev purged rivals from senior party posts, reimposed artistic and intellectual censorship, and adopted a more war-like foreign policy. He wrecked the Paris Summit with Eisenhower in May 1960 by using it as a platform for denouncing American aggression against the USSR. The pilot of an American U-2 spy plane, Francis Gary Powers (1929–1977), had been shot down that month while photographing nuclear test sites in Soviet Kazakhstan. Powers was paraded before the world's press after Eisenhower had publicly denied such missions existed. A humiliated Eisenhower froze relations with Khrushchev for the remainder of his term. Sentenced to 10 years in a Soviet prison, Powers was returned to the United States in 1962 in exchange for a captured Soviet spy.

◆ The Cold War in Crisis: Cuba and Berlin

Before leaving office, Eisenhower approved a CIA attempt to overthrow the Communist regime of Fidel Castro (b. 1926). Castro had been a thorn in America's side since his successful revolution against the pro-American dictator Fulgencio Batista (1901–1973) in 1958-1959. In order not to risk international embarrassment by using American troops, the CIA plan called for training anti-Castro Cuban exiles as an invasion force. When John F. Kennedy (1917–1963) became President of the United States in January 1961, he decided to let the plan go forward. When the poorly trained émigrés waded ashore at the Bay of Pigs in April, they were easily pinned down by local militia units and eventually shot or captured by the regular Cuban army. The popular rising envisioned by the CIA never materialized, and the fiasco convinced Khrushchev he could easily bully Kennedy at the Vienna Summit that July.

When Khrushchev threatened to turn Berlin over to a sovereign East Germany, Kennedy put American troops on alert, and Khrushchev appeared to back down. But a growing crisis in Berlin soon forced him to act. Khrushchev's threats had set off a booming migration to the West. East German citizens were entering Berlin, crossing from East to West, and receiving documents allowing them to immigrate to West Germany where living standards were significantly higher than those in the East and political life was freer. By August, almost 15,000 East Germans—mainly younger, higher-skilled professionals—were migrating each month. On August 12, Khrushchev and East German leader Walter Ulbricht (1893–1973) decided to cut off the brain drain at the source. They ordered construction of the Berlin Wall, a series of fortifications and barriers designed to prevent easy access from East to West Berlin. Even as the wall went up, hundreds of eager refugees plotted to go around, over, or under it. Their narrow escapes and tragic failures provided an unending source of propaganda for the West as long as the Wall stood. Its gun turrets and barbed wire became a visual symbol of the "Iron Curtain" that still divided Europe.

Khrushchev needed a counterbalancing propaganda coup. His economic reforms were in disarray. His push to cultivate the virgin lands of Siberia only resulted in smaller harvests, making a mockery of his boasts to achieve agricultural parity with the United States. At the same time, the American space program was overtaking the Russian. It was clear, as well, that American spending had eliminated the illusory "missile gap."

While the Soviet Union had sufficient Medium Range (MRBM) and Intermediate Range (IRBM) weapons capable of taking out targets in Europe, it did not have nearly enough Inter-Continental Ballistic Missiles (ICBM) capable of hitting the United States to pose a serious threat. But, after the Bay of Pigs incident, Castro had requested military support from the USSR. That request gave Khrushchev the opening he needed. He persuaded Castro to accept Soviet MRBMs and IRBMs in Cuba; those missiles could reach any point in the continental United States except Alaska. Khrushchev would have strategic parity.

Khrushchev's decision forced a face to face confrontation with the United States. In October 1962 American U-2 flights over Cuba revealed the presence of missile bases under construction. President Kennedy's military advisors favored military action to eliminate the weapons, but Kennedy worried about provoking a massive response from the USSR. The President opted instead for a naval blockade: ships heading for Cuba were to be searched for military supplies. The missile bases would remain unusable while negotiations to remove them proceeded. After a few near confrontations between submarine escorted Soviet ships and the blockade line, and the death of one of the two U-2 pilots who had first spotted the missile sites, Khrushchev decided to retreat. After thirteen days of deadlock, the Cuban Missile Crisis was resolved by a secretly negotiated face-saving formula. The Russians would dismantle the missile sites, and the Americans

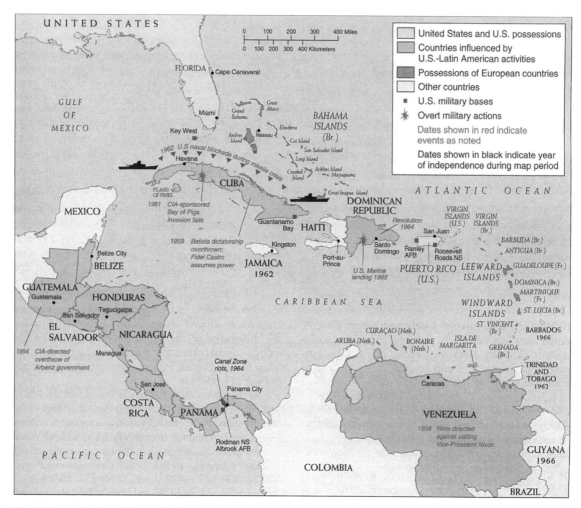

The U.S. in the Caribbean, 1948–1966. U.S. military intervention and economic presence grew steadily in the Caribbean following World War II. After 1960, opposition to the Cuban Revolution dominated U.S. Caribbean policies.
From *Out of Many*, Fourth Edition, (2004), reproduced by permission of Prentice-Hall, Inc.

would pledge never to invade Cuba. In addition, although Kennedy always denied they were part of the deal, six months after the Cuban missile sites were dismantled, obsolete American IRBMs (already scheduled for dismantling) were withdrawn from Turkey.

In the wake of the Cuban Missile Crisis, both sides moved to reduce mutual tensions. A "Hot Line" was installed between the White House and the Kremlin to insure direct communication between the leaders of the two superpowers. In August 1963, the United States, the Soviet Union, and Great Britain signed a *Partial Test Ban Treaty* limiting nuclear weapons testing, if not the size of their arsenals. Neither Khrushchev nor Kennedy was able to follow up on these efforts. Kennedy was assassinated in November 1963, and Khrushchev was forced into retirement in October 1964. Lyndon Baines Johnson (1908–1973) and Leonid Brezhnev (1906–1982) succeeded them. As both sides stepped up weapons development, a new acronym entered the military lexicon: MAD (Mutually Assured Destruction), a condition in which each side had enough weapons to survive a first strike and still annihilate its opponent.

◆ The United States in Vietnam

By 1959, the forces of South Vietnam were disintegrating before a peasant (Viet Cong) revolt supported by Ho Chi Minh in the North. South Vietnamese President Diem was a nationalist who resisted American interference; he was murdered during a military coup in 1963 with US connivance. An alleged attack against American warships in the Gulf of Tonkin in 1964 gave President Johnson the justification he needed to widen American involvement beyond the bounds of the Special Forces "counter-insurgency" units already in place. The Gulf of Tonkin Resolution passed by Congress authorized the protection of American personnel in Vietnam by military means. US Marines sent to protect American air bases from Viet Cong attack in the summer of 1965 were soon used in offensive operations. By December 1967, more than 500,000 American troops were deployed in Vietnam.

As protests against the war flared across the United States, the Johnson Administration continued to fight a war to uphold American prestige against an enemy receiving assistance from both the USSR and Communist China. Johnson predicted final victory in 1968, but that February the Viet Cong launched an offensive throughout the South. The "Tet Offensive" (named for the month in which the Vietnamese celebrated the lunar calendar New Year) was crushed and the Viet Cong infrastructure virtually destroyed. However, the war was continued by the North Vietnamese Army. It soon became clear that American public opinion did not support either the kind of long-term massive military commitment necessary to defeat the North or the nuclear alternative suggested by Presidential candidate Barry Goldwater (1909–1998). By the end of March 1968,

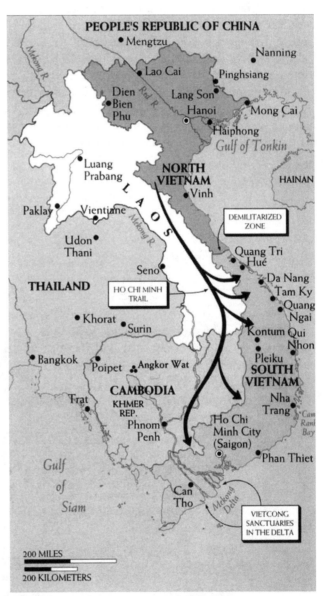

Conflict in Southeast Asia, 1964–1973.
From *The Western Heritage, 6/e, Combined Edition*, by Donald Kagan, Steven Ozment, and Frank M. Turner. Copyright © 1998 by Prentice-Hall, Inc.

Johnson put an end to US troop increases, announced his willingness to negotiate, and declined to stand for re-election. Peace talks began in Paris in May, but quickly stalled.

Republican Richard M. Nixon won the 1968 presidential election. He immediately began to reduce American troop strength in Vietnam. Under his policy of "Vietnamization" the United States stepped up its training and equipping of the South Vietnamese army to enable it to assume the greater share of the fighting. His vision of containment saw regional allies, trained and equipped by the United States, bearing the brunt of local security operations, avoiding the high levels of American troop commitments that set off domestic protests. Nixon was preparing American withdrawal from Vietnam even as his National Security Adviser, Henry Kissinger (b. 1923), struggled to arrange a peace. "Vietnamization" was badly discredited when South Vietnamese forces failed to perform adequately in the June 1970 invasion of Cambodia intended to disrupt North Vietnamese supply lines (the "Ho Chi Minh Trail"), but American withdrawals continued apace. Nixon's announcement in October 1972 that peace was imminent contributed to his landslide re-election, but when the talks appeared to stall that December, he resumed aerial bombing of the North, escalating the use of napalm. Invented by the United States during World War II to burn off the jungle foliage hiding Japanese troops from view, napalm was a mixture of incendiary chemicals

Victims of U.S. napalm attack in Vietnam, June 8, 1972.
Copyright © AP/Wide World Photos

that clung to and set fire to everything it touched. Pictures published by *The New York Times* in 1972 of burned children running from napalm attacks helped consolidate public opinion against the war. By March 1973 agreement was finally reached on what Nixon called "peace with honor" in Vietnam. After 58,000 combat deaths and a serious loss of international prestige, American forces departed Vietnam. In April 1975 a final Northern offensive quickly eliminated all South Vietnamese opposition and unified Vietnam under Communist rule. Nixon and Kissinger would later admit that "peace with honor" had been no more than a means to secure a "decent interval" between the withdrawal of American troops and the inevitable collapse of South Vietnam.

The Rise and Fall of Détente

◆   Building *Détente*

The war in Vietnam did not, however, destroy superpower *détente,* the relaxation of Cold War tensions begun by Kennedy and Khrushchev in the aftermath of the Cuban Missile Crisis. In June 1968, the United States and the Soviet Union signed a *Nuclear Non-Proliferation Treaty* banning the transfer of nuclear arms to other nations. The mutual desire to cut costs kept *détente* alive through political crises that might otherwise have derailed it. Since the Spring of 1968, for example, Alexander Dubcek (1921–1992) had gradually introduced economic and political reform in Czechoslovakia. The "Prague Spring" came to an abrupt end when Russian tanks rolled in that September. Soviet leader Leonid Brezhnev announced that the USSR had the right to carry out unilateral interventions in Eastern Europe to preserve the Warsaw Pact. This "Brezhnev Doctrine (1968)" seemed only to confirm the type of action Soviet troops had been taking in Eastern Europe since 1949.

Despite the issuing of the Brezhnev Doctrine, the strain on the Soviet budget of trying to keep up with American ICBM development made the Soviets willing to negotiate. Similarly, the strain on the political fabric and economy of the United States caused by the prolonged fighting in Vietnam made it willing to deal as well. Strategic Arms Limitation Talks (SALT) began in Helsinki late in 1969. The first treaty (SALT I) emerged in 1972. It placed an upper limit on ICBM deployment. Associated treaties banned nuclear weapons from outer space and the ocean floor, and limited the construction of Anti-Ballistic Missiles (ABM), defensive systems designed to shoot down incoming ICBMs.

Superpower accommodation led to an easing of tensions throughout Europe. In 1970, West German Chancellor Willy Brandt (1913–1992) signed treaties with the USSR and Poland recognizing the German borders drawn in 1945 and expanding economic cooperation with the two Communist states. A similar treaty between West Germany and Czechoslovakia followed. In 1972, the two German states signed a *Basic Treaty* implicitly recognizing each other's existence, and both Germanies were admitted to the United Nations the following year. Brandt's *Ostpolitik* (the politics of normalizing relations with the East) won him the Nobel Peace Prize.

Détente was not limited to US-USSR relations. For more than twenty years, the United States had insisted that Taiwan was the only true Chinese state, but Nixon saw an opening for change in the widening rift in Sino-Soviet relations. The Soviet Union and the People's Republic of China had exchanged fire in a series of border clashes in Manchuria and Central Asia in 1969, and the USSR had begun to deploy MRBMs along its Chinese border. Secretary of State Kissinger met secretly with Mao Tse-tung to prepare for an official presidential visit to Communist China. Nixon's arrival in 1972 paved the way for resumption of normal American-Chinese relations in 1979. Mao's death in 1976 eventually brought Deng Xiaoping (1904–1997) to the leadership of

President Nixon and Zhou Enlai celebrate the beginning of a new era in Chinese-American relations, 1972.
Copyright © AP/Wide World Photos

Communist China. Deng visited the United States that year but US-China relations were off to a rocky start; Congress passed the Taiwan Relations Act (1979) reaffirming America's commitment to maintain Taiwan's independence by supplying it with weapons.

After China, President Nixon went to Moscow, to find the worsening of Sino-Soviet relations made the Soviet Union more willing to put pressure on China to bring the Vietnam peace talks to a speedy conclusion.

By demonstrating that American *détente* could follow either a pro-Soviet or a pro-Chinese path, Nixon and Kissinger were able to improve relations with both. Everyone seemed to benefit. When Nixon signed an agreement to export surplus American grain to the Soviet Union at a discount, vulnerable American farmers were able to stay in business while Brezhnev avoided the expense of trying to reform the USSR's profoundly troubled agricultural sector.

◆   Global Complications

Despite American withdrawal from Vietnam in 1973, *détente* did not move forward as quickly as expected. A fourth Arab-Israeli War in 1973 found the United States and the Soviet Union supporting opposite sides, while an oil shortage created by the Organization of Petroleum Exporting Countries (OPEC) caused the price of crude oil to quadruple and precipitated a world wide recession. The USSR began increasing its military aid to Syria, the Republic of Yemen, and Iraq, all of which counterbalanced American clients in the Middle East such as Israel, Saudi Arabia, and Iran. In 1974, the Soviet Union provided arms to Libya, whose oil-rich revolutionary government began to train and arm a number of terrorist groups hostile to Western governments. The USSR also concluded aid and strategic base agreements with the radical leaders of Ethiopia and Somalia, two East African states in close geographical proximity to Western oil shipment routes from the Persian Gulf. In the bitter aftermath of the oil embargo the spirit of *détente* began to wither.

In 1975, victorious North Vietnam permitted Soviet occupation of the former American naval and air base at Cam Ranh Bay, giving the USSR military access to the Malacca Straits through which oil from the Middle East reached Japan. The Soviet navy, modernized and expanded under Brezhnev, held coordinated global exercises rehearsing measures to paralyze capitalist maritime communications worldwide. Communist coups in Cambodia, Mozambique, and Angola raised anew the specter of international revolution. But, in the aftermath of Vietnam, the United States withdrew into itself. The War Powers Act of 1973 required presidents to gain congressional approval for long-term overseas military deployments not covered by prior treaty or a congressional declaration of war. In 1974, Congress strengthened its oversight of CIA appropriations. And in August 1974, faced with the certainty of impeachment over the Watergate Scandal, Nixon became the first American president to resign his office.

◆ The Rise of Islamic Fundamentalism and the Death of *Détente*

Despite the growing rift, Brezhnev met with Nixon's successor, President Gerald Ford (b. 1913) at Vladivostok where terms for a second round of arms limitation talks (SALT II) were set. The treaty that emerged from those talks in 1979 was signed by the next American President James Earl Carter (b. 1924). Carter believed causes such as environmental development, human rights, and international law should drive American policy. His achievements also included the 1977 treaty that arranged for the gradual return of the Panama Canal to its home nation, the opening of full diplomatic relations with Communist China in 1978, and the *Egyptian-Israeli Peace Treaty* of 1979. He convinced NATO members to increase their military spending by three percent per year for the next decade, and authorized the creation of a Rapid Deployment Joint Task Force (RDJTF) based in the Indian Ocean to protect American interests in the region. Carter's policy seemed justified when the Shah of Iran, one of the most important American allies in the Middle East, fell from power in January 1979.

But Carter had underestimated the degree to which the Iranian revolutionaries, led by the Shi'ite Muslim Ayatollah Ruhollah Khomeini (1902–1989) blamed the United States for everything they detested in the Shah's modernizing but corrupt regime. After Carter permitted a desperately ill Shah to obtain medical treatment in the United States and froze Iranian assets here, demonstrators in Tehran overran the American Embassy in November 1979 and held its staff hostage for over a year. A failed rescue attempt in April 1980 further embarrassed the United States.

For its part, the Soviet Union was also unprepared to deal with the rise of Islamic fundamentalism. A radical Muslim insurgency was gradually undermining the pro-Soviet Communist regime that had ruled Afghanistan since 1974. Brezhnev, fearing the spread of an Islamic revolution to the 100 million Muslims within the Soviet Union, refused to accept the loss of this client state. Ignoring the lessons that might have been learned from the American experience in Vietnam, the Soviet Army launched an invasion of Afghanistan on Christmas Eve, 1979. Brezhnev expected a rapid victory over the Mujihadeen (from *jihad*, "Holy War"), but that failed to materialize.

Because the Iranian crisis had set off a second wave of oil price increases, the United States interpreted Soviet action in Afghanistan as the first step in a drive towards the Straits of Hormuz, through which most of the West's oil was shipped. In his annual State of the Union address, Carter warned the USSR that the United States would use every means necessary, including armed force, to keep this vital waterway secure. He withdrew SALT II from the ratification process, embargoed Russian trade, and boycotted the 1980 Moscow Olympics. Presidential Directive 59, issued that June, substituted the possibility of limited nuclear war for the old strategy of Mutually Assured Destruction (MAD). The United States persuaded NATO to deploy Pershing II mobile MRBMs and Tomahawk cruise missiles at several of its European bases. These projectile weapons, guided by remote control or internal mechanisms, could be launched from ships, planes, submarines, or land-based launchers; they could fly below radar screens and deliver warheads to targets hundreds of miles away or virtually across the street. Europeans, long on the front lines of any such conflict, suddenly learned that their homelands were earmarked as a "limited" nuclear battlefield by their principal ally. The missiles were not scheduled for deployment until 1983, but a popular disarmament movement immediately swept through the Federal Republic of Germany, the Netherlands, and, to a lesser extent, Great Britain. NATO bases were often under siege. The Americans, who had intended to use the planned deployment as a bargaining chip to get the USSR to remove Soviet SS-20 mobile MRBMs already in place in Eastern Europe, felt betrayed by their allies. With NATO in crisis, with American hostages imprisoned, and with the economy in disarray, Carter was swept from office in the elections of 1980. He was followed in office by Ronald Reagan (1911-2004).

Winning and Losing the Cold War
◆ Fighting the "Evil Empire"

Reagan believed that all of America's foreign policy difficulties could be traced to Soviet mischief-making and Carter's weak response to the global Communist threat. He saw the United States as leading a holy crusade against an "evil empire." In his first term in office he increased military spending by 50 percent. Arms were secretly supplied to the Afghan Mujihadeen in far greater numbers than Carter had ever permitted, while the wave of anti-nuclear demonstrations in Europe was simply ignored. But it was in Latin America that the new president's commitment to a confrontational policy was most apparent. In 1979, General Anastasio Somoza (1925–1980), the last ruler of a dynasty that had controlled Nicaragua for over forty years, was overthrown by the leftist Sandinista movement. Carter had begun by aiding the rebels, but cut the aid off once he became convinced that the Sandinistas sought to radicalize all of Central America. In 1980, the Farabundo Martí National Liberation Movement in El Salvador rose up against its pro-US government, with Sandinista support. The Reagan administration began to apply the "Domino Theory" to the Western Hemisphere. Covert aid was provided to the Salvadoran military, to anti-Sandinista rebels (Contras) in Nicaragua, and to any groups claiming antipathy to Communism.

The aid did not stop at the Americas. CIA operatives colluded with South African leaders to destabilize popular Marxist governments in Angola and Mozambique using tribally based counter-revolutionaries. Somalia received the economic and military aid it needed to prolong its war with pro-Soviet Ethiopia. The Reagan administration also declared itself hostile to international terrorism, which it linked to Soviet support. Libya and Iran were named prime offenders, despite the Ayatollah's hostility to Communist atheism. The ever-widening scope of American involvement could not be maintained, however. In 1983 Marines were sent to Beirut to prop up a Christian government in Lebanon opposed by Iran's radical Muslim ally, the Hezbollah. In October, 245 marines died when a Hezbollah suicide bomber destroyed the American headquarters in Beirut. Days later, American forces invaded Grenada and toppled its socialist government, citing an imminent Cuban inspired civil conflict there as justification. American forces soon left both Grenada and Lebanon.

The American missteps were all the more embarrassing because the Soviet Union was in a state of confusion. The Afghanistan War was proving to be a protracted, costly, and demoralizing mistake; the supposedly invincible Soviet Army proved no more successful against the Muslim guerillas than American forces had been against the Vietnamese. Moreover, the trade embargo imposed on the Soviet Union by President Carter cut off the cheap grain imports that had been covering the persistent shortfall in Soviet agricultural yield. The prospect of a renewed arms race threatened the Soviet Union with probable economic collapse.

The unhappy results of socialist central planning were also becoming increasingly apparent in the Warsaw Pact nations. Economic strains jeopardized the very continuation of Communism in Poland, which had financed technological modernization by borrowing money from the West. The global recession resulting from the OPEC embargo deprived Poland of the hard currency earnings with which it planned to pay off its capitalist creditors. It tried to cover itself by discounting the prices of ships, steel, and coal sold abroad, but this required imposing domestic austerity programs, which provoked widespread unrest. Dissent grew stronger after the 1979 visit of Pope John Paul II (born Karol Wojtyla of Poland in 1920). In the port city of Gdansk, Lech Walesa (b. 1944), a shipyard electrician, became one of the leaders of an unofficial trade union that called itself Solidarity. By 1980 Solidarity was coordinating strikes that paralyzed the nation. A frightened government granted Solidarity significant concessions on food and housing prices, wages, and working conditions before the end of the year. But giving the union official recognition and allowing it to extend itself into the agricultural sector only strengthened its resolve. As the Polish economy continued to decline, Walesa used the threat of a general strike to demand political power for Solidarity.

Back in Moscow, the Kremlin was discussing possible Russian intervention in Poland. At first Polish Defense Minister and military Chief of Staff, General Wojciech Jaruzelski (b. 1923) was able to persuade the USSR to hold off by promising to guarantee continued Communist rule. But as the date set for the general strike grew near, Warsaw Pact troops began to mass on Poland's borders. To convince the Soviet Union that an invasion was not necessary, the now Prime Minister Jaruzelski imposed martial law throughout Poland and arrested Solidarity's leaders on December 12, 1981. A severely crippled Solidarity barely managed to survive "underground."

Leonid Brezhnev died in November 1982 after suffering a massive stroke and was succeeded as leader of the USSR by Yuri Andropov (1914–1984), the former KGB chairman. Andropov planned extensive economic and administrative reforms but, even with Politburo support, he was too old and ill to push them past an entrenched bureaucracy despite ample evidence that trying to keep up with the Americans was putting intolerable strains on the Soviet economy.

Then Reagan announced the development of a new Strategic Defense Initiative (SDI), dubbed "Star Wars," to protect the nation from any Soviet ICBM attack. Although most American scientists believed such a system could not work, the very announcement horrified a Soviet leadership that feared an invulnerable United States might be tempted to launch a pre-emptive first strike against the USSR. When NATO carried out the planned deployment of its new Pershing and Tomahawk missiles in November 1983, arms limitation and reduction talks between the two superpowers collapsed. President Reagan showed no concern; he intended to keep up the pressure on the "evil empire."

Adding to the USSR's problems, Andropov died in February 1984 and was replaced by Konstantin Chernenko (1911–1985), a careful and uninspired politician. Many had expected Andropov's successor to be Mikhail Gorbachev (b. 1931). Gorbachev had won considerable esteem for his willingness to tackle agricultural problems while serving as an administrator in the Ukraine in 1982. But despite the Afghanistan morass and the worsening superpower relations, the old guard was not yet ready to pass the baton to a new generation. It was only when Chernenko died in March 1985 that the 54-year old Gorbachev was grudgingly given the authority to address the problems of the Soviet state.

◆ From *Perestroika* to Democracy

Mikhail Gorbachev believed the Soviet Union could not survive unless it reallocated the scarce capital resources previously lavished on the Soviet military. The greatest weakness of the "planned" economy was its lack of room for managerial or independent technological innovation. Decision-making authority remained with the *nomenklatura,* Communist Party loyalists in state posts immune from criticism and dedicated only to self-advancement and personal enrichment. The Soviet Union was in disarray: alcoholism, absenteeism, bribery, and a cynical resignation to a corrupt system were the order of the day. There were perpetual shortages of the most basic goods and foodstuffs, and the futility of the Afghanistan War bred a simmering public resentment.

In order to reconstruct the Soviet system, Gorbachev needed time, domestic support, and improved relations with the West. He could not divert resources from military to civilian uses unless he could slow down the arms race. The Strategic Arms Reduction Talks (START) mandated by the SALT II treaty but abandoned in 1983 had to be revived. Giving approval for the talks to go forward in 1985, Gorbachev met individually with the leaders of the Britain, France, and the United States in November to demonstrate his personal commitment to serious arms control.

He unveiled his domestic programs at the 27th Soviet Communist Party Congress early the following year. Two closely related principles—*Glasnost* (openness) and *Perestroika* (restructuring)—dominated his administration. Under *Glasnost,* the long suppressed critics of the Soviet system were now consulted on reform initiatives. Censorship was relaxed, and the government started telling the truth about its economic problems to the Soviet people. The restructuring of the economy promised under *Perestroika* was to be the result of an open debate on national problems, and would be extended to whatever institution of the Soviet state needed it. A new program of "socialist pluralism" reduced state interference in the economy, allowed spontaneous initiatives helpful to the system, and decentralized industrial management. Desperate to increase agricultural production, Gorbachev even allowed land to be leased to farmers who could sell their crops on the open market. Rules for foreign investment were eased and private ownership of small businesses allowed. *Glasnost* was extended to include discussion of Soviet social problems such as drug and alcohol addiction, prostitution, unsatisfactory working conditions, and housing shortages. After a meltdown at the Chernobyl nuclear power plant in April 1986 polluted the surrounding countryside for miles around, Gorbachev turned *Glasnost* into a campaign against the incompetent *nomenklatura.* He courted Western sympathy by offering to revive human rights discussions and granted well-publicized amnesties to prominent political prisoners. Andrei Sakharov (1921–1989), the designer of the Soviet hydrogen bomb who had become a critic of totalitarian rule, was freed from his internal exile. Gorbachev used the political capital created by such moves to press for another superpower summit.

Gorbachev met Reagan at Reykjavik, Iceland, in October 1986. During the two-day summit meeting, Gorbachev shocked the Americans by suggesting a 50 percent cut in strategic weapons to be followed by their total abolition within ten years. But the summit stalled when Reagan refused to restrict SDI research to the laboratory. His hard line strategy and failure to consult his European allies backfired. The West German government was so incensed it began its own talks with Gorbachev. A scandal over illegal shipments of arms to Contra rebels in Nicaragua funded by secret arms sales to Iran and increasing budget deficits distracted the American government and led to the Republican loss of Congress in the 1986 elections.

Faced with an economy that refused to budge and realizing that the embattled American president needed a diplomatic victory, Gorbachev agreed to a new round of talks in February 1987. The United States and the Soviet Union agreed to destroy an entire class of missiles with ranges up to 3400 miles. On December 8, 1987, Reagan and Gorbachev signed the Intermediate-range Nuclear Forces (INF) Treaty in Washington, the first in a series of dramatic superpower arms control agreements. The first 200 missiles were destroyed before the end of the year. Reagan was able to end his presidency as a peacemaker, and Gorbachev won more time to reform the Soviet Union.

Gorbachev was convinced that only major structural changes could save the Communist experiment. The Soviet army was bogged down in Afghanistan, the Soviet public was growing increasingly disillusioned, and the Soviet economy was becoming increasingly bleak. The very security of the USSR was mocked when a teenage German pilot landed in Red Square in May 1987 as a stunt. Gorbachev announced that Soviet forces were withdrawing from Afghanistan beginning May 1988, and he carried through on that pledge despite considerable opposition. On October 1, 1988, at a special party conference that created a new Soviet constitution, Gorbachev became President as well as General Secretary. Under the new constitution, an elected Congress of People's Deputies assumed the legislative functions of the Communist Party Central Committee. Voters going to the polls in March 1989 found multiple candidates on their ballots for each position, making this the first free election in the Soviet Union's history. This radically democratic procedure was designed to allow Gorbachev to circumvent the Communist Party establishment and appeal directly to the Soviet electorate for support. Having previously replaced two-thirds of his Politburo, Gorbachev's control seemed assured.

In a December 1988 address to the United Nations General Assembly, Gorbachev announced major unilateral cuts in Soviet conventional forces: half a million men and ten thousand tanks would be demobilized. He promised Reagan and his newly elected successor George Bush, Sr. (b. 1924) to strengthen superpower cooperation. He cut military and economic aid to Soviet satellites and client states worldwide. But each concession only served to compound his problems. *Perestroika* had not produced the promised recovery. The poor harvest of 1988 had only aggravated food shortages. The USSR's defeated army was demoralized and impatient for its back pay. And Gorbachev was hated by the very Communist Party whose rule he was attempting to preserve. Opening the Soviet system to reform had only exposed its rotten core.

◆ From Democracy to Dissolution
....

Gorbachev's reforms encouraged the East European satellites to experiment with their own economic and political reform. These experiments were supported by Gorbachev, who needed his trading partners to keep pace with Soviet economic changes. Hungary began to abandon Communism when Janos Kadar retired in 1988. Jaruzelski eased martial law in Poland and opened discussions with the leaders of Solidarity. Gorbachev's problems continued to multiply despite additional military cutbacks and the signing of a trade agreement with capitalist West Germany in May 1989. Hungary scheduled multi-party elections and opened up its borders with Austria. During the summer thousands of East Europeans took advantage of this hole in the Iron Curtain to migrate to the West. In August, the recently legalized Solidarity swept the partially free elections in Poland and formed a coalition government with Jaruzelski. In two key Warsaw Pact nations, the Communist monopoly had come to an end without violence and with the approval of Moscow.

In the German Democratic Republic, General Secretary Erich Honecker (1912–1994) publicly denounced Gorbachev's reforms, but his defiance seemed foolish when Poland and Hungary allowed large numbers of East German citizens to use tourist visas to flee to the West through their territory. Gorbachev's acquiescence encouraged a German "New Forum" party to sponsor rallies against the government. During October 1989 ceremonies honoring the fortieth anniversary of the creation of East Germany, Gorbachev told Honecker not to expect any Soviet assistance if he tried to stem the tide of reform. The Brezhnev Doctrine was dead. Honecker retired on October 18. His successor tried to calm the waters by suspending all travel restrictions. Within hours of the announcement, on November 9, 1989, huge groups of demonstrators began spontaneously to tear down the Berlin Wall, and the next day East German troops completed its demolition. The great symbol of the Iron Curtain was no more; fragments of it could be purchased at souvenir stands.

Berliners tear down the Wall that divided their city for 28 years.
Copyright © Liaison Agency, Inc.

West German Chancellor Helmut Kohl (b. 1930) visited Moscow in January 1990 to begin talks on German reunification.

As the wall tumbled in Berlin, Bulgarian leader Todor Zhivkov (1911–1998) caved in to anti-Communist protesters, scheduling free elections for the following June. In Czechoslovakia, hundreds of thousands of protesters gathered daily in Prague despite attacks by riot police on October 28 and November 17, 1989. Led by the playwright Vaclav Havel (b. 1936) and the old reformer Alexander Dubcek, a "Civic Forum" was forged out of workers, students, professionals, intellectuals, and even army troops. Threats of a general strike forced Gustav Husak (1913–1991), president since 1968, to resign, beginning the transition to democracy. By the end of December, Czechoslovakia's "Velvet Revolution" was complete. At the end of December revolution broke out in Romania, the last of the Warsaw Pact satellites. Its Communist dictator Nicolae Ceausescu (1918-1989) was overthrown and executed on Christmas Day along with his wife Elena.

In June 1990 Bush and Gorbachev met in Washington to sign the START treaty reducing strategic nuclear forces and set the terms for the reduction of conventional weapons. The leaders of NATO used their July summit to announce to the world that NATO and the Warsaw Pact were no longer enemies. During that summer and fall, former enemies cooperated in the First Gulf War (1991) to undo Iraq's invasion of neighboring Kuwait.

By July 1990, Kohl and Gorbachev had come to an understanding. Germany would be reunited and the reunified Germany would remain in NATO with its eastern areas demilitarized and Soviet troops evacuated by 1994. West Germany would assume all of the East's financial obligations to Moscow and provide a loan of five billion Deutschmarks to the Soviet Union. The final treaty was signed on September 12 by the two Germanies and the four Allied powers that had partitioned that nation in 1945. On October 3, 1990, the provinces of East Germany simply became additional *Länder* in the Federal Republic of Germany. The two Germanies had become one.

◆ The End of the Soviet Union

Gorbachev had gambled that economic restructuring would create social and financial progress once he eliminated outside drains on the Soviet economy, but his reforms failed to produce the expected results and his dismantling of the state bureaucracy created serious problems in distribution. Food, clothing, fuel, and industrial materials fell into catastrophically short supply, while rising prices and a black market made a mockery of fixed official salaries and wages. Strikes by Ukrainian coal miners revealed the extent of proletarian discontent and threatened Gorbachev's commitment to political liberalization. An upsurge in religion, occasioned by the thousandth anniversary of the Russian Orthodox Church made it plain that socialist atheism had lost its grip on the Soviet people. Even more ominously, nationalist demonstrations in the Ukraine, Armenia, and Azerbaijan had to be crushed by Interior Ministry troops under KGB command. After permitting free elections in Eastern Europe, Gorbachev now faced similar demands from several of the Soviet republics. When the three Baltic States of Estonia, Latvia, and Lithuania demanded political concessions, an increasingly embattled Gorbachev could do no more than denounce the "virus of nationalism" that threatened to dismember the Soviet Union. The Georgian Republic asserted its right to secede from the USSR in late 1989. Lithuania issued a declaration of independence in 1990. Gorbachev was losing control of the Soviet Union.

By now, Gorbachev was actually far more popular in the West than at home. He was jeered by protesters at the May Day festivities in Moscow's Red Square but cheered by Americans when he met with George Bush later that month. He returned home to find that Boris Yeltsin (b. 1931), the

Gorbachev and Yeltsin before the Russian Parliament as the Soviet Union collapses.
Courtesy of Gamma-Liaison © Shone

newly installed Chairman of the Supreme Soviet of the Russian Republic, had proclaimed Russia's sovereignty. Not only did Yeltsin declare that Russian laws took precedence over those of the USSR, he mocked Gorbachev's latest reform proposals and demanded that the republics be given independent control over taxes and natural resources.

Faced with such a challenge, Gorbachev moved closer to the old bureaucracy and prepared to reassert his control. When violence erupted between indigenous peoples and Russian settlers in January 1991, he permitted the army to crack down on seven republics. Seeking a compromise, Gorbachev prepared a treaty that would create a Union of Sovereign Soviet Republics. Although six republics refused even to vote on its terms, a desperate Gorbachev prepared to put it into effect that August. It was his final gamble, and it failed. Faced with the end of Communist rule, the Soviet military staff, in alliance with sympathetic Party and KGB officials, mounted a *coup d'état* on August 19 and attempted to displace Gorbachev "for reasons of health." The coup attempt collapsed when Yeltsin mobilized popular support and rallied the Russians from atop a tank in front of the Parliament building. Although Gorbachev resumed the Presidency, his power had been shattered. The republics individually seized the offices and assumed the duties of the central government, some even taking the radical step of outlawing the Soviet Communist Party.

Early in December, Yeltsin met with the leaders of Belarus and the Ukraine, and they decided to create a Commonwealth of Independent States (CIS) that would permit all its members to experiment with new forms of government and capitalist economic models. Gorbachev resigned on December 25, 1991, and the Soviet Union was formally dissolved that same day.

In 1993 Russia voted for a new constitution, and Boris Yeltsin won its first presidential elections. With the dissolution of the Warsaw Pact in March 1991 and the Soviet Union that December, the United States became the last remaining superpower. On January 11, 1994, NATO adopted a program of military cooperation with former Soviet satellite states in eastern Europe that led to a formal invitation to Poland, the Czech Republic and Hungary to join NATO in 1997 and a special "Founding Act" of mutual cooperation between NATO and the Soviet Union that same year. A new world order seemed well underway.

For the forty-five years of the Cold War, the United States and the Soviet Union battled for global supremacy. Both recruited allies and satellites protected by military alliances and secured by generous aid packages, in order to promote their respective political and economic systems while containing the spread of the other. This period was marked by alternating confrontation and relaxation as either side probed the strength of the other while recovering from its own missteps. No region of the world escaped the attention of the superpowers or remained immune from their struggle.

The Cold War, however, was only one of the two major consequences of World War II. Our next two chapters deal with the other—the collapse of the great European colonial empires and the emergence of a new world of independent nations trying to catch up to their former masters.

◆ Notes

1. Vital Speeches of the Day, XII (March 15, 1946), 331–335.

2. *Congressional Record,* 80th Congress, 1st Session (Washington, DC: Government Printing Office, 1947), XCIII:1980–1981.

3. *Documenting the Modern World,* edited by George J. Lankevich and Andrea Finkelstein, 2nd edition (Lido Beach, NY: Whittier Publications, 2003), 212.

11

Revolutions in Asia

The empires created by European powers during the nineteenth-century were weakened but not lost as a result of World War I. The territories and colonies lost by Germany and the Ottoman Empire were redistributed to the victors through the Mandate System as laid out in Article 22 of the League of Nations Charter. But the costs of rebuilding their economies after World War II made it increasingly impossible for European powers to maintain their empires. In 1945, only a dozen of the charter members of the United Nations were located in Africa and Asia. By 2003, those two continents boasted the majority of the UN's 191 member states. The course of this transformation and the forces it unleashed is the subject of our remaining chapters. This chapter concentrates on revolution and decolonization within the main geo-political regions of Asia: the Indian Subcontinent, the Far East, Southeast Asia, and the Middle East.

The Decolonization of the Indian Subcontinent

◆ Independence for India

The great Indian poet Rabindranath Tagore (1861-1941), the first Indian to receive the Nobel Prize for Literature, always held western civilization in enormous respect. Tagore believed in the ideals espoused by western liberals, but he was extremely critical of the British Raj that dominated India since 1858 and its attendant racism. So it was not surprising that early in the 1930s Tagore praised Japan for breaking the colonial "spell under which (Asians) lay in torpor for ages." It was a position he maintained until the very end of his life, when he found himself repelled by Japan's own imperial ambitions, authoritarian government, and denial of individual rights. Tagore's literary artistry earned him the admiration of his compatriots, but his constantly shifting and finely modulated positions made him an unlikely candidate for the moral leadership of the campaign for independence. That role fell to his contemporary, Mohandas Gandhi (1869-1948), called the *Mahatma* (Great Soul) by his devoted followers.

Building on his successes in gaining some civil rights for the Indian community in South Africa, Gandhi launched a nationalist crusade in India for which he would spend 2,338 days in jail. The leaders of the Indian independence movement had cooperated with the British during World War I. When that cooperation did not get them the concessions they sought, they were determined not to be let down a second time. With Japanese forces marching across neighboring British Burma, Gandhi launched a "Quit India" campaign that undermined Britain's ability to defend its Asian colonies. The British responded by putting Gandhi and his Congress Party allies behind bars for the duration.

With India needed as a supply base and staging area for Allied efforts against Japan, Sir Richard Stafford Cripps (1889–1952) could only ensure India's cooperation against the Japanese with a promise of postwar independence. Given the amount of mistrust that had built up between ruler and ruler during the British Raj, however, several thousand Indian soldiers in the British colonial forces deserted to the Axis cause after being taken prisoner by the Japanese who also promised India independence. Britain's wartime Prime Minister, Winston Churchill, wanted to keep the empire intact, but when British voters rejected his leadership in 1945, the new Labour government of Clement Attlee (1883–1967) decided to fulfill Cripps's pledge to grant India independence. Lord Louis Mountbatten (1900–1979) was dispatched to New Delhi to oversee the end of the British Raj.

When Mountbatten began his mission late in 1946, the British Empire consisted of over 300 territories scattered across the globe. India, its greatest single treasure, had a population of almost 450 million people, 90 percent of whom were illiterate. Although nationalists like Gandhi spoke in the name of a single people, the population was in fact deeply divided between the Hindu majority, a large (100 million) Muslim minority, and many smaller minorities, such as the Sikhs, who feared for their ways of life in a largely Hindu state. Economic, ethnic, and caste divisions within the Hindu majority further splintered the population.

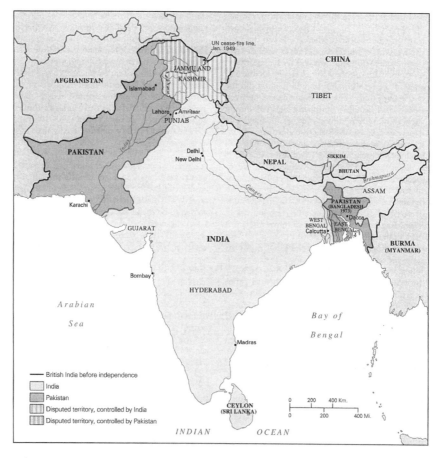

The Partition of British India, 1947.
From *History of World Societies,* Third Edition, (1992), reproduced by permission of Houghton Mifflin.

Despite the best efforts of Mountbatten and Congress Party leader Jawaharlal Nehru (1889–1964), India's freedom became a negotiating nightmare. So deep was the mistrust between the Hindu and Muslim communities that not even Gandhi's influence could bring them together within a single state. Muslim leader Mohammed Ali Jinnah (1876–1948) adamantly demanded the simultaneous creation of an independent Islamic state to be called Pakistan. So, in the summer of 1947, teams of lawyers divided the wealth and resources of the sub-continent between the two rival religions. On August 15, India and Pakistan attained freedom in a blaze of fireworks that could not hide their mutual distrust. The Muslim population was spread throughout British India, although there were very large concentrations of Muslims at the very eastern and western extremes of the territory. In order to contain these two regions within one nation, Pakistan began its existence as a country whose two halves were separated by almost a thousand miles of Indian territory. More than ten million people took to the road across northern India as panicked Hindus and Muslims relocated to live among their fellow co-religionists. Riots and massacres followed as local majorities practiced what would later be called "ethnic cleansing"; at least half a million people died in the civil-religious conflict. No area suffered more intensely than Kashmir, a border province located physically and spiritually between the two new nations. Maharajah Hariandar Singh (1915–1989) of Kashmir was a Hindu, but as more than two-thirds of his people were Muslim he considered bids from both nations. When Pakistani troops entered Kashmir in October, the maharajah decided to join India. The province has been a battleground ever since. The United Nations halted the first bloodshed (1948–1949) and awarded India two-thirds of the disputed territory. UN intervention brought two more border wars (in 1965–1966 and 1971–1972) to a cease-fire, but no permanent settlement was made. An attack on India's Parliament on December 13, 1999, set off a fourth round of fighting because India blamed the attack on Pakistan-based militants supported by Pakistan's intelligence service. The fact that almost 50 percent of the population of Indian Kashmir is Muslim and up to 25 percent of Pakistan's Kashmir is Hindu makes for a difficult peace.

◆   Nehru and the Third World

Jawaharlal Nehru, a loyal disciple of Gandhi, became India's first Prime Minister in 1947. His prestige increased enormously after Gandhi was assassinated by a Hindu fanatic on January 30, 1948, for daring to advocate peace with Muslims. Nehru was determined to chart an independent course for India, adopting a neutral stance during the first years of the Cold War. His main concern was to make India's economy strong enough to meet the demands of its surging population. To avoid the extremes of wealth and poverty that might accompany capitalist development, he followed a socialist model and opted for central planning. His goal was a secular, multi-ethnic, and democratic society with a directed economy.

Britain granted independence to Burma and Ceylon in 1948. The Dutch were forced out of their East Indian possessions, and the over 17,000 islands consolidated themselves into the republic of Indonesia. France was expelled from Southeast Asia in 1954, leading to the creation of Laos, Cambodia, and North and South Vietnam. In 1952 the French sociologist Alfred Sauvy (1898–1990) coined the phrase *Tiers-Monde* (Third World) to describe the underdeveloped lands—newly independent or still colonized—that wished to chart a future free of direction from either the United States or the Soviet Union. These Third World states faced common problems such as population pressures, tribal rivalries, the need for capital investment, lack of infrastructure, and political inexperience.

Nehru believed these Third World states needed to unite in order to influence world affairs and felt India's size and economic potential made it the natural leader of his proposed "non-aligned" bloc that contained over half the world's population. The first formal meeting of this "Third World" took place in April 1955 at Bandung, Java, where President Sukarno (1901-1970) of Indonesia hosted a conference of twenty-nine Asian and African states. Nehru used the Bandung Conference to demand an increased role in world politics for the "Third World," and, as the conference ended, hopes were high that Third World states would acquire political and economic clout reflecting their numbers. But the path to viability and power would prove far more arduous and lengthy than the delegates imagined.

◆ The Nehru Dynasty

Until his death in 1964, Nehru spoke for Third World concerns even as he directed the affairs of India. Domestically, he followed policies of non-alignment, socialist development, and secularism. A treaty signed in 1950 temporarily eased tensions with Pakistan, and allowed Nehru to begin industrialization. He proved to be more successful as a diplomat than as a developer, however, for he was never able to fully mobilize India's human or economic potential. The Marxist orientation of his program failed to raise living standards. Nehru was not above using military force to attain national goals; in 1961 he authorized the army to seize the three Portuguese enclaves remaining on Indian soil. A fading Portugal was easily defeated, but India's military weakness was demonstrated when China humiliated it in a brief border war in the Himalayas in October 1962. Yet the Congress Party never lost its electoral domination and Nehru's leadership was never challenged. So great was Nehru's prestige that after his death, India continued to elect members of his family to lead the country, creating a virtual "Nehru dynasty."

Nehru's heir and Prime Minister of India, Indira Gandhi.
Copyright © CORBIS/Bettmann

After Nehru's death, Lal Bahadur Shastri (1904–1966), another senior member of Gandhi's circle, briefly held the post of Prime Minister until Nehru's daughter Indira Gandhi (1917–1984) assumed the position in January 1966. Mrs. Gandhi (her husband was not related to the Mahatma) had long been Nehru's confidant, and her accession to power within the Congress Party gave her enormous influence. She continued India's participation in the non-aligned movement while pursuing expensive domestic initiatives designed to increase production. Her regime intervened militarily when East Pakistan seceded from West Pakistani control. In a short, successful war India defeated West Pakistan, facilitating the 1971 birth of Bangladesh (the former East Pakistan). That conflict established the military domination of India in the sub-continent but at the price of a continuing arms race between the two powers. Indira Gandhi also authorized the programs that made India the first Third World nation to attain nuclear capability (May 18, 1974). With population gains still outpacing economic growth, she instituted birth control programs that stopped just short of mandatory sterilization. But poverty remained endemic, production lagged, and corruption reached new heights. As an emergency measure, Indira Gandhi assumed dictatorial powers in 1975 and suspended the Indian constitution only to allow free elections two years later. To her surprise, the Congress Party lost its majority, in good measure because of her use of sterilization to control population growth.

Three years of Bharatiya Janata (the "Indian People's Party") rule followed. A Hindu-nationalist party, the Bharatiya Janata attempted to re-establish the traditional Hindu culture discarded in the nation's rush towards modernization. Birth control programs were ended, central planning eroded, and the government encouraged Mahatma Gandhi style local enterprise. But the economy stagnated. In 1980 voters returned Indira Gandhi to the leadership of a weakened nation, in which over seven million people were born into poverty each year as India's ethnic and religious minorities stepped their demands for more autonomy. Hoping to assume her father's international leadership, Mrs. Gandhi hosted a New Delhi conference of Third World nations in March 1983. But separatists continued to threaten India's unity. In June 1984, facing a violent Sikh-nationalist movement, she opted for military action. In a 36-hour battle within the Golden Temple at Amritsar, the center of the Sikh religion, the Indian army crushed the rebel movement. Victory shortly turned to tragedy. On October 31, Indira Gandhi was assassinated by the very Sikh bodyguards she had refused to replace because she believed they were loyal Indians. In scenes reminiscent of 1947, sectarian violence swept the shocked nation and thousands died.

The Nehru dynasty continued to rule India as the Congress Party installed Indira's son Rajiv Gandhi (1944–1991) as Prime Minister. A former airline pilot married to an Italian and with little political experience, Rajiv won office with a record breaking parliamentary majority. The popularity he gained for moderation in settling the Sikh troubles was soon dissipated by his lack of political skill. In 1987 he ordered Indian troops into neighboring Sri Lanka (formerly British Ceylon and independent since 1948) to help it put down a separatist movement by a minority ethnic group, the Tamil. Public disapproval over his intervention and increasing reports of widespread corruption led to the defeat of his party in the 1989 elections. In 1991, while campaigning to return to power, he and sixteen others were killed when a Tamil terrorist committed suicide by detonating a bomb concealed beneath her clothing. But not even this second assassination ended the Nehru dynasty. Despite her loss in the last election, Rajiv's widow Sonia (b. 1947) remains the leading figure within the contemporary Congress Party, and the couple's two children have also pledged to continue Nehru's quest for a secular, socialist, and united Indian state.

Yet India in the new millennium appears far different than the country envisioned by Nehru. Prime Minister Narasimha Rao (b. 1922), governing in the name of Congress (1991-1996), decided to replace state-supported socialism with a free market economy, opening up India to foreign investment. A world-class software industry was created, the tax system simplified, protective tariffs eliminated, and the infamous Indian bureaucracy of 60 million public servants substantially reduced. By implementing the techniques of the Green Revolution in agriculture, India has finally developed the ability to feed itself and even the most rural village has the electricity to run satellite television. But many problems remain. Even though India is a functioning democracy with the world's largest middle-class population, it still has over 300 million illiterate citizens earning less than a dollar a day. The billions spent by the government to test thermonuclear warheads in 1998 and missile delivery systems in 1999 did not contribute to the resolution of India's economic imbalances.

Nor has India successfully resolved its ancient religious and regional rivalries. On December 6, 1992, Hindu mobs, inspired by politicians from the Bharatiya Janata Party, destroyed the Babri Masjid in Ayodhya, one of the most revered sites of Muslim India. Hindu militants complained that the mosque had been erected on the traditional site of the birthplace of Rama, an important hero-turned-god of the Hindu religion. Over 1,000 people were killed in riots following the mosque's destruction. In the 1996 elections the Bharatiya Janata was popular enough to capture the office of Prime Minister, with Atal Bihari Vajpayee (b. 1926) using his inauguration to make several symbolic points: wearing a yellow sash (the color of Hindu nationalism) and taking his oath in Hindi rather than in English as his predecessors had done. But he was out of office just seventeen days later when his party was unable to maintain the coalition that gave it a majority in the Indian parliament. Several other short-lived coalitions followed. Finally, the elections of March 1998 returned the Bharatiya Janata and Atal Bihari Vajpayee to power. The Congress Party candidate, Sonia Gandhi (widow of Rajiv) was defeated. The Bharatiya Janata has apparently rejected Nehru's vision of secular toleration. It has ignored systematic Hindu attacks on India's Muslim and Christian minorities, and, although it has not carried out its promise to erect a temple to Rama on the site of the destroyed Babri Masjid, that promise remains part of the Janata platform. Peace between India's Hindu majority and Muslim minority remain especially important. India's 126 million Muslims make up about twelve percent of India's population of just over one billion people; they are the world's third-largest Muslim population.

◆ Pakistan in the Modern Age

Pakistan (an acronym for **P**unjab, **A**fghan, **K**ashmir, **S**indh, & Baloch**istan**, the provinces of British India having Muslim majorities) dates its birth to August 14, 1947, a day before India's. That birth was marked by the deaths of over half a million Hindus, Muslims, and Sikhs in the slaughter that marked the migrations of minority groups into or out of Pakistan or India. Pakistan's two geographic halves were separated by over a 1000 miles of hostile Indian territory. Its founder, Mohammed Ali Jinnah, died less than a year after its independence, and his successor, Liaquat Ali Khan (1895–1951), was assassinated in 1951 in a failed military coup. Declaring itself an Islamic Republic on March 23, 1956, brought little improvement in its fate. Although its democratic origins have never been completely lost, harsh military regimes have been followed only by inept civilian governments. Both the political and the military elite in Pakistan aspire to lead the Muslim world, and for five decades the state has devoted the largest part of its budget to the army although successive wars with India over Kashmir and Bangladesh have ended in failure.

During most of the 1970s, Pakistan was dominated by Zulfikar Ali Bhutto (1928–1979) and his People's Party, a movement supported largely by poor voters. Bhutto came to power during the crisis that split Pakistan, transforming East Pakistan into the independent state of Bangladesh. The crisis arose in 1970 when East Pakistan was devastated by a cyclone and tidal wave that killed over a quarter of a million people. East Pakistani leaders accused the government in West Pakistan of delaying relief supplies. In the December elections Bhutto's Pakistan People's Party dominated the West while the Awami League won an overwhelming majority in the East. Civil war broke out in March 1971 when East Pakistan declared its independence as Bangladesh. At first it appeared that the rebellion could not succeed, but India intervened in support of Bangladesh and Pakistan surrendered on December 16. Casualties in the brief civil war topped one million.

MOHAMMED ALI JINNAH (1876–1948)

Founder of Pakistan.
Copyright © AP/Wide World Photos

Mohammed Ali Jinnah was born on December 25, 1876, in Karachi, British India, to a well-to-do merchant family. A brilliant student, he passed the matriculation examination of the University of Bombay at the age of sixteen, but instead convinced his father to let him go to England to become a barrister. Arriving in London in 1892, Jinnah trained at Lincoln's Inn and was called to the bar at age nineteen. He also got firsthand experience in English electoral politics when he joined with other Indian students in the successful campaign of Dadabhai Naoroji (1825–1917) to become the first Indian Member of Parliament.

Returning to India in 1896, Jinnah set up a law practice in Bombay. The young lawyer was already a widower for, following Indian custom, a marriage had been arranged before his departure for England, but his bride died soon afterwards. His second wife was the daughter of a Bombay Parsi millionaire, but the marriage was not a success. Jinnah's sister Fatima became his main female confidant.

As a successful member of India's middle-class establishment Jinnah had originally joined the Indian National Congress. But he was also a member of India's Muslim minority. Amidst rising fears that Congress sought a Hindu state rather an inclusive one, an All-India Muslim League had been founded in 1906. At first Jinnah rejected its sectarianism, serving instead on the Imperial legislative Council in 1910. By 1913, Jinnah had joined the Muslim League, but he continued to work for Hindu-Muslim cooperation in a united India. Because of his efforts, both sides approved the constitutional reforms of the 1916 Lucknow Pact, but the Hindu-Muslim alliance proved increasingly rocky. In 1928 Congress rejected Muslim demands for separate electorates, while Muslim League hard-liners refused any compromise with Congress. Jinnah fled to England in disgust, remaining there for five years until he was persuaded to return to India in 1935 to head up a reformed Muslim League. When Congress won an absolute majority in the 1937 elections (held under a new Government of India Act, 1935), it refused to include the League in the formation of Provincial governments. This convinced Jinnah that cooperation with the Hindu majority was fatal to Muslim interests. On March 22-23, 1940, Jinnah's League adopted a resolution calling for the formation of a separate Muslim state, Pakistan.

When the British government decided to withdraw from India in 1947. The colony was split into two nations, a predominantly Hindu India and a predominantly Muslim Pakistan, but Pakistan was a country divided into two pieces, separated by 1,000 miles of India. Mohammed Ali Jinnah, called by his people, *Qa'id-e A'zam* (the Great Leader), became Pakistan's first head of state, but age and cancer sapped his effectiveness. He died on September 11, 1948, in Karachi, now the capital of his new nation. His last year was one of great sorrow over the hundreds of thousands of Indian lives—Hindu and Muslim alike—lost in the civil wars that erupted over partition. His sorrow would have been even greater had he known that Pakistan would itself split into two after a civil war in 1972 or veer from his secularist course into fundamentalism.

Bhutto took office as president in a reduced Pakistan in December 1971. A constitutional reform pushed through in August 1973 split the executive functions into two offices: president (head of state) and prime minister (head of government). Bhutto became prime minister. But the reforms begun by the Bhutto government were ended by a military coup in 1977 led by General Mohammad Zia ul-Haq (1924–1988) who immediately declared martial law. Bhutto was executed in 1979 for conspiring to murder a political opponent. A decade of military rule followed. Zia, a devout Muslim, installed *Sharia* (a law code based upon the *Quran*) as the nation's legal code and squandered Pakistan's meager resources on the military.

After Zia died in a fiery plane crash in August 1988, Ghulam Ishaq Khan (b. 1915) headed up a transitional government as a deeply troubled Pakistan moved to reestablish its democratic framework. That November, Benazir Bhutto (b. 1953) was elected to serve as the first woman prime minister of any Islamic state. Like her father she pledged to serve the interests of the poor, but her policies appeared to benefit only the members of her extended family and the ruling circle within her party. In 1990, Ishaq Khan threw Bhutto's government out of office on charges of corruption. A coalition government headed by Nawaz Sharif (b. 1949) was voted into power. By 1993 Ishaq Khan had tossed out Sharif for corruption as well. Pakistan's Supreme Court invalidated the charges, but Sharif resigned, and Bhutto was voted back into power. Before 1996 was over she was out of power again, and Sharif became Prime Minister once more pending new elections. Those elections in 1997 confirmed Nawaz Sharif and the Muslim League in office for a second time by stoking the fires of extreme nationalism and religious fervor.

A military coup toppled Sharif's government on October 12, 1999. General Pervez Musharraf (b. 1943) became the self-styled "chief executive" of Pakistan, and Sharif was arrested and tried for corruption. Born in India, Musharraf emigrated to Pakistan with his family in the turmoil following independence. He joined an artillery regiment in the Pakistani army and won several military decorations for his role in the 1965 and 1971 border wars with India. Early in 1999, Musharraf backed Pakistani incursions into Kargil, a mountainous region in Indian territory; such campaigns were a good way of diverting public attention from Pakistan's mounting economic problems. When Prime Minister Sharif ordered the army out of Kargil and back into Pakistan in July under pressure from the United States, Musharraf resisted and was dismissed by Sharif. That dismissal led to the coup. Within days, Musharraf had abolished Parliament, replacing it with a six-member National Security Council of hand-picked military and civilian leaders. To attack Pakistan's endemic corruption, he started proceedings to recover billions of dollars in illegal loans made to party cronies under civilian rule. Musharraf also floated offers of negotiations to Indian leaders without withdrawing a single soldier from their joint border or giving any hint when he would return Pakistan to civilian rule. Having fled the country to avoid arrest in 1999, Benazir Bhutto was sentenced in absentia in 2001 and again in 2002 for failing to return to Pakistan to answer a series of corruption charges.

Almost one third of Pakistan's 135 million people live in absolute poverty; its GDP per capita is barely $2,100. It has the highest rate of infant mortality (78.52 deaths per 1000 live births) and the second lowest life expectancy (61.82 years) in Asia. Its literacy rate barely tops twenty-five percent. Its governments, whether military or civilian, have ignored its pressing socio-economic problems, relying instead on appeals to anti-Indian sentiment to stay in power. On May 28, 1998, Pakistan exploded its first nuclear bomb. Each successive Indian test of thermonuclear warheads or missile delivery systems has been met with a similar Pakistani test, and May 28 has become a national holiday, *Youm-e-Takbeer* ("Day of God's Greatness"). Even though its population is only one-seventh the size of India's, Pakistan's army is proportionally larger: in 2002, India had 1.18 million troops on active duty and 528,400 more in reserve; Pakistan had 612,000 troops on active duty and 500,000 in reserve. Both countries have missiles capable of delivering nuclear warheads into Iran, China, Saudi Arabia, or Russia's southern border. Given the unresolved border disputes between the two countries and their ever-escalating military spending, war between India and Pakistan is an ever-present danger threatening the entire region.

The People's Republic of China
◆ Chairman Mao's China

Although China was never actually a colony of any European power, it was still far from being a true nation-state when Mao Tse-tung (1893-1976) proclaimed the installation of the People's Republic of China on October 1, 1949. The Communists won a land so ravaged by Japanese occupation and four years of civil war that it was reduced to operating on the barter system. Over 20,000,000 Chinese died in those wars.

Mao's ultimate aim was the total reorganization of Chinese society, but he could not even take the first steps towards that reorganization until the Communists had consolidated their control over all of China. Mao immediately divided China into six regions under joint military and administrative control. Tibet (autonomous since 1913) and Manchuria were formally integrated into China proper, and a uniform system of taxation imposed. The Communist Party began nationwide campaigns to eradicate opium usage and prostitution. The Marriage Law of 1950 gave Chinese women the right to refuse arranged marriages. It also gave them equal divorce, child custody, and property rights. The Marriage Law reversed centuries of Confucian tradition giving almost unlimited power over the lives of his children to the father of the family. Schools once operated by western missionaries were nationalized, and Mao's version of Communist theory added to the curriculum at every level, but for the first time in Chinese history 60 percent of its children were receiving at least an elementary education. To feed China, Mao ordered the redistribution of agricultural acreage from landlords to peasants in the Agrarian Reform Law of 1950. By 1952 about 43 percent of China's farmlands had been turned over to its poorest peasants and grain production was up 12.6 percent. Without any friends in the international community, China signed a long term *Treaty of Assistance* with Stalin in 1950 that brought China $300 million in credits to spend on Soviet equipment.

These first economic gains gave Mao the confidence he needed to impose tighter political and economic control over China. In the purges of 1951 (the "Five Antis" campaign) directed against capitalists, suspected counter-revolutionaries, and possible dissidents within his own party, Mao oversaw the arrests and execution of almost three-quarters of a million Chinese (including 10 percent of Party members). In 1953 Mao instituted a Stalin-inspired Five-Year Plan, collectivizing some of the re-distributed farmland. The Soviet Union supplied the materials and expertise to begin China's industrialization, as thousands of Chinese students were sent to the USSR to study. Soviet teachers and textbooks aided China's efforts to build a higher education system with free tuition for poorer students. According to the 1953 census, over 582 million people lived in China. By 1956, 64.2 million of them were in primary school, 6.2 in middle school, and 441,000 in secondary schools or colleges.

In 1956, as part of its modernization program, Communist China began using the *Hanyu pinyin wenzi* (Chinese writing system), a new set of rules for rendering the Peking dialect of Mandarin Chinese into a Latin-based alphabet. In the *Pinyin* system, Mao Tse-tung became Mao Zedong, and Peking became Beijing. That same year, a confident Mao encouraged his countrymen to comment on China's progress and suggest ways to further it. "Let a hundred flowers bloom,"

Chairman Mao poses with Chinese students during The Great Leap Forward.
Copyright © CORBIS/Bettmann

he announced; let "a hundred schools of thought contend." Mao was shocked by the intensity of the criticism aimed at the Communist leadership, especially by intellectuals angered over Party interference in scientific research. He responded with a new round of purges.

The Chinese economy was growing, but unevenly; increased industrial output was not translating into as many new jobs as expected and agricultural increases were barely keeping up with population growth. In his second Five-Year Plan (the "Great Leap Forward" of 1958), Mao stepped up the pace of collectivization. To achieve economies of scale, China's 740,000 collective farms were consolidated into 26,425 communes (with about 5000 families each). Communal kitchens and nurseries freed women for additional farm labor. Urban workshops and factories were also turned into communes. China's state industries were soon employing more than 50 million people in fourteen-hour shifts in an effort to make good on Mao's boast that China could "catch up with Britain in 15 years."[1] To mobilize China's youth, "productive labor" was made a mandatory part of the school curriculum at all educational levels.

China lacked both the will and the personnel to carry out such fundamental changes; within a year there was economic chaos. Famine appeared in previously prosperous southern provinces. Conditions grew even worse in 1960. Mao's disapproval of Khrushchev's efforts to "de-Stalinize" the Soviet Union and ease tensions with the west and Khrushchev's disapproval of Mao's saber-rattling over Taiwan led the USSR to withdraw its financial aid from China. Between 1959 and 1961, over 20 million Chinese died of disease and starvation, as Mao continued to export food to prove the success of his revolutionary vision. Only the emergency institution of an "agriculture first" policy by the Party's most senior economist, Chen Yun (1905-1995), avoided more serious trouble. Deng Xiaoping (1904–1997), who would one day become China's leader, was even hinting at a return to the unthinkable—capitalist farming. In 1962 he made a speech claiming that "yellow or white, a cat that catches mice is a good cat."[2]

During the 1960s, China's ideological split with the Soviet Union widened as China consolidated its hold on Tibet and waged a brief but successful border war with India in 1962. Excluded from United Nation's membership because of the American policy of recognizing only Nationalist China, Mao still hoped to make Communist China the future leader of a "Third World" bloc in the UN General Assembly. After the Cuban Missile Crisis in 1962, Mao denounced the Soviet decision to cooperate with the United States on a *Test Ban Treaty* (1963) as cowardly. Determined that China stand on its own, he expended vast resources on a program that produced an atom bomb in 1964, and on factories that created jet fighters in 1970. As he distanced himself from Soviet ties, Mao actually fought a border war against Russian forces along the Ussuri River frontier in 1969.

In May 1966, convinced of the need to revitalize China's revolutionary spirit, Mao launched the undertaking of a "Great Proletarian Cultural Revolution" against the "Four Olds": old ideas, old culture, old customs, and old habits. To carry it out, he authorized the formation of the Red Guards, battalions of secondary school students armed with *Quotations from Chairman Mao* (informally known as *the Little Red Book*). Freed from school responsibilities, the Red Guard were mobilized in 1966 to purge incompetent administrators, punish professorial free-thinkers, and enforce Mao's revolutionary creed. While Mao demonstrated his continuing vitality by taking a highly publicized nine-mile swim in the Yangtze River on July 16, 1966, Deng Xiaoping was exiled to a country village. Twelve million high school graduates were also sent to work on communal farms to be "re-educated" by the peasantry. For nearly ten years most schooling in China stopped at the eighth grade and the few colleges allowed to remain open accepted students on the basis of "work points" rather than grades. By 1968 the outrages perpetrated by Red Guard units were so extreme that Mao had to deploy China's army against them to bring the revolution under

PU YI (1906-1967)

China's last emperor as his abdication was announced (February 12, 1912).
Copyright © CORBIS/Bettmann

P'u-i (known in the West as Henry Pu Yi) was born into an aristocratic Manchu family in Beijing on February 7, 1906. He became the last emperor of the Manchu dynasty that had first conquered China in 1644, but had been in steady decline since the end of the eighteenth century. The Empress Dowager Tz'u-hsi, who had ruled China first through her son and later through her nephew, saw the elevation of the infant Pu Yi as a means of continuing her reign. Already 74 years old, Tz'u-hsi was convinced by her court astrologers that she would live to be 120, but she died on November 15, 1908, just one day after the installation of Pu Yi as Emperor. Within three years, the dynasty had fallen, and a Chinese republic was proclaimed by Sun Yat-sen.

Pu Yi lived a cosseted existence under the republic. He was allowed to remain in the Forbidden City, for centuries the seat of Imperial power, along with his wives, concubines, eunuchs, and other retainers. He was forced to leave Beijing in the mid-1920s by one of the warlords who dominated China in the period, but eventually found a haven in the Japanese concession of Tienjin, a large city close to the capital.

The Japanese government was anxious to legitimize its 1931 conquest of Manchuria, in the northeast corner of the Chinese Republic. Pu Yi's position as the hereditary ruler of the Manchu people offered them a way to do so. In 1934 he accepted Japan's invitation to become emperor of the new state that the Japanese called Manchukuo (literally, land of the Manchus). Pu Yi, who had never exercised any independent authority, may have thought this was the first step in the restoration of his dynasty, but he was easily turned into a puppet of his Japanese masters. They had no difficulty keeping this weak, ignorant, superstitious, and frequently bewildered man entirely under their control. The sale of opium, through which the Japanese financed their occupation, contributed to the addiction and premature death of the Emperor's principal wife.

The Russian conquest of Manchuria in 1945 brought an end both to Manchukuo, and Pu Yi's second reign. The ex-emperor remained in Russian captivity as long as a Soviet domination of Manchuria remained a possibility. He was returned to the People's Republic of China after the success of its communist revolution in 1949, and for years afterward remained a terrified prisoner undergoing "rehabilitation" in camps designed to create loyal citizens. He spent his last years working as a gardener in Beijing before dying of cancer on October 17, 1967. Threatened and harassed by teenaged Red Guards during the Cultural Revolution, Pu Yi barely escaped with his life before the government ordered that the Last Emperor be left in peace. His autobiography, *From Emperor to Citizen,* was never published in China, but appeared in England in 1964–1965.

control. Only Mao's death on September 9, 1976, brought the class warfare to a complete end. By then some ten million lives had been sacrificed to Mao's vision of China's destiny.

◆ Deng Xiaoping and Chinese Modernization

Mao's newly designated successor, Hua Guofeng (b. 1920), and his most dedicated supporters, the "Gang of Four" led by Mao's wife, Jiang Qing (1914–1991), a former movie actress, attempted to continue the Cultural Revolution after his death. After a complicated power struggle, however, the thrice-purged Deng Xiaoping emerged in December 1978 as the new ruler of China. The Gang of Four were tried and convicted in 1980 of plotting to subvert the state. Although Jiang's death sentence was commuted to life imprisonment, she committed suicide in 1991.

Sticking to his "the color of the cat doesn't matter" policy, Deng began a massive restructuring of China's economy through what he called the "Four Modernizations": of industry, agriculture, science, and national defense. A market economy began to replace socialist central planning. Beginning in 1979, a series of agricultural reforms allowed peasants to sell produce raised on their private plots on the open market and, even more importantly, to lease larger tracts of land from the collective farms and keep any produce raised over a contracted minimum. Industries were directed towards consumer production, and a dual system of mixed market and state-set prices was introduced. China was opened up to foreign investment through membership in the World Bank, and special "Enterprise Zones" (beginning with Shenzhen in 1982) were set up as massive experiments in capitalism. China's economy was soon growing at an astounding rate of 9.2 percent per year. By 1995 it ranked as the world's third largest economy.

China's increasing economic strength allowed it to engineer the restoration of territories lost during its long period of weakness. Deng negotiated agreements with Great Britain and Portugal to return Hong Kong (1997) and Macao (1999) to Chinese sovereignty. Tibet's position as a province of China was systematically consolidated despite international protests by Tenzin Gyatso (b. 1935), the 14th Dalai Lama, spiritual and political leader of Tibet. Deng failed only in his attempts to regain control over Taiwan, where the now democratically elected heirs of Chiang Kai-shek still ruled. Nevertheless, by encouraging extensive Taiwanese investment in mainland China, Deng believed that he had advanced the goal of future unification. As China gradually won recognition as a regional superpower, the Deng regime offered military assistance to Pakistan, even though this offended India. Missile technology sold by China to Iran provoked anger in the United States, but relations between the two nations continued even if on an uneasy course. The American government did not approve of China's foreign policy or China's human rights record, but it was loathe to lose access to the world's largest potential market.

Within China, Deng's policies did not work as smoothly. Alarmed by the increase in China's population (it would top one billion in 1982), Deng instituted a one-child per family policy in 1979 that rewarded parents who stayed within the limits but threatened the incomes and freedom of those who did not. The deeply ingrained preference for a son (whose wife would become a worker on the family farm) led to frequent aborting of female fetuses and outright female infanticide. By 1984 Chinese authorities realized that too strict an enforcement of the one-child policy was creating a generation of men without wives, and relaxed the policy.

Even though Deng denounced the excesses of the Cultural Revolution and the Great Leap Forward as serious errors in 1981, the Communist Party was not about to loosen its political grip on China. Deng's regime carried out successive campaigns against "spiritual pollution" (1983), "capitalist thinking" (1985), and "bourgeois democracy"(1987). University students were a particular concern, for the newly reopened school system permitted discussion of political rights. The winding down of the Cold War was bringing democratic reforms to Eastern Europe, and many Chinese dared to believe that Deng's economic liberalization foreshadowed a similar easing of party control. When Soviet President Gorbachev visited Beijing in 1989, he inspired the students to ask for greater political freedom. Throughout the last days of May, a growing crowd of students demonstrating in Beijing's Tiananmen Square was bolstered by workers demanding the right to unionize. But during the night of June 3-4, 1989, Deng sent in troops and tanks to crush the demonstration. As many as a thousand protesters were killed and hundreds more were jailed or fled into exile.

◆   The New China?

Remembering his struggles with the Gang of Four after Mao's death, Deng prepared China for an orderly succession after his own. After the Tiananmen massacre he designated Jiang Zemin (b. 1926), the former Mayor of Shanghai, as his successor. By the time Deng died in 1997, Jiang was able to assume full control of China. Pledged to continue Deng's revitalization, Jiang promised to dismantle the remaining state owned enterprises in order to maintain the pace of transformation. He presides over a China that enjoys social peace, economic prosperity, and great prestige in the world community. China's rapid economic growth has not come without a price. Beijing and Shanghai, like China's other industrial zones have levels of air pollution four to five times higher than those found in Los Angeles, New York, or Tokyo. Nor do all of China's nearly 1.3 billion people share in its new found wealth. Even adjusted for purchasing power parity, China's 2002 Gross Domestic Product per capita is only $4,300, compared to the USA's $36,300. Its urban unemployment rate hovers at ten percent. Like his predecessors, Jiang has punished human rights activists, prevented the organization of alternative political parties, and purged his government of any opposition.

Japan's Economic Miracle

When occupied by American forces in 1945, Japan's productivity had fallen back to 1918 levels. But during the late 1940s, because of rising Cold War tensions, Japan was gradually transformed from a defeated enemy to America's greatest ally in the Far East. Under the tutelage of MacArthur and the American military, Japan approved a constitution that outlawed aggressive war, and pioneered a form of modern capitalist enterprise in which the state directed the energies of entrepreneurs. Adopting the requirements of a democratic state, a parliamentary system with universal male and female suffrage became law in 1947. The Emperor's position was reduced to that of a ceremonial head of state. Effective political power was in the hands of Prime Minister Yoshida Shigeau (1878–1967) who had been arrested by the old regime in June 1945 for advocating a Japanese surrender. Yoshida led the Liberal-Democratic Party (LDP), a coalition of political conservatives and businessmen committed to maintaining Japanese uniqueness while fulfilling American demands for reform. He remained in office until 1954.

When the Cold War turned "hot" in Korea (1950–1953), Japan served as a supply and communications base for American forces. Massive American economic assistance flowed into Japan; capital resources, industrial expertise, and modern equipment eased Japan's transition from a conquered enemy with limited industrial capacity to a valued and technologically advanced partner. A *Security Treaty* signed with the United States in 1951 ended American occupation of Japan and placed it under the protection of the American "nuclear umbrella" even as it maintained Japan's "disarmed" status.

As the nation rebuilt its shattered infrastructure, the Ministry of International Trade and Industry (MITI) began to plan Japan's industrial rebirth. Put in charge of national tax and investment policies, MITI encouraged technology sharing between allied fields and created an export driven economy that cared little for the needs of Japanese consumers. The keys to Japan's "economic miracle" were the foundation laid by American aid during the occupation, long-term planning by a strong bureaucracy, the world's highest savings rate (about 20 percent), and an educated and underpaid labor force. By 1955 Japan had regained pre-war levels of production in textiles, chemicals, and steel. From 1953 to 1973 its economy grew at the rate of 10.5 percent per year. MITI bureaucrats forced production to focus on shipbuilding, machine tools, automobiles, and consumer electronics. In the 1950s the quality of Japanese steel made it the world's largest shipbuilder. In the1960s Japan became synonymous with well-made automobiles, and American manufactures were forced to overhaul America's automobile production to compete.

The oil crises of the 1970s threatened Japan's economic growth, but MITI planning moved Japan's export trade from its exclusive focus on energy guzzling goods to less energy dependent fields such as electronics. In each of these initiatives new *keiretsu* (alliances between independent corporations in related industries) were created to lead the national effort, and product reliability was assured by systems of zero-tolerance quality management. Japanese manufactured goods conquered the consumer world as companies like Toyota, Honda, Sony, Seiko, and Yamaha became known for excellence in production. Their ability to drive American made products out of the marketplace was not without irony. The system of Total Quality Management (involving the workforce in every phase of production) was introduced into Japan by American Dr. W. Edward Deming (1900-1993) during the occupation. A *Sino-Japanese Friendship Treaty* (1978) and *Trade Treaty* (1978) opened the way for Japan to get the coal and oil it needed from Communist China while giving Japan a new market for its industrial exports.

By the 1980s Japan seemed to challenge the United States as the center of worldwide commerce. Its Gross Domestic Product had expanded from $484 billion to over $4.5 trillion, a figure that in 1983 surpassed those of China, India, Pakistan, Australia, and both Koreas combined. Despite world oil shortages and political turmoil, Japan's economy seemed invulnerable to recession. Japan also cultivated its image as a concerned state, becoming the single greatest donor of foreign aid in the world and providing assistance to dozens of developing nations. American citizens watched in disbelief as Japanese investors purchased such prestigious properties as Rockefeller Center in New York and the Pebble Beach Golf Course in California. For a time, the land valuation of Tokyo alone was equal to that of the entire United States. By 1987 nine of the ten largest banks in the world were in Japan.

It was all too good to last. Japan's bubble of speculation and anticipated profits burst because it had been based upon presumed future growth rather than on realistic profit margins. A decline in land values and stock levels began in 1989, and the subsequent recession lasted all during the 1990s. In 1998, prices had fallen by more than 50 percent, and the banking sector of the economy was in ruins. Over 17,500 business had gone bankrupt. As the golden touch of MITI evaporated, Japan's politicians proved unable to cope with a contracting economy. The Liberal Democratic Party, which has been in power for all but ten months since 1955, has been shaken by corruption scandals and has not responded to the challenge. Japan remains the world's second largest economy: its population of just under 127 million people enjoyed a GDP per capita (adjusted for purchasing power parity) of $28,000 in 2002. But it no longer threatens to overtake the United States and faces extended recession. Even its place as the leading economy in Asia is no longer certain as the less well paid labor forces of its Asian neighbors produce more price-competitive goods.

Japan's political place in the international community is as uncertain as its leadership in the ongoing economic development of Asia. On the one hand, Japan's admission into the United Nations in 1956 and the choice of Tokyo for the 1964 Olympics seemed to mark the welcoming back of Japan into the international community. Japan signed the 1968 *Nuclear Non-Proliferation Treaty* in 1970 and contributed $13 billion dollars toward the Gulf War of 1991. The awarding of Nobel Prizes in Literature to Kawabata Yasunari (1899–1972) in 1968 and to Ōe Kenzaburo (b. 1935) in 1994 highlighted the increasing incorporation of Japanese culture into the international scene. However, demonstrations against Japan's refusal to apologize for the atrocities it committed during World War II continued to mar visits abroad by Emperor Akihito (b. 1933) as they had the visits of his father and predecessor, Hirohito, to Britain in 1971 and the United States in 1975. In 1998 British veterans protested their government's decision to give Akihito the Order of the Garter (Britain's highest order of chivalry) during a state visit there. The veterans cannot forget that one-third of the 50,000 British servicemen taken prisoner by the Japanese in the fall of Singapore died in captivity due to ill-treatment while only four percent of the Allied soldiers held prisoner by the Germans died. In 1993, an international tribunal in Switzerland decided that the Japanese government owed at least $40,000 in compensation to every one of the 139,000 Australian, Burmese, Byelorussian, Cambodian, Chinese, Dutch, Filipino, Indonesian, Japanese, Laotian, Malaysian, Taiwanese, and Vietnamese women forced into prostitution by the Japanese military during World War II to service its army.

Japan's modernization has also not been without critics in its own country. As recently as 1995 the Japanese population was shaken by a series of nerve gas attacks in the Tokyo subway system that injured over 5,500 people and killed twelve. The attacks were set off by members of the Aum Shinri-kyō ("Supreme Truth"), a cult combining elements of Buddhism, Taoism, and the worship of Siva (the Hindu god of destruction). Its leader, Matsumoto Chizuo (b. 1955), preached that only a rejection of modernity and a return to the core values of Japan's past would save the Japanese from the apocalypse to come. In the wake of the attacks, the Japanese government outlawed the sect, seized its assets, arrested its leader, and passed laws giving the government greater authority to investigate the financial affairs and political activities of religious groups.

The Asian Tigers

Inspired by the example of a resurgent Japan, four smaller Asian countries adopted modern industrial and financial techniques and joined the ranks of the world's fastest growing economies. Singapore, Taiwan, South Korea, and Hong Kong (before its reintegration into China in 1997) chose to unite political and economic power to control their development. Liberal democracy, with its tradition of vigorous opposition and free competition between interests, was considered an impediment to economic development and to political stability. Instead, these states adopted "authoritarian state capitalism" as a means to economic success. Although ranging in population from only three to forty-five million, the "Asian Tigers" proved that once colonized peoples could equal or exceed the economic performances of their former masters.

Key elements in the success of the Asian Tigers have been their access to capital, careful resource allocation, cheap labor costs, a willingness to copy Japanese techniques, and concentration on the export trade. From 1960 to 1995 South Korea's GDP increased thirty times over, that of Taiwan twenty times, and those of Singapore and Hong Kong fifteen times. Similar techniques were widely implemented across the region, as nations such as Thailand and Malaysia patterned their economic plans on participation in the export trade. In the nineties the pace of expansion fell dramatically, however, as the swelling total of Asian exports joined with those of Japan to create surpluses that depressed the economy of all Asia. The sudden decline of manufacturing and retailing in states such as Thailand and Indonesia caused an international financial panic in late 1997 and its long-range effects are still unclear. One particularly ominous reaction to this financial crisis occurred in largely Muslim Malaysia when its government blamed the crisis on an international Jewish banking conspiracy. Attacks on the ethnic Chinese minority in these states have also risen. The close and frequently secret ties between industry, banks, and government so characteristic of Asian capitalism, and once seen as a special source of its success, are now recognized as among the chief causes of the crisis. Nevertheless, during the last decades of the twentieth century several Asian societies achieved high per capita income levels for their citizens, as they made the transition to modern economies.

◆ Korea: Troubled Peninsula

The Asian version of capitalism has yet to prove its ability to last, but past geo-political tensions also plague this region. No area has endured the ravages of the Cold War longer than Korea, which remains a divided peninsula. The United Nations police action of 1950–1953 ended in stalemate. After the armistice two virtual dictators, Syngman Rhee (1875–1965) in the South and Kim Il Sung (1912–1994) in the North, commanded their respective halves of the country. For the government of South Korea, support from the United States remained vital, as did American military patrol of the demilitarized zone between the two Koreas, in effect since 1953. But Rhee's disdain for democratic procedures bothered Washington, and he lost American support in April 1960 after his army killed over 100 protesters. Rhee lived out his exile in comfort in Hawaii, but his removal hardly altered the situation in Korea. In 1961 General Park Chung Hee (1917-1979) led a military coup and held on to power by supporting American policy in Vietnam. Park wisely directed American economic aid to Korean's industries. But Park gradually lost the support of his right wing followers, and on October 26, 1979, he was assassinated by the Korean intelligence agency. Chun Duo Hwan (b. 1931) maintained South Korea's economic momentum as its next president (1980-1988), but re-instituted martial law. Nevertheless, American pressure combined with Korean dissenters to force the nation's first totally free elections in December 1987. Another military candidate, Roh Tae Woo (b. 1932), was elected (serving 1988-1993), but South Korea had taken its first steps on the road to democracy.

In 1993, as a result of the end of military rule, Kim Young Sam (b. 1927) was elected the first civilian president of South Korea since 1961. Former Presidents Chun and Roh were imprisoned for crimes against those who protested their regimes. Korea's third successive free election was held in 1997, and the voters selected Kim Dae Jung (b. 1924), a former political prisoner, as their president. His efforts towards reconciliation with the North led, in June 2000, to the first face-to-face meeting between the leaders of the two Koreas since the split in 1950. For the first time it seemed possible that the legacy of the Cold War might one day be lifted from the peninsula.

Fulfilling that expectation will depend in large degree on decisions made in North Korea. Kim Il Sung ruled as absolute dictator of North Korea from 1948 until his death in July 1994. Kim never altered his commitment to Marxist-Leninist thought, and, using Chinese aid, he carried out the immediate reconstruction program necessary after the armistice. Ritualistically hailed as the "Dear Leader" of his impoverished state, Kim maintained his armies in a state of wartime alert and in 1993 withdrew his pledge of nuclear non-proliferation. While South Korea's economy was gradually transformed by capitalist enterprise, Kim maintained the planned industry and collective agriculture common to Communist societies despite increasing poverty.

At Kim's death in 1994, power was assumed by his son, Kim Jong Il (b. 1942). In mountainous Korea, the south possesses the most fertile farmland while the north has most of the peninsula's iron and coal. But instead of using those resources for industrial development, the North Korean government squandered them on nuclear weapons production. Agricultural disaster and famine forced Jong's closed society to look outward. North Korea signed agreements with the United States to end nuclear development and permit inspection of its facilities. In return, many Western nations and even South Korea provided foodstuffs to the North. A summit meeting between the leaders of North and South Korea in 2000 led to an agreement allowing for an exchange of family members, making it possible for thousands of Koreans to unite with family members not seen for decades.

But tensions between North Korea and the United States were heightened in 2003 as North Korea publically disavowed its promises not to develop nuclear technology. It reactivated its nuclear program just as the United States was preparing to move into Iraq to remove that state's "weapons of mass destruction." And all the while, US and UN troops continue to patrol the demilitarized zone between the two Koreas.

The Troubled Middle East

The Middle East was fortunate in escaping the worst ravages of World War II. Battles were fought on its periphery, in North Africa, the Caucasus, and Mediterranean waters, but the struggle between Fascism and democracy rarely intruded into its geographic boundaries. Great Britain established military and political control early in 1941 by installing sympathetic governments in Iran and Iraq, and added Egypt to its bloc of cooperating protectorates in 1942. After France fell to German invasion, French mandates dating back to the Versailles Conference were ended; the Free French granted independence to Syria and Lebanon in 1943. Despite some problems in the former mandates, few analysts expected the area to become a major source of world tension for the rest of the century.

◆ From Palestine to Israel

Britain recognized as early as 1946 that its influence in the area was waning and permitted Emir Abdullah (1882–1951) of Trans-Jordan to assume the title of king. But the government of Clement Attlee pursued a different policy in Palestine. Determined to maintain a base "east of Suez," Britain refused to permit free immigration from Europe for Jewish refugees who had survived the Holocaust and were seeking refuge in the Holy Land. It soon faced a guerrilla war waged by Jewish partisans who insisted that the "homeland" promised Jews by Lord Balfour in 1917 should be an independent state. As Arab leaders advanced similar claims to the land beloved by both Abraham and Muhammad, British troops were soon battling both Jewish and Arab terrorists. Early in 1947, Britain decided to turn the vexing issue over to the United Nations. Rival claims to the Holy Land made by 650,000 Jews and 1.2 million Arabs would be adjudicated by the United Nations, successor to the League of Nations that had originally awarded Britain the Palestine mandate.

The United Nations soon realized that the territorial claims of the two sides were irreconcilable. Despite mounting Cold War tensions, the United States and the Soviet Union united in support of partition as the best means of reducing tension in the area. The final UN plan provided for a ten-year customs union, a common currency, and joint economic development in two independent states, one Arab and one Jewish, with Jerusalem under international control. The areas usually referred to as the "Gaza Strip" and the "West Bank" (of the Jordan River) would be part of the Palestinian State. During the General Assembly session of November 29, 1947, all thirteen Arab states rejected the partition proposal that was accepted by the Jews. The Arab League announced it would use force to prevent any division of the mandate, and, as British forces withdrew, the level of internal violence escalated. Hundreds of thousands of Palestinian Arabs fled or were forced to leave their homes even before the State of Israel was declared on May 14, 1948. Within two days Israel won recognition from both the US and the USSR, but found itself at war with invading Arab armies.

Bolstered by international volunteers and using weaponry that even included German *Messerschmitt* aircraft, Israeli forces soon attained military control of more land than envisioned by the UN. The Palestinian Arabs found themselves without a state at all as the Arab nations decided to keep the territories their armies had captured. Egypt took control of the Gaza Strip while Jordan controlled the West Bank. In 1949 the Israelis held democratic elections that made David Ben Gurion (1886–1973) their first Prime Minister. The new state won entry to the United Nations, and American diplomat Ralph Bunche (1904–1971) succeeded in negotiating a cease-fire between the warring parties. Although the city of Jerusalem remained under divided authority, and even while its Arab neighbors boycotted all trade and communication with Israel, Zionists rejoiced that a viable homeland for Jews had finally been created. The Palestinians, however, were still not independent.

◆　The Arab-Israeli Wars

In March of 1945 seven Islamic states (Egypt, Syria, Jordan, Iraq, Lebanon, Saudi Arabia, and Yemen) approved a constitution creating a League of Arab States. Internal disputes nearly tore apart the fledgling league, until its members discovered a unifying principle in their common hatred of Israel. Over the years, the Arab League grew to include Dijoubi, Somalia, Bahrain, Kuwait, Oman, Qatar, Sudan, Libya, Algeria, Mauritania, Tunisia, Morocco, the United Arab Emirates, and the Palestine Liberation Organization. The Ba'th, a Marxist Pan-Arab party, was organized in many states to advocate the unity of Arabs everywhere. The 1951 Ba'th Constitution, however, measured "the value of citizens" only "by the action they take to further the progress and prosperity of the Arab nation" and made no allowance for non-Arab or non-Muslim minorities within its hoped for realm.[3]

Arab militancy increased throughout the region in the 1950s. Libya won its independence in 1951. In 1952 the Free Officers' Movement ousted King Farouk (1920–1965) from the Egyptian throne, ending a dynasty that traced its authority back to Muhammad 'Ali (1769–1849). The new states of the Arab Middle East vied with each other for leadership of the region, creating a volatile situation complicated by Great Britain's desire to regain influence in an area once solidly part of its imperial regime. After its final withdrawal from Iraq in 1955, Britain came to believe that its influence in the region depended entirely on holding the Suez Canal. When the new Egyptian strongman Gamal Abdel Nasser (1918–1970) threatened to seize the waterway, Britain and France developed a scheme to enhance their fading power and deal a blow to rising Arab nationalism. Anticipating Nasser's nationalization of the canal on July 26, 1956, Britain and France conspired with the Israeli government to use the military power of Israel as an excuse for their intervention in the area. After an overwhelming military assault by Israel routed Egyptian forces around the canal, British and French forces parachuted in to "protect" Suez and force Israel back. In the confused negotiations that followed Israel's success and its aftermath, an angry United States humiliated the British and the French by forcing them to withdraw their forces. The British and French

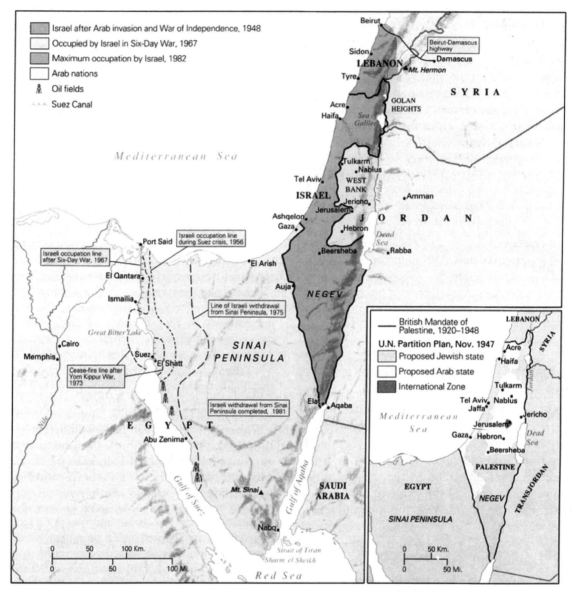

Legend:
- Israel after Arab invasion and War of Independence, 1948
- Occupied by Israel in Six-Day War, 1967
- Maximum occupation by Israel, 1982
- Arab nations
- Oil fields
- Suez Canal

Israeli occupation line during Suez crisis, 1956
Israeli occupation line after Six-Day War, 1967
Line of Israeli withdrawal from Sinai Peninsula, 1975
Cease-fire line after Yom Kippur War, 1973
Israeli withdrawal from Sinai Peninsula completed, 1981

Beirut · Beirut-Damascus highway
Sidon
LEBANON · Damascus
Tyre · Mt. Hermon
SYRIA
Acre · GOLAN HEIGHTS
Haifa · Sea of Galilee
Mediterranean Sea
Tulkarm · Nablus
Tel Aviv · WEST BANK
ISRAEL · Amman
Jericho
Jerusalem
Ashqelon · JORDAN
Gaza · Hebron
Beersheba · Dead Sea · Rabba
El Arish
Auja
NEGEV
Port Said
El Qantara
Ismailia
Great Bitter Lake
Cairo
Memphis · Suez · El Shatt
SINAI PENINSULA
EGYPT
Abu Zenima
Nile
Gulf of Suez
Mt. Sinai
Gulf of Aqaba
Elat · Aqaba
SAUDI ARABIA
Nabq
Strait of Tiran
Sharm el Sheikh
Red Sea

0 50 100 Km.
0 50 100 Mi.

Inset map legend:
- British Mandate of Palestine, 1920–1948
- U.N. Partition Plan, Nov. 1947
- Proposed Jewish state
- Proposed Arab state
- International Zone

LEBANON
SYRIA
Acre · Haifa
Tulkarm · Nablus
Tel Aviv · Jaffa · Jericho
Jerusalem · Dead Sea
Gaza · Hebron
Beersheba
Mediterranean Sea
PALESTINE
EGYPT
NEGEV · TRANSJORDAN
SINAI PENINSULA

0 50 Km.
0 50 Mi.

The Arab-Israeli Wars.
From *History of World Societies*, 3/e, by McKay, Hill, and Buckler. Copyright © 1992 Houghton Mifflin Co. (NY)

had to abandon their dreams of empire as the first United Nations peacekeeping forces were deployed across the Sinai Desert in December 1956 to separate Egypt from the victorious Israeli Army. Nasser resumed his control over the Canal.

Nasser triumphantly reopened the Suez Canal to world trade on April 29, 1957; he claimed that his success showed how emerging nations could overturn the yoke of their colonial past. Along with Marshal Tito of Yugoslavia and Nehru of India, Nasser came to represent the hopes of Third World peoples for an independent stance in the power struggles of the globe. A proponent of Pan-Arabism,

GAMAL ABDEL NASSER (1918–1970)

Egyptian nationalist and Third World leader.
Copyright © Hulton Getty

Gamal Abdel Nasser was born on January 15, 1918, in Alexandria, Egypt. His father was a local postmaster who sent his son to live with an uncle in Cairo to better his education. Nasser soon adopted the nationalism that had earned his uncle s stay in a British prison, taking to the streets to protest the British mandate and getting a scar on his forehead in the process.

After graduating from the Royal Military Academy, Nasser fought in the Egyptian Army during the 1948 Israeli war. Serving in the Sudan, he became one of the founders of the Free Officers, a secret group that aimed to oust both the British and their puppets, the Egyptian royal family. On July 23, 1952, the Free Officers staged a successful *coup d'etat,* replacing King Farouk with a Revolutionary Command Council. Major General Muhammad Naguib (1901-1984) appeared to head the Council, but Nasser kept tight control behind the scenes and emerged in 1954 as the self-proclaimed Prime Minister of Egypt. In June 1956 a controlled plebiscite elected him President.

When the United States and Britain cancelled promised aid for the building of the Aswan Dam in 1956, Nasser nationalized the Suez Canal and earmarked its revenues for hydroelec-

tric development. His action triggered an invasion by Israeli, British, and French forces, but pressure from the United States and the Soviet Union forced their withdrawal from Egyptian soil. Nasser gained immense political prestige in the Arab world for his "victory," and with Soviet military aid, he created the United Arab Republic with Syria in 1958. He hoped eventually to incorporate all Arabs into this state, but it lasted only three years before Syria withdrew in 1961 complaining of Egyptian imperialism. Nasser's dream of Pan-Arab unity was shattered by the rival nationalisms of the Middle East.

Domestically, Nasser's regime was characterized by social reform: land was redistributed, public works like the Aswan Dam began generating hydroelectric power in 1968, and access to education was widened. Egyptian middle class entrepreneurs began to replace the foreign nationals who had dominated the country's economic life since the nineteenth century. But Nasser's rule was repressive; Egypt was essentially a socialist one-party state with little regard for western style civil liberties. Censorship, wiretapping, and political imprisonment were all part of Nasser's authoritarian rule. Islam was recognized as the nation's official religion in Nasser's 1956 constitution, but militant Islamic movements, like the Muslim Brotherhood, were suppressed. Most importantly, Nasser lost control of the Sinai to Israel when he provoked another Arab-Israeli war in 1967.

In the months before his death of a heart attack on September 28, 1970, Nasser brokered a peace agreement between King Hussein of Jordan and Palestinian guerillas quartered there. He also agreed to start an American brokered peace initiative with Israel, although this plan did not bear fruit until his successor, Anwar Sadat, also found military initiatives useless. Despite military defeats and the failure of pan-Arabism, Nasser was an immensely popular figure in Egypt and throughout the Arab world and remains so a generation after his death.

Nasser attempted to form a political union with Syria, but the United Arab Republic (February 1, 1958-September 29, 1961) they created soon collapsed from internal divisions as the Syrians complained that the Egyptians were trying to colonize them. Selling the idea of the UAR to the Egyptians proved almost as difficult; although Egypt's population was over 90 percent Muslim and 99 percent Arabic speaking, Nasser felt he had to launch a massive propaganda campaign to convince his people they were truly Arab. It was an uncertainty he himself had once shared; in his *Philosophy of the Revolution* (1952), Nasser spoke to his fellow Egyptians of the "Arab circle surrounding us."[4] The shared religion of Islam could not always cover over the ethnic diversity of the region.

Like many Third World leaders, Nasser placed his faith in socialism and proudly rejected American developmental aid in favor of that provided by Russia. And all the while, he carefully rebuilt his military forces to prepare an assault on Israel. In May 1967 Nasser convinced Secretary General U Thant (1909–1974) to withdraw all UN peacekeeping units even as he trumpeted his intention of driving Israel into the sea. Faced with the threat of war, Israeli forces carried out a preemptive strike on June 5, 1967. The air forces of Egypt, Jordan, and Syria were destroyed while they were still on the ground, as Israel initiated the most decisive of the several Mid-East wars. Before the imposition of a United Nations cease-fire on June 10, Israeli armies had gained all of Sinai up to the Canal, ousted Arab forces from the West Bank of the Jordan River and East Jerusalem, and expelled the Syrian army from the strategic Golan Heights along its northern border. The Six-Day War established Israel's military domination over an Arab world of over 100 million people, and created a situation in which a triumphant Jewish state was willing to trade land for peace. The Arab League responded with a policy of "three nos": no recognition of the Israeli state, no negotiations, and no peace between the Arabs and Israel. A fourth war in 1973, one begun on Yom Kippur by Nasser's successor Anwar Sadat (1918-1981), put an end to the diplomatic efforts by Israeli Prime Minister Golda Meir (1898-1978) to improve relations between Israel and her Arab neighbors.

◆ Using the Oil Weapon

Even as Israeli armies surrounded and humiliated Egypt's armies in 1973, other members of the Arab coalition were preparing a devastating economic sanction against the western nations that supported Israel during the war. The Arab League decided to utilize their control of 60 percent of the world's oil reserves to punish countries like the United States for providing arms to Israel. The mechanism selected was OPEC, the Organization of Petroleum Exporting Countries, a multinational cartel first organized under Venezuelan leadership in 1960. OPEC had never previously been able to reduce oil production to obtain higher prices, but it now agreed to follow a plan created by the Shah of Iran. By the beginning of 1974, the Mid-Eastern oil producing nations led by Iran and Saudi Arabia managed to quadruple the price of a barrel of crude oil. Gasoline prices soared world wide, inflation increased, and the industrial west entered a period of recession. Yet even OPEC's successful boycott failed to alter the regional power balance within the Middle East. It had no discernible impact on Israeli policy. Nor, thanks to disagreements among its own members, did OPEC ever achieve more than a short-term success.

◆ Revolution in Iran

There was another worldwide rise in oil prices in 1979-1980, but this one was caused by an Islamic Revolution in Iran led by the Ayatollah Khomeini (1902-1989). Shah Muhammad Reza

GOLDA MEIR (1898–1978)

Pioneering Zionist, Prime Minister Meir addresses the Knesset.
Copyright © AP/Wide World Photos

The first female Prime Minister of Israel, Golda Meir was born Goldie Mabovitch on May 3, 1898, in Kiev, Russia. Like many other Jewish families, Goldie's came to the United States to escape Tsarist persecution. Her family settled in Milwaukee, Wisconsin, where elementary school education was free, but textbooks were not. To raise book money, Goldie and her sisters organized the "American Young Sisters Society" to solicit scholarship contributions. After working as a salesclerk and laundress, Goldie Mabovitch trained to be a teacher at the Milwaukee Normal School. She believed in Zionism, the creation of a Jewish state in Palestine, but in the United States she became a democratic socialist and a leader of the local Labor Zionist Party.

She married a sign painter, Morris Myerson, in 1917, and the two Zionists immigrated to Palestine in 1921. The Myersons had two children—Sarah and Menachem—before they separated in 1938. In the 1920s the couple joined a *kibbutz* (farm cooperative), and by 1934 Goldie had become a member of the executive committee (1934) of the *Histadrut* (the General Federation of the Cooperatives). Her growing skills soon made her a leading negotiator with the British who held the mandate for Palestine and were trying to discourage Jewish resettlement. In 1946, she led the Political Department of the Jewish Agency when Britain arrested Jewish war refugees seeking sanctuary in Palestine.

On May 14, 1948, Goldie Myerson was one of the signatories of Israel's *Declaration of Independence,* and became the new nation's first Minister to Moscow. Elected to the *Knesset* (the Israeli parliament), she served as Minister of Labor (1949-1956) and Foreign Minister (1956-1966). She oversaw major programs of housing, road construction, and aid to emerging African nations. During this period she also changed her name to Golda Meir, a more Hebraic form. After the 1967 Arab-Israeli War, she worked with David Ben-Gurion (1886-1973), Moshe Dayan (1915–1981), and Prime Minister Levi Eshkol (1895–1969) to merge several smaller parties into the Labour Party. As a compromise candidate between the party's extremes, Meir became Prime Minister upon Eshkol's death. She campaigned extensively for a diplomatic settlement in the Middle East and a normalization of Israel's relations with West Germany and the Vatican, but the outbreak of another Arab-Israeli War in October 1973 put an end to those efforts. Israel's armies in the field had been caught unprepared for the surprise Arab attack. Although the Arab advance was eventually turned back, Meir's government came under severe public criticism. She resigned her post on April 10, 1974, but remained in office until a successor—General Yitzhak Rabin (1922-1995)—could be chosen in June.

Meir remained an important political figure even in retirement and despite increasing ill health. Only after her death in Jerusalem on December 8, 1978, was it revealed that she had been suffering from leukemia for the past 12 years. Her autobiography, *My Life,* was published in 1975.

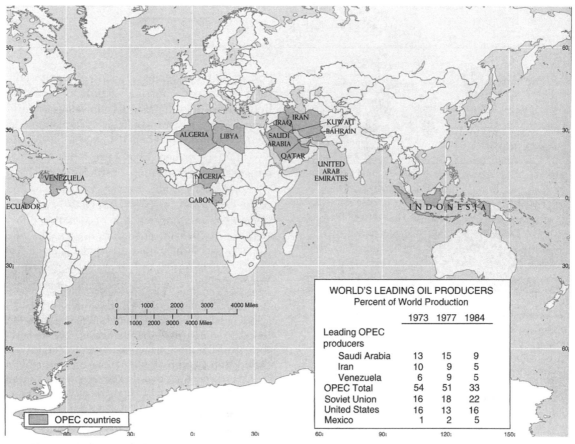

World's Leading Oil Producers.
Reproduced from *Out of Many,* Fourth Edition, (2004), reproduced by permission of Prentice-Hall, Inc.

Pahlavi (1919–1980) had ruled Iran as an ally of the West since 1941. His Prime Minister, Muhammad Mossadeq (1880–1967) attempted to nationalize the British oil industry in Iran and depose the Shah in 1953, but a CIA-supported coup restored Pahlavi to power and returned control of Iran's oil reserves to Britain. The Shah's attempts at rapid modernization led by over 100,000 foreign experts alienated the more traditional elements of the population. Muslim clerics like Khomeini charged the Shah with betraying both his nation and his religion by introducing Western attitudes and customs. The Shah responded by strengthening his secret police and tightening censorship. In January 1978, the Shah's troops opened fire on a student demonstration and set off a national revolt. Popular opinion, abetted by Islamic religious fervor, drove the Shah from Iran in 1979. After the dying leader was treated for cancer in American hospitals, the United States became the target of reprisals by Islamic zealots. In November 1979 student radicals, inspired by Khomeini's preaching, seized the American Embassy in Tehran and held its personnel hostage for 444 days.

As the world watched in amazement, Khomeini consolidated governmental power by condemning the "Great Satan" of the United States. Western music, movies, and female attire were banned, as Iran was turned into an Islamic state in which *Sharia* (Muslim holy law) replaced secu-

Iranian students march against the United States, the "Great Satan" who threatens their revolution, 1979.
Copyright © CORBIS/Bettmann

lar law. Tension between Iran and other Middle-Eastern states limited the spread of Khomeini's version of the Islamic movement, however, and Iran soon found itself in a bitter war against neighboring Iraq.

In Iraq, the Hashemite monarchy had been overthrown in 1958, plunging the country into a decade of coups and counter-coups, until the Ba'th Party succeeded in taking power in 1968. The new regime was formally headed up by President Ahmad Hassan al-Bakr (1914–1982) but behind the scenes real power was increasingly in the hands of his lieutenant, Saddam Hussein (b. 1937), a former law student at Cairo University. Hussein assumed the presidency in 1979 and continued al-Bakr's policy of pressing land claims against neighboring Iran. In September 1980, Hussein's forces attacked Iranian airfields and oil refineries, setting off an Iran-Iraq War that lasted until 1988. Exhaustion brought both sides to the bargaining table. In the worst days of the war, Iran was forced to send 12-year-olds into combat and Iraq used chemical warfare against Iran.

Crude oil prices soared when the Iran-Iraq conflict began, briefly topping $40 a barrel, again demonstrating the vulnerability of modern economies to the oil weapon. But the long-term inability of OPEC nations to agree on production limitations eased the crisis, and oil prices fell dramatically over the next decade as surplus oil was pumped from the ground.

The Iran-Iraq War (1980–1988) was, in part, a contest between two crusading ideologies: Iran's Islamic fundamentalism and Iraq's revolutionary Pan-Arab socialism. But it was also the result of the complex ethnic, religious, and political rivalries that have divided the region for millennia. Farsi, the language of Iran, is a member of the Indo-European Language Family; Arabic, the language of Iraq, belongs to the Semitic Family. The linguistic divide mirrors an ethnic one. Just as divisive is the split within Islam that began with the death of the Prophet Muhammad's son-in-law Ali in 661. The Iranians belong to the Shi'ite division of Islam (the followers of Ali), as do a narrow majority of Iraqis, but the Ba'th Party leadership (and a large minority of Iraqis) belong to the mainstream Sunni division. In the 1970s Iraq's Ba'th leadership expelled 200,000 Shi'ites of Iranian descent and was implicated in the murders of Iraq's native Shi'ite leaders. The Ba'th leadership feared the spread of Shi'ite fundamentalism from Iran to its own oppressed Shi'ite majority would end Ba'th rule of Iraq. Although a moderate reformer, Mohammad Khatami (b. 1943), was elected president of Iran in 1997, his inability to liberalize the regime in the face of clerical opposition did little to allay the concerns of Iraq.

◆   Israel and the Palestinians

Despite the economic traumas caused by successive "oil shocks," Israel's military dominion of the Middle East went unchallenged, and her alliance with the United States remained strong. With only 4,000,000 citizens, the tiny land held the Arab world at bay through a combination of industrialization, military vigilance, and alliances with the West. But military victories had brought the enemy within. At the end of the 1948 wars, the Arab population of Palestine was largely confined to the western bank of the Jordan River, an area controlled by the kingdom of Jordan. Israel had taken the West Bank in the 1967 war, however, making the Palestinian "problem" an Israeli problem. The Palestine Liberation Organization, formed in 1964 to coordinate the efforts of Palestinian guerilla groups against the Jordanian government, shifted its focus to battling the Israeli government. But, because of its earlier efforts, the PLO was expelled from Jordan by King Hussein I (r. 1952–1999) in 1970, forcing it to move to bases in Lebanon.

At Rabat in 1974, the Arab League recognized the Palestine Liberation Organization as the "sole representative" of the Palestinian people. Yasir Arafat (b. 1929), a graduate of Cairo University with a degree in civil engineering and a commissioned officer in Egypt's army in the 1956 war, had become the PLO's leader in 1969. Since the combined might of twenty Arab nations had been unable to defeat Israel in four wars, Arafat orchestrated a campaign of terror bombings and guerrilla attacks against Israeli civilians in the Gaza Strip along the Mediterranean Sea and in settlements located beyond the West Bank of the Jordan River. The most notorious of all PLO terrorist incidents was a systematic massacre of Israeli athletes at the 1972 Olympic Games. Despite many reverses, the PLO recruited an endless supply of fighters from the over sixty camps that still housed Palestinian refugees who had fled from Israeli control in 1948.

Yet regardless of the casualties inflicted by terror attacks, the PLO could not alter a strategic balance that favored Israel. The military expertise of Israel was demonstrated to the world in 1976 when it freed the passengers and crew of a hi-jacked plane in Entebbe, Uganda. In a second, more traditional display of Israeli might, its air force destroyed an Iraqi nuclear installation in 1981. Only after Egyptian President Anwar Sadat made a dramatic decision to visit Jerusalem in 1977, did the frozen politics of the Middle East thaw. Sadat's bold initiative tested Israel's longstanding pledge to exchange land for recognition and peace. President Jimmy Carter of the United States facilitated the negotiating process in 1978 when he brought both sides to a meeting at Camp David, in the Maryland countryside, and virtually forced them to agree. On March 26, 1979, Israel and Egypt signed a treaty that ended 31 years of warfare between them (*Camp David Agreement*). In return for its formal recognition of the State of Israel, the Sinai Peninsula was restored to

Egypt by 1982. Israel received the right to transit the Suez Canal and to purchase oil produced from Sinai wells. Sadat and Israeli Prime Minister Menachem Begin (1913–1992) shared the Nobel Peace Prize for their efforts. As the first Arab to violate the "three no's" policy, Egypt was immediately expelled from the Arab League. Sadat was assassinated on October 6, 1981, by Muslim fanatics who believed he had betrayed the larger Arab cause. His successor, Hosni Mubarak (b. 1928), has ruled as president ever since, despite the efforts of Islamic fundamentalists to destabilize his regime. The peace between Israel and Egypt has endured, but it has not developed deeper roots because of the ongoing confrontation between secular and religious forces within Egypt.

The death of President Sadat seemed to spur Mid-Eastern violence elsewhere. The wounding of Israel's ambassador to Great Britain by PLO agents soon turned the border between Israel and Lebanon into a battle zone, the PLO having retreated to southern Lebanon after its expulsion from Jordan. In June 1982 Israeli forces entered Lebanon, dispersed opposing PLO forces, and rapidly advanced towards Beirut in the fifth Mid-Eastern War. The remaining elements of the PLO were permitted to take refuge in eight separate Arab nations while Arafat established a new center of Palestinian activities in Tunis. Israel retreated from northern Lebanon, but created a "security

Sadat, Carter and Begin at the ceremony announcing the signing of the Camp David Accords (1978).
Copyright © CORBIS

319

zone" in southern Lebanon from which it did not withdraw until 2000. A resurgent PLO began a general uprising in the Israeli-controlled Gaza Strip and West Bank in 1987. This *Intifada* ("uprising") dragged on for seven years, resulting in the death of hundreds of Israelis and Palestinians without settling any of their conflicting nationalist claims.

Defeat convinced Arafat to negotiate. At Madrid in 1988 he seemingly conceded the right of Israel to exist and promised an end to PLO supported terrorism, although the *Intifada* continued. A second round of negotiations in Oslo brought an agreement in 1993 (the "Oslo Accords") that the Palestinians would gradually be granted autonomy within certain areas of the former Palestinian mandate, including the Gaza Strip and portions of the West Bank. In 1994, Jordan signed a peace treaty with Israel, making Jordan only the second Arab nation to do so since the 1948 war. Renewed talks between Israel and Syria were stalled again by the death of Syrian president Hafez al-Assad (1930–2000).

Under the Oslo Accords, some authority was transferred to the newly constituted Palestine Authority in 1997. As its first elected president (1996), Arafat remained the leader of the Palestinian cause. Many Israeli settlements on the West Bank remain to hinder further accommodation, as does Arafat's insistence that the Palestinians achieve formal statehood, and the conflicting claims of both sides to Jerusalem as their "historic" capitals. On the other hand, an ultra-orthodox Jewish fanatic assassinated Prime Minister Yitzhak Rabin (1922–1995) for daring to negotiate away any Israeli land. With a population of 6 million in 2002, a militant Israel still controls the West Bank (home to almost 2.2 million Palestinians). Negotiations between Israel and the Palestine Liberation Organization continue off and on. Perhaps the most important change in the international climate has been the shift in rhetoric under American President George W. Bush (b. 1946) from discussion of an autonomous Palestinian region within Israel to a full Palestinian state. But none of the men who replaced Arafat as nominal leaders of the Palestine Authority has been able to stem the tide of violence.

◆   The Resurgence of Iraq

In August 1990, Iraqi troops invaded Kuwait; the Iraqi army overran the tiny (but oil-rich) state on its southern border in a single day. Fears among western nations and neighboring Arab states that Iraq would make a move towards Saudi Arabia's oil fields created a short lived but unusual coalition between the United States and the Soviet Union, who put aside their Cold war rivalries to push for United Nations Security Council sanctions against Iraq. When these measures failed, the United States headed up a 26-nation coalition of NATO members and Arab states (including Egypt, Saudi Arabia, and Syria) that began bombing Iraq in January 1991. A full scale assault a month later pushed deep into Iraqi territory after clearing the Iraqis from Kuwait: it took only six weeks to force Hussein to the bargaining table. But disagreements between the members of the Gulf War coalition and Iraqi actions prevented consistent enforcement of the conditions imposed on Iraq: "no-fly" zones, destruction of its weapons of mass destruction, and continued United Nations monitoring of facilities to prevent possible reconstruction.

Matters took a drastic turn after the 2002 American invasion of Afghanistan in the wake of the September 11, 2001, bombing of the World Trade Towers in New York. After toppling the Taliban regime in Afghanistan for its support of the al-Qaeda terrorists, the United States began to step up its demands that Iraq destroy its arsenal and reform its government. A resolution put through the United Nations Security Council in 2002 to force Saddam Hussein to readmit the UN weapons inspectors and reveal any remaining stockpiles did not satisfy the United States. Claiming that Iraq was in "material breach" of the resolution for making nothing more than gestures at compliance, the United States tried to push through a second resolution giving a deadline for the use of force in Iraq. The threat of a French veto quashed the resolution before it could be put to a vote, and the United States used the failure of the resolution as an excuse to begin an invasion of Iraq in the spring of 2003. The massive buildup of US forces over the intervening months made it only a matter of weeks before the government of Iraq collapsed, leaving the United States and its ally, Great Britain (the only other permanent member of the UN Security Council to send troops into Iraq), to oversee the rebuilding of the Iraqi government and economy. Whether or not Iraq can be turned into a democratic capitalist state remains to be seen. Many among its Shi'ite majority would like to see an Iran-style fundamentalist Islamic state replace the Ba'th dictatorship, while the Kurds in its northern provinces would like nothing more than to see an independent Kurdish state carved out of the lands the 20 million Kurds occupy in Iraq, Iran, Syria, and Turkey. Neither the United States nor any of the states involved endorse the creation of an independent Kurdistan. Turkey has taken an especially hard line against Kurdish independence because its oil fields are in Turkish Kurdistan. Fears over Kurdish ambitions led Turkey to refuse the United States the use of its air corridors and bases in the attack on Iraq despite Turkey's long membership in NATO.

On May 22, 2003, the United Nations Security Council voted to end economic sanctions against Iraq. The Council also voted to temporarily transfer control of Iraq's oil fields to the United States and Great Britain, as trustees for a fund to rebuild Iraq. These moves allow countries to trade with Iraq and prevents the oil revenues from being seized by Iraq's creditors in payment of its debts. Occupation forces, however, remain subject to continued attacks despite the capture of Saddam Hussein.

The weakness of European economies after World War II made their withdrawal from their former empires inevitable. As this "decolonization" advanced across Asia and the Middle East, a "Third World" gradually took shape. It was a developing world, one that sought an independent role between the Superpower giants fighting their Cold War. Angered by the exploitation they had endured at the hands of capitalist powers, many of the Third World states opted to create socialist economies that ultimately failed to provide the industrialization they sought. Other states resorted, more successfully, to forms of state-directed capitalism, but often at the cost of individual freedom. While economic modernization has preceded apace in the Far East, political Westernization has proved to be an elusive goal in much of Asia as new forms of ethnic and religious nationalism re-awakened ancient conflicts. The next chapters look at the fate of decolonization in Africa and Latin America's struggle against neocolonialism.

◆ Notes

1. J. A. G. Roberts, *A Concise History of China* (Cambridge, MA: Harvard University Press, 1999), 267.

2. Benjamin Yang, *Deng: A Political Biography* (New York: M. E. Sharpe, 1988), 151.

3. *Arab Nationalism*, edited and translated by Sylvia Haim (Berkeley: University of California Press, 1962), 233–241.

4. Haim, *Arab Nationalism*, 230–231.

12

Africa After World War II

In 1945 there were only four independent states in all of Africa (Liberia, Ethiopia, Egypt, and South Africa); today there are more than 50. Faced with the loss of their Asian possessions and dependencies after World War II, European states attempted to hold on to their African colonies without much success. A generation of western-educated African leaders was able to mobilize popular desire for freedom, only to find European economic power continued to cast its shadow over the newly independent African states. For centuries the continent's riches had been exported, its labor expropriated, its agriculture directed into environmental destructive crops profitable to European economies, and its peoples torn apart by colonial borders that ignored traditional ethnic boundaries. If colonial rule brought western technology, government, medicine, and education, it did so without adequately including the native population in those benefits, training them to maintain them, or giving that population a say in how their cultures were to be transformed. Cash-crop economies without adequate industrial infrastructures, the newly independent African states struggled to escape neo-colonial economic woes and the vortex of Cold War politics. This chapter looks at the causes, progress, and results of those struggles.

Ghana

◆ Ghana under Nkrumah

Ghana was a prosperous conglomeration of lands taken by the British from the Asante and their Akan dependencies over a seventy year period in the nineteenth century and enlarged by the addition of half of German Togoland after World War I. Its economy specialized in the production of peanuts, cocoa, and coffee. But despite its prosperity, Ghana was not granted the right to convene its own assembly until 1925. By then Kwame Nkrumah (1909-1972), the missionary-educated son of a goldsmith, had applied to the Government Training College in Accra to become a teacher. Dissatisfied with the limited training available to him there, he left for the United States in 1935 where he received his undergraduate (Lincoln University) and graduate (University of Pennsylvania) degrees in education. His exposure to the theories of Karl Marx and Marcus Garvey, first as a student and later as a professor at Lincoln University, shaped his subsequent career. In 1945 Nkrumah went to London to study law. While there, he and W. E. B. Du Bois co-chaired a Pan-African Congress in Manchester. The Manchester Congress demanded the construction of dams to secure Africa's water supply, financing of native education up to the graduate level, and local political autonomy. A destitute England and a devastated France promised action they had no

Kwame Nkrumah heralds the independence of Ghana as its first Prime Minister, 1957.
Copyright © CORBIS/Bettmann

intention of fulfilling. Despite the services of thousands of African soldiers in World War II, neither power intended to give up their empires without a struggle.

Nkrumah returned home in 1947 to become secretary of the United Gold Coast Convention (UGCC), a new political party organized by westernized Africans. When the group's conservatives resisted Nkrumah's radical program, he formed a rival Convention People's Party (CCP) in 1949 and organized a general strike against English domination. His efforts won him both a jail term and a devoted following. When he was freed in 1951, he was easily elected to colonial office. Over the next few years Nkrumah painstakingly negotiated independence terms from a reluctant Britain. In 1957, with Kwame Nkrumah as prime minister, Ghana became the first sub-Saharan African colony to attain post-war independence.

Under Nkrumah's leadership, Ghana hosted the first Pan-African Conference actually held in the continent in 1958. While Nkrumah spoke eloquently for the cause of continental unity, he soon found himself all too preoccupied by the demands of developing his own country. To do this

Nkrumah decided that Ghana would be "a people's parliamentary democracy with a one-party system" and its economy an agricultural form of socialism. As he argued in his book *Consciencism,* capitalism was "domestic colonialism" and a "multi-party parliamentary system" was just "a ruse for perpetrating" and covering up "the inherent struggle between the 'haves' and the 'have-nots.'"[1]

As part of his plan to implement Consciencism (his name for an agriculturally-based African socialism), Nkrumah quickly ordered the collectivization of the economy. His Second Development Plan, announced in 1959, helped bring the balance of payments deficit up to $125 million before it was abandoned in 1961. He had already forced through a Preventive Detention Act in 1958 that legalized imprisonment without trial; its first victims were Nkrumah's former UGCC allies. Calling himself Ghana's *Osyagefo* ("Blessed Redeemer"), he banned all other political parties, built a cult of personality reminiscent of Stalin's, and declared himself president for life in 1964. Although Nkrumah built schools, hospitals, and hydroelectric facilities, he amassed a huge public debt in doing so. He also destroyed Ghanaian democracy. On February 24, 1966, while traveling to meet Mao Zedong in China, Nkrumah was overthrown by a military coup led by Lt. General Joseph Arthur Ankrah (1915–1992). Nkrumah spent the rest of his life in exile, eventually dying of cancer in Bucharest. Despite Nkrumah's undoubted excesses, his memory is still revered by Ghanaians who remember his early defiance of the British and his creation of a new nation.

◆   Dictatorships and Democracy

A confused decade of economic decline and successive military coups with brief constitutional interruptions followed Nkrumah's ouster. Ankrah, who ruled Ghana as Chairman of the National Liberation Council, was toppled in 1969 by Brigadier Akwasi Afrifa (1936–1979). Nii Amaa Ollenna (b. 1906) managed to take the reigns of power from Afrifa for 25 days in August 1970 before he was followed by the civilian rule of Edward Akufo Addo (1906–1979). Ignatius Kutu Acheampong (1931–1979) took over in 1972 as Chairman of the National Redemption Council, claiming Addo's government was stripping the country's resources. Then Fred W. K. Akuffo (1937–1979) took over in 1978 as Chairman of the Supreme Military Council and made the same charges against Acheampong. Before Akuffo was thrown out he managed to execute three of Ghana's prior military dictators (Afrifa, Addo, and Acheampong). In June 1979, Flight Lieutenant Jerry John Rawlings (b. 1947) took the reigns of government, only to lose them in September when a civilian, Hilla Limann (1934–1998) was allowed to take office as Nigeria's elected president. Then, on December 31, 1981, Rawlings ousted Limann and installed himself as President.

This time Rawlings, the son of a Scottish pharmacist practicing in Accra and a member of the Ewe minority in Ghana, was able to keep control of the country. Under his dictatorial control the economy gradually revived. By 1984 he had abandoned socialism for capitalist development and loans from the International Monetary Fund (IMF) and the World Bank. Associates who opposed this move were subject to purges and executions, but state-owned enterprises were privatized and commerce increased. After giving Ghana a new constitution in 1992, Rawlings was elected president as leader of the National Democratic Congress (NDC) in free elections in December 1996. The constitution did not allow him another term in office. Unlike many dictators, Rawlings decided to abide by the constitution and sit out the 2000 elections. His 1996 vice-presidential running mate, John Evans Atta Mills (b. 1944) did run on the NDC ticket but was soundly defeated by John Kofi Agyekum Kufuor (b. 1938) of the New Patriotic Party (NPP), giving Ghana its first ever orderly transition of power. Kufuor, a member of the Oyoko royal family of Kumasi in the Asante region and a graduate of Oxford University, has a long history of government service. He served as deputy foreign minister (1969–1972) and even briefly as minister for local government under Rawlings. Whether he can maintain the economic growth begun under Rawlings and keep Ghana's fragile democracy alive remains to be seen.

Nigeria

Nigeria, Africa's most populous state and blessed with vast oil reserves, is also a land of thwarted expectations. Taking its name from Africa's third largest river, Nigeria became independent in October 1960 after a century of British rule. Nigeria's first president, Benjamin Azikiwe (1904-1996), was born into an Ibo family that migrated to Northern Nigeria, where his father became a clerk in the Haussa dominated army. Educated in mission schools, Azikiwe (familiarly known as "Zik" to Nigerians) went on to the United States, where he got an undergraduate degree and a certificate in journalism from Columbia University and two master's degrees (from Lincoln University in political science and the University of Pennsylvania in anthropology). He returned to Africa in 1934 to edit a newspaper in Ghana before going back to Nigeria in 1937 to found the *West African Pilot*. Coming up through the ranks of the National Council of Nigeria and the Cameroons (NCNC), he became its president in 1946. The federal elections sponsored by the British in 1959 saw Azikiwe elected governor-general. When Nigeria became a republic in 1963, Azikiwe became its first president, though much power remained in the hands of the prime minister.

◆   The Biafran Secession War

Azikiwe's attempts to get Nigeria's 250 ethnic groups to work together came to an end in 1966, as Nigeria experienced the first of the military coups and civil wars that have marked its history since. With a quarter of all the people in Sub-Sahara Africa, Nigeria's leaders have failed to overcome internal tribal and religious divisions to create a sense of unity between the three largest ethnic groups, the Yoruba, the Ibo, and the Hausa-Fulani. The Yoruba have generally kept to their native religion. Their traditionally militaristic kingdoms in Nigeria's southwest date back some 2500 years and once controlled both Nigeria and Dahomey. The Ibo were largely converted to Christianity in the nineteenth century. They live in what were once independent, commercial villages in Nigeria's southeast, dating back some twelve hundred years. The predominantly Muslim Hausa-Fulani in the north are a blend of two relative newcomers that first established Muslim states in the region in the eleventh and thirteenth centuries. Most, but not all of the Nigerian military's officers are Hausa.

In January 1966, Major General Johnson T. U. Aguiyi-Ironsi (1924–1966) led a coup that overthrew the government of President Azikiwe and murdered two of Nigeria's regional prime ministers. Six months later, Aguiyi-Ironsi (an Ibo) was murdered by a group of Hausa officers who put one of their own, Lieutenant Colonel Yakubu Gowon (b. 1934), in charge. Tensions between the Ibo and Hausa continued to mount. Several Ibo villages along the Hausa-Ibo border were attacked by the Hausa in September, 1966. By May, 1967, the Ibo regional parliament had declared its independence as the state of Biafra (for the Bight of Biafra along its coast). Chukwuemeka Odumegwu Ojukwu (b. 1933), the Ibo military governor of the region, was chosen as the new Biafran president.

Biafra depended on the income from its oil fields to buy food, but the Nigerian military was able to take control of the oil fields early on in the war and systematically starve the Ibo into surrender. The devastation of the Biafran Secession War (1967–1970) ended all hope of Ibo independence.

◆ Nigeria under the Generals

As leader of the reunited country Gowon redrew the regional boundaries within the country to break-up ethnic rivalries. Determined to create a truly united Nigeria, Gowon began using the country's vast oil revenues to rebuild the devastated Ibo homelands. His actions only earned him the distrust of his fellow Hausa. Overthrown in 1975 by Brigadier Murtala Ramat Muhammad (1937–1976), Gowon fled into exile in Britain. Muhammad began a purge of corrupt regional officials that brought him considerable popularity with the Nigerian people, but he was assassinated a year later, leaving the government in the hands of General Olusegun Obasanjo (b.1938), a Yoruba leader. When falling oil prices caused civilian unrest, Obasanjo cracked down on student movements, nationalized land for redistribution, and increased government regulation of the oil industry. Still, he did set Nigeria's government on a course toward civilian rule under an American-style constitution. In an attempt to cut across ethnic divisions, the new constitution required the president and vice-president to win at least 25 percent of the vote in at least two-thirds of Nigeria's new 19 states.

Alhaji Shehu Shagari (b. 1925) became the first elected president of Nigeria's Second Republic in 1979. But changes in the world economy made it difficult for him to achieve any lasting improvements in Nigeria's situation. The world-wide collapse in oil prices in 1982 left Nigeria unable even to meet its short term debts. It could not import the food, medicines, and industrial raw materials it needed. When oil prices were high, millions of people had flooded into Nigeria to escape the poverty of its neighbors. Now, with the massive unemployment resulting from the collapse of oil prices, there were not even enough jobs for the native Nigerians. Shaghari's government ordered all unskilled foreign workers to leave the country at once. Nearly two million people, most of them from Ghana, were forced out within weeks, but the Nigerian economy continued to collapse. Shagari won re-election in 1983. But when the Hausa-dominated military found itself facing budget cuts by year's end as an increasingly desperate Shagari tried to salvage the Nigerian economy, it decided to take matters into its own hands once again. A coup led by Major-General Muhammadu Buhari (b. 1942) deposed Shagari over the New Year's holiday amidst charges of vote fraud and corruption. Buhari initiated an economic austerity plan to rehabilitate Nigeria's credit in the world financial market, but the cuts he had to make in social services to do it made him increasingly unpopular. His overthrow by Major General Ibrahim Badamasi Babangida (b. 1951) in 1985 at first won wide approval among the Nigerian populace.

Babangida was able to put through the austerity measures that had cost his predecessor his office and win further aid from the International Monetary Fund, temporarily stabilizing Nigeria's economy. But these successes did not prevent two failed coup attempts against him in 1986 and 1990. After throwing out the 1992 legislative elections as fraudulent, Babangida promised a gradual return to civilian rule. He allowed presidential elections to be held in 1993, but when the anti-government newspaper publisher Moshood K. O. Abiola (1937–1998) appeared to be winning, Babangida annulled the election. This set off a crisis resolved only when General Sani Abacha (1943–1998), Babangida's Secretary of Defense, seized power in August. When Abiola attempted to take office in 1994, he was arrested and tried for treason along with many of his supporters. Wole Soyinka (b. 1934), the Nigerian playwright who won the Nobel Prize for Literature in 1986, and an Abiola supporter, fled the country to avoid arrest. Another prominent writer, Ken Saro-Wiwa (1941–1995) was not as fortunate. For his attempts to make the Nigerian government share its oil revenues with the Ogoni people in whose region (the Niger River delta) most of Nigeria's oil is located, Saro-Wiwa was arrested and executed in 1995. Former dictator Obasanjo was also arrested in a crack down on all dissident voices. In retaliation the British Commonwealth suspended Nigeria's membership. The United States, the European Union, and the Republic of South Africa all imposed arms restrictions on Nigeria. Despite its $10 billion in annual oil revenues, Nigeria plunged deeper and deeper into poverty as its dictators siphoned off its wealth. Despite mounting protests Abacha remained popular enough among his fellow Hausa (in whose territory most of the oil wealth was spent) to keep control of the government.

◆ Nigerian Elections

Abacha's sudden death from a heart attack in June 1998 created a caretaker government under the leadership of General Abdulsalam Abubakar (b. 1942), Abacha's chief of staff. Abubakar pledged to restore democracy to Nigeria and hold free elections. Under pressure from the United Nations, the United States, the European Union, and demonstrators in his own country, Abubakar agreed to a massive release of political prisoners, including Abiola, Buhari, and Obasanjo. Having survived his earlier arrest, General Olusegun Obasanjo, now leader of the centrist People's Democratic Party (PDP), became president in February 1999. The fact that he had voluntarily given up power during the 1970s was the main cause of his new popularity. With this formal return to democracy, Nigeria was reinstated in the British Commonwealth.

Even though Obasanjo is a member of the Christian minority, he was ardently supported by Northern Muslim leaders. They thought his being a Yoruba would keep that group happy, while his military background would make him a natural ally of the Hausa-dominated military. But they were less than pleased with his attempt to keep the peace by redistributing government contracts among several ethnic groups. Abiola died in July 2002 before he could run for office again, but Muhammed Buhari repositioned himself as the presidential candidate of the All Nigerian People's Party in the 2003 elections. International monitors condemned the April 2003 elections as rampant with fraud but Obasanjo claimed victory and remained in office.

Kenya and Kenyatta

Kenya, an East African British Protectorate since 1895 (and Crown Colony since 1920) was controlled by wealthy expatriate planters whose vast coffee, tea, and cotton estates employed the very Kikuyu from whom these rich farmlands had been taken. Time and again Kikuyu nationalist groups dispatched representatives to London to plead in vain for land reform. Among those sent in 1929 was Jomo Kenyatta (1894–1978). Born Kamau Ngengi and educated in mission schools, he used the pen name *Jomo* ("Burning Spear") *Kenyatta* in his political pamphlets for the Kikuyu Kenya African Union (KAU). In 1952 he was arrested by the British on suspicion of complicity in the Mau-Mau Rebellion (1952–1960) that killed almost a hundred British settlers and 2000 pro-British Africans. The British killed over 11,000 mostly Kikuyu rebels and temporarily confined some 80,000 others in internment camps, but they were unable to contain native nationalism. From his jail cell, Kenyatta oversaw the evolution of the KAU into the multi-tribal Kenya African National Union (KANU). But even when KANU swept the 1962 elections, Kenyatta (released in 1961) was not allowed to form a government. Only in December 1963, four years after the rebellion ended, did Britain grant independence to Kenya and let Kenyatta assume power. Prime Minis-

JOMO KENYATTA (1894–1978)

The Founder of Modern Kenya and Pan-African advocate.
Copyright © CORBIS/Bettmann

Kamau Ngengi, later called Jomo Kenyatta, was born into a Kikuyu farming family in Kenya (then part of British East Africa) sometime around the year 1894. After a childhood illness was successfully treated by missionary doctors, Kamau entered a school run by the Church of Scotland mission. When he graduated from there, he became a government clerk in Nairobi. He quickly became involved in the native protest movement, rising to general secretary of the Kikuyu Central Association (KCA) by 1928. The KCA platform demanded the return of lands expropriated by British settlers, more schools, the end of hut taxes on women, African representation on the colony's Legislative Council, and noninterference with traditional customs (including female circumcision).

After studying for two years at Moscow State University, Kamau moved to London in 1931 and enrolled at the London School of Economics. His anthropology thesis (published in 1938 as *Facing Mount Kenya*) praised traditional African customs. Taking the name Jomo (Burning Spear) Kenyatta, he briefly joined the Commu-

nist Party. Remaining in Britain during World War II, Nkrumah helped Du Bois and Nkrumah organize the 1945 Pan-African Congress in Manchester. There he advocated an agrarian-socialist solution to Africa's land problem.

Back in Kenya in 1947, he became the leader of its newest protest organization, the Kikuyu Kenya African Union (KAU). Because Kenya contained a sizable white population, the questions of independence and land reform were particularly volatile. Whites became the particular target of the terrorist Mau-Mau movement that began in 1952. Arrested in 1952, Kenyatta was sentenced to seven years imprisonment in 1953 for being the Mau-Mau leader, something he always denied. The cost of suppressing the Mau-Mau prompted Britain to concede "one man, one vote" government by 1960. The imprisoned Kenyatta was elected president of the Kenya African National Union (KANU). He became the country's first Prime Minister when independence finally came in 1963.

Within a year he had assumed the Presidency and declared Kenya a one-party state, but this former revolutionary and supposed terrorist soon proved a moderate dictator and capable ruler who included all of Kenya's ethnic groups in his ruling party. He used his power to arrest opponents without trial with great restraint. He also kept his promise that Europeans would continue to have a place in the new nation, as long as they were willing to live as ordinary citizens. The Kenyan economy remained strong under the new president. The former Marxist rejected all socialist experimentation in favor of private entrepreneurship, under the slogan *Harambee* (pulling together). The small but prosperous Indian minority was left unmolested and Western investment encouraged. As a result, Kenya's Gross Domestic Product increased fivefold in the decade after 1971, but much of this new wealth was diverted to Kenyatta's family and friends, leaving most of Kenya's increasing population increasingly poor.

Jomo Kenyatta died on August 22, 1978, in the city of Mombasa.

ter Kenyatta became President Kenyatta when he declared Kenya a republic in 1964. He pressured all politicians to join his KANU organization, making Kenya a one party state. Kenyatta preached socialism, but, in practice, he kept much of the capitalist system he had seen in England. While he crushed his political opponents, he neither nationalized industry nor redistributed land to any great degree. Moreover, in return for aid programs from Western nations, Kenyatta aligned his nation firmly on the American side during the Cold War. While inordinate amounts of Kenya's new wealth ended up in the hands of Kenyatta's family and cronies, Kenya's Gross Domestic Product increased fivefold between 1971 and 1981.

After Kenyatta's death in 1978, Daniel Arap Moi (b. 1924) succeeded him as president and quickly eliminated all hopes that Kenya might become more democratic in spirit. The constitution was altered to create a one-party system, the secret ballot was ended, and the judiciary lost its independence. The position of whites within the state suddenly became more difficult. During the 1980s the economy declined, unemployment rose, and birth rates soared higher than anywhere else in the world. Official corruption was endemic and the capital (Nairobi) became a city of 3,000,000 without public services. Kenya's once-capable health system collapsed under the ravages of the AIDS epidemic. White flight destroyed the remnants of its economy. While Kenyatta had been careful to include members of all of Kenya's ethnic groups in his administrations, Moi markedly favored members of his native Kalenjin group over the majority Kikuyu. Violent clashes between the groups broke out in 1991, 1992, and 1998 over Kikuyu incursion into the Rift Valley, previously a Kalenjin stronghold. It is not surprising that in Moi's last election victory (1997), the vote was split largely among ethnic lines.

In December 2002, however, Moi's handpicked successor, Uhuru Kenyatta (b. 1960), son of Jomo Kenyatta, was defeated at the poles by Mwai Kibaki (b. 1931) and his National Rainbow Coalition (NARC). Having twice been defeated by Moi in elections marked by intimidation and widespread violence, Kibaki's victory gave Kenya its first democratic transition of power since independence. Kibaki promised to review the wide-ranging powers granted to the president in Kenya's current constitution and to set up a panel to review past economic crimes. A graduate of the London School of Economics, Mibaki is expected to keep Kenya on a free-trade path. But Kibaki also has deep ties to KANU and the Kenyan independence movement. His brother Kinyua, a Mau-Mau commander, was killed in the pre-independence uprising. Having himself served as Kenyatta's finance minister and Moi's vice president before breaking with Moi in 1991, it is not clear how much Kenyan government is about to change.

Decolonization in French Africa

◆ Revolution in Algeria

France faced post-war decolonization with a different attitude than did Britain. In 1946 France conferred French citizenship on *all* residents of its colonies and, in 1956, extended independence to both Tunisia and Morocco. However, that policy met its end in France's colony of Algeria. In 1954, just as France was experiencing a humiliating defeat in Indo-China, a National Liberation Front (FLN) began a rebellion against France's presence in Algeria. The FLN leader was Ahmed ben Bella (b. 1916). The son of an Arab-Algerian farmer, Ben Bella had served with distinction in the French armed forces in World War II, winning both the *Croix de Guerre* (1940) and the *Médaille Militaire* (1944). Even though over a million Frenchmen called Algeria home and despite its representation in the French national legislature, Algerian nationalists demanded self-determination. The resulting war for independence (1954–1962) would bring down the Fourth French Republic. The Caribbean writer Franz Fanon (1925–1961), who became the spokesman for the Algerian cause, concluded that the fighting in Algeria was essentially a racial conflict. He alleged that France was only capable of accepting people of color if they gave up their native cultural identities. In *The Wretched of the Earth* (1961), Fanon advocated uncompromising war against colonial oppression, arguing that the French, like the British, had only contempt for non-western cultures.

The increasing violence in Algeria led French voters to elect Charles de Gaulle (1890–1970) to lead their new Fifth Republic in 1958. Most observers were convinced that de Gaulle, leader of the Free French Forces during World War II, would fight to sustain the French Empire. Instead he called for a referendum to determine whether Algeria and France's other remaining colonies wished to become independent or participate in a French-led "association" providing continued aid at the cost of limiting their autonomy. Although Algerian returns indicated that association was the voters' choice, the election had no impact on the rebels. Ultimately, de Gaulle decided to negotiate a settlement considered a sell-out by French-Algerians. After the loss of 300,000 Algerian and 20,000 French lives, Algeria won independence from France on July 5, 1962.

Ben Bella became Algeria's first Prime Minister (1962–1963) and its first President (1963–1965). Under his leadership the new nation nationalized recently discovered oil and natural gas supplies and enacted major educational reforms. Colonel Houari Boumedienne (1927–1978), Ben Bella's Minister of Defense and Vice President, ousted his former comrade after three years, and inaugurated over thirty years of military rule. Algeria was one of the many Arab states that declared war against Israel in 1967, but it never actively participated in the Middle-East wars. Rather, its government concentrated on managing growth as the population of Algeria soared to 28 million. But discontent festered as the oil boom faded and land distribution programs faltered in the 1980s. Voters gave their approval to a multi-party constitutional system in 1989 and finally ended decades of military control. But democratic forms did not create tolerance. In 1991, when the fundamentalist Islamic Salvation Front (FIS) appeared victorious in the parliamentary elections, the government invalidated the results, outlawed the party, and cancelled the presidential elections scheduled for 1992. A military junta, the High State Council (HSC), took over the reigns of government instead. The resulting Islamic insurgency continues to threaten the state with civil war and has already caused over 50,000 deaths. With its economy in a tailspin, Algeria requested and received debt-rescheduling and massive loans from the IMF in 1994 and 1995 after devaluing its currency 50 percent. Unfortunately, these measures did not restore economic order.

General Liamine Zeroual (b. 1941), defense minister under the HSC, was appointed president in 1994. He won 61 percent of the vote in multi-party presidential elections held in November 1995, but the elections were boycotted by the Muslim militants who felt they had been cheated of victory in 1991 and 1992. At his inauguration the former general promised to crack down on the rebels, but his efforts only increased their militancy. Elections were held again in 1999, in the middle of the ongoing war between the fundamentalist rebels and the secular government. With several Muslim groups once again boycotting the elections, Abdelaziz Bouteflika (b. 1937) was elected Algeria's new president. One of the most militant rebel militias, the Salafist Group for Preaching and Combat, has been linked to al-Qaeda. Not surprisingly, in December 2002, the American government announced that it would begin selling military equipment to the Algerian government to help it fight the rebels.

◆ The Ivory Coast

Eventually every former French colony with the exception of Somalia rejected de Gaulle's offer of political "association" with France. France was able to maintain some position in Africa, however, through the Yaounde (1963) and Lome (1975) Declarations that gave its former colonies special trading rights with the European Economic Union. The good will obtained by those privileges made it easier for France to intervene in the internal disputes of its former colonies.

When the Ivory Coast became independent of France in 1960, Felix Houphouët-Boigny (1905-1993) was elected its first president. The son of a Baoulé chief who had taken a medical degree in Senegal, Houphouët-Boigny was an Ivory Coast doctor and planter for almost twenty years before entering politics. In 1944, he took his first political steps, forming a league to protest the effects of French economic restrictions on Baoulé farmers. Houphouët-Boigny became the first African to serve in a French cabinet, and became famous for crusading against the forced labor imposed by French plantation owners on Ivorians. As a French colony, the Ivory Coast was the world's largest producer of cocoa, the third largest coffee grower, and a major source of pineapples and palm oil. For thirty-three years, President Houphouët-Boigny continued the French policy of maintaining high agricultural productivity at the expense of industrial development. He controlled the press, did not permit opposition parties, enjoyed annual vacations in Europe, and constructed vast show projects, including a new capital city at Yamoussoukro and the largest Roman Catholic cathedral in the world. Houphouët-Boigny concentrated on building national pride among the over sixty ethnic groups in his country, and gave the Ivorians political stability along with the second highest per capita income in Africa. Many of his critics said he achieved so much because the "French never left": they called the president a willing servant of colonialism. Nevertheless, the Ivory Coast remained the most prosperous West African State, suggesting that authoritarianism and national development were not mutually exclusive and that an economy did not need extensive industry to thrive.

When Houphouët-Boigny died in 1993 he was succeeded as president by Henri Konan Bédié (b. 1934). Groomed by Houphouët-Boigny to succeed him, Bédié served in several government positions under Houphouët-Boigny, as Ambassador to the United States (1961-1968), Minister of Finance (1968–1977), and President of Parliament (1979- 1993). His first acts as President of the Ivory Republic were to push through exceedingly restrictive laws governing who could run for office. Under the new rules not only the candidate, but also both the candidate's parents had to be native Ivorian. By the time presidential elections were held in 1995, only one of the country's 80 opposition parties was able to get its candidate on the ballot. The weeks leading up to the elections were marked by increasingly violent protests. Not surprisingly, Bédié won hands down.

By 1998, a short economic boom brought on by Bédié's 1994 currency devaluation had collapsed, along with world cocoa prices. Things only got worse the following year when the International Monetary Fund and the European Union put a stop to planned loans to the Ivory Coast because of the corruption and mismanagement they found in its finances. In early December 1999, Bédié tried to short-circuit mounting unemployment and the resulting ethnic violence by ordering the expulsion of some 20,000 Burkina-Faso natives working in the Ivory Coast. By Christmas Eve, Bédié's government was toppled in a military coup led by General Robert Guéï (1941-2002). Guéï promised a quick return to civilian rule but tried to steal the 2000 elections by claiming victory despite evidence that his main rival, Laurent Gbagbo (b. 1945), had actually won. Guéï finally allowed Gbagbo to take office. In an effort to prevent Ivory Coast from suffering through coup after coup, Gbagbo included Guéï in a National Reconciliation Forum together with Bédié and Alassane Dramane Ouattara (b. 1942), a former Deputy Managing Director of the IMF

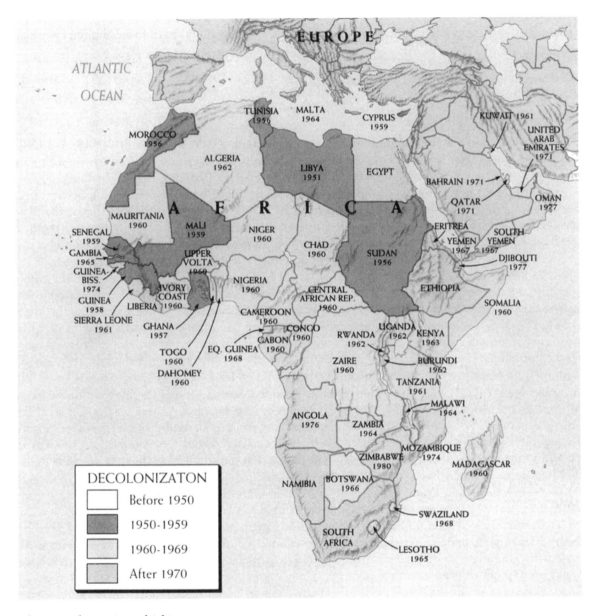

The Transformation of Africa.
From *The Western Heritage, 6/e, Combined Edition,* by Donald Kagan, Steven Ozment, and Frank M. Turner
Copyright © 1998 by Prentice-Hall, Inc.

(1974–1979). Although Ouattara attempted to run for the presidency in 1995 and 2000, he was removed from the ballot because both his parents were not born in the Ivory Coast.

By the beginning of September 2002, however, Guéï withdrew his support from the "national reconciliation" government, charging it with corruption and misrule. Whatever plans Guéï might have had to take over again were short-circuited when he was murdered on September 19, 2002, by unknown assailants. His supporters in the north are still waging a guerilla war against the government of Laurent Gdagbo. Meanwhile, the law that prevented Ouattara from running for office remains in place.

Belgian Africa

◆ From Congo to Zaire

The Belgian Congo suffered mightily under the long personal rule of Leopold II (r. 1865–1909), but succeeding Belgian governments administered it with scarcely more concern for the Congo's potential: in all the native population there was only a single college graduate and a single doctor. Wearied of governing a colony 77 times its own size, Belgium, without preparation or warning, decided to grant freedom to the Congo on June 30, 1960. The first Prime Minister of the new nation was Patrice Lumumba (1925–1961), a missionary-educated former postmaster with a checkered career. In addition to helping found the *Mouvement National Congolais*, he had been a brewery master and had served a year in prison for embezzlement.

Like Britain and France, the Belgian government had found it easier to control a colony when the different native groups within it did not cooperate with each other. When these colonies gained their independence, those native groups became rivals for power. Creating a federal constitution, in which each separate native region maintained some sovereign authority, was highly problematic in such a case. Nigeria's history has been a case in point: if the nation's wealth is only located in one or two of its regions, civil war is often the result. Lumumba thought the Congo, with its over 450 different peoples, would be better off under a "unitary" constitution in which the central government was much stronger than the individual native regions. He soon found himself facing civil war as Katanga, the Congo's richest province, seceded. A three-way power struggle emerged between Prime Minister Lumumba, President Joseph Kasavubu (1910/17?–1969), and Katanga Province's secessionist leader, Moïse Tshombe (1919–1969). The United States, worried about Lumumba's socialism, supported UN intervention in the struggle. In the middle of the fighting, Lumumba was murdered in 1961. An eventual alliance between Kasavubu and Tshombe led to Tshombe's becoming Prime Minister in 1964. But Tshombe only managed to hold on to the office for a year before being ousted in a military coup.

A former army sergeant and newspaper editor, Joseph Mobutu (1930–1997) who served as army chief of staff under Kasavubu, seized power in 1965 and held it for over thirty years. As president, Mobutu renamed the nation Zaire (1971), dubbed himself its "sole guide" (Mobutu "Sese Seko") and utilized Zaire's geographic centrality (it borders on nine other states) to make himself an indispensable supporter of United States policies in Sub-Saharan Africa. He kept power by brutally suppressing all dissenters. Determined to reconstruct his nation from top to bottom, he demanded absolute *"authenticité"*: everyone had to adopt tribal names, wear the *abakos* shirt in place of Western dress, and belong to the single political party he allowed. As long as Mobutu supported CIA programs in Africa, the United States voiced no objections to his authoritarian rule and looked the other way as he and his associates looted the riches of Zaire. The country became an enduring symbol of *kleptocracy,* a government in which ruling bureaucrats became multi-millionaires by looting their nation's coffers. Zaire's army abused the people, the nation's hugely expensive power grids failed to produce electricity, government neglect turned roads back into jungle, and the currency became worthless. When the Cold War ended, Mobutu discovered he was no longer vital to American interests. Without American aid to prop him up, he decided it was time to allow the formation of other political parties. He spent most of his time visiting his French estates, while continuing to control most of Zaire's economy. He returned to Zaire only to encourage the tribal genocide that occurred in Rwanda and Burundi in 1994. When finally overthrown by a rebellion in 1996–1997, Mobutu's personal fortune was estimated at over six billion dollars. He eventually died in exile in Morocco.

◆ Rwanda and Burundi

Zaire's future leadership would actually be determined by events in neighboring Rwanda and Burundi.

Burundi fell under German rule in 1899 and passed to Belgian control in 1916 during World War I. It was given independence by Belgium in 1962. Although the Hutu make up about 85 percent of Burundi's population, the minority Tutsi have controlled the country since its independence, fearing that any power-sharing arrangement with the Hutu would completely disenfranchise them. The new state was rocked by outbreaks of Hutu-Tutsi violence in 1965, 1972, 1988, and 1993, as one ethnic group attempted to wipe out the other. In 1972, ten years after Burundi was given its independence by Belgium, Tutsi soldiers killed over 100,000 Hutu. A similar outburst of ethnic fighting in 1988 resulted in the deaths of hundreds of Tutsi and 20,000 Hutu. In 1993 paratroopers from the Tutsi-dominated army assassinated President Melchior Ndadaye (1953–1993), a Hutu, setting off another round of ethnic warfare. His successor, former Agriculture minister Cyprien Ntaryamira (1956–1994), also a Hutu, died in a mysterious plane crash only a few months after his election by the national assembly. Also killed in the crash was Rwandan president Juvénal Habyarimana (1937–1994). Eighteen more months of Hutu-Tutsi strife ended with a Tutsi military junta taking control of Burundi in July 1996. Half a million people were killed in similar Tutsi-Hutu warfare in Rwanda in 1994. The death of Rwanda's president sparked a struggle for power that ended with the installation of Jean Kambanda (b. 1956) as prime minister of an interim government. Kambanda did nothing to end the slaughter of the Tutsi. That came to an end four months later when a rebel Tutsi army overthrew Kambanda's government. Kambanda fled the country but was arrested in 1997 and extradited to stand trial in Tanzania. Paul Kagame (b. 1957), the Tutsi rebel leader, took charge of Rwanda with Ugandan backing. Kambanda pled guilty to charges of genocide before a UN tribunal in Tanzania on May 1, 1998.

The ethnic violence in Rwanda and Burundi spilled over into Zaire, because there was a large population of Tutsi living in Zaire's Kivu Province. Having barely established peace in their own countries, Rwanda and Burundi were afraid the new violence in Zaire would plunge them into war once again. To stave it off, they sent troops into Zaire in support of the Alliance of Democratic Forces for the Liberation of Congo-Zaire. The Alliance was led by Laurent Desire Kabila (1939–2001), a member of the Luba people of the once-secessionist Katanga province. Neighboring Uganda also sent troops in support of Kabila.

A successful Kabila renamed the country the Democratic Republic of the Congo. He was unable to effect any real economic or social changes because he was faced with a 1998 rebellion fostered by the same governments that had originally backed him against Mobutu. While Zimbabwe, Angola, and Namibia sent troops to his aid, Rwanda, Burundi, and Uganda aided his opponents. Kabila was assassinated on January 16, 2001, by one of his own bodyguards. The Democratic Republic of the Congo returned to civil war and military rule under the leadership of his son, Major-General Joseph Kabila (b. 1970). With the intervention of South Africa in 2001, a cease-fire was brokered between the contending armies. Uganda and Rwanda agreed to a gradual withdrawal of their troops as the United Nations sent in over 5,000 peace-keepers. The cease-fire began to fall apart in 2002 as Uganda delayed withdrawing its troops on the grounds that Rwanda was beefing up its Congo forces rather than reducing them as the agreement stipulated. A new round of ethnic violence broke out that year in the diamond-rich Ituri province. By May, 2003, the United Nations Security Council was considering increasing its own presence in the country as the Democratic Republic of the Congo slid further and further into civil war.

Human Rights in South Africa

Unlike its northern neighbors, South Africa had been an independent state for most of the twentieth century; the Union of South Africa was created in 1910 as a dominion of Great Britain's empire. But independence brought self-government only to its European citizens. Its constitution established white supremacist rule; no natives could serve in the two-house legislature. The Native Land Act of 1913 made it impossible for blacks to own land throughout most of the country, eliminating them as economic competitors to white farmers. During the inter-war period, descendants of the original Dutch settlers assumed increasing power over national policy. After the Second World War, when much of the west was moving away from overt racism, the Afrikaners won complete control of the government. These descendants of the Boers made up only one-fifth of the South African population, and were afraid of being overwhelmed by the black African majority. Led by Daniel Malan (1874–1959) the Afrikaner-dominated National Party took power in 1948 with a mandate to create *Apartheid*, strict racial separation. The Population Registration Act (1950) established race classifications splitting the population up into four groups: whites, blacks, Asians and "colored" (people of mixed parentage). Only whites could vote, mixed marriages were prohibited, and schools were segregated. Since blacks were declared "citizens"of the *bantustans* (native "homelands") created by the 1913 Native Land Act, they were required to carry passports ("passes") when in South Africa. Failure to produce the "pass" led to immediate detention and forced return to the *bantustan*. The Bantu Education Act (1954) ensured an inferior education for blacks and "coloreds," guaranteeing the white majority an unskilled and noncompetitive black labor force. An Anti-Communism Act (1950) allowed the government to interpret any form of protest as Communist subversion, authorizing detention without trial for such offenses. As perfected under Prime Minister Hendrik Verwoerd (1958–1966), the system exploited and humiliated the vast majority of the population in Africa's richest state.

The African National Congress (ANC), a multi-racial organization founded in 1912 by a Zulu Methodist minister John Dube (1871–1946) and Pixley ka Seme (c.1880-1951), an Oxford educated Zulu lawyer and newspaper editor, followed a non-violent Gandhian philosophy as it worked to obtain equal treatment under the law. Its principles were embodied in *The Freedom Charter* (1955) that called for a democratic and multi-racial South Africa. It was soon challenged for the leadership of the struggle against *apartheid* by the breakaway Pan-Africanist Congress (PAC) led by Robert Sobukwe (1924–1978). Sobukwe rejected the ANC's multi-racial character. Founded in 1959, the PAC quickly organized a national demonstration against the "Pass Laws" that turned into an international *cause célèbre* when 69 protesters were murdered at Sharpeville on March 21, 1960. The government blamed both the PAC and the ANC, outlawed both organizations, and began to hunt down their leaders. Some escaped to organize guerilla bases in neighboring countries; others moved underground. Sobukwe and seven ANC leaders were jailed, including Nelson Mandela (b. 1918), a leader of the ANC Youth League, who was sentenced to life in prison. In reaction, the ANC gave up its non-violent tactics for *Umkhono we Sizwe* ("Spear of the Nation") while the PAC adopted the motto POQO ("one settler, one bullet").

In a continuing attempt to separate the races, South Africa forcibly removed 3.5 million blacks to homelands between 1960 and 1983. But violent protests in the Southwest Townships (Soweto) again shook the system in 1976 when South Africa's paramilitary police opened fire on high school and middle school students demonstrating for a better curriculum and against the use of Afrikaans as the language of instruction. Hundreds of teenagers were killed. As international protests mounted, the government attempted to gain support from South Africa's disenfranchised minorities. It tried to appease the Indian (3 percent) and "colored" (9 percent) portions of the population by granting them limited legislative power in a new constitutional structure in 1983. Blacks, some 72 percent of all South Africans, were still ignored. Many observers considered race war inevitable. In the 1980s, Prime Minister P. W. Botha (b. 1916) and the Afrikaner nationalists won support from the United States because of their anti-Communist stance. The American policy of "constructive engagement" basically accepted South Africa's racist system while attempting to mitigate its effects. But protests continued under the leadership of Bishop Desmond Tutu (b. 1931), whose non-violent crusade led to a Nobel Peace Prize.

The South African government attempted to bolster itself by allying with some elements of the black population against others. Chief Mangosuthu Buthelezi (b. 1928), head of *KwaZulu,* and his followers, the *Inkatha* (Zulu Freedom Party), often clashed with ANC rivals. Fomenting violence among blacks did the government little good. International opinion condemned *apartheid,* and American and Common Market sanctions, finally imposed in 1986, greatly damaged the white-dominated economy once the easing of Cold War tensions made it less "necessary" to prop

A new South Africa: Outgong President F. W. DeKlerk, ANC leader and President-elect Nelson Mandela, and Zulu leaders King Goodwill Zwelithini and Chief Buthelezi chart the nation's future after the 1994 elections.
Copyright © CORBIS/Peter Turnley

up anti-Communist South Africa. In 1989 a new Afrikaner leader, Frederik Willem deKlerk (b. 1936), replaced Botha as head of the National Party and surprised the world by working toward a non-racist South Africa. DeKlerk, long a supporter of *apartheid*, lifted the ban on the ANC and began secret negotiations with the still imprisoned Mandela. He arranged for South Africa to give up its control of Namibia, which became an independent state by plebiscite in 1990, and freed Mandela after 27 years in prison. During 1990-1991 most *apartheid* legislation was repealed, and the constitution was altered to permit black voting. Together, deKlerk and Mandela completed the dismantling of *apartheid* and steered South Africa on a democratic course. In recognition of their efforts, they were jointly awarded the Nobel Peace Prize in 1993. Finally, as the last act of a long drama, Mandela was elected president in a free election in 1994.

Mandela, the son of a Thembu chief, set about constructing a truly democratic multiracial state. His most difficult problem was fostering patience among a black electorate that expected to share the prosperity of the largely white-run economy. In addition, he had to cope with lingering violence stemming from black factionalism that verged on warfare. Mandela began new housing, educational, and economic development projects, but the results were less than hoped for by the black majority. South Africa remained a divided nation with a small, white middle class, and large, mostly impoverished black majority.

Thabo Mvuyelwa Mbeki (b. 1942), who served as first executive vice-president under Mandela, was elected president of South Africa in 2000. Holding a Master's Degree in Economics from Britain's Sussex University, Mbeki campaigned vigorously for debt relief for South Africa. But he created world-wide controversy by voicing doubt that HIV causes AIDS and for failing to move quickly enough to stem the epidemic in his country. Even with offers of reduced prices on AIDS medication from drug companies, he did not move to have the government distribute it to infected pregnant women until April 2002. With an estimated twenty-five percent of the nation's adult population HIV-positive, South Africa's road to future economic stability is arduous indeed.

Africa on the World Stage

The year 1960 is sometimes labeled the "Year of Africa." In that year alone seventeen African countries won freedom from colonial fetters. Another ten became independent between 1961 and 1964, and the rest soon afterward. But independence was not *given* to African populations. It had to be wrested from reluctant imperial powers that had done virtually nothing to create conditions favorable to political stability and economic development. Most African nations were woefully unprepared for independence, and suffered from a shortage of trained bureaucrats and administrators, yet all were determined to quickly assume their place in the world community. Many put their faith in dictators: Hastings Banda (1905-1997) ruled Malawi for thirty years. "Emperor" Jean Bedel Bokassa (1921–1996) bankrupted the Central African Republic, and the bloody decade-long reign (1971–1979) of Idi Amin (1925-2003) proved a catastrophe for Uganda. The road from dictatorship to democracy has proved difficult. Kenneth Kaunda (b. 1924) was Zambia's president for 27 years, before he was defeated in Zambia's first ever multi-party elections in 1991. But his democratically elected successor, Frederick Jacob Titus Chiluba (b. 1943) declared a state of emergency in Zambia on October 28, 1997, after a failed coup and ordered Kaunda's arrest two months later, despite the former leader's protest that he had played no part in the coup attempt. Opposition leaders accused Chiluba of staging the coup so he could crack down on the opposition. But Chiluba did step down when his term ended, to be replaced by former vice president Levy Patrick Mwanawasa (b. 1948) on January 2, 2002. Even Ethiopia, the one ancient African kingdom to escape the ravages of nineteenth-century imperialism, fell victim to the coup-

HAILE SELASSIE (1892–1975)

Ethiopia's last Emperor.
Copyright © Hulton Getty

Modern Ethiopia's greatest leader was born on July 23, 1892, as Tafari Makonnen. His father, Ras (prince) Makonnen was a close advisor of Emperor Menelik II, and young Tafari's intelligence caused Menelik to bring him to court at the age of 14. In 1910 Tafari succeeded his father as governor of the province of Harar and began the modernizing policies—expanding government roles at the expense of the feudal nobility—that later marked his reign over the whole country. He also solidified his connections to the throne by marrying Wayzaro Menen, a great-granddaughter of Menelik II.

Menelik's death in 1913 precipitated a political crisis. His grandson and successor, Lij Yasu, was not popular with the country's Christian majority, and Tafari used his royal connections to position himself as the leader of the Christian resistance. In 1917, he put Menelik's daughter Zauditu on the throne with himself as regent and heir. As regent, he instituted modernization and became the champion of an Ethiopian generation hungry for development. He established schools throughout the nation and started a program that sent young Ethiopians abroad for higher education. In 1923 he brought Ethiopia into the League of Nations, and the following year he traveled to Rome, Paris, and London, the first Ethiopian ruler ever to go abroad.

When Zauditu died in 1930, Tafari was crowned Emperor and took the name Haile Selassie (Might of the Trinity). The new Emperor began to build schools, strengthen the power of the police, and eliminate the taxing privileges of the nobility. At the same time he limited parliament's ability to oppose his wishes. In 1935, when the Ethiopian military could not resist an Italian invasion, Selassie went into exile. In June 1936, he gave a dramatic speech to the League of Nations, appealing in vain for the League to impose military sanctions against Italy. The Emperor spent the next four years in London, and was restored to his throne in January 1941 when a combined British-Ethiopian force reclaimed Ethiopia from the Italians.

Haile Selassie ruled as Emperor of his restored kingdom for the next 34 years. In 1955 he issued a new constitution granting universal adult male suffrage, but retained virtually complete autocratic power. He also played a leading role in the creation of the Organization for African Unity, founded in Addis Ababa in 1963. During his long reign, he accepted little outside advice, and, in 1960, an attempted coup was put down by loyal troops. Growing domestic problems—unemployment, inflation, and the beginnings of famine—led a military faction to seize power in September 1974. The Emperor was put under house arrest and died a year later, on August 26, 1975, never having left his palace. The military government claimed his death was due to natural causes, but later evidence pointed to a junta-engineered murder.

dictator syndrome. A military faction seized power from Emperor Haile Selassie (1892–1975) in 1974 and engineered his death a year later. Seventeen years of Marxist military rule under Mengistu Haile Mariam (b. 1946) and the PMAC (Provisional Military Administration Council) came to an end in 1991 only to be followed by years of political infighting and intermittent warfare with Eritrea, which had seceded from Ethiopia in 1993. The first multi-party general elections in Ethiopia's history were held in 1995; a coalition headed by Prime Minister Meles Zenawi (b. 1955) has held office ever since without making much of an impact on the country's endemic poverty. In 1996, Mengistu was put on trial in absentia in Ethiopia for crimes committed during his regime, but since his ouster he has been living in a government-supplied villa in Zimbabwe's capital under the personal protection of Zimbabwe's President Robert Mugabe (b. 1924).

Liberia, the only African nation never to have been anyone's colony (for even Ethiopia was briefly under Italian control during World War II), suffered a similar fate. Its politics were dominated by the descendants of the repatriated African-Americans who had first created Liberia in the nineteenth century. From 1944 to 1971 Liberia was ruled by William Vacanarat Shadrach Tubman (1895–1971). His successor, William Richard Tolbert, Jr. (1913–1980), controlled the country until he was assassinated in April 1980 by Samuel Kanyon Doe (1951–1990), then an army master sergeant from the Krahn ethnic group. While Doe allowed opposition parties to form in 1984, he rigged the 1985 elections to ensure the victory of his National Democratic Party. In 1989, Charles G. Taylor (b. 1948), another descendant of the American settlers, launched an invasion of Liberia from bases in the Ivory Coast. Taylor was a member of Doe's government who had fled to the United States after being charged with embezzlement. Doe was arrested in the United States and held for extradition, but escaped and returned to Africa in 1985 where his rebel group received the backing of Libya and Burkina Faso. Taylor's National Patriotic Front of Liberia (NPFL) was made up largely of the Gio and Mano peoples of Northeast Liberia, who had been persecuted under Doe's regime. Doe was captured and killed by Taylor's forces on September 10, 1990, even as Liberia's neighbors were trying to negotiate an end to the civil war. A UN-brokered peace plan failed as well in 1995. As factions multiplied fighting reached a stalemate. Then, a 1996 Nigerian-brokered cease-fire led to elections on July 19, 1997. The elections were held under the observation of the United Nations, the European Union, and the Organization of African Unity. Former American President Carter was one of the election monitors. Charles Taylor managed to gain enough votes to avoid a run-off election and was inaugurated in August 1997. Nigerian troops left Liberia in 1998. Casualty estimates for the civil war topped a quarter of a million with perhaps another three-quarters of a million people driven into exile. But Charles Taylor's policies only seemed to flame the fires of revolution. With dozens of rebel groups disrupting the country's economic infrastructure, famine began to spread. The largest rebel groups refused to lay down their arms until Taylor was out of office. By the summer of 2003, the country was in such chaos that the United States pressured Taylor to resign by refusing to send any further aid until he did. With 2,300 US Marines floating offshore in three American warships, Taylor resigned, leaving for asylum in Nigeria. Gyude Bryant (b. 1949), a businessman without close ties to either the rebels or Taylor's supporters, was chosen by the various factions as interim leader until elections can be held in 2005. Backed by peace-keeping forces from neighboring West African countries, Bryant's government now has to get all the rebel factions to lay down their arms before Liberia can begin rebuilding itself.

Regardless of the quality of their leadership, all the newly freed African states demanded and won the right to join the United Nations. Led by men such as Nehru, Nasser, and Nkrumah, the Third World coalition began to dominate the deliberations of the General Assembly in New York City. After 1962 the Secretary General of the UN was U Thant. Born and raised in the former

British colony of Burma (now Myanmar), U Thant was sympathetic to the desires of the ex-colonies to obtain restitution for the century of exploitation Africans and Asians had endured under colonialism. Liberation for all remaining colonies, requests for additional developmental aid, restitution for past theft, and an end to neo-colonial economic penetration became common topics of discussion at General Assembly meetings.

Third World delegations to the United Nations organized the *Group of 77* under-developed lands to coordinate their demands. African nations shared not only the common experience of a colonial past but also the harsh failure of efforts to modernize their economies. The continent soon became the most rapidly urbanizing part of the world: in 1960 there were only three cities with a population of a million; by 1998 there were more than thirty. As people abandoned the countryside, these formerly agricultural economies proved incapable of effectively using the billions of dollars in aid provided to them by the United States, the Soviet Union, and Communist China. Large industrial centers often ended up in bankruptcy while proud leaders ignored smaller aid projects that might have been more successful. Endemic corruption led to ever-increasing debt. Since 1970 real per capita income has declined in Africa, and between 1980 and 1990 the continent's share of the world's GDP fell from two to one percent.

The first generation of independent African leaders had shared a vision of Pan-Africanism, but forty-plus years of independence seems to indicate that no single "Africa" can encompass its nearly one billion people. Nationalism's continued attraction threatens the stability of many countries as ethnic minorities agitate for their own domains. In 1963, under the guidance of Nkrumah, Nasser, and Emperor Haile Selassie, the Organization of African Unity (OAU) was created to provide a voice for African concerns, but it proved ineffectual in reducing internal dissent. Perhaps the greatest accomplishment of the OAU was an understanding reached by African states that they would never invade each other's territory, but even that arrangement was shattered by the events in the Congo after 1997. The OAU never became the strong, unifying agency envisioned by its founding fathers: in 1996 alone, fourteen of the fifty-three African states were involved in some type of warfare, and at least eight participated in the 1998 rising against Laurent Kabila. A sad result of these multiple battles are the more than eight million Africans counted among the world's refugees in 1997.

In July, 2002, African leaders met to replace the failed OAU with a new African Union (AU). Its new chairman, President Thabo Mbeki of South Africa, pledged the new union would work to alleviate the lives of ordinary Africans as it tried to forge an African version of the European Union with a regional parliament and central bank. But critics remain unconvinced of the AU's ability to carry out its aims. The leaders of Libya and Kenya were given prominent places at the inaugural ceremonies even though the Union's charter required its members to hold free, multi-party elections. On the other hand, the 53-member union rejected the proposed membership of Madagascar whose leadership, it claimed, took office unconstitutionally.

The relationship between African states and their former colonial masters continues to influence African development. With the cooperation of her former colonies, the French maintain troops in Gabon, the Ivory Coast, Cameroon, Senegal, the Central African Republic, Chad, and Djibouti, and have military cooperation agreements with their neighbors. These forces have been used to evacuate foreign nationals in civil war zones and to maintain cooling-off zones between combatants. While the French government claims to intervene to protect Africa's fledgling democracies, its track record of supporting pro-French leaders, democratic or not, has opened up a continuing debate in African presses as to the need for, or desirability of, France's continued presence in Africa, especially given the commercial concessions the French often demand in return for assistance.

Africa is also developing its own regional powers, Uganda being a case in point. Uganda's Idi Amin was ousted in 1979 by an invasion led by Tanzania's President Julius Kambarage Nyerere (1922–1999). Amin fled to Europe, where he eventually died of leukemia while living in exile in London. In 1980, Amin's place as leader of Uganda was taken by Milton Apollo Obote (b. 1924), a former Ugandan president from the 1960s, in a fraudulent vote. His opponent, Yoweri Kaguta Museveni (b. 1945), was backed by Nyerere, whose government had sheltered Museveni's rebel forces since he had gone into exile in Tanzania when Amin first came to power in 1971. Museveni may have been deprived of victory in 1980, but his National Resistance Movement was strong enough to take the government by force in 1986. Obote fled to exile in Zambia. Museveni, a former Marxist, has spent most of his rule privatizing Uganda's economy. He aims at a "common market" for Africa but rejects multi-party democracy as inappropriate for a pre-industrial society. Museveni sees political parties as doing nothing more than splitting countries along ethnic lines. Not surprisingly, his unopposed ticket won an overwhelming victory in the 2001 elections. Determined to create stability in the region, Museveni has made Uganda a major power broker though military intervention in his neighbors' affairs. In 1990 he sponsored the invasion of Rwandan Tutsi exiles that took control of Rwanda in 1994 after four years of civil war, thus ending the slaughter of Tutsi by the Hutu dictatorship led by Juvénal Habyarimana. Museveni's troops were instrumental in putting Laurent Kabila in power in what was then Zaire. And Museveni supported, and continues to support, the Sudan People's Liberation Army, led by John Garang (b. 1945), against its fundamentalist Muslim regime.

Another potential power bloc is COMESSA (the Community of Sahel-Saharan States), a group founded by Libya in 1998. It consists of Libya, Burkina Faso, the Central African Republic, Mali, Niger, Sudan, Chad, and Eritrea. They held a summit in Chad in February 2000 to coordinated their efforts within the OAU and to mediate the war between Eritrea and a prospective COMESSA member, Djibouti.

Critics of African development unanimously hold that the continent is the Third World's "third world." Real per capita income across the continent declined so steeply in the twenty years between 1970 and 1990 that, by 1990, the total income of all of Sub-Saharan Africa was the same as that of Belgium. Africa is the only area of the globe in which the proportion of children in school is decreasing although it boasts the worlds highest birthrates. A majority of those children who do attend school do not even graduate from grade school. Continental debt tripled in the 1980s to more than $180 billion, a total far surpassing the gross production of all its states. Africa has more that two-thirds of all the AIDS cases in the world. So pervasive are the ravages of that epidemic that in several Sub-Saharan African states more than 25 percent of the adult population is HIV-positive. Demographers are certain that AIDS deaths will cause several African nations to have negative population growth early in the twenty-first century. The loss of the rain forest in nations like Sierra Leone and Ivory Coast has led to flooding, soil erosion, and the resurgence of malaria, while the Sahara Desert continues to spread southwards in an ever-widening arc. As the new millennium begins, Africa contains 35 of the 45 lowest-ranking states on the UN's Human Development Index.

◆ Note
....

1. Kwame Nkrumah, *Consciencism* (New York: Monthly Review Press, 1969), 74 and 100–101.

13

Revolutions in Latin America

No portion of the Third World has been exposed to western influence as long as Latin America. Spain and Portugal maintained vast empires there from the sixteenth century to the revolutions of the early nineteenth century, after which both Great Britain and the United States supported the new Latin American republics as markets for their growing industrial power. Europeans also migrated to Latin America in record numbers in pursuit of investment and employment opportunities. Yet despite substantial gains, Latin America had a total population of only 38 million by 1900, as compared to the nearly 76 million people living in the United States alone.

Jealous of European influence in its own "backyard," an increasingly powerful United States moved quickly to dominate the "banana republics" of the Caribbean Basin, resulting in at least twenty American interventions in the region between 1898 and 1920. Under the umbrella of the Roosevelt Corollary (1904), the United States occupied Haiti (1915–1924), the Dominican Republic (1916–1924), Nicaragua (1926–1933), and sent troops into Honduras six times between 1911 and 1925. In addition the United States held on to a naval base in Cuba, the colony of Puerto Rico, and the Canal Zone in Panama. In the meantime, the regional tradition of *caudillismo* (dictatorial military rule) made a mockery of fine sounding civil rights protections and republican institutions. Again and again across the region, constitutional protections were ignored by a *caudillo* (strong man) who promised stability and order but served only himself, the landed rich, and the clergy. Such behavior seemed to justify outside interference.

The attitude of the United States did not officially alter until President Franklin D. Roosevelt launched a "Good Neighbor" program in 1933 to help Latin America's struggling agricultural economies. Declaring that no state had the right to intervene in the internal affairs of another, Roosevelt withdrew American forces from Haiti and, in 1943, unilaterally abrogated the Platt Amendment (1901) that had authorized continued American intervention in Cuba. One result of Roosevelt's policy was the support most Latin American nations gave to the Allied cause during the Second World War. At the Pan-American Defense Conference in the capital of Brazil just weeks after the Japanese attack on Pearl Harbor, Argentina and Chile were the only countries that did not break off relations with the Axis powers.

Unfortunately for American-Latin American relations, however, the United States once again stepped up intervention in Latin American affairs during the Cold War. The Bay of Pigs invasion of Cuba in 1961 was backed by the CIA, and Cuba was blockaded during the Missile Crisis in 1962. The American Navy put on a show of force in Dominican waters in 1961 to prevent the Trujillo family from interfering with its new government. A marine battalion was positioned off of Haiti in 1963 to prevent damage to American investments there during a period of political unrest. American troops moved into the Dominican Republic in 1965 at the official request of its president to suppress a socialist insurrection. In 1994, American troops were used to return Haitian

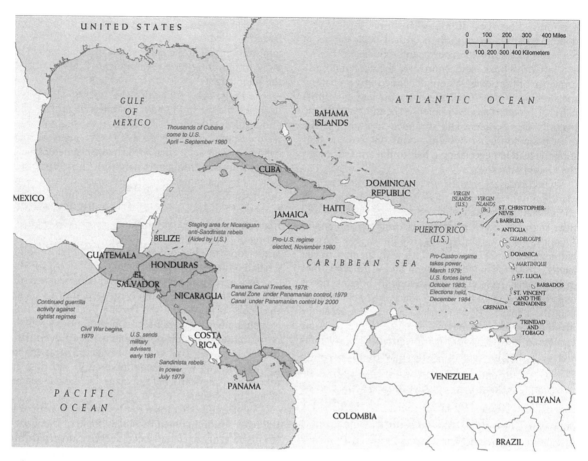

The United States in Central America, 1978–1990. U.S. intervention in Central America reached a new level of intensity with the so-called Reagan Doctrine. The bulk of U.S. aid came in the form of military support for the government of El Salvador and the Contra rebels in Nicaragua.
From *Out of Many,* Fourth Edition, (2004), reproduced by permission of Prentice-Hall, Inc.

President Aristide to office. On December 20, 1989, the United States sent 13,000 troops into Panama (to join the 11,000 already stationed in the Canal Zone) to, as President George Bush put it, "protect American lives, to defend democracy in Panama, to apprehend Noriega and bring him to trial on the drug-related charged for which he was indicted in 1988, and to ensure the integrity of the Panama Canal Treaties."[1] In defense of his actions, President Bush reminded the Congress that, under Noriega's direction, the Panamanian Assembly had declared war on the United States on December 15.

Not all of America's Cold War interventions in Latin America were unilateral. At the request of the Organization of Eastern Caribbean States (OECS), 1,900 US troops joined 300 OECS, Jamaican, and Barbadian troops in an invasion of Grenada on October 25, 1983, overthrowing the socialist revolutionary forces that had murdered Grenada's Prime Minister.

Internally, the region has seen a more marked change. Until the middle of the twentieth century, the Creole elite maintained its socio-political domination and kept control of a disproportionate share of the region's wealth. Today, some fifty years later, rule by *caudillo* appears to be a phenomenon of the past, free market economies have replaced state planning, and personal freedom is more than just a pious promise. The population has grown to half a billion. The standard of living is better overall than it was at mid-century, although a basic maldistribution of wealth continues to haunt the region. As late as the 1980s, 60 percent of Brazil's land was held by only two percent of the population while the top one percent of Paraguay's elite held 80 percent of the arable land.

Argentina: From Perón to Democracy

After attaining its independence from Spain in 1816, Argentina turned to the problems of modernization. Lacking a population trained in the skills required by the Industrial Revolution, the Argentine government offered bounties for skilled immigrants from Europe. In the last decades of the nineteenth century, Argentina accepted so many thousands of European immigrants that Italian was the primary language of one-third of its population and its leaders often spoke French. While some of these new *Peninsulares* reaped the benefits of modernization, many became part of a new urban working class, an economically disenfranchised proletariat seeking socialist reform. Representing both the new middle and working classes, the Radical Party was able to push through political reforms in 1912 that guaranteed a secret ballot and universal male suffrage. Radical Party leader Hipólito Yrigoyen (1852–1933) was elected president in 1916, but his economic policies led to a decade of inflation that eroded his middle-class support.

At the other end of the political spectrum, the Argentine military, its officer class recruited from the old Spanish-creole ranchers, felt that it was not getting a large enough share of government patronage. In league with the dissatisfied middle class, the army overthrew Yrigoyen's government in 1930 and kept control of Argentina through rigged elections until 1943.

Like most of its Latin American neighbors, Argentina's economy was dependent on its sales of raw materials and agricultural products: any change in world commodities markets threatened its economic stability. When Great Britain decided to impose tariffs on goods from outside its own empire in 1932, Argentina's beef exports plummeted. A trade treaty with Britain the following year (the *Roca-Runciman Treaty* of 1933) stabilized the beef market but Argentina's economy was damaged by the concessions it gave to British companies in return.

Argentina's refusal to sever diplomatic relations with Germany at the Pan-American Defense Conference in January 1942 set off a crisis in its government. The military leadership was divided between those who favored an Allied alignment and those who favored closer ties to the so-far victorious Axis Powers. The slow turn of the tide in 1942–1943 from Axis to Allied victories and the fact that many of Argentina's factories were German owned made choosing sides more complicated. President Ramón S. Castillo (1873–1944), who had taken the pro-Axis stance at the Pan-American Defense Conference was overthrown a year later by the anti-Axis general, Arturo Rawson (1885-1952). Rawson only managed to hold office for a few hours before the pro-Axis group put General Pedro Pablo Ramírez (1884–1962) in his place. Ramírez quickly set about creating a one-party state, destroying opposition newspapers, and outlawing opposition political parties. After a series of Allied victories, Ramírez reluctantly decided to sever diplomatic relations with Japan and Germany in January 1994. For that decision, he, too, was thrown out by his own army.

Colonel Juan Domingo Perón (1895–1974), a professed admirer of European Fascist methods, led the *Junta* (coalition) of junior army officers that overthrew Ramírez in February 1944. The Junta remained pro-Axis until Allied victory in Europe seemed imminent. Argentina did not declare war on Germany and Japan until March 27, 1945.

By 1946, with the support of national labor organizations, Perón had advanced from Minister of Labor to President of Argentina, all on promises to favor the working class at the expense of

MARÍA EVA (EVITA) DUARTE DE PERÓN (1919–1952)

Defender of the "descamisados" of Argentina.
Copyright © Hulton Getty

María Eva (Evita) Duarte de Perón, the second wife of Argentine President Juan Perón (1895–1974) was born on May 7, 1919, in the town of Los Toldos and grew up in poverty. As a teenager she moved to the capital city, Buenos Aires, determined to make her fortune as an actress. She had only modest success on the stage and in radio, but her good looks attracted the attention of Colonel Juan Perón, a member of the *junta* controlling Argentina and a widower. In October 1945 Perón was ousted from his position as Vice President, but Evita rallied his support during the crisis, and the couple wed later that year. When Perón campaigned for the Presidency, Evita used her impoverished origins to help win him votes among *los descamisados* (the shirtless ones).

During the six years of Perón's first Presidency (1946-1952) Evita dominated Argentina's health and labor ministries. To subordinate organized labor to her husband's regime, she purged union leaders who opposed her while winning support from the rank and file through generous wage increases. She suppressed the elitist *Sociedad de Beneficiencia,* making enemies of the wealthy women who traditionally patronized it, and replaced it with her own María Eva Duarte de Perón Social Welfare Foundation. Funds for Evita's foundation included money from the national lottery and "voluntary" contributions from unions and businesses. With these resources she built schools, hospitals, orphanages, homes for the elderly, and other charitable institutions. In 1947, Eva won women the vote and equal legal rights with men. In the 1951 elections, over two million Argentine women voted for the first time. The Peronist Party elected six women senators and twenty-four women deputies.

Evita's charitable work convinced the disadvantaged masses of Argentina that she and her husband were devoted to their welfare. In her ostentatious style and expensive clothes, they saw a vision of their own possible success. When she died of cancer on July 26, 1952, it seemed a national catastrophe. Her opponents believed her social welfare foundation had been a scheme to enrich herself from public funds, but they failed to prove their case.

Perón's popularity faded after Evita's death, and his corrupt authoritarian rule collapsed in 1955. But a growing demand for Evita's canonization prompted anti-Peronists to steal her corpse and hide it in Italy for 16 years before its return to the exiled Perón. Perón reclaimed power in 1973, died in office in 1974, and his third wife, Isabel, repatriated Evita's remains in order to bolster her own political power. But Isabelita was no Evita, and a military coup ended the last Perón regime. Removed from the presidential palace, Evita's remains were re-interred in the Duarte family crypt in Recoleta cemetery: she was finally back home.

foreign and native factory owners. But the Axis was not forgotten. One Perónist decision was to permit, and even encourage Nazi war criminals to find refuge in Argentina. Adolf Eichmann (1906–1962), perhaps the most notorious of the war criminals given refuge by Perón, was kidnaped in 1960, transported from Argentina to Israel, and executed for crimes against humanity in 1962. On the other hand, Perón's decision to expropriate five dozen German-owned industrial concerns in 1947 helped ease Argentine-American relations.

Perón's alliance with the laboring *descamisados* (shirtless ones) of Argentina was enormously enhanced by the work of his wife Evita (1919–1952) who created a Social Action Foundation to provide social services and loans to the poor. While Perón nationalized foreign owned corporations, stabilized the debt, and paid off his supporters with higher wages and longer vacations, Evita won a reputation as a "saintly" Madonna. She successfully campaigned to win the vote for women in 1947, even as she got her husband to repress all opposition to his regime. Together, the Peróns made a formidable team. With Evita's help, Perón won an easy reelection in 1952. Evita's untimely death from cancer that same year removed the more charismatic half of the partnership, however. Just as important, Perón's economic policies were beginning to backfire. With European production virtually closed down at the end of World War II, Argentina was able to boost sales of its wheat and beef throughout the world, but when the western European economy revived under the Marshall Plan, Argentina found itself increasingly closed out of the world market. Staggering unemployment and inflation rates of 33 percent forced Perón to re-open Argentina to foreign investment. His 1954 deal giving Exxon the right to develop the oil fields of Patagonia and his simultaneous attack on the Catholic Church angered conservatives within Argentina. A coalition of army officers and middle-class investors forced Perón out of office and into exile in 1955, but succeeding presidents and military regimes were never free of the shadow cast by the ousted leader. Like Robespierre, Perón considered himself the voice of a struggling people striving to become a powerful nation; he believed that violence in the hands of the people was not violence, but justice.

◆ Argentina without Perón: Dictators and Presidents

Major General Eduardo Lonardi (1896–1956), one of the leaders of the revolt against Perón, took office as the Provisional President of Argentina on September 20, 1955. His promise of a restored democracy lasted no longer than he did. One of his own colleagues, Major General Pedro Eugenio Aramburu (1903–1970), took over two months later claiming Lonardi had done nothing to stamp out Perónism. Aramburu threw out Perón's 1947 Constitution, brought back the Charter of 1853 (which limited Presidents to one term in office), and ordered the arrest of thousands of protesters. Representative government was officially restored in 1958 with Arturo Frondizi (1908–1995) as Argentina's new president, although the Perónists had not been allowed to put any candidate on the ballot. Even though Frondizi had won the presidency with socialist support, the United States, deeming him the lesser of two evils, began funneling aid money into Argentina. When Frondizi allowed the Perónists to put up candidates in local elections in 1962, the military had had enough. Even though Frondizi did not allow victorious Perónist provincial governors to take office, the military deposed Frondizi and replaced him with the leader of the Senate, José María Guido (1910–1975).

By barring Communists and Perónists from running candidates for office, the military was able to ensure the election in 1963 of a more moderate leftist, Arturo Illía (1910–1975). Illía tried to stem Argentina's continuing inflation with minimum wage laws and fixed prices for basic commodities, but the only result was increased shortages. When Perónist candidates (running as independents) continued to increase their share of the vote in local elections, the military decided to intervene once again. Juan Carlos Onganía (1914–1995), the commander in chief of the army, led the country from 1966 to 1970. He was followed by General Alejandro Augustin Lanusse (1918–1996). Labor unrest continued to mount; Lanusse agreed to hold elections, and the Perónists nominated Héctor José Cámpora (1909-1980) as a substitute for Juan Perón whose name could not formally be placed on the ballot while he remained in exile. Cámpora took office in May 1973. Perón landed in June, and Cámpora resigned in his favor a month later.

Perón arrived with a new wife, Isabelita (b. 1931), and won 62 percent of the popular vote in a new round of elections that September, but he died shortly thereafter of advanced heart disease. His widow aspired to lead Argentineans as Evita had done, and seized the presidency. In 1976, both Isabelita and her counselor-astrologer were overthrown. Lieutenant General Jorge Rafael Videla (b. 1925) took control. The legislature was dissolved, and martial law was declared. A new era of military rule had begun.

◆ Argentina under the Generals

The "Argentinean process" of government instituted by the military in 1976 entailed the ruthless elimination of all visible opposition on the left. As the number of opponents of the regime who simply disappeared grew beyond 10,000, reports by Amnesty International and a United States investigatory team condemned the excesses of the military. Nevertheless, the regime continued its deadly work even in the face of international outrage and economic decline. Inflation remained at 150 percent and an attempt to devalue the peso in 1981 led to a run on the currency and an escalating foreign debt. The military's response was to change the face of the man in power. Field Marshal Roberto Eduardo Viola (1924–1994) held office for a few months during the fiscal crisis of 1981 before being replaced by General Leopoldo Fortunato Galtieri (1926–2003). Hoping to mobilize national unity by military means, Galtieri revived an old claim to a few small islands off Argentina's southern shores that had been under British control since 1833. The islands, known as the Malvinas in Argentina and the Falklands in Britain, were home to a small community of sheep herders and were without known economic value. But the Argentine military attacked anyway, temporarily seizing the islands. In the brief Falklands War (April–June 1982) the disputed islands were easily recaptured by British forces, revealing the incompetence of Junta rule. Not surprisingly, the Junta decided to replace Galtieri with yet another officer, Major General Reynaldo Bigone (b. 1929) who was put in charge of the transition to civilian rule.

◆ Democracy in Argentina

Free elections were quickly scheduled, and on October 30, 1983, Raúl Alfonsín (b. 1927) became the president of Argentina. By now the rate of inflation was up to 200 percent. Alfonsín's attempt at fiscal reform and his decision to scrap the peso for a new currency—the *Austral*—failed to prevent inflation from soaring above 1,000 percent. Power cuts of up to six hours a day were imposed in an attempt to save Argentina's dwindling resources. Trade treaties were strengthened between Argentina and her neighbors to encourage investment, but the economy continued to spiral downward. Alfonsín was more successful in opening up Argentina politically, trying to make public the army's role in the disappearance of thousands of Argentine citizens between the years of 1976 and 1983. In 1985, Viola was sentenced to 17 years imprisonment for crimes committed under his regime; Galtieri was imprisoned in 1986. But Alfonsín's failure to cure Argentina's financial woes led to his defeat at the polls in 1989. The Perónist candidate, Carlos Saúl Menem

(b. 1930), a former trade union lawyer and Muslim convert to Roman Catholicism, was President of Argentina from 1989 to 1999. He had the military apologize to the nation for its past excesses, and, in return, he pardoned convicted officers and freed jailed ex-commanders. Equally efficiently, Menem abandoned the traditional socialist policies of the Perónist party for privatization and economic austerity. He balanced the budget, won debt rescheduling, and ended the hyperinflation (now topping 15,000 percent) through a currency reform linked to the value of the dollar. He repaired relations with Britain (1992) and brought Argentina into MERCOSUR (1994), a customs union created by Argentina, Brazil, Paraguay, and Uruguay designed to revitalize the region's economy. But problems with Argentina's foreign debt payments set off a new crisis in 1996. To meet it, Menem persuaded the Congress to grant him emergency powers and the right to increase taxes without Congressional approval. He used his emergency powers more frequently and more widely than intended, to quell prison riots in 1976, to quell labor riots in 1997, and to grant amnesty to former Argentine dictators. The 300 presidential fiats Menem issued totaled more than in all previous Argentine history.

The constitutional changes he had initiated in 1994 barred Menem from running for a third consecutive term as president. With Menem disqualified and the Perónist party in disarray, the moderate candidate, Fernando de la Rua (b. 1937), won the presidential elections of 1999. Having inherited an economy once again spinning out of control, Rua froze savings deposits to prevent a run on the banks, slashed government services, laid off thousands of government employees, and set off a full fledged political crisis. Escaping from the presidential palace by helicopter on December 29, 2001, Rua announced his resignation. When the dust settled in January 2002, Eduardo Duhalde (b. 1942), a long-time Perónist, was the new president of Argentina, selected by an emergency constitutional board to fill out the term until the 2003 elections. With unemployment hovering at 21 percent and Argentina's foreign debt equal to more than half of its Gross Domestic Product (which, at $10,200 per capita, is less than one-third that of the United States), there was little Duhalde could accomplish in that short a time.

As for Menem, now an opposition candidate, he was briefly placed under house arrest in June 2002, for involvement in a conspiracy to smuggle arms to Croatia and Ecuador between 1981 and 1985, in violation of a United Nations' arms embargo. Even so, Menem managed to finish first (with 24 percent of the vote) in the first round of presidential elections in April, 2003. Argentina's constitution stipulates that a presidential run-off be held if no candidate receives over fifty percent of the votes cast. As Menem's popularity began to slip in the public opinion polls, he bowed out of the run-off election in May. That left the way clear for another Perónist, Néstor Carlos Kirchner (b. 1950), who got 22 percent of the vote in the first round, to be sworn in as Argentina's new president on May 25, 2003. If nothing else, Kirchner, a former governor in Patagonia, is an example of the multi-ethnic mix in Argentina; his grandparents came from Switzerland and Germany, and his mother is a Croatian from Chile.

Brazil: A Latin American Super Power?

A land of enormous resources, Brazil occupies a third of the territory in the southern half of the Western Hemisphere and has a coastline of over 4600 miles. Its diverse geography ranges from rain forest to savanna to the Andes Mountains. The main stream of the Amazon River system that bisects it draws its waters from seventeen rivers each longer than Europe's Rhine. Hindered in the nineteenth century by a population too small to exploit its natural wealth, Brazil has experienced a reproductive surge that increased its population from 17,000,000 to 176,000,000 by 2002, and did so with less racial strife than any other mixed population in the Americas. But, despite Brazil's fertile land, mineral wealth, and strategic importance, its chaotic politics have made the nation less influential than it might otherwise have been.

Since achieving independence in 1822, Brazil has struggled to overcome the political stranglehold of the plantation owners who controlled its coffee and rubber resources. Sixty percent of Brazil's farmland was owned by only two percent of its population, and sixty percent of all rural Brazilians held no land at all. But coffee brought in hard currency. For much of the twentieth century between 60 and 75 percent of the world's supply of coffee, was produced by Brazil. Even after world commodity prices collapsed in the Stock Market Crash of 1929 Brazil's political system continued to protect the interests of the growers.

Elected President in 1930 Getulio Vargas (1883–1954) established a new constitution in 1934 that included a secret ballot and extended the vote to women, but these liberal measures were severely undermined when Vargas seized dictatorial power three years later. He looked upon himself as a benevolent despot, and consciously attempted to broaden citizen participation in economic life by limiting the power of the landholding elite. Vargas approved the formation of labor unions and spoke movingly of the *estado novo* that would emerge as his initiatives created new domestic industries. During World War II, Vargas joined his nation with the Allies, expanded Brazil's food exports, and saw it become the largest industrial power in Latin America.

But Vargas also muzzled the press and allowed his secret police to torture his opponents. After fifteen years in power, a bloodless coup by the army forced Vargas into retirement and a democracy was established under the wary eyes of the soldiers. Under the new constitution, an elderly Vargas made a comeback, and in 1950 he once again became president. One of his industrial initiatives was to create *Petrobas* (1953), a national oil-exploration corporation that played an essential role in Brazil's subsequent industrial growth. But Vargas still viewed all political activity as a threat. In 1954, faced again with ouster by the military, Vargas wrote a last will affirming his desire to serve Brazil's poor and then committed suicide.

After the demise of Vargas, Brazil struggled for a decade to find a path between despotism and democracy. A former surgeon, Juscelino Kubitschek (1902–1976), used his presidency (1956–1961) to push construction of a new capital city deep in the interior of the nation. *Brasília* was a planned environment in the heart of undeveloped territory, an administrative center so isolated it could only be reached by airplane until the construction of an entirely new road system. Enormous sums were expended to build Brasília and corruption flourished as the new city took shape. Government lending was also central to the development of Brazil's automobile industry, but Kubitschek, wary of alienating the rich, refused to enact the tax increases his programs demanded. From the late 1950s onward a terrible inflation made the life of Brazil's poorest citizens increasingly intolerable.

United as never before, the voters elected João Goulert (1918–1976) of the Labor Party as President (1961–1964). The son of a wealthy rancher but a protégée of Vargas, Goulert committed the government to progressive social legislation that included land redistribution. The richest Brazilians were outraged with such socialist thinking, and in March 1964 the army once more took control. For the next twenty years, a series of military officers held the office of president and transformed Brazil into a virtual police state indifferent to the welfare of its people as the economy continued to disintegrate.

Despite a solid industrial base and agricultural productivity rivaled only by the United States, Brazilian society suffered from overwhelming disparities in personal income, endemic inflation, and a foreign debt that ranked among the world's largest. By 1984 the military was ready to admit it could not solve those problems and allowed voters to elect Tancredo de Almeida Neves (1910-1985) as president. But he was so ill by the time it came for him to take office in March 1985, that

Getúlio Vargas surrounded by the officers whose coup brought him to power in Brazil.
Copyright © CORBIS/Bettmann

his vice president, José Sarney Costa (b. 1930) had to step in as acting president. After Almeida's death on April 21, 1985, Sarney became Brazil's next constitutional president. His 1988 constitution promised liberal reform but did nothing to help Brazil's tenant farmers.

Thousands of desperate farmers began burning down irreplaceable rain forests in order to obtain enough land for independent farming, while millions more moved into Brazil's coastal cities in search of jobs. Their influx into São Paolo created the largest city (16.5 million people) in Latin America, and also one of the most polluted metropolitan areas in the world.

Brazil's transition to democracy resulted in limited but clearly defined progress. In 1989 Brazil organized a plan to salvage the Amazon it had almost destroyed. As part of this change from destroying to preserving its environment, Brazil played host to the 1992 United Nations Earth Summit. There, the Brazilian government criticized rich nations for having a double standard. Having polluted the world while they industrialized, rich countries like the United States now wanted Third World countries to bear the extra expense of having to develop economically without pollution. Brazil challenged the First World to offer alternate plans for Third World growth instead of just lamenting the loss of the rain forest. That same year a consortium of banks arranged the restructuring of Brazil's foreign debt. This removed the terrible threat of default from the political agenda. Although one president died and another was removed for corruption, the constitutional structure adopted in 1984 has proven workable. The inclination of the military to intervene in politics has apparently ended. After his inauguration in 1994, President Fernando Henrique Cardoso (b. 1931), founder of Brazil's center-left Social Democratic Party and a former prisoner under the Junta, managed to reduce both inflation and population growth to below two percent. But he failed to reduce the power of the landlords who control water rights and agriculture in much of Brazil's north. Landless people are both hungry and angry, and the threat of open class conflict is always present. Under its current President, Luiz Ignácio Lula da Silva (b. 1945), a former trade unionist inaugurated January 1, 2003, Brazil remains a country whose Gross Domestic Product per capita is only $7,400. At least twenty-eight percent of its population is under the age of fifteen, and the average life expectancy is only 63.5 years.

Mexico: From Revolution to Democracy

Between 1910 and 1920 over a million Mexicans died in a series of revolutions and civil wars. In 1917, a new constitution was imposed by President Venestiano Carranza (1859–1920) in a move to end the bloodbath by extending economic liberties to Mexico's poor and illiterate population. The two most significant articles of the 1917 Constitution asserted Mexico's national ownership of its mineral, water and sub-soil property resources, and the right of workers to organize. Although Carranza's constitution exalted Mexico's Aztec heritage and praised the glories of *la rasa cosmica* ("the heavenly race"), it kept political power in the hands of the middle classes acting through a strong executive. After a decade of revolution, stability was the condition most desired in Mexico. But despite constitutional guarantees, violence continued to plague Mexican political life with terrible regularity and little was done to actually transfer land from the plantation owners to their tenant farmers. Within a few years of the revolution's end, the mestizo agricultural reformer Emiliano Zapata (1879–1919), the populist rebel Pancho Villa (1878–1923), and Carranza himself were all murdered. Carranza's successor, President Alvaro Obregón (1880-1928) temporarily stabilized the currency by imposing a small tax on the extraction of Mexican oil by foreign corporations, but he failed to curb the political influence of the military before he, too, was assassinated by political opponents.

The man who established the autocratic-democratic tradition that still dominates Mexican political life was Plutarco Elías Calles (1877–1945), a former elementary school teacher and Obregón's handpicked successor. President Calles authorized the creation of a Bank of Mexico, pushed rural road and irrigation projects to completion, and set up a national education system. He was a militant secularist who carried on a long feud with the Roman Catholic hierarchy. Angered by the government's efforts to secularize education and strip the Church of its social and economic power, the Catholic Church closed thousands of its doors and suspended administration of the sacraments to all Mexican Catholics for over two years. Calles focused his governmental reforms on reducing the political activities of army officers, and by 1929 he forced the military into obedience to civilian control. Most vitally, Calles created the *Partido National Revolucionario* (PNR) in 1929. The PNR became the one arena in which political debate was permitted. President Calles merged government bureaucrats, landholders, the growing industrial bourgeoisie, and professionals into a single middle class coalition that had the power to determine Mexico's destiny. The PNR immediately won popular support by confirming all the land seizures peasants had made during the revolution. The Mexican process of land redistribution led many critics, including fearful commentators in the United States, to conclude that Calles' middle-class party was in fact Bolshevik.

After a decade in office, Calles personally selected a president to succeed him and complete the social revolution he had organized. A mestizo, Lázaro Cárdenas (1895–1970) was committed to using the powers of the presidency on behalf of ordinary Mexicans. Although he was not formally a Marxist, Cárdenas did nationalize the railroad system in 1937 in the belief that only public ownership could improve its irregular service. He purged his administration of Calles's men, ended the unofficial persecution of the Church, and built an extensive social welfare system. His government accelerated the breaking up of large landed estates and their distribution to the tenant families who had farmed them for centuries. By 1940 Cárdenas had given away 45 million acres to 750,000 rural farmers and 500 communal corporations.

Cárdenas was determined to act against foreign economic penetration, and in March 1938 he fulfilled the pledge made by Article 27 of the Constitution of 1917 and ordered the nationalization of foreign oil holdings in Mexico. He chose his time well. The industrialized world was awash in oil and his closest neighbor, the United States, could not retaliate because of the Good Neighbor Policy of the Roosevelt Administration. Mexico, under President Cárdenas, became the first developing nation to move against Western economic exploitation. National pride soared after the nationalization and hardly faltered even when American corporations were compensated with $24 million and the British government settled its claims for $80 million. A Mexican corporation, PEMEX, was created to develop national oil reserves and the availability of cheap energy made great contributions to Mexico's industrial development.

Cárdenas also transformed the PNR from a loose federation of state-wide organizations into a truly national party. Eventually renamed the *Partido Revolucionario Institucional* (PRI), it dominated Mexican politics until the end of the twentieth century. Under the leadership of the PRI, Mexico enjoyed the longest period of political stability of any Latin country. But its system of absolute presidential authority for one six-year term could hardly be called democratic when combined with the ability to select one's successor. In 1940 Cárdenas not only selected Manuel Avila Camacho (1897–1955) as his successor, but also manipulated the votes to guarantee his election, as Camacho did in 1946 for Miguel Aleman Valdes (1902-1983), and Aleman did in 1952 for Adolfo Ruiz Cortines (1889–1973), and Ruiz did in 1958 for Adolfo López Mateos (1910–1969). During the extended PRI era, Mexicans outside the protective umbrella of the ruling elite often charged that elections were stolen. Beginning in the 1960s opponents mounted well organized challenges to PRI candidates in gubernatorial elections, but those first attempts ended in failure. The resulting political frustration caused large public demonstrations against the 1964–1970 regime of President Gustavo Díaz Ordaz (1911–1979). In October 1968, the army crushed such a protest just before the Olympic Games were held in Mexico City. Perhaps as many as a thousand university students died in the ensuing violence. The president selected to succeed Ordaz, Luis Echeverría Alvarez (b. 1922), was the official responsible for unleashing the military crackdown. During his administration (1970–1976) tourism collapsed as Mexico adopted more socialist and militantly Third World policies. But the growth of Mexico's population beyond the 100 million mark made general economic progress difficult. Not even the discovery of vast oil reserves was able to reverse the downward trend of the Mexican economy, while border tensions with the United States increased due to the emigration of Mexican nationals northward.

Beginning in 1977, successive PRI presidents, José López Portillo (1920-2004), Miguel de la Madrid (b. 1934) and Carlos Salinas de Gortari (b. 1948) struggled to normalize Mexico's difficult relationship with the United States. When President de la Madrid left office, Mexico's public debt had become second only to that of Brazil's among developing nations. Mexico City, with a population of over 20 million, had become one of the most polluted and dangerous capitals in the world. Police corruption was endemic, and there were rumors of official government participation in the drug trade. Salinas, a Harvard educated economist, was elected president in 1988, but the vote was again tinged with fraud. To restore the troubled economy, Salinas sold off hundreds of state corporations, arrested corrupt union leaders, and signed the *North American Free Trade Agreement* (NAFTA) with the United States in 1993. He promised action against drug lords and permitted free elections that returned three governors from opposition parties. Yet during his term, evidence of police and military involvement in drugs was unearthed. Salinas's tenure ended in scandal as his candidate for president was assassinated, his brother arrested for murder, and his family accounts found to contain $100 million that could not be accounted for. In January 1994, a revolutionary movement called the Zapatistas emerged in the Indian lands in Chiapas province in southern Mexico. The on-going insurrection indicates the immense frustration of the Mexican underclass and ethnic-Indian minority.

PRI Presidential candidate Luis Donaldo Colosio Murrieta (1948-1994) was assassinated on March 23, 1994, and replaced by his campaign manager Ernesto Zedillo Ponce de Léon (b. 1951). Before Zedillo could be inaugurated in December, trouble over the election for governor in Chiapas province further exacerbated that rebellion. One of Zedillo's first actions was to issue an arrest warrant for the self-styled "Sub-Commander Marcos," identified as Rafael Sebastián Guillén Vicente (b. 1957), a former part-time professor who leads the Zapatistas. The Zapatista National Liberation Army (ELZN) claims that they do not intend to impose socialism. Rather, they demand full enforcement of the land laws of the 1917 Constitution, which they see as subverted by the PRI. Peace accords were signed by the ELZN and the Mexican government in 1996 recognizing Zapatista claims for land reform, but Zedillo reneged on the deal six months later under pressure from the World Bank. He sent 60,000 troops into Chiapas and continued to wage a low-level war against sporadic guerrilla attacks.

A Yale-trained economist from a working class family in Mexicali, Zedillo served as education and finance minister under Salinas. As President, Zedillo saved the deteriorating economy by devaluing the peso and negotiating an emergency loan from the United States. Mexico's reviving industrial base was ranked thirteenth in the world by 1998. In 1997, after the PRI lost control of the lower house of the Mexican legislature, Zedillo not only accepted the results but promised that voters in the presidential election of 2000 would have a free choice of candidates. The winner in the 2000 presidential elections was Vicente Fox Quesada (b. 1942), leader of the National Action Party (PAN). The PAN also won two governorships and a controlling majority in Congress. After 71 years in power, the PRI is now a minority party. Fox, a rancher and former chief executive officer of Coca-Cola in Mexico, immediately reached out to strengthen Mexico's economic ties to the United States. A European Union-Mexican free trade agreement heralded closer ties between Mexico and the EU; the agreement phases out tariffs on over 95 percent of Mexico's European trade. This nation of 103 million people has made great progress but many problems remain. While its an average life expectancy is 72, its Gross Domestic Product per capita is only $9,000, trailing behind those of Argentina and Chile.

The Caribbean: The Cold War's Last Battlefield

◆ Cuba

A series of revolutions in Cuba, by the army, labor leaders, and students throughout the first half of the twentieth century ended with former Cuban President Fulgencio Batista (1901–1973) seizing control of the government in 1952. Declaring himself "anti-communist" won Batista acceptance by the United States if not by most Cubans. Fidel Castro (b. 1926) launched his first revolution against Batista's government in 1953, but it took him five more years to unite the various factions opposing Batista and to stage a triumphant march into the Cuban capital (Havana)

Castro leading the guerilla insurrection that seized power in Cuba in 1959.
Copyright © AP/Wide World Photos

on New Year's Day in 1959. The United States was second only to Venezuela in recognizing the legitimacy of Castro's revolution, but by the end of January Castro was already forging closer ties with the Soviet Union. Castro's suspension of the Cuban Parliament and expropriation of a billion dollars of American corporate wealth led to President Eisenhower's decision to sever diplomatic relations with Cuba just before his term ended in January 1961. He also approved plans to oust Castro using Cuban exiles trained by the CIA. Newly inaugurated President John F. Kennedy let the exiles make their move that April only to have the attack (on the Bay of Pigs) routed by Cuba's defense forces. Humiliated by the failure, Kennedy resorted to economic pressure, pledging $10 billion in aid as part of an "Alliance for Progress" to members of the Organization of American States (OAS) in exchange for their willingness to exclude Cuba from membership and join the United States in an economic blockade of Cuba.

Dependent on Soviet economic support and afraid of further American military action, Castro agreed to let the Soviet Union position Medium and Intermediate Range Nuclear Missiles in Cuba, setting off the most nerve-racking crisis of the Cold War, the Cuban Missile Crisis of October 1962. American discovery of the construction of missile launchers led to a standoff: United States blockaded Cuba, the Soviet Union said it would fire on ships whose crews tried to board Soviet vessels, and the United States threatened to launch a nuclear strike in retaliation. The USSR eventually removed its missiles in return for an American pledge not to invade Cuba, but US economic sanctions remained in place.

Castro planned to transform Cuba into a Socialist state, but as early as 1962 the failure of his modernization program and the bite of economic sanctions convinced him that an industrial economy was impossible. Growing diversified agricultural foodstuffs for the world market became Cuba's new goal, but the island gradually returned to its traditional dependence on sugar cane production. After 1975 almost all collective farms focused on this single crop and the revenues produced by sugar exports to Soviet bloc nations. By the 1980s only vast monetary subsidies from Moscow kept the island economy from collapse. In order to reduce Cuba's economic burdens, Castro's army was mobilized to support Soviet Cold War aims in venues such as Ethiopia and Angola; Cuban troops remained in Angola from 1975 until 1988.

The collapse of the Soviet Union in 1991 led to the withdrawal of its economic aid from Cuba and the collapse of the Cuban economy, but the charismatic Castro convinced his people that only America's sanctions, not the defects of his economic planning, kept the island from prospering.

Castro has become the longest reigning ruler in Latin American history. Support for his social reforms has rarely flagged in Cuba, and there are still thousands of dedicated Committees for the Defense of the Revolution located on virtually every block that enforce his decrees. In most areas of human development Cuba set the standard for the entire Latin world. Health and medical reforms initiated by Castro greatly improved the quality of life for most Cubans. Average life expectancy increased from 58 to 76 years during his regime, bringing Cuba very close to the 77.5 average life expectancy enjoyed by the United States. Dedicated teachers soon raised literacy rates to 96 percent, the highest in Latin America. Enormous sums were expended on athletic facilities and performances by Cuba's Olympic athletes thrilled a global audience. Although many rich businessmen had fled the revolution for exile in the United States, the standard of living for the island population improved markedly as long as Soviet aid poured in. In the years since the fall of the Soviet Union, the GDP per capita has plummeted to $2,300, making Cuba one of the poorest nations in the region. Cuba, with a population of 15,500,000, does not possess the oil revenues available to other Latin states, and is hindered by a traditional one-crop economy. Nevertheless, Castro has accomplished more for the well-being of his people than any other regional leader.

Cuba remains socialist in its economics but it is Castro's unique blend of charisma and authority, not his failed materialist philosophy, that has kept his revolution alive for over forty years.

Kennedy's 1962 pledge not to invade Cuba has been honored, but having a Russian ally so close to the United States was a continuing irritant. American interventions in Santo Domingo (1964), Grenada (1983), and even in Haiti during the 1990s were in part driven by fears that "another Castro" might appear. Throughout the 1980s the United States supported the Contra rebellion against the socialist Sandinista government in Nicaragua on the same grounds. The United States, home to many Cuban refugees, paid far more attention to Castro's revolutionary rhetoric than to his more careful diplomacy. But it was undeniable that his chief aide, Che Guevara (1928–1967), died while attempting to foment a popular uprising in Bolivia. Moreover, Mexico's neutrality during the Cold War years was in part due to the fear that Castro-sympathizers might stimulate the simmering discontent of its Indian peoples. Castro manipulated American anxieties in 1980 when he permitted over 100,000 "opponents" of his regime to leave Cuba in a boat-lift to Miami. The "freedom flotilla" allowed Castro to dump derelicts, criminals, the aged, the infirm, and a few free-thinkers on the United States. Castro has always attempted to mobilize regional opinion against continuing American sanctions, and in January 1998 even Pope John Paul II agreed that the world ought to "open itself" to Cuba. Almost fifty years after the success of the revolution, the survival of socialism in Castro's Cuba continues to irritate the United States.

◆   Nicaragua

The second most significant extension of socialism in the Caribbean occurred in Nicaragua during the 1980s. The United States actually occupied that nation from 1926 to 1933, and cooperated with the Somoza dynasty that ruled it afterwards. In 1979, however, a coalition of reformers (the Sandinista National Liberation Front, or FSLN) that included both Roman Catholic and socialist elements succeeded in ousting Somoza and initiating major changes in the political system. In Washington, the administration (1981–1989) of President Ronald Reagan believed that the Sandinista program drew support from Cuba, and was ultimately directed by Moscow. American money was provided to finance a Nicaraguan opposition movement called the Contras, whose goal was to prevent the spread of socialist ideology into new areas of Central America. Daniel Ortega Saavedra (b. 1945), a former bank robber and Sandinista leader elected president in 1984, faced American armed guerrilla forces, harbors mined by the CIA, and economic isolation. The conflict widened to involve both Honduras and El Salvador before a Washington scandal over improperly funded military aid to the Contras forced the United States to pull back from confrontation. Arbitration by Latin nations, and especially work by President Oscar Arias Sánchez (b. 1941) of Costa Rica, ultimately eased the conflict and fostered free elections. In 1990, Violetta Barrios de Chamorro (b. 1929) became president of Nicaragua, and the Sandinistas lost control of the national assembly. Violence, and the inefficiency of the Sandinistas, had wrecked the Nicaraguan economy and the freely cast votes of frustrated voters ended their regime. In 1996, Ortega reemerged as the FSLN candidate for president but was defeated by the conservative politician Arnoldo Alumna (b. 1946). Ortega ran again, and lost again (with 42.3 percent of the vote), in the 2001 elections. With 56.3 percent of the vote Enrique Bolanos Geyer (b. 1928), leader of the PLC (Liberal Alliance Party), a right-center coalition of several parties, became Nicaragua's next president in January 2002. Nicaragua's transition to democracy appears complete, but President Bolanos faces a greater challenge economically. Despite its substantial mineral resources, including gold, Nicaragua's population of 5,024,000 is among the poorest in Latin American with a

Gross Domestic Product per capita of $2,500. With 38.3 percent of its population under fifteen years old and an infant mortality rate of 39.52 deaths per thousand live births, making this economy productive will be a daunting task.

◆ Haiti

Haiti is the second-oldest independent state in the Western Hemisphere. Once a rich agricultural breadbasket, Haiti literally saw its land flow into the sea as a result of antiquated agricultural methods. Politically, the situation was no more stable. Between 1843 and 1915, Haiti had over 25 different constitutions and suffered through 102 coups. United States Marines occupied Haiti from 1915 to1934 in a move designed to protect the approaches to the Panama Canal but, after the Good Neighbor Policy mandated their removal, Haiti resumed its anarchic politics. Stability was achieved in 1957 when Dr. François Duvalier (1907–1971) assumed dictatorial power with the tacit approval of the United States. "Papa Doc" claimed to have no enemies except those of the nation, but if he had no living enemies, it was because he eliminated all such foes by using a secret police called the *Tontons Macoutes*. After completing his first term as president in 1961, Duvalier was reelected by a vote of 1,320,748 to zero. He soon was "President for Life," and in 1971 changed the constitution to permit his son, Jean-Claude Duvalier (b. 1951), to succeed him. But "Baby Doc," as Jean-Claude was called, was forced to flee the island in February 1986. Unfortunately, the end of the Duvalier regime did not improve Haitian government.

Haitian politics has often been a struggle between mulatto middle classes and the vastly larger black and poorer masses. In 1990, in an internationally supervised election, 67 percent of the electorate chose a former priest and advocate of social reform to be their president. Jean-Bertrand Aristide (b. 1953) pledged social revolution, attacked the military, and promised to "cleanse the bureaucracy" while redistributing Haiti's wealth. But his *Lavalas* ("torrent") movement appeared to condone violence and assassination. Within less than a year Aristide was overthrown by a military coup and fled to the United States. As Haitian politicians fell once again into bickering, Aristide maneuvered to gain international support for his ousted regime. In October 1994 he was restored to office by joint United Nations-United States intervention. After completing his term, he officially retired but was accused of undercutting the authority of his elected successor René Préval (b. 1943) who won 87 percent of the vote in the December 1995 elections. Aristide returned to office in 2001 after garnering 91.69 percent of the vote in elections boycotted by the opposition parties because of the violence directed against them during the run up to the campaign.

After almost two centuries of independence, no more than 45 percent of Haiti's population of 7,064,000 is literate. The infant mortality rate is 93.35 deaths per thousand live births, average life expectancy has dropped to 49.55 years, and almost six percent of the adult population is HIV positive. Foreign investment has fled its chaotic economy, and its GDP per capita ($1,700) is the lowest on the continent.

Haiti notwithstanding, Latin American states have made considerable economic and political progress in the decades since World War Two. Despite Castro's continued presence, the *caudillo* style of authoritarian rule personified by Perón, Vargas, and Duvalier and a score of other military leaders has almost vanished from the region. The military have retreated to their barracks and accepted the limitations of constitutional rule. Whether this reflects a permanent change is yet uncertain, because Latin America carries the deserved reputation of having the most convulsive politics in the world: Venezuela and the Dominican Republic alone have had 57 different constitutions between them. Still, Chile ended seventeen years of military rule under General Augusto

Demonstrators call former President Pinochet to account for the prisoners who "disappeared" during military rule in Chile.
Copyright © UPI/Bettmann News Photos

Pinochet (b. 1915) in 1990, and the debilitating strife in Central America seems to have ended. In December 1996 a peace treaty brought an end to 36 years of civil war in Guatemala. The Dominican Republic held free elections in 1996 and 2000. On the other hand, massive strikes in Venezuela brought that country's government to a standstill in 2003, and Bolivia President Gonzalo Sanchez de Lozada (b. 1930) was forced to resign in October 2003 after weeks of protests over food shortages created by his free-market policies.

Those protests are a reminder that Latin American countries still face tremendous economic and social problems—regional trade disputes, pollution, the drug trade, land redistribution, endemic poverty—but as the new millennium began their prospects were higher than at any time since their independence two centuries ago.

◆ Note

1. *Weekly Compilation of Presidential Papers*, 12/25/89.

14

The Twentieth-Century Legacy

The modern world was born in revolutions scientific, national, and industrial. The values those revolutions embodied were spread by the steam engine, the railroad, and the machine gun until there was no place in the world where they were not known, if not always adopted. But the meaning of those words and the societies in which they were born continue to change. What seemed modern in the nineteenth century may be antique today. The only constant seems to be the increasing pace of change. In the twentieth century, humanity added more to its accumulated knowledge than in any previous period of history. We split the atom, landed on the moon, and began deciphering the genetic code. We created vaccines against smallpox, polio, mumps, measles, chicken pox, diphtheria, and tetanus. Our surgeons routinely transplanted corneas, livers, kidneys, bone marrow, and hearts. Lasers facilitated the most delicate brain surgery. Cochlear implants, pacemakers, and artificial valves and joints are turning us into bionic men and women.

But our most heralded triumphs created as many questions as they solved. In 1962, two molecular biologists, Francis Crick (1916-2004) of Great Britain and James Watson (b. 1928) of the United States won the Nobel Prize for their discovery of the double-helix structure of DNA, the genetic code inside every life form. In the decades since their first discoveries in 1953, their work has been used to bio-engineer high-yield, disease-resistant rice in the fight against world hunger, to create sophisticated anti-retro-viral agents in the war against AIDS, to determine guilt or innocence in criminal cases, and to clone animals. A major effort of the Human Genome Project is to identify the genetic variants that predispose people to diseases such as schizophrenia or cancer, but at a conference held in Washington, DC, in July 2001, a debate broke out between the scientists over what would be done with their data. While many genetic variants are uniformly spread throughout the human race, some are linked to different human populations. Fears have been raised that a new form of Social Darwinism might emerge if records were kept of the ethnicity of people donating their DNA for mapping. Other debates have opened up over the possibility of cloning humans and the use of embryonic stem cells in the treatment of genetically transmitted diseases; both challenge some of our most commonly held religious values. The ultimate legacy of the discovery of DNA is its power to alter human evolution.

This chapter looks at the complex legacy—in science, human rights, population, and economic integration—that the twentieth century has left to the twenty-first.

The DNA "Double-Helix," demonstrated by Watson and Crick, opened new biological possibilities, 1953.
Copyright © A. Barrington Brown/Science Source/Photo Researchers, Inc.

Twentieth-Century Science and the Universe of Uncertainty

◆ Physics

The accomplishments of nineteenth-century medicine and technology gave rise to an attitude of confidence and certainty in western culture. While the theories of Lyell and Darwin depicted an ever-changing universe, that change was seen to occur in a discoverable fashion and was popularly believed to be progressive in nature. Evolution was seen as a process of improvement. The work of

Röntgen, Becquerel, and the Curies demonstrated that the world was not so certain a place. Atoms, presumed to be the basic building blocks of all matter, were not necessarily stable. Radioactivity was, after all, evidence of atomic degeneration. Radioactivity seemed to violate the accepted immutability of elements and the assumed distinction between matter and energy. But this aspect of late nineteenth-century physics did not travel beyond the confines of the scientific community to capture the imagination of the general population in the way that Darwin's theories had done. To the world at large, the discoveries in physics were seen chiefly as new medical therapies—the x-ray, chemotherapy—available to the local physician. They were seen as proof of the increasing certainty of medicine rather than as evidence of an uncertain universe. The work of Albert Einstein (1879–1955) and his successors changed that perception.

The son of a German Jewish electrical engineer

Einstein's theories dominated the physics of the 20th Century.
Copyright © American Institute of Physics/Niels Bohr Library

in Switzerland, Einstein had given little evidence of genius during his school days. Unable to find a university post, this graduate of the Swiss Polytechnic Institute supported his family as a patent office clerk. Yet in 1905, at the age of 26, he published three articles in the same issue of the *Annals of Physics* that altered the history of the century (and won him the 1921 Nobel Prize in Physics). The third essay became the Theory of Special Relativity.

Science had already shown that light moved in a straight line and at a constant speed no matter the vantage point. But from this fact, Einstein drew seemingly outrageous conclusions. He demonstrated that, when observed, a moving clock ran more slowly than a stationary one and a moving object shrank in the direction of the motion of light. He used the example of two strokes of lightning hitting a railway embankment at two equidistant points, one in front of and one behind a train moving at a constant speed. An observer outside the train would see the two strokes strike the embankment at the same time, but for someone in the moving train, the front stroke would seem to hit the embankment first. Although such distinctions were important only for objects moving close to the speed of light, Einstein had shown time to be relative. Space, he concluded, was also relative, since the length of material bodies could not be objectively measured, being dependent on the speed at which they were moving in relation to the observer. Time and space were not separate entities but rather joined in a continuum, and both were relative to the position and speed of the measurer. Almost as an afterthought, Einstein added that energy and matter were not different things but different states of the same thing. Indeed, matter could be converted into energy as expressed in the famous formula $E=MC^2$. Matter was stored (latent) energy. Since the energy contained in any object was enormous relative to its mass, a small object could potentially release a tremendous amount of energy. In this formulation the Atomic Age was born.

Einstein now had no difficulty finding a professorial position. At the University of Prague in 1911, he began to assess the workings of gravity within such a world and soon proposed his General Theory of Relativity (1915). His theory can be approached by thinking of objects placed on a rubber sheet: the weight of the objects will cause the sheet to sag. Thus creating a "dimple," or a curve within space/time. Other objects passing by this depression would then roll into it: hence, gravity. Einstein's prediction that light waves were also subject to the force of gravity was proven correct in 1919 by measurements made during an eclipse of the sun. Suddenly Einstein was an international celebrity.

In 1900, Max Planck (1858–1947) had stunned the German Physical Society by presenting a Quantum Theory that challenged all assumptions about the natural world. As he studied the light effects of radiation, Planck noticed the absence of high-frequency light waves and suggested that the exchange of energy between mass and radiation occurred not in a steady stream, but in discrete impulses (quanta). In a sense, the entire universe was blinking on and off. Moreover, such emissions of energy occurred in unpredictable patterns. While Planck's theories caused a great stir in the scientific community, they were not paid much attention in the mass media until Einstein's theories had captured the popular imagination. But even Einstein was disturbed by Planck's work. Einstein found it impossible to believe that the unpredictable whims of subatomic particles could create our intricate universe, and spent most of the rest of his life attempting to find a "Unified Field Theory" that would resolve the seeming contradictions of the laws of gravity and electromagnetism. "The Lord God is subtle," he said, "but malicious he is not." "I shall never believe that God plays dice with the world."[1]

Still more unsettling was the Uncertainty Principle proposed by the German physicist Werner Heisenberg (1901-1976). In 1927, Heisenberg noted it was impossible in principle to simultaneously locate and determine the speed of very small and fast moving sub-atomic particles; the very fact of their being observed would alter their velocity. The science that had once offered certainty was now reduced to substituting relative probability.

◆ Psychology

The nineteenth century had not only inherited a physics of certainty from the Enlightenment, it had also inherited a psychology of rationality. The *philosophes* had seen the human mind as a machine reacting to physical stimuli in a calculating and mechanical fashion. Adam Smith had written of the enlightened (educated) self-interest that underpinned the social division of labor (and was best left unregulated by governments). Jeremy Bentham had written of a "calculus of pleasure" (or, utility). The Romantic Reaction of the nineteenth century had stressed the emotional side of human nature, but had never been able to displace that basic faith in rationality. Auguste Comte and the positivists placed their faith in a human intellectual evolution as guaranteed as that of the Social Darwinists. The work of Sigmund Freud (1856-1939) upset that presumption of certainty as completely as Einstein's destroyed the notion of a fixed universe.

Freud, a lecturer in neuropathology at the University of Vienna, was deeply interested in aspects of the mind that seemed to operate *outside* the control of conscious thought. While using hypnosis to treat "hysteria" (a catchall term for symptoms without apparent physical causes), he found that hypnotic trances often brought out forgotten memories of youthful experiences in his subjects. These memories seemed connected to the hysterical symptoms. Freud speculated that there was an unconscious part of the mind that had a greater potential effect on waking behavior than did rational mentality. His first book, *Studies in Hysteria* (1895), suggested that doctors might be able to focus on the source of a patient's ailment by a method of "free association" (the "talking cure"). Further research led Freud to conclude that dreams depicted, in symbolic form, the desires and conflicts of the unconscious elements of the mind. In *The Interpretation of Dreams* (1899), Freud argued that there were no accidents in mental processes and that the struggle between the conscious and unconscious mind had to be interpreted by an expert analyst. Continuing his work, Freud gradually developed a picture of a human mind divided into three parts: the *Ego* (the mediating center of reason), the *Superego* (the internalized restraints of society), and the *Id* (the "primitive" sexual and aggressive drives). In *Civilization and Its Discontents* (1930), Freud argued that the conflict between humanity's unconscious animal drives and the constraints of society not only caused a vast number of neuroses in troubled people but also threatened civilization itself. Freud argued that the *Id*'s lust for violence could explain why war was so endemic in human history.

Almost from the start, the psychoanalytic movement was divided into factions. Freud's own students remained divided over which "animal" drives played the greatest role in shaping the human personality, the extent to which childhood repression was the key to adult behavior, and the extent to which humans exhibited a "collective" (ethnic, national, or racial) as well as an individual personality. Many of the conditions studied by Freud and his students have also been found to have chemical causes. The modern psychiatrist uses magnetic resonance imaging, psychotropic drugs, electromagnetic shock, and laser surgery as well as Freud's "talking cure." Today, when psychotherapy is used, it is as likely be the short-term behavioral approach as the classic Freudian variety. But the impact of Freud's theories on the wider cultural consciousness remains; people still talk about "Freudian slips," "repression," and "sublimation."

◆ The Existential World

The advances in physics and psychology over the last decades of the nineteenth and first decades of the twentieth did not so much shape the collective consciousness of the twentieth century as reflect it. Though there had been a reaction in the artistic avant garde against nineteenth century optimism and confidence before the turn of the century, the general public did not lose its rose colored glasses until the outbreak of World War One. The inability of the great powers to avoid a global conflagration over the nationalist aspirations of a petty Balkan province, the pointless and ceaseless slaughter in the trenches of the Western Front, the attacks on civilians in violation of all

SIGMUND FREUD (1856–1939)

Sigmund Freud was born into a family of Jewish wool merchants on May 6, 1856, in Freiburg, Moravia, then part of the Austrian Empire. In 1860, Jakob and Amalie Freud took their family to Vienna, but because Jews did not have full political rights in Austria, they settled in the Jewish ghetto. When Freud entered medical school in Vienna, he had to abandon plans to become a research scientist because a quota system limited the number of Jews who could enter the field. He became, instead, a practicing physician interested in mental and emotional problems. Such maladies were then called "nervous" conditions, because people and science believed that unknown nerve damage or brain lesions caused the symptoms. Trying to earn enough money to marry Martha Bernaus, Freud became an aggressive researcher on his own. In 1884, he began testing cocaine's possibilities as a therapeutic drug, impressed by the euphoria it produced. Not knowing it was addictive, he used himself as an experimental subject, but, luckily, never became addicted.

In 1885, Freud went to Paris to study under Jean Martin Charcot (1825–1893), who was using hypnosis to relieve the tremors and paralysis of a malady known as hysteria (symptoms without discernible physical causes). He returned to Austria in 1886, finally well-enough established to marry his Martha. Freud now began to work with Joseph Breuer (1842–1925) whose daily discussions with a young woman suffering from hysterical paralysis (Anna O) suggested her problems arose from repressed childhood fears about sex. In 1895, Freud and Breuer published *Studies in Hysteria,* explaining their new method of "free association."

After the death of his father in 1896, Freud set about analyzing their relationship. His famed book, *The Interpretation of Dreams* (1899), contains the fruits of this analysis. The volume presented to the world his ideas about the complex nature of the unconscious mind, whose drives and fears emerge in disguised form when sleep eliminates the barriers between the rational mind and irrational self. Among his many works were *Three Essays on Sexuality* (1905) discussing the oral, anal, and phallic stages of a child's sexual development, and *The Ego and the Id* (1923) summing up his theory of the tri-partite (Id, Ego, Superego) mind.

The devastation of European society during World War I (1914–1918) helped Freud's ideas about human irrationality gain acceptance. Freud wrote pessimistically of human nature in *Civilization and its Discontents* (1930), but failed to recognize true evil when it threatened his own family. On March 13, 1938, Hitler's forces moved into Austria, but Freud, believing his renown protected him from harm, at first refused to leave. Even after the Nazis ransacked his house, he held to his belief that Nazism was a fleeting excess. Only after his daughter Anna was arrested and briefly held by the Gestapo, did Freud agree to leave his home for exile in London. He was not allowed to take his sisters out of the country, and they eventually died in German concentration camps.

Physicians cannot always cure themselves. Freud successfully overcame a travel phobia but never could cure himself of his addiction to cigars, even after multiple operations for cancer of the mouth. He died in England on September 23, 1939, after deliberately taking a lethal dose of morphine to end the pain of his now inoperable cancer.

the supposed rules of civilization, the overwhelming economic devastation and political stagnation of the eventual peace—all these made the modern mind receptive to the idea of a universe of uncertainty and irrationality.

Two schools of thought developed in reaction to the postwar malaise of the 1920s and the 1930s: existentialism and logical positivism. Each, in its own way, tried to find meaning in what

Explorer of the unconscious mind and founder of Psychoanalysis.
Copyright © Bildarchiv Preussischer Kulturbesitz

seemed to be a random universe. Existentialists embraced the pointlessness of the universe in order to throw down the gauntlet of moral action before it. Existentialism saw people not as finished beings, but as individuals in a state of becoming, obliged to act, to become engaged in life, in order to create their own identities. The French novelist and playwright Jean-Paul Sartre (1905-1980), probably the best known existentialist, believed that we were nothing else but what we made of ourselves. Existentialism was most closely associated in Western Europe with anti-Fascist resistance during World War II and Socialist politics after 1945. "Existence precedes essence" was the existential sound-bite of the undergraduate in the 1960s, but "action creates essence" is a truer summation of existential philosophy.

Existentialism was more of a popular movement than an academic philosophy. Logical positivism, in contrast, was always more influential inside academia than out, but it was equally a response to the seemingly insoluble problem of creating meaning out of an ever-shifting universe. The solution proposed by the logical positivists was to refine ethics into logical propositions as verifiable and reliable as mathematical equations. The founders were Bertrand Russell (1871–1970) and Alfred North Whitehead (1861–1947), two professors at Britain's Cambridge University. Their *Principia Mathematica* (1910–1913) attempted to eliminate imprecision in mathematical logic itself.

These movements echoed through every aspect of modern culture. The French author Marcel Proust (1871–1922) produced the multi-volume *Remembrance of Things Past* (1909–1919), which was both a detailed exposition of past experiences and a study of subjective memory. Proust's masterpiece was the first of the stream of consciousness novels, works in which the thoughts of the protagonist were strung together on the page as casually as in the human mind, in an obvious response to Freudian insights. The most famous practitioner of this technique was the Irish author James Joyce (1882–1941). Joyce's *Ulysses* (1922) was an examination of the lives and thoughts of ordinary Dubliners on one uneventful day in June 1904. The title, an ironic reference to Homer's hero, implied that all of us were on a personal odyssey. The book's uninhibited sexual content led to its being banned in several countries, although its multi-page sentences strung together with little or no punctuation have long caused it to be more referred to than actually read.

An art gallery browser in 1950 could choose between the melting clocks of the Spanish surrealist Salvador Dali (1904–1989), the prismatic fragmentation of a cubist painting by fellow Spaniard Pablo Picasso (1881–1973), the syncopated lines and squares of a geometric painting by Dutch artist Piet Mondrian (1872–1944), and the splattered canvases of the American abstract expressionist Jackson Pollock (1912–1956). Art had turned inward, away from the meaningless universe, to reflect back upon itself. A visit to symphony hall might bring the violent rhythms and unusual beats used by Russian composer Igor Stravinsky (1882–1971) to convey primitive emotions in *Le Sacre du Printemps* or the atonal compositions of the Austrian Arnold Schönberg (1874–1951). Schönberg abandoned melody for an attempt to organize sounds as analytically as geometric painters organized color. In a more popular vein, the nightclub hopper could listen to the latest product of America, "le hot" jazz, a musical form whose essence was an improvisational riff around rather than through a melodic line. Its greatest artists included such African-Americans as Louis "Sachmo" Armstrong (1900–1971) and Edward Kennedy "Duke" Ellington (1899–1974). But Jazz was a world-wide phenomenon by the 1930s. Born in the American South and Mid-West, with roots in the syncopated rhythms brought to the New World from Africa and the Caribbean, Jazz was simultaneously the quintessential American music and the first global music.

Cultural integration became a marked feature of the twentieth century. Hollywood movies and television programs, Coca-Cola, MacDonald's, Rhythm'n'Blues, Rock'n'Roll, Rap, and Superman are international commonplaces, while some of the most prominent conductors and musicians on the western symphonic circuit learned their classical music in Asia. Western culture itself bears a marked non-western influence. "Modern Art" owes as much to Japanese prints and African masks as it does to the western tradition. One-third of the Nobel Prizes for literature since 1960 have gone to writers born in Japan, South Africa, St. Lucia, Mexico, Egypt, Nigeria, Colombia, Chile, Guatemala, and Israel.

Human Rights

While the horrors of the Nazi death camps, revealed in 1945, may have helped discredit the notions of racial superiority and purity so popular in the 1930s, they did not sweep away the barriers to ethnic, religious, and gender equality still found throughout the world. The struggle to break down those barriers was been a major element of the postwar world. It has not been entirely successful.

◆　Civil Rights in the United States

In 1945 the official policy of the richest and most powerful nation on the earth was still that of the 1896 *Plessy v. Ferguson* Supreme Court decision. "Separate but equal" was the law of the land, even though separate was never equal. In the south, all public facilities (including school systems) were segregated. Poll taxes and "literacy" tests prevented African-Americans from registering to vote, and it was against the law for people of different races to marry. While such legal barriers did not exist in the north, more informal forms of discrimination assured white supremacy.

The American armed forces that fought in World War II were officially segregated, although casualties suffered during the first two years of the war had led to piecemeal integration to keep each unit up to strength. After the war, a new militancy on the part of civil rights groups (fueled in part by an infusion of African-American veterans into their ranks) combined with demographic changes to give a new impetus to the campaign for desegregation. The development of synthetic fibers after World War II helped reduce southern cotton acreage from 43 million acres in 1929 to less than fifteen million in 1959. The southern farm population, white and black, fell from 16.2 to 5.9 million in the same period. Three million African-American moved to northern cities between 1940 and 1960 in search of jobs. Able to vote, they helped make African-American demands for civil equality a national political issue. The first public barrier to fall was in the "national pastime," baseball, when, in 1947, Branch Rickey (1881–1965) of the Brooklyn Dodgers broke the major league race barrier by hiring Jackie Robinson (1919–1972) out of the Negro Leagues.

While this opened the floodgates of professional sports to Americans of color, it had the unfortunate side effect of destroying the black-owned enterprises of the Negro Leagues. The other major civil rights victory of the late-1940s came as a result of African-American agitation. A. Philip Randolph, whose threat of a march on Washington in 1941 had brought about the desegregation of the defense plants, had switched his sights to the military itself. His League for Nonviolent Civil Disobedience Against Military Segregation saw its first victory on July 26, 1948, when President Truman issued Executive Order 9981, barring segregation in the armed forces. The military proved to be a major path to African-American advancement over the ensuing decades. Probably the most prominent example of this progress was the appointment of Colin Powell (b. 1937) as the Chairman of the Joint Chiefs of Staff (1989–1993). He would later go on to serve as Secretary of State under President George W. Bush.

Throughout the 1950s the federal government moved gradually to desegregate the military, the federal civil service, and interstate commerce, but the most prominent landmarks of the decade remain the 1954 Supreme Court decision ordering an end to public school segregation and the Montgomery Bus Boycott of 1955–1956. In *Brown v. the Board of Education of Topeka, Kansas* (1954), the Supreme Court declared that segregated schools violated the Fourteenth Amendment. Reversing the "separate but equal" doctrine of *Plessy v. Ferguson,* the Court declared segregation unconstitutional because "separate educational facilities are inherently unequal." The National Association for the Advancement of Colored People (NAACP), which had brought the action on behalf of the parents of Linda Brown (b.1946), rejoiced, although the battle for an integrated educational system had only just begun. Americans who turned on their television sets in 1957 saw paratroopers ordered by President Eisenhower escorting nine black students into Central High School in Little Rock, as Arkansas Governor Orval Faubus (1910–1994) mustered the national guard to keep them out.

Rosa Parks (b. 1913), a member of the Montgomery, Alabama, chapter of the NAACP, was arrested on December 1, 1955, for refusing to give up her seat on a city bus to a white man. Her arrest sparked a black boycott of the city bus lines organized by the newly formed Montgomery Improvement Association led by a local pastor, Martin Luther King, Jr. (1929–1968). For 381 days the African-Americans who made up 70 percent of the bus riders starved the system of its revenues. Adopting the non-violent teachings and tactics that had worked so well for Mohandas Gandhi against the British in India, King's work in keeping the boycott going brought him to national prominence. On December 20, 1956, the Supreme Court declared Montgomery's bus system unconstitutional.

The non-violent arm of the civil rights movement reached its peak in the massive March on Washington for Jobs and Freedom in 1963, supported by a coalition of black organizations, the AFL-CIO, the Protestant National Council of Churches, and the American Jewish Congress. More than 250,000 demonstrators heard King deliver his famous "I Have a Dream" speech on August 28.

Ten years of civil rights legislation and Supreme Court action followed. The Civil Rights Act of 1964 barred discrimination in public accommodations and employment, authorized the attorney-general to withhold federal funds from any state school district that did not desegregate, and created the Equal Employment Opportunity Commission to hear cases of alleged discrimination. The Voting Rights Act of 1965 put the entire registration and voting process under federal control with the introduction of federal examiners in counties where less than fifty percent of minority residents were on the voting lists. As a result, the nationwide number of black voters, which had already risen from 20 to 39 percent between 1960 and 1964, grew to 62 percent in 1971. The Fair Housing Act of 1968 barred discrimination in the selling and renting of real estate. In a series of

Integration, 1957: Black students require a military escort to attend Central High in Little Rock, Arkansas.
Copyright © AP/Wide World Photos

decisions the Supreme Court extended school desegregation to extracurricular activities and ordered the use of mandatory busing to integrate southern and northern schools.

In a period of social upheaval ignited, as well, by protests against American involvement in Vietnam, more militant voices in the civil rights community rejected the non-violent approach to the problems of race in America pioneered by leaders like King. Others even questioned the desirability of assimilation. In California, the Black Panthers repeated Mao Zedong's slogan that "political power comes out of the barrel of a gun." The Black Muslim rejected integration in favor of Black Nationalism, stressing black pride and self-help. It also incorporated an ugly current of anti-white and anti-Semitic bigotry that attempted to give theological credence to the assertion that "the white man is a devil." Malcolm X (1925–1965), one of the most prominent Black Muslim leaders, called Dr. King's 1963 March "the farce on Washington."

The real gains of the civil rights movement began to run up against increased public resentment of the federal re-engineering of society. Malcolm X's murder in 1965, the nationwide rioting and arson in 1967, the murders of New York Senator Robert Kennedy (1925–1968) and Martin

MARTIN LUTHER KING, JR. (1929–1968)

King uses his "I have a dream" speech to campaign for civil rights legislation during the March on Washington (1963).
Copyright © CORBIS/Hulton-Deutsch Collection

The son and grandson of Baptist ministers, the Reverend Dr. Martin Luther King, Jr. was born on January 15, 1929, in Atlanta, Georgia. Receiving his B.A. from Morehouse College in 1948, he went on to Crozer Theological Seminary and Boston University, where he was awarded a Ph.D. in 1955. In Boston, King met Coretta Scott (b. 1927), a student at the New England Conservatory of Music. They married in 1953 and had four children.

While working on his doctoral dissertation, King became pastor of the Dexter Avenue Baptist Church in Montgomery, Alabama. Montgomery's Bus System was segregated (although 70 percent of bus riders were black), and on December 1, 1955, Rosa Parks (b. 1913) was arrested for refusing to give up her seat to a white passenger. Montgomery's black community decided to boycott the transportation system, and King was chosen to lead a campaign that lasted 381 days before the Supreme Court declared Montgomery's bus segregation unconstitutional on December 20, 1956. King survived death threats and the dynamiting of his home to become a national figure.

In 1957 King set up the Southern Christian Leadership Conference (SCLC) to coordinate integration efforts throughout the South. He began a worldwide speaking tour. In India in 1959, he renewed his belief in Mahatma Gandhi's philosophy of non-violence. Appointed co-pastor with his father of the Ebenezer Baptist Church in Alabama, King demonstrated those principles as part of a student sit-in at a segregated lunch-counter in October, 1960. Arrested and sent to Reidsville State Prison Farm, King won release only after the intervention of Democratic presidential nominee John F. Kennedy. It would be only the first of many arrests.

King spent the next three years fighting racial discrimination in the United States. On August 28, 1963, a quarter of a million people gathered near the Lincoln Memorial to hear many civil rights' speakers. But the most famous speech of the March on Washington remains King's. The young pastor evoked a "dream" of a United States in which individuals would be judged "by the content of their character" rather than by "the color of their skin." Awarded the Nobel Peace Prize in 1964, King's true legacy is the Civil Rights Act of 1964 and the Voting Rights Act of 1965 that ended the Jim Crow system.

King's nonviolent methods and his goal of a racially integrated society were not acceptable to other civil rights activists; the Selma March and the Watts Riots in 1965 revealed the growing split within the movement. King himself broadened his concerns beyond integration to oppose American involvement in Vietnam. In March 1968, he was organizing a Poor People's March on Washington when he stopped off in Memphis, Tennessee to support striking sanitation workers. A sniper's bullet ended King's life as he was standing on the balcony outside his motel room on April 4. James Earl Ray (1928-1998) pled guilty to the murder on March 10, 1969, and died in prison.

A champion of human rights in the broadest sense, the Reverend Dr. Martin Luther King, Jr. was the first (and remains the only) private citizen of the United States honored with a National Holiday.

MALCOLM X. (1925–1965)

Advocate of Black Nationalism.
Copyright © CORBIS/Bettmann

Malcolm Little was born on May 19, 1925, in Omaha, Nebraska. During his youth, his home in Lansing, Michigan, was burned by Ku Klux Klan members, his father murdered, and his distraught mother placed in a mental institution. The orphaned teenager went to live with his half-sister in Boston. The deeply troubled teen was soon imprisoned for burglary, but there found the anchor he needed to repair his life. He joined the Nation of Islam, a Black Muslim sect founded by Wallace Fard Muhammad (1877?–1934?) at a Detroit mosque in 1931. Fard, a Saudi immigrant, claimed to be a Messenger sent by Allah to liberate the "Lost-Found Nation of Islam in the West" from its white "slave masters."

Released from prison in 1952, Malcolm Little met Elijah Muhammad (1897–1975) who succeeded Fard as head of the Black Muslims after Fard's mysterious disappearance in 1934. Malcolm took the new surname "X" as way of repudiating the heritage of slavery. A charismatic orator, Malcolm X was largely responsible for the movement's growing membership. During the 1950s he founded numerous mosques across the United States and himself became minister of Mosque Number Seven in Harlem. His *Muhammad Speaks* (1961) became the official publication of the Nation of Islam.

As a Black Nationalist, Malcolm X scornfully rejected the exclusively non-violent methods and integrationist aims of the mainstream civil rights movement. He called for black pride, economic separatism and the legitimate use of violence in self-defense against a racist society. To this end, he advocated the arming of all black men. To white America he was the man who referred to President Kennedy's assassination a "case of chickens coming home to roost." The resulting political furor led to Malcolm's suspension from the Black Muslim movement. Malcolm left the church in March 1964, and in April made a pilgrimage to Mecca. In that Holy City he underwent a conversion to orthodox Islam and repudiated his earlier belief in the inherent evil of all Whites. The obligation to make the *Hajj* (pilgrimage to Mecca) is one of the Five Pillars of Islam; it entails a spiritual rebirth and subsequent renaming. Malcolm X became el-Hajj Malik el-Shabazz.

When he returned to Harlem, there were numerous clashes between his supporters and those of Elijah Muhammad. During a rally of his followers, Malcolm was shot to death on February 21, 1965. Three members of the Nation of Islam were convicted of his murder. But the influence of Malik el-Shabazz continued to grow with the posthumous publication of *The Autobiography of Malcolm X* (1965) based on interviews conducted shortly before his death by Alex Haley (1921–1992), the author of *Roots*. Malcolm's present appeal relies more on his call for black pride and economic self-sufficiency than on the "world brotherhood" he espoused after his return from Mecca. How Malcolm himself would have combined the two can never truly be known.

Luther King in 1968, and the burning of school buses in Boston in 1974 were only symptoms of the larger problem. Removing the legal barriers to integration had not brought an end to discrimination in American society. The Supreme Court began to set limits in the 1970s, refusing to allow busing from one tax jurisdiction to another to prevent the resegregation of inner city schools caused by "white flight" to the suburbs. In 2003 the Supreme Court severely limited the ability of universities to use race-based "Affirmative Action" measures to create diverse student bodies.

While the African-American civil rights movement tended to dominate the news media, other minorities were also agitating for equal opportunity. Although few Hispanics had participated in political life before 1960, this changed with the creation of the Mexican American Political Association (MAPA) at the beginning of the decade. By 1969, however, a more radical political group *La Raza Unida* (The United Race) was formed to fight racism in American life. It was in this period that Cesar Chavez (1927–1993), born to a family of migrant farm workers, founded the National Farm Workers' Association (1962). This militant union began a successful five-year strike and boycott of California grapes in 1965. Joining with the AFL-CIO, Chavez's organization became the United Farm Workers of America (UFW) in 1971. It's aim was to improve the living and working conditions of America's migrant workers. In contrast, the Cuban American community, concentrated in south Florida, was mostly conservative, and loyally supported any candidate who was consistently opposed to the Castro regime.

◆   Women's Rights in the United States

The campaign for equal rights for American women was, by contrast, not the movement of an oppressed minority, but a movement of the oppressed *majority* of the American population (51.20 percent of the population was female according to the 2000 census). In 1900 the average American woman married at age 22, and had three to four children. Campaigners for birth control faced criminal prosecution. Margaret Sanger (1879–1966), the founder of Planned Parenthood (1942), was sentenced to thirty days in the workhouse for opening America's first birth control clinic in 1917. Ratified on August 18, 1920, the Nineteenth Amendment stated that "The right of citizens of the United States to vote shall not be denied or abridged by the United States or by any State on account of sex." But giving women the right to vote made little immediate change in their lives. During the First and Second World Wars women had moved into the workforce in record numbers, to fill the jobs left vacant by departing soldiers, but these gains were temporary. After each war ended, women were expected to surrender their jobs to returning veterans. The 1950s saw a return to a largely male dominated work force, with most women being consigned to unpaid labor as housewives in the newly built and federally subsidized suburbs. But by the late 1960s, new job openings in an increasingly prosperous America attracted many women back into paid employment. More women also began to go to college. Only 35 percent of college undergraduates were women in 1960, but by the 1980s just over half or all graduates were women. Women were also increasingly moving into traditionally male graduate programs in law and medicine.

All this would have important effects on the structure of American family life. By the year 2000 the average American woman had only 2.2 children. The divorce rate rose from only eight percent of all marriages in 1900 to just over 50 percent a century later.

The women's rights movement in the United States received a major impetus from the work of Betty Friedan (b. 1921). A journalist who had left the workplace for the traditional life of a suburban housewife, Friedan wrote an exposé of the pressure on women to conform to the domestic stereotype. Her book, *The Feminine Mystique* (1963), sparked a new militancy among women activists. She organized the National Organization for Women (NOW) in 1967 to channel that militancy into

MARGARET SANGER (1879–1966)

The founder of the American birth-control movement was born Margaret Higgins on September 14, 1879, in Corning, New York, the sixth of eleven children in an Irish working-class family. Her mother's ill health (and eventual death) from the strain of eleven childbirths and seven miscarriages inspired Margaret to seek medical training. She attended Claverack College, where she took nurse's training at the White Plains Hospital. After marrying William Sanger in 1900, she worked as a midwife in the immigrant communities on New York's Lower East Side. High infant mortality rates and infectious disease were common features of life in the crowded tenements, but Sanger was particularly appalled by the frequent deaths from botched illegal abortions. Galvanized by what she saw, Sanger began a lifelong campaign to bring legal contraception to the American woman. Standing in her way was the *Comstock Act* (1873) that made contraceptive literature and devices illegal pornographic materials.

In 1914, Sanger began publishing a monthly magazine, *the Woman Rebel* (later renamed *The Birth Control Review*) advocating birth control and women's rights. Quickly indicted for violating postal obscenity laws, Sanger fled to Europe but returned when the case was dismissed in 1916. She opened up America's first birth control clinic in Brooklyn and was sentenced to 30 days in the public workhouse for operating a "public nuisance." Her first book, *What Every Mother Should Know,* was published that same year (1917). In 1921 she founded the American Birth Control League and served as its president until 1928. Sanger's League merged with other birth control organizations in 1942, becoming the Planned Parenthood Federation of America with Sanger as honorary chairwoman.

Sanger spent considerable time in Europe to escape the mounting political persecution in the States. Her open liaison with J. Noah H. Slee and her advocacy of "free love" did not help her position at home. After a divorce from William Sanger, Margaret married Slee in 1922, but both partners had extra-marital affairs during this "open marriage." The three children that resulted from her two marriages remained in the background as Sanger began a worldwide campaign for contraception and population control. In 1927 she organized the first World Population Conference in Geneva, Switzerland. *My Fight for Birth Control* (1931) and *Margaret Sanger: An Autobiography* (1938) were written to popularize her crusade and keep the issue of birth control before the public. During World War II the practice of birth control became far more common, and Sanger's crusade took on an even greater international dimension. Margaret Sanger became the first president of the International Planned Parenthood Federation in 1953, and took her campaign as far afield as India and Japan.

Back in the United States, her efforts resulted in a relaxation of the *Comstock Act* in 1936 allowing physicians to import and prescribe contraceptives, but the Supreme Court did not strike down a Connecticut law prohibiting the use of contraception (even by married couples) until 1965, when Sanger was 86. The Supreme Court decision extending the right to privacy to cover abortion (*Roe v. Wade*) did not come until 1973, seven years after Sanger's death on September 6, 1966, in Tucson, Arizona.

concrete change. In *Griswald v. Connecticut* (1965) the Supreme Court overturned state laws against the sale of contraceptives to married women, and, in *Roe v. Wade* (1973) it struck down state laws preventing abortions during the first trimester of gestation. The Equal Credit Opportunity Act of 1974 prohibited lenders from discriminating on the basis of gender. But the Equal Rights Amendment, which won the support of a number of state legislatures in 1972 and 1973, ultimately failed to be ratified. The desire to insure equality was, once more, running up against the reluctance to further re-engineer American society.

The Campaigner for a woman's right to birth control with her second son.
Copyright © Sophia Smith Collection

◆   Redefining "Equality"

When the American *Declaration of Independence* (1776) declared all men to be "equal," all that was intended was a narrowly defined equal protection under the law: an equal right to trial by jury and the objective application of criminal and civil law. The right to participate in the making of that law was not even extended to all white men. But it is one of the cardinal features of modern society that the definition of "equal" is always expanding. In 1969, the patrons of the Stonewall Inn, a "gay" bar in New York's Greenwich Village decided they were tired of being harassed by the police and took to the streets. The "Stonewall Riots" set off an ongoing gay and lesbian rights movement. One of the accomplishments of this movement that continues to affect the larger heterosexual community has been the adding of "Domestic Partner" provisions to the employee benefit packages of many local governments and private institutions and an on-going debate over same-sex marriages. In 1990, the Americans with Disabilities Act (ADA) required government offices and private businesses to make all "reasonable accommodations" to insure every American equal access to education, employment, accommodation, and transportation.

◆   Universal Human Rights

In 1948 the United Nations issued *a Universal Declaration of Human Rights,* championed by Eleanor Roosevelt (1884–1962). It declared the equal right of all human beings to "life, liberty and the security of person," protection under the law, presumption of innocence, consensual marriage, education, and freedom of movement, opinion, and assembly. For many, however, it is a declaration honored in name only.

Before World War One, women could vote only in New Zealand, Australia, Finland, Norway, Denmark, and Iceland. By the outbreak of World War Two, women could also vote in the Netherlands, the Soviet Union, Canada, Austria, Czechoslovakia, Germany, Hungary, Poland, Sweden, Luxembourg, the United States, Great Britain, Ecuador, South Africa, Brazil, Thailand, Uruguay, Turkey, Cuba, and Salvador. The Dominican Republic gave women the right to vote during the war, while France, Guatemala, Italy, Japan, Mexico, China, Argentina, South Korea, and Israel extended the franchise to women at war's end or shortly thereafter. Chile, India, and Indonesia granted women the vote in 1949, Pakistan in 1956, Switzerland not until 1971, and Syria not until 1973. Women still cannot vote in some of the more conservative regimes in the Middle East, such as Saudi Arabia and Kuwait.

The right to vote is only the beginning of the road to equality. Even though women gained the right to vote in Brazil in 1932 it was not until 1978 that this largest Roman Catholic country in the world legalized divorce, not until 1988 that a new constitution mandated equality for women, and not until 2001 that the Brazilian Congress passed the legislation that would ensure women real equality within their own families. For the first time husbands would have to share their legal right to make decisions for their children with their wives. Those same husbands would also no longer be able to obtain automatic annulments if they learn their wives were not virgins at the time of their marriage.

In Japan, women were not protected by an equal employment opportunity law until 1985. Not surprisingly, fewer Japanese women have managerial positions or are members of national legislatures than in any other industrialized country. In 2003, 41 percent of all workers in Japan were women, but only 8.9 percent of all managerial positions and 7.3 percent of the national legislature seats were held by women. In the United States, 46.6 percent of all workers, 46 percent of the managers, and 14.3 percent of the Members of both houses of Congress were women in 2003.

The inability of developing nations to catch up with the ever-expanding economies of the industrialized west has often been an aggravating factor in ethnic discrimination. In the 1950s Nasser promised to enrich Egyptian peasants by driving foreign merchants out of the country. Indian minorities were persecuted in and then expelled from Uganda and Tanzania in the 1970s. Chinese minorities in Indonesia, Vietnam, and Malaya have suffered similar fates.

The growth of religious fundamentalism in much of the under-developed world has often been a response to population pressure, growing poverty, and failed economies. Islamic fundamentalism has become the fastest growing social and political movement in the Muslim world. Rejecting the capitalism of their former colonial rulers, many in the Islamic world looked to the Soviet Union for models of social development after World War II, while others became clients of the United States. Plagued by corrupt regimes and inefficient central planning, these governments threatened the traditional values of their societies without improving the lives of their peoples. In contrast, the fundamentalist movement was able to win many supporters among the poor through grassroots organizations, charitable work, and constant preaching against western cultural influences, which they believed encouraged promiscuity and drug use.

Under the leadership of Muammar al-Qaddafi (b. 1942), Libya became an Islamic state in 1969, seeking inspiration not in Socialism, but in the Quran. The Shah of Iran was overthrown a decade later and replaced by a fundamentalist Islamic regime. The Sudan, an area of strong religious fervor since the nineteenth century, became the next site of Islamic revolution. Basing the nation's laws on *Sharia* (Muslim holy law), the new government set off a civil war when it attempted to impose Islam on the largely Christian and animist southern part of the country; the fighting continued into the twenty-first century. By the 1990s this resulted in a revival of the old slave trade, with recalcitrant non-Muslims transported as slaves into the Arab world. Instances of two ancient tribal practices—forced clitoridectomy (female circumcision) and "honor killings" (the murder of female relatives suspected of sexual relations outside of marriage, even if they were forced) have also become increasingly common in fundamentalist Muslim communities.

Pakistan, long troubled by corrupt dictators, a rapidly growing impoverished population, and an illiteracy rate of at least 75 percent, has also begun to adopt *Sharia* as the nation's law. The Pakistani government heralded its nuclear capacity as the "Islamic bomb." The military leaders of Algeria felt obliged to cancel the country's first free elections in 1992 when it appeared Islamic leaders would win. Egypt also barred an Islamic opposition group from participating in its 1995 elections. The multi-ethnic states of Africa are particularly vulnerable to religious tensions. Nine of Nigeria's 36 states have adopted Sharia as their basic law codes, creating tensions in neighboring, mostly Christian, Niger. Christians living in Maradi, a city in Niger just 30 miles north of its border with Nigeria, were attacked by Muslim fundamentalists at the beginning of 2001. On the other hand, Christians controlling the government in the Ivory Coast have turned a blind eye to the destruction of mosques and Muslim owned properties. In India, the growth of Hindu fundamentalism has been fueled by the failure of the secularist Congress Party to solve India's economic problems. The Bharatiya Janata party, which has called for a purified Hindu India, has benefitted from the ongoing distress. Despite the massive shift of population, and terrible massacres that followed the partition of India and Pakistan in 1947, India still had a large Muslim minority (now over 120 million). Hindu militants began to accuse this minority of being responsible for many of the nation's problems, including widespread poverty. Mosques, which during the Mughal ascendancy were sometimes built upon the ruins of demolished Hindu temples, have come under increasing Hindu assault. The 1992 destruction of the oldest Muslim mosque in India (the Babri Masjid) remains a symbol of a divided country.

In Afghanistan, torn by civil war after the failed Soviet invasion, Taliban rebels instituted a fundamentalist Islamic government. As a result, Afghan women were removed from their jobs, denied an education and access to medical care, and threatened with violence if they ventured outside their homes without the supervision of a male relative. Afghan women were only able to return to public life after the ouster of the Taliban by American forces in 2002 and only in those areas enjoying relative freedom from inter-tribal fighting. The most dramatic example of the clash between fundamentalist and secularist culture to date was the attack on the World Trade Center and the Pentagon by Al Qaeda terrorists on September 11, 2001. The result has been American invasions of Afghanistan (the main base for Al Qaeda) and Iraq.

Nor has post-Cold War Europe been immune to ethnic and religious hostilities. The transition to capitalism at the end of the Cold War brought several years of economic hardship to the nations of Central Asia and Central and Eastern Europe. Some of their leaders turned to ethnic nationalism to rally their beleaguered populations. Claims of old betrayals, lost empires, and demands for minority national self-determination combined to set off civil wars in Armenia, Azerbaijan, the former Yugoslavia, and the Kurdish lands of Turkey and Iraq. The Gypsies found themselves under increasing discrimination in the Czech Republic. Even France and Britain began to retreat from the hospitality they had offered to their former colonial populations. And one of the most persistent ethnic-religious divides remains that between the Scots-Protestant and Irish-Catholic factions in Northern Ireland.

The most violent ethnic-religious divide within Europe was that within the former Yugoslavia. Before his death in 1980, Tito had turned Yugoslavia into a federal state with six republics (Serbia, Croatia, Bosnia-Herzegovina, Slovenia, Macedonia, and Montenegro) and two autonomous provinces (Kosovo and Vojvodina) within Serbia. After his death, the country was ruled by a presidency that rotated among the six republics, but Serbia's refusal to give up its seat in 1987 and its rescinding of the privileges of autonomy to Vojvodina and Kosova in 1989 precipitated the breakup of Yugoslavia. A war broke out between the Roman Catholic Croats and Eastern Orthodox Serbs within Croatia when that state declared its independence from Yugoslavia in 1991. That war grew wider when Bosnia-Herzegovina declared its independence the next year. Serbs, Croats and Muslims living in Bosnia slaughtered each other with the support of the Serbian and Croatian armies until NATO air strikes led to peace talks. The resulting Dayton Accords (1995) created a Bosnia with three presidents, one for each ethno-religious group, but some 30,000 NATO troops remain in Bosnia to keep the peace.

September 11, 2001.
Courtesy of Masatomo Kuriya/CORBIS Images

Then the fighting moved to the province of Kosovo in Serbia. 90 percent of Kosovo's population was ethnic Albanian. As the Kosovar Albanians fought to gain their independence, the Serbs fought to keep control of the province. As in the earlier battles in Croatia and Bosnia, each side resorted to "ethnic cleansing" to eliminate its rivals. Once again, it took NATO to bring both sides to the bargaining table. NATO imposed peace accords in 1999 and NATO troops remain on the ground in Kosovo keep the combatants at arms length.

In a post-Cold War World, NATO and the United Nations have been trying to redefine their respective roles. NATO has been acting in part as Europe's policeman. But as the 2003 stalemate over Iraq between France and the United States in the UN Security Council and Turkey's refusal to allow US troops access in the campaign against Iraq made clear, even NATO allies are uncertain of the extent to which NATO troops should be used outside of Europe. Within Europe itself NATO is expanding. In 1999, the Czech Republic, Hungary, and Poland became the first three ex-communist states to join NATO. In November 2002, NATO extended membership invitations to seven more: Bulgaria, Estonia, Latvia, Lithuania, Romania, Slovakia, and Slovenia. While Russia has been given a special auxiliary role, it remains concerned about NATO enlargement, especially into those states (Estonia, Latvia, and Lithuania) which had been part of the Soviet Union (and the Russian empire that preceded it) until 1991 except for a brief period of independence created by the Versailles settlement between the World Wars.

Population

The most basic right in the modern idea of liberty is the right to life, a right that depends, above all, on the food supply. But that supply has to be understood in terms of the population level. Way back in 1798, British economist Thomas Robert Malthus had warned that epidemics, famine and wars were the inevitable effect of population's tendency to increase geometrically in a world where the food supply could only be increased arithmetically. It is easy to say that Malthus was wrong. He believed the only way to increase the food supply was to put more land under cultivation, and the Earth only possessed a limited supply of land. The advances of the Agricultural and Industrial Revolutions of the nineteenth century, multiplied by the Green Revolution's creation of high yield crops through genetic engineering in the twentieth have gone a considerable way to proving that food supplies can be significantly increased. But the question of overall population control still remains.

Ethnic Rivalries in Yugoslavia.
From *The Western Heritage, 6/e, Combined Edition*, by Donald Kagan, Steven Ozment, and Frank M. Turner. Copyright © 1998 by Prentice-Hall, Inc.

The failure of major Latin American and Asian economies to easily adapt to industrial manufacturing has been accompanied by rapid population growth in much of the under-developed world. Medical advances, most especially the use of vaccinations against childhood diseases, combined with increased food production, have resulted in dramatic population growth. World population did not reach the one billion mark until 1800, but jumped to two billion by 1930, four billion by 1975, five billion by 1990, and surpassed six billion in October 1999. Was Malthus right?

The answer is not as simple as the numbers imply. On the one hand, population growth worldwide is actually slowing down. The average annual increase fell from 2.06 percent (1965-1970) to 1.73 percent (1985–1990). This drop occurred in First World, Second World, and Third World nations. The spread of industrialization has set off a worldwide demographic transition to smaller families. But this has not happened evenly across the economic spectrum. Some industrialized countries are undergoing zero population growth; Japan is even experiencing negative population growth, as its birthrate falls beneath the minimum needed to maintain population levels. Crude birth rates remain higher in developing nations than in the world's industrial giants, while medical advances have increased life expectancy worldwide. Population is growing fastest where governments can least afford to feed it. The Chinese nation, encouraged by the Communist party, tripled in size, from 400 million in 1945 to at least 1.2 billion at the end of the millennium. The population of India also tripled, approaching one billion in the same period. The government of Kenya reported eight live births per woman in the 1960s; the average throughout Africa is six.

The First and Third Worlds collide: Shacks and skyscrapers co-exist side by side by side in Bombay, India.
Copyright © Viviane Moore/The Stock Market

Many of the poor in the non-industrialized world, who are born in the countryside, move to the cities as economic refugees. While nineteenth-century urbanization in the West was due to the success of the city-based industrial economy, most of the present growth is the result of the failure of the rural economy. The largest cities in rich nations—London, Tokyo, and New York—are small compared to Mexico City, São Paulo in Brazil, Lagos in Nigeria, or Calcutta in India. In these metropolises the central city is surrounded by ever widening circles of slums and shanty towns, sometimes built on garbage dumps. When the government of Mexico City recently announced proudly that all its inhabitants had drinking water, it meant that everyone was in walking distance of a public spigot. An adequate sewer system has yet to be built for the city, leading to persistent outbreaks of cholera and typhoid.

What can be done to avoid the disasters predicted by Malthus?

A Glimpse Into How the Six Billion Live

	Current Life Expectancy	Fertility Rate Average number of children per woman	Contraceptive Use by percent of currently married women.
Africa	51 Years	5.1	20
Asia	66	2.6	60
Europe	73	1.4	72
Latin America and Caribbean	69	2.7	65
North America	77	1.9	71

Source: United Nations Population Division

Countries or Areas With Highest Infant Mortality Deaths/1,000 live births		Largest Urban Areas Population in millions		Countries With Greatest Immigration 1970–96 Net number, in millions		Oldest Countries Median age of population, 1999.	
Sierra Leone	170	Tokyo	28.2	United States	16.7	Italy	40.2
Afghanistan	151	Mexico City	17.8	Russia	4.1	Japan	40.2
Malawi	128	São Paulo, Brazil	17.3	Saudi Arabia	3.4	Germany	39.7
East Timor	135	Bombay, India	17.4	India	3.3	Sweden	39.7
Lowest		New York	16.5	**Out-migration**		**Youngest**	
Japan	4	Shanghai	14.0	Mexico	−8.0	Uganda	15.0
Singapore	5	Los Angeles	13.0	Bangladesh	−4.1	Niger	15.8
Norway	5	Lagos, Nigeria	12.6	Afghanistan	−4.1	Yemen	15.9
Germany	5	Calcutta, India	12.7	Philippines	−2.9	Congo Republic	15.9
		Buenos Aires	12.3				

Source: United Nations Population Division

With the largest population in the world, and determined to improve the living standard of its citizens, the government of the People's Republic of China took the most drastic measures to slow population growth. Its one child per family rule, enforced by law during the 1970s and 1980s was relaxed in the relative prosperity of the 1990s, but not before it caused some major social realignment. In the traditional Chinese family, children were taught to respect their elders. By making children fewer in number, the one-child policy contributed to the creation of new Western style child-centered families, where spoiled little "emperors and empresses" enjoyed the sole attention of doting parents. More ominous is the fact that the number of female infants who reach adulthood has been severely curtailed. In traditional Chinese culture, married women went to live with their husband's families. The Chinese favored male children over female because sons brought workers into the family circle while daughters left to work for others. Female infanticide, always a problem in times of drought, became increasingly frequent under the one-child rule. Twenty-five years later, the Chinese were faced with too steep a population drop because there was a shortage of brides in some areas for the generation raised under the one-child rule.

The natural checks on population growth have not disappeared with the advance of modern science. The virus that causes Acquired Immunity Deficiency Syndrome (AIDS) long existed among chimpanzees in western central Africa before it spread, with devastating effect, to humans. First diagnosed in 1981, the virus infected over 20 million people by the century's end. While the virus is known on every continent, most of those infected live in Sub-Saharan Africa. Worst hit is Zimbabwe, a country of some eleven million people with less than 1500 physicians. Over one-quarter of the adult population of Zimbabwe was HIV-positive in 1997. Mortality in this area is now so high that population growth has been noticeably slowed and life expectancy has fallen back to under 50 years. Children born in the United States at the turn of the millennium can expect to live into their 80s.

Economic Integration

Free trade has been an aspect of modernization ever since the British Economist Adam Smith first established it as a cornerstone of capitalist economics in his *Wealth of Nations* (1776). In 1819, the Prussians proposed the creation of a *Zollverein* (customs union) among the German states of central Europe to reap the benefits of a larger domestic market. In 1846, the British government adopted an official policy of free trade by repealing the Corn Laws (which had imposed duties on imported grain). In 1918, President Woodrow Wilson of the United States made the removal of trade barriers one of his *Fourteen Points* for a post-war peace. It is time to examine the twentieth-century record.

◆ The European Union

The fierce trade rivalries of the Great Depression were replaced by competing blocks of economic cooperation during the Cold War. The Marshall Plan (1947) was designed to encourage European economic cooperation. In response Norway, Denmark, Sweden, and Iceland formed the Committee on Economic Cooperation (1947) that, with the addition of Finland (1956), evolved into a Nordic Customs Union (NCU) in 1957. The Nordic Union set up a free-trade zone and a labor and credit pool for its members while imposing a common tariff against outsiders. Also in 1957, France, Italy, (West) Germany, and the Benelux states (Belgium, the Netherlands, and Luxembourg) formed the European Economic Community (EEC). The goal of the EEC, often called the Common Market, was the free movement of capital, labor, and goods between members. The EEC continued to grow

**THE EUROPEAN UNION:
MEMBER NATIONS AND
DATES OF ACCESSION
(As of 1996)**

Continental Cooperation: The European Union.
From *The European Scene: A Perspective* by James R. McDonald. Copyright © 1997 by Prentice-Hall, Inc.

over the years. Britain, Denmark and Ireland joined in 1973, Greece in 1981, and Portugal and Spain in 1986. East Germany became part of the Common Market by default, when it was reunited with West Germany in 1990. Austria, Finland, and Sweden joined in 1995.

EEC leaders also hoped someday to create common economic policies and institutions. A major step that direction was taken in 1967 when the EEC became the European Community (EC) with its own executive, judicial, and legislative bodies to which all its members send representatives. The next step was the signing of the *Maastricht Treaty* (1991), which turned the European Community into the European Union (EU) in 1993, by creating a Central Bank and a common currency, the EURO. The treaty also extended European Union citizenship to the citizens of all its member nations. On January 1, 2002, the Euro went into general use in twelve of the fifteen members of the European Union; only Great Britain, Sweden, and Denmark kept their national currencies. Despite the multiple names changes (from Common Market/EEC to EC to EU) a single theme stands out: the desire of Europeans to achieve a market large enough to compete with the United States. The means used to achieve that desire is increased economic integration.

The European has certainly been more successful than its one-time Communist-bloc rival, the Council of Mutual Economic Assistance (COMECON). Three former COMECON countries (NATO members since May 1999)—Hungary, the Czech Republic and Poland– were among the ten new states invited to join the EU in December 2002. The other seven were Cyprus, Estonia, Latvia, Lithuania, Malta, Slovakia, and Slovenia. With Estonia, Latvia, Lithuania, and Slovakia also being asked to join NATO the links between economic and military integration in Europe would appear to be strengthening. But, on the other hand, NATO member Turkey's anger at having its bid for EU membership turned down may mark the beginning of a breach in inter-European cooperation. Valéry Giscard d'Estaing (b. 1926), a former president of France and leader of the project to draft a new constitution for the EU, dismissed Turkey as "not a European country."[2] Turks have taken that as a rejection of their Muslim faith. France's rejection of America's invasion of Iraq in 2003 and Britain's alliance with the United States in that war further threaten the future effectiveness of the EU as well as of NATO.

◆ NAFTA, LAFTA, GATT, and beyond

The United States remains a leading proponent of free trade. Seeing the success of the Common Market and wanting to keep its economic market big enough to compete, the United States began to look for economic partners within its own hemisphere. An American-Canadian free trade agreement was signed in 1988. This was extended to Mexico when Republicans and Democrats joined to support the *North American Free Trade Agreement* (NAFTA). Signed in 1992, ratified in 1993 and put into effect on January 1, 1994, NAFTA provides for the gradual reduction of all trade barriers between the three members. Some tariffs were removed immediately, while others will be phased out over a 15-year period. Although NAFTA has been criticized for the loss of highly paid manufacturing jobs in North America to much lower paid Mexican workers, it has also provided expanded markets for American manufactures. With Chile already in line to join this free trade union, NAFTA may one day embrace all of North and South America.

Latin American nations have not, however, been content to wait for American recognition. Many of them have organized their own customs unions. The Central American Common Market (CACM) united El Salvador, Guatemala, Honduras, and Nicaragua in a free trade union formalized by the *Treaty of Managua* in 1960. Costa Rica joined in 1962. While many of the customs barriers between its members were eliminated, the CACM was not entirely successful because of political tensions between Honduras and El Salvador (which took Honduras out of the CACM from 1971 to 1980) and the problems caused by the Sandinista insurgency in Nicaragua. In 1993, the four original members created a new Central American Free Trade Zone (CAFTZ) designed to reduce tariff barriers between them by the end of the twentieth century.

Argentina, Brazil, Chile, Mexico, Paraguay, Peru, and Uruguay signed a treaty in 1960 setting up the Latin American Free Trade Association (LAFTA). Ecuador, Columbia, Venezuela, and Bolivia joined over the next decade. While tariff barriers were reduced, LAFTA's goal of an integrated economic policy was complicated by the varying levels of economic development among its members; monetary policies appropriate to one level of development were counter productive at other levels. To address this, LAFTA members designed a new organization, the Latin American Integration Association (LAIA) in 1980, substituting bi-lateral trade preference agreements accommodating the different economies within the association. Cuba was admitted to LAIA with observer status in 1986.

In 1966, six members of LAFTA (Bolivia, Chile, Colombia, Ecuador, Peru, and Venezuela) decided to form their own regional subgroup within the larger market to accelerate economic integration and coordinate regional industrial development. The Andean Group (as it is usually known) began its official life in 1969. Venezuela, which backed out in 1969, rejoined the group in 1973 while Chile withdrew in 1976.

In 1994, four LAFTA/LAIA members, Argentina, Brazil, Paraguay, and Uruguay created their own customs union (MERCOSUR - Southern Cone Common Market) within the larger group, removing tariffs on about 90 percent of the goods traded between those countries and erecting a common tariff averaging 12 percent for goods imported from elsewhere. MERCOSUR members also planned to adopt a regional passport, the Andean Migration Card, to facilitate movement of peoples between member states.

In 1967, five former British colonies (Antigua, Barbados, Guyana, Jamaica, and Trinidad and Tobago) joined to form the Caribbean Free Trade Association (CARIFTA). It was designed both to free trade between members and to impose a uniform protective tariff on all trade between members and non-members to support internal industrialization. The *Treaty of Chaguaramas* (1973) set up the Caribbean Community and Common Market (CARICOM) to replace CARIFTA as nine new members (Barbuda, the Bahamas, Belize, Dominica, Grenada, Montserrat, St. Christopher and Nevis, St. Lucia, and St. Vincent and the Grenadines) joined the union. In addition to continuing the policies laid down in the earlier union, CARICOM offers fiscal incentives to investment in its less developed members.

The spread of customs unions has not been limited to Europe and the Americas. Brunei, Cambodia, Indonesia, Laos, Malaysia, Myanmar, the Philippines, Singapore, Thailand, and Vietnam belong to the Association of Southeast Asian Nations (ASEAN). It was formed in 1967 to promote economic, social, and cultural cooperation, and development in the region. Headquartered in Jakarta, Indonesia, it sets regional policy in annual sessions of ministers from member countries. Australia, Brunei, Canada, Chile, China, Indonesia, Japan, Malaysia, Mexico, New Zealand, Papua New Guinea, the Philippines, Singapore, South Korea, Taiwan, Thailand, and the United States belong to the Asia-Pacific Economic Cooperation Group (APEC). It was created in 1989 to further cooperation on trade and investment between nations of the Pacific Rim and with the rest of the world.

The United States has also been an ardent supporter of the 1947 *General Agreement on Tariffs and Trade* (GATT), a treaty signed by most of the world's nations to reduce tariffs and other barriers to international trade as much as possible. Signatories of GATT automatically enjoy Most Favored Nation (MFN) trading status; their goods may enter the markets of all GATT members at rates of duty no less favorable than those applied to similar products from any other member. While the American government certainly believes GATT will favor the spread of American products around the world, it also sees GATT as a way to avoid the political tensions caused by the economic rivalries of the 1930s that helped pave the way for World War II.

While economic integration proceeded fairly smoothly in a Cold War world, it has not had as easy a path in the post-Cold War world. The "triumph of capitalism" may have tied the world more closely together, but it has also made it possible for economic problems in the Far East and South America to reverberate through stock markets around the world. And as the "economic miracles" of Germany, Japan, and the "Asian Tigers" give way to more normal cycles of expansion and recession, there is always the temptation for governments to set up high tariffs in the hope of protecting domestic markets.

Freedom, equality, science, technology, human dignity, and national rights may be key values of the "modern" revolution, but they do not remain unchallenged The ideals of multi-party democracy and a genuine respect for human rights, including freedom of religion, can certainly be found in many more countries than would have subscribed to them in 1750. But the recently emerged democratic governments of Latin America and Africa are neither the dominant form of government in their regions nor necessarily assured of long-lasting success. The rights of racial and ethic minorities, and women, have been enlarged, and assured through legislation, in much of the industrial world. But even in that world, no law can force people to associate with groups against which they hold an irrational prejudice, and in the still developing world those rights have proven much more fragile. The absence of any general war in the second half of the twentieth century has contributed to an unparalleled period of prosperity in the developed world. But while the threat of a general nuclear conflagration has faded with the Cold War, the problem of regional nuclear wars has come to fore as China, India, and Pakistan joined the nuclear club. Human knowledge of the universe continues to increase, but so does the cost of space exploration. Advances in medicine have greatly increased the human life span, but poverty has brought back diseases once thought conquered. A revolution in communications has further contributed to a sense of global community, while the cost of computers threatens to aggravate the rich-poor divide. Industrial pollutants continue to threaten the ozone layer, with the result that global warming, with potentially catastrophic effects on plant and marine life and sea levels, has become a real problem. The warming we see now is, at least in part, the result of nineteenth-century industrialization. Even as western nations take steps to lessen their contributions to global warming, newly industrialized nations step up theirs. This legacy of the Industrial Revolution is a challenge to the twenty-first century: how can people's economic expectations be fulfilled without destroying the climate in which they thrive? The rapid increase of population has prevented real improvement of living standards in much of the non-industrialized world, creating an equally complex problem. One of the most noticeable results of this has been the rejection of much of *modern* culture in favor of a return to *traditionalism*. The rapid growth of a militant fundamentalist movement in much of the Islamic world, and in India, is eloquent testimony to the depths of despair and alienation felt by many of the Earth's poorest millions. It remains for the twenty-first century to determine how all of the world's cultures can be integrated into the new civilization born in the Enlightenment and the Industrial Revolution more than two and a half centuries ago.

◆ Notes

1. *Bartlett's Familiar Quotations*, 15th edition, edited by Emily Morison Beck (Boston: Little, Brown and Company, 1980), 764 [#1] and 763 [#16].

2. *New York Times*, December 15, 2002, L16.

Index